From films specifically tar[...] variety of genres raging thr[...] *tin's Family Film Guide* f[...] rated through the eyes of the author, as a parent. This guide includes:

- Leonard Maltin's own rating system
  (NG=Not Good, VG=Very Good, OK=OK)
  for both older and younger children
- MPAA ratings and ratings explanations
- Category Index

Leonard Maltin's Family Film Guide

LEONARD MALTIN has won the reputation as one of the country's leading film historians and critics as a result of his many books and his regular appearances since 1982 on television's popular syndicated program *Entertainment Tonight*. He is editor of the bestselling annual *Leonard Maltin's Movie & Video Guide* (Signet and Plume) and *Leonard Maltin's Movie Encyclopedia* (Plume), as well as the author of *Of Mice and Magic: A History of American Animated Cartoons* (Plume) and *The Great American Broadcast: A Celebration of Radio's Golden Age* (Dutton). His other titles include *The Disney Films, The Art of the Cinematographer, Music Comedy Teams, Selected Short Subjects (The Great Movie Shorts), The Whole Film Sourcebook,* and *The Little Rascals: The Life and Times of Our Gang* (with Richard Bann). Mr. Maltin hosts a daily syndicated radio program, *Leonard Maltin's Video View*, provides commentary for the Encore cable TV service, and contributes articles regularly to *Modern Maturity*. He is the film critic for *Playboy* magazine, and his articles have appeared in a wide variety of other publications, including *The New York Times,* the *Los Angeles Times, Smithsonian, TV Guide, Variety, Esquire, Disney Magazine, Satellite Direct,* and *Film Comment*. Mr. Maltin and his wife, Alice, are the proud parents of a daughter, Jessica, whose reactions to films and videos have helped inform some of the opinions that he expresses in his new *Family Film Guide*.

Leonard Maltin's
FAMILY FILM GUIDE

EDITED BY LEONARD MALTIN

Associate Editors: Spencer Green, Bill Warren
Consulting Editor: Jessica Bennett Maltin

Contributing Editors:
Cathleen Anderson
Jerry Beck
Rob Edelman
Lawrence Haverhill
Audrey Kupferberg
Michael Scheinfeld
Casey St. Charnez
Patricia Eliot Tobias

A SIGNET BOOK

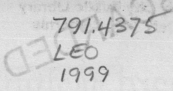

SIGNET
Published by New American Library, a division of
Penguin Putnam Inc., 375 Hudson Street,
New York, New York 10014, U.S.A.
Penguin Books Ltd, 27 Wrights Lane,
London W8 5TZ, England
Penguin Books Australia Ltd, Ringwood,
Victoria, Australia
Penguin Books Canada Ltd, 10 Alcorn Avenue,
Toronto, Ontario, Canada M4V 3B2
Penguin Books (N.Z.) Ltd, 182–190 Wairau Road,
Auckland 10, New Zealand

Penguin Books Ltd, Registered Offices:
Harmondsworth, Middlesex, England

First published by Signet, an imprint of New American Library,
a division of Penguin Putnam Inc.

First Printing, May 1999
10 9 8 7 6 5 4 3 2 1

The MPAA ratings are as follows:

G   For General Audiences
PG   Parental Guidance suggested
PG-13 Not suitable for children under the age of 13
R   Restricted for children under the age of 17

Films released before 1967 do not carry MPAA ratings (although some have received them for reissue purposes).

We have decided that labeling films according to specific age groups is foolhardy, if not downright impossible. So we have divided our ratings into two groups: young children and older children. Only parents can determine whether their 3-to-5-year-old is ready to see a spooky-looking monster. And only a parent has an awareness of whether or not their 10-to-12-year-old is sufficiently mature to handle more sophisticated story material. We hope that these shorthand ratings, amplified by our reviews, will serve as a useful guide to concerned parents.

NG = Not Good for children of this age group
OK = OK for children of this age group
VG = Very Good for children of this age group

If a film title is printed in boldface, you will find a complete review of it in this book.

Introduction

Politicians are fond of talking about "family values," which mistakenly assumes that all families are alike. Moviemakers and moviegoers (like me) know better.

At least one family brought its young child to *Saving Private Ryan*—not because they thought the boy would pay attention, but because it was cheaper than hiring a baby-sitter. They apparently believe that exposing a very young child to graphic, brutal images will do no harm. I disagree.

How well I remember watching with horror as parents took their 4- and 5-year-olds to see the 1989 *Batman* movie—in which young Bruce Wayne sees his parents gunned down on the sidewalk in cold blood. I stood in awe as 5- and 6-year-olds went into the dark of a movie theater to witness *Jurassic Park*—nightmare material if I ever saw it. (Even its creator, Steven Spielberg, said publicly that he wouldn't let his younger children see the film.)

Even more recently, American families flocked to see Adam Sandler's likably goofy comedy *The Waterboy*. Cheerfully heedless of its PG-13 rating, parents and kids laughed together at Sandler's Jerry Lewis–ish antics—and encountered a certain four-letter word twice during the very first scene of the film! (Never mind the sexual humor that turns up later.)

Some parents have simply given up when it comes to monitoring their children's moviegoing. They've succumbed to youthful peer pressure ("All my friends have seen it") and in some cases have talked themselves into believing that there's no real harm in exposing their kids to PG-13 or R-rated action or horror movies. Again, I disagree. When a parent tells me, "My kid has heard all those words," I'm sure it's true. My daughter has heard them, too. But it's one thing to be aware of foul language; it's quite another to condone it. Letting kids, in their formative years, see brainless action movies full of explosions, maimings, and various antisocial behavior may not have an adverse effect on their own lives, but it certainly gives them a warped view of what movies are all about. How are they supposed to receive or accept films that rely more on storytelling or characterizations when their idea of entertainment is things blowing up?

No one can tell parents what's appropriate for their child . . . and no two children are alike. That much is certain.

I speak from firsthand experience. My only child, Jessie, proved to be more sensitive than many of her peers while growing up. When she was very young she watched the G-rated remake of *The Secret Garden* and found the scene in which the young girl's parents are killed (off camera, to be sure) during an uprising in India to be very upsetting. So were the screams and cries down the hall of the eerie old mansion where the orphaned girl goes to live in England.

She almost didn't make it through *Beethoven* on its original theatrical release because she was upset about what the bad guys were going to do to the dogs in a pet shop in the film's opening scene. I assured her that these were bumbling bad guys, and nothing bad would happen. She took my word for it and stayed with the film. Then, when the evil veterinarian (played by Dean Jones) wielded his hypodermic needle, she ran straight to the lobby.

I believe that sensitivities should be respected, not chided. As a child grows and learns more about the world, he or she learns how to deal with upsetting things, in life and in the movies.

At the age of 5, Jessie recoiled in terror while watching the wolves in Disney's *Beauty and the Beast*—and wasn't too crazy about the Beast, either. (Her friends didn't complain.) At 7, she went with a group of friends and my wife to see *Hocus Pocus,* and in the first moments when she saw the Salem witches being hanged, she shot up the aisle. (Her pals made it all the way through.)

That same year, having seen TV commercials for *The Beverly Hillbillies,* she begged me to take her to see it. Noting that it was rated PG, and sensing that it was most likely a silly, benign sort of comedy, I agreed. Early in the film, when the backwoods family comes to Southern California in their beat-up jalopy, drivers on the freeway give them "the finger," and they naively respond in kind. Jessie had never seen this gesture before, so naturally I had to explain it. Then, a sleazy character played by Rob Schneider comes home to vixenish Lea Thompson and the minute he's inside the door, he starts tearing off his pants. This too called for an explanation for my curious daughter.

On the whole, *The Beverly Hillbillies* was pretty much what I expected it to be (only not very good). But I'm not sure I wanted my 7-year-old to know about giving people the finger or about the nature of lust. What's a parent to do?

The situation isn't helped by advertising that misrepresents a film, or commercial tie-ins that create kid appeal for films that aren't kiddie fodder. *Batman Returns* was a typically dark Tim Burton movie, which opened with The Penguin's parents tossing him out of his perambulator into a river! But the blitz of promotion at McDonald's fast-food restaurants encouraged young kids to want to see it. Trailers and commercials for the Disney-released *Jack* indicated a wacky Robin Williams comedy; parents and children alike discovered otherwise when they went to see this melancholy movie, whose moments of mirth were few and far between.

Now, having passed the decade mark, my daughter is more interested in adult films and was attracted to Jim Carrey in *Liar Liar* and Leonardo DiCaprio in *Titanic*. My wife and I would rather she see certain films than have them become forbidden fruit—so long as we watch them together and have a chance to discuss them afterwards.

Even with all the ratings safeguards in place, children of the '90s are being exposed in the movies to a harsher view of life—and a cruder set of sensibilities—than kids of any previous decade. To avoid it all is impossible; to deny its existence is unrealistic.

When I was growing up, in the 1950s and '60s, my parents never had to worry about what I saw when I went to the movies. That's because I attended the last generation of Saturday matinees, when the normal fodder was Francis the Talking Mule and tacky science fiction movies. The same was true for television; the debate back then was over how much TV a kid might watch, not what they might see while the set was on. (Ironically, among the safest viewing a parent can endorse today is cable TV's Nick at Nite, which consists of innocent programming from that same time period. One needn't worry about the likes of *I Love Lucy* or *The Munsters* the way one has to monitor a child's exposure to *3rd Rock from the Sun* or *Married with Children.* Nick also provides a ready response to parents who claim their kids won't watch anything in black-and-white. Does that include *I Love Lucy* and *Bewitched*?)

As a professional film critic, I made another discovery early on in sharing movies with my daughter: good values take precedence over art. I may not have liked a movie, but if it taught a good lesson or promoted the kind of morality I was trying to teach my child, I was glad she saw it. There'd be time for her esthetic sensibilities to develop later on.

A case in point: I saw *The Karate Kid, Part II* when it was new, and dismissed it as a hopelessly corny piece of claptrap. But when Jessie was not quite 3 years old, she discovered it on The Disney Channel one day and fell in love with it. She heard it was being shown again that weekend and wanted me to watch it with her. Then I understood why she liked it so much: the story was simplicity itself, with clearly defined good guys and bad guys. There was a sweet, perfectly chaste puppy-love romance, a cliffhanger rescue climax, and a finale in which the chief bad guy redeemed himself and apologized for his bad behavior. I saw the movie in a whole new light: a perfect film for very young children.

The 1997 remake of *McHale's Navy* with Tom Arnold was roundly booed by most critics—and understandably so. As a comic adventure yarn, it's pretty anemic. But I saw it in the company of two 10-year-old girls who enjoyed every minute. What seemed bland or hokey to me was fresh and engaging for them.

My wife and I saw *Austin Powers: International Man of Mystery,* with Mike Myers, without any children at our side, and found ourselves bored after the one-joke premise wore itself thin. Then we met a friend who told us that her 8-year-old son thought it was the funniest—and coolest—movie he'd ever seen.

It's all in the eye of the beholder.

By definition, then, this book is subjective. Its reviews

express opinions formed by me and my contributing editors. But there is also a degree of objectivity here. We can't pretend to count the number of cusswords in every movie or cite every potentially objectionable moment. What we can do is provide an overall impression of the films we've seen and the impact they may have on children.

I can also steer parents toward a lot of good movies that haven't had the benefit of hype and remind you of older movies that make great entertainment for adults and children alike.

As old-movie aficionados, my wife and I started showing our daughter vintage comedies, musicals, cartoons, and even Westerns when she was quite young and receptive. She immediately responded to Fred Astaire and Ginger Rogers, Laurel and Hardy (or as we know them in our house, Stan and Ollie), The Little Rascals, Betty Boop, Roy Rogers and Dale Evans, and The Lone Ranger.

One day it occurred to me that she might enjoy *Calamity Jane*, because the character is a tomboy; I brought home the cassette and it quickly became a favorite—so much so that when we tried out *The Pajama Game,* she gave it a chance because it starred the same actress she recognized as Calamity, Doris Day.

My wife wanted Jessie to see her all-time favorite movie, *Seven Brides for Seven Brothers,* but our daughter didn't have the patience to wade into the story. So we jumped ahead to the barn-raising musical number, and she was transfixed. She insisted on watching it over and over, and finally got curious enough to want to see the movie from the beginning.

As kids get older, they grow more stubborn and aren't as willing to try something new. But when Jessie—now 11 years old—saw TV ads for the 1997 remake of *Great Expectations,* and I explained that it was a famous story that had been filmed before, she asked if she could see the older version. That night we watched David Lean's classic 1946 movie. There were things that Jessie didn't understand, but she still liked it quite a bit—enough for us to allow her to see the new version that weekend, in spite of its R rating. (Having screened it already, I knew that there were fundamentally two scenes which had earned it the R, and felt that Jessie was mature enough to deal with them.) Walking out of the theater with a close friend, she declared that the old one was better, and brought the friend home to show it to her.

Children who have never eaten anything but McDonald's hamburgers can't be expected to appreciate filet mignon when they first taste it. They must be educated—or weaned, if you prefer—onto better movies, as well. Thanks to home video, the world of film is at your fingertips. Why not share it with your kids?

An important reminder, however: every film is made better when you talk about it with your kids. Is there something in an old movie that they didn't understand? Explain it. Did something in a '50s movie strike them—or you—as being sexist? Talk about changing times and attitudes. Did a violent theme or an unpleasant character make any of you uncomfortable in a brand-new movie? Discuss the reasons why.

Even a bad moviegoing experience can be redeemed if it sparks an honest conversation. Use the film as a springboard for discussion about incidents in your own life and how they might relate to your child's experiences.

Remember that PG doesn't mean "fine for the family." It suggests Parental Guidance. In popular usage, however, PG has come to mean "OK for kids," which simply isn't true. If you don't want your child to hear any four-letter words, or see any violence of any kind, or witness a man and woman going to bed together, you must keep them away from PG films. *Michael*, a fairly benign PG film about a most peculiar angel (played by John Travolta), does have one or two cusswords and involves a budding relationship which leads to a man and woman sharing a room for the night, although nothing is shown. Most parents will find this tolerable nowadays; some might not.

What follows is a book of mini-essays on more than one thousand films. Some of them are obvious family choices; others are films from a variety of genres (comedy, fantasy, musical, Western) that you might not immediately think of for family viewing. Still others are contemporary films that movie studios have aimed at the family trade, for better or worse; if the latter, I say so in plain language. We've even included a handful of R-rated movies (like *Schindler's List*) which have important lessons to teach youngsters who are old enough (or mature enough) to accept them.

My goal is to give an overall impression of each film, as a critic and as a parent. I'll leave the counting of four-letter words to others; I'm more interested in what a child takes away from each movie experience . . . and in trying to steer both children and parents to films they can enjoy together.

My everlasting thanks to a loyal group of contributors: Spencer Green, Michael Scheinfeld, Bill Warren, Rob Edelman, Audrey Kupferberg, Jerry Beck, Casey St. Charnez, Patty Tobias, and Cathleen Anderson. A special word of thanks to Lawrence Haverhill, for coming out of semi-retirement to help me with this project. But most of all, I want to thank my most important collaborators, my wife, Alice, and my daughter, Jessie, who endured this book's long road to completion. I couldn't—and wouldn't—have survived without them.

—Leonard Maltin
Los Angeles, November 1998

A

AARON'S MAGIC VILLAGE
(1995)
Color, 78 minutes
Cast: Voices of Tommy Michaels, Ronn Carroll, Tovah Feldshuh, Steven Newman, Ivy Austin, Harry Goz, Lee Wilkof, Chip Zien, Lewis J. Stadlen, Larry Keith; Fyvush Finkel (narrator)
Directors: Albert Hanan Kaminski (Europe), Buzz Potamkin (U.S.)
Screenplay: Galia Benousilio and Kaminski
Animated musical
Rated G
Young children: OK   Older children: OK

Young Aaron thinks he's going for a nice quiet visit with his Uncle Shlemiel and Aunt Sarah and their three daughters in the peaceful village of Chelm. What he finds instead is a town full of happy fools, blissfully unaware that their magical "Book of Marvels" is being misused by an evil sorcerer who wants to bring a giant Golem to fearsome life. Some vacation.

This European cartoon adaptation of four fables by Isaac Bashevis Singer (1978 Nobel laureate) also involves Aaron with a talking goat, an amnesiac elf, and some forgettable songs by Michel Legrand and Sheldon Harnick.

A sincere but somewhat flat cartoon, it gets better as it goes, with a computer-assisted attack finale. Still, there's a good reason why this film never took off and made a name for itself in theaters.

Fyvush Finkel, from TV's *Picket Fences,* is the familiar voice of the narrator.

ABBOTT AND COSTELLO GO TO MARS (1953)
Black & white, 77 minutes
Cast: Bud Abbott, Lou Costello, Mari Blanchard, Horace McMahon, Jack Kruschen, Robert Paige, Martha Hyer
Director: Charles Lamont
Screenplay: D. D. Beauchamp and John Grant
Science fiction/comedy
Unrated
Younger kids: OK   Older kids: OK

The title's a lie. Bud and Lou don't go to Mars but to Venus, where there are beautiful women so starved for men that they think Lou is cute. Abbott and Costello play handymen (again) who wind up in an experimental rocket with a couple of crooks; they make a false landing in New Orleans at Mardi Gras before going on to Venus.

It takes a while for Bud and Lou—and the movie—to get off the ground, and for those who aren't tuned into their style of humor, the movie can be pretty rough going. Even those who like the team will probably consider this one of their lesser efforts, but younger children, who tend to like silliness, may find it entertaining.

ABBOTT AND COSTELLO MEET CAPTAIN KIDD (1952)
Color, 70 minutes
Cast: Bud Abbott, Lou Costello, Charles Laughton, Hillary Brooke, Fran Warren, Bill Shirley, Leif Erickson
Director: Charles Lamont
Screenplay: Howard Dimsdale and John Grant
Comedy/Action-adventure
Unrated
Younger kids: OK   Older kids: Good

Abbott and Costello play two servants on the pirate island of Tortuga who inadvertently come into possession of a treasure map and get mixed up with the fearsome Captain Kidd (Charles Laughton) and a fetching female buccaneer (Hillary Brooke).

This lowbrow pirate spoof is not one of A&C's better films, but it's given a touch of class by the great Charles Laughton, who once memorably played Captain Bligh in Mutiny on the Bounty, and then Captain Kidd in a 1945 film of the same name. Here he has an opportunity to ham it up to his heart's content.

It's perfectly harmless entertainment for the kiddies, though they'll probably be annoyed by the frequent interruptions for a half-dozen silly songs.

ABBOTT AND COSTELLO MEET DR. JEKYLL AND MR. HYDE (1953)
Black & white, 76 minutes
Cast: Bud Abbott, Lou Costello, Boris Karloff, Craig Stevens, Helen Westcott, Reginald Denny, John Dierkes, Eddie Parker
Director: Charles Lamont
Screenplay: Lee Loeb and John Grant
Comedy/Science fiction
Unrated
Younger kids: OK, with caution   Older kids: OK

In gaslit London, visiting Americans Slim and Tubby (Bud and Lou) are kicked off the police force. Looking for a way to reinstate themselves, they decide to track down the "monster" that's been terrorizing the city. Tubby soon learns it's Dr. Jekyll (Karloff), who turns himself into the monstrous Mr. Hyde to take revenge on his enemies. The expected complications follow.

Though briskly paced, this is well below the standard set by **Abbot and Costello Meet Frankenstein,** although there are some good scenes scattered throughout. Bud and Lou never do any of their famous routines, but at one point, Lou turns into a giant mouse in a derby, and at another, becomes a little fat Mr. Hyde himself.

The Hyde faces are really ugly and could bother the youngest kids; older kids will probably find some amusement in this movie, especially if they're already A&C fans.

ABBOTT AND COSTELLO MEET FRANKENSTEIN (1948)
Black & white, 83 minutes
Cast: Bud Abbott, Lou Costello, Lon Chaney, Jr., Bela Lugosi, Glenn Strange, Lenore Aubert, Jane Randolph
Director: Charles Barton
Screenplay: Robert Lees, Frederic Rinaldo, and John Grant

Comedy/Horror
Unrated
Younger kids: OK, with
    caution   Older kids: VG

Florida deliverymen Chick and
Wilbur (Bud Abbott, Lou Costello) tangle with Dracula (Lugosi), who wants to put Chick's
brain into the body of the Frankenstein Monster (Strange). Larry
Talbot (Chaney), the Wolf Man,
wants to stop this.

A classic of its type, this is one
of the few movies that just about
everyone seems to love. The secret is that the comedy is handled
almost entirely by Abbott and
Costello, who are in peak form,
while the trio of monsters play it
straight. This movie is ideal as an
introduction both to Abbott and
Costello, and to the famous Universal Studios monsters. Bela Lugosi, who created the role of
Dracula, is perfect as the suave
but evil Count. Lon Chaney, Jr.,
who originated the part of the tortured Larry Talbot, once again
finds himself becoming the Wolf
Man when the full moon is bright;
he, too, is just right. And Glenn
Strange fills Boris Karloff's oversized shoes quite well as the Frankenstein monster. There's even a
surprise cameo in the film's final
scene; we won't give it away.

If your kids have never "met"
Abbott and Costello, this is a
great chance to see Bud and Lou
do some of their best routines, including "the moving candle,"
which was first seen in another
scare-comedy, *Hold That Ghost.*

It's well produced, fast paced,
and both funny and suspenseful.
The horror element is just creepy
enough to make the youngest
children uneasy, but they may
love the film as much as you do.

ABBOTT AND COSTELLO MEET THE INVISIBLE MAN (1951)

Black & white, 82 minutes
Cast: Bud Abbott, Lou Costello,
    Arthur Franz, Sheldon
    Leonard, Nancy Guild,
    William Frawley, Adele
    Jergens, Gavin Muir
Director: Charles Lamont
Screenplay: Robert Lees,
    Frederic Rinaldo, and John
    Grant.
Comedy/Science fiction
Unrated
Younger kids: OK   Older kids:
    Good

Newly graduated private eyes
Bud and Lou are hired by a
young prizefighter (Franz) who's
been unjustly accused of murder.
In order to help them find the real
killer, the fighter uses the serum
of a friendly scientist and makes
himself invisible.

Kids will be amused by this
film, one of A&C's better post-
Frankenstein comedies, but the
film has an oddly adult tone, involving drunkenness and sexual
rivalry. The climax is a boxing
match.

But Bud and Lou are in good
form, and there are quite a few
good gags dealing with invisibility.
If you and your kids are A&C fans,
you'll enjoy this one together.

THE ABSENT MINDED PROFESSOR (1961)

Black & white, 97 minutes (also
    available in a computer-
    colored version)
Cast: Fred MacMurray, Nancy
    Olson, Keenan Wynn, Tommy
    Kirk, Ed Wynn, Leon Ames,
    Wally Brown, Alan Carney,
    Elliott Reid, Edward Andrews
Director: Robert Stevenson

3

Screenplay: Bill Walsh, based on a story by Samuel W. Taylor
Comedy/Fantasy
Unrated
Younger children: VG Older children: VG

One of Walt Disney's most successful—and best-remembered—comedy-fantasies, *The Absent Minded Professor* has been eclipsed in its special effects wizardry in the decades since its release, but not in its sure-footed comedy know-how. It's much funnier (and livelier) than its 1997 remake with Robin Williams, **Flubber.**

Fred MacMurray, the engaging comic actor who became a staple of Disney movies in the 1960s, stars as Professor Ned Brainard, who's so distracted by his work that he forgets to show up at his own wedding! (It's not the first time.) While experimenting in his laboratory, he stumbles onto an amazing discovery: a gooey substance that floats, like flying rubber. He names it flubber, and when he applies it to his old Model T car, it flies! He wants to share his excitement with his fiancée (Nancy Olson), but she's gone off with his arch-rival, Shelby Ashton (Elliott Reid), to the Medfield High basketball game. There, Brainard treats the team's sneakers with flubber, and they fly sky-high to win the game. No one believes he's responsible—except for Alonzo Hawk, a local bigwig of dubious character. Hawk determines to get his hands on flubber and make a fortune with it . . . but Professor Brainard takes his Model T to Washington instead.

The Absent Minded Professor may seem a bit naïve to older kids today, but younger ones should still be able to enjoy its broad comedy and imaginative use of special effects. The film was made in black-and-white because the Disney technicians didn't think they could hide their tricks for the color camera. Some years later, the studio computer-colored the original film.

It was followed by a popular sequel, **Son of Flubber,** in 1963.

THE ABYSS (1989)
Color, 145 minutes
Cast: Ed Harris, Mary Elizabeth Mastrantonio, Michael Biehn, Leo Burmester, Chris Elliott, Todd Graff, John Bedford Lloyd
Director: James Cameron
Screenplay: James Cameron
Science fiction/Adventure
Rated PG-13
Young children: No Older children: OK

Scientists and others in an oil-exploration habitat on the bottom of the sea try to find a submarine that disappeared under mysterious circumstances, only to find themselves faced with mysteries and wonders they never expected. The crisis also serves to reunite an estranged husband (Harris) and wife (Mastrantonio).

Spectacularly produced and very suspenseful, this is too intense for young children. Anyone with fears of enclosed spaces will get a real workout here! As with Cameron's later *Titanic,* adults might find some of the romantic elements more than a little corny and some of the plot developments trite. This won't bother youngsters, though.

However, there are some genuinely scary scenes, including a nail-biter in which one of the

4

leading characters literally has to drown in order to be saved. The ending, involving benign and beautiful aliens, might confuse younger children, who might not realize anything so pretty could be powerful and menacing—which, of course, might be a good object lesson.

The laserdisc version is 27 minutes longer, with an expanded, and clearer, ending.

ACROSS THE GREAT DIVIDE (1976)
Color, 100 minutes
Cast: Robert Logan, Heather Rattray, Mark Edward Hall, George "Buck" Flower
Director: Stewart Raffill
Screenplay: Stewart Raffill
Action-adventure/Western
Rated Good
Younger kids: Good Older kids: Good

Produced, directed, and distributed by the same parties responsible for the successful series of *Wilderness Family* films, this wholesome family adventure follows a similar formula, setting kids and animals against the spectacular wilderness scenery of Utah and British Columbia. Robert Logan plays a card shark who leads a pair of orphans across the Rocky Mountains to Oregon to claim a farm they have inherited. Along the way, they survive attacks by mountain lions, wolves, buffalo, and a grizzly bear.

These potentially harrowing incidents are done in such a way that the ultimate safety of the children is never in doubt, and the film also features pro-social depictions of friendly Indians.

THE ADDAMS FAMILY
(1991)
Color, 101 minutes
Cast: Anjelica Huston, Raul Julia, Christopher Lloyd, Elizabeth Wilson, Christina Ricci, Judith Malina, Dan Hedaya, Carel Struycken, Paul Benedict, Christopher Hart, Dana Ivey, Jimmy Workman
Director: Barry Sonnenfeld
Screenplay: Caroline Thompson and Larry Wilson, based on characters created by Charles Addams
Comedy/Horror spoof
Rated PG-13
Younger kids: Too gruesome · Older kids: OK

Happily married Morticia (Huston) and Gomez (Julia) are adoring parents to their children, Wednesday and Pugsley (Ricci and Workman); and they're fabulously wealthy. They're also completely weird, devoted to the strange, the macabre, the horrible; their butler looks like Frankenstein's Monster, and Gomez's valet is a disembodied walking hand called Thing. But they're a fully functional family—until their crooked lawyer (Hedaya) conspires with a greedy client to fleece the Addams Family by passing off the client's son (Lloyd) as the long-lost Addams relative, Uncle Fester.

Based both on the old *New Yorker* cartoons by Charles Addams and the 1960s TV series inspired by the cartoons, *The Addams Family* is surprisingly funny and handsomely produced. The cast rises to the occasion, particularly Huston and Julia, and Sonnenfeld makes an impressive debut as director (having been a notable cinematographer).

There's way too much plot, however, and the movie slows

down whenever the Addams Family is not on screen.

Since the emphasis is on the macabre, as when the Addams children stage a very gory Shakespeare scene at school, this film is rated PG-13 and might send mixed or confusing signals to very young children. But savvy kids (say, from 10 up) will get the joke that the Addamses see things differently from everyone else around them.

A sequel followed and then a made-for-TV movie and a direct-to-video feature.

ADDAMS FAMILY VALUES
(1993)
Color, 101 minutes
Cast: Anjelica Huston, Raul Julia, Christopher Lloyd, Joan Cusack, Christina Ricci, Carol Kane, Jimmy Workman, Carel Struycken, Dana Ivey, Peter MacNicol, Christine Baranski, Mercedes McNab, Nathan Lane, Peter Graves, Tony Shalhoub, David Hyde Pierce
Director: Barry Sonnenfeld
Screenplay: Paul Rudnick, based on characters created by Charles Addams
Comedy
Rated PG-13
Younger kids: OK, with caution   Older kids: VG

This sequel to **The Addams Family** offers further adventures of the uniquely bizarre Addams clan: Morticia gives birth to a bouncing baby boy (complete with moustache, just like his father's), while an evil woman tries to marry Uncle Fester for his money and then knock him off, and Wednesday and Pugsley are sent to a "happy camp" that truly tests their mettle.

Not nearly as popular as the first *Addams* movie, this one is actually funnier, with dark, satiric jibes that adults will appreciate a lot more than their kids will. Happily, the Addams remain the ultimate nonconformists, and—despite all the ghoulish trappings—Gomez and Morticia are helplessly, madly in love with each other and extremely proud of their children.

Some might object to the various, ghoulish ways in which Wednesday and Pugsley try to dispose of their new baby brother or the havoc that the Addams kids wreak at summer camp. Children old enough to get "the joke"—about the family's contrariness—will recognize the violence as extremely stylized and executed with Rube Goldberg–ish panache. Younger kids may find some of it upsetting or confusing.

ADVENTURES IN BABYSITTING (1987)
Color, 99 minutes
Cast: Elisabeth Shue, Maia Brewton, Keith Coogan, Anthony Rapp, Calvin Levels, Vincent D'Onofrio, Penelope Ann Miller, George Newburn, John Ford Noonan, Bradley Whitford
Director: Chris Columbus
Screenplay: David Simkins
Comedy
Rated PG-13
Younger kids: OK, with caution   Older kids: OK

Here's a perfect example of a film that may cause adults to groan, but is bound to entertain kids. Teenage babysitter Chris (Elisabeth Shue) has to help a friend who's stuck at a downtown Chicago bus station. With her three young charges in tow, they leave the safety of the suburbs for the big city, and one mishap after another befalls them, beginning when her car gets a flat and she discovers she left her purse back at the house.

Somehow this leads to being chased by gangsters who run a car-theft ring. The kids hide out (and perform) in a blues club, climb a skyscraper, and eventually outwit the thugs, racing home before their parents return. A nice subplot has little Sara (Maia Brewton), who worships Marvel comic book character Thor, meeting her idol (Vincent D'Onofrio), or so she thinks.

Elisabeth Shue is extremely winning in her first starring role. This marked the directorial debut of screenwriter Chris Columbus, who went on to make **Home Alone, Mrs. Doubtfire,** and *Stepmom.*

However, despite the film's overall kid appeal, parents should pay attention to the PG-13 rating.

THE ADVENTURES OF BULLWHIP GRIFFIN (1967)
Color, 110 minutes
Cast: Roddy McDowall, Suzanne Pleshette, Karl Malden, Harry Guardino, Richard Haydn, Hermione Baddeley, Bryan Russell
Director: James Neilson
Screenplay: Lowell S. Hawley, based on the novel *By the Great Horn Spoon* by Sid Fleischman
Action-adventure/comedy
Unrated
Younger kids: Good   Older kids: VG

"Bullwhip" is the nickname given to a very proper Bostonian butler named Griffin (Roddy McDowall)

who follows his young master out West in the mid 1800s, when Gold Rush fever was at its peak in California. Together and separately, they get mixed up in all sorts of trouble, including being pursued by a villainous judge (Karl Malden) who's after a treasure map.

This is a rollicking Disney-produced Gold Rush spoof filled with some delightful sight gags (particularly during a comical boxing match), clever visual effects by veteran Disney animator Ward Kimball, and even some amusing songs by the Sherman Brothers (of **Mary Poppins** fame). If you're able to get your kids to watch anything resembling a Western, they're sure to enjoy this, which is high-spirited fun for the whole family.

ADVENTURES OF DON JUAN (1949)
Color, 110 minutes
Cast: Errol Flynn, Viveca Lindfors, Robert Douglas, Alan Hale, Romney Brent, Ann Rutherford, Raymond Burr
Director: Vincent Sherman
Screenplay: Harry Kurnitz, based on a story by Herbert Dalmas
Swashbuckler/Action-adventure
Unrated
Younger kids: OK   Older kids: VG

Errol Flynn buckles his swash once again and plants his tongue firmly in cheek for this zesty romp about the life and loves of the legendary Spanish lothario. While working as a fencing master at the court of Queen Margaret (Viveca Lindfors), Don Juan romances every maiden in sight, including the Queen herself, and uncovers a plot by the conniving Duke De

Lorca (Robert Douglas) to depose her.

With Alan Hale as Flynn's sidekick and a rousing Max Steiner score, this conjures up fond memories of Flynn's classic **The Adventures of Robin Hood** and climaxes with an exciting duel that takes place on the steps of the palace. Opulent and colorful, the film features copious swordplay and a bevy of lovely ladies, but it's all very innocent by today's standards.

For years, Errol Flynn's name was associated with pirate films and swashbucklers—like **Captain Blood,** the aforementioned *Robin Hood,* and **The Sea Hawk**. Although they had their lighthearted moments, this was the first time the tone of an entire Flynn adventure was spoofy—and it suited the star, who wasn't as young as he used to be, and whose sometimes scandalous private life had made him seem like a modern-day Don Juan in tabloid headlines of the time.

THE ADVENTURES OF HUCK FINN (1993)
Color, 108 minutes
Cast: Elijah Wood, Courtney B. Vance, Robbie Coltrane, Jason Robards, Ron Perlman, Dana Ivey, Anne Heche, James Gammon, Paxton Whitehead
Director: Stephen Sommers
Screenplay: Sommers, from the novel by Mark Twain
Rated PG
Period adventure/Literary classic
Young children: No Older children: OK, with caution

The story in this Disney production is much the same as in other film versions, with Huck Finn (Elijah Wood) and Jim (Courtney B. Vance) rafting along the Mississippi, encountering colorful and dangerous characters as they go. Writer-director Sommers does darken the tone by including a murderous feud, but this is still bush-league Mark Twain. The definitive movie of this great American novel has yet to be made.

Huck Finn isn't bad as entertainment, but it soft-pedals the book's satire. Twain told such a wonderful story, peopled with terrific, colorful characters and driven by a progressive, picaresque narrative, that it keeps attracting filmmakers—who then shy away from the stronger elements of the novel.

Period slang (including, of course, the word "nigger") is avoided almost completely, and Wood is too young and cute for the role, but he's fun and seems to be having fun as well. Robards and Coltrane are fine as the rascally con men, and unlike many who've played these roles in the past, these actors bring a touch of genuine menace to their parts. Vance does a good job with Jim, but he seems almost too modern for the setting.

We do see Huck learn about many issues, and we learn what leads him to change his mind about slavery and race, but still the film is compromised by the need to make this a jolly kids' adventure.

Younger children are likely to be frightened by Ron Perlman as the brutal Pap Finn and by the subsequent feud scenes, in which deaths occur. This film is primarily for older children, who will enjoy Wood and his ambling thrill ride along the Mississippi.

THE ADVENTURES OF HUCKLEBERRY FINN (1960)
Color, 107 minutes
Cast: Eddie Hodges, Tony Randall, Archie Moore, Patty McCormack, Neville Brand, Buster Keaton, Andy Devine, Judy Canova, Mickey Shaughnessy, John Carradine, Sterling Holloway, Royal Dano
Director: Michael Curtiz
Screenplay: James Lee, based on the novel by Mark Twain
Adventure/Literary classic
Unrated
Younger kids: Good   Older kids: VG

Mark Twain's immortal classic about a mischievous boy's misadventures on the Mississippi River is brought to the screen in this lighthearted version featuring warm performances by Eddie Hodges as Huck and former boxing champion Archie Moore as Jim. The colorful location photography captures the story's picaresque atmosphere, and the supporting cast, headed by Tony Randall as a delightfully roguish con man, is excellent. Adding to the fun is a top-notch roster of veteran character actors, including silent-film comedy star Buster Keaton and Harry Dean Stanton (billed as Dean Stanton) in one of his earliest films.

Those seeking a literal adaptation of Twain or a sharply focused look at racism will not be satisfied with this glossy production, but as children's entertainment it certainly fills the bill.

THE ADVENTURES OF ICHABOD AND MR. TOAD (1949)
Color, 68 minutes
Cast: Voices of Bing Crosby, Basil Rathbone, Eric Blore (Mr. Toad), Pat O'Malley, Claude Allister, John Ployardt, Colin Campbell
Directors: Jack Kinney, Clyde Geronimi, and James Algar.
Screenplay: Erdman Penner, Winston Hibler, Joe Rinaldi, Ted Sears, Homer Brightman, and Harry Reeves, based on "The Legend of Sleepy Hollow" by Washington Irving and *The Wind in the Willows* by Kenneth Grahame
Animated musical
Not rated
Young children: OK, with caution   Older children: VG

This Walt Disney cartoon feature is actually comprised of two separate segments: Kenneth Grahame's delightfully droll *The Wind in the Willows,* narrated by Basil Rathbone (movies' unforgettable Sherlock Holmes), and Washington Irving's spooky *The Legend of Sleepy Hollow*, narrated and sung by Bing Crosby.

The Legend of Sleepy Hollow is often shown around Halloween, and understandably so. It's the story of Ichabod Crane, a schoolteacher in Colonial days who's just come to town and fallen in love with the beautiful Katrina van Tassel. His rival for her affections, the burly Brom Bones, can't get Ichabod out of the way until he learns his weakness: he's terribly superstitious. At a Halloween party, Brom tells the story of the Headless Horseman and so frightens Ichabod that on his lonely ride home that night, he imagines all sorts of terrors along the path. Then he actually sees the Horseman, who laughs as he holds a jack-o'-lantern in his hand and tosses it at the hapless teacher.

The Wind in the Willows (written by Grahame in 1908) is the story of Toad Hall and its eccentric inhabitant, the irrepressible J. Thaddeus Toad, and his friends. There's nothing Mr. Toad likes more than to go riding with his horse and carriage . . . until he sees his first automobile. He becomes so flushed with excitement that he actually steals a motorcar and is arrested, put on trial, and sentenced to prison!

This delightful two-part feature is a treat for children and grown-ups alike. Some of the subtleties of *Willows* will escape young kids, but the constant action should keep them satisfied. The gags in *Sleepy Hollow* are broader, but young ones may find the Headless Horseman climax genuinely scary.

THE ADVENTURES OF MILO AND OTIS (1989)
(originally Koneko Monogatari, or A Vision of Nature on Four Feet)
Color, 76 minutes
Cast: Dudley Moore (narrator)
Director: Masanori Hata
Screenplay: Mark Saltzman, based on a story by Hata
Animal adventure
Rated G
Younger children: VG   Older children: VG

When Milo the yellow kitten falls into a river, his best friend, Otis the dog, sets out to find him. Thus begins their year-long adventure through the Japanese countryside. Not a single human inhabits this film, which is narrated by Dudley Moore, and kids should be enthralled with the seemingly real adventures of these two friends in the wild. Separated at times, occasionally in danger, they eventually make their way home.

Children will have no trouble following the adventures of this cat and dog. Despite some anxious moments along the way, the two are so adorable and have such a great relationship, they will endear themselves to almost everyone. A wonderful film, one that even adults may be surprised to find themselves enjoying.

THE ADVENTURES OF MOWGLI (1996)
Color, 92 minutes
Cast: Voices of Charlton Heston, Sam Elliott, Dana Delany, Ian Corlett, Scott McNeil, Cam Lane, Cathy Weseluck, David Kaye, Alec Willows
Directors: R. Davidov (Russia), Terry Klassen (U.S.)
Screenplay: L. Belokurov (Russia), David Longworth, Allan Stanleigh, Harry Kalensky, and Cordell Wynne (U.S.)
Animated adventure
Unrated
Young children: VG   Older children: VG

Another version of Rudyard Kipling's *The Jungle Book* (1894), assuredly a more conscientious adaptation than Disney's cartoon feature, and bolstered by Russian illustration both stylized and strangely realistic.

The musical snippets, not even quite songs, are wrong, however, and the voices have a rushed, out-of-sync feel that's characteristic of dubbing foreign films. The script tries to be modern but isn't.

However, the continued exotic appeal of the original stories plus the unusual approach to the drawings make it a very interesting movie. Pay close attention or you'll miss the gasp-inspiring touches of artistry and comedy flying by.

THE ADVENTURES OF PINOCCHIO (1996)
Color, 96 minutes
Cast: Martin Landau, Jonathan Taylor Thomas, Genevieve Bujold, Udo Kier, Bebe Neuwirth, Rob Schneider, Corey Carrier, Marcello Magni, Dawn French; voice of David Doyle
Director: Steve Barron
Screenplay: Sherry Mills, Barron, Tom Benedek, and Barry Berman, based on the stories by Carlo Collodi
Fantasy
Rated G
Young children: VG Older children: VG

It might seem difficult—even impossible—to make a film about Pinocchio without copying the work of Walt Disney. But this live-action film succeeds admirably in telling its own version of the story with great charm and imagination. It almost has the feel of a European storybook.

Martin Landau is delightful as the kindly puppet maker Geppetto, a lonely old man who never had the nerve to express his love to his sweetheart, Leona. When he chooses a tree section for his newest carving, he doesn't realize it's the same tree on which he carved his and Leona's initials years ago. This expression of love seems to carry with it a certain power—for from this trunk he carves Pinocchio, who magically comes to life. As soon as he does, the wooden boy gets into mischief, and is kidnaped by the wily Lorenzini, who operates a puppet theater—but secretly turns boys into donkeys so that they may do his bidding. A tiny cricket called Pepe tries to steer Pinocchio onto the straight and narrow path, but it's a tall order.

There are some mildly scary moments involving the villainous Lorenzini, but for the most part *The Adventures of Pinocchio* is a gentle fable, refreshingly free of the cheap, easy type of humor that infects most American kiddie films. Older kids may find it *too* gentle for their taste, but young ones should respond to the amazing special effects that bring Pinocchio to life (courtesy of Jim Henson's Creature Shop).

THE ADVENTURES OF ROBIN HOOD (1938)
Color, 102 minutes
Cast: Errol Flynn, Olivia de Havilland, Basil Rathbone, Claude Rains, Patric Knowles, Eugene Pallette, Alan Hale, Ian Hunter, Una O'Connor
Directors: Michael Curtiz and William Keighley
Screenplay: Norman Reilly Raine, and Seton I. Miller, based on old English legends
Adventure/Literary classic
Unrated
Young children: VG Older children: VG

With King Richard the Lion-Heart away at the Crusades, evil Prince John and his despicable cohorts are mistreating the good people of England and plotting to usurp the throne. Sir Robin of Locksley—Robin Hood, the greatest archer in England—and his band of merry men take shelter in Sherwood Forest and make plans to defeat the tyrants and protect England for King Richard's return. So begins one of the greatest swashbucklers of them all, a thrilling adventure featuring wonderfully drawn characters who perform amazing feats.

No other screen Robin Hood ever has approached the radiance of Errol Flynn, whose good looks, charm, and athleticism make for an ideal hero. Furthermore, the climactic sword fight between Flynn and the villainous Basil Rathbone has never been topped.

Witty dialogue, chaste but true romance, beautiful Technicolor settings, and majestic music by Erich Wolfgang Korngold all add to the enormous entertainment value of this film—truly a classic that can be enjoyed by young and old alike.

Amid all the intrigue of the evildoers, the plucky adventures of the men of Sherwood Forest, and the excitement of clicking and flashing swords, the film never loses sight of its premise that people must defend their right to be free. Don't be surprised if the day after seeing this film, your children temporarily put aside their Power Rangers and cut up the green felt on the pool table to make Robin Hood costumes.

THE ADVENTURES OF THE WILDERNESS FAMILY (1975)
Color, 100 minutes
Cast: Robert F. Logan, Susan Damante Shaw, Hollye Holmes, Ham Larsen, George "Buck" Flower
Director: Stewart Raffill

Screenplay: Stewart Raffill
Action-adventure
Rated G
Younger kids: Good   Older kids: Good

Fed up with the smog and strain of life in Los Angeles, construction worker Skip Robinson (Robert F. Logan) and his wife, Pat (Susan Damante Shaw), pack up their asthmatic daughter Jennifer (Hollye Holmes), their son Toby (Ham Larsen), and their dog and move to a log cabin in the Rockies. There the kids befriend the local wildlife, including a raccoon and a pair of motherless bear cubs, but problems arise when the family has to fend off a pack of wolves and a man-eating grizzly.

This is an idyllic fantasy of chucking it all and moving to the country; the scenery is breathtaking, the performers are attractive, and the naïve and simplistic message (about getting "back to nature") is undeniably appealing. So appealing, in fact, that this low-budget independent film was one of 1975's biggest box-office hits, spawning two sequels and several similarly themed nature films by the same director and cast.

The G rating indicates that the perils encountered by our heroes are mostly benign and resolved with a minimum of fuss.

THE ADVENTURES OF TOM SAWYER (1938)
Color, 77 minutes (some prints run 93 m.)
Cast: Tommy Kelly, Jackie Moran, Ann Gillis, May Robson, Walter Brennan, Victor Jory, Spring Byington, Margaret Hamilton
Director: Norman Taurog
Screenplay: John V. A. Weaver,

based on the novel by Mark Twain

Adventure/Literary classic
Unrated
Younger kids: VG   Older kids: VG

David O. Selznick's lavishly produced Technicolor version of Twain's story is very enjoyable, and while the accent may be a little too heavy on slapstick comedy, children will certainly not object. Tommy Kelly (from the Bronx, of all places!) is perfect as Tom Sawyer, the small town Missouri scamp, and the rest of the film is beautifully cast, right down to the smallest part, with May Robson as Aunt Polly, Walter Brennan as Muff Potter, and Jackie Moran as Huckleberry Finn being the standouts.

All of the book's highlights are lovingly re-created (including the whitewashing of the fence, Tom and Huck attending their own "funeral," and the cave sequence with the murderous Injun Joe), and the entire film is highly evocative of the period—as seen through rose-colored glasses—although some may find the character of Injun Joe (played with villainous gusto by Victor Jory) to be offensive in these "politically correct" times.

THE AFRICAN QUEEN (1951)
Color, 105 minutes
Cast: Humphrey Bogart, Katharine Hepburn, Robert Morley, Peter Bull, Theodore Bikel
Director: John Huston
Screenplay: John Huston and James Agee, based on the novel by C. S. Forester
Action-adventure
Unrated
Younger kids: OK   Older kids: VG

Humphrey Bogart won his only Academy Award for his rich, colorful performance as Charlie Allnut, a gin-guzzling captain of a rickety steam launch who, at the outset of World War I, reluctantly escorts a prim missionary (Katharine Hepburn) through one thousand miles of uncharted African rivers, facing perilous rapids, malaria, and German troops. She deplores his drinking, he calls her a "skinny psalm-singing old maid," and they battle each other as much as the Germans, but she eventually brings out the best in him—courage and fortitude he never knew he had—and vice versa.

This is a superb film in every respect, with equal measures of comedy, action, romance, and adventure, and features crackling dialogue and first-rate photography of the Congo. The chemistry between Bogart and Hepburn is wonderful, making their initially antagonistic but eventually loving relationship credible. Though the film features some mild wartime violence, parents shouldn't have any great concerns; this is a bona fide classic that should appeal to older kids *and* their parents. It may, however, be the first time your kids, like the characters in the movie, encounter leeches!

AFRICA—TEXAS STYLE!
(1967)
Color, 106 minutes
Cast: Hugh O'Brian, John Mills, Nigel Green, Tom Nardini, Adrienne Corri
Director: Andrew Marton
Screenplay: Andy White
Action-adventure/Animal story

Unrated
Younger kids: Good   Older
   kids: Good

Vivid location photography of Kenya and its wildlife highlights this action-filled story about two American cowboys (Hugh O'Brian and Tom Nardini) who are hired by an English rancher (John Mills) to capture and tame the wild game of Africa, which are being massacred by ruthless hunters.

With its conservationist theme and authentic backgrounds, nature lovers should enjoy this production from animal-film specialist Ivan Tors (**Flipper**, *Daktari*, etc.), which was later spun off as the TV series *Cowboy in Africa*. As in most of the movies produced by Tors (and in some cases directed by Andrew Marton, an action-film specialist), the family audience is kept squarely in mind, and there is nothing offensive or overly graphic on screen.

John Mills' daughter Hayley—by this time a major star, thanks to **The Parent Trap** and other Disney movies—appears in a cameo role.

AGAINST ALL FLAGS (1952)
Color, 83 minutes
Cast: Errol Flynn, Maureen
   O'Hara, Anthony Quinn,
   Mildred Natwick, Alice Kelley
Director: George Sherman
Screenplay: Aeneas MacKenzie
   and John Hoffman, based on a
   story by MacKenzie
Swashbuckler/Action-adventure
Unrated
Younger kids: Good   Older
   kids: VG

A somewhat over-age but still sprightly Errol Flynn stars as an 18th-century British naval officer who poses as a renegade in order to infiltrate a pirate stronghold. He clashes with a suspicious buccaneer (Anthony Quinn) who wants to execute him but is saved by a red-haired spitfire named Spitfire (who else but Maureen O'Hara?), whom he naturally romances, and she eventually helps him defeat the pirates.

This enjoyable minor swashbuckler is well mounted and performed with gusto.

It was remade as *The King's Pirate* in 1967.

AIR BUD (1997)
Color, 97 minutes
Cast: Kevin Zegers, Wendy
   Makkena, Michael Jeter, Bill
   Cobbs, Buddy
Director: Charles Martin Smith
Screenplay: Paul Tamasy and
   Aaron Mendelsohn, based on
   the character created by Kevin
   DiCicco
Comedy/Animal story/Sports
Rated PG
Younger children: VG   Older
   children: OK

Buddy the golden retriever—who has the uncanny ability to shoot baskets—escapes from his owner, a mean and incompetent clown named Happy Slappy (Michael Jeter). Soon Buddy finds love, a home, and a basketball career with Josh Framm (Kevin Zegers), a lonely little boy who has lost his father. Together they become the stars of the local basketball team, give a former New York Knicks basketball star (Bill Cobbs) self-respect, and fend off Happy Slappy. "Does he dribble?" asks one adult. "No," comes the answer, "but he might drool a little." With the love of a good dog, Josh becomes well adjusted, and the whole town supports him after the greedy clown tries to regain custody of the now famous Air Bud, team mascot.

What could be better than the story of a boy and his dog? Especially this dog, the basketball-playing Buddy, who does all his own hoop-shooting stunts. The story may be predictable, but it's sweet; there is plenty of slapstick, a few tender moments, plus that great dog and his hoop dreams. A 1998 sequel, *Air Bud: Golden Retriever*, was not nearly as good.

AIRPLANE! (1980)
Color, 86 minutes
Cast: Robert Hays, Julie Hagerty, Robert Stack, Lloyd Bridges, Peter Graves, Kareem Abdul-Jabbar, Leslie Nielsen, Lorna Patterson, Stephen Stucker
Director: Jim Abrahams, David Zucker, and Jerry Zucker
Screenplay: Abrahams and the Zuckers
Comedy
Rated PG
Younger kids: OK   Older kids: VG

Airplane! is a hilarious parody of airplane disaster films and movie disaster sagas in general. The pilots and crew of an airplane are poisoned, and passenger Robert Hays, a former flier himself, is the only one who can land it. Plot, of course, is irrelevant here. The only thing that matters is the non-stop barrage of gags, which just keep coming: bad ones, good ones, puns, one-liners, visual gags, and movie allusions. The cast, happily, delivers everything to deadpan perfection.

There is enough for everyone to laugh at here, but older kids will probably get more of the movie allusions (with a little help from their parents), which range from *From Here to Eternity* to *Saturday Night Fever*. Adults will get a kick out of actors like Stack, Bridges, and Nielsen parodying their own straight, serious cinematic and television personas. Nielsen, in particular, is a delight and began a whole new career as a comedian on the basis of his performance here.

Parents should note that there is some crude, raunchy stuff—fleeting nudity, swearing, and a quite literal interpretation of a classic phrase involving bodily waste hitting the fan. But given some of the ultra-low-brow stuff that passes for comedy today, this is positively restrained by comparison. And even as a parent, you may find yourself laughing too hard to care.

ALADDIN (1992)
Color, 90 minutes
Voice cast: Robin Williams, Scott Weinger, Brad Kane, Linda Larkin, Lea Salonga, Jonathan Freeman, Frank Welker, Gilbert Gottfried
Directors: John Musker and Ron Clements
Screenplay: Clements, Musker, Ted Elliott, and Terry Rossio
Animated feature/Musical
Rated G
Young children: OK   Older children: VG

A young thief named Aladdin, who lives by his wits on the streets of Baghdad, always one jump ahead of the authorities as he steals his meals, falls in love with the beautiful princess, Jasmine, but realizes he can never have her. Finding a magic lamp, he unleashes a Genie who grants him three wishes, and this enables him to masquerade as a prince and romance Jasmine. But he doesn't reckon with the schemes of the Sultan's evil wazir, Jaffar, who will stop at nothing to command the Genie, control the Princess, and rule all of Baghdad.

This is the Disney studio's fastest, funniest animated feature, inspired more by the tone and pace of the old Warner Bros. cartoons than the Disney classics of yore. It has romance and adventure enough to satisfy viewers of all ages, but its trump card is the performance of Robin Williams as the motormouthed Genie, whose stream of chatter is so fast, so funny that even adults may have a hard time absorbing it all.

The most impressionable young children may be frightened by the menacing cave where Aladdin must go to retrieve a treasure . . . and the hero's climactic battle with Jaffar. Otherwise, this is enormously entertaining Arabian Nights fare for all ages.

The great success of this film has led to a TV series and several feature-length sequels, released directly to the home-video market. They all have the same appeal as the initial film, if not its production quality or originality.

ALAKAZAM THE GREAT
(1961)
Color, 84 minutes
Cast: Voices of Frankie Avalon, Dodie Stevens, Jonathan Winters, Arnold Stang, Sterling Holloway, Peter Fernandez
Directors: Osamu Tezuka, Taiji Yabushita, and Daisaku Shirakawa
English-language director: Lee Kresel

Screenplay: Tezuka, Lou Rusoff, and Kresel
Animated feature/Musical
Rated G
Younger kids: OK   Older kids: No

This is a Japanese animated feature based on a Chinese folk tale, but in the preparation of an American release version much of its ethnicity was removed. What's left is a watchable, albeit confusing, cartoon feature that may hold a kid's attention for 84 minutes.

The lead character, a monkey named Alakazam, is a very unlikable chap for most of this episodic film. Crowned King of the Animals, Alakazam becomes arrogant and restless. Sent on a mission of repentance, the monkey king meets a series of new friends and conquers a series of evil characters, including a giant scorpion and an ogre chief. With his newfound wisdom, Alakazam is able to return the love of his faithful girlfriend, Dee-Dee, and live happily ever after.

The original widescreen version is the best way to see *Alakazam the Great,* even on video, and is much superior to the "flat" version widely available. The fantasy sequences are beautifully designed, and the film boasts superb animation and color.

Frankie Avalon sings for Alakazam, but veteran dubbing actor Peter Fernandez (*Speed Racer*) provides his speaking voice. Unfortunately, the rest of the great voice cast is wasted on this production.

ALASKA (1996)
Color, 110 minutes
Cast: Thora Birch, Vincent Kartheiser, Dirk Benedict, Charlton Heston, Duncan Fraser, Gordon Tootoosis

Director: Fraser C. Heston
Screenplay: Andy Burg and
  Scott Myers
Action-adventure
Rated PG
Younger kids: OK   Older kids:
  VG

Dirk Benedict plays a widowed
pilot-for-hire who lives with his
teenage children in Alaska. When
he doesn't return from a routine
air-delivery flight, his kids (Thora
Birch, Vincent Kartheiser) take
off on their own to search for him
in the snowy wilderness.

The story is corny and predictable, but the scenery and photography are spectacular, and some
of the action scenes, such as a
canoe ride down a waterfall, are
exhilarating (if a bit too intense
for the very young). The film also
features a cuddly polar bear cub
who is rescued by the two kids
from the clutches of a thoroughly
evil poacher (Charlton Heston,
the director's father) and becomes
their spiritual guide.

Though Heston gives a robust
performance as the villain (which
grownups may especially enjoy,
given his usual screen image as a
heroic figure), his shooting of the
cub's mother and stalking of the
children may also be too frightening for younger kids.

ALI BABA AND THE FORTY
THIEVES (1944)
Color, 87 minutes
Cast: Maria Montez, Jon Hall,
  Scotty Beckett, Turhan Bey,
  Kurt Katch, Andy Devine,
  Frank Puglia
Director: Arthur Lubin
Screenplay: Edmund Hartman
Action-adventure
Unrated

Younger kids: Good   Older
  kids: Good

After the Caliph of Baghdad is
murdered by the Mongol conqueror Hulagu Khan (Kurt Katch)
and his traitorous henchman Cas-
sim (Frank Puglia), his son Ali runs
away and is taken in by Old Baba
(Fortunio Bonanova) and his band
of noble thieves. The grown Ali
(Jon Hall) tries to regain his rightful throne with the aid of the forty
thieves . . . while romancing Khan's
princess daughter (Maria Montez).

Though pure Hollywood hokum,
this is an enjoyable Arabian Nights
fantasy the whole family will like;
the youngest viewers will be taken
in by the story and amazing sights,
and their parents may enjoy it as
high camp. As with most Hollywood fantasies of this period, it's
completely chaste, innocent, and
bloodless. Filmed in Technicolor at
its most opulent, even garish, its
very attractive stars were reunited
here after costarring in **Arabian
Nights**. And yes, you'll get to hear
someone utter the immortal words,
"Open, Sesame!"

Much of the film's action footage was so good that it was reused
for a 1965 remake called *Sword
of Ali Baba,* with a much older
Puglia playing the same role!

ALICE ADAMS (1935)
Black & white, 93 minutes
Cast: Katharine Hepburn, Fred
  MacMurray, Fred Stone,
  Evelyn Venable, Ann
  Shoemaker, Frank Albertson,
  Hattie McDaniel, Charlie
  Grapewin, Grady Sutton,
  Hedda Hopper
Director: George Stevens
Screenplay: Dorothy Yost,
  Mortimer Offner, and Jane

Murfin, based on the novel by Booth Tarkington
Drama/Literary classic
Unrated
Young children: OK   Older children: VG

Booth Tarkington's Pulitzer prize-winning novel emphasizes the innermost feelings of a young woman who wants to climb the social ladder. Katharine Hepburn is Alice, a girl embarrassed by her shabby home and aching to be accepted by the local society folk.

How much of a stretch is it for today's children to understand how Alice feels as she attends an elegant party in a two-year-old dress, escorted by her brother instead of a boyfriend, to grasp that even when a handsome, wealthy young man shows interest in her, she cannot see past her impoverished surroundings? Feelings of this sort are timeless. A kid whose toes are crowded into worn-out canvas sneakers knows how it feels when his or her classmates show up at school or in a playground in jaunty leather Nikes.

There is a moral to be learned from Tarkington's account: In order to fully evolve as a person, an individual must look beyond money, possessions, and social status.

Hepburn offers one of her most celebrated early-career performances, and the film has several particularly memorable scenes of Alice interacting with her family. Even so, young children might find the whole affair too downbeat to hold their interest.

ALICE IN WONDERLAND
(1951)
Color, 75 minutes
Cast: Voices of Kathryn Beaumont (Alice), Ed Wynn, Richard Haydn, Sterling Holloway, Jerry Colonna, Bill Thompson, Verna Felton, Pat O'Malley.
Directors: Clyde Geronimi, Hamilton Luske, and Wilfred Jackson
Screenplay: Winston Hibler, Bill Peet, Joe Rinaldi, Bill Cottrell, Joe Grant, Del Connell, Ted Sears, Erdman Penner, Milt Banta, Dick Kelsey, Dick Huemer, Tom Oreb, and John Walbridge
Animated feature/Fantasy
Not rated
Young children: VG   Older children: VG

The animated *Alice in Wonderland* takes its title and characters from the immortal work of Lewis Carroll, but adds a distinctive Disney touch.

Alice starts to daydream one lazy afternoon and finds herself following a white rabbit (who sings "I'm Late") down a rabbit hole and into a magical world where everything is topsy-turvy—especially logic, something on which Alice prides herself. Along the way she meets such colorful characters as the smoke ring–blowing caterpillar, The Mad Hatter (who invites her to a wacky tea party), the mad March Hare, the Dormouse, the wily Cheshire Cat, and the vindictive Queen of Hearts. After climbing back through a keyhole and out of the bizarre world of Wonderland, Alice awakens and discovers she's just had an astonishing dream.

Alice in Wonderland is one of Walt Disney's liveliest animated features, but not one of his most endearing. The characters are funny and memorable, but too strident to take to one's heart; we never really get to know Alice, except that she serves the role of straight man opposite The Mad Hatter and all the other bombastic characters in this rogue's gallery of crazies.

The saving grace of *Alice,* aside from its great sense of visual imagination—in the 1970s it was promoted, much like **Fantasia,** as a psychedelic experience!—is a fine array of songs, especially "I'm Late" and "The Unbirthday Song," and a rich gallery of voice talent. If The Mad Hatter sounds familiar to your kids, point out that it's the same man who later played Uncle Albert in **Mary Poppins,** Ed Wynn.

ALL CREATURES GREAT AND SMALL (1974)
Color, 92 minutes
Cast: Simon Ward, Anthony Hopkins, Lisa Harrow, Brian Stirner, Freddie Jones, T. P. McKenna, Brenda Bruce, John Collin, Jenny Runacre
Director: Claude Whatham
Screenplay: Hugh Whitemore, based on the book by James Herriot
Comedy-drama/Animal story
Unrated
Younger children: VG Older children: VG

James Herriot (Simon Ward) is a country veterinarian, fresh from school, who joins a practice with the Farnon brothers, the demanding Siegfried (Anthony Hopkins) and his irresponsible younger brother, Tristan (Brian Stirner). James goes from farm to farm, house to house, treating farm animals and pets, finding that often the owners are more unusual and interesting than the animals that belong to them.

Based on the best-selling memoirs of Alf Wight, who wrote several books under the name James Herriot, this film is quietly amusing and often touching. Because of the very popular public television series also based on Herriot's books, more people may be familiar with Christopher Timothy than Simon Ward as James and Robert Hardy rather than Anthony Hopkins as Siegfried. However, this film has the same warmth, the same true-to-life lessons, and the same gentle humor as the fondly remembered television show.

Followed by a sequel, *All Things Bright and Beautiful* (1979).

ALL DOGS GO TO HEAVEN (1989)
Color, 85 minutes
Cast: Voices of Burt Reynolds, Judith Barsi, Dom DeLuise, Vic Tayback, Charles Nelson Reilly, Melba Moore, Ken Page, Loni Anderson
Director: Don Bluth
Screenplay: David N. Weiss
Animated feature/Musical
Younger kids: OK Older kids: NG

All Dogs Go to Heaven is a strangely downbeat cartoon fantasy that could amuse younger kids while totally confusing older children and parents. Charlie, an unlovable mutt, is killed but finds a way to return to earth and make amends by helping an orphan girl. She has the ability to talk to animals, a talent that Charlie and his dachshund pal, Itchy, use to bet on horse races—in an effort to help the girl find parents.

The story is all over the map. Set in 1930s New Orleans, one moment there's a shoot-out involving ray guns, the next, a ludicrous musical number in the sewer, featuring a giant, singing King Gator. Will kids mind? Probably not, but the result is scarcely worthwhile. Excellent Don Bluth animation is wasted on this pointless film.

Followed by a more coherent theatrical sequel in 1996.

ALL DOGS GO TO HEAVEN 2 (1996)
Color, 82 minutes
Cast: Voices of Charlie Sheen, Sheena Easton, Dom DeLuise, Ernest Borgnine, George Hearn, Bebe Neuwirth, Wallace Shawn
Directors: Paul Sabella and Larry Leker
Screenplay: Arne Olsen, Kelly Ward, and Mark Young
Animated feature/Musical
Rated G
Younger kids: OK   Older kids: OK

A sequel that's much better, story-wise, than its predecessor. Deceased dogs Charlie and Itchy, living the high life in pooch heaven, are assigned to retrieve Gabriel's horn, which has fallen back to earth in a bungled burglary. Evil mutt Carface and demonic cat Red are the culprits in a wild scheme to keep all dogs penned inside Alcatraz. Amid all this, Charlie finds time to woo beautiful Irish setter Sasha with some forgettable songs by Barry Mann and Cynthia Weil.

Younger kids will enjoy the adventure and identify with young David, a little runaway whose endangerment provides Charlie with a chance to redeem himself. The animation is only serviceable but attractive, and the musical sequences stand out artistically with surrealist background designs. The devil character is quite exaggerated in design and movement, and thus nonthreatening to all but the most impressionable young children.

ALL OF ME (1984)
Color, 93 minutes
Cast: Steve Martin, Lily Tomlin, Victoria Tennant, Madolyn Smith, Richard Libertini, Dana Elcar, Jason Bernard, Selma Diamond
Director: Carl Reiner
Screenplay: Phil Alden Robinson and Henry Otek, based on the unpublished novel Me Too by Ed Davis
Comedy/Fantasy
Rated PG
Younger kids: OK   Older kids: VG

Steve Martin is Roger, an idealistic, jazz-playing lawyer whose body (or rather, half his body) becomes possessed by the spirit and soul of Edwina, a cantankerous millionairess. Despite some ribald scenes with Roger adjusting to having control over only half of his body (one in a bathroom where Roger is trying to urinate, and one in a romantic clinch with Tennant), this is an old-fashioned and surprisingly sweet-natured comedy with plot twists and characters that would be right at home in a screwball comedy from the 1930s.

The lawyer and the millionairess become more endearing and complex as the story moves along, and the situations manage to avoid the pitfalls of utter tastelessness. Martin provides a classic comic performance, with one deft physical flourish after another, and Tomlin is a perfect match for him.

Younger kids may not get the

humor of the piece or find it terribly interesting, but older kids should enjoy it.

THE AMAZING PANDA ADVENTURE (1995)
Color, 85 minutes
Cast: Ryan Slater, Stephen Lang, Yi Ding, Huang Fei
Director: Christopher Cain
Screenplay: Jeff Rothberg, Laurice Elehwany, John Wilcox, and Steven Allredge
Animal adventure
Rated PG
Young children: VG   Older children: VG

A 10-year-old American boy (Ryan Slater, younger brother of actor Christian Slater), goes to visit his dad in the Chinese province of Szechwan. There, the Wolong Nature Preserve's colony of panda bears is endangered by poachers, who steal the project's prize cub. It's kids to the rescue, as the boy joins forces with a young Chinese girl (who conveniently works as a translator) to rescue the baby.

Rich location filming is a big plus here, as is the invisible mix of real and make-believe pandas. Furthermore, on the trek nothing really horrible happens to the humans or to those under their protection.

And although the harsh realities of today's Chinese government are known to adults, those same inhumanities are not apparent here, in a movie that will be endearing to anyone who ever slept next to a teddy bear.

AMERICAN GRAFFITI (1973)
Color, 110 minutes
Cast: Richard Dreyfuss, Ronny Howard, Paul Le Mat, Charles Martin Smith, Cindy Williams, Candy Clark, Mackenzie Phillips, Wolfman Jack, Harrison Ford, Bo Hopkins, Kathy Quinlan, Suzanne Somers, Joe Spano, Debralee Scott
Director: George Lucas
Screenplay: Lucas, Willard Huyck, and Gloria Katz
Comedy
Rated PG
Younger kids: OK   Older kids: VG

A few years before a movie called **Star Wars** came along, director-writer George Lucas made this audience favorite about a group of graduating high schoolers searching for answers to life and love during one long night in Modesto, California, circa 1962. This remains one of the great evocations of "the age of innocence" before the Vietnam era, and beautifully captures the self-doubts and worries facing a generation as it makes its way into adulthood.

The structure is episodic, the tone wistful, nostalgic and yet tough all at the same time. As a result, certain nuances might be a bit too subtle for younger children. Older kids should be fascinated by the characters' escapades and realize that the characters' problems and concerns are no different from today's young adults'; only the decor has changed.

The film also provided a veritable who's who of today's top actors with breakthrough roles, along with a flood of soundtrack songs which perfectly evoke the era and—unlike most of today's films that use oldies—are intelligently, subtly woven into the action of the stories. (That's not accidental; Lucas plotted out his story with specific songs in mind for each sequence.)

AMERICAN HOT WAX (1978)
Color, 91 minutes.
Cast: Tim McIntire, Fran Drescher, Jay Leno, John Lehne, Laraine Newman, Jeff Altman, Chuck Berry, Jerry Lee Lewis, Screamin' Jay Hawkins, Moosie Drier
Director: Floyd Mutrux
Screenplay: John Kaye
Musical drama
Rated PG
Young children: OK   Older children: VG

This musical drama of the early years of rock 'n' roll offers up a solid, if somewhat idealized, blend of entertainment and nostalgia. Its screenplay, loosely based on fact, reconstructs the time period leading up to a rock 'n' roll performance organized by legendary disc jockey Alan Freed, who helped introduce the sounds of rhythm and blues to white teenage America in the 1950s.

Such first-generation rock legends as Chuck Berry, Jerry Lee Lewis, and Screamin' Jay Hawkins appear as themselves, and there are takeoffs of acts from Frankie Lymon and the Teenagers to Connie Francis. It seems as if every 1950s rock hit (with the possible exception of "The Purple People Eater") is included on the soundtrack. This is good-time music that young kids respond to just as their parents (and grandparents!) did when it was new.

Most intriguingly, *American Hot Wax* paints a complex portrait of Freed, the controversial daddy of the music. In a potent performance, Tim McIntire cap-

tures the essence of a lonely, solitary man who is harassed by the authorities because he spins Jackie Wilson in place of Pat Boone, "Tutti Frutti" instead of "Tennessee Waltz." In this regard, *American Hot Wax* is a revealing history of early rock 'n' roll, and a time when white teens' dancing to music performed by blacks was, to some, tantamount to a Communist conspiracy.

Viewers of all ages will get a kick out of seeing Jay Leno and Fran Drescher early—and we do mean early—in their careers.

AN AMERICAN IN PARIS
(1951)
Color, 113 minutes
Cast: Gene Kelly, Leslie Caron, Oscar Levant, Georges Guetary, Nina Foch
Director: Vincente Minnelli
Screenplay: Alan Jay Lerner
Musical
Unrated
Young children: OK   Older children: VG

This colorful, Academy Award-winning musical features Gene Kelly as a struggling American painter who romances a pert French shopgirl (the enchanting Leslie Caron) on the streets of Paris (re-created on the back lot at MGM). Despite the various romantic entanglements, the story is Production Code pure, which makes it appropriate for even the youngest viewer.

The "book" of this film, however, will seem boring and remote to younger viewers, who won't understand the idea of a wealthy woman "sponsoring" an impoverished artist or the moral dilemma he faces as a result.

What does work, for viewers of

any age, is the musical numbers, which are buoyant and delightful. When Gene Kelly performs "I Got Rhythm" with a group of French street kids it's impossible not to smile. ("By Strauss," on the other hand, with its gentle ribbing of Viennese waltzes, may simply be a mystery.)

The finale is the stuff of cinema legend: an ornate ballet in which art history comes alive in sequences designed in the styles of Van Gogh, Dufy, Toulouse-Lautrec, Renoir, Rousseau, and Utrillo. Youngsters not only will come away with an awareness of 19th-century French painting, but also will discover that ballet can be beautiful.

For his work in this film, Kelly was presented an honorary Academy Award "in appreciation of his versatility as actor, singer, director, and dancer, and specifically for his brilliant achievements in the art of choreography on film."

There may be other Kelly films that kids can relate to more easily, but if you start them off with just the musical highlights, they may become interested enough to want to learn some of the story, too. If that fails, revert to **Singin' in the Rain.**

AN AMERICAN TAIL (1986)
Color, 80 minutes
Cast: Voices of Phillip Glasser (Fievel), Dom DeLuise, Madeline Kahn, Christopher Plummer, Cathianne Blore, John Finnegan, Nehemiah Persoff
Director: Don Bluth
Screenplay: Judy Freudberg and Tony Geiss
Animated feature/Musical
Rated G

Younger kids: OK   Older kids: OK

This animated parable about a family of Russian-Jewish mice immigrating to U.S. at the turn of the century will intrigue younger kids, who will clearly identify with lead character, Fievel Mousekewitz. Separated from his parents during a storm at sea, the little mouse gets a true American experience as he wanders the back alleys of New York in search of his parents. Meeting a series of multi-ethnic friends and foes, Fievel wanders from one episode to another until a tear-filled reunion with his family.

The New York characters Fievel befriends are stereotyped caricatures, to say the least: Henri (with an excellent song "Never Say Never," sung by Christopher Plummer), a French pigeon, Italian street mouse Tony Toponi, con artist Warren T. Rat, and a vegetarian cat named Tiger (Dom DeLuise). Don Bluth provides his usual superior visuals, and the songs by Barry Mann, Cynthia Weil, and James Horner are excellent—including the hit "Somewhere Out There"—but the story is surprisingly predictable and doesn't seem to know how to come to a satisfying conclusion. (There are at least two false endings.)

This was the first animated effort of Steven Spielberg's Amblimation and was followed by a sequel, **An American Tail: Fievel Goes West.**

AN AMERICAN TAIL: FIEVEL GOES WEST (1991)
Color, 74 minutes
Cast: Voices of Phillip Glasser (Fievel), James Stewart, Dom DeLuise, Amy Irving, Jon

23

Lovitz, John Cleese, Nehemiah Persoff

Directors: Phil Nibbelink and Simon Wells

Screenplay: Flint Dille

Animated feature/Musical

Rated G

Younger kids: OK Older kids: NG

This lightly plotted film picks up where *An American Tail* left off. After two years in New York, circa 1887, and having discovered that the streets are *not* "paved with cheese," the Mousekewitz family decides to move west. There, villainous Cat R. Waul lures them into his evil schemes. Little Fievel foils his plans with the help of his vegetarian cat friend, Tiger, and an over-the-hill canine marshal named Wylie Burp.

All the western clichés are enacted in full animation (the O.K. Corral shoot-out finale, Tiger captured by "Indian" prairie dogs, etc.). The film has a faster pace than the original and some nice musical numbers, plus the added delight of hearing Jimmy Stewart as the old but still valiant Wylie Burp. As before, this is aimed mostly at younger kids, who will identify with young Fievel's personality and actions.

Followed by a TV series (also available on video), *Fievel's American Tales.*

AMISTAD (1997)
Color, 152 minutes
Cast: Morgan Freeman, Anthony Hopkins, Matthew McConaughey, Nigel Hawthorne, Djimon Hounsou, David Paymer, Pete Postlethwaite, Stellan Skarsgård, Anna Paquin, Tomas Milian, Austin Pendleton

Director: Steven Spielberg

Screenplay: David Franzoni

Historical drama

Rated R

Younger kids: No Older kids: OK, with caution

Steven Spielberg's first "serious" follow-up to the Holocaust epic **Schindler's List** tackled an equally provocative and daring subject: the 1839 mutiny on the Spanish slave ship *La Amistad*, in which fifty-three African slaves, led by the imposing Cinque (Hounsou) revolted and took over the vessel. Once apprehended, the slaves were put on trial in the American colonies and defended by, first, a real estate attorney (McConaughey) and later by former president John Quincy Adams (Hopkins), who successfully argued the case before the Supreme Court.

The film is scaled to be a masterpiece, and the scenes depicting the initial revolt and the middle passage (the journey that the slaves made from Africa to the Caribbean) are fierce, bloody, and wrenching, unforgettably conveying the physical degradations suffered by the slaves. These scenes are unquestionably too intense for young children to watch . . . and in fact will cause stomach knots in viewers of any age.

The courtroom drama, however, is far less compelling; we learn precious little about the slaves' point of view or the psychological effects that slavery has upon them. The slaves—particularly Cinque, impressively played by Hounsou—are portrayed with dignity, and even allowed to speak in Mende, their native African language, but the film dwells upon matters of property and the intellectual definitions of slavery, which are of historical interest but may well bore younger (and older) kids. It's frustrating that a film with so many dramatic high points can also have so many lulls.

Still, even with its faults, this is a worthy film about an oft-forgotten time in our history.

ANASTASIA (1997)
Color, 94 minutes
Cast: Voices of Meg Ryan (Anastasia), John Cusack, Kelsey Grammer, Christopher Lloyd, Angela Lansbury, Hank Azaria, Bernadette Peters
Directors: Don Bluth and Gary Goldman
Screenplay: Susan Gauthier, Bruce Graham, Bob Tzudiker, and Noni White, based on the play by Marcelle Maurette as adapted by Guy Bolton, and the screenplay of Arthur Laurents
Animated feature/Musical
Rated G
Younger kids: OK   Older kids: OK

Although it takes some major liberties with the historic facts upon which the story is based, Fox Animation's *Anastasia* is an entertaining and ambitious cartoon musical, one of the best from former Disney animator Don Bluth (**An American Tail**).

Girls between the ages of 7 and 12 will particularly enjoy this "rags to riches" story of an orphan named Anya who is determined to learn her true identity. In Russia of the early 20th century, Anya falls in with two rogues, Dimitri and Vladimir, who hope to groom the girl and pass her off as the long-lost Princess Anastasia, only survivor of the Romanoff family. Evil sorcerer Rasputin learns that the girl actually *is* the Princess Anastasia and tries to destroy her, leading to some exciting action sequences, particularly one on a runaway locomotive. The emotional climax comes when Anastasia must prove herself to her grandmother, the Dowager Empress. Mild comedy relief comes in the form of two sidekicks, Anya's pup, Pooka, and Rasputin's bat, Bartok.

Cut from the same cloth as many recent Disney features, *Anastasia* has songs by Lynn Ahrens and Stephen Flaherty (who wrote the score for Broadway's *Ragtime*), beautiful CinemaScope landscapes and full character animation. While there's nothing "revolutionary" about *Anastasia* and nothing particularly memorable either, it has the right stuff to entertain kids. (Only their parents might question some of the warping of history, or the fact that the leading characters sound awfully contemporary for a story that takes place in the 1920s.)

Older children might even be curious enough to want to learn more about the real story of Anastasia.

ANCHORS AWEIGH (1945)
Color, 140 minutes
Cast: Frank Sinatra, Kathryn Grayson, Gene Kelly, Jose Iturbi, Dean Stockwell, Pamela Britton, Billy Gilbert, Rags Ragland, Edgar Kennedy, Grady Sutton, Henry Armetta
Director: George Sidney
Screenplay: Isobel Lennart, based on a story by Natalie Marcin

Musical
Unrated
Young children: OK   Older
    children: OK

This bright World War II–era musical follows the antics—romantic and otherwise—of two sailors on shore leave in Hollywood. One (Frank Sinatra) is gawky, grinning, and girl-shy, while the other (Gene Kelly) is a Don Juan. The story takes many detours, some engaging (as the sailors befriend and baby-sit a pretty girl's kid brother, played by Dean Stockwell) and some strained.

Youngsters will delight as Kelly, in a cleverly devised, technically dazzling sequence, dances with an animated Jerry (of Tom and Jerry cartoon fame). The sheer technique of this number may have been surpassed in recent years, but not its infectious spirit of fun.

Kids also should savor the zany contributions of three wonderful (but mostly forgotten) character comedians who brightened scores of films during Hollywood's Golden Age: Billy Gilbert, Edgar Kennedy, and Grady Sutton.

And anyone could understand why the boyish Frank Sinatra was so appealing at this time, when bobby-soxers swooned over him; just watch him sing the wistful "I Fall in Love Too Easily."

Alas, *Anchors Aweigh* is weighed down by too much plot, much of it just plain silly. But with the marvels of video, you can fast-forward to "the good stuff" and still derive great pleasure from its many wonderful musical moments.

ANDRE (1994)
Color, 94 minutes
Cast: Keith Carradine, Tina
    Majorino, Chelsea Field,
    Shane Meier, Aidan
    Pendleton, Keith Szarabajka,
    Joshua Jackson; voice of
    Annette O'Toole
Director: George Miller
Screenplay: Dana Baratta, based
    on the book *A Seal Called
    Andre* by Harry Goodridge
    and Lew Dietz
Animal adventure
Rated PG
Younger children: VG   Older
    children: VG

Andre is a delightful family outing, set in the 1960s, about a harbormaster (Keith Carradine) in Rockport, Maine, who lives in a seaside home with his wife, three children, and a passel of animals. The youngest daughter, Toni (played by the adorable Tina Majorino), has trouble relating to other children and gets along much better with her pets. But even she is unprepared for the arrival one day of a seal who's been separated from his family. Dad agrees that they can nurse the seal, Andre, back to health, but when he's well, Toni can't bear to let him go. Meanwhile, a brutish fisherman keeps needling Carradine because he believes that seals are his natural enemy. In the end, it's Andre himself who decides his fate.

Andre dodges many of the clichés of animal stories and has more than a few surprises in store for young viewers . . . along with the irresistible and often hilarious antics of its aquatic star, played by Tory the Sea Lion. The very real human conflicts that arise over the protection of the seal give the story some substance, as well.

26

To that end, there are some language and violence along the way that merit a PG rating instead of G.

Believe it or not, this is based on a true story; be sure to have your kids watch the closing credits, when actual home movies of Andre and the family that took care of him are shown.

THE ANDROMEDA STRAIN
(1971)
Color, 130 minutes
Cast: Arthur Hill, David Wayne, James Olson, Kate Reid, Paula Kelly
Director: Robert Wise
Screenplay: Nelson Gidding, from Michael Crichton's novel
Science fiction/Drama
Rated G
Younger kids: Too cerebral   Older kids: OK

When a virus carried to Earth by a returning probe kills everyone in a small town except a baby and an old man, a team of scientists is isolated in an underground complex to find a way of preventing the spread of the deadly disease.

The story goes on too long, and the ending is a disappointment, but it's very carefully worked out and features strong production values and good performances.

Children who are interested in science might well find themselves caught up in the occasionally suspenseful plot. The unusual musical score by Gil Melle is a plus.

ANGELS IN THE OUTFIELD
(1951)
Black & white, 99 minutes
Cast: Paul Douglas, Janet Leigh, Keenan Wynn, Donna Corcoran, Spring Byington, Ellen Corby, Lewis Stone, Bruce Bennett, Marvin Kaplan, Jeff Richards; voice of James Whitmore
Director: Clarence Brown
Screenplay: Dorothy Kingsley and George Wells, based on a story by Richard Conlin
Comedy/Fantasy/Sports
Unrated
Younger kids: Good   Older kids: VG

A delightful comic fantasy that was said to be President Eisenhower's favorite movie, this is about the Pittsburgh Pirates baseball team and how it goes from worst to first when the prayers of an orphan (Donna Corcoran) are answered by the Angel Gabriel and his team of invisible all-stars. Paul Douglas gives a gem of a performance as the team's irascible manager, whose hilariously foul-mouthed tirades are translated into harmless gibberish, and Janet Leigh is charming as a suspicious reporter whose stories spark an investigation by the baseball commissioner.

Clarence Brown's lighthearted direction strikes just the right balance between heavenly whimsy and cynical comedy. The magic here is that we never actually see the angels who help the baseball players—we must use our imagination. (The 1994 remake, needless to say, was heavy on special effects.)

There are some funny cameos by the likes of baseball greats Ty Cobb and Joe DiMaggio, as well as Bing Crosby, who was part owner of the real Pirates at the time.

ANGELS IN THE OUTFIELD (1994)

Color, 102 minutes
Cast: Danny Glover, Tony Danza, Brenda Fricker, Ben Johnson, Joseph Gordon-Levitt, Milton Davis, Jr., Christopher Lloyd, Jay O. Sanders
Director: William Dear
Screenplay: Holly Goldberg Sloan, based on the script by Dorothy Kingsley and George Wells
Comedy/Fantasy/Sports
Rated PG
Younger kids: Good   Older kids: VG

This sentimental remake of the much subtler 1951 film is a perfectly pleasant minor-league fantasy, although it's been thoroughly Disneyfied in every respect—from the use of the Disney-owned California Angels baseball team and the heavy-handed special effects to the shameless tearjerking involving foster kids, coldhearted parents and dying players.

The story is essentially the same as the original, about a lousy baseball team that gets divine assistance, but instead of the invisible angels of the first version, we get to see them strut their mischievous stuff via digital wizardry, led by a mugging Christopher Lloyd as the chief angel.

The performances, like the movie, are corny but good-natured, headed by Danny Glover as the stereotypical "gruff but lovable" manager, whose salty language earns the film its PG-rating, and young Joseph Gordon-Levitt (who later starred in the TV series *3rd Rock from the Sun*), who's quite appealing as the 11-year-old whose prayers about both his family and his team are ultimately answered.

ANNE OF AVONLEA (1987)

Color, 230 minutes
Cast: Megan Follows, Colleen Dewhurst, Jonathan Crombie, Dame Wendy Hiller
Director: Kevin Sullivan
Screenplay: Kevin Sullivan, based on the books by Lucy Maud Montgomery
Comedy-drama/Literary classic
Unrated
Younger children: OK   Older children: VG

Megan Follows returns to play an older Anne Shirley, who continues getting into scrapes, but remains as enchanting as ever. As she grows up and learns new lessons about life, Anne struggles with love and her own unpredictable temper. In her quest to become a teacher, she leaves Avonlea for a while but continues to spar with her archenemy and love interest, Gilbert Blythe (Jonathan Crombie).

Based on several of Lucy Maud Montgomery's sequels to **Anne of Green Gables,** this production is true to the spirit of the books. Anne Shirley is one of the great female role models in children's literature, and all of the episodes in this series do her justice. Set in turn-of-the-century Canada, this thoughtful and beautiful production is flawless. Children who have read the books will love the video of this and its predecessor. Children who fall in love with these videos will want to read the books and learn even more about Anne's adventures.

ANNE OF GREEN GABLES
(1934)
Black & white, 79 minutes
Cast: Anne Shirley, Tom Brown, O. P. Heggie, Helen Westley, Sara Haden
Director: George Nicholls, Jr.
Screenplay: Sam Mintz, based on the novel by Lucy Maud Montgomery
Comedy-drama/Literary classic
Unrated
Young children: VG Older children: VG

Lucy Maud Montgomery's spunky, red-haired young heroine comes to life in this retelling of the famous children's novel. This is a thoroughly enjoyable, heartfelt version of orphan Anne's story as she is transferred from an asylum in Nova Scotia to Green Gables, which is the Prince Edward Island farm of Marilla and Matthew Cuthbert, an elderly brother and sister. Since the crotchety sister had "ordered" a boy, she constantly threatens to send poor pig-tailed Anne back to the institution, and only through her natural charm does Anne win a home on the Cuthbert farm.

While most children will prefer the 1985 made-for-television movie for its color, detail, and beautiful scenery, many also will want to take a look at this early version, which offers fine entertainment, with wonderful performances and equally beautiful location settings—even if they are photographed in "old-fashioned" black-and-white!

Incidentally, the delightful young actress who plays the leading character had been using the stage name Dawn O'Day, but with this film assumed the name of Anne Shirley (the name of her character in the story) for the rest of her life.

In 1940, RKO produced a follow-up based on Montgomery's novel *Anne of Windy Poplars*, in which Shirley also starred. It isn't nearly as good as the first film.

ANNE OF GREEN GABLES
(1985)
Color, 199 minutes
Cast: Megan Follows, Colleen Dewhurst, Richard Farnsworth, Patricia Hamilton, Schuyler Grant, Jonathan Crombie
Director: Kevin Sullivan
Screenplay: Sullivan and Joe Wiesenfeld, based on the book by Lucy Maud Montgomery
Comedy-drama/Literary classic
Unrated
Younger children: OK Older children: VG, particularly for girls

When dreamy, impulsive orphan Anne Shirley is adopted unwillingly by brother and sister Matthew and Marilla Cuthbert—who really wanted a boy who would work for them—she changes their lives. Despairing of her red hair and freckles, longing for a "kindred spirit," Anne creates accidental havoc as she, the Cuthberts, and the community adjust to each other. She dyes her hair—green—gets her best friend drunk, and grows into an exceptional young lady.

Set in the small Canadian town of Avonlea on Prince Edward Island, this period piece is a faithful adaptation of the beloved Lucy Maud Montgomery novel.

As Anne, Megan Follows manages to bring this literary character to life just the way devoted readers have imagined her. In fact, the entire cast is ideal: Colleen Dewhurst as the gruff Marilla, Richard Farnsworth as her soft-hearted brother Matthew, Schuyler Grant as Anne's kindred spirit, Diana, and Jonathan Crombie as her nemesis, Gilbert Blythe. Although younger children will enjoy Anne's wild adventures, sad moments at the end may be tough. A delight from beginning to end.

Sequel: **Anne of Avonlea.**

ANNE (1982)
Color, 128 minutes
Cast: Albert Finney, Carol
  Burnett, Aileen Quinn,
  Bernadette Peters, Tim Curry,
  Ann Reinking, Geoffrey
  Holder, Edward Herrmann,
  Lois DeBanzie, Peter Marshall
Director: John Huston
Screenplay: Carol Sobieski,
  based on the stage production
  by Thomas Meehan, Charles
  Strouse, and Martin Charnin
  inspired by Harold Gray's
  comic strip *Little Orphan
  Annie*
Musical
Rated PG
Young children: VG Older
  children: OK

The Broadway musical *Annie* has become a staple of theater groups and large-scale touring companies, which is only natural, since it's ideal family entertainment and has served as many youngsters' first exposure to the wonders of a Broadway musical.

Alas, the movie version is a heavy-handed, ill-conceived, badly rewritten adaptation of that show.

Aileen Quinn is a fine choice in the title role of a Depression-era foundling who survives the "hard-knock life" at Miss Hannigan's

orphanage to find refuge (and a dreamlike existence) in the palatial home of billionaire Daddy Warbucks. Albert Finney, best known for his varied dramatic performances on stage and film, is warm and engaging here, and even gets to sing and dance.

But the talented Carol Burnett plays the mean Miss Hannigan with too much acid (which can work on stage, where a caricature is acceptable). When she and her criminal cohorts (Bernadette Peters, Tim Curry) sing about landing on "Easy Street," we simply don't care.

Worst of all, a melodramatic cliffhanger finale puts Annie in real peril, has Miss Hannigan suddenly (and unbelievably) changing her tune, and offers no real satisfaction.

Younger kids may enjoy *Annie* just the same, with its colorful characters and sets, and lively songs. (Parents will have to identify Franklin D. Roosevelt and explain other references to life in the 1930s.) Older kids could likely have the same complaints as their parents and feel that all the happy goings-on are hollow underneath.

Because of the villainy, and the jeopardy that befalls Annie, the film is rated PG and could cause some mild upset in the youngest viewers.

ANTZ (1998)
Color, 82 minutes
Cast: Voices of Woody Allen,
  Sharon Stone, Sylvester
  Stallone, Gene Hackman,
  Danny Glover, Jennifer Lopez,
  Christopher Walken, Anne
  Bancroft, Dan Aykroyd, Jane
  Curtin, John Mahoney
Directors: Eric Darnell and Tim
  Johnson

Screenplay: Todd Alcott, Chris Weitz, and Paul Weitz
Animated feature/Adventure
Rated PG
Young children: OK, with caution   Older kids: VG

This delightful, imaginative computer-animated feature film tells the story of Z (with the voice and comic personality of Woody Allen), a worker ant who feels insignificant. A chance meeting with Princess Bala (Sharon Stone) inspires him to do bigger, better things with his life . . . and to do what ants are trained not to do, namely, buck the system. This interferes with the nefarious plans of General Mandible (Gene Hackman), who cares nothing about the ant colony and only about his quest for power.

With a winning screenplay, ideal voice talent, and an eyeful of sights we've never yet seen on screen, *Antz* is great fun from start to finish. It relies on themes and story principles that have never failed yet—rooting for the underdog, breaking the rules to do what you believe, etc.

The film was not conceived with a kiddie audience in mind; much of its humor will go over youngsters' heads, especially Z's asides and Woody Allen–ish banter. But more important, there is real violence in a key battle scene between ants and fearsome-looking termites, which may upset the youngest members of your family.

APOLLO 13 (1995)
Color, 139 minutes
Cast: Tom Hanks, Bill Paxton, Kevin Bacon, Gary Sinise, Ed Harris, Kathleen Quinlan, Miko Hughes, David Andrews, Chris Ellis, Joe Spano, Xander Berkeley, Marc McClure, Tracy Reiner, Brett Cullen; Walter Cronkite (narrator)
Director: Ron Howard
Screenplay: William Broyles, Jr., and Art Reinert, from the book *Lost Moon* by Jim Lovell and Jeffrey Kluger
Drama/Space travel
Rated PG
Younger kids: VG   Older kids: VG

Apollo 13 is an engrossing recreation of the 1970 Apollo moon mission, which was cut short by an oxygen tank explosion and nearly ended in tragedy for astronauts Jim Lovell (Hanks), Fred Haise (Paxton), and Jack Swigert (Bacon). Director Ron Howard keeps patriotic sentiments to a minimum (for the most part) and concentrates instead on the tension involved in Mission Control's efforts to figure out the best way to return the men home safely.

As history and as drama, *Apollo 13* is irresistible, with an excellent ensemble cast and an often documentarylike feel, which heightens the suspense. Kids interested in science will naturally thrill to the absolutely convincing period detail and special effects, not to mention the scenes inside the space capsule, which were filmed aboard an Air Force plane in actual weightless conditions. They will also appreciate the portrayals of the Houston technicians and crew members who work together as a team and the various improvised plans they devise to help the astronauts—a triumph of brain power under the worst imaginable pressure.

The other interesting, and sobering, element of the film is the public's almost complete indifference to the Apollo 13 mission, even though it took place a mere eight months after man had landed on the noon. (This is depicted most forcefully in a scene where NASA execs reveal that, unknown to the astronauts, a live satellite feed inside the capsule is not being carried by any of the networks.) Only when the astronauts are in danger does the public show any interest, a horrible irony given today's blasé attitude toward NASA and the space program, except in tragic situations like the Challenger explosion or unusual ones, like the return of John Glenn to space.

Apollo 13 is a great movie that also serves as a superb history lesson.

AN ARABIAN ADVENTURE (1979)
Color, 98 minutes
Cast: Christopher Lee, Milo O'Shea, Puneet Sira, Oliver Tobias, Emma Samms, Peter Cushing, Mickey Rooney, Capucine
Director: Kevin Connor
Screenplay: Brian Hayles
Action-adventure/Fantasy
Rated G
Younger kids: Good   Older kids: VG

All of the familiar Arabian Nights elements are assembled in this lavishly mounted British-made fantasy of Old Baghdad, including flying carpets, evil sorcerers, a genie in a bottle, an imprisoned princess, and a street waif with a scene-stealing pet monkey. Christopher Lee stars as the wicked caliph Alquazar, who keeps his good "double" trapped in a mirror while searching for a magical

rose with the power to make its owner omnipotent.

The film borrows elements from a number of others, including **The Thief of Bagdad, The Wizard of Oz, Snow White and the Seven Dwarfs,** and even **Star Wars,** but the special effects are convincing and the cast seems to be having a ball, especially Mickey Rooney as an Oz-like wizard.

Good clean fun for young and old alike.

ARABIAN KNIGHT (1995)
Color, 72 minutes
Cast: Voices of Vincent Price, Matthew Broderick, Jennifer Beals, Eric Bogosian, Jonathan Winters, Clive Revill, Toni Collette
Director: Richard Williams
Screenplay: Williams and Margaret French
Animated feature/Musical
Rated G
Younger kids: OK   Older kids: OK

Spectacular stylized animation overwhelms this modest tale of a love-struck cobbler caught up in an adventure in ancient Baghdad. Evil magician ZigZag (a wonderful vocal performance by Vincent Price) has eyes for Princess Yum-Yum and her father's kingdom, and plots to snare them both with the help of a flea-bitten Thief and a horde of loutish monsters.

Ornate visuals take precedence over story, and kids may find the artistic details fascinating (tiny fleas intricately animated around the Thief, M. C. Escher–like background paintings, etc.). But while the film is pleasant enough to watch, it has no endearing characters and is easily forgotten, despite all the obvious effort that went into it. In production for over two decades, the film was taken out of director Williams' hands in its final year and the soundtrack was rewritten and re-voiced (except for Price). The Thief was originally a silent character; now he chatters away nonstop, with no rhyme or reason. Similarly, the musical sequences feel shoehorned into the production.

ARABIAN NIGHTS (1942)
Color, 86 minutes
Cast: Jon Hall, Maria Montez, Sabu, Leif Erickson, Turhan Bey, Billy Gilbert, Shemp Howard, John Qualen, Thomas Gomez
Director: John Rawlins
Screenplay: Michael Hogan and True Boardman
Action-adventure
Unrated
Younger kids: OK   Older kids: OK

Arabian Nights is definitely not faithful to its source, but it *is* entertaining escapism, with Jon Hall as the heir to the throne of the Caliph, who's ousted by his evil half-brother (Leif Erickson) and fights back with the aid of the beautiful Scheherazade (Maria Montez), his loyal servant (Sabu), and the elderly Aladdin (John Qualen) and Sinbad (Shemp Howard).

When the bright, charismatic Indian boy Sabu left England after making **The Thief of Bagdad**, and completed **The Jungle Book** in Hollywood for producer Alexander Korda, he was signed by Universal Pictures to costar in this deft, fast-moving blend of romance, action, and comedy. No longer the star, he was now the featured sidekick for Hall and Montez, who became a popular team in a string of kitschy 1940s costume dramas and were dubbed "The King and Queen of Technicolor." This was their first screen teaming.

This film and its follow-ups were no match for the dazzling *Thief of Bagdad,* but they remain light, amusing entertainment that the whole family can enjoy.

Comedy relief, incidentally, is provided by comic veteran Billy Gilbert and by Shemp Howard, who later joined his brother Moe as one of the Three Stooges.

ARACHNOPHOBIA (1990)
Color, 109 minutes
Cast: Jeff Daniels, Harley Jane Kozak, John Goodman, Julian Sands
Director: Frank Marshall
Screenplay: Don Jakoby and Wesley Strick
Science Fiction/Thriller
Rated PG-13
Younger kids: No   Older Kids: Good

A newly discovered species of spiders ends up in a typical small American town, where it quickly interbreeds with the local population, producing scads of nasty hybrids. The local doctor, Jeff Daniels, who suffers from the phobia of the title (fear of spiders), has to take on the creepy crawlers with the help of a gung ho exterminator, John Goodman.

This fast-paced comic thriller may be too intense for younger children (hence the PG-13 rating), but the older ones should have a great time, especially if they can demonstrate to their squirming parents that *they* aren't afraid of those icky bugs. But they might leave the lights on that night. . . .

THE ARISTOCATS (1970)
Color, 78 minutes
Cast: Voices of Eva Gabor, Phil Harris, Sterling Holloway, Scatman Crothers, Paul Winchell, Lord Tim Hudson, Vito Scotti, Thurl Ravenscroft, Nancy Kulp, Pat Buttram, George Lindsay, Monica Evans, Carole Shelley, Hermione Baddeley
Director: Wolfgang Reitherman
Screenplay: Larry Clemmons, Vance Gerry, Ken Anderson, Frank Thomas, Eric Cleworth, Julius Svendsen, and Ralph Wright, based on a story by Tom McGowan and Tom Rowe
Animated feature
Rated G
Younger kids: VG   Older kids: VG

The Aristocats was the first animated feature to be made by the Disney studio following the death of Walt Disney (although he had reportedly given his approval to the project), and it's a pretty entertaining and enjoyable one by 1970s standards. Set in 1910 Paris, the story centers on an eccentric old lady who wills her entire estate to her beloved pet cat, Duchess, and Duchess' three kittens. Edgar, the scheming butler who's next in line for the inheritance, catnaps the animals and dumps them into a river in the French countryside, but they're rescued by a carefree alley cat named Thomas O'Malley, who falls in love with Duchess and helps her regain her fortune. Along the way, the high-class felines have a high old time with the swinging Thomas and his wild pals, including Scat Cat and his jazz band.

The animation might be a cut below the finest Disney cartoons, while the story is highly reminiscent of **Lady and the Tramp** (1955), with the cultured Duchess falling for the streetwise Thomas, as well as **One Hundred and One Dalmatians** (1961), transposing the kidnapped animal plot from England to France, but kids will be having too much fun to care, particularly during the high-spirited "Ev'rybody Wants to Be a Cat" musical number.

The characters are amusing and the voice characterizations are all top-notch, especially Phil Harris (the voice of Baloo the Bear from **The Jungle Book**) as the rakish Thomas, Sterling Holloway (the original Winnie the Pooh) as a friendly mouse named Roquefort, and Scatman Crothers (a worthy last-minute replacement for Louis Armstrong) as the hipster Scat Cat.

THE ARRIVAL (1996)
Color, 109 minutes
Cast: Charlie Sheen, Ron Silver, Lindsay Crouse, Teri Polo, Richard Schiff, Tony T. Johnson, Leon Rippy, Buddy Joe Hooker
Director: David Twohy
Screenplay: David Twohy
Science fiction/Mystery
Rated PG-13
Younger kids: Too intense   Older kids: Good, but scary

A dedicated radio astronomer with the wonderful name of Zane Ziminski (Sheen) discovers evidence that aliens have infiltrated the human race. In Mexico, he encounters a botanist (Lindsay

34

Crouse) who's concerned that the planet's climate is changing. It turns out their concerns have the same source: aliens are trying to alter Earth's atmosphere to suit their own race. That this will wipe out humanity is of no concern to them.

Tense, amusing, and very well written, *The Arrival* will please adults as well as older kids; it's an intelligent updating of themes from science fiction movies of the 1950s. The last third is more slow paced than the rest of the film, but the climax and a surprise ending are satisfying.

Most of the effects are excellent, particularly for a modestly budgeted movie, and the actors are well cast and convincing. The scares (along with a smattering of adult language) are potent enough to have earned this a PG-13 rating, so proceed with caution.

AROUND THE WORLD IN 80 DAYS (1956)
Color, 167 minutes
Cast: David Niven, Shirley MacLaine, Cantinflas, Robert Newton, and an all-star cast
Director: Michael Anderson
Screenplay: S. J. Perelman, John Farrow, and James Poe, based on the novel by Jules Verne
Adventure/Comedy
Rated G
Younger kids: Good   Older kids: Good

Mike Todd's Oscar-winning super-production of Jules Verne's novel is a prime example of the kind of epic movie "they just don't make anymore," and offers cameos by an incredible array of more than 40 guest stars, with everyone from Buster Keaton and Marlene Dietrich to Frank Sinatra and John Gielgud (a novelty that will obviously be of greater interest to parents than children).

David Niven stars as Phileas Fogg, a Victorian gentleman who makes a bet that he can go around the world in eighty days and sets off with his servant Passepartout (Cantinflas). By train, boat, balloon, stagecoach, rickshaw, and even elephant, they travel to France, Spain (where Passepartout fights a bull), India (where they rescue a princess, played by Shirley MacLaine, who joins them on their adventures), Hong Kong, and America (where their train is attacked by Indians).

Though the film hasn't aged very well, it still has enough comedy, action, and spectacular travelogue-style photography (courtesy of the 70mm Todd-AO widescreen process) to provide three hours of fine family entertainment. Some of the globe-trotting escapades and the irresistible race to beat the clock are timeless elements that may stay in young viewers' minds for years to come.

AT SWORD'S POINT (1952)
Color, 81 minutes
Cast: Cornel Wilde, Maureen O'Hara, Robert Douglas, Dan O'Herlihy, Alan Hale, Jr., Robert Douglas, Gladys Cooper
Director: Lewis Allen
Screenplay: Joseph Hoffman, based on a story by Aubrey Wisberg and Jack Pollexfen
Swashbuckler/Action-adventure
Unrated
Younger kids: Good   Older kids: Good

Cornel Wilde makes a dashing son of D'Artagnan in this well-paced swashbuckler with a novel twist: the main characters are the children of the original four musketeers, including a daughter (Maureen O'Hara). The story centers on a plot by a scheming duke (Robert Douglas) to seize the throne from the aging queen (Gladys Cooper), who rallies the junior musketeers to come to her defense.

There's plenty of action and sword fights, while the depiction of O'Hara's character as an equal who wields a mean sword, rather then being just another damsel in distress, should especially appeal to young girls.

AUNTIE MAME (1958)
Color, 143 minutes
Cast: Rosalind Russell, Forrest Tucker, Coral Browne, Fred Clark, Roger Smith, Peggy Cass, Joanna Barnes, Patric Knowles, Pippa Scott, Lee Patrick, Willard Waterman
Director: Morton DaCosta
Screenplay: Betty Comden and Adolph Green, based on the novel by Patrick Dennis and the play by Jerome Lawrence and Robert E. Lee
Comedy
Unrated
Younger kids: OK   Older kids: VG

Rosalind Russell gives the performance of her life, re-creating her famous stage role as a madcap Roaring Twenties eccentric who lives life to the fullest. Based on Patrick Dennis's autobiographical novel, Mame's colorful antics are seen through the eyes of her orphaned 10-year-old nephew, Patrick, whose life becomes a whirlwind of parties with his Auntie's bohemian friends, much to the consternation of the conservative trustee (Fred Clark) of the boy's estate.

As the years progress, Mame perseveres through the stock market crash and the Depression by marrying a Southern oil man (Forrest Tucker), which inspires the film's funniest scene, in her participation in a fox hunt, and later hilariously breaks up Patrick's engagement to a snooty Connecticut debutante.

Though the film is a sparkling comedy that should appeal to the whole family, it also deals with some serious issues (albeit in a humorous way), such as the anti-Semitism of Patrick's fiancée and her "really top-drawer" family.

Auntie Mame is a wonderful character whose motto is "Life is a banquet, and most poor suckers are starving to death." Younger kids may find this too long to endure; older kids should enjoy being introduced to her; they may find themselves wishing they had someone like her in their lives.

Auntie Mame was later turned into the Broadway musical *Mame*, which was filmed in 1974 with Lucille Ball in the title role. Although everybody loves Lucy, the film is not very good.

AU REVOIR, LES ENFANTS (1987)
Color, 103 minutes
Cast: Gaspard Manesse, Raphael Fejto, Francine Racette, Stanislas Carre de Malberg, Philippe Morier-Genoud, Francois Berleand, Irene Jacob
Director: Louis Malle
Screenplay: Louis Malle
Autobiographical drama
Rated PG
Young children: No   Older children: VG

Au Revoir, Les Enfants is about that point in time, if such a moment can be measured, at which childhood inevitably and irrevocably ends. This heartbreaking, unforgettable autobiographical drama from Louis Malle tells the story of Julien Quentin, a spirited 11-year-old prankster. The time is World War II, and Julien attends a rural Catholic boarding school in Occupied France. Even though he is coming of age in time of war, he has been protected from the horrors of the outside world.

Nevertheless, Julien senses something unusual about a new classmate: a sweet-faced, bushy-haired, exceptionally intelligent boy called Jean Bonnet. Jean is a Jew, in hiding at Julien's school . . . and Julien is oblivious to what Jean knows all too well: in Occupied France, it is highly dangerous—and nearly always fatal—to be Jewish.

Au Revoir, Les Enfants is a story of heroes and villains and anti-Semitism, of those who will risk their all to shelter the needy and those who will collaborate with the enemy to fill their pockets or gain a false sense of power.

It is a powerful, highly personal work of art based on writer-director Malle's own experiences during the war and should be considered must viewing for mature children. They are almost certain to raise questions that parents should deal with during (and after) the film.

THE AUTOBIOGRAPHY OF MISS JANE PITTMAN (1974)
Color, 110 minutes
Cast: Cicely Tyson, Barbara Chaney, Richard Dysart, Katherine Helmond, Michael Murphy, Odetta, Thalmus Rasulala
Director: John Korty
Screenplay: Tracy Keenan Wynn, based on the novel by Ernest J. Gaines
Historical drama
Unrated
Young children: OK   Older children: VG

This superb made-for-television movie is a landmark of its type. It chronicles the life of a strong, dignified 110-year-old former slave, offering a rich slice of American history from the Civil War through the Civil Rights Movement.

The film opens in 1962, with a young white journalist requesting to tape an interview with the elderly Miss Jane. She begins reminiscing about a lifetime filled with narrow escapes and personal tragedies, and with racism both blatant and subtle. For the most part, Jane is a sharp-eyed onlooker, not a partaker in history. As she ages, however, she develops an insight into the world of African-Americans and how they have fared in her lifetime. Meanwhile, she relishes life's simple pleasures, one of which is baseball. Of course, one of her great latter-day heroes is Jackie Robinson.

The Autobiography of Miss Jane Pittman is the story of a survivor. As she ages, Miss Jane manages to make history herself. In an especially stirring sequence, she becomes the first black person to drink out of a "Whites Only" water fountain.

This film puts a human face on the civil rights struggle in America and serves as a valuable history lesson for children and adults alike.

37

B

BABAR: THE MOVIE (1989)
Color, 70 minutes
Cast: Voices of Gordon Pinsent, Gavin Magrath, Elizabeth Hanna, Sarah Polley, Chris Wiggins, Stephanie Ouimette, John Stocker
Director: Alan Bunce
Screenplay: Peter Sauder, J. D. Smith, John De Klein, Raymond Jaffellice, and Alan Bunce, based on the books by Jean and Laurent de Brunhoff
Animated feature/Musical
Rated G
Younger kids: OK   Older kids: NG

Jean and Laurent de Brunhoff's famous children's book hero, Babar the elephant, stars in this pleasant, occasionally delightful, feature-length adventure. The film opens on the day of the Elephantland Victory Parade, and Babar explains to his children, by way of a bedtime story flashback, the origins of the celebration. Back on his first day as boy king of Elephantland, Babar learns of a rhinoceros attack, and with the help of his girl Celeste, a wisecracking monkey and an Australian crocodile, the heroic pachyderm defeats his foes at the very gates of his city.

An engaging storyline that's sure to appeal to young children makes up for strictly serviceable animation. The film's earnest messages (one good turn deserves another; friendship is the best pol-icy) are carefully woven into plot, and there are a couple of enjoyable (if unmemorable) songs. The film's character designs are taken from the original books' illustrations and are sure to be familiar to Babar fans.

BABE (1995)
Color, 92 minutes
Cast: James Cromwell, Magda Szubanski; voices of Christine Cavanaugh, Miriam Margolyes, Danny Mann, Hugo Weaving, Miriam Flynn, Russie Taylor, Evelyn Krape, Roscoe Lee Browne (narrator)
Director: Chris Noonan
Screenplay: Noonan and George Miller, based on the book *The Sheep-Pig* by Dick King-Smith
Comedy/Fantasy/Animal story
Rated G
Younger kids: VG   Older kids: VG

Babe is an absolutely charming tale about the title character, an orphaned pig who is adopted by quiet Farmer Hoggett (Cromwell). As Babe learns to adapt to life on Hoggett's farm and interact with the other animals there, he discovers his true calling—herding sheep!—and defies all expectations by making it come true.

What might seem at first like a cutesy excuse for a children's film turns out to be a classic piece of entertainment for everyone, with more profound things to say about identity and self-worth than most so-called "serious" films. Special-effects wizards succeed spectacularly in making the farm animals "talk" to each other by use of animatronics and computer graphics, but this sleight of hand is not meant to dazzle or call attention to itself. It is simply a part of the whole magical atmosphere that helps define each character and make the farm world absolutely believable.

Children should love Babe, a winning and plucky hero who believes in himself and the seriousness of his quest. Parents will certainly appreciate a character who respects the feelings of others and learns the importance of cooperation—not to mention good manners. The youngest children may be upset by the fate of Babe's mother, who's taken off to be slaughtered, but this fact of life is handled so honestly (along with Babe's lingering sadness) that it becomes an integral part of the film's great appeal.

BABES IN TOYLAND (see March of the Wooden Soldiers)

BABE: PIG IN THE CITY
(1998)
Color, 97 minutes
Cast: Magda Szubanski, James Cromwell, Mary Stein, Mickey Rooney, Julie Godfrey; voices of E. G. Daily, Danny Mann, Glenne Headly, Steven Wright, Stanley Ralph Ross, Russie Taylor; narrated by Roscoe Lee Browne
Director: George Miller
Screenplay: Miller, Judy Morris, and Mark Lamprell, based on characters created by Dick King-Smith
Fantasy adventure/Animal story

Rated G
Young children: OK Older children: OK

They couldn't leave well enough alone; that's why there's a sequel to *Babe,* a film that didn't need one. While this second film is entertaining enough, it can't touch the original for charm and quiet invention. What's more, it places its beloved star—and assorted other animals—in almost constant peril, which may make some of the youngest members of the audience a bit uncomfortable.

Farmer Hoggett and his wife owe the bank so much money that they're going to lose their farm, so Mrs. Hoggett takes Babe to the city for a lucrative personal appearance. But nothing goes right, and Babe winds up on his own in the Big City (an amalgam of every major metropolis on the planet), chased by a pit bull, wedged into a clown act, pursued by scowling animal handlers, etc. All along, his distraught human owner is going through troubles of her own, but eventually they are reunited.

Babe is as charming as ever, and those three singing mice are as funny and endearing as they were in the first film. (Adults will get a special kick out of their musical selections.)

But did we really need to see the addled clown (played by Mickey Rooney) carried off on a stretcher, gasping for life? Or watch a fire ignite in a children's hospital ward? Or witness a dog nearly drowning? What were the filmmakers thinking?

BABY BOOM (1987)
Color, 103 minutes
Cast: Diane Keaton, Sam Shepard, Harold Ramis, Sam Wanamaker, James Spader
Director: Charles Shyer
Screenplay: Shyer and Nancy Myers
Comedy
Rated PG
Younger kids: OK   Older kids: Good

Diane Keaton stars in this superficial but irresistibly entertaining story about a workaholic Manhattan executive named J.C. whose life is turned upside down when a baby is unexpectedly dumped in her lap after the death of a distant relative. J.C. tries to get rid of the "disruption" to her fast-track life but is unable to, and after her live-in boyfriend (Harold Ramis) walks out on her and a ruthless male colleague (James Spader) steals one of her prized accounts, she quits the rat race and moves up to Vermont. There she finds romance with a dreamy veterinarian (Sam Shepard) and starts up a successful baby-food business, which eventually brings her back to New York for a showdown with her old company.

This is a sweet feminist fantasy about "having it all" that cleverly skewers the yuppie lifestyle of the late '80s and benefits enormously from its charming cast, not the least of which are the adorable twins used to portray the baby.

While this is an out-and-out comedy, with Keaton in fine comic form, the movie might spark some discussion within your family about the pressures of balancing motherhood (or fatherhood) and a career.

Rated PG for some mild language, there is really nothing objectionable here for kids.

BABY . . . SECRET OF THE LOST LEGEND (1985)
Color, 95 minutes
Cast: William Katt, Sean Young, Patrick McGoohan, Julian Fellowes, Kyalo Mativo
Director: B. W. L. Norton
Screenplay: Clifford and Ellen Green
Action-adventure/Fantasy
Rated PG
Younger kids: OK, with caution   Older kids: Good

When an American paleontologist (Sean Young) living in Africa with her sportswriter husband (William Katt) discovers a baby brontosaurus, they risk their lives to save the dino and its family from a ruthless rival paleontologist (Patrick McGoohan).

This Disney fantasy borrows liberally from such films as **King Kong** and **E.T. The Extra-Terrestrial** but gets by on the cute and cuddly creatures. It does, however, contain a surprisingly large amount of mayhem and sexual elements for a purported family film, including realistic gun battles, as well as some *National Geographic*–style nudity, and stereotyped depictions of "savage" natives.

THE BABY-SITTERS CLUB (1995)
Color, 85 minutes
Cast: Schuyler Fisk, Bre Blair, Rachel Leigh Cook, Larisa Oleynik, Tricia Joe, Stacey Linn Ramsower, Zelda Harris, Peter Horton, Ellen Burstyn, Brooke Adams, Bruce Davison
Director: Melanie Mayron
Screenplay: Dalene Young,

based on the book series by Ann M. Martin

Drama

Rated PG

Younger children: VG, with caution   Older children: VG

Seven girls, led by the resourceful Kristy (Schuyler Fisk), who've already organized a successful baby-sitting cooperative, decide to expand by running a day-care camp during summer vacation. This is easier said than done, especially when several of the girls develop personal problems that distract them from the job at hand.

Preadolescent girls are likely to respond to this movie, as they have to Ann M. Martin's hugely popular books and the subsequent cable-TV series.

The key story element in this feature film, beyond the usual ups and downs of dealing with little kids, upsetting a fussbudget neighbor, and maintaining friendship through good times and bad, has to do with the return of Kristy's long-absent father and his insistence that she not tell anyone that he's in town. This leads to many questions and dilemmas for the girls, the most vexing being "When is it wrong to keep a secret?"

The seriousness of this subplot and of a parallel story about another girl trying to grow up too fast (and going on a date that can only lead to trouble) put this film in PG territory. That only means that the subject matter is inappropriate—one might say irrelevant—for younger kids.

BABY TAKE A BOW (1934)

Black & white, 76 minutes

Cast: Shirley Temple, James Dunn, Claire Trevor, Alan Dinehart, Ray Walker, Dorothy Libaire, Ralf Harolde, James Flavin

Director: Harry Lachman

Screenplay: Philip Klein and E. E. Paramore, Jr., based on the play *Square Crooks* by James P. Judge

Melodrama

Unrated

Young children: VG   Older children: VG

In this touching melodrama about a family that is struggling to attain a comfortable lifestyle, Shirley Temple plays the daughter of a reformed ex-convict who is being framed by a jewel thief and hounded by an overzealous policeman. As the plot builds, the little tyke becomes the recipient of stolen loot, and at another point she is taken hostage. This is an engrossing, excitement-packed story, but always one that is geared to a family audience, so the events never become too intense for children to enjoy.

One of the more cheerful scenes occurs when Shirley sings a number called "On Accounta I Love You" with her dad, who is played by soft-voiced, charming James Dunn (her costar in several early films). Parents should also note that the character of the threatening policeman occasionally comes on strong.

BACK TO THE FUTURE (1985)

Color, 116 minutes

Cast: Michael J. Fox, Christopher Lloyd, Crispin Glover, Lea Thompson, Wendie Jo Sperber, Thomas F. Wilson

Director: Robert Zemeckis

Screenplay: Zemeckis and Bob Gale

Science fiction/Comedy
Rated PG
Younger kids: OK   Older kids: VG

Teenager Marty McFly helps his scientist friend Doc Brown test his time machine—which is mounted in a DeLorean, a once-fashionable luxury car—and winds up back in the 1950s, when his own parents were his age.

Fast-paced (almost manic at times) and very funny, this box-office hit should be a lot of fun for the whole family. Everyone will particularly enjoy Christopher Lloyd's wacky scientist, but Fox is just as good as the confused central character.

When he's in the 1950s, the girl who will be his own mother when she grows up is strongly attracted to him, but this is very playful and is not likely to bother mothers or their sons. (Although it might confuse them a bit!) Parents are more likely to be asked about various elements of '50s life—such as a full-service gas station where a battery of attendants rush out to service a car that pulls in for a fill-up! Kids who love written science fiction will be pleased to realize that the time-travel ideas in the film (and its two sequels) are intelligently developed.

BACK TO THE FUTURE PART II (1989)
Color, 107 minutes
Cast: Michael J. Fox, Christopher Lloyd, Lea Thompson, Thomas F. Wilson, Joe Flaherty, Elisabeth Shue
Director: Robert Zemeckis
Screenplay: Zemeckis and Bob Gale
Science fiction/Comedy
Rated PG
Younger kids: OK   Older kids: OK

This sequel picks up exactly where the first film ended, with the excitable Doc Brown (Lloyd) telling Marty McFly (Fox) and his girlfriend Jennifer (Shue) that they have to come with him to the future. They arrive in 2015 in time for Marty to impersonate his own grandson (also Fox) and prevent a robbery planned by Griff (Wilson), grandson of Biff (also Wilson), who'd made life miserable for Marty's father back in 1955. However, while they are straightening this out, Biff overhears them, and uses the DeLorean time machine to go back to 1955 with a sports almanac, which he forces on his younger self.

When Marty and the others return to their own time of 1985, they discover that Biff used the almanac to bet on sporting events and become fabulously rich; Hill Valley is now a sinkhole of depravity, presided over by Biff, who married Marty's mother Lorraine (Thompson) after having his father murdered back in 1973. Doc realizes the only way to set things right is to return again to 1955 and destroy the almanac before Biff can use it, but of course nothing in time travel is ever that simple.

Very sophisticated about its time-travel gimmicks, this is an interesting but surprisingly downbeat film, very dark and even unpleasant. It's not only missing the joyful freneticism of the first movie, but it doesn't come to a conclusion, opting instead to leave viewers with a cliffhanger ending. The only good news about that is that Part III is so much fun.

Because the scenes in the altered 1985 are pretty grim, this sequel might bother younger children, but older ones will be more likely to take it as it goes and be eager to see the third film of the trilogy.

BACK TO THE FUTURE PART III (1990)
Color, 118 minutes
Cast: Michael J. Fox, Christopher Lloyd, Mary Steenburgen, Lea Thompson, Thomas F. Wilson, Elisabeth Shue, Matt Clark, Richard Dysart, Pat Buttram, Harry Carey, Jr., Dub Taylor, James Tolkan, Marc McClure, Wendie Jo Sperber
Director: Robert Zemeckis
Screenplay: Zemeckis and Bob Gale
Science fiction/Comedy/Western
Rated PG
Younger kids: OK   Older kids: VG

Just as the second had, the third in the series follows hard on the heels of its predecessor, at the end of which Marty learned that his friend Doc Brown had evidently been killed back in 1885. Marty is now stuck in 1955, but a note from Doc leads him to the DeLorean, which Doc hid in 1885 for Marty to find. (When you're dealing with time travel, effects routinely precede causes.) Hoping to save his friend, Marty uses the time machine to go back to 1885 himself, when Hill Valley was part of the Old West. He does find Doc, but the DeLorean has sprung a leak, and finding sufficiently powerful fuel is difficult. Furthermore, Doc falls for pretty schoolmarm Clara Clayton (Steenburgen) and isn't so sure he wants to go back to the future after all. Meanwhile, Marty has made a new enemy, Buford "Mad Dog" Tannen (Wilson), ancestor of the other Tannens who caused him and his father trouble in the earlier films. Everything finally comes to hinge on whether Doc can get a steam locomotive to go fast enough to propel the DeLorean through the time barrier.

When Marty arrives in 1885, the film becomes a wonderfully astute spoof of and salute to Westerns. But it doesn't evade its science fiction responsibilities and is even more action-packed than the second entry. Even with the somewhat downbeat nature of Part II, these three films together could be ideal viewing for a family, perhaps on a weekend when the weather keeps everyone indoors. The only drawback: Children are likely to clamor for a *fourth* film.

THE BAD NEWS BEARS (1976)
Color, 102 minutes
Cast: Walter Matthau, Tatum O'Neal, Vic Morrow, Joyce Van Patten, Jackie Earle Haley, Alfred W. Lutter
Director: Michael Ritchie
Screenplay: Bill Lancaster
Comedy/Sports
Rated PG
Younger kids: OK   Older kids: VG

A terrible Little League baseball team gets a chance at the championship when a grouchy coach (Matthau) takes over and brings on a star pitcher (Tatum O'Neal), who happens to be a girl. This very entertaining comedy revels in (but does not exploit) the quirks and idiosyncrasies of different types of kids. It is also a well-observed examination of the darker side of competition, with parents who live through their children and push them into winning at all costs, acting more like kids than the kids themselves. This is reflected in Matthau's chewing out a player for not allowing himself to get hit by a pitch, and—in the film's most powerful scene—when a rival coach strikes his own son for accidentally throwing a wild pitch at a batter.

Some parents will be shocked at the little kids' frequent use of profanity; if that's a concern, cross this film off your list.

The sequels that followed—*The Bad News Bears in Breaking Training* (1977), *The Bad News Bears Go to Japan* (1978)—were, to put it charitably, less inspired.

BALTO (1995)
Color, 74 minutes
Cast: Voices of Kevin Bacon, Bridget Fonda, Bob Hoskins, Phil Collins, Jim Cummings, Jack Angel, Danny Mann, Robbie Rist, Donald Sinden
Director: Simon Wells
Screenplay: Cliff Ruby, Elana Lesser, David Steven Cohen, and Roger S. H. Shulman
Animated feature
Rated G
Younger kids: OK   Older kids: OK

Balto is a winning animated adventure with much for children of all ages and their parents to enjoy. The movie is based on the true story of an Alaskan sled dog who, in 1925, led a team across six hundred miles of Arctic tundra to deliver antitoxin to the diphtheria-stricken children of Nome.

Balto is an outcast half-breed (part husky, part wolf) who is vying for the affection of Jenna, a beautiful husky belonging to a little girl taken ill. Balto faces many challenges, not the least from Steele, an egotistical bully and rival for Jenna's affections. When Steele's team, carrying the medicine, gets lost, Balto comes to the rescue to lead them home—by way of an ice cave avalanche, a ferocious black bear attack, cracking thin ice, and treachery from Steele.

The animation, from Steven Spielberg's Amblin Entertainment, is excellent, but more important, the story wrings all the drama out of this exciting story—without forgetting to inject bits of humor for punctuation. A first-class effort.

BAMBI (1942)
Color, 69 minutes
Cast: No voices credited
Director: David Hand; story director: Perce Pearce
Screenplay: Larry Morey (story adapter), George Stallings, Melvin Shaw, Cal Fallberg, Chuck Couch, and Ralph Wright (story development), based on the book by Felix Salten
Animated feature
Unrated
Young children: VG, with caution   Older children: VG

Bambi is one of Walt Disney's genuine classics. It is also a touchstone of early moviegoing for several generations, who recall first seeing it—and how they responded to the now famous scene in which Bambi's mother is killed. (How kids of the 1940s and '50s would have responded to the parallel scene in **The Lion King,** which is far more explicit—and lengthy—can only be imagined.)

The theme of *Bambi* is nature and the turning of the seasons; its underlying message is that life goes on, no matter what. Come rain or snow, forest fire or death, life continues as it must, and the creatures of the forest must find a way to survive and prevail.

What keeps Bambi from becoming a nature-study lecture, or a heavy-handed message movie, is its infectious sense of humor, personified in the character of Thumper. Whenever the film threatens to take itself too seriously, there is the adorable young rabbit, whose comments are so funny—so recognizably childlike and mischievous—that you can't help but laugh.

Because the story follows Bambi and his friends Thumper and Flower (the skunk) from infancy through adulthood, the story is designed to attract and hold young viewers. That's why the loss of Bambi's mother—even though it happens quickly, off-screen—is so devastating. But one couldn't ask for a better, more reasoned resolution, as the Great Prince (Bambi's father) quietly indicates to Bambi that it is time to move on.

The climactic forest fire is almost as upsetting. Bambi's life is threatened by vicious dogs as he tries to save the life of his beloved Faline, and then he dashes and dodges through the forest with flames licking at his heels.

All ends well, but not before viewers have gone through a heart-pounding experience alongside the forest creatures they have come to know and love.

The pastoral music of *Bambi* may date it more than anything in the story, but it's so beautifully woven into the tapestry of the film that children will likely accept it as they wouldn't in some other context.

Bambi is a beautiful film that can create a childhood memory to last a lifetime. But it would be cruel to show it to young children without being there to guide them along and soothe them in its most upsetting moments.

THE BANDIT OF SHERWOOD FOREST (1946)
Color, 86 minutes
Cast: Cornel Wilde, Anita Louise, Jill Esmond, Edgar Buchanan, Henry Daniell
Directors: George Sherman and Henry Levin
Screenplay: Wilfrid H. Pettit and Melvin Levy, based on the novel *Son of Robin Hood* by Paul A. Castelton
Swashbuckler/Action-adventure
Unrated
Younger kids: Good   Older kids: VG

When the young king of England is threatened by the machinations of a dastardly regent (Henry Daniell), Robert of Nottingham (Cornel Wilde), the son of Robin Hood, gallops back to Sherwood Forest with his bow and arrow to save the day, and also finds time to win the hand of a beautiful maiden (Anita Louise).

Aimed squarely at juveniles, this is a fairly routine but action-packed swashbuckler made enjoyable by its color photography and practiced supporting cast, including Edgar Buchanan as a comical Friar Tuck and the reliably nasty Daniell and George Macready as heavies.

THE BAND WAGON (1953)
Color, 112 minutes
Cast: Fred Astaire, Cyd
  Charisse, Oscar Levant,
  Nanette Fabray, Jack
  Buchanan, James Mitchell
Director: Vincente Minnelli
Screenplay: Betty Comden and
  Adolph Green
Musical
Unrated
Young children: OK   Older
  children: VG

Here is one of the most stylish movie musicals of all time. Fred Astaire is cast as an aging movie star whose box office returns have slipped. Seeking new worlds to conquer, he decides to star in a Broadway musical. Along the way, there are some entertaining dialogue, comedy with a theatrical flavor, and several absolutely wonderful musical numbers, including the immortal "That's Entertainment." "A Shine on Your Shoes," a tuneful tap-dance number performed by Astaire with LeRoy Daniels at a 42nd Street arcade, is a standout. The young-sters also will enjoy "Triplets," a comedy piece sung by Astaire, Nanette Fabray, and Jack Buchanan dressed up as toddlers sporting a whole lot of attitude!

This movie musical is justly considered a classic. Its story and dialogue may be a bit sophisticated for the youngest viewers (though in no way objectionable), but they're sure to come alive during the musical numbers. If you have a laserdisc or DVD, start by showing the kids "Triplets" or "A Shine on Your Shoes," and chances are they'll want to see more.

**BARNEY'S GREAT
ADVENTURE** (1998)
Color, 75 minutes
Cast: George Hearn, Shirley
  Douglas, Trevor Morgan, Kyla
  Pratt, Diana Rice
Director: Steve Gomer
Screenplay: Stephen White
Kiddie fantasy
Rated G
Young children: VG   Older
  children: No

Kids past kindergarten age will find *Barney's Great Adventure* a great big bore. But this feature-length version of the smash-hit TV show is not designed for them, let alone older siblings. It is expertly fashioned for their kid brothers and sisters, those in the 2-to-5 age range, who have come to know and adore the lovably goofy Big Purple Dinosaur.

The plot involves Barney and a trio of kids who are visiting their grandparents' farm and what happens when they become involved with a large, magical egg that has fallen from the sky. However, the story is secondary to Barney's mere presence; his target audience will be captivated as he sings, dances, and puts forth a cheery message regarding the power of imagination and the importance of feeling compassion.

BATHING BEAUTY (1944)
Color, 101 minutes
Cast: Red Skelton, Esther
  Williams, Basil Rathbone,
  Ethel Smith, Xavier Cugat,
  Lina Romay, Harry James
Director: George Sidney
Screenplay: Frank Waldman
Musical comedy
Unrated
Young children: VG   Older
  children: VG

A real period piece, with something for everybody.

In her debut as a swimming movie star, Esther Williams plays a teacher at a girls' school. Her new but estranged husband (Skelton) elbows his way in as the only male student. The whole movie seems constructed just to get Red into a tutu for ballet class, and it's all very silly.

But there are musical guest stars, some swell numbers, that always eye-popping MGM Technicolor, and naturally, a huge aquacade finale. If that's not enough, there's a sweetly naive opening title card that says, "We don't know if this story actually happened—but if it did happen, it couldn't happen in a nicer place than California."

This is the kind of colorful, innocent musical comedy that younger kids can thoroughly enjoy—even if some of the "names" are foreign to them and the 1940s trappings a bit of a mystery. Older kids might even appreciate some of the kitsch value here.

In her heyday, the beautiful Williams (who trained to compete in the 1940 Olympics but never got her chance because of the war in Europe) promoted swimming and diving internationally, inspiring many to take to the water. Similarly, seeing this movie now might induce one to start going to the municipal pool. Esther, still doing laps daily, would approve.

BATMAN (1966)
Color, 105 minutes
Cast: Adam West, Burt Ward, Burgess Meredith, Cesar Romero, Frank Gorshin, Lee Meriwether, Neil Hamilton
Director: Leslie Martinson
Screenplay: Lorenzo Semple, Jr.
Superhero action-adventure
Unrated
Younger kids: Good   Older kids: Good

The 1960s *Batman* TV series was notable for its campy humor and clever pop-culture satire—not to mention its pop-art/comic strip exclamations of POW!, BAM!, etc. This big-screen feature, designed to cash in on the show's enormous success, isn't as ingenious as the series at its best, and if anything, seems to be aimed much more directly at kids. The plot brings together The Penguin (Burgess Meredith), The Joker (Cesar Romero), The Riddler (Frank Gorshin), and Catwoman (Lee Meriwether), who team up to destroy Batman (Adam West) and Robin (Burt Ward) in a quest for world domination.

There's some mild comic-strip violence, but it's all very innocuous, particularly compared to the later series of *Batman* films.

BATMAN (1989)
Color, 126 minutes
Cast: Michael Keaton, Jack Nicholson, Kim Basinger, Michael Gough, Jack Palance, Robert Wuhl, Pat Hingle, Billy Dee Williams, Jerry Hall
Director: Tim Burton
Screenplay: Sam Hamm and Warren Skaaren, based on characters created by Bob Kane
Superhero action-adventure
Rated PG-13
Younger kids: Use caution   Older kids: Good

Eccentric billionaire Bruce Wayne, disguised as Batman, battles crooks in dark, brooding Gotham City.

One such crook (Nicholson) annoys his boss (Palance) who orders him killed, but it backfires: chemicals drive the guy crazy and turn him into the Clown Prince of Crime, The Joker, complete with white face, red lips, and green hair. Batman has to take on The Joker while trying to keep attractive reporter Basinger from learning his secret identity.

If you or your kids are into comic books and superheroes, you've probably seen this giant hit several times. It's ideal fare for teenage boys, who've always identified with the outsider nature of superheroes; teenage girls will like it as well, because this entry is surprisingly romantic, in a way that manages to be exotic and completely harmless at once.

The problem with Tim Burton's dark, nightmarish vision of *Batman* is that it isn't appropriate for young kids, even though they may clamor to see it. In one flashback, Bruce Wayne sees his parents gunned down on the street in cold blood. In another, The Joker (who's acquired his bizarre face by a bath in acid!) and his henchman invade a Gotham City museum and deface the art treasures inside.

The film earns its PG-13 rating; take heed, save this until your kids are a little older and you'll be glad you did.

BATMAN & ROBIN (1997)
Color, 130 minutes
Cast: George Clooney, Chris O'Donnell, Arnold Schwarzenegger, Uma Thurman, Alicia Silverstone, Michael Gough, Pat Hingle
Director: Joel Schumacher
Screenplay: Akiva Goldsman, based on characters created by Bob Kane
Superhero action-adventure
Rated PG-13
Younger kids: OK   Older kids: OK

Strident, flashy, and hollow, the fourth Batman movie suffers from overkill in every department, including an overhyped new Batman (George Clooney), *two* flamboyant villains (Arnold Schwarzenegger as Mr. Freeze, Uma Thurman as Poison Ivy), teen sidekicks (Chris O'Donnell as Robin, Alicia Silverstone as Batgirl), and shrill and incoherent action scenes. It's mindlessly entertaining comic-book stuff, but way too long, and the net effect is like being trapped inside a hyperactive pinball machine that won't turn off.

In addition to the usual violence, there's the spoofy sexuality of Poison Ivy to deal with, and the eerie notion of Mr. Freeze keeping his dead wife in a water chamber, but these are fairly harmless next to the brain-numbing noise and action—and a story that has little if any coherence.

BATMAN FOREVER (1995)
Color, 121 minutes
Cast: Val Kilmer, Tommy Lee Jones, Jim Carrey, Nicole Kidman, Chris O'Donnell, Michael Gough, Pat Hingle, Drew Barrymore, Debi Mazar, Rene Auberjonois, Joe Grifasi
Director: Joel Schumacher
Screenplay: Lee Batchler, Janis Scott Batchler, and Akiva Goldsman, based on characters created by Bob Kane
Superhero action-adventure
Rated PG-13
Younger kids: No   Older kids: OK

Not only does Batman (played this time by Kilmer) have another pair of villains to fight, but in this installment he gains a partner in the youthful Robin (O'Donnell). A goofy scientist (Carrey) becomes the deranged supervillain The Riddler, who joins forces with the literally half-good, half-bad Two-Face (Jones) to wreak havoc on Gotham City. In the midst of this chaos, Bruce Wayne finds time to romance psychologist Kidman both as himself and as Batman.

Director Joel Schumacher radically changed direction for the series; where Burton's Gotham City and Batman were dark and brooding, Schumacher's city is lit in vivid neon, and Batman now makes wisecracks. (Of the Batmobile he remarks, "Chicks dig the car.") The movie edges closer to the bogus-camp quality of the 1960s TV show, though Schumacher still takes part of the film seriously.

Two-Face, one of the best villains from the comics, is turned into an imitation Joker in Jones' over-the-top portrayal, but trying to play a campy character alongside Jim Carrey is an exercise in futility. Carrey's Riddler is flamboyant in the extreme, but after a while the film becomes so manic it's too much to take.

Kidman's character is the most engaging and the most interesting in the film, as she explores the mystery of Batman/Bruce Wayne.

While nowhere near as dark as the first two *Batman* movies, this one also earned a PG-13 for its action violence.

BATMAN RETURNS (1992)
Color, 126 minutes
Cast: Michael Keaton, Michelle Pfeiffer, Danny DeVito, Christopher Walken, Michael Gough, Pat Hingle, Michael Murphy, Christi Conaway, Vincent Schiavelli, Andrew Bryniarski, Jan Hooks, Paul Reubens
Director: Tim Burton
Screenplay: Daniel Waters, based on characters created by Bob Kane
Superhero action-adventure
Rated PG-13
Younger kids: No   Older kids: Good

This time, Batman is confronted by a pair of super villains: the sleek, sensuous Catwoman (Pfeiffer) and the grotesque Penguin (DeVito), who's out for revenge on the notable families of Gotham City. The Catwoman wants revenge, too, on the corrupt millionaire (Walken) who tried to have her killed, but to her own surprise she becomes romantically interested in Batman.

One of the most bizarre films ever to come from a major studio, this is even stranger than the first *Batman* film. Sensitive children, even teenagers, might find the freakish Penguin a bit more than they can take. But teenage girls should enjoy the character of Catwoman, one of the few superheroes (or villains, in her case) to cross gender lines in appeal, especially as played by Michelle Pfeiffer, who starts out as a mousy secretary and then gets "empowered" by her transformation into the superfeline. The settings are more elaborate than in Burton's first *Batman* movie, but they're also darker and even more Gothic.

Burton's twisted sensibilities (and sense of humor) don't click with everyone, but chances are that older kids will find this intriguing. As with **Batman,** this film is inappropriate for younger children; the scene near the beginning when The Penguin's parents abandon him by tossing his baby carriage off a bridge is genuinely upsetting.

*batteries not included (1987)
Color, 105 minutes
Cast: Hume Cronyn, Jessica Tandy, Frank McRae, Elizabeth Pena, Michael Carmine, Dennis Boutsikaris, Tom Aldredge, Jane Hoffman, John DiSanti, John Pankow, MacIntyre Dixon
Director: Matthew Robbins
Screenplay: Brad Bird, Matthew Robbins, Brent Maddock, and S. S. Wilson, from a story by Mick Garris
Fantasy
Rated PG
Younger children: Perhaps
   Older children: OK (offensive language)

Tiny flying saucers from outer space visit New York City. Benign, humorous, and whimsical, these "little guys" who like to fix things consume electricity. When they befriend the inhabitants of a condemned apartment building, particularly the senile Faye (Jessica Tandy), they manage to solve everyone's problems. They also multiply, creating funny-looking hamburger-shaped babies.

The creatures are adorable, and the special effects are first-rate, but the story is an obvious mix of cloying sweetness and occasionally forced humor. And was it really necessary to tell this simple story using adult language? From Steven Spielberg's Amblin Productions, *batteries not included* is nothing special, but it may be an

acceptable way to kill 105 minutes if you aren't overly sensitive to four-letter words.

BATTLE FOR THE PLANET OF THE APES (1973)
Color, 92 minutes
Cast: Roddy McDowall, Claude Akins, Natalie Trundy, Severn Darden, Lew Ayres, Paul Williams, Austin Stoker, Noah Keen, France Nuyen, John Huston, John Landis
Director: J. Lee Thompson
Screenplay: John William Corrington and Joyce Hooper Corrington, from a screen story by Paul Dehn, based on ideas created by Pierre Boulle
Science fiction/Adventure
Rated G
Young children: OK   Older children: OK

The rebellion of the intelligent apes against humanity, shown in the previous installment, led to atomic war, and much of the Earth—the Planet of the Apes to be—has been reduced to a wasteland. McDonald (Austin Stoker), a human being, works with Caesar (Roddy McDowall), the chimpanzee hero of this and the previous film, to try to ease tensions between the human beings and the apes. But even among the apes themselves, the chimpanzees, gorillas, and orangutans are often at odds.

Caesar visits a ruined city inhabited by a handful of human survivors, led by Kolp (Severn Darden), to try to learn more about what his parents said upon their escape from the Planet of the Apes. Meanwhile, ambitious gorilla warlord Aldo (Claude Akins), who hates all human beings, is itching to take over from Caesar and to kill every human in sight.

This is pretty lackluster, with terrible dialogue throughout. There's a feeling of everyone just going through their paces. However, the very ending of the film *almost* answers the big questions: Can the oppressive society we saw in the very first movie be averted? Can humans and apes get along?

This was the last of the **Planet of the Apes** movie series, though it was followed by a short-lived TV series that didn't link itself very closely to the movies in terms of plot. Episodes of that series were combined to make synthetic "movies" that are shown on TV under the following titles: *Farewell to the Planet of the Apes, Forgotten City of the Planet of the Apes, Life, Liberty and Pursuit on the Planet of the Apes, Treachery and Greed on the Planet of the Apes.* Avoid these.

BATTLING BUTLER (1926)
Black & white, 71 minutes
Cast: Buster Keaton, Sally O'Neil, Snitz Edwards, Francis McDonald, Mary O'Brien, Tom Wilson, Eddie Borden
Director: Buster Keaton
Screenplay: Paul Gerard Smith, Albert Boasberg, Lex Neal, and Charles Smith, based on the musical play *Battling Butler*
Comedy/Silent classic
Unrated
Young children: VG   Older children: VG

While far from Buster Keaton's very best, this clever silent comedy feature is still loaded with laughs. Buster stars as Alfred Butler, a wealthy wimp who heads off to the country with his valet (Snitz Edwards, a popular silent-screen character actor who is one of the funniest-looking men ever to appear in the movies). Alfred meets and falls in love with a mountain girl whose relatives want no "weaklings" in the family. It so happens that a champion boxer named Alfred "Battling" Butler shares our hero's name. The fun starts when, in order to win his beloved, the scrawny Butler impersonates the battling one.

You just know that the phony Battling Butler eventually will be called upon to show off his pugilistic "expertise." This is where Keaton gets to display his mastery of physical comedy, as he is unable to enter the ring without getting his entire body caught in the ropes!

The film has many clever sight gags as the milquetoast millionaire and his valet offer their idea of "roughing it" with the most elaborate camping-out setup you've ever seen.

Like all good silent comedies, this one is a treat for the whole family.

BEAN (1997)
Color, 90 minutes
Cast: Rowan Atkinson, Peter MacNicol, Pamela Reed, Harris Yulin, Burt Reynolds, John Mills, Richard Gant, Tricia Vessey
Director: Mel Smith
Screenplay: Richard Curtis, Robin Driscoll, and Rowan Atkinson
Comedy
Rated PG-13
Younger kids: OK, with caution   Older kids: VG

Mr. Bean is a comic character who would have been right at

home in the era of silent movies. In fact, he hardly speaks at all. He is a likable bumbler, a childlike everyman, whose curiosity gets the better of him at inopportune moments, and who has a knack for getting into trouble. In this story, he is sent as the unlikely representative of England's Royal National Gallery to accompany the priceless painting "Whistler's Mother" to its new home, in a southern California museum. The museum's gallery director (Peter MacNicol) makes the mistake of inviting Mr. Bean to stay with him and his family, and from that point on, one catastrophe follows another.

Mr. Bean is a very funny character, but this patchwork film is little more than a series of skits loosely tied together. The PG-13 rating derives from some double-entendre gags which might go over the heads of younger kids, a brief look at a centerfold-style poster, and a gag in which Bean is given "the finger" by a motorcyclist and, innocently thinking it's a positive greeting, employs the gesture himself thereafter. On the whole, this is a lightweight, funny film that kids and parents can both enjoy. (Parents will think about the consequences of Bean's destructive actions more than kids, but that's probably taking this film more seriously than anyone should.)

Some of these same skits were originally presented on television; they and others can be better enjoyed in the many video compilations of Rowan Atkinson's television series and specials.

THE BEAR (1989)
Color, 92 minutes
Cast: Bart the bear, Douce the cub, Jack Wallace, Tcheky Karyo, Andre Lacombe
Director: Jean-Jacques Annaud
Screenplay: Gerard Brach, from the novel by James Oliver Curwood
Animal adventure
Rated PG
Young children: VG, with caution   Older children: VG

James Oliver Curwood's venerable 1917 novel *The Grizzly King* is transposed to widescreen as a remarkable wildlife adventure starring Bart the bear, an animal actor with all the charisma and star appeal of the greats from Lassie to Trigger.

Bart portrays an adult Kodiak in the British Columbia forests of 1885. There he befriends a cub orphaned by a rock slide and teaches him how to fend off a hungry puma and how to avoid a pair of pelt-hungry bear hunters. *The Bear* celebrates the magnificence of nature and the unpredictability of life. The scene in which the young cub loses his mother is wrenching; his need to survive on his own is the impetus for the story.

The first thing you see in the movie is the legend, "All scenes depicting injury to animals have been simulated," and that caveat is crucial. With movie magic (and a little help from Jim Henson's Creature Shop) the filmmakers create the illusion of shootings and other injuries. The fact that these scenes are not real doesn't change the fact that in the context of the film they *seem* real.

Younger kids and animal lovers of all ages may have a few anxious moments. Older kids should love the film.

THE BEAST FROM 20,000 FATHOMS (1953)
Black & white, 80 minutes
Cast: Paul Christian (Hubschmidt), Paula Raymond, Cecil Kellaway, Kenneth Tobey, Donald Woods, Lee Van Cleef
Director: Eugene Lourié
Screenplay: Fred Freiberger, Louis Morheim, Eugene Lourié, and Robert Smith
Science fiction/Monster thriller
Unrated
Younger kids: Good   Older kids: Good

This moderately low-budget movie, an independent film purchased by Warner Bros., set the form for all the monster-on-the-loose movies of the 1950s and remains one of the best of the breed.

Atomic explosions awaken a dinosaur in the Arctic; after sinking a ship or two, it arrives in New York and stomps up Wall Street, eating policemen and smashing buildings. For all that, children, especially boys, will love the beast. Be sure to tell them that this dinosaur, a "rhedosaurus," is fictional, or they'll wear themselves out digging through reference books.

Ray Harryhausen's special effects are primitive by today's standards, but only technically; the Beast has a vivid personality and creates convincing havoc. This was inspired by Ray Bradbury's short story of the same title (later retitled "The Foghorn").

Note: Younger children might find some elements, such as the disease the Beast spreads and its spectacular demise amid the framework of a burning roller coaster, hard to take without a lot of parental reassurance.

BEAU GESTE (1939)
Black & white, 114 minutes
Cast: Gary Cooper, Ray Milland, Robert Preston, Brian Donlevy, Susan Hayward, J. Carrol Naish, Albert Dekker, Broderick Crawford, Donald O'Connor
Director: William Wellman
Screenplay: Robert Carson, based on the novel by P. C. Wren
Action-adventure
Unrated
Younger kids: OK   Older kids: VG

Beau Geste is a rousing action yarn (copied scene-for-scene from the superior 1926 silent version, which starred Ronald Colman) about the adventures of three English brothers, who join the French Foreign Legion over a matter of family honor and clash with a sadistic sergeant. Gary Cooper, Ray Milland, and Robert Preston are excellent as the devoted brothers, but a snarling Brian Donlevy steals the film with his chilling portrayal of the brutal sergeant (for which he won an Oscar nomination).

This is old-fashioned, stiff-upper-lip adventure at its best. Viewers who saw this, or the silent film, at an impressionable age will never forget certain elements of the story: an unforgettably eerie opening featuring a platoon of dead soldiers frozen at their stations at a deserted fort . . . the willingness of the Geste brothers to sacrifice their lives for each other, without question . . . and the concept of a "Viking funeral," established in the film's early scenes (where we see the Geste brothers as boys).

The violence is discreet by modern standards, and the depiction of Arabs is old-fashioned, to say the least, but the story is still stirring.

The story was remade again in 1966, and then parodied by Marty Feldman in *The Last Remake of Beau Geste* (1977), which borrowed footage from this version.

BEAUTY AND THE BEAST
(1946)
Black & white, 95 minutes
Cast: Jean Marais, Josette Day, Marcel Andre, Mila Parely, Nane Germon
Director: Jean Cocteau
Screenplay: Cocteau, based on the fairy tale by Mme. Leprince de Beamont
Fantasy
Unrated
Younger kids: OK   Older kids: VG

French poet-playwright Jean Cocteau directed this visually stunning version of the classic fairy tale about the beautiful country girl Belle (Josette Day) who offers herself to the Beast (Jean Marais) in order to save her impoverished father's life. But as a hostage in the Beast's palace, Belle is treated with such kindness that she eventually falls in love with him and he's magically transformed back into a Prince.

Featuring exquisite photography, art direction, and makeup, the film captures the true poetic quality of fantasy with a lyrical flow of surreal sounds and images, achieved with an utter simplicity and directness (all the more impressive because of the arduous wartime conditions under which it was made).

This would make a fascinating comparison piece for kids who know the 1991 Disney cartoon feature well. Its sophisticated artistry may be over the heads of young children, but those old enough to read subtitles should find it as enchanting as adults.

BEAUTY AND THE BEAST
(1991)
Color, 85 minutes
Cast: Voices of Paige O'Hara, Robby Benson, Jerry Orbach, Angela Lansbury, Richard White, David Ogden Stiers, Jesse Corti, Rex Everhart
Directors: Gary Trousdale and Kirk Wise
Screenplay: Linda Woolverton
Animated feature/Musical
Rated G
Young children: VG, with caution   Older children: VG

In this Disney update of the classic story, Belle is a young woman who thinks more of books than she does of people. She has no use for Gaston, the handsome local bully who fancies himself a ladies' man. When her inventor father is captured by a Beast who occupies a desolate castle in the woods, she bravely goes to the castle and offers herself in her father's place. Thus Belle finds herself prisoner in an enchanted environment where all the household objects—from a clock to a candelabra—have come to life and befriend her. They explain that the Beast was once a Prince; unless he finds true love before the last petal falls from a rose preserved in the castle, he will remain a beast forever. When Belle refuses to submit to his brow-beating, the ferocious creature begins to soften, and they begin to genuinely care for each other. But Gaston and his gullible friends in the village cannot leave well enough alone.

Beauty and the Beast is a highly successful and satisfying adaptation of a "tale as old as time," energized by an ideal song score and peppered with wonderful supporting characters, including the very French candelabra, Lumière (voiced by Jerry Orbach), who sings "Be Our Guest," and the very British teapot, Mrs. Potts (voiced by Angela Lansbury), who sings the lovely title song.

The Beast himself might be off-putting to the youngest members of your family, and there is a scene in which Belle is threatened by wolves that is also cause for concern.

More important, the film sends a valuable message about not judging a person by his appearance: The Beast, in fact, has a tender heart, while the good-looking Gaston turns out to be a cruel and worthless character.

BEBE'S KIDS (1992)
Color, 74 minutes
Cast: Voices of Faizon Love, Nell Carter, Tone Loc, Rich Little, Vanessa Bell Calloway, Wayne Collins, Jr., Jonell Green, Marques Houston
Director: Bruce Smith
Screenplay: Reginald Hudlin
Animated feature
Rated PG-13
Young kids: OK, with caution   Older kids: OK

Bebe's Kids is based on the late comedian Robin Harris' hilarious experiences with misbehaving kids and is the first animated film

to be aimed specifically at inner-city youngsters and black audiences. A trip to the amusement park provides the serviceable plot, as we follow Robin's frantic first date with single mom Jamika, her small son, and three bratty neighborhood youngsters—Bebe's kids. Boys and girls will connect with Bebe's rowdy brood as they stand up to authority and generally take over Fun World and turn it upside down.

The film is a refreshing change from the usual animated fairy tales and musical epics, and is set in contemporary times, with identifiable characters who could be of any color. Although everyone can relate to situations presented here, *Bebe's Kids* definitely presents an urban African-American point of view. Clever dialogue, attractive visuals, and slick animation make this winning entertainment, but some of the material is not really suitable for younger children, hence the PG-13 rating.

BEDKNOBS AND BROOMSTICKS (1971)
Color, 117 minutes
Cast: Angela Lansbury, David Tomlinson, Roddy McDowall, Sam Jaffe, Cindy O'Callaghan, Roy Snart, John Ericson, Reginald Owen, Tessie O'Shea, Bruce Forsyth
Director: Robert Stevenson
Screenplay: Bill Walsh and Don DaGradi, based on the book by Mary Norton
Musical/Fantasy
Rated G
Young children: VG   Older children: VG

In the wake of **Mary Poppins,** the Disney studio concocted this charming musical-comedy-fantasy, in which children costar with colorfully eccentric adults and actors consort with animated characters. The setting is a rural village in England during the early years of World War II, where Miss Price (Angela Lansbury), an eccentric unmarried lady, resides in a large house with Cosmic Creepers, her pet cat. Miss Price has been studying witchcraft via a correspondence course, but the war has shut down her school. Undaunted, Miss Price pursues its headmaster (who in reality is an incompetent magician) and seeks the data that will allow her to learn the secret of a spell. Along the way, she also opens her home to a trio of children who have been sent to the country to avoid the danger of the London blitz.

The story here is serviceable, the songs entertaining, but it's the special effects that give *Bedknobs and Broomsticks* its special kick. From Miss Price flying on a broomstick to an entire bed taking to the sky, there are many delights in this film, especially when the group goes underwater to the "beautiful, briny sea" and comes into contact with a gallery of animated ocean creatures. There's also a frantic soccer game involving live and cartoon players.

While not nearly as enchanting as *Mary Poppins*, *Bedknobs and Broomsticks* is still an entertaining diversion that will especially appeal to younger viewers. Angela Lansbury is a delight to watch, as always.

BEETHOVEN (1992)
Color, 89 minutes
Cast: Charles Grodin, Bonnie Hunt, Dean Jones, Nicholle Tom, Christopher Castile, Sara Rose Karr, Oliver Platt, Stanley Tucci, David Duchovny, Patricia Heaton, Laurel Cronin, O-Lan Jones
Director: Brian Levant
Screenplay: John Hughes
Comedy/Animal story
Rated PG
Younger children: OK, with caution   Older children: OK

A Saint Bernard puppy escapes from the clutches of an evil and myopic veterinarian (Dean Jones), who cruelly uses animals in his vicious experiments, and finds his way into the Newton home. As far as George Newton (Charles Grodin) is concerned, a fuzzy little puppy is one thing, but when it grows up to be a two-hundred-pound, slobbering, havoc-wreaking dog he loses all patience. Of course, in time the dog becomes a godsend to the Newton family—even cranky George—and after another near miss with the diabolical doctor, they all settle in for a loving, sloppy life together.

Beethoven isn't a masterpiece, but it's silly fun set in a not quite real suburbia. Lots of laughs during those moments when the dog is tipping over tables and knocking down unpleasant guests. Best of all, the film illustrates how this loving animal changes a family's life for the better—and even wins over the disgruntled dad.

One warning for small children: The opening scene of a dognapping may upset sensitive kids. Moreover, Dean Jones (yes, *that* Dean Jones) may scare kids witless as the creepy vet. The best way to deal with this is to keep reminding your little ones that both the vet and his henchman are quite likely to "get theirs" before the film is over.

The language is more raw than necessary, and some scenes are violent. Proceed with caution.

BEETHOVEN'S 2ND (1993)
Color, 86 minutes
Cast: Charles Grodin, Bonnie Hunt, Nicholle Tom, Christopher Castile, Sara Rose Karr, Debi Mazar, Christopher Penn, Ashley Hamilton, Danny Masterson, Catherine Reitman, Maury Chaykin, Heather McComb
Director: Rod Daniel
Screenplay: Len Blum
Comedy/Animal story
Rated PG
Younger children: OK   Older children: OK

The high jinks in suburbia continue with the Newtons and their rambunctious Saint Bernard, Beethoven. In this outing, Beethoven falls in love and becomes a dad. Once again, there's a villain: This time it's avaricious Debi Mazar, who wants to steal and then sell all those bouncing puppies.

More of the same combination of messy slapstick, hints of danger, and sitcom sentimentality as the first film, without the real fright that it had. Although there are some laughs and moments of suspense, this isn't as good as the first—just more of the same. A safe, bland, stale sequel.

BEETLE JUICE (1988)
Color, 92 minutes
Cast: Michael Keaton, Alec Baldwin, Geena Davis, Catherine O'Hara, Jeffrey Jones, Winona Ryder, Glenn Shadix, Sylvia Sidney, Robert Goulet, Dick Cavett, Annie McEnroe
Director: Tim Burton
Screenplay: Michael McDowell and Warren Skaaren
Fantasy/Comedy
Rated PG
Younger kids: OK, with caution   Older kids: VG

A newly deceased young couple (Baldwin and Davis) are destined to haunt their fine old New England home for 125 years, so when a new couple (O'Hara and Jones) move in with their black-clad, melodramatically morbid daughter (Ryder) and redecorate, the ghosts are horrified. For help, they turn to bizarre, impish spirit Betelgeuse (Keaton), an otherworld specialist in scaring away the living.

At its best, this truly unusual movie is hilarious, and Keaton, unrecognizable with a gray fright wig, rotting teeth, and a clown's taste in clothes, is frantically funny as the unbridled Betelgeuse (pronounced "beetle juice," hence the title). At other times, the movie stumbles over its awkward plot, never director Tim Burton's strong suit.

But as usual with the imaginative Burton, the film looks wonderful, with strange sight gags, a cheerful approach to the macabre and death itself, and a great cameo role for Sylvia Sidney as a social worker in the Beyond.

There are too many strange faces, monsters and weirdness for the very young, but kids from 10 up are likely to love the movie, and have certainly been prepared for it, since the movie spun off a TV cartoon series that your children have almost certainly seen.

THE BELLBOY (1960)

Black & white, 72 minutes
Cast: Jerry Lewis, Alex Gerry, Bob Clayton, Sonny Sands, Milton Berle, Walter Winchell
Director: Jerry Lewis
Screenplay: Jerry Lewis
Comedy
Unrated
Young children: VG   Older children: VG

Jerry Lewis had already been a box-office headliner for a decade and a solo success (since splitting up with longtime partner Dean Martin) for four years when he suddenly decided to become a one-man band.

While standing around the lobby of Miami's Fontainebleu Hotel, the idea of a quick comedy about an incompetent bellboy occurred to him. He needed to fulfill a contract with Paramount Pictures for a new movie, and this would be it, providing he could deliver the finished product quickly. He decided to write, produce, and direct, as well as star.

The result is one of his best movies, a joke-a-minute assemblage of comic vignettes, featuring celebrity pals and movie stars in guest appearances.

Interestingly, in this virtually plotless comedy, Jerry is almost completely silent, favorably recalling the great pantomime comedians of yore. If kids of the Jim Carrey generation haven't yet encountered Jerry Lewis, this would be a good place to start. The mostly visual gags are sure to please both young and old.

BELLS ARE RINGING (1960)

Color, 127 minutes
Cast: Judy Holliday, Dean Martin, Fred Clark, Eddie Foy, Jr., Jean Stapleton, Ruth Storey, Dort Clark, Frank Gorshin
Director: Vincente Minnelli
Screenplay: Betty Comden and Adolph Green, based on the musical play by Betty Comden, Adolph Green, and Jule Styne
Musical
Unrated
Young children: OK   Older children: VG

There is something about Judy Holliday that particularly appeals to children. Maybe it's her mischievous grin and her round clown eyes, or her infectious, comic voice. As with Danny Kaye, she inspires youngsters to laugh out loud at her silliness and comic business. This musical offers Holliday in one of her best roles, which she originated on Broadway, as a switchboard operator at a telephone answering service (Susanswerphone) who falls in love with one of the company's clients, just from hearing his voice. Although she is an attractive young woman, her client believes she is an elderly grandma type. Eventually they meet and fall in love, but only through a circuitous route which involves many funny incidents.

Two songs, "Just in Time" and "The Party's Over," provide dreamy romantic interludes, while there also are hilarious scenes involving comical racehorse bookies who take over the telephone service. There's also a dentist who prefers writing songs—using dental equipment! While some of the script might be over children's heads, the basic story is fun—and so are the stars.

BENEATH THE PLANET OF THE APES (1970)

Color, 95 minutes

Cast: James Franciscus, Charlton Heston, Kim Hunter, Maurice Evans, Linda Harrison, Paul Richards, Victor Buono, James Gregory, Jeff Corey, Natalie Trundy, David Watson

Director: Ted Post

Screenplay: Paul Dehn, based on ideas created by Pierre Boulle

Science fiction/Adventure sequel

Rated G

Young children: Scary Older children: OK

Having learned that the planet of the apes is really Earth of the 40th century, with his own civilization wiped out by nuclear war, astronaut Taylor (Charlton Heston) literally disappears into the Forbidden Zone. (He falls through the face of a cliff as if it was smoke.) Meanwhile, another expedition from Taylor's own time goes awry just as his did, stranding astronaut Brent (James Franciscus) on the ape planet. By an impressive coincidence, Taylor's mute human friend Nova (Linda Harrison) rides up just at this moment and leads the astronaut to the ape city, where he, too, is befriended by chimpanzees Zira (Kim Hunter) and Cornelius (David Watson).

Inside the Forbidden Zone, Brent and Nova find an underground civilization of mutated human beings living in the ruins of New York City and worshipping a nuclear device. Elsewhere, the more militaristic apes are planning to revive warfare by attacking the worshippers of the bomb.

The first of the sequels to **Planet of the Apes** is mostly a re-play of the first film, married to the hackneyed concept of mutated survivors of a nuclear war. It's well made but surprisingly unimaginative and full of absurd, time-worn, and dull ideas.

If your kids liked *Planet of the Apes,* they may want to see the sequel, but they'd be better off skipping ahead to the next follow-up, **Escape from Planet of the Apes.** If they do watch this one, be warned: there is a shocking moment (for young kids) in which the mutants pull off human masks. What's more, the ending is very bleak and downbeat.

BENJI (1974)

Color, 85 minutes

Cast: Higgins the Dog, Patsy Garrett, Allen Fiuzat, Cynthia Smith, Peter Breck, Frances Bavier, Terry Carter, Edgar Buchanan, Tom Lester, Christopher Connelly, Deborah Walley

Director: Joe Camp

Writer: Joe Camp

Animal story/Drama

Rated G

Younger children: VG Older children: OK

Viewers follow the dog Benji (Higgins the Dog) on his regular daily rounds in a small Southern town: visiting two children whose father doesn't want them to have a dog, chasing a cat, waking up the local café owner who gives him a bone, and getting advice on romance from a cop. Then he adjourns to his "home," an abandoned mansion. Soon Benji finds himself a girlfriend, but when crooks invade his house, Benji has to become a hero to save the children and dog he loves.

Filmed almost entirely from the

viewpoint of the dog, *Benji* is a gentle (if prosaic) film that even the youngest child should appreciate. The dog, who became a big star in the 1970s, may look familiar to parents; he was featured for several seasons on television's *Petticoat Junction*. In fact, several of this film's cast members were familiar faces at the time from their respective TV series (*Petticoat Junction*, *The Andy Griffith Show*, and *Green Acres*).

It was followed by a sequel, *For the Love of Benji* (1977), an entertaining romp set in Athens; *Oh! Heavenly Dog* (1980), in which comic actor Chevy Chase inhabited Benji's body; and *Benji the Hunted* (1987), an unsuccessful attempt at a comeback for the canine star.

BENNY & JOON (1993)
Color, 98 minutes
Cast: Johnny Depp, Mary Stuart
    Masterson, Aidan Quinn,
    Julianne Moore, Oliver Platt,
    CCH Pounder, Dan Hedaya,
    Joe Grifasi, William H. Macy
Director: Jeremiah Chechik
Screenplay: Barry Berman, from
    a story by Berman and Leslie
    McNeil
Comedy-drama
Rated PG
Younger children: No   Older
    children: OK, with caution

Joon (Mary Stuart Masterson), a mentally disturbed painter, and her protective brother, Benny (Aidan Quinn), win the quirky Sam (Johnny Depp) in an offbeat poker game. Joon soon falls in love with Sam, an illiterate savant who idolizes silent film clowns Buster Keaton and Charlie Chaplin. Benny, predictably, objects to this relationship, even though his constant watchfulness over his little sister has kept him from getting on with his own life. Joon is traumatized by Benny's reaction, but ultimately Joon and Sam decide they belong together—juggling, painting, smashing potatoes with a tennis racket, and making grilled cheese sandwiches with the iron.

All the characters in *Benny & Joon* are delightfully eccentric, and most are good at heart; what's more, many scenes feature very funny visual gags. Still, parents should know that the film has several disturbing elements, including references to Joon and Sam's sexual relationship, Joon's tendency to start fires, and a very unsettling scene in which Joon becomes violent on a bus and is committed to a hospital. Screenwriter Barry Berman has created an unforgettable group of oddball characters and sprinkled his script with absurdist humor. But this one's only for the most mature children, if parents are comfortable with the material.

THE BICYCLE THIEF (1947)
Black & white, 90 minutes
Cast: Lamberto Maggiorani,
    Lianella Carell, Enzo Staiola,
    Elena Altieri
Director: Vittorio De Sica
Screenplay: De Sica, Cesare
    Zavattini, Oreste Biancoli,
    Suso D'Amico, Adolfo Franci,
    Gherardo Gherardi, and
    Gerardo Guerrieri, based on a
    story by Zavattini and a novel
    by Luigi Bartolini
Drama
Unrated
Younger kids: No   Older kids:
    VG

The Bicycle Thief is one of the classics of world cinema, about a man's desperate search for his stolen bicycle, which he needs for his job. Winner of a special Oscar, it's often hailed as the epitome of Italian cinema's Neo-realist movement—which utilized authentic locations, largely nonprofessional casts, and a documentarylike technique to depict realistic slices of everyday life. It's also an extremely moving portrayal of a father-and-son relationship.

Lamberto Maggiorani gives a superbly restrained performance as the father, and as his son, Enzo Staiola is refreshingly free of cloying sentimentality. (Both were amateur actors.) The story of *The Bicycle Thief* is so simple, so elemental that mature children should respond as strongly as adults—and find it just as affecting. It's probably too sad and too difficult to explain for younger kids. Even older children will need some sense of historical context about the Italian people's struggle to survive in the days following World War II.

The mournful music and poetic photography create an indelible sense of alienation and despair as the pair wander through the gloomy city, but there is also some irony and humor, and by the end, the problems of these "ordinary little people" have attained the force and universality of a Greek tragedy.

BIG (1988)
Color, 102 minutes
Cast: Tom Hanks, Elizabeth Perkins, John Heard, Jared Rushton, Robert Loggia, David Moscow, Jon Lovitz, Mercedes Ruehl, Josh Clark, Tracy Reiner

Director: Penny Marshall
Screenplay: Gary Ross and Anne Spielberg
Comedy/Fantasy
Rated PG
Younger kids: VG   Older kids: VG

Josh, a dejected 12-year-old boy, wishes he was "big" . . . and then wakes up to find himself magically transformed into a 30-year-old man (with his 12-year-old mind intact). Forced to leave home, "Josh" soon finds himself facing the real world, and almost as quickly becomes the vice president of development for a major toy company. He even has a romance with an executive (Perkins) at the company who is charmed by his honesty and lack of guile. But something's got to give: he can't live in two worlds at once, both a child and an adult.

The rare instance of a "high concept" Hollywood fantasy idea becoming a beautifully realized, and even touching, film, with Hanks perfectly capturing all the emotional and physical awkwardness of a boy trapped in an "adult" body. It examines the loss of innocence and skillfully avoids cheap gags and mawkishness, and deals with adult themes of sexuality with great sensitivity and great humor. (There is one curious question to ponder after the movie is done, however: How will David deal with the rest of his life as a kid again, having seen what he could be like as an adult?)

Young children may find some of the plot developments confusing, especially where the love interest is involved. They will also be saddened by certain scenes—Josh feeling alone in the city and starting to cry, and a moving moment when he goes home and his own mother doesn't recognize him.

A good companion piece for this is *Vice Versa,* another 1988 body-switching movie, with Judge Reinhold and Fred Savage, that was actually pretty good.

BIG RED (1962)
Color, 89 minutes
Cast: Walter Pidgeon, Gilles Payant, Emile Genest, Janette Bertrand, Doris Lussier
Director: Norman Tokar
Screenplay: Louis Pelletier, based on a novel by Jim Kjelgaard
Drama/Animal story
Unrated
Young children: VG, with caution   Older children: VG

Big Red is a fine, understated Walt Disney production, set and filmed in Canada, about a boy's relationship with a dog. Unlike so many films of the 1990s, it isn't told in bold strokes but takes its time, allowing us to learn about its characters bit by bit. Some contemporary kids, who are accustomed to having stories laid out for them, ready-made, on a platter, may not take to this brand of storytelling at first. But if they give it a chance, they may find *Big Red* quite satisfying.

Rene Dumont is an orphan who lands a job with a rich but lonely dog breeder named James Haggin (Walter Pidgeon). Haggin has his eye on a beautiful Irish setter in his kennel named Big Red, but no one can get anywhere with the stubborn animal . . . until Rene comes along. Rene and Big Red become inseparable, to the point where Haggin fears that the youngster will be too dependent on the animal. This leads to the first of several crises that test both the boy's courage and the dog's constitution.

Big Red is filled with incident, but it doesn't telegraph where it's going at every turn; that's one of the refreshing things about the film. Neither its story nor its characters are easily pinned down at first; it's based on one of Jim Kjelgaard's popular juvenile novels of the 1950s, many of which deal with his favorite breed, Irish setters.

There are some highly emotional scenes in which Red is placed in peril; this is bound to upset some children, especially younger ones who can't foresee that since this is a Disney film, everything is going to be OK.

BILL & TED'S BOGUS JOURNEY (1991)
Color, 91 minutes
Cast: Keanu Reeves, Alex Winter, William Sadler, Joss Ackland, George Carlin, Pam Grier
Director: Peter Hewitt
Screenplay: Chris Matheson and Ed Solomon
Science fiction–fantasy/Comedy
Rated PG
Younger kids: NG   Older kids: OK

The premise of this sequel is grimmer than the original: Robot duplicates of Bill and Ted arrive from the future and kill our heroes, who go to Hell. (In fact, the original title of the film *was* "Bill & Ted Go to Hell.") However, they make a deal with the Grim Reaper, amusingly played by William Sadler, who eventually teams up with them in their effort to get back to their girlfriends on Earth.

Bill and Ted are even dumber here than in the first film—which may be hard to believe—but their escapades are, if anything, a bit cleverer, involving close encounters with everyone from Albert Einstein to the Easter bunny! There are also more special effects, which may score this higher for older kids.

BILL & TED'S EXCELLENT ADVENTURE (1989)
Color, 90 minutes
Cast: Keanu Reeves, Alex Winter, George Carlin, Bernie Casey
Director: Stephen Herek
Screenplay: Chris Matheson and Ed Solomon
Science fiction/Comedy
Rated PG
Younger kids: Of little interest Older kids: Good

Two amiable, airheaded pals, high school students Winter and Reeves, are told by Carlin, a visitor from the future, that it is so important for them to pass their history exam that he is giving them the use of a time machine. So they bat about through history, gathering up an assortment of celebrities, including the likes of Abraham Lincoln, Joan of Arc, and Aristotle.

Surprisingly well written, this might actually be of more interest to adults than kids, but there's fun to be had for the older ones. The younger kids won't find much of interest for them here, but it's harmless enough. The humor never quite works as well as it keeps promising to, and ten years later, the teenage slang is already dated, but the types well played

by Reeves and Winter are timeless.

Followed by a sequel of similar merit: **Bill & Ted's Bogus Journey**.

BILLY ROSE'S JUMBO (1962)
Color, 123 minutes
Cast: Doris Day, Stephen Boyd, Jimmy Durante, Martha Raye, Dean Jagger, Joseph Waring, Lynn Wood
Director: Charles Walters
Screenplay: Sidney Sheldon, based on the Broadway musical by Ben Hecht and Charles MacArthur
Musical/Circus
Unrated
Young children: VG   Older children: VG

Seeing *Billy Rose's Jumbo*, a long-in-coming screen version of the 1935 Broadway musical with songs by Richard Rodgers and Lorenz Hart, is the cinematic equivalent of a trip to the big top.

Billy Rose's Jumbo does have a story, which charts the plight of a touring circus operated in the days prior to World War I by Pop Wonder (played by the ever-delightful Jimmy Durante, who also appeared in the original production). Its primary attraction is Jumbo, a multitalented elephant. Unfortunately, Pop tends to fritter away the show's profits by gambling. Meanwhile, his pert daughter, Kitty (Doris Day), hires virile circus veteran Sam Rawlins (Stephen Boyd) to work both in front of the customers and behind the scenes. She doesn't know that Sam is the offspring of Pop's rival, who is scheming to gain control of the circus.

Despite the dramatics, and an inevitable romance between Kitty and Sam, the spotlight here is on the circus. Its sheer scope is captured by the legendary director-choreographer Busby Berkeley. While there are romantic numbers (most memorably "The Most Beautiful Girl in the World"), quite a few of the songs ("Circus on Parade," "What Is a Circus," "Sawdust, Spangles and Dreams") feature a big top theme. And there's plenty of broad comedy, provided by Durante and the great, rubber-faced Martha Raye.

This is an entertaining dose of cotton candy with something to please every member of the family. If not among the best movie musicals, it is certainly among the most colorful.

THE BIRDS (1963)
Color, 120 minutes
Cast: Tippi Hedren, Rod Taylor, Jessica Tandy, Suzanne Pleshette, Veronica Cartwright
Director: Alfred Hitchcock
Screenplay: Evan Hunter, loosely based on the story by Daphne du Maurier
Science fiction/Suspense
Unrated
Younger Kids: No Older Kids: OK

As a prank, spoiled heiress Hedren delivers a pair of lovebirds to Taylor in his small California coastal town, and soon thereafter, birds of all species begin attacking and killing local residents. They seem to be after Hedren in particular.

One of Alfred Hitchcock's most famous films, *The Birds* is not among his very best; the first half is very talky, and the talk isn't very interesting. But when the bird attacks start, the film becomes memorably terrifying. The attacks are so different from one another that each is a standout: the crows silently massing on the jungle gym in a schoolyard, the sparrows bursting out of a chimney, the seagulls attacking the diner.

Definitely too intense for younger children, but older ones, once they get past all the boring stuff at the beginning, could well be mesmerized. (The attacks still terrify some *adults*.) Kids used to explosive resolutions to "monster" movies may well be disappointed with the quiet finale, too.

The film, incidentally, does not have a musical score, but instead uses the cries of birds, electronically modified and "arranged" by master composer Bernard Herrmann.

THE BLACK ARROW (1948)
Black & white, 76 minutes
Cast: Louis Hayward, Janet Blair, George Macready, Edgar Buchanan, Rhys Williams, Paul Cavanagh
Director: Gordon Douglas
Screenplay: Richard Schayer, David P. Sheppherd, and Thomas Seller, based on the novel by Robert Louis Stevenson
Swashbuckler/Action-adventure
Unrated
Younger kids: OK Older kids: VG

The Black Arrow is an exciting and entertaining story about a young knight (Louis Hayward) who returns from the Wars of the Roses to learn that his uncle has murdered his father to seize the House of York. The uncle (played by the deliciously evil George Macready) then frames a neighboring lord for the crime and tries to force the man's daughter to marry him, but she's saved by the heroic knight.

This is a top-flight swashbuckler with convincing performances and vigorous action as the hero takes on the villain and his henchmen with sword, dagger, lance, crossbow, and battle-axe. As with other films of this period, the climactic battle for supremacy is memorably exciting—but not gory. Louis Hayward starred in such other swashbucklers as **The Man in the Iron Mask** and **Captain Pirate.** The story was remade for television in 1985.

BLACKBEARD THE PIRATE (1952)
Color, 99 minutes
Cast: Robert Newton, Linda Darnell, William Bendix, Keith Andes, Torin Thatcher, Richard Egan, Irene Ryan
Director: Raoul Walsh
Screenplay: Alan LeMay
Swashbuckler/Action-adventure
Unrated
Younger kids: OK Older kids: Good

After his stint as Long John Silver in Disney's **Treasure Island** (1950), Robert Newton was somewhat typecast in similar parts; none was hammier than his eye-rolling portrayal of Blackbeard (who actually wears firecrackers in his beard!) in this lively swashbuckler. Here he shivers his timbers and matches wits with another famous pirate, Henry Morgan (Torin Thatcher), who has supposedly reformed and earned a commission from the King of England to capture the scourge of the Caribbean.

Director Raoul Walsh keeps the bloodthirsty action coming fast and furious, with some swordplay that is surprisingly violent for its time and may be inappropriate for the very young. Kids who enjoyed *Treasure Island* may like seeing Newton as another roaring pirate, and those with sharp eyes will recognize Torin Thatcher as the villain from **The 7th Voyage of Sinbad.**

BLACK BEAUTY (1994)
Color, 85 minutes
Cast: Sean Bean, David Thewlis, Jim Carter, Peter Davison, Alun Armstrong, John McEnery, Eleanor Bron, Peter Cook, Andrew Knott; voice of Alan Cumming
Director: Caroline Thompson
Screenplay: Caroline Thompson
Animal story/Literary classic
Rated G
Young children: OK Older children: VG

Anna Sewell's 1877 novel, written from her sickbed, is the life story of a patient, suffering horse who moves from owner to owner in 19th-century England. It was the first book to make people realize that animals are God's creatures, too, and deserve respect and care.

This is the third and best screen treatment, made on location in England, and the only one that allows Beauty to narrate, just as in the book (which is subtitled "The Autobiography of a Horse").

The sensitive screenwriter of **Edward Scissorhands** and **The Nightmare Before Christmas** here makes her debut as writer-director with an atmospheric, if episodic, tale that runs him through the full course of what life can serve up, from benevolence to mistreatment.

The brutality that animals often face will make the movie difficult to watch for little ones, especially those that care about pets. (In spite of the G rating, those scenes can be fairly upsetting.)

Otherwise, this classic about the ups and downs of equine existence—from coach horse to cart horse—will interest all. It's a handsome production with an excellent cast.

Oh, and fear not: it ends well.

THE BLACK CAULDRON
(1985)
Color, 82 minutes
Cast: Voices of Grant Beardsley, John Hurt, Susan Sheridan, Freddie Jones, Nigel Hawthorne, Arthur Malet, John Byner, narration by John Huston
Directors: Ted Berman and Richard Rich
Screenplay: David Jonas, Vance Gerry, Berman, Rich, Joe Hale, Al Wilson, Roy Morita, Peter Young, Art Stevens, Rosemary Anne Sisson, and Roy Edward Disney, based on the five novels of the series *The Chronicles of Prydain* by Lloyd Alexander.
Animated feature/Fantasy/ Action-adventure
Rated PG
Younger kids: Good   Older kids: VG

Disney's 25th animated feature, *The Black Cauldron* is an engaging (if not particularly memorable) sword-and-sorcery fantasy, based on the enduringly popular novels by Lloyd Alexander, set in a mythical English countryside, about a teenage pig-keeper named Taran who dreams of becoming a mighty knight. After learning about a mystical black cauldron that can give its owner great power, Taran sets off on a perilous quest to find the object and keep it out of the hands of the evil Horned King. He is accompanied by Hen Wen, his clairvoyant pig, an old minstrel, a beautiful princess, and Gurgi, a funny forest creature they meet along the way.

Filled with swashbuckling action, fire-breathing dragons, skeleton warriors, and magic swords, kids (especially young boys) are sure to enjoy this adventure. Even though the story lacks the old Disney warmth and heart, the production is opulent and the animation is impressive (it was originally filmed in a 70mm widescreen format), featuring some razzle-dazzle lighting effects and colorful explosions.

The voice cast, which includes some distinguished British actors and John Huston as the narrator, is also very good, particularly John Hurt as the villainous Horned King, whose creepy character looks and sounds a lot like the sinister Emperor Palpatine from **Star Wars.** John Byner's work as Gurgi adds sure-fire comic relief.

This is the only Disney cartoon to ever receive a PG rating, based on some fantasy violence and "scary" imagery involving witches, goblins, and the Horned King that might be considered frightening for the very young, but it's mild stuff compared to most of today's TV cartoons for kids.

THE BLACK PIRATE (1926)
Color, 85 minutes
Cast: Douglas Fairbanks, Billie Dove, Anders Rudolf, Donald Crisp
Director: Albert Parker

Screenplay: Lotta Woods and
Jack Cunningham, based on a
story by Elton Thomas (pseud.
of Douglas Fairbanks)
Action-adventure/Swashbuckler/
Silent classic
Unrated
Younger kids: Good   Older
kids: VG

Silent-screen action hero Douglas
Fairbanks stars in this fun swashbuckler that's given added sparkle
by virtue of its being photographed in an early Technicolor
process. Fairbanks plays a nobleman who becomes a pirate in order
to avenge the death of his father
and rescue a princess (Billie Dove),
but the story is really just an excuse for Fairbanks to display his
prowess at spectacular stunts and
acrobatics: single-handedly capturing an enemy vessel, flying
through the air on a ship's sail
(one of the most famous stunts in
movie history), swimming to his
underwater hideout, being made
to walk the plank—and escaping—and engaging in countless
duels with rival buccaneers.

If your kids can be persuaded
to try a silent movie—or if, by
some happy chance, they've already made that discovery—this is
one they're bound to enjoy.

THE BLACK SCORPION
(1957)
Black & white, 85 minutes
Cast: Richard Denning, Mara
Corday, Carlos Rivas, Mario
Navarro.
Director: Edward Ludwig
Screenplay: David Duncan and
Robert Blees
Science fiction/Monster
Unrated
Younger kids: Too dull   Older
kids: Likewise

An American geologist and his
Mexican partner are investigating
the aftermath of recent volcanic
activity in the heart of Mexico
when they learn that the geologic
disturbances freed gigantic scorpions from their underground lair,
and the scorpions ravaging the
countryside. Eventually, one last
scorpion, bigger than the rest, attacks Mexico City.

Mostly dull and dreary, this obvious rehash of the far better
Them! is enlivened by outstanding stop-motion monsters, the
work of the great Willis O'Brien,
of **King Kong** fame, and his partner, Peter Peterson. Oddly, the
film was released before the effects were completed, so what attacks Mexico City is generally the
featureless, blacked-out matte of
a scorpion without the model
being inserted.

If your kids are into special effects, particularly from a historic
standpoint, this otherwise hum-
drum film is ideal for them; they'll
watch with one finger on the fast
forward button, but they'll look at
the scorpion scenes over and over
again. And you might do the
same thing.

THE BLACK SHIELD OF
FALWORTH (1954)
Color, 99 minutes
Cast: Tony Curtis, Janet Leigh,
David Farrar, Barbara Rush,
Herbert Marshall
Director: Rudolph Maté
Screenplay: Oscar Brodney,
based on the novel *Men of
Iron* by Howard Pyle
Swashbuckler/Action-adventure
Unrated
Younger kids: OK   Older kids:
Good

Tony Curtis, at his handsomest, stars in this swashbuckling tale of medieval England, though with his New York accent he seems a trifle out of place amid the largely British cast. Curtis plays Myles, the son of a disgraced knight, who goes to the court of King Henry IV (Ian Keith) in an effort to prove that his late father was not a traitor. The cocky youth becomes a squire, then trains for knighthood and, with the aid of the Earl of Mackworth (Herbert Marshall) and Prince Hal (Dan O'Herlihy), thwarts a conspiracy against the king by the wicked Earl of Alban (David Farrar). In the process, Myles restores his family's good name and wins the heart of Mackworth's daughter, the lovely Lady Anne (Curtis' then-wife Janet Leigh).

This juvenile romp is generally fun and has plenty of action and romance, all of it G rated by today's standards. Fans of Jamie Lee Curtis might get a kick out of seeing her mother and father when they were young.

novel, which follows the adventures—and friendship—of a young boy and an imposing stallion who meet on a remote island after an ocean liner has sunk. This is a rarity among boy-and-his-pet stories: It's told simply, eloquently, poetically, and reaches near-mythic heights. It conveys a clear, childlike awe for nature and, amazingly, never gets sticky or manipulative. It's a feast for the ears and for the eyes (courtesy of cinematographer Caleb Deschanel) that captures the grace of movement as few other films have ever done.

As a bonus, Mickey Rooney turns in a wonderful performance, as the horse trainer who befriends the young boy, and conjures up memories of his own part in another classic family film, **National Velvet.**

Parents might want to be aware that in the opening scenes, a ship sinks and the hero loses his father. The sequence is quite realistic and may be upsetting to smaller children.

THE BLACK STALLION
(1979)
Color, 118 minutes
Cast: Kelly Reno, Mickey
    Rooney, Teri Garr, Clarence
    Muse, Hoyt Axton, Michael
    Higgins
Director: Carroll Ballard
Screenplay: Melissa Mathison,
    Jeanne Rosenberg, and
    William D. Wittliff, based on
    the novel by Walter Farley
Animal story/Drama
Rated G
Younger kids: VG   Older kids:
    VG

The Black Stallion is a beautiful adaptation of the classic children's

THE BLACK STALLION
RETURNS (1983)
Color, 93 minutes
Cast: Kelly Reno, Vincent
    Spano, Allen Goorwitz
    (Garfield), Woody Strode,
    Ferdinand Mayne, Jodi
    Thelen, Teri Garr
Director: Robert Dalva
Screenplay: Richard Kletter and
    Jerome Kass
Animal adventure
Rated: PG
Younger kids: OK   Older kids:
    OK

The Black Stallion Returns is a disappointing sequel that lacks the charm and magic of the original, but still makes for decent children's entertainment. The corny story concerns the now-teenage Alec (Kelly Reno) pursuing some thieves who have stolen his stallion and taken it to Morocco to participate in a horse race.

The photography of the Sahara desert and other African locations is impressive, but the film substitutes routine action and lowbrow comedy for the poetic qualities that made the first film so special. Kelly Reno is back in the leading role, but the warm presence of Mickey Rooney is very much missed.

The language which earned this a PG rating may not be suitable for the youngest viewers.

THE BLACK SWAN (1942)
Color, 85 minutes
Cast: Tyrone Power, Maureen O'Hara, Laird Cregar, Thomas Mitchell, George Sanders, Anthony Quinn, George Zucco
Director: Henry King
Screenplay: Ben Hecht and Seton I. Miller, based on the novel by Rafael Sabatini
Swashbuckler/Action-adventure
Unrated
Younger kids: Good   Older kids: VG

From the pen of novelist Rafael Sabatini (**Captain Blood, The Sea Hawk**) comes another lusty pirate saga, with Tyrone Power in peak form as an aide to Henry Morgan (Laird Cregar), the notorious former buccaneer who is appointed governor of Jamaica with a directive to rid the island of his former cronies. Two of them are played by George Sanders and Anthony Quinn, who revel in their roles as

swaggering renegades who refuse to reform, while Maureen O'Hara is rescued from their clutches by Power.

This is one of the most entertaining swashbucklers ever made, offering generous portions of high adventure, swordplay, and romance, and is extremely well produced, with superb, Oscar-winning Technicolor cinematography (by Leon Shamroy). Like many Hollywood escapist adventures, this was not aimed specifically at kids, but rather a general audience, which is why it holds up so well today and can entertain both parents and children.

BLANK CHECK (1994)
Color, 93 minutes
Cast: Brian Bonsall, Karen Duffy, James Rebhorn, Jayne Atkinson, Michael Faustino, Chris Demetral, Miguel Ferrer, Michael Lerner, Tone Loc, Rick Ducommun, Alex Zuckerman, Debbie Allen
Director: Rupert Wainwright
Screenplay: Blake Snyder and Colby Carr
Comedy
Rated PG
Younger children: OK   Older children: OK

Cross **Richie Rich** with **Home Alone** and you get *Blank Check*, a derivative kids comedy with nothing special in its account.

Eleven-year-old Preston (Brian Bonsall) is feeling the pressures of his roughneck siblings, his penny-pinching parents, and his free-spending friends. When fugitive criminal Quigley (Miguel Ferrer) damages Preston's bike with his auto, he hands the boy a half-completed check and dashes off before police arrive. The clever lad cashes the check for one million dollars, buys a local mansion, and stocks it full of video games and high-tech gizmos. When Quigley and his men catch on to the boy who emptied his ill-gotten bank account, they fall prey to many *Home Alone*–like booby traps trying to break into his mansion.

Bonsall, of TV's *Family Ties*, is believable, and the other actors are adequate. Kids will enjoy the spending spree scenes—who wouldn't?—but the rest of the film may strike even youngsters as being awfully familiar.

Bad language and the threats of the villains make this a PG title.

THE BLOB (1958)
Color, 86 minutes
Cast: Steve McQueen, Aneta Corseaut, Earl Rowe, Olin Howlin
Director: Irvin S. Yeaworth, Jr.
Screenplay: Theodore Simonson and Kate Phillips, from an idea by Irvine H. Millgate
Science fiction/Monster thriller
Unrated
Younger kids: No   Older kids: Good of its kind

A small, fallen meteor pops open, revealing a mobile blob of protoplasm that has only one goal: to devour as many people as possible, growing with each new victim. The movie takes place entirely in one night. Steve McQueen (billed as Steven, at the beginning of his career) is the leader of a group of teenagers who try to rouse the townspeople to the alien danger in their midst.

The odd, almost jokey tone of the movie keeps this dated, low-budget thriller watchable today, but it's not going to be anyone's favorite film. Older kids might be amused by the overage teenagers, but could also be interested in the very basic nature of this movie's monster: it moves, it eats, and that's it.

A word of warning: the 1988 remake is R-rated.

BLOCK-HEADS (1938)
Black & white, 58 minutes
Cast: Stan Laurel, Oliver Hardy, Billy Gilbert, Patricia Ellis, Minna Gombell, James C. Morton, James Finlayson, Harry Woods, Tommy Bond
Director: John G. Blystone
Screenplay: Charles Rogers, Felix Adler, James Parrott, Harry Langdon, and Arnold Belgard
Comedy
Unrated
Young children: VG   Older children: VG

This Laurel and Hardy comedy opens during World War I. The boys are soldiers on the front lines, and as Ollie goes "over the top," Stan is ordered to remain behind and guard the trench. He does so—for the next twenty years! When they're finally reunited, Stan tells his old pal, "You know how dumb I used to be? Well, I'm better now."

But not quite. The rest of the film shows Stan and Ollie getting into all sorts of jams, from a misunderstanding with Ollie's wife to an altercation with a tough-guy neighbor. Then there's the time Stan leaves the gas on too long in the kitchen. . . .

Block-Heads is short and sweet, an easygoing, very funny film that coasts on the delightful personalities of its stars and has an ample supply of sight gags to keep things lively. It will please Laurel and Hardy fans of all ages.

THE BLUE BIRD (1940)
Color, 88 minutes
Cast: Shirley Temple, Spring Byington, Nigel Bruce, Gale Sondergaard, Eddie Collins, Sybil Jason, Jessie Ralph, Helen Ericson, Johnny Russell, Laura Hope Crews
Director: Walter Lang
Screenplay: Ernest Pascal, based on the play by Maurice Maeterlinck
Fantasy/Allegory
Unrated
Young children: OK   Older children: OK

In this lavish, highly unusual fantasy film, a selfish brat—played by Shirley Temple—and her brother embark on a quest to locate the Bluebird of Happiness, just as the world around them is being shattered by war. In a dreamlike state, the children visit the kingdoms of the Past, Luxury, and the Future, where they witness fanciful and exotic people and events as they search for the elusive bird.

This is a haunting fairy tale, which occasionally may be frightening to younger children. It features aspects of death and the "unliving," in the forms of deceased grandparents and babies who are waiting to be born. Some children, of all ages, will find this film off-putting for its eerie quality, as well as its unusual, allegorical story. On the other hand, some will be intrigued by the film's special effects, which feature a spectacular forest fire, children leaping into the air by magic, and animals turning into human beings.

As a historical note, this elaborate Technicolor production was launched after Shirley's studio, 20th Century-Fox, refused to loan her to MGM, which wanted her to star in their production of **The Wizard of Oz.** Film buffs have always regarded *The Blue Bird* as Fox's answer to *Oz,* though it's not nearly as good a film.

BLUE HAWAII (1961)
Color, 101 minutes
Cast: Elvis Presley, Joan Blackman, Angela Lansbury, Roland Winters, Iris Adrian
Director: Norman Taurog
Screenplay: Hal Kanter, based on a story by Allan Weiss
Romantic comedy/Musical
Unrated
Young children: VG   Older children: VG

This friendly Elvis Presley vehicle casts the King of rock 'n' roll as Chad Gates, a young man who's just been released from the military (as Elvis had in real life). He returns to his native Hawaii, where his snooty mother (Angela Lansbury) demands that he associate only with those who are wealthy and white, wed a girl of his class, and take a job with her husband's stuffy company. Chad, of course, has other ideas regarding how to live his life.

Elvis sings the title hit, as well as one of his loveliest numbers, "Can't Help Falling in Love," in this colorful, lighthearted film. Although it's quite entertaining and innocuous, it spelled a change for Elvis' film career and led to a string of increasingly fluffy, insubstantial movies—quite a change from his gritty pre-Army image.

Kids who want to understand Elvis' great appeal will certainly get a dose of his effortless charm in this movie.

THE BODY SNATCHER
(1945)
Black & white, 77 minutes
Cast: Boris Karloff, Bela Lugosi, Henry Daniell, Edith Atwater, Russell Wade, Rita Corday, Sharyn Moffett, Donna Lee, Robert Clarke
Director: Robert Wise
Screenplay: Carlos Keith (pseud. of Val Lewton) and Philip MacDonald, from the short story by Robert Louis Stevenson
Horror/Drama
Unrated
Younger kids: Boring, then scary   Older kids: OK

In 19th-century Edinburgh, dedicated doctor Daniell is forced to buy bodies stolen from a cemetery by a sardonic cab driver (Karloff) in order to conduct medical experiments. When the bodies in the cemetery run out, the cab driver turns to murder.

Stevenson's short story was based on the true story of Burke and Hare, real-life body snatchers; producer Val Lewton and director Robert Wise add a touch of macabre poetry to the events. The excellent performances, particularly from Karloff and Daniell, handsome if budget-conscious production design, and a bravura climax result in what's probably the best horror movie of the 1940s.

Made for adults, the film is over the heads of younger kids, who still shouldn't be allowed to sit through it, because of the very frightening climax. This almost genteel film is far removed from the horror movies of the 1980s

and 1990s, so while teenagers won't be bothered by it, they may not be very interested, either. However, those with a taste for older films or who have already been impressed by the movies of Val Lewton may appreciate its quality.

BOGUS (1996)
Color, 111 minutes
Cast: Whoopi Goldberg, Gérard Depardieu, Haley Joel Osment, Nancy Travis, Denis Mercier, Andrea Martin, Ute Lemper, Sheryl Lee Ralph
Director: Norman Jewison
Screenplay: Alvin Sargent, based on a story by Jeff Rothberg and Francis X. McCarthy
Fantasy
Rated PG
Young kids: No   Older kids: OK

A young boy who lives with his mom has his world shattered when she's killed in an auto accident. With no other relatives to call on, he is sent to live with his godmother (Whoopi Goldberg) in Newark, New Jersey. She has no use for a child in her life and pays little attention to him . . . so he conjures up an imaginary friend named Bogus (Gérard Depardieu). As Bogus becomes increasingly real (and important) to the boy, his godmother is forced to become more involved in his life—as he seems to have no sense of reality or responsibility.

This attempt to create a modern-day fable would seem to have all the right ingredients, but it just doesn't work. The death of the mother is very upsetting, and Bogus' friendship with the boy never takes on that magical feeling one keeps hoping for.

Bogus is an odd, melancholy film, in spite of good performances all around. It's long, slow, and ultimately unsatisfying.

THE BOHEMIAN GIRL (1936)
Black & white, 75 minutes
Cast: Stan Laurel, Oliver Hardy, Antonio Moreno, Jacqueline Wells (Julie Bishop), Darla Hood, Mae Busch, James Finlayson, William P. Carleton, Thelma Todd, Zeffie Tilbury
Directors: James W. Horne and Charles Rogers
Screenplay: Alfred Bunn, based on the opera by Michael Balfe
Comedy
Unrated
Younger children: VG Older children: VG

As in **The Devil's Brother,** Laurel and Hardy found an ideal setting for their comedy in a vintage opera. This time they play gypsies who raise a girl who has been abducted—unbeknownst to them. (She is played, as a youngster, by Darla Hood of The Little Rascals.) It turns out the girl is the daughter of a wealthy and powerful nobleman, but there are many twists and turns before she is restored to her rightful home.

Of course, the plot is not nearly as important as the gags, which are plentiful and involve some of the duo's usual gallery of comic costars, including the pop-eyed James Finlayson and the shrewish Mae Busch, who plays Ollie's manipulative wife.

Kids may grow impatient with some of the remaining songs from Balfe's opera, but any time Stan and Ollie are on screen, *Bohemian Girl* springs to life. Laurel and Hardy fans will find much to cherish here—from great routines like Stan playing "fingers" and sucking too much wine instead of bottling it—to throwaway lines, such as Stanley announcing that he's going to his zither lesson.

BOPHA! (1993)
Color, 120 minutes
Cast: Danny Glover, Malcolm McDowell, Alfre Woodard, Marius Weyers, Maynard Eziashi, Malick Bowens, Grace Mahlaba
Director: Morgan Freeman
Screenplay: Brian Bird and John Wierick, based on the play by Percy Mtwa
Drama
Rated PG-13
Young children: No Older children: VG

Bopha! is a taut drama which tells the story of Master Sergeant Micah Mangena (Danny Glover), a black policeman in a South African township. To many—and, in particular, his country's political radicals—Mangena is little more than an Uncle Tom, a tool of the white ruling class and a symbol of the status quo.

Mangena's world is destined to fall apart, however, and he will undergo a crisis of conscience, set into motion when his son, whom he expects to follow in his footsteps, takes part in a revolt against the policies of a local, white-run school.

Bopha!, which in the Zulu language means "arrest" or "detain," is an insightful allegory that examines the impact of apartheid on the individual, the family, and the community.

Danny Glover and Alfre Woodard (who plays the policeman's strong yet justifiably fearful wife) also costarred as Nelson and Winnie Mandela in the highly recommended made-for-cable feature *Mandela* (1987).

Bopha! contains strong language and scenes of violence that may be upsetting even to older children. Parents (or teachers) should be on hand for a viewing of this film, as it cries out for a discussion of apartheid.

BORN FREE (1966)
Color, 95 minutes
Cast: Virginia McKenna, Bill Travers, Geoffrey Keen, Peter Lukoye, Omar Chambati, Bill Godden, Brian Epsom, Robert Cheetham
Director: James Hill
Writer: Gerald L. C. Copley, based on books by Joy Adamson
Animal story/Drama
Unrated
Younger children: OK Older children: OK

Born Free is the true story of game warden George Adamson (Bill Travers) and his wife Joy (Virginia McKenna), who adopt an orphaned lion cub in Africa and raise it. When Elsa, the lion, grows too big, the Adamsons are supposed to turn her over to a zoo, but decide instead that they will prepare Elsa to return to the wilderness—an environment this tame lion has never known.

Set in Kenya, *Born Free* was a huge success when it came out in 1966 (and even spawned a hit record with its title tune). The exotic locations, fine nature photography and timeless appeal of the story should keep the whole family involved from beginning to end. The film has dated somewhat, but that shouldn't deter children from appreciating the scenic beauty or the captivating tale of the baby lion raised in captivity and trained by humans to become, once again, a wild lion.

Followed by a sequel, *Living Free*.

THE BORROWERS (1997)
Color, 86 minutes
Cast: John Goodman, Jim Broadbent, Mark Williams, Celia Imrie, Hugh Laurie, Ruby Wax, Bradley Pierce, Flora Newbigin, Tom Felton
Director: Peter Hewitt
Screenplay: Gavin Scott and John Kamp, from the novels by Mary Norton
Fantasy adventure
Rated PG
Young children: OK Older children: OK

The Clock family—you know, the little ones who live under the clock in the hall—might be the last of their miniature kind if evil developer Ocious Potter (Goodman) has his way with the wrecking ball. Can the little people defeat that big fat nasty? In how many painful ways?

And will fans of Mary Norton's immensely popular fantasy series even recognize their cherished characters?

This movie seems more like "*Little Home Alone*" than *The Borrowers*, but the entirely convincing special effects bring the story up to date, while offering action-packed hairsbreadth stunts and escapes. It's not a great movie, but it's entertaining, and young ones certainly won't object to the vigorous slapstick scenes as the Borrowers do battle with the bad guy.

This is actually the third version of the 1952 Carnegie Medal–winning novel. The 1973 video production with Eddie Albert is charming and now on tape. A 1993 British miniseries did incorporate more of the book's details onto the TV screen.

This latest, biggest edition is not Norton's text inviolate, interpolating characters from various books from the series into a new scenario.

Still, it could well send youngsters to the library for the tale and its sequels: *The Borrowers Afield*, *Afloat*, *Aloft*, and *Avenged*.

THE BOY AND THE PIRATES (1960)

Color, 82 minutes
Cast: Charles Herbert, Susan Gordon, Murvyn Vye, Paul Guilfoyle, Joseph Turkel
Director: Bert I. Gordon
Screenplay: Lillie Hayward and Jerry Sackheim
Swashbuckler/Fantasy
Unrated
Younger kids: Good   Older kids: Good

This is a likable fantasy designed primarily for preteen boys, who should enjoy the story if they can look past the nondigital special effects. It's about a 10-year-old boy (Charles Herbert) who, after finding a genie in a bottle, is magically transported back to Blackbeard's pirate ship, where he has various adventures and rescues a young girl (Susan Gordon).

It's no great shakes but a pleasant juvenile swashbuckler from a more innocent period of moviemaking, with enjoyable performances from Murvyn Vye (the original "pore Jud" in Broadway's *Oklahoma!*) as Blackbeard

and menacing character actor Timothy Carey as a member of his crew.

A BOY NAMED CHARLIE BROWN (1969)

Color, 85 minutes
Cast: Voices of Peter Robbins, Pamelyn Ferdin, Glen Gilger, Andy Pforsich, Sally Dryer, Erin Sullivan
Director: Bill Melendez
Screenplay: Charles M. Schulz
Animated musical
Rated G
Younger kids: OK   Older kids: OK

The first of four feature-length movies based on Charles M. Schulz's *Peanuts* comic strip is clearly the best of the bunch. A simple storyline merely serves to introduce us to Charlie Brown, Lucy, Linus, Snoopy, et al., with many classic moments from the *Peanuts* repertoire reprised for the big screen.

As for the plot: beleaguered Charlie Brown becomes the class spelling champ and is goaded into entering the National Spelling Bee in New York City. Linus and Snoopy join Charlie Brown in the big city for a few misadventures.

Kids can identify with Charlie Brown's insecurities, while parents will laugh at Lucy's ruthlessness.

Animation here is only a notch better than the *Peanuts* TV specials. Rod McKuen wrote four featured songs, which are serviceable; jazz pianist and composer Vince Guaraldi wrote and performed the background score, as he did for so many of the Peanuts television specials.

If you're going to see (or own) one *Peanuts* movie, this one has the most to offer.

This film was followed by other feature-length Peanuts features, all of similar quality: *Race for Your Life, Charlie Brown*; *Bon Voyage, Charlie Brown*; and *Snoopy Come Home*.

A BOY TEN FEET TALL
(1963)
Color, 118 minutes
Cast: Edward G. Robinson, Fergus McClelland, Constance Cummings, Harry H. Corbett
Director: Alexander Mackendrick
Screenplay: Dennis Cannan, based on the novel *Sammy Going South* by W. H. Canaway
Adventure
Unrated
Younger kids: Good, with caution   Older kids: VG

When the parents of a 10-year-old boy named Sammy (Fergus McClelland) are killed in an air raid during the Suez crisis in 1956, the lad embarks on an arduous journey from Port Said to see his aunt who lives thousands of miles away in Durban, South Africa, armed only with a toy compass. Along the way, he falls in with a Syrian thief who tries to exploit him, as well as a rich American tourist, but eventually winds up being guided by a kindly old diamond smuggler (Edward G. Robinson), with whom he develops a deep bond of friendship.

This is a wonderful British family film (originally titled *Sammy Going South*), dealing with Sammy's emotional growth, that also offers plenty of adventure filmed in striking locations. It also features one of Edward G. Robinson's best performances. (Kids who've never seen him as *Little Caesar* may still know his face and voice, since he was caricatured in so many vintage Warner Bros. cartoons!)

It's a sensitive treatment of childhood, although the opening bombing scene where the boy's parents are killed is quite harrowing, and the physical hardships he endures during his trek are treated in a realistic manner.

THE BOY WHO COULD FLY
(1986)
Color, 114 minutes
Cast: Lucy Deakins, Jay Underwood, Bonnie Bedelia, Fred Savage, Colleen Dewhurst, Fred Gwynne, Mindy Cohn, Janet MacLachlan, Louise Fletcher
Director: Nick Castle
Screenplay: Nick Castle
Fantasy/Drama
Rated PG
Younger children: OK   Older children: OK

This is an unusual fantasy drama–love story about an autistic boy and the friendship that heals his scarred soul.

New neighbor Milly (Deakins) takes an interest in teenage Eric, a boy who doesn't speak and spends hours sitting on his roof, imagining he can fly. They attend classes together, go on school trips, and eventually, she gets Eric to open up and talk. At one point, a bump on the head has Milly fantasizing that Eric can fly—and their bond grows deeper.

He and Milly are separated when Eric's drunken uncle (Fred Gwynne) commits the boy to a mental institution. When Eric show's up at Milly's window a few nights later, she's totally convinced of his flying abilities.

The title suggests a fun-loving fantasy, but this is really a small, sweet relationship film. Adults may be uncomfortable with the transition from believable drama to wish-fulfillment dream, but this may be its prime attraction to adolescent viewers. (The younger ones may respond more to kid brother Fred Savage and his problem with neighborhood bullies.)

The actors bring great warmth and sincerity to their roles and help compensate for some of the story's weaknesses.

THE BOY WITH GREEN HAIR (1948)
Color, 82 minutes
Cast: Dean Stockwell, Pat O'Brien, Robert Ryan, Barbara Hale, Dwayne Hickman
Director: Joseph Losey
Screenplay: Ben Barzman and Alfred Levitt, based on a story by Betsy Beaton
Drama/Fantasy
Unrated
Younger kids: OK Older kids: VG

Thirteen-year-old Dean Stockwell gives one of the best performances ever by a child actor in this one-of-a-kind antiwar parable about an unwanted young war orphan named Peter who becomes a social outcast and a symbol of protest when his hair inexplicably turns green. The story is told in flashback as the boy relates his strange tale to a doctor (Robert Ryan). Peter explains how he was shunted from one relative to another before being taken in by a kindly ex-vaudevillian he calls Gramp (Pat O'Brien). One day, after washing his hair, he's shocked to discover that it has

turned bright green. A doctor tells him there's nothing medically wrong with him, but the adults in his community shun him out of fear that he's "contagious," and the kids at school tease him for being different.

When the distraught Peter runs away to the woods, he has a mystical encounter with a group of war orphans who tell him that his hair turned green as a reminder to adults that war is bad, especially for children, and that he must tell them all about it.

This film is really an allegory about tolerance aimed at grownups, but the message is so clear and the simple symbolism of the boy's green hair so striking that it's certain to make a strong impression on children. They will also relate to the feelings of a boy who is lonely and misunderstood. *The Boy With Green Hair* marked an impressive directorial debut for Joseph Losey, who just a few years later was blacklisted as a Communist; forced to leave the United States, he continued his career in England.

BOYZ N THE HOOD (1991)
Color, 107 minutes
Cast: Larry Fishburne, Ice Cube, Cuba Gooding, Jr., Nia Long, Morris Chestnut, Tyra Ferrell, Angela Bassett, Whitman Mayo
Director: John Singleton
Screenplay: John Singleton
Drama
Rated R
Young children: No Older children: VG, with caution

Boyz N the Hood is, quite simply, one of the most blistering explorations of ghetto life in contemporary urban America ever put on film. It was written and directed by John Singleton, who was all of 23 years old when the film came to theaters.

Singleton tells the story of Furious Styles, a divorced African-American attempting to raise his son, Tre, in South Central Los Angeles. Furious tries to steer the boy away from the myriad temptations and violence of the streets. That he is fighting a losing battle is one of the sad, harsh truths of this perceptive drama. Meanwhile, Tre—who wants to do the right thing—is caught between his parents and their conflicting values.

Boyz N the Hood tackles such issues as fatherly neglect in the black community and the prevalence of liquor stores in a neighborhood that can ill afford to have its young people out of control.

There may be violence to spare in *Boyz N the Hood,* but it is neither gratuitous nor exploitative; as with the language, it is an intrinsic part of the society it depicts.

Parents must decide whether or not these ingredients place the film off-limits for their children. This film is appropriately rated R not only because of violence, but street language and sexual situations as well. Even so, it sends a potent and necessary message about personal responsibility that impressionable adolescents need to hear.

THE BRADY BUNCH MOVIE
(1995)
Color, 90 minutes
Cast: Shelley Long, Gary Cole, Michael McKean, Jean Smart, Henriette Mantel, Christopher Daniel Barnes, Christine Taylor, Paul Sutera, Jennifer Elise Cox, Jesse Lee, Olivia Hack, Reni Santoni
Director: Betty Thomas
Screenplay: Laurice Elehwany, Rick Copp, Bonnie Turner, and Terry Turner, based on characters created by Sherwood Schwartz
Comedy
Rated PG-13
Younger kids: OK Older kids: VG

The story of a lovely lady, her three golden-haired daughters, and a man named Brady with three boys of his own . . . you probably know the rest. This big-screen adaptation of the super-square TV sitcom is updated to the '90s and finds the Brady clan still mired in '70s TV-land optimism and their own squeaky-clean world. It's a one-joke movie, but the joke is surprisingly durable.

Many of the subplots in the film are cobbled together from actual *Brady Bunch* episodes (Marcia getting hit in the nose with a football . . . trying to get The Monkees' Davey Jones to appear at a school dance), and fans will have fun noting the exact recreations of the Brady homestead, as well as cameo appearances by former cast members.

However, you do not need to be intimately familiar with the show to get the jokes. The larger comic point is the juxtaposition of TV-defined cultural blandness against the realities of today's world, and seeing squares like the Bradys emerge triumphant from one modern-day scrape after another is amusing and often quite pointed. It also helps to have a cast that is totally immersed in its roles. The standouts here are Cox, as the eternally tortured Jan, and Cole, who is frighteningly dead-on as Mr. Brady.

There are some hints at nastier '90s stuff, such as a girl who has a serious crush on Marcia (this may take some explaining to younger kids and is partially responsible for the PG-13 rating) and some bullies who threaten Peter. The double-entendre jokes will appeal more to older viewers and, with luck, sail over younger kids' heads.

This movie was followed by a sequel that, amazingly, took the same basic joke into even funnier and cleverer territory.

THE BRAVE LITTLE TOASTER (1987)
Color, 80 minutes
Cast: Voices of Deanna Oliver, Jon Lovitz, Tim Stack, Thurl Ravenscroft, Phil Hartman
Director: Jerry Rees
Screenplay: Jerry Rees and Joe Ranft, based on the book by Thomas M. Disch
Animated feature/Musical
Rated G
Younger kids: OK Older kids: OK

A charming little film with fresh ideas, a funny script, and good animation. In a country cabin, a group of household objects are left behind when a beloved family moves to the city. Determined to reunite with the boy they belong to, the brave Toaster, a cowardly Lamp, a powerful Vacuum Cleaner, a noisy Radio, and an electric Baby Blanket leave the house and embark on a journey filled with danger. Quicksand, thunderstorms, and homesickness test their courage.

They end up in a repairman's spare parts bin, but escape and eventually find their "master's" home (on the same day he goes back to the country to retrieve them). Challenged by modern high-tech appliances who throw him and his friends into a junkyard, the Toaster saves the day in a climactic battle with an evil electromagnet.

Missing the production polish of a Disney or Bluth presentation, *Toaster* is nonetheless an entertaining, original outing that demonstrates the potential of animation storytelling by using inanimate household objects (as opposed to the usual mice, cats, and dinosaurs). The character design is original and pleasing, and the voices are great fun to listen to—all the more so for parents who may recognize Jon Lovitz as the talkative Radio or Thurl Ravenscroft (the longtime voice of Tony the Tiger) as the curmudgeonly Vacuum Cleaner. There are also some hip gags involving visual and vocal caricatures of everyone from Jack Nicholson to Peter Lorre!

Followed eleven years later by a direct-to-video sequel, *The Brave Little Toaster Goes to Mars* (1998)

THE BRAVE ONE (1956)
Color, 100 minutes
Cast: Michel Ray, Rodolfo Hoyos, Fermin Rivera, Elsa Cardenas, Carlos Navarro
Director: Irving Rapper
Screenplay: Harry Franklin and Merrill G. White, based on a story by Dalton Trumbo
Animal story/Drama
Unrated
Younger kids: Good Older kids: VG

Writing under the pseudonym Robert Rich, blacklisted writer Dalton Trumbo won a Best Original Story Oscar for this heartwarming variation on the old boy-and-his-dog yarn. The story here deals with a Mexican peasant boy (Michel Ray) who saves the life of a bull calf. He names the bull Gitano and rears it as a pet, but when it's selected for the bullring, the boy goes to Mexico City to save it, eventually getting an audience with the President in an attempt to win Gitano a pardon.

Though unabashedly sentimental, the film is very nicely made, featuring some exciting bullfight sequences and excellent photography, while the nick-of-time rescue finale is a guaranteed tearjerker for both adults and children.

BREAKING AWAY (1979)
Color, 100 minutes
Cast: Dennis Christopher, Dennis Quaid, Daniel Stern, Jackie Earle Haley, Barbara Barrie, Paul Dooley, Robyn Douglass, Hart Bochner, Amy Wright, John Ashton, Pamela Jayne (P. J.) Soles
Director: Peter Yates
Screenplay: Steve Tesich
Comedy-drama/Sports
Rated PG
Younger kids: OK   Older kids: VG

Breaking Away is a living definition of the movie term "a sleeper," which is to say a film without big stars or surefire, promotable ingredients that goes on to win a big audience just the same. The film deals with four friends who have graduated high school in Bloomington, Indiana, and are confused about what the future holds in store for them.

One of the quartet, Dave (Dennis Christopher), is a bicycling enthusiast who lives to ride with his Italian racing idols, much to the consternation and bewilderment of his car-salesman father (Dooley).

This is a small film with a lot to say about the frustrations of growing up, of dreams unfulfilled, subjects that may be best appreciated by older kids. It provides a sympathetic view of working-class people, and the antagonisms between the four young men and the college students at Indiana University, who condescendingly call the Bloomington locals "cutters," referring to the Bloomington natives who cut limestone for a living. Even more impressive is the relationship between Dave and his father, which grows from puzzlement to gradual understanding. The climactic bicycle race, pitting the four "cutters" against University students, is a special treat.

BRIAN'S SONG (1971)
Color, 73 minutes
Cast: James Caan, Billy Dee Williams, Jack Warden, Judy Pace, Shelley Fabares, Bernie Casey, David Huddleston, the Chicago Bears
Director: Buzz Kulik
Screenplay: William Blinn, based on *I Am Third,* a memoir by Gale Sayers
Biographical drama/Sports
Unrated
Young children: OK   Older children: VG

Brian's Song remains one of the most touching made-for-television movies ever produced: a deeply felt, based-on-fact story of fellowship and admiration that extends beyond its professional football setting.

The scenario charts the evolving relationship between a pair of Chicago Bears running backs: legendary Hall of Famer to be Gale Sayers (Billy Dee Williams) and Brian Piccolo (James Caan), who at an all-too-young age is fated to fight a losing battle with cancer. That Sayers is black and Piccolo is white only adds to the drama, as their shared humanity and deep friendship transcend race.

The film is superbly acted, not only by Billy Dee Williams and James Caan but by Jack Warden as George Halas, the Bears' fabled coach. However, while the football fans in the family will savor the film's setting and there are touches of warmth and humor throughout, the depiction of Piccolo's plight may be disturbing to younger viewers.

Brian's Song deservedly won an Emmy Award as Best Dramatic Program of 1971.

BRIDE OF FRANKENSTEIN
(1935)
Black & white, 75 minutes
Cast: Boris Karloff, Colin Clive, Ernest Thesiger, Valerie Hobson, Elsa Lanchester, Una O'Connor, Dwight Frye
Director: James Whale
Screenplay: William Hurlbut and John R. Balderston
Horror/Science fiction
Unrated
Young children: OK, with caution   Older children: VG

This first sequel to **Frankenstein** begins with an unusual prologue: Lord Byron and Percy Shelley are pestering Mary Wollstonecraft (Lanchester) to continue her tale of Frankenstein and his Monster, and she obliges.

Unknown to his creator, Henry Frankenstein (Clive), the Monster (Karloff) has, like him, survived the fire in the old mill. While the Monster wanders the countryside, frightened yet menacing to those around him, Dr. Frankenstein is confronted by an old teacher, Dr. Pretorious (Thesiger), who wants him to engage in a new project: creating a female monster from the bodies of the dead.

This is an undisputed horror classic—witty, suspenseful, scary, beautifully made, with touches of surrealism and occasional religious imagery. All great horror movies have a few indelible images; this one has many, some frightening, some unexpectedly poignant, as when it (briefly) looks as though the fugitive Monster might find a life as the companion to a kindly, blind hermit (O. P. Heggie) who welcomes him in, teaches him the pleasures of smoking cigars, and even gets him to speak. (This sequence, incidentally, is affectionately parodied in Mel Brooks' **Young Frankenstein**.) The scene of the Bride's creation is one of the most amazing in all of movie history—set to the memorable music of master film composer Franz Waxman.

If your children like older movies, this masterpiece of Hollywood horror could be right up their alley. It's scary, but not too scary, and the horror is somehow enhanced by director Whale's eccentric sense of humor. Children might identify with Karloff's forlorn but deadly Monster; his brilliant performance is the best of his career, and one of the best in horror movie history. But the flamboyant Thesiger is also wonderful, and the climax is satisfactorily apocalyptic.

Younger children may not understand what's going on, and the imagery might disturb them, although it's not really a gruesome film.

THE BRIDES OF DRACULA (1960)
Color, 85 minutes
Cast: Peter Cushing, David Peel, Yvonne Monlaur, Martita Hunt, Freda Jackson, Miles Malleson, Mona Washbourne, Michael Ripper, Andree Melly
Director: Terence Fisher
Screenplay: Peter Bryan, Edward Percy, and Jimmy Sangster
Fantasy horror/Melodrama
Unrated
Younger kids: No Older kids: OK

Dr. Van Helsing (Cushing), who destroyed Count Dracula in **Horror of Dracula,** here encounters one of Dracula's disciples, Baron Meinster (Peel), a vampire so corrupt he attacks his own mother! Mainly, however, he's after a young woman (Monlaur) and other students at a girls' school.

One of the very best Hammer films, *The Brides of Dracula* is stylish, eerie, and as fast paced as an action film. Cushing is the ideal hero: intelligent, resourceful, compassionate, and completely dedicated to the eradication of vampires. Though made on a budget, the period settings are lush, the costumes excellent, and the score outstanding. All in all, the very model of a horror movie of its period.

Younger kids could be badly scared by this film, which works its effects through film craftsmanship rather than gore. The films from the British Hammer studio have been rereleased (and rediscovered) on video in recent times; if your older kids have caught onto them, they will greatly appreciate being introduced to *The Brides of Dracula.*

BRIGADOON (1954)
Color, 108 minutes
Cast: Gene Kelly, Van Johnson, Cyd Charisse, Elaine Stewart, Barry Jones, Hugh Laing, Albert Sharpe, Eddie Quillan
Director: Vincente Minnelli
Screenplay: Alan Jay Lerner, based on the musical play by Alan Jay Lerner and Frederick Loewe
Musical
Unrated
Young children: VG Older children: VG

Lerner and Loewe's stage success translates beautifully to the screen with Gene Kelly and Cyd Charisse as two true lovers who almost miss their chance to spend their lives together. As the story goes, Brigadoon is a Scottish village that comes to life for only one day each one hundred years. It just so happens that American tourist Kelly is walking through the Highlands on the very day that Brigadoon wakes up. The plot involves his romance with Charisse, a native daughter of the elusive town, and his efforts to make their love affair permanent, a major feat considering the come-and-go ways of Brigadoon.

Although MGM chose to shoot this film on a conservative budget, using sound stages rather than locations, this is still a beautiful film to behold. When Kelly and Charisse perform their lilting, romantic dance duet to "The Heather on the Hill," you can use your imagination and almost smell the heather! Several of the Scottish scenes are picturesque and whimsical in nature, but others show deep emotion. For example, a rebellious young man from the village tries to escape, even though his departure would mean the end of Brigadoon! (Scenes of Kelly back in New York City, drinking at a bar with a business crowd, might bore the younger members of the family, but there is nothing sensitive or objectionable here.)

When people talk about the "magic" of Hollywood musicals, a special feeling one doesn't often find in modern films, this is what they're talking about. Even though *Brigadoon* is not highly rated among the MGM musicals, it still has qualities that set it apart from all the rest.

BRIGHT EYES (1934)
Black & white, 83 minutes (also available in computer-colored version)
Cast: Shirley Temple, James Dunn, Judith Allen, Lois Wilson, Jane Withers, Theodor von Eltz, Charles Sellon, Jane Darwell
Director: David Butler
Screenplay: William Conselman, based on a story by David Butler and Edwin Burke
Comedy/Melodrama/Musical
Unrated
Young children: VG Older children: VG

This time Shirley Temple is an adorable tot whose widowed mother is forced to work as the maid in a household of snooty, nouveau riche folks. Shirley's father had been an aviator, so she spends lots of time in and out of airplanes in the company of Loop, her dad's flying friend. Younger children should be cautioned that the story includes the death of Shirley's mother, followed by a sugary discussion with Loop about Mommy joining Daddy up in Heaven.

In spite of the gooey melodramatic sequences, the film is a treat for the whole family, particularly young children. Shirley has several very funny sequences with Jane Withers, who plays an outrageously comical spoiled brat with oversized hair ribbons and an oversized pout to match. Above all, this is the film in which the golden-haired tot introduces her most famous song, "On the Good Ship Lollipop," during a birthday party held in her honor on a taxiing airplane.

BRIGHTY OF THE GRAND CANYON (1967)
Color, 89 minutes
Cast: Joseph Cotten, Pat Conway, Karl Swensen, Dick Foran, Jason Clark
Director: Norman Foster
Screenplay: Norman Foster
Animal adventure
Unrated
Young children: VG Older children: VG

Based on true accounts of a lone little burro who wandered the North Rim's Bright Angel Trail and who became the fictionalized hero of Marguerite Henry's 1953 novel, this faithful adaptation of the book features some movie actors from Hollywood's Golden Age and location vistas no soundstage could ever hope to duplicate.

Nicknamed Brighty by the turn-of-the-century prospector who befriended him, the shaggy gray burro is orphaned when a heartless claim jumper murders the old man. Then Brighty—attacked by a mountain lion but rescued by a kindly miner—helps brings the killer to justice.

Author Henry, normally a horse person (she also wrote *Misty of Chincoteague* and *The Medicine Hat Stallion*), makes the sights, sounds, and smells of the Canyon ring true. It's must reading, and viewing of course, for animal lovers . . . and for every family that went to the Canyon last summer.

A BRONX TALE (1993)
Color, 119 minutes
Cast: Robert De Niro, Chazz
  Palminteri, Lillo Brancato,
  Francis Capra, Taral Hicks,
  Katherine Narducci, Joe Pesci
Director: Robert De Niro
Screenplay: Chazz Palminteri,
  based on his one-act play
Drama
Rated R
Young children: No Older
  children: VG with caution

A Bronx Tale, which marked the directorial debut of Robert De Niro, is a film that seethes with emotion. Set in the 1960s, it depicts the coming of age of a young Italian-American on the streets of the Bronx, where two adults vie for the lad's attention and respect: Lorenzo, his honest and hardworking father, a bus driver, and Sonny, a flashy local tough guy.

A Bronx Tale perceptively explores the psyche of a young boy attempting to define himself. One of the keys to the story is the way Lorenzo desperately attempts to maintain the deference of his son.

Sure, Sonny maintains a flashy lifestyle and has more money in his pocket than Lorenzo might earn in a year. It would be easy for the boy to cast has father aside and emulate Sonny. But Lorenzo, an anonymous working man who rises each morning and goes to work in order to support his family, is in his own modest way a hero, a man worthy of the deepest admiration.

As the years pass, the Italian-American neighborhood in which the story is set is encroached upon by the black community. In this regard, the film pointedly examines the roots of racism amid the changing face of urban America.

The street language and moments of (often frightening) violence are fully in keeping with the tone and setting of the story but may make parents uncomfortable unless they feel their children can handle these elements and appreciate the message the film has to offer.

THE BUCCANEER (1938)
Black & white, 124 minutes
Cast: Fredric March, Franciska
  Gaal, Margot Grahame, Akim
  Tamiroff, Walter Brennan,
  Anthony Quinn
Director: Cecil B. DeMille
Screenplay: Edwin Justus Mayer,
  Harold Lamb, C. Gardner
  Sullivan, Jeanie Macpherson,
  and Grover Jones, based on
  the novel *Lafitte the Pirate* by
  Lyle Saxon
Swashbuckler/Action-adventure
Unrated
Younger kids: OK Older kids:
  Good

Fredric March gives a spirited performance as the legendary French pirate Jean Lafitte in this sprawling Cecil B. DeMille epic. Set in the early 1800s, the story concerns Lafitte and his band of buccaneers coming to the aid of General Andrew Jackson (Hugh Sothern) and fighting for the American cause against the British in the Battle of New Orleans.

Long but lots of fun, this features liberal dashes of action, romance, and spectacle, and is an exciting history lesson to boot, if one doesn't take it too literally. Among those in the huge supporting cast is Anthony Quinn, who later directed a 1958 remake of the story starring Yul Brynner, which was produced by his then-father-in-law DeMille.

BUCK PRIVATES (1941)
Black & white, 82 minutes
Cast: Bud Abbott, Lou Costello, Lee Bowman, Alan Curtis, The Andrews Sisters, Jane Frazee, Nat Pendleton, Samuel S. Hinds, Shemp Howard
Director: Arthur Lubin
Screenplay: Arthur T. Horman and John Grant
Comedy
Unrated
Younger children: VG   Older children: VG

This was Abbott and Costello's first starring movie. The time was right for a military comedy, since the United States had reactivated the draft in 1940 (even before entering World War II).

But that's just background information to tell your kids. The reason to show them *Buck Privates* today is to introduce them to Abbott and Costello—the slick con man and his perpetual patsy—at their funniest. Times may have changed, but their patter routines, honed to perfection

during years of performance on stage, are as hilarious as they ever were—whether it's Lou unable to understand the directions of a drill sergeant ("Throw your chest out!" "I'm not through with it yet!") or Bud asking for the loan of $50. (Lou only has $40, but Bud says that's OK, he can owe him the remaining $10.)

There's one great bit after another in *Buck Privates,* punctuated by a perfunctory plot and a handful of music numbers, including The Andrews Sisters performing their delightful hit, "The Boogie-Woogie Bugle Boy of Company B." Fans of The Three Stooges will also recognize Shemp Howard in a supporting role.

If your kids take to the comedy of Abbott and Costello, they might want to follow up by watching *In the Navy,* made the same year, which has almost as many great routines . . . and before long, they'll be up to **Abbott and Costello Meet Frankenstein.**

BUCK PRIVATES COME HOME (1947)
Black & white, 77 minutes
Cast: Bud Abbott, Lou Costello, Tom Brown, Joan Fulton (Shawlee), Nat Pendleton, Beverly Simmons, Don Beddoe, Don Porter, Donald MacBride
Director: Charles Barton
Screenplay: John Grant, Frederic I. Rinaldo, and Robert Lees, based on a story by Richard Macauley and Bradford Ropes
Comedy
Unrated
Young children: VG   Older children: VG

Here is a rare instance in which a sequel actually outdistances the original in entertainment value. *Buck Privates Come Home* returns Bud Abbott and Lou Costello to the roles of Slicker Smith and Herbie Brown that they created six years earlier. Just as the original **Buck Privates** showed us how these two goofs wound up in the Army by accident, this film—released at a time when countless Americans were ending their careers as soldiers after serving their country in World War II—follows Slicker and Herbie as they're mustered out of the service and try to readjust to life on the home front. Along the way, they try to sneak a young French orphan into the United States.

Nat Pendleton returns as their flustered sergeant, and the film is full of funny gag sequences, leading up to a climactic chase scene that's worth the price of admission. With more story value (and fewer patter routines) than *Buck Privates,* this sequel is a grade-A comedy, especially for Abbott and Costello fans.

BUDDY (1997)
Color, 84 minutes
Cast: Rene Russo, Robbie Coltrane, Peter Elliott, Alan Cumming, Paul Reubens
Director: Caroline Thompson
Screenplay: Thompson, based on the book *Animals Are My Hobby* by Gertrude Davies Lintz
Animal story/True-life
Rated PG
Younger children: OK, with caution   Older children: OK

Rene Russo stars as a real-life woman, Gertrude Lintz, who in the 1920s gathered an amazing menagerie of animals at her vast Long Island home . . . none more unusual than a baby gorilla she decided to raise herself as if it were human. The ape, Buddy, does begin to behave very much like a child, but Lintz refuses to deal with the fact that he is still an animal who is capable of violent outbursts.

Who wouldn't be attracted to a film in which an enormous ape behaves like an affectionate child? *Buddy* would seem to have everything going for it.

The film is very sweet, and Russo's character is immensely likable, but the story loses steam halfway through and moves so lackadaisically toward its finale that kids (especially younger ones) are likely to squirm in their seats. A dramatic scene where the frustrated ape lashes out at his mistress may momentarily jar younger viewers.

THE BUDDY HOLLY STORY
(1978)
Color, 113 minutes
Cast: Gary Busey, Don Stroud, Charles Martin Smith, Will Jordan, Maria Richwine, Conrad Janis, Albert Popwell, Amy Johnston, Jim Beach, Fred Travalena, Dick O'Neill, Stymie Beard
Director: Steve Rash
Screenplay: Robert Gittler, based on the book by John Coldrosen
Musical biography
Rated PG
Young children: VG   Older children: VG

Back in the late 1950s, a bespectacled Lubbock, Texas, native named Buddy Holly delighted young audiences with such vintage rock 'n' roll classics as "Peggy Sue," "That'll Be the

Day," and "Oh Boy," all of which he composed. However, this multitalented young man did not live beyond his early twenties. On February 3, 1959, Holly, along with fellow rock 'n' rollers Ritchie Valens (whose life story is told in **La Bamba**) and The Big Bopper, died in a plane crash. (That date is immortalized in Don McLean's anthem "American Pie" as "the day the music died.")

Holly's life and times are recounted in this solid biography, which charts his youth in Lubbock, his conflicts with those who felt his music was too "black" in nature, and his ascent to stardom. Gary Busey has the role of his career as Holly. Like his onscreen partners Don Stroud and Charles Martin Smith, he actually performs Holly's music; he also earned a Best Actor Academy Award nomination.

Those who were around when Holly achieved stardom will be enamored of *The Buddy Holly Story*. For those who are too young to remember him, the film serves as an entertaining history lesson about a young man with a dream, whose music inspired The Beatles and many other rock 'n' rollers who followed in his footsteps.

Young kids should enjoy this story as much as anyone but must be warned about the sadness of Holly's demise.

BUFFY THE VAMPIRE SLAYER (1992)
Color, 86 minutes
Cast: Kristy Swanson, Donald Sutherland, Paul Reubens, Rutger Hauer, Luke Perry, Michele Abrams, David Arquette, Mark DeCarlo, Stephen Root, Candy Clark
Director: Fran Rubel Kuzui
Screenplay: Joss Whedon
Fantasy horror/Comedy-drama
Rated PG-13
Younger kids: No Older kids: OK

Poor Buffy (Swanson). About to graduate from high school, she has already decided on her future: she will go to college, tour Europe, marry Christian Slater, and die. Instead, a strange old guy (Sutherland) reveals that she is the latest of a long line of young women chosen by destiny to kill vampires. But the king of the Los Angeles vampires (Hauer) learns about her from his head flunky (Reubens) and sets out to slay the slayer.

Director Kuzui errs in having the vampires be comic rather than real menaces, which means it's hard to regard the spunky Buffy as a genuine hero. Any bozo could take out *these* bloodsuckers. But the cast is very good (especially Swanson), the idea is fresh and funny, and overall the movie's a lot of fun.

Writer Whedon seized control of his property and turned it into the popular TV series; there, the teenagers still crack wise and worry about zits, but the menaces are truly dangerous. He knows the trick of comedy horror: play the horror straight, and the comedy stands out in relief. If your kids are already fond of the series, they'll enjoy the movie, too, but will probably conclude that the series is better.

THE BUGS BUNNY/ROAD RUNNER MOVIE (1979)
Color, 92 minutes
Cast: Voices of Mel Blanc, Arthur Q. Bryan
Director: Chuck Jones

Screenplay: Michael Maltese and
  Chuck Jones
Animated feature
Rated G
Younger kids: OK Older kids:
  OK

Less a movie than a compilation
of classic cartoons and sequences
of Chuck Jones' animation for
Warner Bros. A bridging device
has Bugs Bunny giving us a tour
of his mansion, discussing his origins, and expounding on the topic
of humor and chases. Five cartoons are shown complete (*Hare-
way to the Stars*, *What's Opera,
Doc?*, *Duck Amuck*, *Bully for
Bugs*, *Rabbit Fire*) along with ex-
cerpts from many others.

The framework for this film is
merely an excuse to show some
great cartoons; parents (and kids)
would do better to simply find another tape that has those cartoons
intact and skip the window
dressing.

a bug's life (1998)
Color, 94 minutes
Cast: Voices of Dave Foley,
  Julia Louis-Dreyfus, Kevin
  Spacey, Phyllis Diller, David
  Hyde Pierce, Denis Leary,
  John Ratzenberger, Richard
  Kind, Hayden Panettiere,
  Jonathan Harris, Madeline
  Kahn, Bonnie Hunt, Brad
  Garrett, Michael McShane,
  Roddy McDowall
Director: John Lasseter; co-
  director Andrew Stanton
Screenplay: Stanton, Donald
  McEnery, and Bob Shaw, from
  a story by Stanton, Lasseter,
  and Joe Ranft
Animated feature
Rated G
Young kids: VG Older kids:
  VG

The Pixar company's follow-up to
Toy Story is possibly even better:
a delightful computer-animated
fable with a solid story, terrific
characters, and an endless supply
of clever and funny ideas.

The colony on Ant Island is
under pressure because every
year Hopper and his greedy grass-
hoppers arrive to take their (un-
fair) share of the ants' storehouse
of food. And this year, the ants
have come up short—made worse
by the well-meaning Flik's fum-
bling. Now Hopper is demanding
a fresh supply, which will cut into
the ants' own winter provisions.

Flik, whose ideas never seem to
work out, hatches yet another
scheme—to hire some big, tough
insects to protect them from the
ravaging Hopper. He goes off on
a mission to find some protectors
and mistakenly hires a troupe of
circus performers instead!

a bug's life is the kind of film so
rich in ideas that even a sharp-eyed
adult can't take it all in with one
viewing. Kids will delight at the
imagination on display here, as
well as the gags and often hilarious
vocal performances of the cast.

While the character of Hopper
is definitely mean and threatening, there is nothing to unduly
frighten the youngest viewers;
once they're immersed in the insect world, they're going to love
every bit of it.

BUGSY MALONE (1976)
Color, 93 minutes
Cast: Scott Baio, Florrie Dugger,
  Jodie Foster, John Cassisi,
  Martin Lev
Director: Alan Parker
Screenplay: Alan Parker
Comedy/Musical
Rated G

Younger kids: OK   Older kids: OK

This elaborate musical parody of 1930s gangster films—cast entirely with children—is certainly one of the more peculiar movies of all time. Writer-director Alan Parker gets points for the sheer feat of pulling it off. The gangster clichés are played relatively straight—bootlegging, machine-gunning, and warfare over gangland turf—and all of the more sinister implications of the genre remain, except for the fact that the players are kids and so their props are not the usual ones: soft drinks stand for booze, cream pies for bullets.

It's fun for a while, but the novelty quickly begins to pale. Older kids who are familiar with Jodie Foster from other movies may especially enjoy her mature-beyond-her-years portrayal of a jazz-age floozie, an interesting companion piece to her mature-beyond-her-years prostitute in the very adult film *Taxi Driver,* released the same year.

BUTCH CASSIDY AND THE SUNDANCE KID (1969)
Color, 112 minutes
Cast: Paul Newman, Robert Redford, Katharine Ross, Strother Martin, Henry Jones, Jeff Corey, George Furth, Cloris Leachman, Ted Cassidy, Kenneth Mars, Christopher Lloyd
Director: George Roy Hill
Screenplay: William Goldman
Western/Comedy-drama
Rated PG
Younger kids: OK   Older kids: VG

Paul Newman and Robert Redford teamed up for the first time in this box-office smash about the misadventures of two of the Old West's most colorful outlaws. Set at the turn of the 20th century, Newman plays the affable Butch, the leader of the infamous Hole-in-the-Wall Gang, and Redford is his quick-draw sidekick Sundance. Accompanied by Sundance's girlfriend, Etta (Katharine Ross), they make their way across the country robbing trains and banks, but find that times have changed and eventually wind up in South America.

The film has action and excitement galore, along with magnificent widescreen photography and a jaunty score (including "Raindrops Keep Fallin' on My Head"), but it's the low-key comic chemistry between Newman and Redford and the bantering Oscar-winning script by William Goldman that have made it an enduring classic. (In fact, this film inspired many an imitation, with too many filmmakers trying to achieve its delicate balance between serious action and light-hearted dialogue.)

Kids may find it intriguing—and perhaps a bit unsettling—that the "heroes" of this movie are in fact outlaws whose choice of career may mean an unhappy ending. The blurred lines of good and bad (as opposed to likable and unlikable) may spark some interesting conversation as well.

The violence is of a fairly mild Western variety, and there is one memorable profanity during the famous leap-off-the-mountain-into-the-river scene.

BYE BYE BIRDIE (1963)
Color, 112 minutes
Cast: Dick Van Dyke, Janet Leigh, Ann-Margret, Maureen Stapleton, Bobby Rydell, Jesse

Pearson, Ed Sullivan, Paul
Lynde
Director: George Sidney
Screenplay: Irving Brecher,
based on the musical by
Michael Stewart, Charles
Strouse, and Lee Adams
Musical
Unrated
Young children: VG   Older
children: VG

Youngsters may know Dick Van
Dyke best from the classic 1960s
TV series *The Dick Van Dyke
Show,* or from his role as Bert in
Mary Poppins. But his liveliest
screen role just may be in this ef-
fervescent adaptation of the hit
Broadway musical.

The actor re-creates the role he
originated on stage: Albert Peterson, a songwriter who pens a
farewell tune that Conrad Birdie,
an Elvis-like rock idol, will sing to
a fan on *The Ed Sullivan Show*
before he is inducted into the military. While poking gentle fun at
all the hoopla over Elvis "the Pel-
vis," and the phenomenon of adolescent girls screeching at the
sight of a greasy-haired rock 'n'
roller, *Bye Bye Birdie* is an entertaining musical by any standards
and a nostalgic mirror of a more
innocent time.

Fans of the original show (and
even kids who may have seen, or
participated in, revivals or school
productions) will notice certain
changes, many of which have to
do with the fact that the film was
trying to build up budding star
Ann-Margret.

But such vibrant songs as "Put

on a Happy Face," "A Lot of Living to Do," "Kids" (the parental
complaint voiced by the hilarious,
put-upon father Paul Lynde), and
the wild dance at the Shriners'
convention (featuring Janet Leigh,
whom today's kids may know best
as the mother of Jamie Lee Curtis) retain all the vigor and vitality
that made them so successful on
stage.

An expanded television remake
aired in 1996 starring Jason Alexander and Vanessa L. Williams.

BY WAY OF THE STARS
(1992)
Color, 150 minutes
Cast: Zachary Bennett, Tantoo
Cardinal, Gema Zamprogna,
Jan Rubes, Michael Mahonen
Director: Allan King
Screenplay: Marlene Matthews
Western
Rated PG
Young children: VG, with
caution   Older children: VG

The Canadian frontier of the 19th
century is the setting for this unusual and satisfying action tale
about young Lukas Beinmann
and his trail west. Way west, since
he starts out in Prussia!

Lukas crosses Europe, the At-
lantic, and uninhabited America
in search of his long-lost father.
The journey holds Indians and
battles, but also romance and
insight.

The epic length allows us
enough time to become involved
with the characters, as we would
reading a good book. There's
some frontier-style violence but
nothing out of the ordinary.

C

CADDIE WOODLAWN (1988)
Color, 106 minutes
Cast: Scanlon Gail, Season
  Hubley, Conrad Janis, Nick
  Ramus, James Stephens,
  Parker Stevenson, Betsy
  Townsend, Emily Schulman
Director: Giles Walker
Screenplay: Joe Wiesenfeld and
  Richard John David
Children's classic
Unrated
Young children: VG   Older
  children: VG

In 1865 Dunnville, Wisconsin, red-
headed tomboy Caroline Augusta
Woodlawn, age 11, torments her
snobby cousin from Boston, becomes jealous of her adored older
brother's object of affection, constantly defies her parents, and always shows up late for dinner.

But she also has a pure heart
and a will to follow her own conscience, no matter what it tells
her. Thus she comes between her
prairie community and a nomadic
tribe of Dakotas when rumors of a
neighboring Sioux uprising cause
the settlers to fear for their lives.

As mischievous as Pippi Longstocking and as resourceful as
Laura Ingalls Wilder, Caddie was
a real woman who died at 86 and
was immortalized in a 1935 New-
bery Award–winning novel by
Caddie's own granddaughter, Carol
Ryrie Brink. Every incident in
this movie actually happened to
Caddie as you see it.

This is one of the better made-
for-TV offerings for kids, and well
worth watching with the entire
family.

Count your blessings.

CALAMITY JANE (1953)
Color, 101 minutes
Cast: Doris Day, Howard Keel,
  Allyn McLerie, Philip Carey,
  Dick Wesson, Gale Robbins
Director: David Butler
Screenplay: James O'Hanlon
Musical/Western
Unrated
Younger kids: VG   Older kids:
  VG

Doris Day is the ultimate tomboy in
this boisterous musical about real-
life Wild West heroine Calamity
Jane, who matches wits (and guns)
with Wild Bill Hickok (Howard
Keel). Calamity actually likes Bill as
a friend but feels a pang of jealousy
when a well-dressed, ultra-feminine
entertainer (Allyn McLerie) comes
to Deadwood Gulch and steals his
attention.

Feminists may wince at some of
the '50s attitudes embodied in the
song "A Woman's Touch" and in
the story thread about Calamity
becoming more ladylike. But none
of that mutes in any way the rambunctious appeal of the title character or the impact of the way she's
played by Doris Day, who's great
fun to watch. Preteen girls should
especially enjoy this. The tuneful
score includes "Whip Crack-
Away" and the Oscar-winning
"Secret Love."

THE CALL OF THE WILD
(1935)
Black & white, 81 minutes
Cast: Clark Gable, Loretta
    Young, Jack Oakie, Reginald
    Owen, Frank Conroy
Director: William Wellman
Screenplay: Gene Fowler and
    Leonard Praskins, based on
    the novel by Jack London
Action-adventure
Unrated
Younger kids: Good   Older
    kids: VG

The first sound version of Jack
London's oft-filmed adventure
classic is considerably toned down
from the book, playing up the romance and softening the St. Bernard's wildness, but is still highly
enjoyable, especially for dog lovers.
Clark Gable is properly stalwart as
the Yukon gold prospector who,
with his comic sidekick Shorty
(Jack Oakie), battles a villain
(Reginald Owen) who wants to
steal his gold. Loretta Young is
the woman whom he rescues from
the snow after she's abandoned
by her husband.

Filmed on location in the wintry
Pacific Northwest, the film vividly
captures the harsh atmosphere of
the turn-of-the-century Klondike
and makes for dandy entertainment. The clear-cut heroism and
villainy here make this fun to
share with young kids, while older
ones might be more entertained
by contemporary versions of the
same story.

THE CAMERAMAN (1928)
Black & white, 69 minutes
Cast: Buster Keaton, Marceline
    Day, Harold Goodwin, Harry
    Gribbon, Sidney Bracey,
    Edward Brophy
Director: Edward Sedgwick
Screenplay: Richard Schayer,
    based on a story by Clyde
    Bruckman and Lew Lipton
Comedy/Silent classic
Unrated
Young children: VG   Older
    children: VG

Plenty of privileged moments may
be found in this, Keaton's final silent feature. Buster plays a lovesick clodhopper who is attempting
to establish himself as a newsreel
cameraman—and win the hand of
the girl he idolizes. Needless to
say, he is the most inept cameraman who ever worked in movies—and while there are many
roadblocks in his path, he eventually emerges triumphant. There's
even an orangutan at his side to
add laughs in almost every scene.

The film is crammed with imagination, clever sight gags, and lots
of chuckles. In one inspired sequence, Buster and his camera
are seen at Yankee Stadium,
where he pantomimes the various
physical movements of a pitcher
and eventually runs the bases
after belting an inside-the-park
home run.

Watching Keaton create celluloid poetry as a solitary figure in
the vast stadium is at once wistful,
charming, and even awe-inspiring.
The sequence was actually filmed
on location in the Bronx, and
there are other moments that take
advantage of actual New York
City locations.

Kids of all ages should have a
great time watching this one.

THE CANDIDATE (1972)
Color, 109 minutes
Cast: Robert Redford, Peter
    Boyle, Don Porter, Allen
    Garfield, Karen Carlson,
    Melvyn Douglas, Quinn

Redeker, Michael Lerner,
Kenneth Tobey
Director: Michael Ritchie
Screenplay: Jeremy Larner
Political satire
Rated PG
Young children: No Older
children: VG

Here is one of the best of all
modern-era political movies. The
message: Anyone running for office
today, no matter how sincere,
is fated to become a superficial
creature of the media, to be sold
to the public like cereal or bathroom
tissue. *The Candidate* tells
the story of Bill McKay, an idealistic
young liberal lawyer who attempts
to maintain his integrity
while running for the United
States Senate. Without fully realizing
it, he is manipulated by
media types and power brokers
who have their own agendas for
getting him into office.

Will McKay be elected? Will he
have sold his soul to do so?

The Candidate offers a visionary
portrait of the manner in which
meaningless words and phrases,
press agent puffery, and spin doctoring
have come to replace purposeful
political debate—and how
image has replaced content in the
American electioneering process.

It is ideal viewing—and a
springboard for conversation—for
older children and their parents.
Some language and behavior
make it inappropriate for younger
kids, who wouldn't understand
much of the drama in any event.

CANDLESHOE (1977)
Color, 101 minutes
Cast: David Niven, Helen Hayes,
Jodie Foster, Leo McKern,
Vivian Pickles, Veronica
Quilligan, Ian Sharrock
Director: Norman Tokar
Screenplay: David Swift and
Rosemary Anne Sisson, based
on the novel *Christmas at
Candleshoe* by Michael Innes
Comedy-drama
Rated G
Younger children: VG Older
children: Good

Casey (Jodie Foster) arrives at
the estate of Lady St. Edmund
(Helen Hayes), pretending to be
her long-lost granddaughter. Actually,
she's a young con artist
sent by Bundage (Leo McKern) to
ferret out some rare coins. Lady St.
Edmund's semi-scrupulous champion
is Priory (David Niven), who
puts on multiple disguises to help
Lady St. Edmund save her estate,
which also has the effect of thawing
Casey's tough demeanor.

David Niven is delightful in this
minor Disney comedy, and parents
will enjoy revisiting Jodie
Foster's career as a child actress.
Candleshoe was made toward the
end of the time when family films
were meant for children of all
ages. Nothing offensive here, with
a few laughs thrown in, and some
life lessons, too. These days, it
may be too tame for older children,
with its Aesop-like moral
and its mild comedy.

CAPTAIN BLOOD (1935)
Black & white, 119 minutes
Cast: Errol Flynn, Olivia de
Havilland, Basil Rathbone,
Lionel Atwill, Ross Alexander,
Guy Kibbee, J. Carrol Naish
Director: Michael Curtiz

Screenplay: Casey Robinson, based on the novel by Rafael Sabatini
Swashbuckler/Action-adventure
Unrated
Younger kids: OK   Older kids: VG

Errol Flynn became a star with this film, his first swashbuckler, and one of the all-time greats. He plays an Irish doctor who's wrongly condemned for high treason after treating a wounded rebel and is exiled to an English colony in the West Indies by the tyrannical King James II. He's then sold into slavery and purchased by a sadistic plantation owner (Lionel Atwill), whose beautiful daughter (Olivia de Havilland) naturally falls in love with him. But when Spanish pirates attack the island, Blood escapes and becomes a buccaneer himself, forming an uneasy alliance with a treacherous French pirate (Basil Rathbone), which ends with a spectacular duel to the death.

This has action and adventure to spare, with director Michael Curtiz staging some exciting sea battles and sword fights, while Flynn and the 19-year-old de Havilland provide genuine romantic sparks in the first of their eight costarring films. Here's one that may well have the whole family cheering.

CAPTAIN HORATIO HORNBLOWER (1951)
Color, 117 minutes
Cast: Gregory Peck, Virginia Mayo, Robert Beatty, James Robertson Justice, Denis O'Dea, Terence Morgan, Richard Hearne, James Kenney, Stanley Baker, Christopher Lee
Director: Raoul Walsh
Screenplay: Ivan Goff, Ben Roberts, and Aeneas MacKenzie, based on the novel by C. S. Forester
Action-adventure/Drama
Unrated
Young children: VG   Older children: VG

This colorful sea epic focuses on the heroic exploits of Captain Horatio Hornblower, the most famous fictional sea officer in British literature. This feature follows the steadfast hero on two exploits. The first adventure involves the Captain's mission to deliver arms to a South American dictator who is an enemy of Spain, which then was England's rival. Just as the arms are delivered, England changes its hostile policy towards Spain and makes that nation its ally, which puts Hornblower and his crew in drastic straits. Later, Hornblower leads a sea battle against Napoleon's fleet. In between, the Captain makes time for a romance with the beautiful Lady Barbara, sister to the Duke of Wellington.

Action in this film comes fast and furious, and includes sword fighting, cannon blasts, gun battles, and even a flogging, which is handled discreetly. Throughout these escapades, Captain Hornblower remains strong, brave, and dignified. He is a true hero and patriot, and Gregory Peck was the perfect choice to play him (except, of course, for the fact that he is American, not British).

Incidentally, *Star Trek*'s creator, Gene Roddenberry, often said that he based the character of Captain James T. Kirk on Hornblower!

CAPTAIN JANUARY (1936)
Black & white, 75 minutes
Cast: Shirley Temple, Guy Kibbee, Slim Summerville, Buddy Ebsen, June Lang, Sara Haden, Jane Darwell
Director: David Butler
Screenplay: Sam Hellman, Gladys Lehman, and Harry Tugend, based on the story "The Lighthouse at Cape Tempest" by Laura E. Richards
Comedy/Melodrama/Musical
Unrated
Young children: VG Older children: VG

Here is a story to capture the fancy of children who crave adventure. Shirley Temple plays a young waif who was rescued from a shipwreck by a kindly old Maine sea captain who operates a lighthouse. He names his beloved foundling Star and, along with his unemployed seafaring friends, teaches her to dance and sing, and spit into the wind!

Interrupting this picture of paradise is the arrival of a stern new truant officer who tries to separate Star from her adoptive father and put the little girl into school. (As Shirley herself might say, "Oh, my goodness!") What follows is a struggle of good guys versus meanies, interspersed with fine song and dance numbers. The best one is "At the Codfish Ball," which Shirley performs with wonderfully eccentric dancer and singer Buddy Ebsen, decades before he played Jed Clampett on *The Beverly Hillbillies*.

This is one of Shirley's most entertaining vehicles, featuring unusual characters and beautiful shoreline settings.

CAPTAINS COURAGEOUS (1937)
Black & white, 116 minutes
Cast: Freddie Bartholomew, Spencer Tracy, Lionel Barrymore, Melvyn Douglas, Mickey Rooney
Director: Victor Fleming
Screenplay: John Lee Mahin, Marc Connelly, and Dale Van Every, from the novel by Rudyard Kipling
Adventure/Literary classic
Unrated
Young children: OK Older children: VG

A snobby young brat—suspended from school for lying and cheating—is taken on an ocean voyage by his widowed father. One day, in heavy fog, he falls overboard and is picked up by a Massachusetts fishing boat that won't be heading back to port for several months. At first the boy is angry and aloof—but in time he begins to make himself useful and becomes a part of the crew, enjoying the camaraderie as well as the hard work. He grows especially close to Manuel, the kindhearted Portuguese fisherman who saved his life, and during those long weeks at sea, the boy learns self-reliance, the value of honest work, and the true meaning of friendship.

This outstanding film earns the right to be called a family classic. It has heart and honest sentiment, and offers a straightforward look at the lives of fishermen and their dedication to their work. Some of the story is prettified in the slick MGM manner—Melvyn Douglas as the father is too good to be true—but a few minor compromises are a small price to pay for the rich rewards this movie has to offer. Freddie Bartholomew's performance doesn't date one bit, nor does Spencer Tracy's. The finale, in which Manuel dies heroically, insisting that his young friend be spared the sight of his injuries, may require some explaining—and is, as intended, quite sad. The film may leave sensitive viewers, young and old, with a lump in their throats.

CAPTAIN SINDBAD (1963)
Color, 85 minutes
Cast: Guy Williams, Heidi Bruhl, Pedro Armendariz, Abraham Sofaer, Bernie Hamilton
Director: Byron Haskin
Screenplay: Samuel B. West and Harry Relis
Action-adventure/Fantasy
Unrated
Younger kids: Good   Older kids: VG

Sindbad (Guy Williams) falls in love with a princess (Heidi Bruhl) whose father is under the spell of a villainous wizard (Pedro Armendariz) who is trying to force the princess to marry him. Sindbad sets out to destroy the tyrant, but to do so, he must first battle fire-breathing monsters with multiple heads and face other fantastic perils in order to reach an ivory tower where the wizard keeps his heart locked away so as to remain invincible!

This is pure kiddie-matinee fantasy stuff, but it's fairly well done, with good special effects and imaginative creature designs (although quite different from the stop-motion effects by Ray Harryhausen that set the standard for this kind of film in the 1950s).

Many viewers will know Guy Williams from his television stints in the title role of Walt Disney's *Zorro* and as Prof. John Robinson in *Lost in Space*.

CAROUSEL (1956)
Color, 128 minutes
Cast: Gordon MacRae, Shirley Jones, Cameron Mitchell, Barbara Ruick, Claramae Turner, Robert Rounseville, Gene Lockhart, Audrey Christie, Susan Luckey, William Le Massena, John Dehner, Jacques D'Amboise, Richard Deacon
Director: Henry King
Screenplay: Phoebe and Henry Ephron, based on the musical play by Richard Rodgers and Oscar Hammerstein III, as adapted by Benjamin F. Glazer from *Liliom* by Ferenc Molnar
Musical
Unrated
Young children: OK   Older children: VG

One of the most beautiful screen adaptations of a Rodgers and Hammerstein stage musical, *Carousel* also is one of their most complex stories. The plot involves the love affair between Billy Bigelow, a rough-edged carnival worker and thief, and Julie Jordan, an innocent young woman who works in the mill in a New England town. After a brief courtship, Billy marries Julie and tries to keep to an honest path. Despite his good intentions, he soon begins to treat her abusively, and then agrees to take part in a robbery—a crime that will lead to his death. As the fantasy musical begins, Billy has been dead for several years. He is polishing stars in the heavens and hoping to make a onetime visit back to earth to help out his teenage daughter, who is terribly unhappy.

This is a family-oriented story, but the themes rise far above typical musical subject matter. In addition to showing summer courtships, carnival lights, and cheerful celebrations such as a clambake, the story deals with honesty, criminality, marital commitment, death, afterlife, orphans, spousal abuse, and finally, faith in God in the face of adversity. These elements are best dealt with in Rodgers and Hammerstein's songs, including "What's the Use of Wondrin'," "You'll Never Walk Alone," and "If I Loved You," as well as a remarkable tour de force called "Soliloquy" in which Billy expresses his feelings about becoming a father. This musical might sound like a complicated kettle of fish, but it is a uniquely wonderful work that pleases and inspires as it entertains.

Family members who have seen and enjoyed **Oklahoma!**, released the previous year, will recognize the two leading performers, golden-voiced Shirley Jones and Gordon MacRae, who were reunited here. If you're a Rodgers and Hammerstein fan, you also might want to seek out the documentary *Rodgers and Hammerstein: The Sound of Their Music*, which explores their many film adaptations, and includes recordings made by Frank Sinatra, who was scheduled to play Billy Bigelow in *Carousel*.

CASEY'S SHADOW (1978)
Color, 116 minutes
Cast: Walter Matthau, Alexis Smith, Robert Webber, Murray Hamilton, Andrew A. Rubin, Stephen Burns, Michael Hershewe, Susan Myers, Harry Caesar, Whit Bissell
Director: Martin Ritt
Screenplay: Carol Sobieski, based on the short story "Ruidoso" by John McPhee
Sports/Comedy-drama
Rated PG
Younger kids: Good Older kids: VG

Casey's Shadow is old-fashioned family entertainment that's leisurely paced and very low key, but ultimately emerges as a flavorful and enjoyable piece of Americana. Walter Matthau is delightful in a role that Wallace Beery might have played in the 1930s: gruff but softhearted Cajun quarter horse trainer Lloyd Bourdelle. While trying to raise his three sons in near poverty, a colt of championship lineage is born on his ranch. Bourdelle's youngest son, Casey (Michael Hershewe), for whom the horse is named, develops a close bond with it. Convinced that he has a champion, Bourdelle trains the horse for the forthcoming million-dollar-purse All-American Futurity race for 2-year-olds at Ruidoso, New Mexico, on Labor Day. As Casey's Shadow continues to excel at tryouts, a wealthy horse owner (Alexis Smith) tries to buy it, but Bourdelle spurns her offer, and some unscrupulous competitors (Robert Webber, Murray Hamilton) try to sabotage the horse.

This all leads to a climactic race, of course, but there is a bittersweet finale that, like the rest of the film, downplays the typical clichés of this sentimental genre. The film is packed with documentary details of the horse-racing milieu. The offbeat, Southern small-town atmosphere is vividly communicated, thanks to fine performances and refreshing outdoor photography.

There is a small amount of salty language, courtesy of the colorful Bourdelle, and an explicit foal-birthing sequence. The story should appeal to all age groups, since it's as much about the relationships among the three brothers and their father as it is about horse racing.

CASPER (1995)
Color, 101 minutes
Cast: Christina Ricci, Bill Pullman, Cathy Moriarty, Eric Idle, Amy Brenneman, Ben Stein, Don Novello, Ben Stein; voices of Malachi Pearson, Joe Nipote, Joe Alskey, Brad Garrett
Director: Brad Silberling
Screenplay: Sherri Stoner and Deanna Oliver
Comedy/Fantasy
Rated PG
Young children: OK, with caution   Older children: OK

Harvey Comics' famous junior spook made his live-action film debut in this elaborate movie, a funhouse ride set in an old mansion inhabited by a human family and a not-human family. When the two collide, the story begins.

A widowed therapist (Dr. Harvey, played by Bill Pullman) and his daughter, Kat (Christina Ricci), move into Whipstaff Manor, ostensibly to start a new life. But he's also there on a mission to exorcise the house's shades: Casper, the ghost of a 12-year-old boy who died many years ago, and his three late uncles, Stretch, Stinky, and Fatso. Kat and Casper hit it off immediately, though the dead kid's relatives

continue to detest the living. A subplot about searching for treasure propels the narrative.

Casper was a great success, and kids seem to love it, but there are troubling elements in it from an adult point of view. Turning the comic-book and animated-cartoon character into the ghost of an actual 12-year-old boy gives the film a melancholy air, abetted by the fact that Dr. Harvey can't seem to get over the death of his wife. (This cuts no ice with the three ghoulish ghosts, who taunt him by pretending to make her materialize in one cruel scene.)

The treasure-hunt subplot, involving greedy Cathy Moriarty and her dim-bulb husband Eric Idle, adds a mean-spirited human character to the mix.

Uncritical kids may have no trouble with any of this—especially because so much of the film focuses on the little girl and tells the story from her and Casper's point of view. What's more, the special effects are sensational. But when all is said and done, *Casper* plays fast and loose with the audience's emotions, making far too many tasteless jokes about death and dying. Even the climactic appearance of the dead mother—now an angel—is a cruel bone to throw to children in the audience (especially kids who may have lost parents already).

This has been followed by a pair of direct-to-video sequels: *Casper: A Spirited Beginning* and *Casper and Wendy*.

CAT BALLOU (1965)
Color, 96 minutes
Cast: Jane Fonda, Lee Marvin, Michael Callan, Dwayne Hickman, Tom Nardini, John Marley, Reginald Denny, Jay

C. Flippen, Arthur Hunnicutt,
Bruce Cabot
Director: Elliott Silverstein
Screenplay: Walter Newman and
Frank R. Pierson, based on
Roy Chanslor's novel *The
Ballad of Cat Ballou*
Western/Comedy
Unrated
Young children: OK · Older
children: VG

Cat Ballou is bustin' out all over
with good humor, as a virginal
frontier gal forms an outlaw gang
to avenge the murder of her
rancher pa. A lusty free-for-all
follows in this adaptation of Roy
Chanslor's 1956 comic novel *The
Ballad of Cat Ballou*. Wandering
minstrels Nat "King" Cole and
Stubby Kaye tunefully apprise us
of the salient plot points during
the course of the movie, as innocent Catherine (Jane Fonda) becomes fugitive Cat, placing her
trust in a band of reluctant would-
be cutthroats.

Lee Marvin received a Best
Actor Academy Award for his rollicking dual roles as the noseless
hired gun Strawn, who's working
for the greedy railroad, and the
drunken gunslinger Kid Shelleen,
who's precariously perched atop
his cross-legged horse.

But Fonda, showing surprising
ability as a light comedienne, is
also memorable. (Whatever happened to her?)

Cat Ballou is a romp the whole
family can enjoy. Even if your
kids haven't seen the Western
conventions being parodied here,
they'll enjoy the outsized gags
and performances.

CAT PEOPLE (1942)
Black & white, 73 minutes
Cast: Simone Simon, Kent
Smith, Tom Conway, Jane
Randolph, Jack Holt
Director: Jacques Tourneur
Screenplay: DeWitt Bodeen
Horror/Drama
Unrated
Young children:
Marginal Older children: OK

A young woman (Simon) comes
to fear that she is the descendant
of a strange tribe whose women
turn into fierce black leopards
when angry.

Those few words about the
story are accurate enough, but fail
to do *Cat People* justice. Despite
a few failings, it's a strong, potent,
and frightening horror drama
(rather than melodrama), with
emphasis on the characters and
the mood. Although there's nothing at all graphic about the movie,
there are several sequences that
are still as frightening as the day
they were completed, such as
when Irena's romantic rival (Randolph) is alone in a swimming
pool, with the never-quite-seen
shape of a giant cat moving about
in the shadows.

This is typical of the film: we
only once briefly glimpse the pro-
tagonist after one of her transformations. (This may come as a
disappointment to contemporary
kids who expect to see everything—but it's a perfect example
of how our imagination can produce scares as vivid as anything
the movies can show us.)

Cat People was the first of a series of low-budget but intelligent
horror movies made for RKO by
Val Lewton, one of the few producers in movie history whose influence was greater than that of

the directors who worked with him. Yet his eye for talent was astute enough that several of his directors, including Tourneur, Robert Wise, and Mark Robson, went on to distinguished careers of their own.

Younger children may find the film boring, but older ones should enjoy it.

Note: Avoid the R-rated 1982 remake, which isn't very good.

CATS DON'T DANCE (1997)
Color, 76 minutes
Cast: Voices of Scott Bakula, Jasmine Guy, Natalie Cole, John Rhys-Davies, Kathy Najimy, George Kennedy, Hal Holbrook, Don Knotts, Rene Auberjonois, Ashley Peldon
Director: Mark Dindal
Screenplay: Roberts Gannaway, Cliff Ruby, Elana Lesser, and Theresa Pettengill
Animated feature/Musical
Rated G
Younger kids: OK   Older kids: OK

A brightly colored animated musical comedy set in 1930s Hollywood. Danny, a song and dance cat from Indiana, comes to Tinsel Town and quickly learns that movieland animals are treated as second-class citizens. The best roles go to humans, especially child star Darla Dimple, who treats her animal costars like dogs.

Danny convinces a showbiz menagerie consisting of a goat and fish dance team, a soprano hippo, a cute penguin, a swashbuckling turtle, an elephant composer, and a beautiful kitty named Sawyer to put together an act using his songs. Darla sabotages the animals at every turn, but her final

attempt to discredit the bunch in front of an audience of Hollywood's who's who exposes her true nature once and for all.

Wonderfully cartoony character designs hark back to an earlier style of Hollywood animation—but the melancholy aspects of this small-town-boy-goes-to-Hollywood saga are at odds with the cheerful look of its "stars." Most of the characters are failures, has-beens, and outcasts. What's more, the gentle ribbing of old-time (and newtime) Hollywood will likely go over the heads of younger kids. Trying to satisfy a broad, multigenerational audience, *Cats Don't Dance* winds up truly pleasing no one.

CAVEMAN (1981)
Color, 92 minutes
Cast: Ringo Starr, Barbara Bach, John Matuszak, Shelley Long, Dennis Quaid, Avery Schreiber, Jack Gilford
Director: Carl Gottlieb
Screenplay: Gottlieb and Rudy de Luca
Comedy
Rated PG
Younger kids: OK   Older kids: OK

Caveman is a silly but engaging comedy about a thoughtful prehistoric caveman named Atouk (Ringo Starr), who forms his own tribe from members of other caves. This is a harmless collection of loosely connected skits and *Flintstones*-type Stone Age gags, but a good deal of them work, and some of them actually strive to capture the spirit of classic physical comedy routines. Atouk learns to walk upright and discovers fire . . . a group of cavemen try to carry a dinosaur egg up a hill, find it's too big, and are driven backwards down the hill and up another hill right behind them . . . a blind caveman bumps into a dinosaur, etc.

Ex-Beatle Starr is just right as the inquisitive caveman, and it's only appropriate that he should be involved in a sequence where music is created. Most impressive and funny are the stop-motion dinosaurs created by Jim Danforth and David Allen; they are lovingly detailed, full-blooded characters in their own right, including a Tyrannosaurus Rex that gets drunk and a lizard that howls at the moon like a wolf.

There are a few off-color jokes, but on the whole, kids should enjoy this along with their parents.

CHARIOTS OF FIRE (1981)
Color, 123 minutes
Cast: Ben Cross, Ian Charleson, Nigel Havers, Nick Farrell, Alice Krige, Cheryl Campbell, Ian Holm, John Gielgud, Lindsay Anderson, Patrick Magee, Nigel Davenport, Dennis Christopher, Brad Davis
Director: Hugh Hudson
Screenplay: Colin Welland
True-life drama/Sports
Rated PG
Younger kids: OK   Older kids: VG

This engrossing, beautifully made drama is based on the true story of two runners on the 1924 British Olympic track team: Eric Liddell (Charleson) and Harold Abrahams (Cross), and the different motivations which drive them to compete. Liddell, a Scottish missionary, runs for God because he can "feel His pleasure" when he

does so. Abrahams, whose father is a wealthy Lithuanian Jew, runs to fight English anti-Semitism.

Although the highlights of the film are the running sequences, it is not who wins the races that is important to the filmmakers, but what running means to these men. (Despite what a viewer might expect, the only race between Liddell and Abrahams comes in the middle of the film; they never meet again in competition after that.) Abrahams is consumed with winning to shame his detractors, while the devout Liddell refuses to run a qualifying race on Sunday, upsetting the heads of the British Olympic committee.

This all may be a bit too heady for younger kids, but older kids should relate to the pressures faced by these young men from without and within, and how running helps them achieve their goals. Besides this, there is the stunning photography, which turns physical exertion into high drama, the impeccable production, and of course, the now famous music by Vangelis, which is so important to the often poetic pace and tone of the film.

Younger children will likely find this film boring and obscure. (Some adults did, too.)

CHARLOTTE'S WEB (1972)
Color, 94 minutes
Cast: Voices of Debbie Reynolds (Charlotte), Paul Lynde, Henry Gibson, Rex Allen, Danny Bonaduce, Agnes Moorehead, Don Messick, Herb Vigran
Directors: Charles A. Nichols and Iwao Takamoto
Screenplay: Earl Hamner, Jr., based on the book by E. B. White

Animated feature/Musical
Rated G
Younger kids: OK   Older kids: OK

E. B. White's award-winning book makes a successful leap to the screen courtesy of veteran cartoon producers William Hanna and Joseph Barbera. While not up to Disney standards, the film has enough moments of charm to keep its young audience involved.

The story follows the adventures of a barnyard pig named Wilbur. Concerned over his fate, a spider named Charlotte befriends him, weaving words of encouragement in her web. These words spare Wilbur from the slaughterhouse and turn him into a celebrity at the county fair, thus saving his life. In return, Wilbur, with some help from Templeton the rat, takes it upon himself to protect Charlotte's offspring.

Veteran Disney songwriting duo Richard M. and Robert B. Sherman provide nine songs, but none of them has the magic to make them memorable. The characters are well animated, but designed and drawn in a flat, conventional way, not very different from Hanna-Barbera's standard TV fare. The producers did, however, remain faithful to the book's message of friendship and salvation, and this is one of their better efforts.

CHEAPER BY THE DOZEN
(1950)
Color, 85 minutes
Cast: Clifton Webb, Jeanne Crain, Myrna Loy, Betty Lynn, Edgar Buchanan, Barbara Bates, Mildred Natwick, Sara Allgood, Anthony Sydes, Roddy McCaskill, Norman Ollestad, Carol Nugent, Jimmy Hunt, Teddy Driver, Betty Barker
Director: Walter Lang
Screenplay: Lamar Trotti, based on the novel by Frank B. Gilbreth, Jr., and Ernestine Gilbreth Carey
Comedy
Unrated
Younger children: OK   Older children: VG

Efficiency experts Frank and Lillian Gilbreth (Clifton Webb and Myrna Loy) raise their twelve children using the methods they preach to others. This period film, set at the turn of the 20th century, is episodic in nature and based on the real-life experiences of the renowned Gilbreths, who revolutionized modern industrial procedures.

Older children will sympathize with oldest daughter, Ann (Jeanne Crain), when her father insists on chaperoning her to a school dance. Every scene is full of humor and charm, and affords today's youngsters an opportunity to glimpse another time and a different kind of life. But this is no outmoded story; Lillian Gilbreth is an equal partner in her husband's business, and among their acquaintances is a birth-control advocate. All presented with delicate 1950s sensibilities, of course.

Cheaper by the Dozen and its sequel, the more feminist-oriented *Belles on Their Toes,* are just two of many fine pictures made about turn-of-the-century families during the 1940s and 1950s, including **Meet Me in St. Louis, I Remember Mama,** *On Moonlight Bay*, **Life With Father,** and **A Tree Grows in Brooklyn**. This is one film parents probably won't mind watching with their children, as it presents the events from both the parents' and the children's perspectives.

Be forewarned, however: there may be some tears by the finish. Younger children may not be ready for that experience.

CHEETAH (1989)
Color, 84 minutes
Cast: Keith Coogan, Lucy Deakins, Collin Mothupi, Timothy Landfield, Breon Gorman
Director: Jeff Blyth
Screenplay: Erik Tarloff, John Cotter, and Griff Du Rhone, based on the book The Cheetahs by Alan Caillou
Animal adventure
Rated Good
Younger kids: Good   Older kids: VG

Cheetah is a wholesome Disney film about two American teens (Keith Coogan, Lucy Deakins) who accompany their scientist father (Timothy Landfield) and medical worker mother (Breon Gorman) to Kenya, where they befriend a Masai urchin (Collin Mothupi) and adopt an orphaned baby cheetah, who is later kidnapped by poachers.

The simple storyline is formulaic, but the cheetah is adorable, the location photography of Africa and its wildlife is impressive, and the film offers a worthy message for kids about respect for nature and tolerance of other cultures. Good guys and bad guys are clearly defined, but the trickier issues of different civilizations are dealt with straightforwardly and in a non-condescending manner.

A side note: Young leading man Keith Coogan is the grandson of Jackie Coogan, who was introduced to movie audiences in Charlie Chaplin's silent film comedy classic **The Kid** (1921). Jackie went on to become one of the biggest stars in the world, and in later years—much heavier and balder!—played Uncle Fester on *The Addams Family* television series.

THE CHIPMUNK ADVENTURE (1987)
Color, 90 minutes
Cast: Voices of Ross Bagdasarian, Janice Karman, Dody Goodman, Susan Tyrell, Frank Welker, Anthony DeLongis
Director: Janice Karman
Screenplay: Janice Karman and Ross Bagdasarian
Animated feature/Musical
Rated G
Younger kids: OK   Older kids: NG

The famous singing Chipmunks, Alvin, Simon, and Theodore, make their feature-film debut in this lightweight vehicle. The Chipmunks and their female counterparts, The Chipettes, are sent on a race around the world by two con artists, who use the singers to smuggle diamonds hidden within chipmunk dolls. Taking separate routes, the chipmunks find opportunity at each locale for mild danger (killer sharks off South America, a "temple of doom" in Egypt, etc.) or colorful rock 'n' roll musical sequences.

Animation and production values are superior to Chipmunk TV episodes, and the musical sequences have a real spark. The characters are surrogate kids with positive attitudes and should appeal to the younger ones in the audience. Unfortunately, the thin storyline has little to offer those over 10 years old.

CHITTY CHITTY BANG BANG (1968)
Color, 142 minutes
Cast: Dick Van Dyke, Sally Ann Howes, Lionel Jeffries, Gert Frobe, Anna Quayle, Benny Hill, James Robertson-Justice, Robert Helpmann, Heather Ripley, Adrian Hall, Barbara Windsor
Director: Ken Hughes
Screenplay: Roald Dahl and Ken Hughes, based on the book *Chitty Chitty Bang Bang: the Magical Car* by Ian Fleming
Musical/Fantasy
Rated G
Young children: VG   Older children: NG

Ian Fleming is fondly recalled as the creator of 007, James Bond. However, he also is the author of the fanciful fiction on which this musical is based. It tells of a poor, miserably ineffectual inventor who remodels a beat-up old car into a spanking new auto, which he calls Chitty Chitty Bang Bang. He then conjures up a tale in which the car has magical powers, and can soar across the sky like a bird.

Chitty Chitty Bang Bang is pleasant but hardly a classic, in spite of calling on the talents of the songwriters responsible for **Mary Poppins,** along with its male star, Dick Van Dyke. Nonetheless, it will entertain kids who are young enough to giggle at the sound of the film's title—and the names of its various characters (Caractacus Potts, Truly Scrumptious, and Baron and Baroness Bomburst of Vulgaria, to mention just a few).

THE CHOSEN (1982)
Color, 108 minutes
Cast: Maximilian Schell, Rod Steiger, Robby Benson, Barry Miller, Hildy Brooks, Ron Rifkin, Val Avery
Director: Jeremy Paul Kagan
Screenplay: Edwin Gordon, based on the novel by Chaim Potok
Drama
Rated PG
Young children: No   Older children: VG

This intelligent drama, set in 1940s Brooklyn, spotlights the evolving friendship between two Jewish adolescents. They are products of polar-opposite cultures and diverse views regarding the practice of religion, but they are both strongly affected by their relationship with their fathers.

Reuven Malter has been brought up as a Reform Jew and is assimilated into American culture. Danny Saunders is Hasidic. To Reuven, Danny's 19th-century garb and side curls—not to mention his unique sense of community with other Hasids—are exotic and fascinating. Meanwhile, Danny is intrigued by Reuven's more open worldview and the diversity of knowledge available to him. As the boys become friends, the film reveals the contrasting personalities and religious and political beliefs of their fathers, and the impact each has on his son.

The Chosen is a cogent, worthwhile drama of religion and dogma, politics and father-son relations. It opens up many opportunities for discussion, including the question of whether one sector of a religious group is superior to another.

A CHRISTMAS CAROL (1938)

Black & white, 68 minutes

Cast: Reginald Owen, Gene Lockhart, Kathleen Lockhart, Terry Kilburn, Barry Mackay, Lynne Carver, Leo G. Carroll, Lionel Braham, Ann Rutherford

Director: Edwin L. Marin

Screenplay: Hugo Butler, based on the novella by Charles Dickens

Drama/Fantasy/Literary classic

Unrated

Young children: VG   Older children: VG

A Christmas Carol is, arguably, Charles Dickens' most celebrated work. This is no small statement, considering that the author's other books include *The Pickwick Papers, A Tale of Two Cities, David Copperfield, Oliver Twist, Bleak House, Little Dorrit,* and *Great Expectations.*

A Christmas Carol has long been a staple of the Christmas season, as it celebrates human kindness, redemption, and forgiveness. This handsome version of the story, produced by MGM, is ideal viewing at holiday time. Character actor Reginald Owen has one of his best-ever roles as miserly Ebenezer Scrooge (kids may enjoy learning that the same actor, nearly thirty years later, played Admiral Boom in **Mary Poppins**). He is surrounded by a choice cast and picturesque period flavor.

As with all versions of this story, young children may find some of the ghostly visions to be unsettling.

Connoisseurs understandably prefer the 1951 British version with Alastair Sim, but taken on its own terms, this one is quite good.

A CHRISTMAS CAROL (1951)

Black & white, 86 minutes (also available in computer-colored version)

Cast: Alastair Sim, Kathleen Harrison, Jack Warner, Michael Hordern, Mervyn Johns, Hermione Baddeley, John Charlesworth, Glyn Dearman, George Cole, Miles Malleson, Ernest Thesiger, Peter Bull, Hugh Dempster, Patrick Macnee

Director: Brian Desmond Hurst

Screenplay: Noel Langley, based on the novella by Charles Dickens

Drama/Fantasy/Literary classic

Unrated

Young children: VG   Older children: VG

This scrupulously rendered, deeply felt British adaptation of the Dickens holiday perennial is even better than the 1938 Hollywood version. Many people believe it to be the definitive filming of the story.

This is due in large part to Alastair Sim's rich portrayal of Ebenezer Scrooge. The wily character actor holds nothing back in his delineation of Scrooge as a flinty, unyielding miser and misanthrope. His horror at seeing his past (and future) depicted so vividly seems genuine. That's why his transformation, in the story's final scenes, is so satisfying . . . and why his unbridled joy is all the more delightful. He even surprises himself!

There have been many other good adaptations of this story,

which is all but foolproof, including a half-hour Mickey Mouse featurette, a television special with Mister Magoo, a made-for-TV movie with George C. Scott, and a full-fledged musical starring Albert Finney called **Scrooge**. In fact, just about the only variation on this Dickens classic that doesn't work is the mean-spirited, wrongheaded comedy *Scrooged*, starring Bill Murray.

A CHRISTMAS STORY (1983)
Color, 98 minutes
Cast: Peter Billingsley, Darren McGavin, Melinda Dillon, Ian Petrella, Scott Schwartz, Tedde Moore; voice of Jean Shepherd (narrator)
Director: Bob Clark
Screenplay: Jean Shepherd, from a story in his book *In God We Trust, All Others Pay Cash*
Comedy
Rated PG
Young children: VG   Older Children: VG

Here is a genuine rarity, a perfect movie.

What's more, it's a film that can amuse and entertain children on one level and adults, who will get even more from it, on another. That's because it's humorist Jean Shepherd's reminiscence of childhood, so it speaks to both generations.

The voice of the narrator is Shepherd himself, a legendary figure to radio listeners who became addicted to his wonderfully rambling tales in the 1950s and '60s, and readers of his subsequent short stories and books. Kids may think that he's copying the style and format of the popular TV series *The Wonder Years*,

when it fact that show was influenced by Shepherd.

An ideally cast Peter Billingsley is the boy growing up in the Midwest during the early 1940s. All he wants for Christmas is a BB gun, but his mother (Melinda Dillon) laments, "You'll put your eye out with that thing!" His father (Darren McGavin) isn't a bad sort, but he tends to complain a lot, cursing a blue streak in a wonderful form of gibberish.

There isn't much story here; it's more a series of vignettes about the slings and arrows of childhood, from a humiliating encounter with a department store Santa Claus to falling over in the snow and not being able to get up because your clothing is so bulky.

It's hard to think of any family member who wouldn't relate to at least some of this; the comedy here is all based on truth, exaggerated for effect.

A long-awaited sequel to *A Christmas Story* finally came out in 1994, titled *It Runs in My Family* (also known as *My Summer Story*) with Charles Grodin miscast as the father and Kieran Culkin as the kid. It has its moments but can't hold a candle to this gem of a movie.

A CHUMP AT OXFORD (1940)
Black & white, 63 minutes
Cast: Stan Laurel, Oliver Hardy, Forrester Harvey, Wilfred Lucas, Forbes Murray, Peter Cushing, Charlie Hall
Director: Alfred Goulding
Screenplay: Charles Rogers, Felix Adler, and Harry Langdon
Comedy
Unrated

Young children: VG   Older
children: VG

This film is divided into two sections. In the first, Stan and Ollie take a job as maid and butler—with Stan as Agnes the maid. When Stan is told to serve the salad "undressed" he does exactly that.

But it's the rest of the film that sets *A Chump at Oxford* apart from all other Laurel and Hardy comedies. The boys help catch a bank robber, and as a reward are sent to Oxford University in England to catch up on their education. At first, they fall victim to student pranksters, but then a chance bump on the head transforms Stan into a completely different personality: Lord Paddington, hailed as the greatest scholar and athlete in the history of the school! What's more, he has no memory of Ollie, whom he insists on referring to as "Fatty, old thing."

If you and your family have fallen in love with Laurel and Hardy, then you owe yourselves the treat of watching this film, just to see Stan become a totally different character!

Kids might not understand all the trappings of life at an ancient, tradition-bound university like Oxford, but that's part of what makes this film so intriguing. What's more, it's great fun.

CINDERELLA (1950)
Color, 74 minutes
Cast: Voice of Ilene Woods,
  William Phipps, Eleanor
  Audley, Rhoda Williams,
  Verna Felton, Luis Van
  Rooten
Directors: Wilfred Jackson,
Hamilton Luske, and Clyde
  Geronimi
Screenplay: Kenneth Anderson,
  Ted Sears, Homer Brightman,
  Joe Rinaldi, William Peet,
  Harry Reeves, Winston Hibler,
  and Erdman Penner, from the
  original story by Charles
  Perrault
Animated feature
Unrated
Young children: VG   Older
  children: VG

Cinderella is one of Walt Disney's most enchanting animated features. It tends to be overshadowed by its forerunner, **Snow White and the Seven Dwarfs,** but it is an excellent film that can stand on its own against any competition.

There is also a tendency in recent years to put down the character of Cinderella, especially in contrast to such contemporary female Disney heroines as Belle in **Beauty and the Beast** or Pocahontas. But unlike Snow White, who is indeed waiting for her prince to come, Cinderella shows great strength of character—she's no wimp. Faced with tragedy (the death of her beloved father) and dire straits (having to work as a slavey for a cruel stepmother and two horrible stepsisters), she makes up her mind to adopt a cheerful attitude and not let life get her down. She is brave and resourceful, a young woman worthy of our admiration and applause.

Certainly she hopes for someone to rescue her and take her away from her life of drudgery. But she doesn't whine; instead, she sings, "A Dream Is a Wish Your Heart Makes," one of Disney's loveliest, most touching songs.

While Cinderella wins our empathy, it is her tiny sidekicks, Jaq and Gus, who keep us laughing throughout the film, as they attempt to help their friend and try to outwit their natural foe, the housecat. The scene in which all the household birds and animals come together to create a ball gown for Cinderella is one of the most delightful in all of Disneydom.

Cinderella is one of those films that has you rooting for its good-guy characters every step of the way—which is why you share their heartbreak at every setback. The way the finale is played out, with its double twist, is especially ingenious at manipulating our emotions.

THE CIRCUS (1928)
Black & white, 72 minutes
Cast: Charlie Chaplin, Merna Kennedy, Allan Garcia, Betty Morrissey, Harry Crocker, Henry Bergman
Director: Charles Chaplin
Screenplay: Charles Chaplin
Comedy/Silent classic
Unrated
Young children: VG Older children: VG

The Circus may not be Charlie Chaplin's best feature, but it's irresistibly enjoyable, and chock-full of laughs. It doesn't have the lingering poignancy of **City Lights** or the memorable set pieces of **The Gold Rush**; it's just a wonderfully entertaining, funny movie.

Its story is sweet and simple: The Little Tramp is mistaken for a pickpocket, takes refuge in a circus, and falls in love with a bareback rider.

Chaplin was honored with a special Academy Award for "versatility and genius in writing, acting, directing, and producing" *The Circus*. It would be hard to find a funnier film today.

CITY LIGHTS (1931)
Black & white, 86 minutes
Cast: Charlie Chaplin, Virginia Cherrill, Harry Myers, Hank Mann, Florence Lee, Henry Bergman
Director: Charles Chaplin
Screenplay: Charles Chaplin
Comedy/Silent classic
Unrated
Young children: VG Older children: VG

Just as Hollywood was embracing the talking picture, Charlie Chaplin made this funny and touching silent comedy-romance. Here, The Little Tramp falls for a blind flower girl, and attempts to obtain money for the operation that will restore her sight. She is overwhelmed by his attentions but has mistaken him for a wealthy customer, and he can't bear to tell her the truth. This leads him into many misadventures, including a bout in the boxing ring, and an on-again, off-again friendship with a drunken millionaire (who never recognizes Charlie when he sobers up).

In the hands of a less-talented filmmaker, this might have been unbearably maudlin. But Chaplin transforms the story into a heartfelt look at the essence of what it means to love another human being.

He also memorably illustrates a concept that is as radical today as in 1931: Physical beauty is ultimately fleeting and irrelevant when measuring a person's worth. Parents who are sensitive to issues of alcohol abuse might have concern about the drunken millionaire, but Chaplin presents him in a broadly comic fashion—and shows the true effect that liquor can have on someone.

If your kids have never experienced a film that can make them laugh, then cry, perhaps it's time to try *City Lights*.

CITY SLICKERS (1991)
Color, 112 minutes
Cast: Billy Crystal, Daniel Stern, Bruno Kirby, Patricia Wettig, Helen Slater, Jack Palance, Noble Willingham, Josh Mostel, Tracey Walter, David Paymer, Jeffrey Tambor, Bill Henderson
Director: Ron Underwood
Screenplay: Lowell Ganz and Babaloo Mandel, based on a story by Billy Crystal
Comedy/Western
Rated PG-13
Younger kids: OK   Older kids: VG

Billy Crystal, Daniel Stern, and Bruno Kirby saddle up for fun and adventure as three buddies from New Jersey who ride roughshod through their assorted midlife crises by going on a two-week cattle drive from New Mexico to Colorado. Along the way, they indulge their childhood fantasies and "find their smiles" again, while learning some valuable life lessons from a grizzled trail boss (Jack Palance) who looks like a "saddlebag with eyes."

This slick comedy hits the bull's-eye with some real belly laughs as long as it sticks to its basic premise, but it wanders off the trail whenever it tries to get serious and sentimental. Palance easily steals the film as a genuine

cowboy and deservedly won a Best Supporting Actor Oscar for his role.

While in no way aimed at the family audience, this has definite appeal for older kids. However, there is enough profanity and crude humor along the trail to have earned this a PG-13—which should signal a warning for parents.

CLASH OF THE TITANS (1981)
Color, 118 minutes
Cast: Harry Hamlin, Judi Bowker, Laurence Olivier, Claire Bloom, Maggie Smith, Burgess Meredith, Ursula Andress, Sian Phillips
Director: Desmond Davis
Screenplay: Beverley Cross
Mythological adventure/Fantasy
Rated PG
Young children: OK   Older children: OK

This star-studded film about Greek gods serves as an excuse to frame some spectacular animation effects by the man responsible for such classic fantasy films as **7th Voyage of Sinbad.**

Harry Hamlin plays Perseus, the half human son of the Greek god Zeus (Laurence Olivier). Determined to save Andromeda (Judi Bowker), the cursed daughter of queen Cassiopeia (Sian Phillips), he tames the flying horse Pegasus, faces Medusa, the snake-headed woman whose gaze turns men to stone, and rescues Andromeda from the giant sea monster Kraken.

This was the last movie to feature special effects by the great Ray Harryhausen, master of stop-motion animation. Before computer graphics became commonplace and opened a whole new world of special effects possibilities, he created small jointed figures and moved them one frame at a time to produce the illusion of motion.

Even though *Clash of the Titans* is his most star-laden film, it's not Harryhausen's best; it's hampered by a somber, episodic story of no great interest. But scattered throughout the film are some of Harryhausen's finest creations, such as the winged horse Pegasus, the giant Kraken, and the scary, red-lit Medusa. Here, instead of being a beautiful woman, the snake-haired menace is a monster with the scaly upper torso of a woman and the lower body of a snake. She's so believably rendered by Harryhausen's hands that she's very likely to frighten younger children.

Older children who like fantasy adventures will find this one rather pokey but will enjoy the special-effects sequences, when the movie springs to life.

CLOSE ENCOUNTERS OF THE THIRD KIND (1977)
Color, 135 minutes (but see below)
Cast: Richard Dreyfuss, Francois Truffaut, Teri Garr, Melinda Dillon, Bob Balaban, J. Patrick McNamara, Warren J. Kemmerling, Cary Guffey, Lance Henriksen, Josef Sommer
Director: Steven Spielberg
Screenplay: Steven Spielberg
Science fiction/Epic
Rated PG
Younger kids: OK, with caution   Older kids: OK

The life of an ordinary guy (Dreyfuss) is changed forever when he sees some UFOs and becomes obsessed with details about them. His wife (Garr) and children finally leave him, but he can't shake his obsession. Meanwhile, a French UFO researcher (Truffaut) in the U.S. and a single mom (Dillon) whose young son (Guffey) is carried off by a UFO have their own problems.

Spielberg's famous movie is nearly perfect family entertainment, with its dazzling special effects, engaging characters, broad-based action (some scenes were shot in India), and sheer magnificence of scale. Its major weakness is a willingness to sweep so many unusual occurrences up into this one story; good thing it was made before the legends about Roswell, New Mexico, became famous.

Younger kids might be disturbed, not by the toylike UFOs and very friendly aliens, but by the estrangement between Dreyfuss and his family, which is realistically depicted. When little Cary Guffey is abducted, he's not scared for a moment, so these scenes might upset *older* people more than children.

Spielberg has tinkered with the film several times since it was originally released; a "special edition" runs 132 minutes, while various broadcast-TV versions are longer than the original film. This remains one of the few big science fiction hits of the last thirty years not to spawn at least one sequel!

CLUELESS (1995)
Color, 97 minutes
Cast: Alicia Silverstone, Stacey Dash, Brittany Murphy, Paul Rudd, Donald Faison, Breckin Meyer, Jeremy Sisto, Justin Walker, Elisa Donovan, Dan

Hedaya, Wallace Shawn,
  Twink Caplan; Julie Brown
Director: Amy Heckerling
Screenplay: Heckerling, inspired
  by the novel *Emma* by Jane
  Austen
Comedy
Rated PG-13
Younger kids: No   Older kids:
  VG

Clueless follows the adventures of
Cher, an extremely popular (and
well-dressed) Beverly Hills teen,
who thinks she is wise in the ways
of love—and enjoys playing
matchmaker for friends and
teachers alike—until she is smitten herself and doesn't know what
to do. This sharp, modern updating of Jane Austen's *Emma* is actually more faithful in tone and
spirit than many serious-minded
"period" adaptations.

One of the novelties of *Clueless*
is writer-director Amy Heckerling's invention of Beverly Hills
jargon for her cutting-edge teens
to speak. It works not only in
rooting the characters, but also
creates an environment apart
from the "normal" world.

Alicia Silverstone's Cher is a
completely winning heroine: self-
absorbed, to be sure, overly con-
scious of status and fashion, but
in her own way a role model who
is more than willing to help others
less fortunate than she. Dan Hedaya also makes an impression as
her gruff father, who turns out to
have a heart as big as his daughter's. Another pleasant surprise:
It's comforting to see a teenage
character in a movie who looks
out for her father's best interests
and genuinely cares about him.

In depicting modern teens, there
is both language and behavior that
is inappropriate for younger chil-

dren, but older kids will recognize
the drugs, drink, and sexual advances at a party to be genuine,
not exploitive. Besides, Cher
manages to rise above it all.

COCOON (1985)
Color, 117 minutes
Cast: Don Ameche, Wilford
  Brimley, Hume Cronyn, Brian
  Dennehy, Jack Gilford, Steve
  Guttenberg, Maureen
  Stapleton, Jessica Tandy,
  Gwen Verdon, Herta Ware,
  Tahnee Welch, Barret Oliver
Director: Ron Howard
Screenplay: Tom Benedek, from
  a story by David Saperstein
Science fiction/Comedy-drama
Rated PG-13
Younger kids: No   Older kids:
  OK, with caution

Art (Ameche), Ben (Brimley),
and Joe (Cronyn), retired and living in Florida, regularly sneak
into an abandoned estate to swim
in its luxurious pool. However,
unknown to them, a team of
friendly aliens—disguised as people—rent the estate to resuscitate
the members of an expedition to
Earth that took place ten thousand years in the past. They were
forced to cocoon themselves, and
now these cocoons are in the
pool, which is charged with reju-
venating energy. The energy
works wonders on Art, Ben, and
Joe, and they kick up their heels in
various ways. With the permission
of Walter (Dennehy), friendly
leader of the aliens, they introduce the "fountain of youth" to
their wives (Stapleton, Tandy, and
Verdon), but then things begin to
get out of hand.

Fantasy disguised as science
fiction, *Cocoon* is well acted by a

great cast of talented older stars. It's more than a bit condescending to the idea of aging (to prove his vim and vigor, Ameche break-dances) and sometimes calculatedly sentimental. Still, it is undeniably ingratiating and entertaining. If your kids can stand the thought of watching a movie with nothing but old fogeys in it, they're likely to enjoy this unexpected smash hit. (The film may also serve to introduce them to some extraordinarily talented actors.)

Note: There's an emphasis on sex, both human and alien; while it's almost entirely offscreen, it does make it questionable for younger kids. They may also have some questions about the concept of "cheating death." After all, real-life grandparents can't escape the inevitability of death by flying off to outer space.

COCOON: THE RETURN
(1988)
Color, 116 minutes
Cast: Don Ameche, Wilford
  Brimley, Courteney Cox,
  Hume Cronyn, Jack Gilford,
  Steve Guttenberg, Barret
  Oliver, Maureen Stapleton,
  Elaine Stritch, Jessica Tandy,
  Gwen Verdon, Tahnee Welch,
  Linda Harrison, Tyrone
  Power, Jr., Herta Ware, Brian
  Dennehy
Director: Daniel Petrie
Screenplay: Stephen McPherson
  and Elizabeth Bradley
Science fiction/Comedy-drama
Rated PG
Younger kids: OK   Older kids:
  OK

The three couples who left Earth with friendly aliens in **Cocoon** return to Florida when their friends decide to raise the cocoons with hibernating aliens from the bottom of the sea. Elsewhere, a scientist has been experimenting on one of the cocoons, which ultimately opens; the scientist makes friends with the alien that emerges.

What was warm in *Cocoon* is stickily sentimental here; furthermore, there's not really very much of a plot, and most of the old-folks-acting-young jokes from the original are trotted out again to weak effect. Fortunately, this time the ending suggests that getting old is a natural part of the human condition and doesn't have to be avoided by fleeing into outer space—but this doesn't offset the weakness of the rest of the movie.

If your kids liked the original film, they'll clamor to see this one. It won't hurt them, but it may leave them dissatisfied.

COLLEGE (1927)
Black & white, 65 minutes
Cast: Buster Keaton, Ann
  Cornwall, Flora Bramley,
  Harold Goodwin, Snitz
  Edwards, Carl Harbaugh, Sam
  Crawford
Director: James W. Horne
Screenplay: Carl Harbaugh and
  Bryan Foy
Comedy/Silent classic
Unrated
Young children: VG   Older
  children: VG

This Buster Keaton comedy is loaded with his patented physical humor and has more than one magical moment. Buster stars as Ronald, his high school's "most brilliant scholar." At his graduation, he proceeds to lecture his classmates on the "Curse of Athletics." Mary, the girl of Ronald's dreams, tells him his speech is ridiculous.

At Clayton College, Ronald realizes that in order to win his fair maiden he will have to immerse himself in athletics. What follows is a series of clever slapstick skits in which our hero attempts to master the basics of several sports, earn the love of Mary, and show up an obnoxious rival suitor.

Leaning more on sight-gag set pieces (Buster attempting to work as a soda jerk or trying his hand at pole-vaulting) than on plot, *College* is breezy fun that's sure to have kids of all ages laughing out loud.

THE COLOSSUS OF NEW YORK (1958)
Black & white, 70 minutes
Cast: John Baragrey, Otto Kruger, Mala Powers, Ross Martin, Charles Herbert, Robert Hutton, Ed Wolff
Director: Eugene Lourié
Screenplay: Thelma Schnee
Science fiction/Melodrama
Unrated
Younger children: OK, with guidance   Older children: OK

When his brilliant humanitarian son is killed, scientist Kruger saves his brain and installs it in a giant mechanical body, like a robot. (Though why a robot, or a mechanical body, would need a voluminous cloak is anyone's guess.) The Colossus tries to befriend his own young son (Herbert), but gradually his humanity slips away.

This slow, ponderous movie—matching its title character—certainly wears its heart on its sleeve. It's obvious, but children usually like the obvious, making this better for younger kids than older ones.

Little boys who like robots already will adore the character, and some kids might be moved by the sad ending. But The Colossus is intended to be frightening, and it is—even if mildly so.

COLOSSUS: THE FORBIN PROJECT (1970)
Color, 100 minutes
Cast: Eric Braeden, Susan Clark, Gordon Pinsent, William Schallert, Leonid Rostoff, Georg Stanford Brown
Director: Joseph Sargent
Screenplay: James Bridges, from the novel by D. F. Jones
Science fiction/Suspense
Rated PG
Younger kids: Too boring   Older kids: OK

In the near future, the defense of the United States is turned over to a huge computer called Colossus, the brainchild of Dr. Charles Forbin (Braeden). The computer cannot be turned off and is housed in an impregnable mountain. But no sooner has Colossus gone into operation than it issues a warning: "There is another system." The Russians have created a supercomputer of their own, and the two want to be linked to each other. This creates an even more powerful computer that starts issuing demands, making nuclear threats, and resorting to killing whenever it wishes.

By today's standards, the computer technology in this movie is primitive, but the issues it deals with are still timely and will be recognized as such by older children. This is a sober and serious movie, avoiding sensationalism and keeping everything within the bounds of reasonable speculation. This leads to a bleak but faintly hopeful climax that might disturb kids more used to films where everything is neatly wrapped up; still, this is not a concept to be avoided.

If anything, the movie is *too* sober and serious, tending toward the ponderous. The story thread about a phony affair that leads to a real one is just plain silly. (There's a bit of near nudity here.) Computer-loving kids will grin knowingly about the ancient technology, but are also likely to be engrossed by the story.

CONEHEADS (1993)
Color, 88 minutes
Cast: Dan Aykroyd, Jane Curtin, Michelle Burke, Michael McKean, Jason Alexander, Lisa Jane Persky, Chris Farley, David Spade, Phil Hartman, Dave Thomas, Sinbad, Jan Hooks, Michael Richards, Jon Lovitz, Kevin Nealon, Adam Sandler, Garrett Morris, Laraine Newman, Tim Meadows, Julia Sweeney, Ellen DeGeneres, Parker Posey, Tom Arnold, Peter Aykroyd
Director: Steve Barron
Screenplay: Dan Aykroyd, Tom Davis, Bonnie Turner, and Terry Turner
Comedy/Science fiction
Rated PG
Younger kids: VG   Older kids: VG

Two pointy-headed aliens (Aykroyd and Curtin) from the planet Remulak arrive on Earth intent on conquest, but plans go awry. Despite their weird heads, shuffling walk, bizarre habits and speech patterns, they successfully pass themselves off as immigrants from France and move into the suburbs. Years later, they're still there, good neighbors, happily married, and with a mildly troublesome teenager (Burke) who's more human than she is a Conehead. But there's trouble brewing: not only is the Immigration and Naturalization Service on the trail of our heroes, but there's a ship on the way from Remulak to find out why the Coneheads didn't fulfill their original mission.

The very thin series of sketches from television's *Saturday Night Live* is unexpectedly turned into a warm, touching family comedy. Not all of the jokes work equally well, but the concept certainly does. The Coneheads are a decent family, hard workers, and liked by their neighbors; finding positive family and social values in a goofy, satiric science fiction comedy is a real treat.

Children especially seem to like this film; it's full of gags, the Coneheads themselves are funny to look at, and the script is built upon the one idea that seems to endear more stories to children than any other: outsiders can fit in without giving up the traits that made them outsiders in the first place.

Your kids are likely to love this one, and you're likely to enjoy it yourself. (If nothing else, you can have a grand time spotting all the guest stars.)

CONGO (1995)
Color, 108 minutes
Cast: Laura Linney, Dylan Walsh, Ernie Hudson, Tim Curry, Grant Heslov, Joe Don Baker, Joe Pantoliano, Lorene Noh, Misty Rosas, Mary Ellen Trainor, Bruce Campbell
Director: Frank Marshall
Screenplay: John Patrick

Shanley, from Michael Crichton's novel
Adventure/Thriller
Rated PG-13
Younger kids: Too intense Older kids: OK, with caution

When the son of her electronics billionaire boss disappears in the Congo, Karen Ross (Linney) sets up an expedition to continue his search for high-grade diamonds. She's joined by primatologist Peter Elliott (Walsh), whose 8-year-old gorilla charge, Amy, wants to return to the jungle and later by greedy adventurer Herkemer Homolka (Curry), who's on the trail of King Solomon's Mines. They're guided on the dangerous expedition by "great white hunter" Monroe Kelly (Ernie Hudson), who happens to be black. After various perils, they arrive at the Lost City of Zinj, which is protected by mysterious, murderous guards. . . .

Adults will find *Congo* too familiar, with flat characters and dialogue, routine action, and a curiously truncated climax; we barely get a glimpse of the fierce and intelligent gray apes that guard Zinj. The effects are adequate at best.

While you should pay attention to the PG-13 rating—the climax is intense and scary, and there is some strong language—most movie-savvy kids from 10 to 16 should have a grand time with *Congo,* partly because of Amy, the young gorilla.

Children will forgive lapses in realism that might bother older viewers, and won't be familiar with the clichés.

A CONNECTICUT YANKEE IN KING ARTHUR'S COURT
(1949)
Color, 107 minutes
Cast: Bing Crosby, Rhonda Fleming, William Bendix, Cedric Hardwicke, Henry Wilcoxon, Murvyn Vye, Virginia Field, Richard Webb, Joseph Vitale, Alan Napier, Julia Faye
Director: Tay Garnett
Screenplay: Edmund Beloin, based on the novel by Mark Twain
Musical/Fantasy/Literary classic
Unrated
Young children: VG Older children: VG

The ever-popular Mark Twain novel was easily adapted into a musical vehicle for the easygoing charm of Bing Crosby. He plays Hank Martin, a Connecticut Yankee who works as a blacksmith and one day suffers a blow on the head. When he regains consciousness, he finds himself centuries back in time, in Merrie Olde England and in the court of King Arthur (Cedric Hardwicke). He is captured by Sir Sagramore (William Bendix), a knight who brings him before the King himself. Then there is Alisande La Carteloise (Rhonda Fleming), the monarch's pretty, red-haired niece, to whom Hank is predictably attracted.

Younger children should go for the fantasy aspect of the story, which is played lightly and for laughs, and relish the manner in which Hank utilizes his "modern-era" knowledge to confound and dazzle his hosts. The elaborate Technicolor production features a handful of pleasant if forgettable songs.

Twain's story was previously filmed in 1921 and 1931 (notably, with Will Rogers in the lead), and has been remade and reworked countless times since.

CONQUEST OF THE PLANET OF THE APES
(1972)
Color, 88 minutes
Cast: Roddy McDowall, Don Murray, Natalie Trundy, Hari Rhodes, Severn Darden, Ricardo Montalban
Director: J. Lee Thompson
Screenplay: Paul Dehn, based on ideas created by Pierre Boulle
Science Fiction/Sequel
Rated PG
Young children: Iffy Older children: OK

Twenty years after the deaths of Cornelius and Zira, the two civilized chimpanzees who escaped the future destruction of the Earth by traveling into the past, their son, Caesar (Roddy McDowall), arrives in a large city in the company of kindly circus owner Armando (Ricardo Montalban), who's hidden him from the government for years.

As predicted by Cornelius in **Escape from the Planet of the Apes,** a plague has killed all the cats and dogs in the world. People adopted monkeys and apes as pets, then, as the intelligence of gorillas, chimpanzees, and orangutans increased, began using them in other ways. The society into which Caesar is unwillingly thrust treats apes as slaves, torturing the frightened creatures into submission. The Governor (Don Murray) learns that Caesar can talk and fears that he will lead rebellion against human society.

Some elements of Paul Dehn's otherwise clever script are a little hard to swallow, and there's really not very much plot. Dehn does intend the oppressed apes to stand in for oppressed human beings the world over, now and in the past, but most audiences—and children are the most receptive—will take this film as the entertaining melodrama it is. Thompson directs forcefully, making good use of Century City, a lavish commercial development in Los Angeles. The climactic rebellion of the apes is very dramatic and exciting . . . too intense and violent for the youngest viewers.

CONTACT (1997)
Color, 153 minutes
Cast: Jodie Foster, Matthew McConaughey, Tom Skerritt, James Woods, David Morse, John Hurt, Angela Bassett, William Fichtner, Rob Lowe, Jake Busey
Director: Robert Zemeckis
Screenplay: James V. Hart and Michael Goldenberg, from the novel by Carl Sagan, based on a story by Sagan and Ann Druyan
Science fiction/Drama
Rated PG
Young children: No Older children: VG

Ever since she was a child (inspired by her father, Ted), Ellie Arroway (Foster) has been fascinated with the idea of communicating with other worlds. As an adult, she's a respected astronomer working on SETI, the Search for Extra-Terrestrial Intelligence, eagerly listening to one star after another.

One night she actually picks up a signal from space, emanating from the star Vega. At first it's simple, but soon Ellie and others discover page after page of diagrams which turn out to be designs for a colossal machine to carry one human passenger "out there"—but where?

Contact is one of the best science fiction dramas of recent times and an excellent film to share with older children, for two reasons: First, it celebrates scientific research, making it seem both passionately romantic and desperately necessary. Second, it has a genuine sense of wonder, which we share with the story's main character, so vividly portrayed by Jodie Foster. At a time when movies hurl razzle-dazzle special effects in our face at every opportunity, here is a rare instance of a film that finds genuine excitement in the unknown.

The film may be too long for some kids; many adults felt the same way. It has one sexual episode, some mild language, and one particularly upsetting scene of intense action.

COOL RUNNINGS (1993)
Color, 98 minutes
Cast: Leon, Doug E. Doug, John Candy, Rawle D. Lewis, Malik Yoba, Raymond J. Barry, Peter Outerbridge, Paul Coeur
Director: Jon Turteltaub
Screenplay: Lynn Siefert, Tommy Swerdlow, Michael Goldberg, from a story by Siefert and Michael Ritchie
Comedy/True-life/Sports
Rated PG
Young children: VG Older children: VG

Here is a perfect feel-good movie based on a true story of some naive Jamaicans who decide to enter the Winter Olympics as a bobsled team! (They've never even seen snow before.) Their coach is a once proud, now disgraced athlete (John Candy) who believes in the team—and sees in their quest for victory a chance to redeem himself. The young men work hard, earn the cheers of their countrymen, and do their best to compete with almost everything working against them.

To give away more of the story would be a crime. And while that story may be formulaic from an adult point of view, it's also surefire, with a heartening message about spirit, perseverance, and teamwork.

The young actors who play the bobsledders are absolutely ideal. We believe in them and their struggle, and we care what happens to them.

One minor quibble: the scene where one of the athletes psyches himself up by calling himself a "mean muther" in the mirror. Was this absolutely necessary?

THE CORN IS GREEN (1945)
Black & white, 114 minutes
Cast: Bette Davis, John Dall, Joan Lorring, Nigel Bruce, Rhys Williams, Rosalind Ivan, Mildred Dunnock, Gwyneth Hughes, Arthur Shields
Director: Irving Rapper
Screenplay: Casey Robinson and Frank Cavett, based on the play by Emlyn Williams
Drama
Unrated
Young children: OK Older children: VG

This touching drama tells the story of Miss Lilly Moffatt, an aging schoolteacher who comes to live in a backward Welsh mining town. She is appalled to find that the people around her are illiterate and hopelessly poor, so Miss Lilly opens a school and offers to teach reading and writing to anyone willing to learn. The story deals with her struggle to keep the school afloat and her impact on the life of a rough-hewn but brilliant young miner.

The Corn Is Green is a beautifully realized story that emphasizes the way education can expand minds and alter lives. Even more to the point, it dramatizes the impact a single dedicated and self-sacrificing instructor may have on a student who is disadvantaged because of his environment.

It is one of Bette Davis' best roles; some thirty years later, her contemporary Katharine Hepburn played the same part in a television remake of the story.

CORRINA, CORRINA (1994)
Color, 114 minutes
Cast: Whoopi Goldberg, Ray Liotta, Tina Majorino, Don Ameche, Wendy Crewson, Larry Miller, Erica Yohn, Jenifer Lewis, Joan Cusack
Director: Jessie Nelson
Screenplay: Jessie Nelson
Drama
Rated PG
Young children: OK   Older children: VG

Back in the 1950s, everybody had two parents. Or at least that was what our television sets told us. On *Ozzie and Harriet*, *Leave It to Beaver*, *Father Knows Best*, and other sitcoms, kids had both a mother (who stayed at home and baked cookies all day) and a father (who was never too busy at work to offer sage advice to his offspring). Of course, in the 1950s as today, there were single-parent households. But they were rarely depicted on television or in the movies.

The subject of single parenthood back when everybody liked Ike is explored in *Corrina, Corrina*, a poignant and perceptive reminiscence. It is the story of a newly widowed Jewish advertising man and his vulnerable young daughter, and how they get on with their lives. Writer-director Jessie Nelson neatly tosses a curve ball into her story when she has the widower become romantically involved with the black woman he hires as a housekeeper. (This would still raise eyebrows today, but an interracial affair— let alone marriage—at that time was extremely controversial.) The film pointedly depicts how the deep feelings and understanding two people may come to share ultimately transcend religion, class, or color.

Corrina, Corrina is a "nice" film that doesn't hammer its racial issues too hard and works better as entertainment than as a social history. Still, it does reflect some of the attitudes of that period and offers a bittersweet and entertaining story that all family members can enjoy.

Young children who have lost a parent may find the film too upsetting.

THE CORSICAN BROTHERS (1941)
Black & white, 112 minutes
Cast: Douglas Fairbanks, Jr., Ruth Warrick, Akim Tamiroff, J. Carrol Naish, H. B. Warner, Henry Wilcoxon
Director: Gregory Ratoff
Screenplay: George Bruce and Howard Estabrook, based on

the novel by Alexandre
Dumas
Swashbuckler/Action-adventure
Unrated
Younger kids: OK   Older kids:
  VG

Douglas Fairbanks, Jr., admirably
carries on his father's swashbuckling tradition in this plush production of Alexandre Dumas's classic
tale about Siamese twins who are
separated at birth and grow up
not knowing each other, but remain spiritually tied all the same.
When they're reunited, they wreak
vengeance on the tyrannical robber baron (Akim Tamiroff) who
killed their parents and stole their
estate, and both fall in love with
the same woman (Ruth Warrick).
  Fairbanks is ideal in the dual
role, convincingly portraying the
physical and emotional telepathy
between the brothers, which adds
a fascinating aspect to the melodramatic derring-do. It's a fascinating concept—that when one
brother is injured, the other feels
pain—which could spark an interesting family conversation. You'll
also be amazed at the skill of the
"trick photography" in this film,
which was made decades before
CGI and digital effects made such
special effects commonplace.

**THE COUNT OF MONTE
CRISTO** (1934)
Black & white, 119 minutes
Cast: Robert Donat, Elissa
  Landi, Louis Calhern, Sidney
  Blackmer, Raymond Walburn,
  O. P. Heggie, Irene Hervey
Director: Rowland V. Lee
Screenplay: Philip Dunne, Dan
  Totheroh, and Rowland V.
  Lee, based on the novel by
  Alexandre Dumas

Swashbuckler/Action-adventure
Unrated
Younger kids: OK   Older kids:
  VG

While Alexandre Dumas's novels
have served as the basis for many
excellent swashbucklers, and there
have also been several fine versions of *The Count of Monte
Cristo*, perhaps no other film adaptation of his work is equal to
this superbly entertaining 1934
production. Robert Donat (in his
only American-made film) is brilliant as Edmond Dantes, the innocent Frenchman who's framed for
treason and railroaded to prison
without a trial. After rotting in his
dank, dark cell for thirteen years,
Dantes escapes with the aid of an
old friar (O. P. Heggie) and, after
becoming rich from a treasure he
finds on the island of Monte
Cristo, plots an elaborate revenge
on the three men who framed
him.
  Extravagantly produced, wonderfully acted, and packed with
plentiful action and rich characters, this is a first-class film that's
faithful to the spirit of the book
and remains one of Hollywood's
quintessential adventure films.
Donat is a superb actor, who is
best remembered as the star of
1939's **Goodbye, Mr. Chips**.

COURAGE MOUNTAIN
(1990)
Color, 98 minutes
Cast: Juliette Caton, Joanna
  Clarke, Nicola Stapleton,
  Charlie Sheen, Jan Rubes,
  Leslie Caron, Jade Magri
Director: Christopher Leitch
Screenplay: Weaver Webb, based
  on a story by Fred Brogger
  and Mark Brogger
Adventure

Rated PG
Young children: OK   Older
  children: No

Courage Mountain is a below average family film that's even more
disappointing in that it's a sequel
to the beloved Heidi story.

Teenage Heidi (Juliette Caton)
leaves behind Grandfather (Jan
Rubes) and Peter (a miscast
Charlie Sheen) to further her education at a finishing school in
northern Italy. Headmistress Miss
Hillary (Leslie Caron) befriends
Heidi, who has a rough time due
to her rural upbringing.

When World War I breaks out,
Heidi and friends are put up at a
local orphanage, whose evil keep-
ers have the girls work in a sweat
shop. Heidi's escape through the
snow-covered Alps provides the
suspense and adventure, and is
the catalyst for some thrilling sequences of a ski rescue led by
boyfriend Peter.

Clearly a kiddie film, not meant
to be considered seriously, *Courage Mountain* is a time-filler for
younger ones only.

THE COURT JESTER (1956)
Color, 101 minutes
Cast: Danny Kaye, Glynis Johns,
  Basil Rathbone, Angela
  Lansbury, Cecil Parker,
  Mildred Natwick, Robert
  Middleton, John Carradine
Directors: Norman Panama and
  Melvin Frank
Screenplay: Norman Panama and
  Melvin Frank
Swashbuckler/Comedy
Unrated
Younger kids: VG   Older kids:
  VG

This Danny Kaye vehicle is first
and foremost one of his funniest

comedies, but it's also a top-notch
swashbuckler that is as good as it
is because it takes its action-
adventure elements seriously. Kaye
is hilarious as a medieval servant
who, in the guise of a jester, becomes involved in a rebellion
against the tyrannical king. The
excellent cast includes the re-
doubtable Basil Rathbone as an
evil baron, while the witty script
deftly combines songs, gags, duels,
and intrigue with highly felicitous
results. The film also contains
Kaye's all-time classic routine,
where he has to remember a secret message that involves the
phrase "The pellet with the poison's in the vessel with the
pestle. . . ."

This film is so good that anyone
can enjoy it at face value, but if
your kids have seen other swashbucklers, they'll particularly savor
the parody elements of this one.

The witty songs by Sammy
Cahn and Kaye's wife, Sylvia
Fine, include "They'll Never Out-
fox the Fox" and "Maladjusted
Jester."

THE COURTSHIP OF
EDDIE'S FATHER (1963)
Color, 117 minutes
Cast: Glenn Ford, Ronny
  Howard, Shirley Jones, Stella
  Stevens, Dina Merrill, Roberta
  Sherwood, Jerry Van Dyke
Director: Vincente Minnelli
Screenplay: John Gay, based on
  the novel by Mark Toby
Comedy/Drama
Unrated
Younger kids: Good   Older
  kids: VG

Glenn Ford stars as a recent widower trying to raise his 6-year-old
son Eddie (Ronny Howard) on
his own in this wholesome family

120

comedy with lots of laughs and a few tears. When Dad starts to date again, he has a brief romance with a ditsy beauty (Stella Stevens) and eventually becomes engaged to a glamorous fashion consultant (Dina Merrill), but little Eddie has his own ideas about the opposite sex—including his belief that large busts and "skinny eyes" indicate that a woman is mean. He tries to fix Dad up with their girl-next-door neighbor (Shirley Jones).

This is not strictly a kid's movie, as it has serious undertones about dealing with loss, but children are sure to relate to Eddie's precocity, and 9-year-old Howard is irresistibly cute. (The TV series spawned by this movie was more deliberately designed as family entertainment.)

COVER GIRL (1944)
Color, 107 minutes
Cast: Gene Kelly, Rita Hayworth, Phil Silvers, Lee Bowman, Jinx Falkenburg, Leslie Brooks, Eve Arden, Otto Kruger, Jess Barker, Anita Colby, Curt Bois, Edward Brophy, Thurston Hall, Shelley Winters
Director: Charles Vidor
Screenplay: Virginia Van Upp, Marion Parsonnet, and Paul Gangelin, based on a story by Erwin Gelsey
Musical
Unrated
Young children: VG   Older children: VG

For a story that is mainly composed of froth and flounce, there is plenty of spice to this entertaining musical, which casts Gene Kelly as the owner of a small musical comedy theater in Brooklyn, where Rita Hayworth is his featured performer and girlfriend. Hayworth wants to be a model for fashion magazine covers, and when she gets her opportunity, Kelly conspires to keep his gal in Brooklyn. Predictably, Hayworth responds by falling into the arms of another man, and so the story goes. . . .

What makes this musical appealing to the family, particularly to adolescent girls, is the style with which the story is presented. There are fine songs, especially "Long Ago and Far Away" and "Sure Thing." The musical routines are energetic and fun to watch, particularly the one featuring Kelly dancing on a darkened street with his alter ego, who's come to life from a reflection in a storefront window. There's an energy and lightheartedness to the film that transcends the hokey story, the familiar battle of the sexes.

One nice twist has Hayworth playing her own grandmother in flashback. Additionally, Phil Silvers, known to baby boomers as television's Sergeant Bilko, contributes fine comedy touches in the role of Genius, Kelly's and Hayworth's loyal friend.

THE COWBOYS (1972)
Color, 128 minutes
Cast: John Wayne, Roscoe Lee Browne, Bruce Dern, Colleen Dewhurst, Slim Pickens, Lonny Chapman, A. Martinez, Robert Carradine, Allyn Ann McLerie
Director: Mark Rydell
Screenplay: Irving Ravetch, Harriet Frank, Jr., and William Dale Jennings
Western
Rated PG

Young children: No Older
  children: OK

Controversial in its time (and de-
batable still) is this seemingly ordinary oater with the Duke. It's
actually a disguised Vietnam-era
treatise on violence.

In 1877, Wyoming Territory,
aging cattle rancher Will Anderson is deserted by gold-fevered
ranch hands when it's time for the
four-hundred-mile drive to market. His only recourse is to train
and hire a crew of schoolboys,
ages 9 to 15, promising "a summer ahead you'll remember to
your dying day."

And then some. The journey
from tenderfoot to cowboy is a
deadly one, strewn with the car-
casses of stampeded herds and the
graves of those who don't make it
to the end of the trail.

The theme of the movie is the
familiar one about what it takes
to survive in the Old West. How
that existence is maintained
through bloodshed will be the
topic of tonight's discussion.

Aside from the "necessity" of
killing, there is a scene in which
the boys visit a madam and her
"girls" for an introduction to sex
that may not please parents. *The
Cowboys* is a good example of a
film that grown-ups might want to
watch first, before recommending
to their kids.

CREATURE FROM THE
BLACK LAGOON (1954)
Black & white, 79 minutes
Cast: Richard Carlson, Julia
  (Julie) Adams, Richard
  Denning, Whit Bissell,
  Antonio Moreno, Nestor
  Paiva, Ricou Browning, Ben
  Chapman
Director: Jack Arnold

Screenplay: Harry Essex and
  Arthur Ross
Science fiction/Monster
  adventure
Unrated
Younger kids: OK Older kids:
  OK

Looking for fossils of a half-
human, half-fish prehistoric animal, an expedition travels up the
Amazon to the (fictional) Black
Lagoon and finds there's one of
these creatures still alive. The
Gill-Man wants them to go away
and leave him alone . . . then he
glimpses Julia Adams in a white
bathing suit . . .

Nearly the archetypal man-in-a-
monster-suit movie, this often-
imitated film still has the power
to thrill kids, who'll sympathize
with the Creature, no matter how
many faces he crushes. For one
thing, the monster suit itself is so
well-designed that, strangely, it
transcends itself: it looks real but
also like something from your
dreams. Moreover, the underwater scenes are eerily hypnotic.

Both in terms of writing and
acting, the film seems dated now,
and while children might laugh at
some of the straight-faced dialogue, they'll still be mesmerized
by the Creature.

This was originally shown in
3-D, accounting for some of the
more forced-looking elements,
such as the bats in a cave.

Followed by **Revenge of the
Creature** and **The Creature Walks
Among Us.**

THE CREATURE WALKS
AMONG US (1956)
Black & white, 78 minutes
Cast: Jeff Morrow, Rex Reason,
  Leigh Snowden, Gregg Palmer,
  Don Megowan

Director: John Sherwood
Screenplay: Arthur Ross
Science fiction/Monster
Unrated
Younger kids: OK   Older kids:
   OK

The Gill-Man is found alive and well in a Florida swamp, but in fending off attack, he's severely burned. He turns out to have human skin under his scales (and to be much larger with them gone); without his gills, he can no longer breathe in the water. Taken to San Francisco, he stands glumly around a cage, protecting some sheep, until briefly springing into action at the end.

The last of the three Creature films is slow going, but if children have seen the first two, they may want to try this one, too. Be prepared for them to be puzzled by the inconclusive ending, in which the altered Creature is last seen standing by the ocean. Adults will be puzzled why Universal-International so pointlessly changed their first great monster since the Wolf Man.

THE CREEPING UNKNOWN
(see **The Quatermass Xperiment**)

THE CRIMSON PIRATE
   (1952)
Color, 104 minutes
Cast: Burt Lancaster, Nick
   Cravat, Eva Bartok, Torin
   Thatcher, James Hayter, Leslie
   Bradley, Margot Grahame,
   Noel Purcell, Christopher Lee
Director: Robert Siodmak
Screenplay: Roland Kibbee
Swashbuckler/Action-adventure/
   Comedy
Unrated
Younger kids: OK   Older kids:
   VG

Burt Lancaster is at his acrobatic best in this good-natured swashbuckling spoof that's both funny and exciting. With a twinkle in his eye and a sparkle on his teeth, Lancaster plays a buccaneer who, along with his mute sidekick (Lancaster's real-life pal and former circus partner Nick Cravat), is hired by the Spanish to quell West Indian revolutionaries but falls in love with the rebel leader's beautiful daughter (Eva Bartok) and promptly switches sides.

Beautifully filmed in color in the Mediterranean, it's a nonstop delight with numerous tongue-in-cheek action scenes, highlighted by the finale in which the 18th-century pirates utilize primitive machine guns, tanks, submarines, and balloon bombers, which they have invented. If your kids enjoy this, they should also enjoy **The Flame and the Arrow,** which features more acrobatic action with Lancaster and Cravat.

"CROCODILE" DUNDEE
(1986)
Color, 98 minutes
Cast: Paul Hogan, Linda
   Kozlowski, John Meillon,
   David Gulpilil, Mark Blum
Director: Peter Faiman
Screenplay: Paul Hogan, Ken
   Shadie, and John Cornell,
   based on a story by Hogan
Comedy/Action
Rated PG-13
Younger kids: OK, with
   caution   Older kids: VG

Affable Aussie Paul Hogan stars in this sleeper hit about a bush country tour guide from Down Under whose tall tales about being a legendary crocodile hunter bring him to the attention of an attractive New York reporter (Linda

Kozlowski), but who experiences culture shock when he agrees to return with her to the asphalt jungles of the Big Apple.

Though generally predictable, this old-fashioned fish-out-of-water tale is disarmingly enjoyable, thanks to Hogan's genuine charisma and some funny gags involving Dundee's introduction to "civilization." He sleeps on the floor and washes his socks in the bathtub of his fancy hotel room, tangles with muggers, transvestites, and the reporter's wimpy, conniving boyfriend. The film contains some off-color language, sexual gags involving hookers, and violence . . . just potent enough to earn it a PG-13.

THE CRUCIBLE (1996)
Color, 123 minutes
Cast: Daniel Day-Lewis, Winona Ryder, Joan Allen, Paul Scofield, Bruce Davison, Rob Campbell, Jeffrey Jones, Peter Vaughan, George Gaynes, Karron Graves, Charlayne Woodard, Frances Conroy
Director: Nicholas Hytner
Screenplay: Arthur Miller, based on his play
Historical drama
Rated PG-13
Younger kids: OK, with caution   Older kids: VG

The Crucible is a gripping adaptation of Arthur Miller's 1953 morality play, which used the infamous witch trials of 17th-century Salem, Massachusetts, as a metaphor for the equally insidious Communist "witch hunt" of the 1950s. The story begins with teenage girls dancing in the woods. One of them, Abigail Williams (Winona Ryder), lusts for farmer John Proctor (Daniel Day-Lewis) and drinks a voodoo charm in the hopes of killing his wife, Elizabeth (Joan Allen). The girls are caught, and Abigail claims to have been influenced by the Devil. When Proctor finally rebuffs Abigail, her accusations of witchcraft fly around the Salem village and several innocent people—including Elizabeth—are targeted as being witches themselves.

The Crucible works well in a classical way, as it slowly gathers momentum and builds to its tragic and all-too-inevitable conclusion. The direction is straightforward and powerful, the acting excellent, particularly from Allen and from Paul Scofield as Judge Danforth, the inquisitor who is sent to rid the town of the Devil's influence. The drama is inherently interesting for its historical value, and parents can explain to their children how it echoes the times in which it was originally written. But the film and the play are more than a simple transcription of Joseph McCarthy's (and the House Un-American Activities Committee's) goings-on and deal with far greater, universal themes. Director Hytner noted that the issue of lies and hysteria swaying an all-too-gullible public is more pertinent than ever in the present era of religious fundamentalism and child molestation trials.

The necessity (and difficulty) of maintaining one's personal honor, even in the face of overwhelming odds, is a constant element in most of Miller's work.

Much of The Crucible's content is too adult in nature to be easily explained to young children; it is ideally suited to older kids, however, who will probably recognize from their own experiences the power of a lie, and how quickly its poison can spread.

CRY-BABY (1990)
Color, 85 minutes
Cast: Johnny Depp, Amy Locane, Susan Tyrrell, Polly Bergen, Iggy Pop, Ricki Lake, Traci Lords, Kim McGuire, Darren E. Burrows, Troy Donahue, Mink Stole, Joe Dallesandro, Joey Heatherton, David Nelson, Patricia Hearst, Willem Dafoe, Stephen P.H. Mailer
Director: John Waters
Screenplay: John Waters
Comedy/Satire
Rated PG-13
Younger children: No   Older children: OK, with caution

This campy pop musical may be a bit too edgy for the younger crowd—who will perhaps enjoy it the most. Its minimalist plot pays homage to variety of inspirations: **West Side Story, Rebel Without a Cause, Jailhouse Rock,** *The Wild One,* etc.

In 1954, Cry-Baby (Johnny Depp) is leader of The Drapes, a motorcycle gang; he has fallen in love with Allison (Amy Locane), a girl from the right side of the tracks. This sparks a war between The Drapes and The Squares, led by Baldwin (Mailer), whom Allison was dating.

This may be John Waters' most accessible film, though not as much fun (or outrageous) as the unconventional filmmaker's previous epic, **Hairspray.** The story is just an excuse for musical numbers, which enthusiastically take over the show. Kids will get a kick out of characters and costumes, but there is some language and humor that's distinctly not kiddie variety.

THE CRUSADES (1935)
Black & white, 123 minutes
Cast: Loretta Young, Henry Wilcoxon, Ian Keith, C. Aubrey Smith, Katherine DeMille, Joseph Schildkraut, Alan Hale
Director: Cecil B. DeMille
Screenplay: Harold Lamb, Waldemar Young, and Dudley Nichols, based on Lamb's book *The Crusade, Iron Men and Saints*
Action-adventure/Historical
Unrated
Younger kids: OK   Older kids: Good

This prodigious spectacle has all of the pomp and pageantry that one would expect from a Cecil B. DeMille epic about the Holy Wars. Its two hours are over-stuffed with action, religion, romance, and massive battle scenes that boggle the mind. Henry Wilcoxon stars as King Richard Lion-Heart, who embarks on his holy crusades and has to rescue his beloved wife (Loretta Young), Queen Berengaria, when she's kidnapped by Muslim infidels.

It may be overlong and ponderous at times, and certainly shouldn't be used in place of a history book (a caveat well applied to DeMille movies in general, which had blithe disregard for facts), but it's certainly entertaining.

CRY, THE BELOVED COUNTRY (1951)
Black & white, 111 minutes
Cast: Canada Lee, Charles Carson, Sidney Poitier,

Geoffrey Keen, Reginald
  Ngeabo, Joyce Carey
Director: Zoltan Korda
Screenplay: Alan Paton, based
  on his novel
Drama
Unrated
Young children: No   Older
  children: VG

This moving story, filmed and set
in South Africa, deals with a simple, country minister who is
forced to make his first trip to the
big city—Johannesburg—because
he is concerned about his son.
Following Absalom's trail, he
eventually discovers that the boy
has turned to petty crime and is
involved in a murder. The dead
man turns out to be the son of the
prosperous white landowner who
has never really given the reverend much thought. Through circumstance and tragedy, these two
men—both brokenhearted fathers—are drawn together.

The first film adaptation of
Alan Paton's novel is in some
ways superior to the recent remake. Its story is told with a simplicity and directness that only
add to its power. What's more,
the passage of time has given the
film a period context. Finally, it
showcases a young actor in one of
his first prominent roles: Sidney
Poitier, who would go on to become America's preeminent black
movie star.

The film stars a fine (if mostly
forgotten) American actor named
Canada Lee as Rev. Kumalo; he
delivers a poignant and memorable performance as the naïve cler-
gyman whose dreams are shattered.
Cry the Beloved Country is an
excellent film to share with mature children; if you want a more
contemporary slant on the same

story, the 1995 remake is also
quite good.

CRY, THE BELOVED COUNTRY (1995)
Color, 120 minutes
Cast: Richard Harris, James Earl
  Jones, Charles S. Dutton, Vusi
  Kunene, Leleti Khumalo, Ian
  Roberts, Dambisa Kente, Eric
  Miyeni
Director: Darrell James Roodt
Screenplay: Ronald Harwood,
  based on the novel by Alan
  Paton
Drama
Rated PG-13
Young children: No   Older
  children: VG

Here is a literate, beautifully
acted version of Alan Paton's celebrated novel in which two very
different men become linked
amid the racism and bloodshed of
South Africa during the late
1940s. One is the Rev. Stephen
Kumalo, an aging Zulu Anglican
priest (James Earl Jones). The
other is James Jarvis, a prosperous farmer and white supremacist
(Richard Harris).

The story is set into motion
when Rev. Kumalo is called to Johannesburg, where his sister and
brother reside. Eventually, he
learns that his son, Absalom, has
become a petty criminal who may
be linked to the murder of a white
man: Arthur Jarvis, a staunchly
anti-apartheid social reformer.

Arthur, of course, is the son of
James Jarvis.

Despite the evolving politics in
South Africa today, *Cry, the Beloved Country* remains a relevant,
universal story of the tragedy of
racism and blind hatred. The fine
performances of its two familiar
stars (Jones and Harris) are

matched by the African actors who fill out the cast.

Cry, the Beloved Country contains incidents and emotional moments that would be too intense for younger children. There is also some strong language.

CURLY TOP (1935)

Black & white, 75 minutes (also available in computer-colored version)

Cast: Shirley Temple, John Boles, Rochelle Hudson, Jane Darwell, Rafaela Ottiano, Esther Dale, Arthur Treacher, Etienne Girardot, Maurice Murphy

Director: Irving Cummings

Screenplay: Patterson McNutt and Arthur Beckhard, based (without credit) on the novel *Daddy Long Legs* by Jean Webster

Comedy/Melodrama/Musical

Unrated

Young children: VG   Older children: VG

This charming tale follows two parentless sisters as they travel from a grim institutional facility to a luxurious, loving home. The younger of the girls is Curly Top, a spunky child played with zest by Shirley Temple. While she makes mischief at the orphanage, her older sister is relegated to do the chores of a drudge. Their journey from the orphanage starts when the handsome trustee of the facility adopts the sisters in the name of a fictitious client and places them with an aunt at his beautiful Long Island home.

Although the beginning of the film might be quaint for today's juvenile audiences, the subsequent scenes of the girls in their opulent household—with a comical British butler played to perfection by Arthur Treacher—ought to charm even the most resistant viewer. Additionally, there is a pleasant and sometimes complicated romance between the trustee and the older daughter, which should appeal to adolescent girls. The highlight of the film is Shirley singing "Animal Crackers in My Soup," a song with which she was associated even into adulthood.

THE CURSE OF FRANKENSTEIN (1957)

Color, 83 minutes

Cast: Peter Cushing, Robert Urquhart, Hazel Court, Christopher Lee, Valerie Gaunt, Paul Hardtmuth

Director: Terence Fisher

Screenplay: Jimmy Sangster, from the novel *Frankenstein; Or, a Modern Prometheus* by Mary Shelley

Horror/Literary classic

Unrated

Younger kids: Too scary   Older kids: For horror fans

Wealthy Victor Frankenstein (Cushing) is determined to create a Creature from the bodies of the dead and to bring it to life, no matter what this takes. He ruthlessly kills an old mentor (Hardtmuth) just to get his brain, but in a quarrel with his associate (Urquhart), Victor accidentally damages the brain, and the Creature that results is a shambling, hideous killer.

Horror movies were thought to be dead by the late 1950s and were replaced by the more up-to-date science fiction genre. Then the old Universal horror classics were released to television, and around the same time, this colorful, violent thriller appeared in theaters. It was a smash hit and revived the horror genre. It also established Hammer, the British production company, and its stars, Peter Cushing and Christopher Lee, who went on to lifelong careers in the genre, often as co-stars.

Definitely too gruesome for younger kids, it may be too gory even for the older ones—and there's a strong undercurrent of sex as well. But teenagers, if used to modern horror movies, might enjoy watching this trendsetter.

THE CURSE OF THE CAT PEOPLE (1944)
Black & white, 70 minutes
Cast: Simone Simon, Kent
  Smith, Jane Randolph, Ann
  Carter, Eve March, Julia
  Dean, Elizabeth Russell,
  Erford Gage, Sir Lancelot
Directors: Robert Wise and
  Gunther von Fritsch
Screenplay: DeWitt Bodeen
Drama/Horror/Fantasy
Unrated
Young children: OK   Older
  children: OK

RKO insisted that producer Val Lewton come up with a sequel to the hit *Cat People,* but instead of the thriller they expected, he and his team gave them this serious, moody fantasy about a little girl and her imaginary playmate. There is no curse, nor are there any cat people!

Oliver Reed (Smith), the hero of **Cat People,** is married to the Good Girl (Randolph) from the movie, and they have a young daughter named Amy (Carter). She's a quiet, lonely child and begins imagining that Irena (Simon), Oliver's first wife, meets her in the garden behind the family home. Little Amy also becomes involved with an elderly recluse and her bitter, grown daughter.

One of the most serious and realistic dramas about childhood ever attempted by a major studio, the film is inconsistent (Amy is not always credible as a character), but the scenes with the angry adult daughter (Russell) are unexpectedly powerful, and everything concerning Amy and her imaginary friend, Simon, has a delicate, ethereal quality, like a dream.

A side note of interest: Sir Lancelot, a famous Calypso singer, plays probably the least stereotyped black character to appear in any Hollywood movie of this period.

Even though the central character is very young, this isn't really a film for younger kids; it's too serious—and occasionally quite scary—though it's not really a horror movie. More thoughtful older children, who are already examining their own earlier years, might well be caught up in the movie's delicate spell.

CURSE OF THE DEMON (1957)
Black & white, 95 minutes
  (some prints run 83m.)
Cast: Dana Andrews, Peggy
  Cummins, Niall MacGinnis,
  Maurice Denham, Athene
  Seyler, Liam Redmond,
  Reginald Beckwith, Ewan
  Roberts
Director: Jacques Tourneur
Screenplay: Charles Bennett and
  Hal E. Chester, from the story
  "Casting the Runes" by M. R.
  James
Horror/Suspense
Unrated

Younger kids: Very scary Older kids: OK, but still scary

Skeptical psychologist Andrews arrives in England intent on debunking witchcraft, demonology, and the like, but he becomes involved in a mystery: a series of deaths that increasingly suggest to him that demons exist and that one is after him.

Although barely noticed when it was first released, this movie (known as *Night of the Demon* in England) is now rightly regarded as one of the most persuasive and frightening horror movies ever made. Andrews is only fair as the hero, but the rest of the cast is very good, particularly Niall MacGinnis as Julian Karswell, who unleashes the demon of the title—a power that once set free, he cannot control.

Though hampered by a limited budget, director Tourneur uses sound effects, distorting lenses, and carefully staged scenes to build a powerful sense that the supernatural is real and waiting just around the corner. The demon of the title is glimpsed a few times, but the low budget prevents it from being particularly convincing. Still, the film itself is very persuasive. Your teenagers are likely to be surprised and impressed that a film from the olden times can be so effective.

THE CURSE OF THE WEREWOLF (1961)
Color, 91 minutes
Cast: Oliver Reed, Clifford Evans, Yvonne Romain, Catherine Feller, Anthony Dawson, Hira Talfrey, Richard Wordsworth
Director: Terence Fisher
Screenplay: John Elder (pseud. of Anthony Hinds), from the novel *The Werewolf of Paris* by Guy Endore
Horror
Unrated
Younger kids: Strong stuff Older kids: OK

The movie opens with a lengthy prologue depicting how a werewolf can be created, but most of the film is about Leon (Reed), an earnest young man who unknowingly becomes a monster when the moon is full.

Set in 18th-century Spain, this movie has a different look from other Hammer films of the period, but is still well produced on a low budget, with a strong cast and good direction by Fisher. Young people often feel alienated, so they might well identify with the tragic Leon, well played by Reed.

Less intense and gruesome than more recent horror movies, it's also better made, with more emphasis on characters, courage, and fate.

Note: There is a rape near the beginning of the film, but it occurs offscreen.

D

DADDY LONG LEGS (1955)
Color, 126 minutes
Cast: Fred Astaire, Leslie Caron, Terry Moore, Thelma Ritter, Fred Clark, Charlotte Austin, Larry Keating, Kathryn Givney, Steven Geray, Ray Anthony Orchestra
Director: Jean Negulesco
Screenplay: Phoebe and Henry Ephron, based on the novel and play by Jean Webster
Musical
Unrated
Young children: VG   Older children: VG

The story of this deluxe musical comedy begins when a wealthy American businessman adopts an orphaned girl during a trip to France. Rather than identify himself as her benefactor, he prefers to remain distant from her. He places her at the best schools and even arranges for her to become his niece's roommate. For years, the girl writes letters to her "Daddy Long Legs," but he never reads them. Instead, he has his office staff respond to her every need. Eventually she grows up. One day they meet, and—as the Oscar-winning song says—"Something's Gotta Give!" It does, and they fall in love.

The story is quite charming and innocent; however, taking into account headlines of father figures who make advances towards teenage innocents, some adolescents might be startled by an adoptive father kissing his custodial daughter. It's important to remember that this romance was produced during the age of innocence and merely intends to impart a Cinderella tale, complete with a happy ending.

The story was filmed before—without songs—in 1919 and 1931, and in 1935 as a Shirley Temple vehicle, **Curly Top**.

DAMN YANKEES (1958)
Color, 110 minutes
Cast: Tab Hunter, Gwen Verdon, Ray Walston, Russ Brown, Shannon Bolin, Nathaniel Frey, Jimmie Komack, Rae Allen, Robert Shafer, Jean Stapleton
Directors: George Abbott and Stanley Donen
Screenplay: Abbott, based on the musical play by Abbott and Douglass Wallop, based in turn on Wallop's book *The Year the Yankees Lost the Pennant*
Musical/Fantasy
Unrated
Younger kids: OK   Older kids: VG

This rousing musical fantasy was a smash hit on Broadway, and makes a good transition to the screen. It is the saga of Joe Boyd, an aging, forever-frustrated Washington Senators rooter who says one night that he'd sell his soul to see his beloved team get one good long-ball hitter. With that, a mys-

130

terious Mr. Applegate appears to consummate just such a deal. Joe is magically transformed into slugging all-American boy Joe Hardy—"Shoeless Joe from Hannibal, Mo." Hardy is promptly signed by the Senators and becomes their savior as they rise in the standings and chase the dreaded New York Yankees for the American League flag.

Tab Hunter has one of his best roles as Hardy, while Ray Walston is a delight as Mr. Applegate, the Devil. Gwen Verdon is at her sexiest as Lola, a temptress in Applegate's employ who is ordered to occupy Joe's mind when he realizes how much he misses his former life.

Some of the story points in *Damn Yankees,* including its great empathy for the middle-aged Joe and his wife, may make it seem remote to younger children, while its sexuality (in the person of Lola, who's a caricature of a vamp) may seem unsuitable. But the musical numbers, including "(You Gotta Have) Heart," "Shoeless Joe," and the climactic mambo, all staged by the great Bob Fosse, are tough for viewers of any age to resist.

Aging baby boomers will appreciate the presence of Jean Stapleton in a supporting role, employing the very same voice she used over a decade later as Edith Bunker on *All in the Family.*

A DAMSEL IN DISTRESS
(1937)
Black & white, 98 minutes
Cast: Fred Astaire, George Burns, Gracie Allen, Joan Fontaine, Reginald Gardiner, Ray Noble, Constance Collier
Director: George Stevens
Screenplay: P. G. Wodehouse, Ernest Pagano, and S. K. Lauren, based on the novel by Wodehouse
Musical
Unrated
Young children: VG   Older children: VG

Here is one 1930s Fred Astaire musical that does *not* feature Ginger Rogers as his romantic interest and dance partner. When *A Damsel in Distress* was made, both reportedly were tiring of their constant onscreen teaming. But Rogers' absence from the cast does not mean that *A Damsel in Distress* is lacking in charm. For one thing, the original music was composed by George and Ira Gershwin and includes such standards as "Nice Work If You Can Get It" and "A Foggy Day." For another, Astaire is still here and in top form.

The story involves Jerry Halliday, an American musical comedy star who becomes immersed in romantic tomfoolery in Merry Olde England with aristocratic Lady Alyce Marshmorton (Joan Fontaine). However, what makes *A Damsel in Distress* extra special is the presence of George Burns and Gracie Allen, who are cast as Halliday's publicist and his imbecilic secretary. Youngsters may only know Burns as an ancient presence on television and in latter-day movies. Here, kids may get a chance to see the team of Burns and Allen when they were one of America's best-loved comedy duos and experience Gracie's unique way of driving George crazy.

Along the way, Astaire, Burns, and Allen get to romp in the famous "Fun House" sequence, performed in a carnival setting

131

with the three principals on roller skates. This routine alone (which won an Academy Award) is enough to delight youngsters of all ages.

DANCES WITH WOLVES
(1990)
Color, 181 minutes
Cast: Kevin Costner, Mary McDonnell, Graham Greene, Rodney A. Grant, Floyd Red Crow Westerman, Tantoo Cardinal, Robert Pastorelli, Charles Rocket, Maury Chaykin
Director: Kevin Costner
Screenplay: Michael Blake, based on his novel
Western/Drama
Rated PG-13
Younger kids: No   Older kids: VG

Kevin Costner made an impressive, Oscar-winning directorial debut with this epic Western that won a total of seven Oscars, including Best Picture. Costner also gives a fine performance as a disillusioned U.S. cavalry lieutenant who's sent to a remote outpost in the frontier in 1863. Discovering that it's been abandoned, he befriends some nearby Sioux Indians and eventually deserts his post and becomes a part of their tribe.

Beautifully filmed in the grandiose style of epic Westerns of the past, with spectacular photography and including a breathtaking buffalo stampede, the sympathetic portrayal of Native Americans and the depiction of their brutal treatment at the hands of the American government is what sets this film apart from vintage Hollywood Westerns.

It is long (three hours—or if you see Costner's revised version on video, four hours), uncompromising, and highly graphic in depicting the violence of the times. There is strong language and some sexual content as well. Even older children will be disturbed by its (historically accurate) chronicle of the Indians' suicide . . . yet this is not a downbeat film but rather a celebration of a great people.

Children who do see this film should be reassured that no animals were actually injured during production; the incredibly realistic scenes of buffalo slaughter were accomplished with movie magic.

DARBY O'GILL AND THE LITTLE PEOPLE (1959)
Color, 93 minutes
Cast: Albert Sharpe, Janet Munro, Sean Connery, Jimmy O'Dea, Kieron Moore, Estelle Winwood, Walter Fitzgerald, Denis O'Dea
Director: Robert Stevenson
Screenplay: Lawrence E. Watkin, suggested by the Darby O'Gill stories of H. T. Kavanagh
Fantasy
Unrated
Young children: OK, with caution   Older children: VG

Darby O'Gill and the Little People is one of Walt Disney's most beguiling fantasies.

Albert Sharpe is ideally cast as Darby, a born tale-spinner with a wink in his eye who works as a caretaker on the governor's estate. He can't bear to tell his daughter Katie that he's been replaced by a younger man. (Never mind that the replacement, Michael McBride, has eyes for Katie—and vice versa.) One night, Darby falls down a well and finds himself in the land of leprechauns. King Brian explains that he brought Darby there to spare him having to confront his daughter, but Darby isn't grateful and manages to escape. King Brian follows, launching a battle of wits as the old man tricks the leprechaun into granting him three wishes—while the wily King plays some tricks of his own. When an accident leaves Katie with a serious injury, however, the tricks turn serious.

This delightful tale is not only a wonderful fantasy, but one of the most ingenious special-effects films ever devised. That's because the most incredible effects are virtually invisible. The leprechauns blend in with full-sized actors so convincingly that your eye is fooled; you stop looking for the illusion and accept it completely . . . whether it's King Brian hoisting himself onto a bedpost to speak to Katie and Michael while they're sleeping, or Darby playing his fiddle as scores of leprechauns dance with glee. (Perhaps the ultimate illusion is the movie's setting, which is unmistakably Ireland—but was in fact recreated in Southern California!)

THE DARK CRYSTAL (1983)
Color, 94 minutes
Cast: Jim Henson, Kathryn Mullen, Frank Oz, Dave Goelz, Brian Muehl, Jean Pierre Amlel, Kiran Shah
Directors: Jim Henson and Frank Oz
Screenplay: David Odell and Henson
Fantasy
Rated PG
Young children: No   Older children: VG

In another world, where there are three suns and no humans, the evil Skekses and the peaceful Mystics continue to play out their primeval battle for dominance, using the gentle Gelfling people as pawns. There, little Kira and Jen embark on a heroic quest to return a missing shard to the great gemstone called The Dark Crystal, which guards the mood of the universe.

Imaginative design ideas permeate this remarkable movie, which is enacted entirely by sophisticated puppets and visionary puppeteers. Leave it to Jim Henson and his team to come up with something completely original and unusual. Because it is so different, the film takes some time to warm up to—but it's worth the effort.

The somber, simple fable has no laughs, but there is a lot of heart beneath the grotesque character designs, and youngsters will find a worthwhile moral to the fablelike story.

This is truly a one-of-a-kind work that deserves more recognition. The littlest ones might find some of the fairy-tale ingredients a bit scary.

D.A.R.Y.L. (1985)
Color, 99 minutes
Cast: Barrett Oliver, Mary Beth Hurt, Michael McKean, Kathryn Walker, Colleen Camp, Josef Sommer, Ron Frazier, Steve Ryan, Danny Corkill, Amy Linker
Director: Simon Wincer
Screenplay: David Ambrose, Allan Scott, and Jeffrey Ellis
Science fiction/Family adventure
Rated PG
Younger kids: Tense, but OK   Older kids: OK

Ten-year-old Daryl (Oliver), found in the North Carolina woods, ends up in the care of foster parents (McKean and Hurt); over the next few months, they become a close-knit family. He proves to be amazingly adept at everything, from mathematics to baseball—but when his "real parents" reclaim him, we learn that Daryl is really D.A.R.Y.L. (Data Analyzing Robot Youth Lifeform). He's not a robot, but a cyborg: his body, conceived in a test tube, is perfectly human, but he has a computer mind. Then the military decides to terminate the D.A.R.Y.L. project. . . .

This polished and underrated movie is a fine choice for sci-fi-loving kids, and even their parents will enjoy it. Daryl doesn't have any computer intellect other than his mind, making his triumphs especially satisfying and believable. Barrett Oliver is excellent in the title role, and the rest of the cast matches him.

DAVID COPPERFIELD (1935)
Black & white, 130 minutes
Cast: Freddie Bartholomew, Frank Lawton, W. C. Fields, Lionel Barrymore, Madge Evans, Roland Young, Basil Rathbone, Edna May Oliver, Maureen O'Sullivan, Lewis Stone, Elizabeth Allan, Lennox Pawle, Elsa Lanchester, Una O'Connor, Jessie Ralph
Director: George Cukor
Screenplay: Howard Estabrook and Hugh Walpole, based on the novel by Charles Dickens
Drama-comedy/Literary classic
Unrated
Young children: VG Older children: VG

No, this isn't a biography of the popular contemporary magician. It's a handsome, heartfelt rendition of Charles Dickens' autobiographical 1850 novel, which in an earlier day was a staple on the reading lists of schoolchildren everywhere.

David Copperfield is the saga of a boy whose mother is widowed before he is born; we follow his journey from youth through adulthood, and meet an incredible variety of colorful characters, both kind and cruel. (Remember that Dickens wrote most of his lengthy novels in serialized form; that's why they have so many episodes within their lengthy narratives.)

W. C. Fields is a delight in period garb as Micawber, the princely pauper who befriends young David and gives him excellent advice; Basil Rathbone is chillingly good as Mr. Murdstone, David's cruel stepfather; Roland Young is perfect as the odious (and perfectly named) Uriah Heep; and Edna May Oliver is unforgettable as David's imposing (but still loving) Aunt Betsey Trotwood.

Several screen versions of *David Copperfield* have been produced over the years, from a 1911 silent version to a 1970 made-for-television movie. But this is still the one to see: a panoramic story of life, with all its joys and sorrows, filled with characters one can never forget.

It might even inspire some viewers to read Dickens' wonderful book.

DAVY CROCKETT AND THE RIVER PIRATES (1956)
Color, 81 minutes
Cast: Fess Parker, Buddy Ebsen, Jeff York, Kenneth Tobey, Clem Bevans

Director: Norman Foster
Screenplay: Tom Blackburn and
    Norman Foster
Action-adventure
Rated G
Younger kids: OK Older kids:
    Good

Davy Crockett may have been
killed at the Alamo in real life,
but that didn't stop Walt Disney
from bringing him back for some
more episodes of the hit TV
show, which were then re-edited
into this feature-length sequel to
**Davy Crockett, King of the Wild
Frontier.**

The lighthearted first half of the
film finds Davy (Fess Parker) and
sidekick Georgie (Buddy Ebsen)
taking on Mike Fink (Jeff York),
the rascally "King of the River"
in a keelboat race down the Ohio
and Mississippi rivers to New Orleans. The second segment is
much more serious (and a little violent), as Davy tries to prevent
war with the Indians and discovers that some white bandits
are dressing as Indians and raiding ships. While not quite as fresh
as the original, this is still good
fun for kids (and nostalgic adults).

**DAVY CROCKETT, KING OF
THE WILD FRONTIER** (1955)
Color, 93 minutes
Cast: Fess Parker, Buddy Ebsen,
    Basil Ruysdael, Hans Conried,
    William Bakewell, Kenneth
    Tobey
Director: Norman Foster
Screenplay: Tom Blackburn
Action-adventure
Rated PG
Younger kids: VG Older kids:
    Good

This is a feature-length version of
three episodes from the *Disney-*

land TV show about the legendary frontiersman Davy Crockett.
The series created a pop-culture
phenomenon in 1955, with virtually every young boy in the country donning a coonskin cap and
singing its theme song, "The Ballad of Davy Crockett," which became a nationwide hit.

Fess Parker plays Crockett,
whose adventures (with sidekick
Georgie Russel, played by Buddy
Ebsen) include making peace with
Indian leader Chief Red Stick
(Pat Hogan), ridding a town of an
outlaw, running for Congress and
opposing Andrew Jackson's bill
depriving Indians of land rights,
and joining a group of Texans in
their fight against Mexico at the
Alamo.

Though necessarily episodic in
nature, this is an enjoyable pioneer adventure that's nicely made
(Disney had the foresight to shoot
the series in color even though it
aired in black-and-white) and well
acted by its amiable cast, headed
by Parker.

A DAY AT THE RACES
(1937)
Black & white, 109 minutes
Cast: Groucho, Chico, and
    Harpo Marx, Maureen
    O'Sullivan, Allan Jones,
    Margaret Dumont, Sig
    Rumann
Director: Sam Wood
Screenplay: Robert Pirosh,
    George Seaton, and George
    Oppenheimer, based on a
    story by Pirosh and Seaton
Comedy/Musical
Unrated
Younger kids: Good Older
    kids: VG

This follow-up to the Marx Brothers' **A Night at the Opera** is almost

135

as good as that classic, featuring some hilarious comic set pieces, including the "Tootsie-frootsie Ice Cream" skit and a hysterically funny medical examination scene, but it's padded with some superfluous (if lavish) musical numbers and a dull romance between Allan Jones and Maureen O'Sullivan.

Groucho plays Dr. Hugo Z. Hackenbush, a horse doctor who's mistakenly hired to run a financially troubled sanitarium that's in danger of being taken over by some bad guys. While Harpo and Chico help raise money with their racehorse for the sanitarium's sweet owner (O'Sullivan), Groucho romances the hypochondriac socialite Mrs. Upjohn (the priceless Margaret Dumont), and is wooed by a seductive villainess (Esther Muir) who ends up being plastered with wallpaper for her troubles.

The script is very funny and the brothers are in top form (having honed their material on the stage before filming began), but the film does contain some racial stereotypes in the depiction of black characters around the racetrack. There is also one production number ("All God's Chillun Got Rhythm") in which the Marxes perform in blackface.

The parts may be greater than the whole, but *A Day at the Races* is the kind of film that will have you and your family laughing out loud, and those moments are precious enough to forgive the film its shortcomings.

A DAY IN OCTOBER (1990)
Color, 97 minutes
Cast: D. B. Sweeney, Kelly Wolf, Daniel Benzali, Tovah Feldshuh, Ole Lemmeke
Director: Kenneth Madsen

Screenplay: Damian F. Slattery
Drama
Rated PG-13
Young children: No Older children: VG, with caution

Here is one of those not-to-be-missed sleepers. It's a film that "slipped through the cracks" but is well worth discovering, both for its entertainment value and its enlightened, uncompromising point of view.

A Day in October, based on actual events, is a World War II drama set in Nazi-occupied Copenhagen. It tells the story of Sara Kublitz, a young Jewish woman who brings a stranger—Niels Jensen, a wounded resistance fighter—into her home. This act of compassion disrupts her close-knit family.

Sara's action presents a dilemma for her father, Solomon, an educated and cultured bookkeeper who has chosen to ignore the Nazi domination of his country and maintain a business-as-usual order within the confines of his home. He believes that if he and his loved ones remain silent about the harsh realities in their midst, they will be spared by the Nazis.

A Day in October is a sharp morality tale about the necessity to speak out and act up when confronted by evil.

This is mature subject matter, and inappropriate for younger children; there is also some violence in the unfolding of the story.

THE DAY OF THE DOLPHIN
(1973)
Color, 104 minutes
Cast: George C. Scott, Trish Van
Devere, Paul Sorvino, Fritz
Weaver, John Dehner, Severn
Darden, Edward Herrmann,
Paul Korkes, John David
Carson, Leslie Charleson,
Victoria Racimo
Director: Mike Nichols
Screenplay: Buck Henry, from
the novel by Robert Merle
Science fiction/Aquatic
adventure/Animal story
Rated PG
Younger kids: Marginal Older
kids: OK

The title may suggest a Disney-
style animal adventure dealing
with porpoises, but this is really a
serious film for adults, dealing
with dolphin researcher Scott and
his wife Van Devere, who've
raised a dolphin to speak English
at their isolated Florida research
base. Now the dolphin has a mate
who's learning English from him.

Until this point, the movie is
consistently interesting, and the
talking dolphins (voiced by Buck
Henry) are amusing and endearing.
Then it turns into a routine thwart-
the-assassination plot—sort of *The
Dolphin Who Knew Too Much*—
and peters out completely at the
end.

Nonetheless, children who adore
dolphins, and there are many, may
want to see this movie. Since the
dolphins survive—this isn't *Old
Yeller At Sea*—there's no reason
to stop them other than the fact
that the film doesn't live up to its
initial promise.

THE DAY OF THE TRIFFIDS
(1963)
Color, 93 minutes
Cast: Howard Keel, Nicole
Maurey, Janette Scott, Kieron
Moore, Mervyn Johns, Janina
Faye
Director: Steve Sekely
Screenplay: Philip Yordan, from
the novel by John Wyndham
Science fiction/Suspense
Unrated
Younger kids: No Older kids:
OK

A meteor shower not only ends up
blinding everyone who watches it,
but brings with it seeds of walking,
carnivorous plants. The disaster is
worldwide, but the film focuses on
an American seaman (whose eyes
were bandaged from an operation) in England and France, and
a couple at a lighthouse off the
English coast.

John Wyndham's fine novel is
given hit-and-miss treatment, with
some elements added (the pair at
the lighthouse who discover the
triffids' "weakness") that don't
help the story in the slightest. But
there are some very effective moments, and the basic idea is still
fascinating.

Younger kids won't get much
out of it, and there are some horror moments involving the plants'
attacks on human beings. The
special effects—and the very appearance of the walking plants—
are highly variable.

THE DAY THE EARTH
STOOD STILL (1951)
Black & white, 92 minutes
Cast: Michael Rennie, Patricia
Neal, Hugh Marlowe, Billy
Gray, Sam Jaffe
Director: Robert Wise
Screenplay: Edmund H. North,

from a short story by Harry
Bates
Science fiction
Unrated
Younger kids: OK   Older kids:
VG

A flying saucer lands in the middle of Washington, D.C., and a mysterious but human-looking alien, Klaatu, emerges, only to evade authorities and go incognito among the citizens of the city. He hopes to learn more about the human race and becomes friendly with a widow and her young son.

This science fiction classic is almost as effective and entertaining today as it was when it was first released, nearly half a century ago. The dialogue is a little corny at times, and not all the acting is as good as that of the two leads, but the special effects still work, and Gort the robot will still scare the bejabbers out of children—who will love him for it anyway.

This is a quintessential example of a classic film that adults can enjoy alongside their kids, seeing it for the first time or rediscovering it after many years.

Main drawback: For weeks, expect to hear your children saying, "Gort! Klaatu barada nikto."

THE DEADLY MANTIS (1957)
Black & white, 79 minutes
Cast: Craig Stevens, William
Hopper, Alix Talton, Donald
Randolph
Director: Nathan Juran
Screenplay: Martin Berkeley
Science fiction/Monster
Unrated
Younger children: Too
scary   Older children: Not
scary enough

A nuclear explosion in the Antarctic improbably flips an iceberg over in the *Arctic,* freeing a giant praying mantis, which promptly starts eating hapless people, mostly in stock footage. The usual types race to stop the giant insect, which is making its way toward Manhattan.

It was inevitable that the "big bug" movies of the 1950s would finally get around to the mantis, an impressive, eerie-looking predator even at its natural size of a couple of inches. But the movie underuses its long green menace and spends too much time following the activities of the lead actors, who understandably look rather bored. The effects are uneven but generally good, an important consideration for monster movie fans.

Younger children might find the big roaring bug too much to take, while older kids will long for more scenes with the mantis. It's way below par for its studio, Universal-International, but if your children really like these old giant insect movies, they'll demand to see this one too.

DEAD OF NIGHT (1945)
Black & white, 102 minutes
Cast: Mervyn Johns, Roland
Culver, Frederick Valk, Sally
Ann Howes, Googie Withers,
Basil Radford, Naunton
Wayne, Michael Redgrave,
Judy Kelly, Anthony Baird,
Miles Malleson
Directors: Basil Dearden, Robert
Hamer, Charles Crichton, and
Alberto Cavalcanti
Screenplay: John Baines,
T. E. B. Clarke, and Angus
Macphail, from stories by
E. F. Benson, John Baines,
and H. G. Wells

Fantasy-Horror/Short stories
Unrated
Young children: No   Older
   children: OK

Mr. Craig (Mervyn Johns) arrives at a country home for the first time, but soon puzzles those gathered there by claiming to have dreamed the entire event—repeatedly—and revealing that something horrible happens at the end of the dream. While a psychiatrist (Valk) scoffs, the others each tell about personal incidents that may have been supernatural.

One man tells how a dream of an undertaker (Miles Malleson) may have saved his life. Young Sally (Sally Ann Howes) tells about how, while at a local Christmas party, she may have encountered a sad young ghost. The story of Mrs. Courtland (Googie Withers) involves an antique mirror; in it, her husband, but only her husband, could see a room from the previous century.

Foley, who owns the country house, tells a whimsical tale of two golfing friends (Basil Radford and Naunton Wayne) who play a round of golf to see who will win the hand of the woman they both love.

Finally, the psychiatrist grudgingly admits he, too, has a story. A talented ventriloquist (Michael Redgrave) is convinced that his dummy has a mind of its own—and that the mind is evil. . . .

The movie returns to the original group for an ending that has influenced many anthology films since.

This classic film (which is truly worthy of that adjective) will have little appeal for younger kids, but older children who are open-minded enough to try something both old and British will be well rewarded. The framing story has an ending that's nothing less than brilliant, and the sequence about the ventriloquist is one of the greatest short horror stories ever filmed, with an astonishing performance by Michael Redgrave. If you and your family like stories of the supernatural, this movie should be considered a must.

DEAD POETS SOCIETY
(1989)
Color, 128 minutes
Cast: Robin Williams, Robert
   Sean Leonard, Ethan Hawke,
   Josh Charles, Gate Hansen,
   Dylan Kussnian, Allelon
   Ruggiero, James Waterston,
   Norman Lloyd, Kurtwood
   Smith, Lara Flynn Boyle
Director: Peter Weir
Screenplay: Tom Schulman
Drama
Rated PG
Younger kids: OK, with
   caution   Older kids: VG

Robin Williams plays English teacher John Keating, who returns to his alma mater, a conservative New England prep school, in 1959. He inspires his students to look beyond the boundaries of their neatly proscribed lives and "seize the day." Some of the students take his message to heart and revive the Dead Poets Society, a secret club Keating himself had participated in when he was a student, whose members gather at night to read poetry. But while the young men embrace Keating's life lessons, the school's stuffy administration is not amused.

Young adults will certainly relate to this story of nonconformity and the need to follow one's muse, and Williams is the perfect choice as the man who opens their hearts and minds. However, events outside of the classroom are less compelling and believable, and the plot often becomes ham-handed, especially in its depiction of adults as being uniformly blind to children's needs and feelings. (This is demonstrated, quite melodramatically, when one student commits suicide.)

However, the film is worthwhile in promoting the use of imagination and celebrating the liberating joys of poetry. Of course, most students are not lucky enough to have Robin Williams as their teacher, but the message is still loud and clear.

DEEP IMPACT (1998)
Color, 125 minutes
Cast: Robert Duvall, Tea Leoni, Elijah Wood, Vanessa Redgrave, Morgan Freeman, Maximilian Schell, James Cromwell, Ron Eldard, Jon Favreau, Laura Innes, Mary McCormack, Charles Martin Smith, Kurtwood Smith, Leelee Sobieski
Director: Mimi Leder
Screenplay: Michael Tolkin and Bruce Joel Rubin
Disaster movie
Rated PG-13
Young children: No   Older children: VG

As a comet streaks toward a head-on collision with Earth, three plot lines form a microcosm of American reaction to impending doom: the young amateur astronomer (good Wood) who discovered the New York-sized ball of flying, flaming ice;

the MS-NBC reporter (vapid Leoni) who stumbles onto the government's secret preparations for extinction; and the old-time astronaut (dependable Duvall) who goes along for the ride on a NASA strike force to attempt planetary salvation from space and turns out to be more useful than his younger colleagues thought possible.

Although there are some decent special effects, the movie is really a study in apocalyptic fiction, like **When Worlds Collide.** It's not so much about what's going to happen as what humanity is thinking and feeling about the absence of a future, and how to prepare for it. (Leoni, for instance, has to come to terms with her father, from whom she's been estranged.) Young people will especially relate to the story involving Elijah Wood and his determination to include his girlfriend among the "chosen survivors."

Therefore, viewers expecting a noisy blockbuster (for instance, the same year's dumber version of a similar story, *Armageddon*) may be frustrated that the big bangs come more from the emotional impact than from Industrial Light and Magic. Little ones won't understand why everyone else in the room is looking for tissues.

THE DEFIANT ONES (1958)
Black & white, 97 minutes
Cast: Tony Curtis, Sidney Poitier, Theodore Bikel, Charles McGraw, Cara Williams, Lon Chaney, Jr.
Director: Stanley Kramer
Screenplay: Harold Jacob Smith and Nathan E. Douglas (pseud. of Nedrick Young)
Drama

Unrated
Young children: OK   Older
children: VG

Back in 1958, *The Defiant Ones* was viewed as ultimate word on relations between the races. It still impresses today, as it tells the story of two convicts who escape, chained together, from an overturned prison van. One, Noah Cullen (Sidney Poitier), is black; the other, John "Joker" Jackson (Tony Curtis), is white—and the two share an immediate and intense dislike. But while they are fleeing the authorities, they cannot elude each other and are forced to face up to their own prejudices as they depend upon each other for their very survival.

The experiences Cullen and Jackson share as they race through the backwater swamps and fields allow each one to come to view the other as a human being; gradually, they develop a mutual respect.

The Defiant Ones is representative of the integrationist films of the period in that the black character is defined in terms of his relationship to whites (rather than his fellow blacks or black culture and society), and ultimately sacrifices his freedom.

Still, the drama is potent and the performances by Poitier and Curtis are as impressive as ever. This is one of the key films that vaulted Poitier to superstardom.

The violence is mild by today's standards, and there is no bad language, but the intensity of the drama might be too much for very young children. For older kids, *The Defiant Ones* is as much a time capsule of liberal American attitudes in the late 1950s as it is a parable about race relations.

DESTINATION MOON (1950)
Color, 91 minutes
Cast: Warren Anderson, John Archer, Tom Powers, Dick Wesson
Director: Irving Pichel
Screenplay: Robert A. Heinlein and Rip Von Ronkel, loosely based on Heinlein's novel *Rocketship Galileo*
Science fiction/Drama
Unrated
Younger kids: OK   Older kids: OK

A visionary scientist convinces some millionaires to finance the first expedition to the Moon.

Everything is presented very clearly, but what was cutting-edge science when the movie was made now seems musty, even archaic. It *is* a handsome film, with good special effects and a fine score by Leith Stevens. (There's also a guest appearance by Woody Woodpecker.) If your children enjoy older movies, and are interested in the science of space travel, this is a very good way of introducing them to the early history of space exploration.

This film also has a niche in movie history as the first science fiction film by the famous producer George Pal, who started out making animated Puppetoons and went on to produce **War of the Worlds, Conquest of Space,** and **The Time Machine**.

THE DEVIL RIDES OUT
(1968) (aka **The Devil's Bride**)
Color, 95 minutes
Cast: Christopher Lee, Charles Gray, Nike Arrighi, Leon Greene, Patrick Mower, Gwen Ffrangcon-Davies, Sarah Lawson, Paul Eddington
Director: Terence Fisher

Screenplay: Richard Matheson, from the novel by Dennis Wheatley
Period horror/Suspense
Unrated
Younger kids: Too scary Older kids: OK

In the 1920s, with the help of his friend Rex (Greene), occult expert Duc de Richleau (Lee) tries to prevent his protégé, Simon (Mower), and the beautiful Tanith (Arrighi) from being inducted into a cult of Satanists headed by the sinister Mocata (Gray).

Exciting, fast-paced horror from the reliable Hammer studios is a cut above even their usual high standard; the script understands the occult and takes it seriously, but mixes in romance, car chases, and other elements as well. The special effects are somewhat below the level of the rest of the film, which could curl the lips of more knowing teens; those who get into the story, however, will enjoy this well-made thriller, much less gory or sexy than the usual Hammer film.

THE DEVIL'S BROTHER
(1933) (aka **Fra Diavolo**)
Black & white, 88 minutes
Cast: Stan Laurel, Oliver Hardy, Dennis King, Thelma Todd, James Finlayson, Henry Armetta
Directors: Hal Roach and Charles Rogers
Screenplay: Jeanie MacPherson, based on the opera *Fra Diavolo* by Daniel F. Auber
Comedy
Unrated
Young children: VG Older children: VG

In 18th-century Italy, a bold bandit known as Fra Diavolo (The Devil's Brother) roams the countryside, stealing fortunes while mingling with the wealthy, pretending to be the Marquis de San Marco. Meanwhile, two less colorful bandits rob the life savings from Stanlio and Ollio, who decide that if that's the way things are, they'll become bandits, too. Who should they try to rob but Fra Diavolo himself?

This delightful comic opera gives Stan and Ollie the opportunity to play some wonderfully funny routines against a colorful period backdrop. The result is one of their very best feature films.

There are many memorable moments in *The Devil's Brother,* including a hilarious scene in which Stan gets happily soused on wine and another where he sets Ollie off into an incurable laughing jag. (There's also a sequence in which Stan is ordered by Fra Diavolo to hang his friend, one of many oddly macabre moments in Laurel and Hardy's work . . . but of course, nothing goes right.)

But best of all is Stan's eye-hand game, known as kneesie-earsie-nosie. It drives the innkeeper character crazy, and it will likely have your kids imitating Stan for days—weeks—maybe years to come!

THE DIARY OF ANNE FRANK
(1959)
Black & white, 170 minutes
Cast: Millie Perkins, Joseph Schildkraut, Shelley Winters, Richard Beymer, Lou Jacobi, Gusti Huber, Diane Baker, Ed Wynn
Director: George Stevens
Screenplay: Frances Goodrich and Albert Hackett, based on

their stage play inspired by Anne Frank's diary
Drama
Unrated
Young children: OK   Older children: VG

During World War II, the German army occupied the Netherlands, and Jews who resided there were issued one-way tickets to concentration camps. Between 1942 and 1944, a girl named Anne Frank avoided this fate by hiding in a small, cramped Amsterdam attic with her relatives, another family, the Van Daans (including her first love, young Peter Van Daan), and Mr. Dussel, an aged dentist.

Eventually, Anne and her fellow captives were betrayed, and she died of typhus in a concentration camp in 1945. At the time, she was all of 16 years old.

Her story is one of the most enduring of the Holocaust. It might never have been known had Anne not recounted her feelings and experiences in a diary, which was published in 1947 and went on to become one of the most celebrated personal journals of the 20th century.

Her years in hiding are recounted in *The Diary of Anne Frank,* a life-affirming drama, which was first a hit Broadway play and then lovingly (and painstakingly) adapted for the screen. The film is quite long, and not all of its incidents will have equal relevance or resonance for young viewers, but those flaws are overridden by the tremendous power of the material itself.

Despite her predicament and her fate, Anne's story is one of self-discovery and eternal hope. It remains—and shall always be—must reading (and must viewing) for everyone Anne's age, and even younger children are captivated by the story of her life. Despite the nearly three-hour length and the fact that the story is told through dialogue more than action, *The Diary of Anne Frank* remains a mesmerizing experience.

DICK TRACY (1990)
Color, 104 minutes
Cast: Warren Beatty, Madonna, Al Pacino, Glenne Headly, Charlie Korsmo, Mandy Patinkin, Charles Durning, Paul Sorvino, William Forsythe, Seymour Cassel, Dustin Hoffman, Dick Van Dyke, Catherine O'Hara, James Caan, Michael J. Pollard, Estelle Parsons, James Tolkan, R. G. Armstrong, Kathy Bates
Director: Warren Beatty
Screenplay: Jim Cash and Jack Epps, Jr., based on the comic strip by Chester Gould
Action-adventure/Fantasy
Rated PG
Younger kids: VG   Older kids: VG

This big-budget adaptation of Chester Gould's classic comic strip about a square-jawed detective and his rogue's gallery of nemeses is brought to the screen in bold, colorful style. Dick Tracy is pitted against crime boss Big Boy Caprice (an unrecognizable Al Pacino), who works with other underworld figures to frame Tracy. In the meantime, the detective must contend with a tough street kid (Korsmo) and the amorous advances of singer Breathless Mahoney (Madonna), while his steady Tess Trueheart (Headly) keeps hoping he will settle down.

Dick Tracy is one of the more satisfying comic strip (or comic book) translations ever put on screen, with fantastic care and attention paid to the sets, costumes, cinematography, and especially the makeup. Director Warren Beatty also employs an admirably straightforward tone that does not mock the source material. The story is rather square, and so is Beatty as the hero, but both are more than compensated for by the look of the film and the parade of fantastic gargoyles and villains, led by Al Pacino's outrageous Big Boy. (Dustin Hoffman's Mumbles runs a close second.)

There is some cops-and-robbers violence, most of it as stylized as the comic strip on which the film is based. Younger kids unfamiliar with Dick Tracy—in any medium—and his famously freakish villains may require a few words of introduction.

DIMPLES (1936)
Black & white, 78 minutes (also available in a computer-colored version)
Cast: Shirley Temple, Frank Morgan, Helen Westley, Berton Churchill, Stepin Fetchit, Robert Kent, Delma Byron, Astrid Allwyn, Julius Tannen, The Hall Johnson Choir
Director: William A. Seiter
Screenplay: Arthur Sheekman and Nat Perrin
Historical comedy/Melodrama/Musical
Unrated
Young children: VG   Older children: VG

In this moving story which takes place in the mid-19th century, little Shirley Temple plays a plucky street waif named Dimples who leads a ragtag life of poverty in the care of her beloved grandfather, a failed actor turned petty thief. Most members of the family will recognize the actor playing the grandfather as Frank Morgan, who three years later would achieve screen immortality in the title role of **The Wizard of Oz.**

Here, Dimples is fated to win stardom on the stage as Eva in a fictitious, first-ever production of *Uncle Tom's Cabin,* and will earn the adoration of an adopted family. Through it all, she will retain the love of her wayward grandfather. However, at one point, the grandfather arranges to leave Dimples in the home of a rich woman who offers him $5,000, prompting the little girl to fear that she is being sold. Several other times during the film, the grandfather comes close to being arrested and taken to jail for his misdemeanors. Moments such as these may concern small children; however, the script generally handles details that might frighten youngsters with sensitivity.

In the course of the play being presented within the movie, there are scenes in which white actors don blackface makeup. Because this practice was traditional in minstrel shows and vaudeville acts through the early part of the 20th century but no longer is considered acceptable, a discussion explaining this theatrical custom might be in order.

DOCTOR DOLITTLE (1967)
Color, 144 minutes
Cast: Rex Harrison, Samantha Eggar, Anthony Newley, Richard Attenborough, Peter Bull
Director: Richard Fleischer

Screenplay: Leslie Bricusse, based on stories by Hugh Lofting
Musical/Animal story
Rated G
Younger kids: VG   Older kids: VG

Rex Harrison stars as the man who could "talk to the animals" in this big-budget musical fantasy based on Hugh Lofting's children's stories. Although the film was a major commercial flop when it was first released, it received nine Academy Award nominations, including Best Picture, and won two (for visual effects and the "Animals" song), and is a prime example of the kind of lavish but gentle family entertainment that just isn't made anymore (for proof, just see the crude 1998 Eddie Murphy remake).

Harrison is delightful as the whimsical veterinarian living in the Victorian English village of Puddleby-on-the-Marsh. Dolittle is more at home among animals than humans and has the ability to speak with 498 of them in their own languages, having been taught by his parrot, Polynesia. Accompanied by his faithful human friends Emma (Samantha Eggar), Matthew (Anthony Newley), and Tommy (William Dix), the kindly doctor embarks on a series of wondrous adventures around the world in search of such fantastical creatures as the Giant Pink Sea Snail, the Giant Lunar Moth, and of course, the beguiling two-headed llama called Pushmi-Pullyu.

The film is slow-moving and way overlong, but kids can fast-forward past the acres of dialogue to enjoy all of the animals on dis-

play, as Dolittle's house is a virtual menagerie, overflowing with dogs, horses, pigs, and birds, and his voyage to the South Seas is charming and imaginative.

DOCTOR X (1932)
Color, 77 minutes
Cast: Lionel Atwill, Fay Wray, Lee Tracy, Preston Foster, John Wray, Harry Beresford, Arthur Edmund Carewe, Leila Bennett, Robert Warwick
Director: Michael Curtiz
Screenplay: Robert Tasker and Earl Baldwin, from the play *The Terror* by Howard W. Comstock and Allen C. Miller
Science fiction/Horror
Unrated
Young children: No   Older children: OK

Several people have been killed (and partly eaten) during full moons. Reporter Lee (Tracy) is on the trail, which leads to the laboratory of Dr. Xavier (Atwill), whose daughter Joan (Fay Wray) catches Lee's roving eye. Xavier suspects that someone from his medical academy is the killer, so he sets a trap designed to expose the mysterious murderer/cannibal.

Despite its age, if seen in the right mood, this movie can still raise the hackles on a viewer's neck. Director Curtiz uses the two-strip Technicolor process to good effect, with a lot of emphasis on copper and poisonous greens. The plot, as writer Robert Bloch pointed out, is revealed with two words: synthetic flesh. The makeup in this sequence, the work of Perc Westmore and Ray Romero, is satisfactorily horrible.

This looks like an antique to most adults, but to children this could well be taken as something fresh and interesting. However, while it is not graphic (except for the makeup, really a mask), it is indeed creepy, and shouldn't be shown to younger kids without supervision.

DOUBLE HAPPINESS (1994)
Color, 100 minutes
Cast: Sandra Oh, Stephen Chang, Allanah Ong, Frances You, Callum Rennie
Director: Mina Shum
Screenplay: Mina Shum
Drama
Rated PG-13
Young children: No Older children: VG

This charming and insightful coming-of-age tale paints a portrait of Jade Li, a young woman of Chinese heritage who resides with her immigrant parents and kid sister in Canada. Jade's elders cling to an Old World culture in which children are expected to obey Mom and Dad without question. They are pressuring Jade to find a boyfriend and get married; by their standards, a woman of 22 who has not found a man to protect her is doomed to be an old maid.

However, Jade has other ideas. She is an aspiring actress whose one desire is to win an Academy Award. She is intent on pursuing a career and living her own life. Jade loves her parents and does not want to hurt them, but she knows she will be miserable if she stifles her desires and suffers through life as an obedient wife. She is attempting to strike a balance, and this is no easy task.

While the characters in *Double Happiness* are Chinese, director-screenwriter Mina Shum depicts the struggles that might occur within any family in which parent and child have clashing agendas. To her credit, Shum does not paint Mr. and Mrs. Li as stodgy and one-dimensional Old World villains. They simply have their way of living and thinking, and want what they feel is best for the daughter they love.

There are also bright touches of humor in *Double Happiness*. Some of the cleverest spotlight the fact that despite Jade's Asian "look," she is thoroughly Westernized, a product of the culture in which she came of age.

Adolescents should relate to this film quite easily, but parents should be aware that in addition to some strong language, there is one scene of a sexual nature.

DOWN ARGENTINE WAY (1940)
Color, 90 minutes
Cast: Don Ameche, Betty Grable, Carmen Miranda, Charlotte Greenwood, J. Carrol Naish, Henry Stephenson, Katharine Aldridge, Leonid Kinskey, Chris-Pin Martin, The Nicholas Brothers
Director: Irving Cummings
Screenplay: Darrell Ware and Karl Tunberg, from a story by Rian James and Ralph Spence
Musical
Unrated
Young children: VG Older children: VG

This bright, picture-postcard-pretty musical serves to mirror America's Good Neighbor Policy toward Latin America in the 1940s. It begins with a mini-travelogue of Argentina and introduces the Brazilian Bombshell, Carmen Miranda, whose infectious songs and equally vibrant personality made her an overnight sensation. She's still delightful to watch (and listen to) today—and her colorful costumes are especially eye-catching for kids.

Betty Grable, who was destined to become World War II's most celebrated pinup girl, is cast here as Glenda Crawford, an American vacationing "down Argentine way." Comical and romantic complications arise as she falls for a rich horse breeder named Ricardo Quintana. He is played by Kenosha, Wisconsin's, very own Don Ameche; this was a time when very American Hollywood actors could be assigned roles as Latinos or Europeans and no one would bat an eye. The story twists and turns on its way toward a happy ending, with plenty of screen time for a number of scene-stealing character players and comedians, including the vivacious, long-legged Charlotte Greenwood as Grable's outgoing aunt.

Another highlight of *Down Argentine Way* is the spectacular acrobatic dancing of The Nicholas Brothers, Fayard and Harold, who appear in a dazzling specialty number.

DRACULA (1931)
Black & white, 80 minutes
Cast: Bela Lugosi, Helen
  Chandler, David Manners,
  Dwight Frye, Edward Van
  Sloan, Herbert Bunston,
  Frances Dade, Joan Standing
Director: Tod Browning
Screenplay: Garrett Fort and
  Dudley Murphy, from the
  Hamilton Dean play based on
  the novel by Bram Stoker
Horror/Melodrama
Unrated

Young children: Some scary
  scenes Older children: OK

English businessman Renfield (Frye) arrives at the Transylvanian castle of the mysterious Count Dracula (Lugosi), who is actually a vampire—one of the living dead who has staved off true death for centuries by drinking the blood of the living. He attacks Renfield and makes him his slave; then the two go to England. Renfield, now insane, becomes a patient in the asylum of Dr. Seward (Bunston), while Dracula begins to prey on the young blood of London. He befriends Seward and turns Lucy (Dade), a friend of Seward's daughter, Mina (Chandler), into a vampire. When Dracula targets Mina as well, the wise Dutch metaphysician Van Helsing (Van Sloan) is summoned.

Until *Dracula*, horror movies were not regarded as a separate genre. Although it had predecessors, this film, a worldwide sensation, made it clear that it was something entirely different. With **Frankenstein** following later in the year, Universal Pictures was established as the home of horror movies.

Today, *Dracula* seems stagy and slow, though the opening scenes in the castle still have an eerie power, and Lugosi's performance, copied and parodied though it has been, remains very effective. ("I never drink . . . wine.") Even though younger children may not react to Lugosi, they could well be scared by Frye's bizarre performance as the mad Renfield. Older children who like horror movies will want to watch this at least once, if only as a historical curiosity. They might prefer the Spanish-language version, also released in 1931 and starring Carlos Villar as the Count; shot on the same sets at night, it is actually a better-made film. It's also available on video, in a subtitled print.

In addition to the legion of imitations and the several remakes, this spawned a few direct sequels, the first of which was *Dracula's Daughter.*

DRACULA (1958) (see **Horror of Dracula**)

DRACULA—PRINCE OF DARKNESS (1966)
Color, 90 minutes
Cast: Christopher Lee, Barbara Shelley, Andrew Keir, Francis Matthews, Suzan Farmer, Charles Tingwell, Thorley Walters, Philip Latham
Director: Terence Fisher
Screenplay: John Sansom
Horror/Sequel
Unrated
Young children: No   Older children: If used to horror movies

Two English couples, traveling in the Carpathian Mountains, are given shelter in an old castle. Unbeknownst to them, it was the home of the vampire Count Dracula, whose devoted servant (Latham) kills one of the travelers and uses his blood to bring Dracula (Lee) back to life.

Robust Hammer horror, exciting and well-made, with particularly good performances by Andrew Keir and Barbara Shelley. It's not up to the level of its predecessor, **Horror of Dracula,** partly because Dracula has no dialogue, turning Lee into nothing more than a looming presence . . . but he looms very well indeed.

Overall, it's a good horror movie from its period.

Definitely too gruesome for youngsters, it might even be too strong for teenagers, more because of sensuality than blood (there is no nudity). However, if your kids have become hooked on Hammer horror and/or Christopher Lee, they're likely to make your life miserable until you let them see this one. Be sure to watch it with them.

Followed by *Dracula Has Risen From the Grave.*

DRAGONHEART (1996)
Color, 108 minutes
Cast: Dennis Quaid, David Thewlis, Pete Postlethwaite, Dina Meyer, Julie Christie, Lee Oakes, John Gielgud; voice of Sean Connery
Director: Rob Cohen
Screenwriter: Charles Edward Pogue
Medieval fantasy/Comedy-drama
Rated PG-13
Young children: OK, with caution   Older children: OK

Here is a rare and noble attempt to invent a fairy-tale adventure in the classic tradition.

The knight Bowen (Dennis Quaid) is training Prince Einon (Lee Oakes) in knightly virtues and skills, but when Einon's father the king, a brutal tyrant, dies, the boy eagerly seizes the crown and is accidentally pierced by its points. His mother, Aislinn (Julie Christie), takes him to the lair of her old friend, a mighty dragon, who gives the boy half his own heart to save his life. But Einon turns out to be every bit as much of a selfish, bloodthirsty tyrant as his father and enslaves the peasants to rebuild a castle. Convinced that it was the heart of the dragon that corrupted Einon, the embittered Bowen spends the next twelve years killing every dragon he finds, always for a sack of gold.

But when he squares off against one more dragon, he and the beast—yes, the dragon talks, in Sean Connery's voice—reach a stalemate. Impressed by each other's prowess, they form an uneasy alliance. The dragon, whom Bowen names Draco after the constellation, pretends to raid a village; for a fee, Bowen offers to slay the dragon, a deed carried out with a great deal of satisfying spectacle. Eventually, it falls to these unlikely partners to challenge King Einon.

The dragon doesn't just have the voice of Sean Connery; through the skills of the computer-animation experts at Industrial Light & Magic, it also has his gestures and facial expressions. As a result, Draco is the most convincing dragon in movie history. The movie is more appealing when it's light and funny than when it's serious, but for many, it does capture much of the feeling of a great fairy tale. It has a pure-hearted hero, a dastardly villain, heroines, comic relief, sword fights, warfare, castles—and a romantic heart.

Children and many adults will adore Draco and have a good time with the film, although the ending is tragic. The dragon dies, and sensitive youngsters should be prepared for this possibility early on.

DRAGONSLAYER (1981)
Color, 109 minutes
Cast: Peter MacNicol, Caitlin Clarke, Ralph Richardson, John Hallam, Peter Eyre, Albert Salmi, Chloe Salaman
Director: Matthew Robbins
Screenplay: Hal Barwood and Matthew Robbins
Fantasy/Adventure
Rated PG
Younger children: Too scary Older children: OK

The ancient dragon Vermithrax Pejorative has been raiding the small country of Urland; the King's only defense is to sacrifice virgins to the beast. After the sorcerer Urland (Ralph Richardson) is apparently killed attempting to aid the people of Urland, his over-ambitious apprentice, Galen (Peter MacNicol), lets the Urlanders believe he can defeat the dragon himself.

This attempt at creating an authentic-sounding myth is redolent with interesting names (even the dragon has a name) and founded in part on the "Sorcerer's Apprentice" myth. But it's compromised by borrowing elements from **Star Wars** (the sorcerer who returns from the dead) and other latter-day movies. The dramatics are uneven, and the story is very grim for a fantasy; for example, a brave princess is eaten alive by baby dragons (fortunately for us, most of this occurs offscreen).

The dragon is realized mostly by a computer-enhanced version of stop-motion animation, and it is an unqualified success, accounting for one of the greatest dragons in movie history. It even has its own wicked, proud personality and does all the things a good dragon should do: it flies, breathes fire, and crawls on its belly like a reptile.

The movie is too darkly serious for most children under 10, and those over that age will be impatient with the first third or so. But after that, with Galen at the center of the movie, courageously bearding the dragon in its den, teenagers who like fantasy thrillers are likely to enjoy this one a lot.

DRAGONWORLD (1994)
Color, 86 minutes
Cast: Sam Mackenzie, Brittney Powell, John Calvin, Lila Kaye, John Woodvine, Andrew Kier
Director: Ted Nicolaou
Screenplay: Suzanne Glazener Naha and Ted Nicolaou, based on a story by Charles Band
Action-adventure/Fantasy
Rated PG
Younger kids: Good   Older kids: VG

This low-budget, direct-to-video children's film is a surprisingly pleasant and enjoyable fantasy about a 5-year-old orphan named Johnny who goes to Scotland to live with his grandfather and discovers a dragon, whom he names Yowler and raises as a pet. Fifteen years pass and after his grandfather dies, Johnny has to pay back taxes on his estate, so he reluctantly agrees to lease Yowler to a theme park for thirty days. Then he discovers that the park's deceitful owner is exploiting the dragon and plans to keep him.

The story may be a blatant rip-off of **Mighty Joe Young,** but kids certainly won't mind, as the splendid special-effects work and stop-

motion animation convincingly bring the dragon to life.

DR. DOLITTLE (1998)
Color, 85 minutes
Cast: Eddie Murphy, Ossie Davis, Oliver Platt, Peter Boyle, Richard Schiff, Kristen Wilson, Jeffrey Tambor, Kyla Pratt, Raven Symone; voices of Norm Macdonald, Ellen De Generes, Albert Brooks, Chris Rock, John Leguizamo, Garry Shandling, Gilbert Gottfried
Director: Betty Thomas
Screenplay: Nat Mauldin and Larry Levin, based on the Doctor Dolittle stories by Hugh Lofting
Comedy-Fantasy/Animal story
Rated PG-13
Young children: If they must   Older children: OK

As a boy, John Dolittle discovers that he can talk to animals—and they seem to want to talk to him. His parents discourage this apparent fantasy, and he suppresses his gift. Years pass, and he grows up to be a busy, successful doctor in San Francisco; when he nearly runs over a dog with his car, the canine says something to him. Though he denies it at first, he eventually comes to realize that he has regained his rare gift—though for him it seems more of a curse, causing complications with both his family and his career.

This is about as far from Hugh Lofting's whimsical stories as one could possibly get. Most of the laughs in this disappointing (and surprisingly flat) film derive from the funny voices of the various animals and a parade of body-function jokes. It's unlikely that one will ever hear the words *butt* and *ass* so many times again in a single motion picture. Since kids seem to respond to this humor, they will almost surely enjoy the film more than their parents, though Murphy is likeable and energetic, and some of the voice performances are amusing.

DRIVING MISS DAISY (1989)
Color, 99 minutes
Cast: Jessica Tandy, Morgan Freeman, Dan Aykroyd, Patti LuPone, Esther Rolle
Director: Bruce Beresford
Screenplay: Alfred Uhry, based on his play
Comedy-drama
Rated PG
Younger kids: OK   Older kids: VG

A gentle, leisurely adaptation (which won Oscars for Best Picture, Actress, Screenplay, and Makeup) of Alfred Uhry's prize-winning play about a black chauffeur named Hoke who's hired to drive a wealthy, older (and feisty) Jewish woman in the South, circa 1948. As the years go by, their friendship grows, slowly but surely. Though this is more of a character study than an overt examination of racism and prejudice, the ever-deepening relationship between Hoke and Miss Daisy subtly reflects the changes going on around them in society.

Parents will want to fill in some of the background of those changing times, the Civil Rights era, for younger children who are not aware of it. The film makes its points quietly and tactfully, and the performances of Tandy and Freeman—who both bring out the full complexities of their characters—never ask for easy sympathy and keep things from drifting too close to sentimentality.

DR. JEKYLL AND MR. HYDE (1931)
Black & white, 98 minutes
Cast: Fredric March, Miriam Hopkins, Rose Hobart, Holmes Herbert, Halliwell Hobbes, Edgar Norton
Director: Rouben Mamoulian
Screenplay: Samuel Hoffenstein and Percy Heath, from the novella by Robert Louis Stevenson
Science fiction–horror/Literary classic
Unrated
Younger kids: Too sophisticated   Older kids: OK

Dashing, sincere Dr. Jekyll (March) is engaged to the genteel Muriel (Hobart) but is also momentarily attracted to Ivy (Hopkins), an earthy girl of the streets. He continues with his research into the duality of human nature, and one night proves it: he drinks a potion he's created and is transformed into the lusty, hedonistic Mr. Hyde, who promptly goes in search of Ivy. Jekyll is torn between the release from society's strictures provided by the potion and his sincere desire to do good.

The best film version so far of the famous Stevenson novella, Mamoulian's elaborate production is full of imaginative touches, including long, slow lap dissolves, and the bravura transformation sequence. (Wally Westmore's makeup is actually simple, but totally changes March's handsome face to that of a beast—and he looks worse every time he changes.) As Jekyll, March gives a mannered, theatrical performance, but as Hyde, he's brilliant—scary, funny, and unbridled. This won him an Academy Award as Best Actor.

Definitely too adult for younger children and pretty scary at times, the movie might appeal to older kids who are comfortable with the conventions of movies from the 1930s. It really is one of the few horror movies that while not at all gruesome is primarily intended for adults.

DR. JEKYLL AND MR. HYDE (1941)
Black & white, 127 minutes
Cast: Spencer Tracy, Ingrid Bergman, Lana Turner, Donald Crisp, Ian Hunter, Barton MacLane, C. Aubrey Smith, Peter Godfrey
Director: Victor Fleming
Screenplay: John Lee Mahin, from the earlier script by Samuel Hoffenstein and Percy Heath, based on the novella by Robert Louis Stevenson
Science fiction–horror/Literary classic
Unrated
Younger kids: Of little interest   Older kids: OK

This remake follows the plot of the 1931 entry rather than going back to the Stevenson novella, but somehow ends up running half again as long. Dr. Jekyll (Tracy) is attracted to two women, his naive society fiancée (Turner) and a more sensual woman (Bergman) from the streets. When his potion unleashes Mr. Hyde, he finds a way to deal with both of them—but then begins changing even without taking the potion.

MGM's elaborate, expensive version of *Dr. Jekyll and Mr. Hyde,* starring one of the great actors of all time and two of the screen's most beautiful women, is not an improvement on the 1931 Paramount film; it adds a lot of Freudian imagery and does have an excellent performance by Ingrid Bergman, but as a horror movie, it's very mild. Hyde looks so much like Jekyll you wonder why he isn't instantly recognized as the good doctor. In a reverse of Fredric March from 1931, Tracy is excellent as Jekyll, but embarrassingly hammy as Hyde.

This isn't as intense as the 1931 version, so it's mostly acceptable for younger kids, but they'll find little of interest in it. Older kids who love film classics will respond to it, but there's no point in showing it to kids who are crazy about *Scream.*

DRUMS ALONG THE MOHAWK (1939)
Color, 103 minutes
Cast: Henry Fonda, Claudette Colbert, Edna May Oliver, John Carradine, Jessie Ralph, Arthur Shields, Robert Lowery, Ward Bond
Director: John Ford
Screenplay: Lamar Trotti and Sonya Levien, based on the novel by Walter Edmonds
Adventure/Historical
Unrated
Younger kids: OK   Older kids: VG

John Ford's chronicle of Colonial life during the Revolutionary War is a stirring and beautifully made piece of Americana. Henry Fonda and Claudette Colbert play newlyweds settling in the Mohawk Valley in upstate New York who have to deal with Indian attacks and British troops while trying to establish a farming community.

Wonderfully acted, with a superb supporting cast that includes scene-stealing Edna May Oliver as a feisty spinster, this frontier saga is richly atmospheric—even though it was actually filmed in Utah—and vividly captures a sense of time and place with unerring realism. It's also a period of history not often depicted in films. Younger kids might be bored, but it's a true classic, and a must for history-minded teens.

DUCK SOUP (1933)
Black & white, 68 minutes
Cast: Groucho, Chico, Harpo, and Zeppo Marx, Margaret Dumont, Louis Calhern, Edgar Kennedy, Raquel Torres
Director: Leo McCarey
Screenplay: Bert Kalmar, Harry Ruby, Arthur Sheekman, and Nat Perrin
Comedy
Unrated
Younger kids: Good   Older kids: VG

The Marx Brothers go to war in *Duck Soup,* an inspired lunatic blend of slapstick, satire, songs, and surrealism that is considered to be one of the funniest movies ever made. Groucho plays Rufus T. Firefly, who becomes the head of the mythical republic of Freedonia with the aid of wealthy dowager Mrs. Teasdale (Margaret Dumont). Trentino (Louis Calhern), the ambassador from neighboring Sylvania, intends to take control of Freedonia by marrying Mrs. Teasdale, but faces competition from the impudent Firefly, so he assigns a dancer (Raquel Torres) to seduce Firefly. Also working

for Trentino are two incompetent spies, Chicolini (Chico Marx) and Pinky (Harpo Marx), who spend most of their time fighting with a lemonade stand vendor (Edgar Kennedy). Eventually, Firefly declares war on Sylvania, leading to a riotous battle in which Chicolini and Pinky defect and fight for Freedonia.

Director Leo McCarey, who got his start working on Laurel and Hardy silent shorts, had a real genius for visual humor, and his freewheeling style obviously brought out the best in The Marx Brothers, resulting in what is arguably their masterpiece. *Duck Soup* has been streamlined for maximum laughs by eliminating any type of romantic subplot and cutting out Harpo and Chico's usual harp and piano solos. Groucho gets to fire off some of his most immortal one-liners at the expense of the gallant Margaret Dumont ("I hear they're going to tear you down and put up an office building"), but the most famous comic set pieces, such as the lemonade-stand fights, the Paul Revere parody (where Pinky rides through town spying on pretty girls and ends up in bed with his horse!), and the all-time classic fake-mirror scene, are all visual in nature and highly reminiscent of silent comedies.

The mirror sequence is a brilliant, two-and-a-half-minute masterpiece of timing that's played in complete silence. Chicolini and Pinky disguise themselves as Firefly to steal the war plans, wearing identical nightshirts, caps, glasses, fake mustaches, and cigars. After Pinky accidentally shatters a mirror, he pretends the mirror's still there and mimics Firefly's every move and facial expression. (Fans of *I Love Lucy* may recall an episode in which Lucille Ball recreated this routine with guest star Harpo Marx.)

Duck Soup is a masterpiece of nonsense humor, and a perfect introduction to The Marx Brothers for every member of the family.

DUMBO (1941)

Color, 66 minutes
Cast: Voices of Edward Brophy,
    Verna Felton, Cliff Edwards,
    Herman Bing, Sterling
    Holloway
Director: Ben Sharpsteen
Screenplay: Dick Huemer and
    Joe Grant, based on a book
    by Helen Perl
Animated feature
Unrated
Young children: VG, with
    caution Older children: VG

Have you ever been made fun of? Have you ever felt like an outsider? Have you ever been separated from a parent?

Everybody has had at least one of these experiences . . . which is why we can all relate to *Dumbo,* one of Walt Disney's sweetest and most heartfelt animated features.

When Mr. Stork delivers a baby to circus elephant Mrs. Jumbo, and the baby turns out to have oversized ears, everyone taunts him (and his mother)—except a jaunty little mouse named Timothy. He and Dumbo become fast friends, and Timothy tries to coax his pal out of his shyness. But Dumbo gets into one predicament after another until Timothy convinces him that he can fly—and the little fellow makes good.

The most wrenching scene in *Dumbo* comes after Dumbo makes a mess of a trained elephant act in the circus and, as a result of the ensuing melee, Mrs. Jumbo is decreed to be a "mad elephant." Locked away, she can't be with her beloved Dumbo, but he comes to her at night and to the strains of the lullaby "Baby Mine" she cradles him in her trunk (through the bars of her cage) and encourages him to wipe his tears away. It's a tender scene that wrings tears out of viewers young and old.

Another high point of the film comes when Dumbo accidentally drinks some liquor and starts seeing things. This becomes the incredible sequence "Pink Elephants on Parade," in which the Disney artists outdid themselves; twenty-five years later, the results would have been called psychedelic.

In a climactic scene, Timothy and Dumbo come upon some black crows who sing the delightful song "When I See an Elephant Fly." There has been some criticism of these characters as stereotypes, but what they are in fact is caricatures. Anyone who can't enjoy this number should be told to simply lighten up.

Dumbo is a delight, but it also provides an emotional roller coaster, especially for sensitive kids; parents should be aware of this and not try to suppress their children's feelings. There's nothing wrong with a good cry.

DUNSTON CHECKS IN (1996)

Color, 85 minutes
Cast: Jason Alexander, Faye
    Dunaway, Eric Lloyd, Rupert
    Everett, Graham Sack, Paul
    Reubens, Glenn Shadix,
    Nathan Davis
Director: Ken Kwapis
Screenplay: John Hopkins and
    Bruce Graham

Comedy/Animal story
Rated PG
Younger children: VG   Older
  children: OK

Dunston is an orangutan who creates both monkeyshines and misunderstandings in this breezy and entertaining comedy.

Jason Alexander stars as Robert Grant, a widower who lives with his two kids, Kyle (Eric Lloyd) and Brian (Graham Sack), at the fancy hotel where he works as manager. His boss is the demanding Mrs. Dubrow (Faye Dunaway), who's received a tip that a representative of a prestigious travel/hotel guide is coming to the hotel. Since no one knows who this person will be, or what they'll look like, everyone is expected to be on their toes so the hotel will make a good impression.

One new guest, a Lord Rutledge (Rupert Everett), puts on a good front, but turns out to be a thief who uses his well-trained orangutan Dunston to do all his dirty work; the agile animal clambers all over the hotel to steal jewelry and other possessions. Kyle befriends the much-abused Dunston, but no one believes that he's found a simian friend, and that's where trouble begins to brew.

Dunston Checks In is a farce, and everyone gets into the spirit of the piece. It's light, entertaining, and often very funny.

Very young kids might be upset when Dunston's owner mistreats him, but this is merely a setup for the bad guy to get his comeuppance later on. There are a few innuendoes along the way, but they're played broadly and shouldn't be offensive to anyone.

E

AN EARLY FROST (1985)
Color, 100 minutes
Cast: Gena Rowlands, Ben
  Gazzara, Sylvia Sidney, Aidan
  Quinn, D. W. Moffett, John
  Glover, Sydney Walsh
Director: John Erman
Screenplay: Ron Cowen, Daniel
  Lipman, and Sherman Yellen
Drama
Unrated
Young children: No Older
  children: VG

A successful young Chicago lawyer must make a fateful trip back
home to conservative rural Pennsylvania because he's gay and has
contracted AIDS. Now he has to
break the news to his family. The
parents don't take it well. The father
goes into denial while the mother
heads straight for fear; grandma is
the sensible fulcrum who brings the
coming family bereavement into
the right perspective.

The first television movie ever
to deal with the then new spectre
of HIV, *An Early Frost* received
fourteen Emmy nominations and
won for Best Script. Strangely, it
hasn't dated at all. Perhaps that's
because the wrenching questions
this movie raises still haven't
been answered.

Mature children who have
heard about this deadly virus or
who have questions about it could
do well to approach the subject
through this dramatic film. It is
the kind of movie they should see
alongside their parents, as it will

inevitably be a springboard for
lively discussion afterward.

EARTH VS. THE FLYING SAUCERS (1956)
Black & white, 82 minutes
Cast: Hugh Marlowe, Joan
  Taylor, Donald Curtis, Morris
  Ankrum, Tom Browne Henry,
  John Zaremba
Director: Fred F. Sears
Screenplay: George Worthing
  Yates and Bernard Gordon
Science fiction/Suspense
Unrated
Younger kids: OK Older kids:
  OK

Just as the title says: flying saucers
from outer space attack the Earth,
bent on conquest. Scientist Marlowe leads the team trying to defeat the alien invaders.

This lower-budgeted imitation of
War of the Worlds is almost as entertaining as its model, thanks to a
fast pace, a plot with at least one
good twist, and terrific special effects by the great Ray Harryhausen.

The flying saucers occasionally
seem even more real than the
actors as they flit about with grim
purpose and deadly rays. At the
climax, all heck (this *is* the 1950s)
breaks loose as the aliens attack
Washington, D.C. Tim Burton
used some of the imagery for his
much later **Mars Attacks!**

If your kids are accustomed to
black-and-white movies and have
no problems with somewhat dated
dialogue, they're likely to have a

ball with this one. It's scary, but not too scary; all the right people survive, and it ends happily.

EASTER PARADE (1948)
Color, 103 minutes
Cast: Fred Astaire, Judy Garland, Peter Lawford, Ann Miller, Jules Munshin, Clinton Sundberg, Jennie LeGon
Director: Charles Walters
Screenplay: Sidney Sheldon, Frances Goodrich, and Albert Hackett, based on an original story by Frances Goodrich and Albert Hackett
Musical
Unrated
Young children: VG   Older children: VG

There are seventeen—count 'em, seventeen—Irving Berlin songs in this terrific holiday musical about a song and dance act in vaudeville. The action takes place between Easter Sunday, 1911, and Easter Sunday, 1912. Fred Astaire and his dancing partner Ann Miller split, so he brings in Garland to train as his new partner. Garland falls for Astaire, but he still has his mind on Miller, and all the while a handsome young playboy is romantically interested in both the women.

While the plot is quick paced and entertaining, it's really just an excuse for all the wonderful songs. They include the title number, performed during the annual Easter Parade on Fifth Avenue in New York City, "Shaking the Blues Away," with Miller doing her famous fast tapping, and the legendary number "A Couple of Swells," which presents Astaire and Garland as two hoboes expounding on their preferred lifestyle.

Easter Parade is great fun for all ages . . . and too good to be shown just at Easter time. For younger viewers, it may be particularly interesting to see how Judy Garland had grown up since **The Wizard of Oz.**

THE EDUCATION OF LITTLE TREE (1997)
Color, 117 minutes
Cast: James Cromwell, Tantoo Cardinal, Joseph Ashton, Mika Boorem, Christopher Heyerdahl, Chris Fennell, Graham Greene
Director: Richard Friedenberg
Screenplay: Richard Friedenberg, based on the novel by Forrest Carter
Drama
Rated PG
Younger children: OK   Older children: OK

In 1935, Little Tree (Joseph Ashton) goes to live with his grandparents in their Tennessee mountain home. There the young orphan begins to learn about his Cherokee heritage. His grandparents, a Cherokee grandmother and a white grandfather who has taken on Cherokee ways, give him moccasins so he can feel the trail beneath his feet, show him how to catch fish with his hands, and give him a poetic appreciation for nature. They also get him involved in the family business, moonshining.

Little Tree comes to distrust Christians, to resent the prejudice against his people, and to resist attempts to assimilate him into white society. When he is taken from his grandparents and put in the Notched Gap School, a Dickensian state-run institution for Indian children, he rebels.

Slow moving and somber, *The Education of Little Tree* works overly hard to make its point, that

Little Tree's real education comes from his people, not from a demeaning and barren school.

Small children may become bored early on; older children are likelier to become involved, as the film is well made and well acted, but they will probably see the moral coming long before the film ends.

There are some uses of mild profanity and a few intense scenes.

EDWARD SCISSORHANDS
(1990)
Color, 100 minutes
Cast: Johnny Depp, Winona
    Ryder, Dianne Wiest, Vincent
    Price, Alan Arkin, Anthony
    Michael Hall, Kathy Baker,
    Conchata Ferrell, Caroline
    Aaron, Dick Anthony
    Williams
Director: Tim Burton
Screenplay: Caroline Thompson,
    based on a story by Thompson
    and Burton
Fantasy
Rated PG-13
Younger kids: OK, with
    caution   Older kids: VG

Edward Scissorhands is the enchanting story of a manmade creature (Johnny Depp) who lives in an old, spooky mansion and has long scissors instead of hands, because his creator (Vincent Price) died before they could be installed. The creature is discovered by Peg, an Avon Lady, who takes him to live with her family in the wilds of suburbia.

Tim Burton's funny, gentle twist on the Frankenstein legend substitutes bright, Day-Glo–colored communities for the dark and brooding villages of Bavaria, but still focuses on the trials and tribulations of the freakish outsider: Edward at first is welcomed into the happy neighborhood and dazzles everyone with his ability to cut hair and shape topiary animals, but he falls in love with Peg's daughter Kim (Winona Ryder) and is soon perceived as a threat by her boyfriend, Jim (Anthony Michael Hall). Edward is framed for a robbery, and soon the neighbors' emotions turn ugly, just as Kim begins to understand and even love him.

This element of fear, and the delicate, fragile way Depp plays Edward, could be upsetting to smaller children, as could the poignant death of Edward's creator. Little ones also won't understand the satiric elements of the movie. Older kids, especially sensitive ones, should love it.

Overall, the film resembles a fairy tale, with appropriate light and dark elements, and there are many magical moments, particularly when Edward shears ice to form a sculpture and makes snow. Composer Danny Elfman matches the mood with a poetic, haunting score.

ELEPHANT BOY (1937)
Black & white, 80 minutes
Cast: Sabu, W. E. Holloway,
    Walter Hudd, Allan Jeayes,
    Bruce Gordon, D. J. Williams
Directors: Robert Flaherty and
    Zoltan Korda
Screenplay: John Collier, Akos
    Tolnay, and Marcia de Sylva,
    based on the novel *Toomai of
    the Elephants* by Rudyard
    Kipling
Adventure/Animal story
Unrated
Younger kids: OK   Older kids:
    Good

Famed documentarian Robert Flaherty (*Nanook of the North*) codirected this early-day docudrama, filmed on location in India. It has lost some of its freshness and originality, but should enchant kids who enjoyed the live-action version of *The Jungle Book.*

The Kipling story is about a young Indian boy (Sabu, making his film debut) called Little Toomai who dreams of being a great elephant hunter like his father and grandfather before him. Little Toomai and his beloved elephant, Kala Nag, accompany his father and a team of British authorities on a search for a herd of wild elephants, but his father is killed during a tiger attack, and Kala Nag is given to a new master who beats it, causing it to go on a rampage. When the man threatens to kill Kala Nag, Little Toomai flees into the jungle with the animal and eventually becomes a hero.

Initially shot as a documentary, but later altered to incorporate a fictional plot, the resulting film is a bit awkward, but the animal and wildlife photography is delightful, including shots of the elephants bathing in a river, romping through the jungle, and lifting Sabu into the air.

The 12-year-old Sabu, who was a former stableboy at the court of an Indian maharajah, was cast in the film after being discovered by the filmmakers and gives a charmingly natural performance. He went on to appear in a number of similar films, including **The Thief of Bagdad** and **The Jungle Book.**

AN ELEPHANT CALLED SLOWLY (1969)
Color, 91 minutes
Cast: Bill Travers, Virginia McKenna, George Adamson, Vinay Inambar, Joab Collins
Director: James Hill
Screenplay: Bill Travers and James Hill

Action-adventure/Animal story
Rated G
Younger kids: VG   Older kids: VG

Born Free stars Bill Travers and his wife, Virginia McKenna, portray themselves in this fictionalized travelogue that features some magnificent African wildlife photography. While housekeeping for some friends in Kenya, the couple is "adopted" by a trio of friendly elephants, the youngest of which they name Pole Pole, which is Swahili for "slowly." After visiting with the game warden whom Bill portrayed in *Born Free* (and whose lions starred in that movie), they try to train the elephants so that they can return to the wild; there are also encounters with various other animals, including some tame rhinos.

The story is not very dramatic, but it's quite wholesome, and kids will adore the menagerie of cute animals on display.

THE ELEPHANT MAN (1980)
Black & white, 125 minutes
Cast: Anthony Hopkins, John Hurt, Anne Bancroft, John Gielgud, Wendy Hiller, Freddie Jones, Michael Elphick, John Standing, Phoebe Nicholls, Kathleen Byron, Kenny Baker, Patricia Hodge
Director: David Lynch
Screenplay: Lynch, Christopher DeVore, and Eric Bergren
Drama/Biography
Rated PG
Younger kids: No   Older kids: VG

The true story of John Merrick, a hideously deformed man, who lived in turn-of-20th-century London. After years of being exhibited as a sideshow freak by a brutish, drunken man named Bytes (Jones), he is rescued by Frederick Treves, a compassionate surgeon who brings him to a hospital where he is allowed to stay. Eventually, Merrick reveals a noble and dignified soul to Treves and the hospital workers; soon he becomes the toast of high society.

Given the subject matter, this film could have been overly harsh or overly sentimental, but fortunately, it is neither. Director Lynch and cinematographer Freddie Francis use great visual imagination in creating an industrial England with an atmosphere of ominous, lurking threat, as it must have been perceived by Merrick. However, the emotional focus is on the innocent soul of John Merrick himself, and John Hurt beautifully conveys the character's sweetness through all of the (excellent) makeup he wears.

The physical deformity of Merrick is not exploited for cheap thrills or shocks; in fact, the point is frequently made that the behavior of almost everyone around Merrick is far more grotesque than he is initially perceived to be. (Even Treves wonders at one point whether he is exploiting Merrick, as the sideshow owner did.)

Younger children will be alarmed by the degradation the main character must endure, but the whole film is handled with extraordinary sensitivity and parents will appreciate a story that examines the beauty *inside* a person, waiting to be acknowledged.

THE EMIGRANTS (1971)
Color, 148 minutes
Cast: Max von Sydow, Liv Ullmann, Eddie Axberg, Pierre Lindstedt, Allan Edwall, Monica Zeterlund, Hans Alfredson
Historical drama
Rated PG

THE NEW LAND (1972)
Color, 161 minutes
Cast: Max von Sydow, Liv Ullmann, Eddie Axberg, Hans Alfredson, Monica Zeterlund, Per Oscarsson
Historical drama
Rated PG

Director: Jan Troell
Screenplays: Troell and Bengt Forslund, based on four novels by Vilhelm Moberg
Young children: No Older children: VG

The Emigrants chronicles the exodus of a group of simple but stoic Swedish peasants from the Old World to the New at the midpoint of the 19th century. They are headed by Karl Oskar (Max von Sydow), a farmer, and his perpetually pregnant wife Kristina (Liv Ullmann), who leave their native land to escape religious persecution and the ravages of a drought. They sail across the ocean and then travel by steamboat and railroad to the Midwest, where they settle in Minnesota.

Detailed in this deliberately paced and lushly photographed film are births, illnesses, and deaths: the events of life.

A sequel, *The New Land,* further charts the story of Karl Oskar and Kristina as pioneers living out a rugged American experience.

Both films stirringly reflect on American history as first they explore the reasons why individuals chose to abandon their native lands and cross oceans to a new world and then depict the struggles inherent in immigrant existence. While life in America clearly is preferable to what the settlers left behind, their new country is no utopia. (As they travel across the country, for example, Karl Oskar and Kristina become aware of the presence of slaves.) And there is an ever-present tension between Indians and the Swedes, who are in their own way "imperialists."

The Emigrants and *The New Land* are the stories of human beings who wish for a better life and attempt to translate their dream into reality. They are sagas of hope and survival.

The Emigrants and *The New Land* have been edited together, dubbed into English for American television, and retitled *The Emigrant Saga.*

Parents should be aware that despite the seemingly benign PG rating, these films dramatize the harshness of life in this period. There is a scene of an Indian slaughter and mass execution, and there's one incident in which Karl kills and guts an ox in order to warm his son.

EMMA (1996)
Color, 111 minutes
Cast: Gwyneth Paltrow, Jeremy Northam, Toni Collette, Greta Scacchi, Juliet Stevenson, Alan Cumming, Polly Walker, Ewan McGregor, James Cosmo, Sophie Thompson, Phyllida Law.
Director: Douglas McGrath
Screenplay: Douglas McGrath, based on the novel by Jane Austen
Comedy/Literary classic
Rated PG

Young children: No   Older children: VG

Here is an amusing and appealing adaptation of Jane Austen's 19th-century comedy of manners (which was cleverly updated to contemporary Beverly Hills in **Clueless**).

Emma (Gwyneth Paltrow) is a spirited and determined young woman who enjoys playing the role of matchmaker for those around her . . . but curiously, she has no sense of her own feelings and desires, and hasn't a clue about the feelings of the men around her.

Emma is a perfect story for adolescent girls who are beginning to deal with their own romantic inclinations. It also carries a not-so-subtle message about meddling in other people's lives.

THE EMPIRE STRIKES BACK (1980)
Color, 124 minutes (also 127m.)
Cast: Mark Hamill, Harrison Ford, Carrie Fisher, Billy Dee Williams, Anthony Daniels, David Prowse, Peter Mayhew, Kenny Baker, Frank Oz, Alec Guinness, Kenneth Colley, Julian Glover; voice of James Earl Jones
Director: Irvin Kershner
Screenplay: Leigh Brackett and Lawrence Kasdan, from a screen story by George Lucas
Science fiction space opera/ Romantic adventure
Rated PG
Young children: OK, with caution   Older children: OK

While on a wintry planet, Luke Skywalker (Hamill) is visited by the spirit of Ben Kenobi (Guinness), who tells him he must go to the Dagobah System and complete his training to become a true Jedi Knight with the Jedi master Yoda. The Empire strikes the rebel base on the icy world, and Luke heads for Dagobah with droid R2-D2 (Kenny Baker). In his speedy craft, the *Millennium Falcon*, Han Solo (Ford) flees with Princess Leia (Fisher), his co-pilot Chewbacca the Wookiee (Mayhew), and whining droid C-3PO (Daniels). After several adventures, during which they begin to fall in love, Han and Leia end up in the cloud city of Bespin, ruled by Han's old friend and rival Lando Calrissian (Williams). But villainous Darth Vader (Prowse), the Dark Lord of the Sith, has plans of his own.

The first sequel (but fifth chapter) of the Star Wars saga is bigger and grander than **Star Wars** itself, and many consider it the best of the series so far. The romance between Han and Leia, though well played, seems perfunctory and doesn't get very far. The real story here is about Luke Skywalker, his Jedi training with the wizened little Yoda (voiced and performed by Muppet veteran Oz, whose other alter egos include Miss Piggy and Fozzie Bear), and the terrible thing Luke learns from Darth Vader.

Should your kids watch this? The only way to prevent them from seeing it would be to lock them in a padded cell from age 4 to age 18. The Star Wars movies are more full-bodied than the Star Trek sagas, the background details are richer, and George Lucas is actually going somewhere with all this; he has a climax in mind (as proved by the release of Chapter 1 in 1999). The three films so far could hardly be better suited for preteens and teenagers; sure, there are some slightly questionable scenes, mostly involving violence, and there

is a definite dark side to this chapter, but the scope of the tale, the excitement the movies engender and the sense of belonging to a massive saga are actually healthy and cathartic for kids, like the classic mythological tales which inspired Lucas in his writing.

ENEMY FROM SPACE (see **Quatermass II**)

ESCAPE FROM THE PLANET OF THE APES (1971)
Color, 98 minutes
Cast: Roddy McDowall, Kim Hunter, Bradford Dillman, Natalie Trundy, Eric Braeden, William Windom, Sal Mineo, Albert Salmi, Jason Evers, John Randolph, Harry Lauter, M. Emmet Walsh, Ricardo Montalban
Director: Don Taylor
Screenplay: Paul Dehn, based on ideas created by Pierre Boulle
Science fiction/Comedy-drama
Rated G
Young children: OK   Older children: OK

Even though **Beneath the Planet of the Apes** ended with the Earth being destroyed, it seems that, like the hero of a cliffhanging serial, three survivors jumped aside at the last moment. Intelligent chimpanzees Milo (Sal Mineo), Zira (Kim Hunter), and her husband, Cornelius (Roddy McDowall), have somehow managed to come from the ape-dominated future to the present day.

Zira and Cornelius charm the world and become media celebrities. However, when cold-blooded presidential advisor Dr. Hasslein (Braeden) learns that the apes have come from a time when human beings are the inferior species, he fears that Zira and Cornelius are but the first step on the road to the downfall of mankind—especially when Zira admits she's pregnant. . . .

This is easily the best of the sequels to **Planet of the Apes**; it's fast, light on its feet, and amusing, although it does become very serious toward the end, with some deaths that may upset young viewers. Paul Dehn's script is not just clever, it's wise and imaginative, and sets up the last two films very neatly. The performers, particularly McDowall and Hunter, are very good, too.

The next film in the series was **Conquest of the Planet of the Apes.**

ESCAPE TO WITCH MOUNTAIN (1975)
Color, 97 minutes
Cast: Eddie Albert, Ray Milland, Donald Pleasence, Kim Richards, Ike Eisenmann, Walter Barnes, Reta Shaw, Denver Pyle, Alfred Ryder
Director: John Hough
Screenplay: Robert Malcolm Young, based on a book by Alexander Key
Science fiction
Rated G
Younger children: VG Older children: OK

One of the better Disney live-action films of the 1970s, this film focuses on two orphans (Kim Richards, Ike Eisenmann) with telekinetic powers who are pursued by an evil millionaire (Ray Milland) who wants to exploit their unusual abilities.

The children have amnesia about their past, but thanks to a map found in the girl's metallic compact case and her dreams that recall a memory of an accident at sea, they slowly piece together the mystery. Jason (Eddie Albert), an old-timer wandering the country in his camper, befriends the children and helps them find their way home to Witch Mountain, with the bad guys in pursuit.

Director John Hough leads an attractive cast through the supernatural doings to an unexpected conclusion. The special effects may seem simplistic today, but for their time they were excellent and still serve the movie's purpose well. The screenplay efficiently combines chases, effects, humor, and mystery in a satisfying way.

This being a family-oriented Disney film, the menace never becomes too intense, and the film is suitable for all ages.

Followed by a sequel, **Return From Witch Mountain** (1978).

ETHAN FROME (1993)
Color, 107 minutes
Cast: Liam Neeson, Patricia Arquette, Joan Allen, Tate Donovan, Katharine Houghton
Director: John Madden
Screenplay: Richard Nelson, based on the novella by Edith Wharton
Drama/Literary classic
Rated PG
Young children: No Older children: VG

This quietly compelling version of the Edith Wharton novella tells, in flashback, the story of the title character, a compassionate yet poverty-stricken farmer (Liam Neeson) in 19th-century New England. Not only does Ethan Frome toil his land with little financial reward; he has the misfortune to be wed to Zeena, a bitter, domineering older woman (Joan Allen). Then Mattie Silver (Patricia Arquette), Zeena's impoverished young cousin, comes to live with the Fromes. Mattie and Ethan are destined to become involved . . . but it is not fated for them to find happiness.

This respectful (if not especially inspired) adaptation of *Ethan Frome* is both a morality tale and a love story in which passion overcomes suppressed emotion. Older children who have read the book, most likely as a school assignment, may be interested to see the book brought to life. Others will likely find it too austere.

E.T. THE EXTRA-TERRESTRIAL (1982)
Color, 115 minutes
Cast: Dee Wallace, Henry Thomas, Peter Coyote, Robert MacNaughton, Drew Barrymore, K. C. Martel, Sean Frye, Erika Eleniak
Director: Steven Spielberg
Screenplay: Melissa Mathison
Science fiction/Comedy-drama
Rated PG
Young children: VG   Older children: VG

A tubby little alien is accidentally left behind when his spaceship, which has landed near an American suburb, has to flee to avoid men who seem to be searching for them. The alien (eventually called E.T.) becomes friendly with 10-year-old Elliott (Thomas), whose father recently abandoned the family. Elliott hides the alien, who has some miraculous powers, in his house, eventually enlisting the aid of his older brother (MacNaughton) and younger sister (Barrymore). However, in the streets outside, unmarked vans still prowl, and E.T.'s desire to

"phone home" eventually becomes a powerful need.

Some elements of the story don't bear close examination (such as E.T.'s magical powers or his unexplained death and resurrection), but this worldwide smash hit is such a charming, even sweet experience that few are going to hold a little thing like logic against it. It's at once a low-brow comedy and a sweepingly lyrical tale of friendship; it's also quite suspenseful at times.

Few filmmakers understand or relate to the world of contemporary American kids the way Steven Spielberg does here. All the children in *E.T.* seem genuine, which is why kids in the audience can relate to them so well. (The very occasional four-letter word, which bothered some parents when the film came out, is also part of that believability—like it or not.)

This is, understandably, Spielberg's best-loved movie, with moments that can make any viewer—young or old—dissolve into tears. (In this, the filmmaker was immeasurably aided by composer John Williams, whose score has become a classic in its own right.)

E.T. The Extra-Terrestrial certainly earns the right to be called a family classic.

EVER AFTER (1998)
Color, 122 minutes
Cast: Drew Barrymore, Anjelica Huston, Dougray Scott, Patrick Godfrey, Megan Dodds, Melanie Lynskey, Timothy West, Judy Parfitt, Jeroen Krabbé, Jeanne Moreau
Director: Andy Tennant
Screenplay: Susannah Grant, Tennant, and Rick Parks
Fairy tale/Adventure

Rated PG-13
Younger kids: OK, with caution
   Older kids: VG

Contemporary kids should be delighted by this modern twist on the Cinderella tale, with a very appealing Drew Barrymore in the leading role. It's a feminist slant on the fairy tale, in which Cinderella turns out to be braver and pluckier than her prince charming (Dougray Scott), who's nice and good-looking but a bit of a wimp. Our heroine also teaches him a thing or two about humanity, setting an example by genuinely caring about the people around her, regardless of their station in society.

Anjelica Huston is deliciously mean as the stepmother, and is matched by the snooty Megan Dodds as her insufferable, constantly preening daughter Marguerite. (The other daughter, played by Melanie Lynskey, is actually sympathetic to poor Cinderella.)

Some occasional four-letter words and scenes in which a lascivious landowner neighbor expresses his lust for Cinderella no doubt earned this a PG-13 rating. Those moments are fleeting, but they do give the film a more "adult" atmosphere. Still, the film is certain to entertain older children, who will be rooting for Cinderella (and hissing the villainesses) just as in every rendering of this timeless tale.

EVIL OF FRANKENSTEIN
(1964)
Color, 86 minutes
Cast: Peter Cushing, Peter
   Woodthorpe, Duncan Lamont,
   Sandor Eles, Katy Wild, David
   Hutcheson, Kiwi Kingston

Director: Freddie Francis
Screenplay: "John Elder"
   (Anthony Hinds)
Science fiction–horror/Sequel
Unrated
Younger kids: Too
   gruesome   Older kids: OK

This entry in the loosely linked Frankenstein series from Hammer combines elements from their earlier films, notably Peter Cushing as the obsessed Dr. Frankenstein, and ideas from the old Universal Frankenstein series of the 1930s and '40s. For example, the clumsy makeup on the Monster (Kingston) here resembles Jack Pierce's design for Boris Karloff from way back in 1931, and as with a couple of films in that series, the Monster is first found frozen in ice.

This time, Frankenstein tries to revive the damaged brain of his monster with the help of an unscrupulous hypnotist (Woodthorpe), who has nasty ideas of his own.

Cushing is, as always, splendid as the fanatic scientist—intense, driven, and dynamic—and the production values are impeccable. The film itself, however, is below the level of the Hammer Frankenstein series. Still, if your monster-loving teen has already become devoted to these films, this will be a must-see.

Followed by **Frankenstein Created Woman.**

EXPLORERS (1985)
Color, 109 minutes
Cast: Ethan Hawke, River
   Phoenix, Jason Presson,
   Amanda Peterson, Dick
   Miller, Robert Picardo, Dana
   Ivey, Meschach Taylor, Mary
   Kay Place
Director: Joe Dante
Screenplay: Eric Luke

Rated PG
Science fiction/Comedy
Younger kids: OK   Older kids: OK

A boy who's crazy about science fiction teams up with a new friend who's crazy about science in hopes of building a spaceship. With a third kid, they actually do, and zoom off to some comic adventures with friendly aliens.

The first half of the movie captures childhood yearnings for adventure as well as any film ever has; it's imaginative, fast paced, and full of the sense of wonder always created by the very best science fiction adventures. Adults, but perhaps not children, are likely to be let down once the daring trio boards the alien spaceship because the film suddenly turns into a raucous spoof of 20th-century culture. Though this is radically different from the first half, it's still very clever and entertaining; it's just that the transition is something of a shock.

Director Dante says that when he meets fans, this is the film of his they most often cite as their favorite.

F

FAHRENHEIT 451 (1966)
Color, 111 minutes
Cast: Oskar Werner, Julie Christie, Cyril Cusack, Anton Diffring, Jeremy Spenser, Bee Duffell
Director: François Truffaut
Screenplay: Truffaut and Jean-Louis Richard, from the novel by Ray Bradbury
Science fiction/Literary classic
Unrated
Younger kids: Of little interest Older kids: OK

In the future, all books have been banned; the duty of firemen like Montag (Werner) is in fact to burn books whenever they are found. When Montag meets schoolteacher Clarisse (Christie), who looks very much like his wife Linda (also Christie), his view of his repressive society begins to change. He even starts reading books. . . .

If your older kids have already discovered the works of Ray Bradbury, this is an ideal film for them; though flawed (and considered cold and aloof by some critics), it still remains the best filmed version of his work. Even for others, however, the story's strongly stated message—that books are part and parcel of a free society—comes through loud and clear, and could stimulate interesting family discussions.

This was the only English-language film made by famed French director François Truffaut;

it's not his best, but in this case, good intentions really do help make up for some defects.

FAIRY TALE: A TRUE STORY (1997)
Color, 97 minutes
Cast: Florence Hoath, Elizabeth Earl, Paul McGann, Phoebe Nicholls, Peter O'Toole, Harvey Keitel, Bill Nighy, Tim McInnerny
Director: Charles Sturridge
Screenplay: Ernie Contreras, based on a story by Albert Ash, Tom McLoughlin, and Contreras
Fantasy/Drama
Rated PG
Younger children: No Older children: VG

In England during World War I, a young girl comes to stay with her cousin, whose brother's death several years before has left a void in the family. The two girls become fast friends, and while playing at the bottom of their garden, discover a colony of real live fairies. They borrow a camera and take photographs, which come to the attention of Sir Arthur Conan Doyle (Peter O'Toole), the noted author of Sherlock Holmes and expert on extranormal phenomena. He and his friend the great magician Harry Houdini (Harvey Keitel) come to visit the girls, to see if there has been a hoax—or if indeed they have made a magical discovery. Meanwhile, a cynical reporter is determined to break the story, and penetrates the shroud of secrecy that has surrounded the girls' identities since the publication of their photos.

Fairy Tale: A True Story is indeed based on events that made worldwide news in 1917. As such, it requires some explanations for children, especially younger children; the film will be even more meaningful if your kids know a bit about the characters of Conan Doyle and Houdini.

Told at a deliberate pace, *Fairy Tale* will bore smaller kids, and also put them off, as there are scenes showing soldiers injured in the war (one with terrible facial scars) and others where the spirit of the dead brother is invoked. In fact, *Fairy Tale* is the kind of film that may appeal more to adults who are young at heart than children themselves.

THE FALLEN IDOL (1948)
Black & white, 94 minutes
Cast: Ralph Richardson, Michele Morgan, Bobby Henrey, Sonia Dresdel, Jack Hawkins, Bernard Lee
Director: Carol Reed
Screenplay: Graham Greene, from his story "The Basement Room"
Drama
Unrated
Young children: OK   Older children: VG

The consequences of one's actions must be examined in advance so as to alter the dreadful effects that might arise otherwise.

That's what happens when an ambassador's son, a little boy who adores his father's butler, helps cover up what he thinks is the murder of the butler's wife. Instead, he draws the police's attention to the innocent man.

Told in large part from the child's perspective, what was simply an accident is wrongly aggrandized into a homicide charge that seems inescapable.

The Fallen Idol is a thriller, but it's also an engrossing study of the surrogate father relationship between Richardson, the servant, and Henrey, his idolator. Mature youngsters will find it fascinating, because so much of the story is seen from the boy's point of view.

THE FALL OF THE HOUSE OF USHER (see House of Usher)

FAME (1980)
Color, 134 minutes
Cast: Irene Cara, Lee Curreri, Eddie Barth, Laura Dean, Paul McCrane, Barry Miller, Gene Anthony Ray, Maureen Teefy, Antonia Franceshi, Anne Meara, Albert Hague
Director: Alan Parker
Screenplay: Christopher Gore
Musical/Drama
Rated R
Younger kids: OK   Older kids: G

This rousing musical drama follows a diverse group of students during their four years at New York's High School of Performing Arts, as they begin the journey toward fame and success. Among the wannabe stars: talented, illiterate dancer Leroy (Gene Anthony Ray), tough singer Coco (Irene Cara), musician Bruno (Lee Curreri), Puerto Rican stand-up Ralph (Barry Miller), and sensitive homosexual Montgomery (Paul McCrane).

Given the time frame and the

numerous characters, the film is understandably episodic in structure, leaving more than a few loose ends untied. It also lapses into cliché more often than not, and sometimes into the totally unbelievable, as when Coco is "tricked" into making a pornographic movie. Even the grittiness of the New York milieu occasionally feels like an updated Mickey Rooney–Judy Garland musical, with kids literally dancing in the streets.

Despite its faults, however, *Fame* does capture the energy of the young students and their need to perform and express themselves, all driven by Michael Gore's pulsating Oscar-winning score. Kids interested in the arts will no doubt relate to the pains these young men and women must go through to fulfill their dreams.

Also worth noting is the depiction of the student-teacher relationships, particularly the bond between Leroy and Mrs. Sherwood (Anne Meara), an English teacher who refuses to let his academic career just slide by. Ray, Curreri, and Hague re-created their roles for the later TV series, which considerably watered down the more vibrant aspects of the film.

Parents should take this movie's R rating seriously: in language, behavior, and incident, *Fame* is not for younger children.

FANTASIA (1940)
Color, 120 minutes
Cast: Deems Taylor (narrator); Leopold Stokowski, conducting the Philadelphia Orchestra
Directors: Samuel Armstrong, James Algar, Bill Roberts, Paul Satterfield, Hamilton Luske, Jim Handley, Ford Beebe, T. Hee, Norman Ferguson, and Wilfred Jackson
Story direction: Joe Grant and Dick Huemer
Animated musical
Unrated
Young children: OK   Older children: VG

Fantasia will stimulate some children and bore others. It's two hours long, and some of its segments are livelier than others, but with the advent of home video parents can determine which pieces work best for their family. No child should be denied the experience of watching this landmark film.

The highlight of *Fantasia* for many audiences, young and old, is "The Sorcerer's Apprentice," starring Mickey Mouse as a lowly magician's assistant who dreams of wielding great power over the waters of the ocean, and gets carried away. It was this segment, a visualization of a famous piece of music by Paul Dukas, that inspired Walt Disney to go further and produce a series of animated sequences based on some of the world's greatest music.

Tchaikovsky's *Nutcracker* Suite is a colorful treat, as dancing mushrooms and thistles frolic to his famous themes. Stravinsky's *Rite of Spring* becomes an accompaniment to the roaming of dinosaurs from the beginning of time. "The Dance of the Hours" is a delightful ballet performed by hippos, alligators, and ostriches. And "Night on Bald Mountain" is a fearsome display of evil during a night of deviltry broken only by the coming of dawn.

These are the strongest sections of *Fantasia* from a youngster's point of view. Beethoven's *Pastoral* Symphony is considerably sleepier (even for adults), and Shubert's "Ave Maria" is stiffly reverent.

There has never been another film quite like this one, although the Disney studio has worked for many years to produce *Fantasia 2000*, a long-promised sequel. Some children are bound to consider it medicine, as some audiences did in 1940 . . . but the best segments of the film still have the power to do what Walt Disney envisioned so many years ago, to introduce people to great classical music and fire their imagination with stimulating visual ideas.

FANTASTIC VOYAGE (1966)
Color, 100 minutes
Cast: Stephen Boyd, Raquel
   Welch, Edmond O'Brien,
   Donald Pleasence, Arthur
   O'Connell, William Redfield,
   Arthur Kennedy
Director: Richard Fleischer
Screenplay: Harry Kleiner
Science fiction/Adventure
Unrated
Younger kids: VG   Older kids:
   VG

A famous scientist needs urgent medical attention, so a group of doctors aboard a submarine are miniaturized and injected into the comatose man's bloodstream, to try to get to the root of the problem. Naturally, there's a saboteur among them, and they only have an hour to complete their task.

It's dated now, though the characters were always thinly drawn and the plot predictable (you can probably pick the saboteur out of the cast list without seeing the movie), but this is still an entertaining adventure that should be fun for all. Older kids may curl a lip at the "old-fashioned" special effects but will be caught up in the story anyway.

FAR FROM HOME: THE ADVENTURES OF YELLOW DOG (1995)
Color, 80 minutes
Cast: Mimi Rogers, Bruce
   Davison, Jesse Bradford, Tom
   Bower, Joel Palmer
Director: Philip Borsos
Screenplay: Philip Borsos
Adventure/Animal story
Rated PG
Younger kids: OK, with
   caution   Older kids: Good

Another "boy and his dog" tale, but a fairly rugged and effective one, thanks to a refreshingly unsentimental script. Set in British Columbia, the story is about 14-year-old Jesse (Jesse Bradford) and his recently adopted stray Golden Labrador, who have to make their way home through the Canadian wilderness after being separated from the boy's father when their boat capsizes in the waters off the coast.

Adults will find it predictable, but most kids will get a kick out of the resourcefulness and self-reliance shown by Jesse and his smart pup, while delighting in their "gross" adventures in the woods, which include eating bugs and mice. Some young children, however, may be frightened by some scenes of the boy and his dog in peril.

A FAR OFF PLACE (1993)
Color, 105 minutes
Cast: Reese Witherspoon, Ethan
   Randall (Embry), Sarel Bok,
   Maximilian Schell, Jack

Thompson, Robert Burke,
Patricia Kalember
Director: Mikael Salomon
Screenplay: Robert Caswell,
Jonathan Hensleigh, and Sally
Robinson, based on the novels
A Story Like the Wind and *A
Far Off Place* by Laurens van
der Post
Adventure
Rated PG
Younger kids: OK Older kids:
Good

Two teens—a game warden's
daughter (Reese Witherspoon)
and a visiting city boy (Ethan
Randall)—along with a youthful
Bushman guide (Sarel Bok) and a
dog, are pursued across 1,000
miles of the Kalahari desert by
ruthless elephant poachers who
have killed the teens' parents.

Beautifully photographed, this
leisurely paced Disney film is a
fine adventure for older children
who will appreciate its environmental message, but it contains disturbing scenes of animal slaughter
that are too intense for children
under 10. (This after the kids'
parents are murdered!) A number
of critics remarked on this anomaly in a family-oriented film—
from Disney, no less.

FATHER OF THE BRIDE
(1991)
Color, 105 minutes
Cast: Steve Martin, Diane
Keaton, Martin Short,
Kimberly Williams, Kieran
Culkin, George Newbern,
B. D. Wong
Director: Charles Shyer
Screenplay: Shyer and Nancy
Myers, based on a screenplay
by Frances Goodrich and
Albert Hackett from the novel
by Edward Streeter

Comedy
Rated PG
Younger kids: Good Older kids:
VG

Steve Martin and Diane Keaton
step into the shoes of Spencer
Tracy and Joan Bennett in this
perfectly pleasant, if unremark-
able, remake of the 1950 Vincente
Minnelli classic about a panicked
father's reaction to his daughter's
upcoming wedding. Martin plays
George Banks, an upper-middle-
class L.A. businessman who goes
apoplectic when his daughter,
Annie (Kimberly Williams), reveals that she's engaged. Annie's
mother, Nina (Diane Keaton), is
thrilled, but George can't deal
with losing his "baby." A disastrous meeting with their wealthy future in-laws only further irritates
him. George then finds himself
practically going bankrupt at the
hands of their flamboyant wedding
consultant, Franck Eggelhoffer (a
hilarious Martin Short), whose
elaborate plans include a cake that
costs more than George's first car.

Society has changed a lot since
1950, but this remake draws on
the same values of wholesome
suburban domesticity and middle-
age anxiety that made the original
film so appealing. Steve Martin
may lack Spencer Tracy's consummate delivery and skill at expressing befuddled exasperation,
but he makes up for it with his
talent for pratfalls and physical
comedy, such as in the scene
where he's terrorized by his in-
laws' dogs and falls into their
swimming pool. The script has
been shrewdly updated for baby
boomers, and the women's roles
have been made more modern, so
that the mother now works and
the daughter is studying to be an

architect, but deep down, the film yearns for a return to the idealized good old days when families stayed together and every problem could be solved with a heart-to-heart talk.

And what's wrong with that?

The PG rating is for some mild language.

FATHER OF THE BRIDE PART II (1995)
Color, 106 minutes
Cast: Steve Martin, Diane Keaton, Kimberly Williams, George Newbern, Martin Short, Eugene Levy, B. D. Wong, Jane Adams
Director: Charles Shyer
Screenplay: Nancy Meyers and Shyer, based on the movie *Father's Little Dividend,* written by Albert Hackett and Frances Goodrich
Comedy
Rated PG
Younger children: OK Older children: VG

This enjoyable domestic comedy picks up where the first film left off. George (Steve Martin) is feeling old and useless, and tries to find ways to be more youthful. He goes so far as to suggest to his wife (Diane Keaton) that they move to a condo at the beach, and they reluctantly decide to sell their house. When he finds out that his precious daughter, Annie, is going to have a baby, he freaks out . . . but that news is topped by the announcement that his wife is pregnant, too.

Martin Short returns as Franck, the flamboyant, vaguely European character who this time supervises the designing of the baby's room. He adds broad comedy relief to the gentler brand of

humor that permeates the rest of the picture.

It can be safely said that if you liked **Father of the Bride** you'll like *Father of the Bride Part II* just as much. Some of the situations (particularly dealing with George's midlife crisis) will go over the heads of the youngest viewers, and there are a few four-letter words, but most of the family will find something to relate to in the various crises and complications encountered by the Banks family.

FERNGULLY . . . THE LAST RAINFOREST (1992)
Color, 76 minutes
Cast: Voices of Tim Curry, Samantha Mathis, Christian Slater, Robin Williams, Tone-Loc, Jonathan Ward, Robert Pastorelli, Cheech Marin, Tommy Chong
Director: Bill Kroyer
Screenplay: Jim Cox
Animated feature/Musical
Rated G
Younger kids: VG Older kids: VG

One of the best of the recent non-Disney animated features, *FernGully . . . the Last Rainforest* is a delightful fantasy that includes an important (if unsubtle) environmental lesson. The evil spirit Hexxus, imprisoned in an enchanted tree, is released by workers who are leveling the rain forest. One of the hard hat crew, Zak, is reduced to pixie size by a winged sprite, Crysta, so he can see firsthand what his work is destroying. With the help of the fairy kingdom and a whacked-out laboratory escapee named Batty, the battle commences against the forces of evil.

Excellent animation and a good story will hold children's interest . . . and parents will enjoy listening to the vocal performances on the soundtrack. Tim Curry (Hexxus) and Tone-Loc (as a threatening lizard) stand out with their songs and performances, while Robin Williams is as funny as ever as the brain-fried bat, which will give parents the incentive to enjoy this cartoon feature alongside their kids.

A less-enchanted direct-to-video sequel, *FernGully II: The Magical Rescue*, was released in 1997.

FERRIS BUELLER'S DAY OFF (1986)
Color, 103 minutes
Cast: Matthew Broderick, Alan Ruck, Mia Sara, Jeffrey Jones, Jennifer Grey, Cindy Pickett, Lyman Ward, Edie McClurg, Charlie Sheen, Del Close, Virginia Capers, Louis Anderson, Max Perlich, T. Scott Coffey, Kristy Swanson
Director: John Hughes
Screenplay: John Hughes
Comedy
Rated PG-13
Younger kids: OK, with caution   Older kids: OK

This upbeat comedy chronicles the adventures of Ferris Bueller (Matthew Broderick), who decides to take the day off from high school and roam downtown Chicago with his friend Cameron (Ruck) and girlfriend Sloane (Sara) in tow. Meanwhile, the school principal (Jones) suspects something is up, and is determined to catch Bueller playing hooky. . . .

In other words, another slick but entertaining slice of high school life from the John Hughes Teenage Daydream Factory, with all of the expected components in place: a clever, likable central character, dim-witted parents and authority figures, and a feel for the trials and tribulations of young-adult life. There are some attempts at moral insights as Ferris inspires Cameron to stand up for himself and notes that "life moves pretty fast—if you don't stop once in a while and look around, you could miss it."

Mainly, though, it's an excuse for kids to root for a wily teen as he gets away with murder. As usual, the deck is stacked against all adults, to the point where Cameron destroys his materialistic father's prized Ferrari, and we are supposed to cheer him for it because we are told Dad doesn't pay enough attention to Cameron. Kids will no doubt lap it up, while some parents may groan and consider Ferris something of a jerk.

FIDDLER ON THE ROOF (1971)
Color, 181 minutes
Cast: (Chaim) Topol, Norma Crane, Leonard Frey, Molly Picon, Paul Mann, Rosalind Harris, Michele Marsh, Neva Small, (Paul) Michael Glaser
Director: Norman Jewison
Screenplay: Joseph Stein, based on the musical play by Joseph Stein, Jerry Bock, and Sheldon Harnick, based in turn on the stories of Sholem Aleichem
Musical
Rated G
Young children: VG   Older children: VG

This lavishly produced musical, based on the long-running Broadway hit, tackles the serious social issue of religious persecution (and the less solemn problem of a younger generation trying to break with tradition), while it entertains with moving songs and clever storytelling. Perhaps its greatest achievement is that it takes a story about very specific people and makes it absolutely universal.

The setting is the village of Anatevka in Czarist Russia. Although the community has a host of splendid, diverse characters, the focus of the story is Tevye, a poverty-stricken Jewish milkman who has five unmarried daughters. While he struggles to feed his family, marry off his girls, and keep the spark of Judaism going within the household, he and the other Jews in Anatevka experience hatred from some of their neighbors and even undergo a violent pogrom.

While the story has a serious edge to it, the marvel of Joseph Stein's screenplay (adapted from his book for the Broadway stage) is the way it incorporates humor, homespun philosophy, and a deep sense of humanity. Much of the music celebrates the life and spirit of the Jewish community as a group and as individuals. The songs include "To Life," "Anatevka," "Sunrise, Sunset," and Tevye's comically sweet duet with his wife, "Do You Love Me?"

While the violence that breaks up a wedding scene is frightening, it is styled in such a way as not to be off-putting to children. On the other hand, a dream sequence in which dead ancestors come back to life might scare smaller children, even though it is depicted in a theatrical fashion.

The Tevye of *Fiddler on the Roof* bears little resemblance to the more solemn Tevye of the Sholem Aleichem stories, on which the musical is based. Because the younger generation of Anatevka includes several independent, tradition-breaking characters, this film will be of particular interest to teenagers.

FIELD OF DREAMS (1989)
Color, 107 minutes
Cast: Kevin Costner, Amy Madigan, Gaby Hoffmann, James Earl Jones, Timothy Busfield, Ray Liotta, Burt Lancaster, Frank Whaley, Dwier Brown
Director: Phil Alden Robinson
Screenplay: Robinson, based on the novel *Shoeless Joe* by Ray Kinsella
Drama/Fantasy/Sports
Rated PG
Young children: OK Older children: VG

This sweet fantasy-drama is a wonderful film, a compelling tale that expresses a heartfelt love for (and keen understanding of) baseball. Here, the game is not so much an athletic endeavor as a way of life that serves as a link between generations. Furthermore, it offers a simple, clearly defined connection to all that is good about America.

Kevin Costner gives one of his best performances as Ray Kinsella, an Iowa farmer, husband, and father. One day, while in his fields, he hears an unearthly voice that tells him, "If you build it, he will come." Kinsella soon figures out that "it" is a baseball field, which he promptly constructs amid his corn stalks. Once it is complete, the ghosts of the legendary Shoeless Joe Jackson and his Chicago Black Sox teammates come to

Kinsella's field of dreams. All are long-deceased, and all have been wandering aimlessly through the netherworld. Now, finally, they have a place in which to play their beloved game.

One of the highlights of *Field of Dreams* is the presence of an aged Burt Lancaster as Moonlight Graham, a one-game major league wonder who went on to spend his life as an obscure small-town doctor. As the scenario plays itself out, the point is made that Old Doc Graham need not have won fame as a big leaguer to have enjoyed a rich, full, and useful life.

With each new development, someone else finds peace and/or redemption by coming to Costner's field of dreams and renewing their love affair with baseball.

Younger children will not understand all of these fantasy elements—nor will they recognize names like Shoeless Joe, who was disgraced in the "fixed" 1921 World Series. But if parents help them through these moments, they too may fall under the film's magic spell.

THE FIFTH ELEMENT (1997)
Color, 127 minutes
Cast: Bruce Willis, Gary Oldman, Milla Jovovich, Ian Holm, Chris Tucker, Luke Perry, Brion James, Tiny Lister, Lee Evans, Maiwenn Le Bresco, John Neville
Director: Luc Besson
Screenplay: Besson and Robert Mark Kamen
Science fiction
Rated PG-13
Younger kids: No Older kids: OK, with caution

In 1914, archaeologists in Egypt make a discovery about a danger to the Earth that will occur in the future. In 2259, the danger arrives in the form of a colossal talking asteroid, carrying "anti-life" that will wipe out our planet. The complicated plot involves adorable, regenerated Jovovich, tough former soldier (now cabdriver) Willis, and exotic talk show host Tucker. Meanwhile, evil Oldman conspires with various aliens in an effort to speed the advent of "anti-life."

Intensely colorful, fast-paced, and imaginative, *The Fifth Element* is unlike any other science fiction movie ever made. As bizarre, even silly, as some of the elements of the movie may be, director Besson keeps them all of a piece and part of his singular vision of the future (a none-too-optimistic view, to be sure).

It's too intense in some sections for any but the most battle-hardened younger kids. The sexual elements of the film, brief though they are, helped earn this a PG-13 rating; Jovovich is glimpsed naked, and there is a hefty dose of foul language and violence. With it all (or perhaps because of it), teenagers are likely to love the film. Adults may be turned off by some of its excesses and eccentricities.

THE FIGHTING PRINCE OF DONEGAL (1966)
Color, 112 minutes
Cast: Peter McEnery, Susan Hampshire, Tom Adams, Gordon Jackson, Andrew Keir, Donal McCann
Director: Michael O'Herlihy
Screenplay: Robert Westerby, based on the novel *Red Hugh, Prince of Donegal* by Robert T. Reilly
Swashbuckler/Action-adventure

Unrated
Younger kids: OK   Older kids: VG

Young children: VG   Older children: VG

The Fighting Prince of Donegal is an exhilarating Disney swashbuckler about the 16th-century Irish Prince Hugh O'Donnell (Peter McEnery), who tried to unite the clans of Ireland and free them from British oppression. When the elder Prince Hugh of Donegal dies, young Hugh becomes head of the clan, but is imprisoned by the British because of an old legend that "when Hugh succeeds Hugh, Ireland shall be free." Wicked British officer Captain Leeds (Gordon Jackson) then seizes Donegal castle and captures Hugh's mother and his sweetheart from prison, but Hugh escapes and, after beating Leeds in a duel, forces him to sign a treaty with Ireland.

Filmed in England on a lavish scale, this is a full-blooded action film that's a cut above the normal juvenile Disney treatment of such stories. McEnery is a pleasing hero, and Jackson a despicable villain. And if there's a pinch of history lesson here along with the fun, no one can complain.

FINIAN'S RAINBOW (1968)
Color, 145 minutes
Cast: Fred Astaire, Petula Clark, Tommy Steele, Don Francks, Keenan Wynn, Barbara Hancock, Al Freeman, Jr., Ronald Colby, Dolph Sweet
Director: Francis Ford Coppola
Screenplay: E. Y. Harburg and Fred Saidy, based on the musical by Harburg and Burton Lane
Musical/Fantasy
Rated G

Fred Astaire (older but no less charming than he was in his starring films of the 1930s and '40s) offers a made-to-order performance in this elaborate adaptation of a classic Broadway musical as Finian McLonergan, an Irish rapscallion who, with his daughter, Sharon (pop singing star Petula Clark), moves to the American South with a pot of pilfered leprechaun gold. Finian's plan is to bury it; because he has settled near Fort Knox, he is convinced the treasure will multiply. Meanwhile, Finian is unaware that a leprechaun named Og (Tommy Steele) has followed him to America with the intention of reclaiming the fortune. If he does not do so, Og is destined to turn mortal.

The songs, from "How Are Things in Glocca Morra?" to "That Come-and-Get-It Day" to "Old Devil Moon," remain charming. However, *Finian's Rainbow* is more than just a bewitching bit of Irish blarney. It is a show with a social conscience, as it involves a bullying, racist good-old-boy Southern politician (Keenan Wynn) and a bright young African-American scientist (Al Freeman, Jr.) who finances his experiments by toiling as the politician's servant.

While the social commentary was dated even by late 1960s standards—the show opened in New York in 1947—its message remains relevant today, and the show's high spirits are ageless.

FIRST KID (1996)
Color, 101 minutes
Cast: Sinbad, Brock Pierce, Blake Boyd, Timothy Busfield, Art La Fleur, Robert

Guillaume, Lisa Eichhorn,
James Naughton, Fawn Reed,
Bill Cobbs, Zachery Ty Bryan
Director: David Mickey Evans
Screenplay: Tim Kelleher
Comedy
Rated PG
Younger kids: VG   Older kids:
VG

Sinbad is an ideal comic hero in
this bull's-eye comedy about a
hang-loose Secret Service agent
on the White House detail who
gets the worst job in town: guard-
ing the bratty son (Brock Pierce)
of the President of the United
States. They soon form a bond,
however, and become good
friends. The agent teaches him to
box, and even helps his young
charge in his first contact with a
girl at school. But the agent is forever putting himself (and his already dubious reputation) at risk
in order to help the First Kid have
a good time.

A film with heart, a good story,
and a healthy dose of slapstick
comedy, *First Kid* benefits most of
all from an immensely likable Sinbad in the lead and an appealing
performance by Brock Pierce in
the title role.

The subplot about a disgruntled
ex–Secret Service agent gets a bit
seamy and might be intense for
very young children (including a
scene where a bullet is fired and
the camera takes the bullet's
point of view!). There is a smattering of foul language and a brief
scene of partial nudity, as well,
which make the PG rating accurate and appropriate.

FIRST MEN IN THE MOON
(1964)
Color, 103 minutes
Cast: Edward Judd, Lionel
Jeffries, Martha Hyer
Director: Nathan Juran
Screenplay: Nigel Kneale and
Jan Read, from the novel by
H. G. Wells
Science fiction/Adventure
Unrated
Younger kids: VG   Older kids:
VG

In the Victorian era, an eccentric
scientist invents an anti-gravity
metal that takes him, a neighbor,
and a young woman to the Moon.
There, they encounter monsters
resembling giant caterpillars and a
race of insectlike lunar inhabitants.

H. G. Wells' lightly comic novel
has had the comedy quotient increased, sometimes to an irritating
degree, but generally speaking, this
is a lively, colorful adventure that
would be good fun for family viewing, especially if watched in a
wide-screen (letterboxed) format.
Younger children might get a little
restless waiting for the fun to start,
but once the spherical ship takes
off for the Moon, they'll be right
with the story. The special effects
by Ray Harryhausen are not as
plentiful as in his other films, but
they're just as well done.

**FIVE MILLION YEARS TO
EARTH** (see **Quatermass and
the Pit**)

**THE 5,000 FINGERS OF DR.
T.** (1953)
Color, 89 minutes
Cast: Peter Lind Hayes, Mary
Healy, Hans Conried, Tommy
Rettig, John Heasley, Robert
Heasley, Noel Cravat, Henry
Kulky

Director: Roy Rowland
Writer: Ted Geisel (Dr. Seuss)
  and Allan Scott
Fantasy/Musical
Unrated
Younger children: Pretty
  scary   Older children: VG

In this, the only Hollywood feature film written by Dr. Seuss, Bart (Tommy Rettig) lives with his widowed mother (Mary Healy). He wants to play baseball, but she insists that he must practice the piano because his piano teacher, Dr. Terwilliker (Hans Conried), will be by soon to give Bart a lesson. Bart's best friend is handyman Mr. Zabladowski (Peter Lind Hayes, real-life husband of Mary Healy). While practicing, Bart has a wild, surrealistic nightmare about a preposterous fantasy land in which the piano teacher, Dr. T., has kidnapped 500 children, forcing them to play the world's largest piano and wear beanies.

The 5,000 Fingers of Dr. T. may be responsible for frightening a generation of children away from piano lessons! At the same time, it's a memorable flight of fancy with images that linger long after the film is over. (No one is likely to forget the beanie hat each student is forced to wear, with five rubber fingers sticking out on top, for instance.)

One would like to salute this as a great movie, which it is not, but it has too many good ingredients not to be recommended. That superb character actor Hans Conried has the role of a lifetime as the mad Dr. T. If only Healy and Hayes were more charismatic as the grown-ups, if only the songs were better . . . Still, *Dr. T.* is certain to make an impression on kids if they're not too young to

be scared by the nightmarish aspects of the story.

THE FLAME AND THE ARROW (1950)
Color, 88 minutes
Cast: Burt Lancaster, Virginia Mayo, Robert Douglas, Aline MacMahon, Nick Cravat
Director: Jacques Tourneur
Screenplay: Waldo Salt
Swashbuckler/Action-adventure
Unrated
Younger kids: Good   Older kids: VG

Burt Lancaster is a sort of Robin Hood of medieval Italy in this bouncy swashbuckler that delightfully mixes exuberant action and tongue-in-cheek humor. Lancaster plays Dardo, a rebel who lives in the mountains and taunts the cruel Hessian warlord Ulrich (Frank Allenby). When Ulrich captures Dardo's son, he retaliates by abducting Ulrich's beautiful niece Anne (Virginia Mayo), who falls in love with him, of course. This heated rivalry climaxes with a siege of the castle with Dardo and his cohorts disguised as a troupe of acrobats (one of whom is Nick Cravat, Lancaster's real-life former circus partner, who, as in **The Crimson Pirate,** plays his mute sidekick).

Adults will understand the tongue-in-cheek nature of the film, while kids may take it more seriously, but everyone should have a great time. This is great fun, and a perfect companion piece to the better-known *The Crimson Pirate.*

FLAMING STAR (1960)
Color, 91 minutes
Cast: Elvis Presley, Barbara Eden, Steve Forrest, Dolores Del Rio, John McIntire

Director: Don Siegel
Screenplay: Clair Huffaker and Nunnally Johnson, based on the novel by Huffaker
Western/Drama
Unrated
Younger kids: OK   Older kids: VG

Believe it or not, this Elvis Presley vehicle is a serious and dignified racial Western in which he only sings two songs (and none after the first ten minutes). In a role reportedly intended for Marlon Brando, Elvis is quite convincing as a half-breed Indian who's torn between his full-blooded Indian mother (Dolores Del Rio, in an excellent performance) and his white father (John McIntire) during a range war between his own tribe and a group of Texas settlers.

Managing to balance rugged action with an honest look at prejudice, *Flaming Star* is Elvis' best nonmusical movie, holding equal appeal for Presley fans, Western aficionados, and movie-lovers young and old.

FLASH GORDON (1980)
Color, 110 minutes
Cast: Sam J. Jones, Melody Anderson, Topol, Max von Sydow, Ornella Muti, Brian Blessed, Timothy Dalton, Peter Wyngarde, Mariangela Melato
Director: Mike Hodges
Screenplay: Lorenzo Semple, Jr.
Science fiction/Fantasy
Rated PG
Young children: VG, with caution   Older children: VG

Both a homage to and a spoof of Alex Raymond's celebrated comic-strip creation of the 1930s, this big-scale production is an opulent space opera in which the indefatigable Ming the Merciless (Emperor of Mongo) once again tries to conquer Earth. Only New York Jets quarterback Flash, his perennial squeeze, Dale Arden, and stalwart scientist Dr. Zarkov stand in the way of interstellar warfare.

This campy film is crammed with hearty character turns: Muti's sultry Aura, Blessed's robust Vultan, Dalton's flighty Prince Barin, and especially von Sydow's full-tilt Ming ("I did it for my grandkids," the actor later explained). Fabulous sets look like Radio City Goes to Mars. Queen's mock-epic score adds greatly to the tone of the film.

This is good fun for three or four generations of relatives to watch together, just to compare notes against the original Larry "Buster" Crabbe movie serials (which are still so enjoyable). But perhaps the reason this film never became a huge success was that kids were left out of the joke. **Star Wars,** after all, was completely earnest in its storytelling (even though it had a hearty sense of humor). Young people who'd never seen the vintage movie serials couldn't be expected to understand a spoof of them—and probably wouldn't want to make fun of them in any case. It's much more satisfying to actually get involved with characters and identify with them than it is to mock.

There is some mild sexual suggestiveness, and outer space–style violence, which earned the film a PG rating.

FLIGHT OF THE NAVIGATOR (1986)
Color, 98 minutes
Cast: Joey Cramer, Paul

Reubens (voice only),
Veronica Cartwright, Cliff de
Young, Sarah Jessica Parker,
Matt Adler, Howard
Hesseman, Robert Small,
Albie Whitaker, Jonathan
Sanger
Director: Randal Kleiser
Screenplay: Michael Burton and
Matt MacManus
Science fiction/Adventure
Rated PG
Younger kids: OK Older kids:
OK

Twelve-year-old David (Cramer)
is knocked unconscious in the
woods behind his family's home.
When he comes to, he discovers
his family no longer lives there
and that eight years have passed—
although he hasn't aged a day.
Eventually, it's learned this has to
do with his being captured as a
specimen by a friendly, intelligent
flying saucer, which took David to
its home planet, then returned
him to Earth. He didn't age because he was traveling at the
speed of light. Now the government and the flying saucer both
want David, for different reasons.

The opening is almost a classic
childhood fantasy: What happens
if, while you are gone, your parents move away and don't tell
you? Unfortunately, after this
imaginative start, the story heads
straight into familiar territory,
with unscrupulous government
agents and friendly, toylike aliens.
The special effects are good, with
the mirrored surface of the flying
saucer especially well rendered.

Younger kids won't be bothered by the familiarity of the plot;
the boy is the hero and has exciting (but not scary) adventures.
Older ones may fidget. (And so
might you.)

THE FLINTSTONES (1994)
Color, 92 minutes
Cast: John Goodman, Elizabeth
Perkins, Rick Moranis, Rosie
O'Donnell, Kyle MacLachlan,
Halle Berry, Elizabeth Taylor,
Dann Florek, Richard Moll,
Irwin Keyes, Jonathan
Winters, Harvey Korman,
Elaine Silver, Sheryl Lee
Ralph, Jean Vander Pyl, The
B-52's, Laraine Newman, Jay
Leno, Sam Raimi, Joe
Barbera, Bill Hanna
Director: Brian Levant
Screenplay: Tom S. Parker, Jim
Jennewein, and Steven E. de
Souza, based on the Hanna-
Barbera animated series
Comedy/Fantasy
Rated PG
Younger children: OK Older
children: OK

Meet the Flintstones: Fred (John
Goodman) and Wilma (Elizabeth
Perkins), and their neighbors, the
Rubbles, Barney (Rick Moranis)
and Betty (Rosie O'Donnell).
Embezzler Cliff Vandercave (Kyle
MacLachlan) tries to use Fred in
his scheme to steal from the Slate
Gravel Company. Of course, he
and his assistant, Rosetta Stone,
played by Halle Berry, are
thwarted.

Many critics dealt harshly with
this elaborate feature film, but
what can one rightly expect of a
live-action feature based on a
half-hour cartoon series? It's
pleasant, if uninspired, and does
manage to capture the spirit of
the durable animated series
(which, in turn, got its inspiration
from Jackie Gleason's *Honey-
mooners* skits and series).

Baby boomer parents may be
as caught up in this film as their
kids are but for different reasons.

For kids, there are loads of puns, lots of silly prehistoric gags, and plenty of action and color. Parents will probably enjoy revisiting a childhood cartoon favorite come eerily to life. And if they watch closely enough, they may see *Flintstones* creators Joe Barbera and Bill Hanna as a man in a "Mersandes" and a board room executive, respectively.

FLIPPER (1996)
Color, 96 minutes
Cast: Paul Hogan, Elijah Wood, Chelsea Field, Isaac Hayes, Jessica Wesson, Jonathan Banks
Director: Alan Shapiro
Screenplay: Alan Shapiro
Adventure/Animal Story
Rated PG
Younger children: VG   Older children: OK

This updated fish tale is passable entertainment for youngsters who've had their fill of **Free Willy** sequels. Sandy (Elijah Wood) is a victim of divorce and has been sent to live in Coral Key for the summer with his sea hermit Uncle Porter (Paul Hogan). Sandy reluctantly joins his uncle on a fishing trip where they witness the local bad guys shooting at dolphins. Sandy saves them, and one of the sea creatures follows him home. Sandy adopts him as a pet and names him Flipper. Flipper saves the day when he discovers the bad guys' plot to dump toxic waste off the coast. Lots of underwater shenanigans and appealing characters make up for the almost nonexistent plot.
Flipper, like its movie and TV predecessors, is aimed strictly at kids, so the level of menace in the movie is muted, as is the action

component. The puppy-love subplot, and the natural appeal of both Elijah Wood and everybody's favorite Aussie, Paul Hogan, make this a natural for younger kids. Older viewers are likely to find it all too bland.

FLIRTING (see **The Year My Voice Broke**)

FLOWER DRUM SONG (1961)
Color, 133 minutes
Cast: Nancy Kwan, James Shigeta, Juanita Hall, Jack Soo, Miyoshi Umeki, Benson Fong, Reiko Sato, Patrick Adiarte, Kam Tong, Victor Sen Yung, James Hong
Director: Henry Koster
Screenplay: Joseph Fields, based on the musical by Richard Rodgers, Oscar Hammerstein II, and Fields from the novel *The Flower Drum Song* by C. Y. Lee
Musical
Unrated
Young children: VG   Older children: VG

This overlong but entertaining Rodgers and Hammerstein musical is set in San Francisco's Chinatown. It is the story of sweet, servile Mei Li (Myoshi Umeki), who, with her father, stows away on board a ship headed from Hong Kong to San Francisco. She is anxious to come to America because the mother of nightclub owner Sammy Fong (Jack Soo) has chosen Mei Li as her son's "picture bride." Sammy, however, does not wish to marry; in fact, for the past five years he has been stringing along his sweetheart, flirtatious showgirl Linda Low (Nancy Kwan).
The scenario goes on to involve

Wang Ta (James Shigeta), an Americanized college student whose wealthy Old World father, Wang Chi-Yang, wants him to wed a "picture bride," too. Upon meeting Mei Li, Wang Chi-Yang deems that she will be the perfect mate for his son.

Flower Drum Song is effective as a story of the conflict between older and younger generations, and the Old World versus the New, with tradition pitted against an ever-changing culture. It's also fascinating for its depiction of Linda, a classic pre-feminist heroine who "enjoys being a girl" and relishes her identity as a decorative sex object. Indeed, Linda's one goal in life is to lasso herself a rich husband. (This may spark some interesting family conversation!)

The score doesn't have timeless hits like most other Rodgers and Hammerstein musicals, but they are bouncy, flavorful, and express the characters' feelings with grace and charm. Kids and parents alike should enjoy this film.

FLUBBER (1997)
Color, 93 minutes
Cast: Robin Williams, Marcia Gay Harden, Christopher McDonald, Raymond Barry, Clancy Brown, Ted Levine, Wil Wheaton, Edie McClurg; voice of Jodi Benson
Director: Les Mayfield
Screenplay: John Hughes and Bill Walsh
Comedy/Fantasy
Rated PG
Younger kids: OK   Older kids: OK

Professor Philip Brainard, of Medfield College, is the living embodiment of an absentminded professor.

He's so distracted by his work that he keeps forgetting about his own wedding! But one day he stumbles onto an amazing discovery, which he calls flubber (short for "flying rubber"). His fiancée (Marcia Gay Harden) will no longer speak to him and even goes to the school's big basketball game with his romantic rival, Wilson Croft (Christopher McDonald). In order to impress her with his invention, he applies flubber to the team's sneakers, which sends them bouncing to an amazing victory. But the person most impressed is a sinister businessman (Raymond Barry) whose son attends Medfield. He wants to steal the substance and exploit its money-making potential . . . and that's where the plot thickens.

Robin Williams would seem to be the ideal person to rediscover flubber in this remake of Disney's 1961 comedy hit **The Absent Minded Professor**. But in fact the constraints of the role make him more a straight man than comedian, and John Hughes' wrongheaded script treats the whole film in much the same manner. It's actually dull at times and forgoes some of the best comedy set pieces from the original movie.

Kids of the '90s will no longer be astonished to see a car fly—as small fry of an earlier generation were when Fred MacMurray took flight—but the flubberized basketball game is still good for laughs, the best laughs in the film, in fact.

Still, it's a far cry from a classic comedy—another case of Hughes "improving" a movie by rewriting it into oblivion, as he did with **Miracle on 34th Street** and **101 Dalmatians**.

The villainy is fairly sinister,

and the slapstick violence is the cause of the PG rating, along with a few four-letter words.

FLUKE (1995)
Color, 95 minutes
Cast: Matthew Modine, Nancy Travis, Eric Stoltz, Max Pomeranc, Comet (Fluke), Barney (Rumbo); voice of Samuel L. Jackson (Rumbo)
Director: Carlo Carlei
Screenplay: Carlei and James Carrington, based on the novel by James Herbert
Animal story/Comedy-drama
Rated PG
Younger children: OK, with caution   Older children: OK

This unusual dog story, more dramatic and artful than most, will appeal to all ages. The story begins with a fatal car crash that sends the soul of young family man Thomas Johnson (Matthew Modine) through a tunnel of light . . . and a rebirth as a puppy named Fluke. Scavenging the streets of Atlanta, Fluke is adopted by a homeless woman for a short time before her death, then is befriended by fellow lost canine, Rumbo (voice of Samuel L. Jackson). Rumbo teaches Fluke the proper way to urinate on the street and how to beg for food at restaurants.

Fluke recalls much of his former life and decides to seek out his human family. When he's held captive in a cosmetics laboratory, Fluke is rescued by Rumbo, who puts his life on the line. Fluke tries to fit in with his family and make good with his former business partner. Shot from a dog's point of view, the film tries to impart a Capra-esque message: enjoy the life you have.

Young kids will find this film entertaining, but parents should be warned: there are quite a few deaths of likable characters in the course of the story, and this will naturally upset children, especially sensitive ones. (Didn't this concern the filmmakers at all?) There is also a rather intense dog attack in one scene.

Fluke is played by Comet, familiar to many kids from the popular *Full House* TV series.

THE FLY (1958)
Color, 94 minutes
Cast: Al (David) Hedison, Patricia Owens, Vincent Price, Herbert Marshall, Charles Herbert, Kathleen Freeman
Director: Kurt Neumann
Screenplay: James Clavell, from the short story by George Langelaan
Science fiction–horror/ Melodrama
Unrated
Younger kids: No   Older kids: OK

A happily married scientist (Hedison) is trying to find a way to transmit objects through space, like TV signals, but when he tries out his "matter transmitter" on himself, something goes terribly wrong.

The movie is structured like a mystery: the husband keeps his head covered with a black scarf, and we—like his wife—become intensely curious to find out what's under it. The movie's surprise is well known enough by now that it's safe to reveal he has the enlarged head of a housefly, while a fly has ended up with his head in miniature form.

Some of the dialogue is dated, and the very last scene, involving

Price, Marshall, and a spiderweb, often sends people into gales of laughter, but children might not react this way. The "unmasking" scene still carries a wallop, and the focus on a (formerly) happy family has the potential of involving children in a way that might disturb them. Older kids who are used to horror movies, however, will take it in stride.

Caution: The remake, directed by David Cronenberg, is a better movie, but it's rated R, and with good reason.

FLY AWAY HOME (1996)
Color, 107 minutes
Cast: Anna Paquin, Jeff Daniels, Dana Delany, Terry Kinney
Director: Carroll Ballard
Screenplay: Robert Rodat and Vince McKewin, based on an autobiography by Bill Lishman
Drama/Adventure/Animal story
Rated PG
Young children: OK Older children: VG

Fly Away Home is a thoughtful and entertaining story that will charm both children and their parents. When her mother is killed in an auto accident, 13-year-old Amy Alden (Anna Paquin) is dispatched to rural Ontario to live with her father (Jeff Daniels), an eccentric inventor who is well meaning but ill equipped to raise an adolescent girl. Amy proceeds to retreat into her own solitary world but one day rescues some goose eggs from a marsh near her father's property. The eggs soon hatch, and Amy becomes godmother to a flock of goslings. Her father then explains that because they have no mother, he and Amy will have to find a way to teach these geese

to fly south for the winter. This becomes an amazing adventure for father, daughter, and their feathered friends.

Fly Away Home is an intelligent and compassionate movie, inspired by the real-life experiences of a man who did indeed find a way to "imprint" young geese. Amy is a difficult character to play, but Anna Paquin (who earned an Oscar for *The Piano*) offers a beautifully nuanced performance.

Parents should be aware, however, that the death of Amy's mother in the first scene of the film is, naturally, quite upsetting.

FOLLOW THE FLEET (1936)
Black & white, 110 minutes
Cast: Fred Astaire, Ginger Rogers, Randolph Scott, Harriet Hilliard, Astrid Allwyn, Harry Beresford, Lucille Ball, Betty Grable
Director: Mark Sandrich
Screenplay: Dwight Taylor and Allan Scott, based on the play *Shore Leave: A Sea-going Comedy in Three Acts* by Hubert Osborne
Musical
Unrated
Young children: VG Older children: VG

Fred Astaire trades in his top hat, tie, and tails for a sailor suit in this charming musical comedy, cast as Bake Baker, a sailor on shore leave in San Francisco who crosses the path of (and summarily romances) Sherry Martin (Ginger Rogers), his ex–dance partner. Meanwhile, a parallel affair unfolds involving Bake's sailor pal Bilge Smith (Randolph Scott) and Sherry's sister, Connie (Harriet Hilliard, who was to marry bandleader Ozzie Nelson and become the 1950s' perfect mom on TV's *Ozzie and Harriet*).

The plot is a simple Hollywood concoction, with romance, misunderstanding, and reconciliation. But the actors are charming, and the musical numbers a treat.

Irving Berlin, one of America's foremost songwriters, provided a perfect score, with songs both silly and sublime. "We Joined the Navy" gets things off on the right foot. (The sailors joined up to see the world, but what did they see? They saw the sea.) It's followed by a goofy "I'm Putting All My Eggs in One Basket," perhaps the most nonsensical routine in Astaire and Rogers' partnership. But the dramatic highlight is the duo's rendition of "Let's Face the Music and Dance."

This, like so many of their best numbers, tells a story through dance . . . a point worth making to young viewers who've grown up with MTV imagery. Here, Ginger plays a woman so down on her luck that she's thinking of killing herself until Fred steps in and lightens her thoughts through a romantic swirl of dance steps and the lovely lyrics of Berlin's song.

If you pay close attention, you'll see a young, blond Lucille Ball in one scene.

FOLLOW THE RIVER (1995)
Color, 93 minutes
Cast: Sheryl Lee, Eric Schweig, Ellen Burstyn, Tim Guinee, Renee O'Connor
Director: Martin Davidson
Screenplay: Jennifer Miller
Adventure
Rated PG
Young children: OK, with caution   Older children: VG

James Alexander Thom's 1981 historical novel about an actual pioneer woman who escaped from Indian captivity in 1755 is the source of this well-acted, location-photographed adventure film.

Mary Draper Ingles was 23 and expecting her third baby when Shawnees raided her peaceful Virginia Colony township, murdering many and kidnapping her. She was but one of an estimated two thousand homesteaders abducted during the French and Indian Wars.

Resolute and undaunted by her months of imprisonment, she managed to flee her captors, only to face a thousand miles of the uncharted Ohio Valley, fighting her way back to a husband who might or might not still be alive.

Did she make it? Well, let's simply say that this exhausting wilderness story is proof of the indomitable human spirit.

Mary's rugged odyssey may be too strong for younger viewers to take.

FOOTLOOSE (1984)
Color, 107 minutes
Cast: Kevin Bacon, Lori Singer, John Lithgow, Dianne Wiest, Christopher Penn, Sarah Jessica Parker, John Laughlin, Elizabeth Gorcey, Frances Lee McCain, Jim Young, Brian Wimmer
Director: Herbert Ross
Screenplay: Dean Pitchford
Musical/Drama
Rated PG
Young children: VG   Older children: VG

This lightly likable drama with music should be endearing to preteens on up to kids who are the ages of the story's characters. It is set in a small, ultra-religious (and ultimately, not so all-American) Midwestern town where the word of Shaw Moore (John Lithgow), a hellfire-and-brimstone preacher, is the rule. Moore has deemed that dancing and rock 'n' roll are verboten because, as the preacher pronounces, they are "obscene" and akin to "easy sexuality and relaxed morality."

Enter Ren McCormack (Kevin Bacon), who has just moved to the area from the big city. Ren is fun-loving and amiably aggressive, but he is not trusted, simply because he is an outsider. Like any normal teen, he likes rock 'n' roll and loves to boogie. He will not sit still for the preacher's ban and institutes a campaign to convince the town's adults to permit a high school prom. Adding to the conflict: the pretty girl with whom Ren becomes involved is the daughter of Preacher Moore.

Footloose features a lively soundtrack, sparked by the Deniece Williams hit "Let's Hear It for the Boy." Essentially it's a throwback to all those mid- and late-1950s low-budget rock 'n' roll movies in which adults expressed grave suspicions about the negative influence of this music—except this one is better made and filled with likable performances.

FORBIDDEN PLANET (1956)
Color, 98 minutes
Cast: Walter Pidgeon, Leslie Nielsen, Anne Francis, Jack Kelly, Warren Stevens, Robby the Robot
Director: Fred McLeod Wilcox
Screenplay: Cyril Hume, loosely based on William Shakespeare's *The Tempest*
Science fiction/Suspense adventure

Unrated
Younger kids: Good   Older kids: VG

In the future, the flying saucer–like spaceship C-57-D arrives from Earth on Altair-4, a distant planet, to investigate what became of a previous expedition. The crew finds a scientist and his beautiful daughter, as well as his servant/handyman Robby the Robot—and a baffling mystery not only concerning the rest of the previous expedition but the wise and noble race, called the Krel, that used to inhabit the planet. (They were wiped out in a single night, ages ago.) Beneath the surface of the planet, their machines still operate.

Still one of the best science fiction films ever made, this remains fascinating for almost everyone, despite some inept moments of humor and rather plodding direction. The special effects hold up perfectly, the mystery is intriguing, and the screenplay is surprisingly rich in detail. Some elements of the story may require explanation, even to older kids. Get ready to look up *id* in your dictionary.

It's occasionally scary for younger kids, but they should handle it fine with parents in the room. If possible, this should be seen only in a letterboxed, or CinemaScope print. The screenplay is loosely based on Shakespeare's *The Tempest* (English teachers take note), and the movie's influence on the later *Star Trek* is obvious.

Contemporary moviegoers may need to remind themselves that the Leslie Nielsen who stars here and barely cracks a smile is the same actor who's become associated almost exclusively with wacky comedy (**Airplane!**, *Naked Gun*, *Mr. Magoo*) in the 1980s and '90s.

FOREVER YOUNG (1992)
Color, 102 minutes
Cast: Mel Gibson, Jamie Lee Curtis, Elijah Wood, Isabel Glasser, George Wendt, Joe Morton, Nicholas Surovy, David Marshall Grant
Director: Steve Miner
Screenplay: Jeffrey Abrams
Romance/Science fiction
Rated PG
Younger children: OK (some coarse language)   Older children: OK

In 1939, when test pilot Daniel McCormick's girlfriend is injured and becomes comatose, he volunteers for an experiment in cryogenics, allowing himself to be frozen for a year rather than have to wait to see if she will recover. Decades later, after being forgotten in a warehouse, he is accidentally unfrozen by two little boys and then tries to adjust to a life in which nothing is familiar.

This old-fashioned tearjerker, despite its improbabilities and uneven script, is redeemed by the charisma of its star, Mel Gibson, and his character's interaction with a young boy (Elijah Wood) who wants to fly.

The language makes it unsuitable for very young children, but it should appeal to any older child with a sense of the romantic.

FORREST GUMP (1994)
Color, 142 minutes
Cast: Tom Hanks, Gary Sinise, Robin Wright, Sally Field, Mykelti Williamson, Rebecca Williams
Director: Robert Zemeckis
Writer: Eric Roth, based on the novel by Winston Groom
Drama
Rated PG-13
Younger children: NG   Older children: OK, with caution

Forrest Gump is a fable about an innocent—a man who is slow of mind but swift of feet. Forrest has been told by his loving mother (Sally Field) that life is like a box of chocolates; you never know what you're going to get. That proves to be true, as Forrest, through sheer inadvertence, manages to bump into most of the key historical events of the 1960s and '70s, meeting three presidents along the way, serving in Vietnam, and uncovering the Watergate burglary. The love of his life, aside from his mother, is his childhood friend Jenny, a restless spirit who finally settles down with Forrest when it's almost too late.

More sentimental than Winston Groom's satiric novel, this hugely popular movie (propelled by the hugely popular Tom Hanks) focuses on a likable simpleton, who proves to have more courage and integrity than most of the people around him. Because of this, the character of Forrest has a great appeal to curious adolescents.

But, as the film explores the canvas of American life in the '60s and '70s, it inevitably offers adult language and situations, nudity, sex, and unremitting violence (in the Vietnam segment). We see drunks, druggies, and prostitutes.

For all that, it remains a highly moral film, and if your older children are anxious to see it and you're willing to expose them to the darker side of life it depicts,

they will take away indelible
memories of the good man who
serves as the foundation of the
story.

4D MAN (1959)
Color, 85 minutes
Cast: Robert Lansing, Lee
  Meriwether, James Congdon,
  Robert Strauss, Edgar Stehli,
  Patty Duke
Director: Irwin S. Yeaworth, Jr.
Screenplay: Theodore Simons
  and Cy Chermak
Science fiction/Suspense
Unrated
Younger kids: OK, with
  caution   Older kids: OK

Daring scientist Tony (Congdon)
is trying to find a way to allow
one solid object to pass through
another. But it's his staid older
brother Scott (Lansing), also a
scientist, who comes up with the
means, which he uses on himself.
He now has the power to walk
through walls, which causes him to
age rapidly. He can regain youth,
however, by moving through other
people; they die of old age, and
he gets younger. When Scott goes
insane, Tony tries to find a way
to stop him.

This is really a science fiction
variation on the vampire theme,
but it is particularly well written,
with strong, convincing performances by the leads. Younger
children are not likely to be bothered too much by the scary
scenes, and the shaky special effects might make experienced
teens curl a jaded lip. But this
little-known movie is a solid piece
of sci-fi storytelling, so it could click
with more imaginative older kids.

FOUR FACES WEST (1948)
Black & white, 90 minutes
Cast: Joel McCrea, Frances Dee,
  Charles Bickford, Joseph
  Calleia
Director: Alfred E. Green
Screenplay: Graham Baker and
  Teddi Sherman, from the
  Saturday Evening Post
  novelette *Paso par Aqui (They
  Passed This Way)* by Eugene
  Maniove Rhodes
Western
Unrated
Younger children: OK   Older
  children: VG

Fugitive McCrea, a reluctant outlaw who turned to robbery to save
his father's ranch, is pursued by
determined but honest sheriff Pat
Garrett (Bickford). When he in-
terrupts his getaway to nurse a
stricken Mexican family back to
health, he's captured and must
face the law.

A heartfelt story about atone-
ment, this Western with a moral
may still reach out to young viewers. The turning point takes place
at New Mexico's Inscription
Rock, where for nearly five centuries travelers crossing the Spanish
trails on their way to the new
American West have stopped to
carve their names. The site is now
preserved and protected by the
National Park Service.

Note: This absorbing character
study once made Ripley's "Believe It or Not" newspaper col-
umn, as Hollywood's only Western
in which not a single gunshot is
fired. These days, it's hard to
imagine such a thing.

Incidentally, the stars (McCrea
and Dee) were married in real
life.

THE FOUR FEATHERS (1939)
Color, 115 minutes
Cast: John Clements, Ralph
  Richardson, C. Aubrey Smith,
  June Duprez, Allan Jeayes
Director: Zoltan Korda
Screenplay: R. C. Sherriff, Lajos
  Biro, and Arthur Wimperis,
  based on the novel by
  A. E. W. Mason
Action-adventure
Unrated
Younger kids: OK   Older kids:
  VG

This is the best version of A. E. W.
Mason's classic novel about courage and cowardice, and stands as
the quintessential British adventure movie. John Clements stars
as Faversham, a young army officer who, after resigning his commission in 1898, is branded a
coward by three officers as well
as his fiancée (June Duprez). To
prove them wrong, Faversham
goes to Egypt and joins the Sudan
campaign, disguising himself as a
native to help the British army.

Though the old-fashioned story
gets melodramatic and the stiff-
upper-lip sentiments about tradition and honor are *veddy* British
(along with some now antiquated
attitudes toward colonialism), the
film is notable for its fine supporting cast (particularly Ralph Richardson as a blinded officer and C.
Aubrey Smith as a long-winded
tale-spinner), and especially for
its stupendous action scenes.
Filmed in dazzling Technicolor on
location in the Sudan with thousands of extras, the battles between the British and the native
"Fuzzy Wuzzies" are brilliantly
done, creating a sweeping tapestry of breathless impact.

**THE FOUR HUNDRED
BLOWS** (1959)
Black & white, 99 minutes
Cast: Jean-Pierre Léaud, Patrick
  Auffay, Claire Maurier, Albert
  Remy, Jeanne Moreau
Director: François Truffaut
Screenplay: Truffaut and Marcel
  Boussy
Drama
Unrated
Younger kids: OK   Older kids:
  VG

Former film critic François Truffaut helped to start the French
"New Wave" and made one of
the most auspicious directorial de-
buts in movie history with this
shattering, autobiographical film
about a lonely and neglected 12-
year-old who wanders the streets
of Paris committing petty crimes
and eventually winds up in a reform school for juvenile delinquents. The young Jean-Pierre
Léaud is perfect as Truffaut's
alter ego Antoine Doinel, a character which he and the director
would revisit in several subsequent films.

This is a beautiful film, both poetic and realistic at the same time,
examining the joy and pain of adolescence. It's one of the best
films ever made about childhood,
treating it in a mature and understanding manner that never suc-
cumbs to sentimentality.

It's too mature, in fact, for
young children, but adolescents
who don't mind reading subtitles
may fall under its spell.

THE FOUR MUSKETEERS
(1975)
Color, 108 minutes
Cast: Michael York, Oliver
  Reed, Richard Chamberlain,
  Frank Finlay, Faye Dunaway,

Charlton Heston, Raquel
Welch, Christopher Lee,
Geraldine Chaplin
Director: Richard Lester
Screenplay: George MacDonald
Fraser, based on the novel by
Alexandre Dumas
Swashbuckler/Action-adventure
Rated PG
Younger kids: OK   Older kids:
VG

The swashbuckling three musketeers (Oliver Reed, Richard Chamberlain, Frank Finlay) and their
comrade, D'Artagnan (Michael
York), attempt to protect King
Louis XIII (Jean-Pierre Cassel) and
his queen (Geraldine Chaplin)
from the scheming Cardinal Richelieu (Charlton Heston) and his per-
fidious accomplice, Milady de
Winter (Faye Dunaway).

Director Richard Lester's follow-up to his 1974 hit **The Three
Musketeers** is much more somber
in tone (even though the two films
were shot simultaneously) but is
still great fun, with equal measures of pratfalls, action, and suspense. Dunaway is especially good
as the vengeance-seeking Milady,
whose mysterious past is revealed.
Parents should know that the film
is rife with sexual innuendo and
double entendre, all in the spirit
of fun.

THE FOX AND THE HOUND
(1981)
Color, 83 minutes
Cast: Voices of Mickey Rooney,
Keith Mitchell, Kurt Russell,
Corey Feldman, Pearl Bailey,
Pat Buttram, Sandy Duncan,
Dick Bakalyan, Paul Winchell,
Jack Albertson, Jeanette
Nolan

Directors: Art Stevens, Ted
Berman, and Richard Rich
Screenplay: Larry Clemmons,
Berman, Peter Young, Steve
Hulett, David Michener,
Burny Mattinson, Earl Kress,
and Vance Gerry, based on
the book by Daniel F. Mannix
Animated feature
Rated G
Young children: VG   Older
children: OK

This easygoing Disney animated
feature represented a transition
from the "old guard" of animators and story men to a new generation of talent.

The story is simple: an orphaned baby fox named Tod and
a puppy named Copper become
best of friends one summer, but
things change the following spring
as the puppy grows into an expert
hunting dog and is taught to
hate foxes.

This gentle film comes alive
during an exciting climax involving Tod's battle with a ferocious
grizzly bear. Mild comedy relief is
provided by two mixed-up birds
who are chasing a caterpillar, while
the songs favor Big Mama Owl, a
warmhearted character voiced by
entertainer Pearl Bailey.

No one can compete with the
Disney studio when it comes to
fashioning cute, appealing characters, and that's what comes
through most of all in *The Fox
and the Hound.* Young children
are bound to enjoy watching Tod
and Copper, though those same
youngsters might find the climactic fight with the grizzly bear a
bit intense.

FRA DIAVOLO (see **The
Devil's Brother**)

FRANCIS (1949)
Black & white, 91 minutes
Cast: Donald O'Connor, Patricia
  Medina, ZaSu Pitts, Ray
  Collins, John McIntire
Director: Arthur Lubin
Screenplay: David Stern, based
  on his novel
Comedy
Unrated
Younger kids: Good   Older
  kids: Good

This was the first in a series of
crowd-pleasing escapist comedies
about the misadventures of a talking Army mule named Francis
and his amiable if none-too-bright
G.I. pal (Donald O'Connor).
  O'Connor stars as newly com-
missioned lieutenant Peter Stirling, who gets lost behind enemy
lines in Burma during World War
II and is rescued by the loqua-
cious jackass. When Peter tries to
tell his superiors about the amazing Francis, they don't believe
him, since Francis stubbornly refuses to speak to anybody but
Peter. The lieutenant is thrown
into the psychiatric hospital for
observation.
  Francis is silly but still irresistibly amusing, thanks to a good
comedy-fantasy premise and the
convincing trick work that actually makes it look like Francis is
talking. Today it would all be
done with digital animation, but
back in the '40s and '50s, director
Arthur Lubin (who later put his
expertise to use by creating the
Mr. Ed TV series) got the mule
to move his mouth by putting
chewing gum and tobacco in its
mouth. (He also relied on photo-
graphic and editing tricks.)
  Francis's voice is provided by
character actor Chill Wills, who puts
the whole thing over with a wry,
folksy drawl and cracker-barrel
charm. Most of the movie's laughs
arise from the fact that Francis is
smarter than all of the human soldiers (including a young Tony Curtis, billed here as Anthony).
  Though dated in its wartime
service humor and containing
some Japanese stereotypes, kids
should still enjoy the film's basic
concept and the uproarious scenes
featuring the wisecracking mule.
  If you and your family want to
see more of Francis, all seven of
his starring films are available on
video: **Francis Goes to the Races,**
*Francis Goes to West Point, Francis
in the Big Town, Francis Joins the
Wacs, Francis in the Navy,* and the
final entry, *Francis in the Haunted
House,* in which Mickey Rooney replaced Donald O'Connor.

**FRANCIS GOES TO THE
RACES** (1951)
Black & white, 88 minutes
Cast: Donald O'Connor, Piper
  Laurie, Cecil Kellaway, Jesse
  White, Barry Kelley
Director: Arthur Lubin
Screenplay: Oscar Brodney and
  David Stern, based on a story
  by Robert Arthur and
  characters created by Stern
Comedy
Unrated
Younger kids: Good   Older
  kids: Good

Francis Goes to the Races is the
second entry in the whimsical series about Francis the talking
mule and picks right up where the
first one left off. After telling his
stuffy bank manager boss about
Francis' abilities, Peter (Donald
O'Connor) is fired from his job
and winds up staying at a horse-
breeding ranch where Francis recognizes a thoroughbred called Sir

Gallant as one of his distant relatives. While Francis cheers up the "emotionally frustrated" horse, Peter becomes smitten by a different Frances (Piper Laurie), the pretty granddaughter of the ranch's owner (Cecil Kellaway). Using tips straight from the mule's and horses' mouths, Peter makes a small bundle at the racetrack, which rouses the interest of the racetrack detective (Jesse White) as well as a gambler named Mallory (Barry Kelley), neither of whom believes that Francis is a talking tout.

This is innocuous fluff, but in some ways it's funnier than the original film, since we already know about Francis and we can get right to the farcical plot. Cecil Kellaway as the kindly grandfather and the inimitable Jesse White as the exasperated track dick provide some excellent comic support, while Chill Wills (the voice of Francis) is in fine form. The well-trained mule speaks in pig Latin at one point, and in a comic highlight, the usually tight-lipped animal gets drunk and starts blabbing to everyone in sight.

The comedy is on a pretty juvenile level, but there are some outlandish compensations for adults, such as a truly surreal sequence where Francis psychoanalyzes an insecure horse while it's lying on a straw "couch."

FRANKENSTEIN (1931)
Black & white, 70 minutes
Cast: Colin Clive, Mae Clarke, John Boles, Boris Karloff, Edward Van Sloan, Frederick Kerr, Dwight Frye, Lionel Belmore
Director: James Whale
Screenplay: Francis Edward Faragoh, Garrett Fort, and John L. Balderston, from the play by Peggy Webling, based on Mary Shelley's novel *Frankenstein; Or, a Modern Prometheus*
Horror/Literary classic
Unrated
Younger kids: Too scary Older kids: OK

Alone in a stone tower, Henry Frankenstein (Clive), a young scientist, pieces together parts salvaged from dead bodies and brings his creation (Karloff) to life. Unknown to Frankenstein, his hunchbacked assistant (Frye) has provided him with a deranged criminal brain instead of the perfect one he sought. The Monster kills the assistant and flees from the tower, then ravages the countryside.

Frankenstein will seem primitive to many contemporary viewers, both young and old; its filmmaking style is prosaic, and it cries out for a music score (which, in the days of early talkies, was a rarity). But it still has the power to impress and frighten; in fact, some sequences are still quite powerful, particularly the scenes in the tower and when Dr. Frankenstein confronts his creation in the old mill at the end. Boris Karloff's brilliant performance is still disturbing in its strange blend of sympathetic innocence and menace. Nowhere is this more evident than in the famous scene—censored for many years—in which he meets a young girl who's too sweet and innocent to be afraid of him. He responds to her kindness with childlike glee, but doesn't understand that while the flower petals they toss into the pond will float, a little girl will not.

Moments like this make *Frankenstein* off-limits for younger children, even after all these years.

Older children, on the other hand, may find the film a fascinating antique. Just when they're tempted to dismiss it as boring or slow, a scene will come up that could haunt them for years to come. It's important to point out to movie-savvy kids that *Frankenstein* (released the same year as **Dracula** by the same studio, Universal Pictures) virtually invented what we know as the horror movie.

It was followed by a long line of sequels.

FRANKENSTEIN CREATED WOMAN (1967)
Color, 92 minutes
Cast: Peter Cushing, Susan Denberg, Thorley Walters, Robert Morris, Duncan Lamont, Peter Blythe, Barry Warren, Derek Fowlds
Director: Terence Fisher
Screenplay: "John Elder" (Anthony Hinds)
Science fiction–horror/Sequel
Unrated
Younger kids: No Older kids: Marginal

In this perfunctory entry in the Hammer Frankenstein series, Dr. Frankenstein (the reliable Cushing) is experimenting with capturing souls at the moment of physical death. When his assistant Hans (Morris) is unjustly executed and his crippled, deformed fiancée, Christina (Denberg), drowns herself in grief, Frankenstein revives Christina and infuses her with Hans' soul. Christina, now beautiful, seeks revenge on those who really committed the crime Hans was executed for.

Frankenstein takes a backseat to the movie's events, helplessly watching while Christina carries out Hans' gory revenge. As with most of the later Hammer films, while there's no nudity, this does emphasize sex to a degree that might worry some parents.

Followed by **Frankenstein Must Be Destroyed!**

FRANKENSTEIN MEETS THE WOLF MAN (1943)
Black & white, 74 minutes
Cast: Lon Chaney (Jr.), Bela Lugosi, Ilona Massey, Patric Knowles, Lionel Atwill, Maria Ouspenskaya, Dennis Hoey, Dwight Frye
Director: Roy William Neill
Screenplay: Curt Siodmak
Science fiction–horror
Young children: OK, with caution Older children: OK

Werewolf Larry Talbot (Chaney) learns from the old gypsy woman (Ouspenskaya) who befriended him in **The Wolf Man** that he can never die. Desperate, Talbot searches for Dr. Frankenstein, who knew the secrets of life and death. Frankenstein, however, is long dead—but his Monster (Lugosi) still lives. Talbot convinces Frankenstein's descendant Elsa (Massey) and her friend Dr. Mannering (Knowles) to help him find death, but, of course, things don't work out so smoothly.

In the previous entry in the series, **The Ghost of Frankenstein,** the Monster ended up with the brain of the evil Ygor, so this movie was originally shot with the Monster still having Ygor's brain and voice. Advance audiences didn't like that, so all scenes of the Monster speaking were removed. This probably helped give *Frankenstein Meets the Wolf Man* the liveliest pace of any film in the classic Universal monster series. It's great fun. Lugosi wasn't suited to play Frankenstein's Monster, but Chaney gives a vigorous, committed performance as the troubled Larry Talbot, one of his best in a horror movie.

Unlike most Universal horror movies of this period, this one is occasionally pretty scary, particularly in the opening scene. While it's mostly a lively adventure, younger kids might find some of it rough going—though a parent nearby would most likely smooth over the bumps.

It was followed by **House of Frankenstein.**

FRANKENSTEIN MUST BE DESTROYED! (1969)
Color, 97 minutes
Cast: Peter Cushing, Simon Ward, Veronica Carlson, Thorley Walters, Freddie Jones, Maxine Audley, Geoffrey Bayldon, George Pravda
Director: Terence Fisher
Screenplay: Bert Batt
Science fiction–horror/Sequel
Rated PG
Young children: No Older children: Maybe

Fleeing authorities, Dr. Frankenstein (Cushing) takes up residence in the boardinghouse managed by Anna (Carlson), then blackmails Karl (Ward), her doctor fiancé, into helping him with his sinister experiments in transferring brains from one body to another. But this time, the result is no monster, but a man who's deeply horrified by what Frankenstein has done.

The best in the Hammer Frankenstein series, this intense, even shocking movie examines themes usually only lightly touched on in other entries. In other Hammers, Frankenstein himself has occasionally been sympathetic, but here he's a cruel, soulless zealot, and Cushing is forceful in the role. This is pretty strong stuff, today as much as when the film was made. Even if your kids have come to love Hammer and Peter Cushing, check this one out yourself first.

Warning: Some versions include a brutal and unnecessary (though not graphic) rape scene.

FREAKY FRIDAY (1977)
Color, 98 minutes
Cast: Jodie Foster, Barbara Harris, John Astin, Patsy Kelly, Dick Van Patten, Vicki Schreck, Sorrell Booke, Ruth Buzzi
Director: Gary Nelson
Screenplay: Mary Rodgers, based on her novel
Comedy/Fantasy
Rated G
Young children: VG Older children: VG

The talented writer Mary Rodgers (daughter of renowned Broadway composer Richard Rodgers) was hired by the Disney studio to adapt her own novel, *Freaky Friday,* and while the idea of a grown-up and youngster switching places has been done many times, this remains one of the very best. Credit for that must go to Rodgers and to the two talented actresses who star in this film, teenage Jodie Foster and Broadway veteran Barbara Harris.

Harris plays a busy mother who thinks her teenage daughter has a pretty carefree life; similarly, her daughter thinks her mom gets off easy. When, by magic, they switch personalities for a day, they both learn better. The fun here is watching Harris, an adult, act like a kid, and vice versa.

Adults may be disappointed that the story winds up, in typical Disney fashion of the day, with a slapstick car chase, but kids probably won't mind. What counts is the fun of the premise and the delightful way it's carried out by its stars.

Freaky Friday was remade by Disney for television in 1995 with Shelley Long and Gaby Hoffmann.

FREE WILLY (1993)
Color, 112 minutes
Cast: Jason James Richter, Lori Petty, Michael Madsen, Jayne Atkinson, Michael Ironside, August Schellenberg, Richard Riehle, Mykelti Williamson
Director: Simon Wincer
Screenplay: Keith A. Walker, Corey Blechman, and Tom Benedek, based on a story by Walker
Adventure/Animal story
Rated PG
Younger kids: Good   Older kids: Good

When delinquent 12-year-old street kid Jesse (Jason James Richter) is ordered to perform community service cleaning up an aquatic theme park, he forges a special bond with a lonely orca named Willy who is thought to be untrainable. But Jesse is able to get through to Willy—and vice versa—and then has to rescue the whale when he discovers that the unscrupulous park owner plans on doing away with it for the insurance money.

The first of three Willy adventures (so far) is the best of the series, and though the script is formulaic (especially from an adult point of view), this is a warm-hearted family film with good performances, beautiful Pacific Northwest scenery, and a nice moral for kids about friendship and maturity. The occasional use of four-letter words earned this a PG rating; young children may also be sensitive to the danger that both Willy and his young pal find themselves in before the inevitable happy ending. *Free Willy 2* and *3* are, for the most part, more of the same.

FRIENDLY PERSUASION (1956)
Color, 140 minutes
Cast: Gary Cooper, Dorothy McGuire, Anthony Perkins, Marjorie Main, Richard Eyer, Walter Catlett, Robert Middleton, (Peter) Mark Richman, William Schallert
Director: William Wyler
Screenplay: Michael Wilson, based on the novel by Jessamyn West
Drama
Unrated
Younger kids: OK   Older kids: VG

This is a fine, homespun piece of Americana about the ethics of violence, focusing on a Quaker family in 1862 Indiana whose peaceful existence is threatened by the Civil War. When a Union officer arrives to recruit soldiers for the army, the family's son (Anthony Perkins) is torn between his religious beliefs and the fear that he'll be thought a coward. Over the objections of his devout mother (Dorothy McGuire),

195

he joins up when word comes that Southern raiders are approaching.

William Wyler's meticulous direction captures a real sense of time and place. The cast couldn't possibly be better; Gary Cooper gives one of his warmest performances as the family patriarch, and Perkins is ideal in his second film appearance. The young man's ethical dilemma is sure to strike a responsive chord in any viewer old enough to understand what he's going through.

THE FRISCO KID (1979)
Color, 122 minutes
Cast: Gene Wilder, Harrison Ford, Ramon Bieri, Val Bisoglio, George Ralph DiCenzo, Leo Fuchs, Penny Peyser, William Smith, Jack Somack
Director: Robert Aldrich
Screenplay: Michael Elias and Frank Shaw
Western/Comedy-drama
Rated PG
Younger kids: OK, with caution   Older kids: OK

Gene Wilder stars as Avram Belinsky, a Polish rabbi who travels from his homeland to San Francisco to head a new congregation and marry the daughter of a prominent citizen. Unfortunately, once he arrives in America, Belinsky is robbed and winds up working on a railroad gang. Eventually he teams up with an unlikely partner, outlaw Tommy Lillard (Ford), who grudgingly helps the rabbi get to his destination.

A curious comedy, to say the least, especially coming from director Robert Aldrich, who was known mainly for tough melodramas and brutal action films, *The Frisco Kid* does have its oddball

charms. The tone and Wilder's performance are broad enough to keep kids entertained, along with the presence of Harrison Ford. But the heart of the film is the amusing clash of cultures between naïve, Orthodox Belinsky and tough-talking Lillard.

Their friendship evolves in interesting ways. Even as he learns to adapt to the West's wild ways, the rabbi always remains firm in his religious beliefs, and it pays off a number of times, especially when he and Lillard are captured by Indians who are impressed not only by Belinsky's courage in the face of certain death but by his dancing!

Parents will appreciate the serious, thoughtful examination of violence that also runs through the film: Belinsky is forced to kill a villain and must wrestle with the consequences of his actions, and later manages to defeat an adversary without resorting to bloodshed at all. He does, however, have to adopt one of his outlaw partner's less endearing epithets (parents be warned).

FROM THE MIXED-UP FILES OF MRS. BASIL E. FRANKWEILER (1973) (aka The Hideaways)
Color, 105 minutes
Cast: Ingrid Bergman, Sally Prager, Johnny Doran, George Rose, Richard Mulligan, Georgann Johnson, Madeline Kahn
Director: Fielder Cook
Screenplay: Blanche Hanalis, based on the novel by E. L. Konigsburg
Comedy/Suspense
Rated G
Younger children: OK   Older children: OK

Claudia (Sally Prager) and her little brother Jamie (Johnny Doran) run away from home and set up housekeeping in New York City's Metropolitan Museum of Art. They bathe themselves—and their clothes—in a fountain and sleep in an exhibit, somehow managing to avoid the security guards. A mystery soon presents itself to the fugitives in the form of a statue that may or may not have been created by Michelangelo. Determined to find the statue's true origin, the kids meet up with the very rich and very eccentric Mrs. Basil E. Frankweiler (Ingrid Bergman), who helps them in more ways than one.

Although nothing special, *From the Mixed-up Files of Mrs. Basil E. Frankweiler* is a pleasant enough diversion, and children who have read the well-known book may enjoy seeing it come to life.

THE FRONT (1976)
Color, 94 minutes
Cast: Woody Allen, Zero
    Mostel, Herschel Bernardi,
    Michael Murphy, Andrea
    Marcovicci, Remak Ramsay,
    Joshua Shelley, Lloyd Gough,
    Danny Aiello, Charles
    Kimbrough
Director: Martin Ritt
Screenplay: Walter Bernstein
Comedy-drama
Rated PG
Young children: No Older
    children: VG

This poignant comedy-drama offers a basic course in the whos, whats, and whys of the infamous Hollywood blacklist of the 1950s, when successful show business personalities and creators were forced to go underground because

they were accused of being Communists. Woody Allen stars as Howard Prince, a none-too-bright New Yorker who is enlisted by Alfred Miller, a newly blacklisted writer and his old high school buddy, to serve as a "front." In order for Alfred to continue in his profession, Howard's name will appear on the screenplays he submits for production. The ruse works, and Prince soon finds himself fronting other writers and lauded as a brilliant new scenarist.

While plenty of comedy is mined from this premise, the sadness and irony of the situation are never soft-pedaled. This is reflected in the character of Hecky Brown (Zero Mostel), a rotund comic who is unable to deal with his lot as a blacklistee. The fate of the vulnerable Hecky serves as a reminder of how the blacklist destroyed the lives of people whose only crime was being liberal and humanist in a time of reactionary conservatism. (It's important to point out to younger viewers that while some of the blacklisted artists were indeed Communists, others suffered merely because they associated with the wrong people, attended rallies, or were seen in the wrong place at the wrong time.)

Adding to the potency of *The Front* is the knowledge that director Martin Ritt, screenwriter Walter Bernstein, and cast members Mostel, Herschel Bernardi, Joshua Shelley, and Lloyd Gough all were blacklisted in real life during the 1950s. Their names are cited in the film's end titles.

Although first and foremost an entertaining movie, *The Front* also serves as a perfect introduction to a fascinating—and profoundly sad—period of recent

American history. It will have little or no appeal for younger kids and does contain one prominent four-letter word in a key climactic scene. For children who are interested in (or might even be studying) this period, the film will dramatize and personalize what might otherwise seem an abstract concept.

FUN & FANCY FREE (1947)
Color, 73 minutes
Cast: Edgar Bergen, Charlie McCarthy, Mortimer Snerd, Luana Patten
Director: Ben Sharpsteen
Screenplay: Homer Brightman, Harry Reeves, Ted Sears, Lance Nolley, Eldon Dedini, and Tom Oreb; "Bongo" based on a story by Sinclair Lewis
Animated feature
Rated G
Younger kids: VG   Older kids: VG

Mickey Mouse, Donald Duck, and Goofy appear together in *Fun & Fancy Free*, a slim but entertaining Disney animated feature comprised of two cartoons linked together by host Jiminy Cricket. The first is "Bongo," about a mistreated circus bear who runs away and falls in love with a female bear he meets in the woods. The second story is "Mickey and the Beanstalk," with ventriloquist Edgar Bergen relating the classic fairy tale to his dummies Charlie McCarthy and Mortimer Snerd, along with Disney child star Luana Patten. Jiminy watches as Edgar tells them a story about three starving farmers—Mickey Mouse, Donald Duck, and Goofy—who are so impoverished

that they have to sell their cow. Mickey brings home some magic beans and plants them, and while they're sleeping, a giant beanstalk begins to grow, carrying the three of them up into the clouds. Once there, they come upon a castle and do battle with Willie the Giant.

"Bongo," which is based on a story by Pulitzer Prize–winning novelist Sinclair Lewis, is definitely the lesser of the two cartoons. Although it's pleasantly animated and charmingly narrated and sung by Dinah Shore, the story is maudlin and innocuous. The second segment is much better. Mickey, Donald, and Goofy's battles with the giant are very funny, as is character actor Billy Gilbert's characterization of Willie (featuring his trademark sneezing-fit routine) and his rendition of "Fe, Fi, Fo, Fum." The segment is beautifully animated, particularly when the beanstalk grows into the sky and carries the sleeping trio along with it, and in the scene where they try to eat Willie's food and Goofy gets stuck in a giant plate of Jell-O.

The live-action footage with Edgar Bergen and his dummies—who, it should be pointed out to younger viewers, were tremendous stars on radio at the time—is sometimes quite amusing, especially during some of Charlie McCarthy's surprisingly nasty wisecracks (urging Donald to kill the cow, calling Bergen a ham, and comparing his storytelling to a sleeping pill). As always, Cliff "Ukulele Ike" Edwards is wonderful as the voice of Jiminy. The voice of Mickey was provided by Walt Disney himself.

Fun & Fancy Free is a relatively

minor Disney work, but it's still enjoyable.

FUNNY FACE (1957)
Color, 103 minutes
Cast: Fred Astaire, Audrey Hepburn, Kay Thompson, Michel Auclair, Robert Flemyng, Virginia Gibson, Suzy Parker, Ruta Lee
Director: Stanley Donen
Screenplay: Leonard Gershe
Musical
Unrated
Young children: OK   Older children: VG

Adolescents and teenage girls in particular will be attracted to this well-mounted musical romance with a score by George and Ira Gershwin. The story concerns a middle-aged fashion magazine photographer (Fred Astaire) and his attraction to a lovely young model (Audrey Hepburn). Here, for a pleasant change, the model is no airhead, but a free-spirited intellectual. When first introduced, she is working as a clerk in a Greenwich Village bookshop. For a time she becomes caught up in the whirl of the Paris fashion world, in a segment which provides a dazzling depiction of the City of Light. There even is a number called "Bonjour Paris" sung by Astaire, Hepburn, and flamboyant magazine editor Kay Thompson (who, by the way, was the creator of the classic children's book *Eloise*), as the trio dances from one famous Paris site to another.

As the plot moves along, Hepburn sours on the superficiality of high fashion and falls back into her old bookish habits, including attending a kooky meeting of pseudo-intellectual Empathetical-

ists, who are satirically depicted as a beat-generation group in black turtleneck shirts. Otherwise, Givenchy fashions dominate this May–December romance. Top numbers include "Think Pink," an energetic piece featuring Thompson in the offices of the fashion magazine, "How Long Has This Been Going On?," and the melodic tender finale "'S' Wonderful," performed by Astaire and Hepburn.

While the film is wildly colorful, it is also stylized and sophisticated and probably not of great interest to younger kids. Teenage girls, on the other hand, seem to have a great affinity for Audrey Hepburn.

FUNNY GIRL (1968)
Color, 155 minutes
Cast: Barbra Streisand, Omar Sharif, Walter Pidgeon, Kay Medford, Anne Francis, Lee Allen, Gerald Mohr, Frank Faylen
Director: William Wyler
Screenplay: Isobel Lennarts, based on her Broadway play
Musical/Biography
Rated G
Young children: OK   Older children: VG

When Barbra Streisand sings "I'm the Greatest Star (but No One Knows It)" she's playing someone else, but the lyrics seem to embody the emotions Streisand must have felt as a young woman determined to make it in show business. That's why this role was so perfect for her—and why it made her a bona fide star, first on Broadway, then in Hollywood. This was her film debut, and for it she won an Academy Award as Best Actress.

Funny Girl is the bittersweet story of Fanny Brice, a homely girl from the tenements who rose to become one of America's best-loved comediennes and entertainers in the 1920s and '30s. Along the way, she fell in love with a suave gambler named Nick Arnstein (Omar Sharif), who would break her heart more than once with promises unkept.

Fanny worked for the fabled Broadway producer Florenz Ziegfeld (Walter Pidgeon), who was known for his opulent productions featuring beautiful women in elegant and improbable costumes. This film re-creates some of those Ziegfeld production numbers, which are fun to see, but there's no question where the focus of attention always goes: Streisand is incomparable in her renditions of such songs as "People" and "Don't Rain on My Parade," as well as some of Fanny Brice's famous numbers, "My Man" and the comic "Second Hand Rose."

Adolescents who've been bitten by the show-business bug will find this movie a special treat . . . but it's good entertainment for any audience (if not particularly trustworthy as biography). Younger kids may find the running time a problem and may squirm during the plottier portions of the picture.

It was followed in 1975 by a mediocre sequel called *Funny Lady*.

THE FURTHER ADVENTURES OF THE WILDERNESS FAMILY (1978)
Color, 105 minutes
Cast: Robert Logan, Susan D. Shaw, Heather Rattray, Ham Larsen, George "Buck" Flower
Director: Frank Zuniga
Screenplay: Arthur R. Dubs
Adventure
Rated G
Younger kids: Good   Older kids: Good

As the title indicates, this sequel to 1975's sleeper hit **The Adventures of the Wilderness Family** follows the continuing exploits of the Robinson family, who fled the city to live in a log cabin amid the splendor of the Rocky Mountains. This time around, they have to deal with avalanches, pneumonia, wolf attacks, and other natural hazards, but as expected, everything turns out all right in the end.

None of this is handled in a realistic manner that would scare small children, who'll enjoy the presence of dogs, bears, raccoons, and other friendly critters, and the magnificent scenery is expertly photographed by John Hora (**Gremlins**).

G

GAMERA, THE GUARDIAN OF THE UNIVERSE (1995)
Color, 96 minutes
Cast: Tsuyoshi Ihara, Akira Onodera, Ayako Fujitani, Shignobu Nakayama, Yukijiro Horatu, Takateru Manabe, Yumi Kameyama
Director: Shusuke Kaneko
Screenplay: Kazunori Ito
Science fiction/Monster
Unrated
Young children: Marginal   Older children: OK

Strange birdlike creatures attack—and eat—people on a small island near Japan. Scientists investigate and eventually capture the three creatures, placing them in a huge covered baseball stadium. A mysterious floating atoll is also investigated, yielding small, comma-shaped metal objects and an obelisk that disintegrates. A colossal turtle emerges from the sea and attacks the bird-creatures at the stadium, then disappears into the water again, after inflicting damage. Inscriptions from the obelisk provide names for the creatures: the turtle is Gamera, and the bird creatures are Gyaos.

The military and government want to use Gyaos against Gamera, but others are convinced that both were created centuries ago by a now lost race and that Gamera was created to protect humanity from the voracious Gyaos.

Back in the 1960s, Daiei's Gamera was a kind of second cousin to Godzilla from Toho studios, so when Toho revived Godzilla in 1985, eventually someone brought back Gamera. The surprise was that this movie is the very model of a modern *kaiju eiga* (Japanese for this kind of movie). Excellent effects, fine production values, good acting, and a solid story make this an entertaining film for almost anyone. Yes, it's about a giant fire-breathing flying turtle, but the treatment here is reasonable, logical, and actually mature. A genuine surprise and a rare treat for fans of this kind of movie.

Because Gyaos (there's eventually just one) is a potent menace, young children might find the movie pretty scary, although she mostly eats people offscreen.

GANDHI (1982)
Color, 188 minutes
Cast: Ben Kingsley, Candice Bergen, Edward Fox, John Gielgud, Trevor Howard, John Mills, Martin Sheen, Rohini Hattangandy, Ian Charleson, Athol Fugard, Roshan Seth, Saeed Jaffrey, John Ratzenberger, Geraldine James, Michael Hordern, Marius Weyers
Director: Richard Attenborough
Screenplay: John Briley
Historical drama/Biography
Rated PG
Younger kids: OK   Older kids: OK

Director/producer Attenborough spent over twenty years bringing this epic tale of Mohandas K. Gandhi to the screen; this multiple-Oscar-winning film follows Gandhi's transformation from lawyer to world spiritual leader and his quest for peace and freedom for India. It's a long film, but worthwhile as good old-fashioned epic storytelling, and Ben Kingsley is utterly convincing and captivating in the title role of the Mahatma. It is less impressive as history, however, with some issues simplified, many of the more complex elements of Gandhi's life left unexplored, and most of the supporting characters reduced to a parade of luminary cameos (Candice Bergen as Margaret Bourke-White, John Gielgud as Lord Irwin, etc.).

Knowing this, the film can be viewed as an entertaining primer on Gandhi's life and a forum for parents to discuss the methods of nonviolence and civil disobedience that Gandhi employed against the British Empire. Parents should also be aware of several violent set pieces, including a protest at the Dharsana Saltworks in 1930, where Gandhi's followers received beatings without retaliating, and the 1919 Amritsar massacre, in which over a thousand Indian citizens—men, women and children—were wounded or killed.

THE GAY DIVORCEE (1934)
Black & white, 107 minutes
Cast: Fred Astaire, Ginger
   Rogers, Alice Brady, Edward
   Everett Horton, Erik Rhodes,
   Eric Blore, Betty Grable
Director: Mark Sandrich
Screenplay: George Marion, Jr.,
   Dorothy Yost, and Edward
Kaufman, from the musical
   Gay Divorce by Dwight
   Taylor, Kenneth Webb, and
   Samuel Hoffenstein
Musical
Unrated
Young children: VG   Older
   children: VG

The Gay Divorcee is the very first film costarring Fred Astaire and Ginger Rogers, who first danced together in the previous year's *Flying Down to Rio* and caused a small sensation.

Astaire plays American dancer Guy Holden, who arrives in London at the tail end of a vacation and is attracted to Mimi Glossop (Rogers), who is unhappily married. Mimi wants a divorce, but given the laws of that era, she has to be caught with another man—which is where professional correspondent Rodolfo Tonetti (Erik Rhodes) comes in. . . .

But forget the plot. What makes this film so delightful is not just the interplay of the main characters and the wonderful comic actors who support them, but the outstanding musical numbers. In "A Needle in a Haystack," Astaire dances by himself and gracefully establishes the boundaries of his screen persona. The seventeen-minute extravaganza "The Continental" features Astaire and Rogers along with a battery of others doing 1930s-style dance formations. Best of all is "Night and Day," a romantic highpoint in which Astaire and Rogers dance by themselves in a ballroom.

The story elements of *The Gay Divorcee* may confuse (or even bore) some kids, but the musical numbers are still great to watch. The secret of Astaire and Rogers' work together was that they told a story through their dances, which is why those numbers hold up so well.

GAY PURR-EE (1962)
Color, 86 minutes
Cast: Voices of Judy Garland, Robert Goulet, Red Buttons, Hermione Gingold, Paul Frees, Morey Amsterdam, Mel Blanc
Director: Abe Levitow
Screenplay: Dorothy and Chuck Jones
Animated Feature/Musical
Rated G
Younger kids: OK   Older kids: OK

This is an odd, adult-skewed animated feature that may leave kids confused. Conceived by legendary Warner Bros. cartoon director Chuck Jones and his wife, directed by Jones collaborator Abe Levitow, and one of the last creative gasps from the innovative UPA studio, *Gay Purr-ee* is a strange blend of Hollywood cartoon, Broadway musical, and French art lesson.

Judy Garland provides the voice of Mewsette, a French farm cat who runs away to Paris in the 1890s, seeking fame and adventure. Her boyfriend, Jaune Tom (Robert Goulet), follows but is detoured to Alaska, where he stumbles upon a fortune in gold. Meanwhile, Mewsette becomes the darling of Paris society and an inspiration to the great artists of the day: Cezanne, Monet, Degas, Toulouse-Lautrec, Van Gogh, Picasso, et al. Jaune Tom returns to Paris to be with his true love but must first save Mewsette from catnappers in a climactic battle aboard a speeding train.

Colorful, stylish animation can't save the slow-moving story. Kids may wish for more action and fewer love songs (even though they're written by Harold Arlen and E. Y. Harburg, who wrote the songs for **The Wizard of Oz**).

Gay Purr-ee, with its pedigree, should be a lot better than it is. Most kids are likely to find it a bore.

THE GENERAL (1927)
Black & white, 74 minutes
Cast: Buster Keaton, Marion Mack, Glen Cavender, Jim Farley, Frederick Vroom, Charles Smith, Frank Barnes, Joseph Keaton, Mike Donlin
Directors: Buster Keaton and Clyde Bruckman
Screenplay: Al Boasberg and Charles Smith, based on William A. Pittenger's Civil War narrative *Daring and Suffering: A History of the Great Railway Adventure (The Great Locomotive Chase)*
Comedy/Silent classic
Unrated
Young children: VG   Older children: VG

Not only is *The General* Keaton's most ambitious film, but it is arguably his masterpiece. The setting is the Civil War, and the story (based on real incidents of the period) casts Buster as Johnnie Gray, a Southern train conductor who loves The General, his locomotive, almost as much as he adores Annabelle, his sweetheart. Johnnie attempts to enlist in the army but is spurned because his skills as an engineer are deemed more valuable to the Confederate cause. Thinking him a coward, Annabelle shuns Johnnie. But he is fated to prove his gallantry as enterprising Union spies steal his locomotive and kidnap Annabelle, and Johnnie sets out to recover both The General and the girl.

The General is loaded with classic Keaton moments, but all within the context of an exciting story that never stops to take a breath; in fact, much of the story takes place on a moving railroad train. It is this solid foundation—along with Buster's incredible ingenuity—that makes *The General* something more than a "mere" slapstick comedy. (Some thirty years later, Walt Disney produced a serious version of the same story, titled **The Great Locomotive Chase**.)

Comedies, silent or otherwise, do not come any better than this one.

GENTLEMAN'S AGREEMENT (1947)
Black & white, 118 minutes
Cast: Gregory Peck, Dorothy McGuire, John Garfield, Celeste Holm, Anne Revere, June Havoc, Albert Dekker, Jane Wyatt, Dean Stockwell, Sam Jaffe
Director: Elia Kazan
Screenplay: Moss Hart, based on the novel by Laura Z. Hobson
Drama
Unrated
Younger children: No Older children: VG

In its time, this was a groundbreaking examination of a subject that was seldom discussed in an open forum and never tackled onscreen: anti-Semitism in America. *Gentleman's Agreement* even won an Academy Award as Best Picture. Some feel that it has not held up well in the more than fifty years since it was made, but it is still worth seeing (especially for children), as it lays out its case in clear, simple terms.

Gentleman's Agreement is the story of Phil Green, a widowed writer who poses as a Jew while researching a series of magazine articles on anti-Semitism. "I'll be Jewish," Green declares, as he conjures up his angle for the series. "All I've got to do is say it. I've even got a title: 'I Was Jewish for Six Months.' Hmm. Dark hair, dark eyes . . . I'll just call myself Phil Greenberg."

Green's experiences as he plays the role of Jew and encounters prejudice firsthand are surprising and revealing. In one of the most affecting scenes, Green's tearful young son reveals that he was called a "dirty Jew" and "stinking kike" in the school yard. In another, more subtle sequence, Green's well-meaning but clueless girlfriend notes how she and others at a dinner party were shocked by the racist blatherings of one of their fellow guests, yet none of them dared to speak out.

Gentleman's Agreement may no longer seem "hard-hitting" to adult viewers, but it still serves as a good introduction for intelligent children to a social problem that has never really gone away.

GEORGE OF THE JUNGLE (1997)
Color, 91 minutes
Cast: Brendan Fraser, Leslie Mann, Thomas Haden Church, Richard Roundtree, John Cleese, Greg Cruttwell, Abraham Benrubi, Holland Taylor, John Bennett Perry; Keith Scott (narrator)
Director: Sam Weisman
Screenplay: Dana Olsen and Audrey Wells, from a story by

Dana Olsen, based on
characters developed by Jay
Ward
Comedy/Adventure
Rated PG
Younger kids: OK, with
caution   Older kids: OK

An amiable Tarzan spoof, the 1960s Jay Ward television cartoon series is best remembered for its theme song—which expectedly gets quite a workout in this live-action version. Fraser is perfectly cast as the simpleminded, loin-cloth-wearing jungle king who gets along with all his animal friends and feels the first stirrings of human emotions when he comes into contact with lovely Ursula (Leslie Mann), an American on safari.

It's too bad the people who made *George* didn't have (a) Jay Ward's sharp sense of humor and (b) the ability to tell a good story. For instance, George's friend and confidant, an ape named Ape, is voiced by the British actor/writer/Monty Python member John Cleese, who is given virtually nothing funny to say! Ursula's goonish fiancé (Thomas Haden Church) is portrayed as an obnoxious idiot from his first moment on camera and remains a tiresome, one-note character thereafter. By the film's climax, the director and writers resort to any cheap joke they can think of—mostly involving body parts, passing gas, etc.—to get a laugh, which of course works with kids as the primary target audience.

Given its source material, the amiable tone of the film, and the utter likability of Fraser and Mann, this should have been much better. Or perhaps it should have remained a five-minute car-

toon segment on TV, as it was meant to be.

Kids won't share these adult-type complaints, and with luck, the younger ones won't get the jokes about George being especially well endowed.

GHIDRAH, THE THREE-HEADED MONSTER (1964)
Color, 81 minutes
Cast: Yosuke Natsuki, Yuriko
   Hoshi, Hiroshi Koizumi,
   Takashi Shimura, Emi Ito,
   Yumi Ito, Akiko Wakabayashi,
   Akihiko Hirata, Kenji Sahara,
   Haruo Nakajima, Shoichi
   "Solomon" Hirose
Director: Ishiro Honda
Screenplay: Shinichi Sekizawa
Science fiction/Monster/Comedy-
   drama
Unrated
Young children: OK   Older
   children: OK

A princess (Wakabayashi) disappears from her plane just before assassins blow it up and turns up later in the streets of Tokyo, claiming to be a Martian. She warns that Earth is in deadly peril from some mysterious force. Meanwhile, Godzilla and Rodan reappear and wreak some havoc, mostly aimed at each other. Then a huge egglike object hatches in the mountains, and Ghidrah, the Three-Headed Monster, is born. He flies about blasting everything with his lightning-bolt breath. **Mothra**'s tiny twins (the Ito sisters) are persuaded to summon the giant caterpillar to Japan, so Mothra can try to talk—yes, *talk*—Godzilla and Rodan into ganging up on the very mean Ghidrah.

It was in this movie that Godzilla changed from a menace to

Protector of the Earth, since, at the climax, he and the other monsters do get together to defeat the golden dragon, Ghidrah. It's also with this film that the bizarre humor that so endears these films to people of all ages began to turn up—with the monsters, not the human beings. Godzilla and Rodan occasionally laugh, and when the Mothra twins are translating, they're shocked by Godzilla's "bad language."

This movie is perfectly suitable for almost all children, who'll get a kick out of it. There are good guys (Godzilla, Rodan, and Mothra), a spectacular bad guy (Ghidrah), lots of colorful action, explosions, and lumbering fights. What more could a bored 10-year-old want?

This was followed by *Monster Zero* (aka *Godzilla vs. Monster Zero*).

GHOSTBUSTERS (1984)
Color, 107 minutes
Cast: Bill Murray, Dan Aykroyd, Sigourney Weaver, Harold Ramis, Rick Moranis, Annie Potts, William Atherton, Ernie Hudson, Slavitza Jovan
Director: Ivan Reitman
Screenplay: Dan Aykroyd and Harold Ramis
Fantasy comedy/Horror
Rated PG
Young children: OK, with caution   Older children: VG

When their funding is cut off, three university professors team up to form a professional "ghostbusting" team, which garners a surprising amount of business. Stantz (Aykroyd) and Spengler (Ramis) take their work seriously, but the wisecracking Venkman (Murray) is far less devoted to their job. In fact, he loses them the task of exorcising the refrigerator belonging to attractive Dana (Weaver) when he makes a pass at her. Otherwise, the Ghostbusters do great business and become famous, eventually adding Zeddemore (Hudson) to their team.

Dana, however, has bigger problems than a possessed refrigerator; she and her nerdy neighbor Louis (Moranis) live in a supernaturally significant apartment building, and both are possessed by arcane entities. Meanwhile, an overzealous government agent (Atherton) shuts down the grid that holds in all the ghosts our heroes have been collecting—and Dana's apartment building and the escaped ghosts add up to a potential worldwide catastrophe. Who you gonna call?

This smash hit spawned a sequel and an animated TV series, but you should still turn to the original movie for the most fun and games. Writers (and costars) Aykroyd and Ramis not only know the "scare" comedies that preceded them, but supernatural literature and parapsychology jargon as well. The film is great fun as a comedy and a treat for the eyes, with fabulous special effects (supervised by Richard Edlund). It also plays fair with the supernatural elements; you don't have to park your brains under the seat for this one.

While most of the ghosts, including Slimer, are played for comedy, there are some genuinely scary elements, such as the helldogs, that will spook younger children. But as with other movies, the presence of a parent will work wonders. There are also some mildly risqué moments when the possessed Dana makes advances

206

toward Venkman. Older children will think they've died and gone to movie heaven.

GHOSTBUSTERS II (1989)
Color, 102 minutes
Cast: Bill Murray, Dan Aykroyd, Sigourney Weaver, Harold Ramis, Rick Moranis, Ernie Hudson, Annie Potts, Peter MacNicol, Harris Yulin, David Margulies, Kurt Fuller, Janet Margolin
Director: Ivan Reitman
Screenplay: Dan Aykroyd and Harold Ramis
Fantasy/Comedy/Horror
Rated PG
Young children: Scary   Older children: OK

The Ghostbusters are again approached by Dana (Weaver), who is having supernatural problems involving her baby, Oscar. Our heroes find a river of slime flowing beneath the streets of New York; it feeds on the negative attitudes of New Yorkers and is getting more and more powerful. Dana, who works at a museum, is further disturbed by a painting of Vigo the Carpathian that's being restored by her creepy boss, Janosz (MacNicol). Vigo, a sorcerer, possesses Janosz from beyond the grave, and tries to use him to seize Oscar, so that Vigo can transfer his malignant spirit to the baby.

These two story elements never really come together, except in the most haphazard way, making this entry sloppier and less interesting than the first. Also, an annoying amount of time is spent just getting the Ghostbusters back together and on the shaky relationship between Venkman (Murray) and Dana.

However, adolescents will hardly be bothered by these defects and will happily wallow in the comedy and special effects, both of which are plentiful. Peter MacNicol is particularly funny as the possessed but still nerdy Janosz, and the special effects are even slicker than in the first film. Though the kids may not like this as much as they did the first one, they'll still have a good time.

THE GHOST OF FRANKENSTEIN (1942)
Black & white, 67 minutes
Cast: Lon Chaney (Jr.), Bela Lugosi, Cedric Hardwicke, Ralph Bellamy, Lionel Atwill, Evelyn Ankers, Janet Ann Gallow, Barton Yarborough
Director: Erle C. Kenton
Screenplay: W. Scott Darling, from a story by Eric Taylor
Science fiction–horror/Suspense
Unrated
Young children: Marginal   Older children: OK

Evil Ygor (Lugosi) digs Frankenstein's Monster (Chaney) out of the sulfur pit into which he fell in **Son of Frankenstein,** and takes him to Ludwig (Hardwicke), *another* son of Frankenstein, who's horrified to finally encounter his father's creation. However, he becomes convinced that if he can replace the Monster's criminal brain with that of a decent man, he will justify his father's research. Ygor and Ludwig's conniving associate (Atwill) have ideas of their own.

Like many Universal horror movies of the 1940s, this was never intended to be particularly frightening; instead, it's a kind of science fiction thriller with the Frankenstein Monster at its core.

As such, it still works pretty well today.

Children might be disturbed by the brain the Monster himself decides should be placed in his square cranium . . . but given that this *is* a horror movie, it's otherwise not likely to bother kids from 8 up.

This was followed by **Frankenstein Meets the Wolf Man.**

THE GIANT BEHEMOTH
(1959)
Black & white, 79 minutes
Cast: Gene Evans, Andre Morell, Jack MacGowran, Maurice Kaufman, Henry Vidon, Leigh Madison
Director: Eugene Lourié
Screenplay: Eugene Lourié
Science fiction/Monster
Unrated
Younger kids: Probably not   Older kids: OK

Another prehistoric monster rises from the sea to menace another city; this time, it's London. The dinosaur here has radioactive eyes and occasionally burns people to death rather than stepping on them. This results in scary makeup effects (only one, really) that could disturb younger children.

Thanks to the stop-motion effects of the great Willis O'Brien (of **King Kong** fame) and Pete Peterson, the Behemoth is convincingly real most of the time; the nonanimated effects by others are definitely inferior. The movie itself is standard stuff, not bad for this kind of thing.

G.I. BLUES (1960)
Color, 104 minutes
Cast: Elvis Presley, Juliet Prowse, Robert Ivers, Leticia Roman, Ludwig Stossel, James Douglas, Arch Johnson
Director: Norman Taurog
Screenplay: Edmund Beloin and Henry Garson
Musical/Romance
Unrated
Young children: VG   Older children: VG

In the late 1950s, adolescent America was all aflutter as Elvis Presley, the era's premier rock 'n' roll idol, was inducted into the military. This lightly likable musical comedy was his comeback effort, and traded on the notoriety of his highly publicized Army hitch.

It also marked a turning point in Elvis' movie career. In contrast to his sometimes surly, hip-shaking pre-Army persona (see **Jailhouse Rock** for the ultimate example), he's considerably toned down and more of an all-American boy.

The scenario mixes reality with fiction. Elvis is cast as Tulsa McCarthy, a guitar-playing soldier who is stationed in West Germany (just as Elvis was). Along the way, Tulsa becomes involved in a romance with a standoffish cabaret singer (Juliet Prowse) and performs ten songs, including "Wooden Heart," "Tonight Is So Right for Love," "Blue Suede Shoes," and the title tune.

G.I. Blues may not be the greatest musical in Hollywood history. But it's still entertaining and offers a peek at Presley at a key point in his still-evolving career.

GIGI (1958)
Color, 116 minutes
Cast: Leslie Caron, Maurice Chevalier, Louis Jourdan, Hermione Gingold, Jacques

Bergerac, Eva Gabor, Isabel Jeans, John Abbott
Director: Vincente Minnelli
Screenplay: Alan Jay Lerner, based on the novel by Colette
Musical
Unrated
Young children: VG   Older children: VG

Based on Colette's novel of a *fin de siècle* Parisian girl who is trained to be a courtesan by her aunt and grandmother, this musical is entertaining, with fine production values, a good cast, and a wonderful score. It even won nine Academy Awards, including Best Picture. However, as family entertainment it comes with the caveat of having to explain a society in which a teenage girl is prepared for a life as a wealthy man's mistress.

As the older women take great pains to teach Gigi how to walk with a book on her head and take her place among the elegant ladies of Paris, some of the family may give up on the movie. Don't! There is too much to savor here. Just keep in mind that Gigi will overcome her lot in life, and then try to sit back and enjoy the film. (Besides, many of the plot points of this sophisticated musical will fly over the heads of young children.)

If you've already dived into the world of musicals, your kids may recognize Leslie Caron as the young costar of **An American in Paris**, **Lili,** and **The Glass Slipper**.

Legendary French musical star Maurice Chevalier practically steals the movie away from the other stars with his rendition of "Thank Heaven for Little Girls" and in a duet with Hermione Gingold called "I Remember It Well."

GLORY (1989)

Color, 122 minutes
Cast: Matthew Broderick, Denzel Washington, Cary Elwes, Morgan Freeman, Jihmi Kennedy, Andre Braugher, John Finn, Donovan Leitch, John David Cullum, Bob Gunton, Cliff DeYoung, Jane Alexander, Raymond St. Jacques
Director: Edward Zwick
Screenplay: Kevin Jarre, based on the books *Lay This Laurel* by Lincoln Kirsten and *One Gallant Rush* by Peter Burchard, and the letters of Robert Gould Shaw
Historical drama
Rated R
Young children: No   Older children: VG, with caution

A heretofore little-known slice of American history comes alive in *Glory,* a breathtaking drama which tells the story of the 54th Massachusetts Regiment: America's first unit of African-American soldiers, which went into battle in the Civil War. Its scenario is partially based on the recollections of Colonel Robert Gould Shaw (Matthew Broderick), the unit's young, white commanding officer.

The soldiers of the 54th are a conglomeration of free Northerners and runaway slaves who volunteer to fight against the Confederacy. However, not all their battles are against the enemy. As they train, they must deal with the abject racism of their white comrades; they are not provided with uniforms (or even shoes) and only reluctantly given rifles.

The dramatic intensity increases as the personalities of the individual recruits and their life histories emerge, and as the group as a whole is molded into a crackerjack fighting unit that is anxious to prove its competency in battle.

Glory is brilliantly photographed and staged, and features a gallery of memorable characters and performances. Denzel Washington won an Academy Award as Best Supporting Actor for his portrayal of an angry young man.

Parents should know that for all its many virtues, *Glory* is an extremely violent and upsetting film. Like all great war movies, this one does not traffic in make-believe violence, but captures all the agony and heartbreak of battle.

THE GNOME-MOBILE (1967)
Color, 90 minutes
Cast: Walter Brennan, Matthew
    Garber, Karen Dotrice,
    Richard Deacon, Tom Lowell,
    Sean McClory, Ed Wynn,
    Jerome Cowan, Charles Lane
Director: Robert Stevenson
Screenplay: Ellis Kadison, based
    on the book by Upton Sinclair
Fantasy
Unrated
Young kids: VG   Older kids:
    VG

The Gnome-Mobile was one of the last films Walt Disney personally produced. It's also one of his best comedy fantasy films, and why it isn't better known is something of a mystery.

Veteran character actor Walter Brennan stars as D.J. Mulrooney, a lumber tycoon who takes his niece and nephew into a magnificent redwood forest for a picnic. There, they encounter a two-foot gnome named Jasper who asks for their help in finding a new home for his tiny clan, which has been cut off from other gnomes. D.J. agrees to help—but Jasper's irascible 943-year-old grandfather, Knobby (also played by Brennan), raises a fuss when he learns that his benefactor is the same man he blames for ruining the forest.

This colorful story never stops to take a breath, with gags, chases, and special effects galore. The colors are bold and beautiful, and the performances just right, with Brennan ideal in a dual role and the delightful kids from **Mary Poppins**, Karen Dotrice and Matthew Garber, as his grandchildren.

The Gnome-Mobile deserves to be rediscovered and enjoyed by a new generation. Younger children should especially like it.

THE GODS MUST BE CRAZY (1981)
Color, 109 minutes
Cast: Marius Weyers, Sandra
    Prinsloo, N!xau, Louw
    Verwey, James Uys
Director: Jamie Uys
Screenplay: Jamie Uys
Comedy
Rated PG
Young children: VG   Older
    children: VG

This out-of-nowhere sleeper hit from South Africa shattered box-office records across the globe—and for good reason. It is a screamingly funny comedy that is filled with clever sight gags. Its sense of the absurd transcends language or culture, and is universal in appeal—just like the very best comedies of the silent-film era.

The Gods Must Be Crazy opens in the Kalahari Desert, where a bushman named Xi (hilariously played by N!xau) is off on a hunting trip. It just so happens that an empty Coca-Cola bottle is casually tossed out of the window of a small airplane flying overhead. The bottle lands near the bushman, and he becomes convinced it has fallen from the heavens! Xi eventually sets out on an odyssey in which he seeks to return the bottle to the "gods."

The film might have taken a patronizing attitude toward Xi and his fellow tribesmen, seeing them as primitives who are so set apart from "civilization" that they cannot differentiate between a pop bottle and a religious icon. However, the whites in the story (who come into play as Xi goes off on his journey) turn out to be just as preposterous as the tribesmen.

Furthermore, Xi responds to his various challenges with a simple logic that makes his character endearing.

The whole family will enjoy this engaging film.

GODZILLA, KING OF THE MONSTERS (1954)

Black & white, 81 minutes
Cast: Raymond Burr, Frank Iwanaga, Takashi Shimura, Momoko Kochi, Akira Takarada, Akihiko Hirata, Haruo Nakajima
Directors: Ishiro Honda and Terrell O. Morse, Sr.
Screenplay: Takeo Murata and Honda, from a story by Shigeru Kayama
Science fiction/Monster melodrama
Unrated

Young children: Intense at times   Older children: OK

American reporter Steve Martin (Burr) is visiting Tokyo when strange fire from the sea incinerates several ships. All too soon, the source of the fire is revealed: Godzilla, a four-hundred-foot-tall prehistoric monster, evidently revived by radiation. It comes ashore at Tokyo and ravages the city with its sheer size and its fiery breath. Can anything stop the scaly colossus?

Well, yes, actually: a reclusive scientist (Hirata) has invented the "oxygen destroyer" that removes all oxygen from water and thereby (?) turns everything within range into a skeleton, and this is done to Godzilla. Which means that in the twenty-one Japanese Godzilla films that followed, it was a *different* monster. This small fact will surprise and probably annoy your monster-loving children, who may also be surprised to learn that Godzilla was *never* green.

The world came to love this big bad-tempered monster from the Pacific depths, particularly as the movies stopped imitating American originals (the debts to **King Kong** and **The Beast From 20,000 Fathoms** are obvious). The film has a dark but almost elegiac tone, not about Godzilla, but about the helplessness of mankind in the face of his monstrous onslaught. The cast is large, and the American-filmed scenes (directed by Terrell O. Morse, Sr.) are surprisingly well integrated into the Japanese footage.

This and its immediate sequel, called *Gigantis, the Fire Monster* in the U.S., were very serious films intended for adults, but Toho, the production company, realized that the main audience was children and tailored subsequent films to them. When this initial series died out, a new one was launched, beginning with another direct sequel to this movie, but those were aimed at a somewhat older audience.

Very young children will be disturbed that their old pal Godzilla is, here, a terrible, destructive monster for sure, but they'll probably want to see the film anyway. *Godzilla* was remade, Hollywood-style, in 1998.

GODZILLA 1985 (1984)
Color, 87 minutes
Cast: Raymond Burr, Keiju Kobayashi, Ken Tanaka, Yasuko Sawaguchi, Shin Takuma, Eitaro Ozawa, Taketoshi Naito, Warren Kemmerling
Director: Koiji Hashimoto
Screenplay: Shuichi Nagahara
Science fiction/Monster
Rated PG
Young children: OK, with caution   Older children: OK

Almost thirty years after their last Godzilla movie, Toho pictures made this elaborate sequel to/remake of the first picture. The American distributor severely cut the film, adding scenes starring Raymond Burr in the same role he had in the American-shot scenes for the original. These scenes are jokey, almost contemptuous, and completely at odds with the Japanese scenes.

The destruction of a Japanese fishing boat leads to the realization that Godzilla has somehow revived and is heading for Japan. An encounter with a Soviet nuclear submarine causes the monster to become even larger, but the Japanese government's news blackout results in the Russians believing the Americans were responsible for the sub disaster. The Japanese are forced to reveal that Godzilla has returned, and claim they have a secret weapon that will destroy the giant monster. The Soviets, however, surreptitiously prepare their own nuclear missile, just in case.

The American version of the film retains most of the special effects, which are pretty good for a movie of this nature (and really what most people want to see anyway). It's not as good as some of its own sequels, but children won't care; they just want to see Godzilla breathe fire and knock over buildings. There's plenty of both here.

GODZILLA VS. KING GHIDORA (1991)
Color, 103 minutes
Cast: Anna Nakagawa, Megumi Odaka, Isao Toyohara, Kiwako Harada, Tokuma Nishioka, Robert Scottfield, Tushio Tsuchiya
Director: Kazuki Omori
Screenplay: Kazuki Omori
Science fiction/Monster action
Unrated
Young children: Too intense   Older children: OK

In 1984, Toho Pictures of Japan revived the most famous giant monster of all, Godzilla, in a brand-new series that bore no relation to the long-running series following **Godzilla, King of the Monsters.** In these new films, Godzilla was almost always a fierce, almost demonic menace, rather than the "defender of the Earth." Some of the new films re-created a few of Godzilla's old opponents, including this surprisingly sharp, entertaining movie—ideal fare for a monster-loving 13-year-old.

Time travelers from the 23rd century come to Japan of 1992 with a warning. Back in 1944, an islandful of Japanese soldiers had been saved by a dinosaur that wiped out invading Americans; ten years later, a nuclear test turned that dinosaur into Godzilla. The visitors from the future tell the leaders of present-day Japan that Godzilla, who feeds on nuclear power, will eventually leave Japan uninhabitable. They advise wiping Godzilla from history.

A trio of contemporary Japanese go with future woman Emi (Anna Nakagawa) back to 1944, where, after the dinosaur saves the troops, they teleport the wounded creature to the bottom of the Bering Sea. Meanwhile, Emi releases three cute but artificial batlike creatures onto the island in 1944. When our heroes return to 1992, they discover that the visitors from the future (except Emi) did all this to create King Ghidora, a terrible, golden, three-headed dragon destined to destroy Japan—which, by the 23rd century, will have become the most powerful nation on Earth.

Kids in their early teens, particularly those already getting into science fiction books, will be a receptive audience for this well-produced epic, which blends originality with elements "inspired" by the American *Terminator* movies. Not only are Koichi Kawakita's special effects generally very good, particularly in the city-destroying scenes, but the plot keeps

springing one intriguing surprise after another, right up until the final fadeout.

It's a shame this film never received a theatrical release in the United States; it's fast paced, intelligent, and lavish. Sure, it's about a giant, fire-breathing monster, but it never plays down to its audience. It is widely available on video, albeit in a somewhat muddy print.

GODZILLA VS. THE THING
(1964) (aka *Godzilla vs. Mothra*)
Color, 88 minutes
Cast: Akira Takarada, Yuriko Hoshi, Hiroshi Koizumi, Yu Fujiki, Kenji Sahara, Emi Ito, Yumi Ito, Jun Tazaki, Yoshifumi Tajima, Haruo Nakajima
Director: Ishiro Honda
Screenplay: Shinichi Sekizawa
Science fiction/Monster thriller
Unrated
Young children: OK, with caution   Older children: OK

After a hurricane, a gigantic egg washes up on a Japanese beach, and a pair of unscrupulous businessmen (Sahara and Tajima) lay claim to it. The twins (the Ito sisters) from Mothra Island appear with Mothra, and beg for the return of the egg, which was laid by Mothra, but the businessmen refuse. Godzilla erupts from land where he was accidentally buried and begins another reign of destruction. Two reporters (Takarada, Hoshi) and a scientist (Koizumi) convince the twins to ask the weakened Mothra to battle Godzilla.

One of the best Japanese monster films (*kaiju eiga*), this handsome production is well structured, intelligent, and features some of the best special effects work of master Eiji Tsuburaya. The fairy tale elements of **Mothra** blend surprisingly well with the monster mayhem of **Godzilla** (yet to become Protector of the Earth), and the fight between a colossal moth and a dinosaur plays far better than you might expect.

Like *Mothra*, this is a physically beautiful movie, with excellent use of subdued color, fine widescreen photography (by Hajime Koizumi) and one of the best scores by Akira Ifukube, who worked on many of these movies. Even Haruo Nakajima, who wore the Godzilla suit most often, seems more inspired: he moves like a great beast, not the tough but clownish figure Godzilla would become with the next movie, **Ghidrah, the Three-Headed Monster.**

Young children may be brokenhearted by Mothra's eventual fate in this film (and even you may be moved, so well is this scene handled by director Honda). But there's a surprise ending that should have everyone cheering.

GOING IN STYLE (1979)
Color, 96 minutes
Cast: George Burns, Art Carney, Lee Strasberg, Charles Hallahan, Pamela Payton-Wright
Director: Martin Brest
Screenplay: Martin Brest
Drama
Rated PG
Young children: No Older children: VG

This simple, straightforward, and endearing comedy-drama tells the story of three aged pals who share a dingy flat in Queens, New York,

and pass their hours withering away on a park bench. As much to break the monotony of their lives as add to their paltry social security checks, they conspire to rob a bank!

Going in Style is more than just a film about a trio of likable senior citizens who scheme to pull off a caper. It explores many facets of aging in American society, from the problems of dealing with government agencies to the overwhelming feeling of loneliness that overtakes older people who have lost their mates and are separated from their families.

What keeps this movie from wallowing in melancholy is the clever script and the enormous likability of its stars—the incredible comedian turned actor George Burns, the delightful Art Carney, and the legendary acting teacher Lee Strasberg—and the uplifting nature of their friendship.

Many children feel a special kinship with older people; it is these youngsters who will most appreciate *Going in Style*. Some salty language and adult situations—not the least of which is death—make this inappropriate for younger kids.

GOLD DIGGERS: SECRET OF BEAR MOUNTAIN (1995)
Color, 94 minutes
Cast: Christina Ricci, Anna Chlumsky, Polly Draper, Brian Kerwin, Diana Scarwid, David Keith
Director: Kevin James Dobson
Screenplay: Barry Glasser
Adventure
Rated PG
Young children: VG Older children: OK

214

Beth (Christina Ricci) and her widowed mother move to the Pacific Northwest and try to make a fresh start. At first Beth fears that she's moved to "the sticks," but then she meets Jody (Anna Chlumsky), a girl with a bad reputation who nevertheless becomes Beth's closest friend. During summer vacation Jody leads Beth on an adventure in search of a mystery woman (and her supposed cache of gold) long hidden inside nearby Bear Mountain.

A simple film aimed at preadolescent girls, *Gold Diggers* gains its strength from the substantial appeal of its two talented stars. Their presence and chemistry together make the film watchable for its target viewers—although even young kids may find the story's resolution somewhat disappointing.

There is some suspense along the way, including a cliffhanger-style scene of Beth in peril . . . and tension of another kind as it's revealed that Jody has an alcoholic mother with an abusive boyfriend. That facet of the story may cause some uncomfortable moments for the youngest viewers (and is why the film is appropriately rated PG).

THE GOLDEN SEAL (1983)
Color, 95 minutes
Cast: Steve Railsback, Michael Beck, Penelope Milford, Torquil Campbell, Seth Sakai
Director: Frank Zuniga
Screenplay: John Groves, based on the novel *A River Ran Out of Eden* by James Vance Marshall
Adventure
Rated PG
Younger kids: Good   Older kids: Good

This is an unpretentious and enjoyable animal film about a young boy named Eric (Torquil Campbell) who lives on one of the remote Aleutian Islands off the Alaskan coast with his parents. When Eric finds a "mythical" golden seal that's been pursued for years because of the $10,000 bounty on its pelt, he tries to shelter the creature from bounty hunters including his own father (Steve Railsback).

Predictable plotting is uplifted by the story's mystical undertones and some truly spectacular nature photography, particularly of a ferocious storm known as a "williwaw." Mild language earned this a PG rating.

THE GOLDEN VOYAGE OF SINBAD (1974)
Color, 104 minutes
Cast: John Phillip Law, Caroline Munro, Tom Baker, Douglas Wilmer, Gregoire Aslan
Director: Gordon Hessler
Screenplay: Brian Clemens
Action-adventure/Fantasy
Rated G
Younger kids: Good   Older kids: VG

Special-effects maestro Ray Harryhausen created some of his most imaginatively bizarre creatures for this highly entertaining and captivating old-fashioned children's adventure. Accompanied by the Vizier (Douglas Wilmer), a young boy (Kurt Christian), and a beautiful slave girl (Caroline Munro), Sinbad (John Phillip Law) sets sail in search of the Fountain of Destiny, battling the wicked Koura (Tom Baker) and his horde of mythical demons.

The story is typical Arabian

Nights fantasy, but the effects are dazzling, as Harryhausen's stop-motion "Dynamation" process (created frame-by-frame, long before the age of computer effects) brings to life a ship's figurehead, a multi-armed sword-wielding statue of the goddess Kali, a one-eyed centaur, and a ferocious gryphon.

THE GOLD RUSH (1925)
Black & white, 82 minutes
Cast: Charlie Chaplin, Georgia Hale, Mack Swain, Tom Murray
Director: Charles Chaplin
Screenplay: Charles Chaplin
Comedy/Silent classic
Unrated
Young children: VG Older children: VG

The Gold Rush arguably is Charlie Chaplin's greatest early feature. This classic places The Little Tramp in the Yukon during the heyday of gold-rush fever, where he struggles for survival, contends with a roly-poly fellow prospector, and falls for a dance hall girl who is anything but demure.

You will find several of Chaplin's funniest and most famous comedy routines in *The Gold Rush.* One that virtually defines his comic aesthetic is the sequence in which the Tramp, starving but heroically attempting to put on a happy facade, transforms an old, cooked shoe and its laces into a feast fit for royalty. In another scene, he performs a charming dance with a pair of dinner rolls!

There's also a genuine cliff-hanging climax, in which Charlie and his prospector pal teeter on the edge of a precipice in their log cabin.

Chaplin also laces his film with poignancy, as the lonely Little Tramp mistakes the flighty friendship of the dance hall girl for genuine affection.

The Gold Rush is a joy to watch, again and again, for young and old alike.

GONE WITH THE WIND (1939)
Color, 222 minutes
Cast: Clark Gable, Vivien Leigh, Leslie Howard, Olivia de Havilland, Thomas Mitchell, Barbara O'Neil, Victor Jory, Laura Hope Crews, Hattie McDaniel, Ona Munson, Harry Davenport, Ann Rutherford, Evelyn Keyes, Butterfly McQueen, Rand Brooks, Eddie "Rochester" Anderson, George Reeves
Director: Victor Fleming
Screenplay: Sidney Howard, based on the novel by Margaret Mitchell
Drama
Unrated
Young children: No Older children: VG

This is Hollywood filmmaking at its best. The epic-length Civil War–era romance has taken hosts of awards and honors, and it is often considered to be the greatest film ever made. Under the supervision of fabled producer David O. Selznick, the four-hour film was culled from the pages of Margaret Mitchell's runaway bestseller. Yet even beyond the lavish production values and wonderful acting, this movie is far and away the greatest piece of storytelling ever to grace the screen.

The scenario follows Scarlett, a flirtatious, unyielding beauty, from a romantic teenager living in splendor on her family's antebellum plantation in Georgia through the horrors of the Civil War, when she acquires a ruthless, iron will, and then later, into the Reconstruction period, in which she displays survival techniques that make her appear selfish and shameless. Scarlett O'Hara is a red-blooded heroine for the ages, and Rhett Butler, the man she truly loves, remains one of literature's most exciting heroes. (The willful, scheming nature of Scarlett has been the subject of much discussion in recent years by feminists, who debate her place in popular culture—and the consciousness of millions who have watched her.)

Younger children who will scarcely sit still for a two-hour film couldn't be expected to wade through this one; if they try to, however, they may be upset by some death scenes (one involving a child), the famous "birthing" sequence, and some of the harsher moments depicting the horrors of the Civil War. There is also the issue of slavery to be dealt with, as *GWTW* depicts only loyal servants who seem utterly content with their lot in life.

For all these reasons, the film is better suited to older children and will be best appreciated in the company of their parents.

GOOD BURGER (1997)
Color, 95 minutes
Cast: Kel Mitchell, Kenan Thompson, Sinbad, Abe Vigoda, Shar Jackson, Dan Schneider, Jan Schweiterman, Carmen Electra, Shaquille O'Neal
Director: Brian Robbins
Screenplay: Dan Schneider, Kevin Kopelow, and Heather Seifert, based on characters created by Schneider, Kopelow, and Seifert
Comedy
Rated PG
Younger kids: OK   Older kids: OK

Kids who know and enjoy Kenan and Kel, the genial young performers on TV's Nickelodeon show *All That,* form a built-in audience for this easy-to-take feature film, though it's not likely to win any awards for excellence in story development.

Kenan plays a high school student whose summer vacation plans are disrupted when he has an accident (with his mother's car) and causes $1,900 worth of damage to a vehicle belonging to his long-suffering teacher (Sinbad). He is forced to take a summer job at Good Burger, a scruffy fast-food operation where the front-counter orders are taken by likable dimwit Kel ("Welcome to Good Burger, home of the good burger, may I take your order?"). Their misadventures focus on a growing competition with the massive new fast-food enterprise opening across the street, Mondo Burger.

Good spirits make up for a connect-the-dots script in this simplistic comedy aimed strictly at a juvenile audience. *Hell* is the strongest word uttered—and that only happens once. The violence is mostly oafish and cartoonlike. Only a sequence set in an insane asylum might raise a few parents' eyebrows, but its darker implications will probably sail over the heads of small fry.

Good Burger is much like fast food itself—not terribly nourishing, but kids like it anyway.

GOODBYE, MR. CHIPS (1939)
Black & white, 114 minutes
Cast: Robert Donat, Greer
 Garson, Paul von Hernreid
 (Henreid), Terry Kilburn, John
 Mills, Judith Furse, Lyn
 Harding, Milton Rosmer
Director: Sam Wood
Screenplay: R. C. Sherriff,
 Claudine West, and Eric
 Maschwitz, based on the novel
 by James Hilton
Drama/Literary classic
Unrated
Young children: VG Older
 children: VG

Arthur Chipping, the hero of
James Hilton's *Goodbye, Mr.
Chips,* was an earlier generation's
prototypical movie schoolteacher:
shy, endearing, and ever-devoted
to "all my boys." Chipping, who
is nicknamed "Chips," is a schoolmaster at Brookfield, an English
public school. The story recounts
his difficult early years at Brookfield, his unlikely courtship and
marriage to a vivacious young
woman, and how he ages into a
dearly loved figure at his school.
There is much drama and emotion as Chipping mixes with and
affects the lives of his young men
across the decades.

Goodbye, Mr. Chips is a highly
sentimental film, which may be
out of step with today's young
viewers—but perhaps the younger,
less cynical kids of today will still
be charmed by its simplicity and
sincerity. And who among us
wouldn't love to have a teacher as
caring and concerned as Chipping?

Robert Donat's performance as
Mr. Chips is so beautifully realized that, back in 1939, it beat out
Clark Gable's Rhett Butler for
the Best Actor Academy Award.

Thirty years later, the story was
remade as a musical, which
floundered despite a fine cast
headed by Peter O'Toole.

GOOD NEWS (1947)
Color, 83 minutes
Cast: June Allyson, Peter
 Lawford, Patricia Marshall,
 Joan McCracken, Ray
 McDonald, Mel Torme,
 Donald MacBride
Director: Charles Walters
Screenplay: Betty Comden and
 Adolph Green, based on the
 Broadway musical by Lew
 Brown, Buddy G. DeSylva,
 Frank Mandel, and Lawrence
 Schwab
Musical
Unrated
Young children: VG Older
 children: VG

This cheery and underrated MGM
musical is not just a rehash of the
Broadway play of the late 1920s
(which was filmed in 1930); it's an
affectionate parody of all those
sis-boom-bah college stories of
the period.

Either way, it's great fun to
watch, with June Allyson as the
poor, plain-Jane student who's
working her way through school,
and Peter Lawford as the football
star of Tate College, who's under
the thumb of his latest girlfriend—and can't get himself to
admit that he's really falling in
love with June.

Beside the overall good cheer,
the film is peppered with lively
production numbers, including
the infectious "Ladies' Man," the
unbelievably energetic "Pass That
Peace Pipe," and the delightful
special-material number (written
especially for this film by the
clever Comden and Green) "The

French Lesson," in which Allyson gives Lawford a crash course in language skills. The big finale is the original show's hit number "The Varsity Drag." There are also some pretty ballads like "Just Imagine" and "The Best Things in Life are Free."

Whether or not they understand the subtle satire of this script, kids are bound to enjoy the spirited music and comedy of *Good News*.

A GOOFY MOVIE (1995)
Color, 78 minutes
Cast: Voices of Bill Farmer, Jason Marsden, Jim Cummings, Kellie Martin, Rob Paulsen, Wallace Shawn
Director: Kevin Lima
Screenplay: Jymn Magon, Chris Matheson, and Brian Pimental, from a story by Magon
Animated feature/Musical
Rated G
Younger kids: VG   Older kids: VG

Goofy is an embarrassment to his young son, Max, who finally gets up the nerve to ask the girl of his dreams to go to a Powerline concert and party. When the boy gets in trouble with his school principal, Goofy decides to take Max on a father-son fishing trip, as a way of bonding. Max is upset and annoyed, but during the course of their adventure, he and Goofy grow closer . . . and Max comes to appreciate his resourceful, lovable dad.

Neither as ambitious or as elaborate as most Disney animated features, *A Goofy Movie* has just one thing in its favor: it's delightful.

A thoroughly winning piece of family entertainment, it deals head-on with the fact that "The Goof" is an old-fashioned character by putting him at odds with his ultra-contemporary kid and fashioning a plot in which the two come to love and respect one another.

The songs are fun, the animation is very good, the situations believable (in some cases exciting), and the laughs plentiful. It's ideal family entertainment.

THE GOONIES (1985)
Color, 114 minutes
Cast: Sean Astin, Josh Brolin, Jeff Cohen, Corey Feldman, Ke Huy Quan, Kerri Green, Martha Plimpton, John Matuszak, Anne Ramsey, Joe Pantoliano
Director: Richard Donner
Screenplay: Chris Columbus, based on a story by Steven Spielberg
Action-adventure
Rated PG
Younger kids: OK   Older kids: Good

Executive producer Steven Spielberg wrote the story for this boisterous children's film about a group of small-town kids searching for buried treasure. While trying to save their houses from being razed by a developer, four friends (Sean Astin, Josh Brolin, Corey Feldman, Ke Huy Quan) discover a treasure map and embark on an adventure that takes them into an underground network of secret passageways filled with obstacle courses.

This is a slick roller-coaster ride of a movie that plays like a suburban kiddie version of Spielberg's *Indiana Jones* movies, while judiciously sprinkling in elements from some Errol Flynn swashbucklers and even an old Our Gang/Little Rascals comedy, *Mama's Little Pirate.* The small amount of violence is comical in nature, but some of the teens' swearing is realistically crude. There is also a boogeyman-type character, played by the late football star John Matuszak, who is threatening at first, then lovable.

GORGO (1961)
Color, 78 minutes
Cast: Bill Travers, William Sylvester, Vincent Winter, Bruce Seton
Director: Eugene Lourié
Screenplay: John Loring and Daniel Hyatt
Science fiction/Monster adventure
Unrated
Younger kids: VG Older kids: VG

A couple of adventurers capture a dinosaur in the Irish Sea and take it back to London to exhibit at an amusement park. However, they eventually learn that the dinosaur, dubbed Gorgo, is merely a baby, and his much larger mother is on her way to rescue him.

For all the scoffing about giant monster movies of the 1950s and early '60s, a hefty number of them are well-made thrillers that hold up on their own terms even today. Children always seem to enjoy watching dinosaurs and other big creatures knock buildings down and send crowds screaming; a psychiatrist could make a lot out of this, suggesting that kids, who often feel powerless, identify with the monsters. Be that as it may, kids do love these movies and might like this one best of all. Not only does Gorgo's mama wreak impressive havoc on London, but there's the mother-son story at the heart of it, a subplot involving a young boy who befriends Gorgo, and the novelty of having the monsters get away scot-free at the end.

THE GORGON (1964)
Color, 83 minutes
Cast: Peter Cushing, Christopher Lee, Richard Pasco, Barbara Shelley, Michael Goodliffe, Patrick Troughton, Jeremy Longhurst
Director: Terence Fisher
Screenplay: John Gilling, from a story by J. Llewellyn Devine
Horror/Suspense
Unrated
Younger kids: Scary Older kids: OK

In the Balkan village of Vandorf in 1910, a young man and later his father, Professor Heitz, both die by being turned to stone from the gaze of a Gorgon, a female figure with snakes in her hair. Heitz's other son, Paul (Pasco), and the dashing Professor Meister (Lee) realize that a curse is transforming a local woman into the Gorgon by night, but Dr. Namaroff (Cushing), who knows the secret, refuses to talk.

This scrambles the Greek legends of the Gorgon with standard Hammer Films middle-European imagery to reasonably good effect, thanks to a strong cast and handsome production values. Slower moving than most Hammers, and constructed as a mystery, this will appeal primarily to pre- and early teens who have clicked with Hammer and/or the great team of Peter Cushing and Christopher Lee.

GORILLAS IN THE MIST
(1988)
Color, 129 minutes
Cast: Sigourney Weaver, Bryan
  Brown, Julie Harris, John
  Omirah Miluwi, Iain
  Cuthbertson, Constantin
  Alexandrov, Waigwa Wachira,
  Iain Glen, David Lansbury,
  Maggie O'Neill
Director: Michael Apted
Screenplay: Anna Hamilton
  Phelan; story by Phelan and
  Tab Murphy
Biographical drama/Animal story
Rated PG-13
Young children: No   Older
  children: VG

Older children who are intrigued by
animals will not want to miss this engrossing drama. It is the story of
Dian Fossey, a woman with a deep
feeling for animals, who became
profoundly upset by the knowledge
that the mountain gorillas of central
Africa were facing extinction. And
so, in 1967, Fossey (with no particular scientific training) settled in
Rwanda and set about chronicling
the plight of these gorillas.

Fossey confronts the apes and
eventually connects with them, as
she uncannily copies their behavior.
As the years pass, she becomes one
of the world's most celebrated authorities on the mountain gorilla.

The film is not recommended
for younger children. They will be
disturbed by the violence (which
is a natural part of the story) and
the transformation of Fossey from
dedicated investigator to reclusive
crusader. She ends up treasuring
her relationships with the gorillas
over all else and becomes fanati-
cally obsessed with protecting
them, to the point where she turns
off even those who are in the best

position to assist her. (Sigourney
Weaver is completely believable in
this difficult role; the scenes in
which she first approaches the gorillas are incredible.)

Then there is the fact that in
1985, Fossey was murdered, most
likely by one of the many people
she alienated in her quest to safe-
guard the animals.

GO WEST (1925)
Black & white, 69 minutes
Cast: Buster Keaton, Howard
  Truesdale, Kathleen Myers,
  Ray Thompson
Director: Buster Keaton
Screenplay: Raymond Cannon,
  based on a story by Keaton
Comedy/Silent classic
Unrated
Young children: VG   Older
  children: VG

Buster meets the wild and woolly
West in this low-key but very enjoyable silent comedy. He plays the
appropriately named Friendless, a
dude who finds himself toiling—in-
eptly, of course—on an Arizona
cattle ranch. His one true friend is
Brown Eyes, a cow who has been
shunned by a large herd of cattle.

Anyone who ever has felt alone
in the world will relate to Friendless. But it's unlikely that any
children will have experienced
some of the adventures he gets
into—including a stampede down
the main street of a city!

Go West is not considered one
of Keaton's best comedies, but it's
still fun to watch and should have
widespread appeal to kids.

THE GRAPES OF WRATH
(1940)
Black & white, 129 minutes
Cast: Henry Fonda, Jane
  Darwell, John Carradine,

Charley Grapewin, Dorris
Bowden, Russell Simpson,
John Qualen, O. Z.
Whitehead, Eddie Quillan,
Zeffie Tilbury, Darryl
Hickman, Ward Bond, Charles
Middleton, Tom Tyler, Mae
Marsh, Jack Pennick
Director: John Ford
Screenplay: Nunnally Johnson,
from the novel by John
Steinbeck
Drama/Literary classic
Unrated
Young children: VG   Older
children: VG

The Grapes of Wrath is the
tragic but ultimately uplifting
saga of "Okies," the drought-
stricken Dust Bowl farmers
whose land dried to death in the
depths of the Great Depression
of the 1930s. In search of a modern promised land, ruined homesteaders by the thousands joined
as one with other stricken hope-
fuls, all desperate to find new
lives in California. To get there,
they drove to the western termi-
nus of a yellow brick road called
Route 66.

Their will to live was immortalized in John Steinbeck's Pulitzer
Prize–winning tribute to the triumph of pioneer spirit over national hardship. His book, its title
taken from a line in Julia Ward
Howe's "Battle Hymn of the Republic," made household names
of the family Joad and preacher
Jim Casey. Their journey is riveting, now and forever.

This is a story of ordinary people and their extraordinary experiences, of poverty and triumph,
of moral commitment and moral
outrage. The Okies were not part
of a distant past when the film

was made; today, their story is a
part of 20th-century history, beautifully brought to life by director
Ford.

John Ford's heartfelt film won
Oscars for himself and for Jane
Darwell as the undefeatable Ma
Joad. His second unit captured
monochrome images of the real
Route 66, location shots that are,
today, historically valuable docu-
ments.

The book should be required
reading and the film required
viewing for every American. Just
so we remember.

THE GRASS HARP (1996)
Color, 107 minutes
Cast: Edward Furlong, Sissy
Spacek, Piper Laurie, Jack
Lemmon, Walter Matthau,
Nell Carter, Mary
Steenburgen, Roddy
McDowall, Charles Durning
Director: Charles Matthau
Screenplay: Stirling Silliphant
and Kirk Ellis, based on the
autobiographical novella by
Truman Capote
Drama
Rated PG
Young children: No   Older
children: VG

Despite its big-name cast, *The
Grass Harp* is a small-scale film.
Set in a pre–World War II Southern town, it is a simple, straightforward, coming-of-age tale. Upon
the death of his parents, Collin
Fenwick (Edward Furlong) comes
to live with his two maiden aunts,
who couldn't be more different
from each other. Verena (Sissy
Spacek) is a successful but nar-
row-minded businesswoman who
is concerned with making profits
and owning people. Her sister,

Dolly (Piper Laurie), is a gentle soul whose emotions are right on the surface; she exerts a great influence on young Collin as she draws out the boy's feelings.

During the course of the film, Collin meets a great many eccentric and colorful characters, both at home and in town. He participates in a variety of adventures, including running away and living in a tree house.

Collin, of course, will grow up to be a writer. And Dolly, Verena, and all the other characters who pass through his life are destined to, in Collin's words, "shape my life as a storyteller."

The Grass Harp is a mellow and humanistic film, filled with wonderful performances. (Best of all: Piper Laurie as the ethereal Aunt Dolly.) Some of its tenderest moments come when Charlie Cool (Walter Matthau, whose son directed the film), a wizened widower and retired judge, talks of his late wife, the meaning of love, and how difficult and elusive it is to find.

For younger children this may be too wispy and difficult to understand; more mature, older children will find much to savor here.

GREASE (1978)
Color, 110 minutes
Cast: John Travolta, Olivia Newton-John, Stockard Channing, Jeff Conaway, Didi Conn, Eve Arden, Sid Caesar, Joan Blondell, Edd Byrnes, Alice Ghostley, Dody Goodman, Lorenzo Lamas, Dinah Manoff
Director: Randal Kleiser
Screenplay: Brontë Woodard, based on the Broadway play by Jim Jacobs and Warren Casey

Musical
Rated PG
Younger kids: OK   Older kids: VG

Grease is a fantasy musical about high school life in the '50s (based on a long-running Broadway show) and rates high as utter escapism. The boys and girls are one-dimensional stereotypes, but they're very likable, and the songs ("Greased Lightning," "Hopelessly Devoted to You," "You're the One That I Want") are infectious. A serious-minded parent might object to the "message" that a solid, straight-arrow girl like Olivia Newton-John has to trash herself up in order to win the cool guy on campus. There is also the subplot about tough-talking Rizzo (Stockard Channing) fearing that she's pregnant—a topic parents would have to explain to younger viewers. But it would be foolish to take anything in this film much more seriously than one would an *Archie* comic book.

GREAT BALLS OF FIRE!
(1989)
Color, 102 minutes
Cast: Dennis Quaid, Winona Ryder, Alec Baldwin, Lisa Blount, Trey Wilson, John Doe, Steve Allen, Stephen Tobolowsky, Lisa Jane Persky, Joshua Sheffield, Mojo Nixon, Michael St. Gerard, Peter Cook, Joe Bob Briggs
Director: Jim McBride
Screenplay: McBride and Jack Baran, based on the book *Great Balls of Fire* by Myra Lewis and Murray Silver, Jr.
Musical biography
Rated PG-13
Young children: No   Older children: VG, with caution

This entertaining biography charts the rise to fame—and fall from grace—of Jerry Lee Lewis, a twice-married, Louisiana-born hell-raiser who was blessed with the ability to play a mean boogie-woogie piano. He won acclaim with such raucous, let-it-all-hang-out classics of early rock 'n' roll as "Whole Lotta Shakin' Goin' On" and the title number. But Jerry Lee forfeits his chance to rival Elvis Presley's success when he marries Myra, his cousin, who is all of 13 years old!

Unlike too many rock 'n' roll biographies, *Great Balls of Fire!* does not deify its subject. In fact, the film is almost a cartoon, with a wild performance to match by Dennis Quaid. It doesn't offer any tangible reasons for Lewis' self-destructive tendencies, but it does show us a good time, and it has many lively musical sequences that capture the spirit of the time.

Parents will have to decide whether or not they approve of their kids—however mature—watching this film, which is rated PG-13 for its sexual content. Any film in which a grown man is sexually attracted to a 13-year-old girl (even though he goes on to marry her) is not standard family fare.

THE GREAT DICTATOR
(1940)
Black & white, 128 minutes
Cast: Charlie Chaplin, Paulette
    Goddard, Jack Oakie,
    Reginald Gardiner, Maurice
    Moscovich, Billy Gilbert,
    Henry Daniell, Emma Dunn,
    Bernard Gorcey
Director: Charles Chaplin
Screenplay: Charles Chaplin
Comedy-satire
Unrated

Young children: VG   Older
   children: VG

In 1940, America was maintaining its isolationist stand, remaining on the sidelines as Europe was engulfed in war. Adolf Hitler was seen as a menace, but the true horror of his Nazi crimes was yet to be revealed. Few Americans had the audacity to take a stand as publicly as Charlie Chaplin did with this lampoon, which deftly mixes satire and political commentary.

This was also Chaplin's first talking picture—a genuine milestone in the career of a man whose distinctive look and eloquent pantomime had made him beloved around the world.

Unwilling to discard the character of The Little Tramp completely, he decided to play dual roles in this film, as a Jewish barber (the Tramp reborn), and his look-alike, Adenoid Hynkel, dictator of Tomania. Adding to the lunacy is Jack Oakie, who matches Chaplin with his broadly funny performance as a Benito Mussolini clone: Benzino Napaloni, head honcho of Bacteria.

The Great Dictator could well serve as a historical introduction to this period for young people. Although laced with comedy and satire, Hynkel's quest for world domination (symbolized by his famous ballet with an oversized balloon globe) is genuine, and the scenes of Hynkel's soldiers harassing the people of the Jewish ghetto make their point quite well. The Barber's closing speech, a plea for tolerance and world peace, was considered premature by some in 1940—before most Americans felt any involvement in the European "situation"—and out of step with the rest of the film by many critics, but carries great weight today.

THE GREAT ESCAPE (1963)
Color, 168 minutes
Cast: Steve McQueen, James Garner, Richard Attenborough, Charles Bronson, James Coburn, David McCallum, Donald Pleasence, Gordon Jackson
Director: John Sturges
Screenplay: James Clavell and W. R. Burnett, based on the book by Paul Brickhill
Action-adventure/War
Unrated
Younger kids: NG Older kids: VG

The Great Escape is one of the great action-adventure movies of the 1960s, relating in hypnotic and spine-tingling fashion the fact-based story of how a motley group of prisoners of war, including a stalwart British officer (Richard Attenborough) and a cocky American (Steve McQueen), worked to plot a massive escape from a maximum-security Nazi prison camp by digging an elaborate series of tunnels. This is taut, humorous, and exhilarating entertainment, though not sheer escapism, as its realistic depiction of the prison camp—and its bittersweet ending—are a sobering reminder of the true cost of war.

The large, international cast is superb, but the standout is McQueen; it's easy to see why this cemented his status as a superstar.

The subject matter and some specific scenes in this film make it off-limits for younger children. It's also quite long.

THE GREATEST SHOW ON EARTH (1952)
Color, 153 minutes
Cast: Betty Hutton, Charlton Heston, Cornel Wilde, Dorothy Lamour, Gloria Grahame, James Stewart, Lyle Bettger, Henry Wilcoxon, Lawrence Tierney
Director: Cecil B. DeMille
Screenplay: Fredric M. Frank, Barre Lyndon, and Theodore St. John, based on a story by Frank, St. John, and Frank Cavett
Circus/Comedy-drama
Unrated
Younger kids: Good Older kids: VG

Cecil B. DeMille's three-ring circus extravaganza is a heaping helping of corny melodrama and glitzy showmanship that's somehow impossible to resist. Charlton Heston plays the swaggering circus manager who has "sawdust in his veins," barking out orders to his crew of performers, including his aerialist girlfriend (Betty Hutton), the conceited French rival (Cornel Wilde) she starts to fall for, a cruel elephant trainer (Lyle Bettger), and a mysterious clown (James Stewart) with a dark secret who never takes off his makeup.

Like most of DeMille's movies, this may not be art, but it's hugely enjoyable; it also comes with the pedigree of having won an Academy Award as Best Picture (despite the complaints of critics and movie lovers ever since, who don't think it worthy of the honor).

From a youngster's point of view, there are plenty of authentic Ringling Bros.–Barnum & Bailey circus acts (along with some patently faked ones with stars in front of obvious rear projection), some amusing guest-star cameos, a host of story lines that are clearly drawn and easy to follow, and even a spectacular train wreck. There are images that kids may never forget—from an aerialist falling to the ground to a car driving toward a train on the railroad tracks. It's great fun "for children of all ages," as they say under the big top.

GREAT EXPECTATIONS
(1946)
Black & white, 118 minutes
Cast: John Mills, Valerie Hobson, Bernard Miles, Francis L. Sullivan, Finlay Currie, Martita Hunt, Anthony Wager, Jean Simmons, Alec Guinness, Ivor Barnard, Freda Jackson, Torin Thatcher
Director: David Lean
Screenplay: Ronald Neame, Lean, Anthony Havelock-Allan, Kay Walsh, and Cecil McGivern, based on the novel by Charles Dickens
Drama/Literary classic
Unrated
Young children: VG   Older children: VG

All the wonder, mystery, humor, and high drama of Charles Dickens' *Great Expectations* come gloriously alive in this classic adaptation.

This is the story of Pip, a poor young orphan who becomes enamored of the haughty Estella, ward of the spinsterish Miss Havisham, and the manner in which a mysterious patron ensures that Pip grows up to become a gentleman of means.

This *Great Expectations* is expertly detailed and perfectly paced;

one cannot imagine a more ideal adaptation of a fabled work of fiction, or a more flawless filmic introduction to an important work of literature. All of Dickens' characters are vividly realized, from Pip and Estella, both as children and adults, to Miss Havisham and Magwitch, an escaped convict. The cast is simply perfect (although today's kids may get a special kick out of knowing that the ebullient young Herbert is played by the same actor who, thirty years later, would become Obi-wan Kenobi in **Star Wars**).

Great Expectations has been filmed a number of times. A Hollywood version (with a mostly British cast) was released in 1934, a made-for-television movie was aired in 1974, and a TV miniseries followed in 1989, with Jean Simmons, the Estella of 1946, now cast as Miss Havisham. Then, in 1998, a modern-day adaptation was filmed with Gwyneth Paltrow, Ethan Hawke, Robert De Niro, and Anne Bancroft.

But none of them can top this British-made feature. Two years after the film's release its director, David Lean, made **Oliver Twist,** another surefire adaptation of a Dickens classic.

THE GREAT LOCOMOTIVE CHASE (1956)
Color, 85 minutes
Cast: Fess Parker, Jeffrey Hunter, Jeff York, John Lupton, Eddie Firestone, ·Kenneth Tobey
Director: Francis D. Lyon
Screenplay: Lawrence E. Watkin
Action-adventure
Unrated
Younger kids: OK   Older kids: Good

Based on the same historical incident that inspired Buster Keaton's seriocomic **The General,** this sturdy Walt Disney action yarn takes a completely serious approach to the story, while focusing the account on James J. Andrews (Fess Parker), the Union spy who stole a Confederate train during the Civil War. Jeffrey Hunter portrays the relentless Confederate conductor, William A. Fuller, who valiantly takes off in pursuit of Andrews and his band of raiders.

This is an exciting and visually impressive movie (especially in widescreen) that faithfully and realistically re-creates the locomotives of its era, as well as the fervor of the two sides fighting America's Civil War. Walt Disney loved trains and that is evident from this production, which should entertain young and old—but especially train lovers of all ages.

THE GREAT MOUSE DETECTIVE (1986)
Color, 80 minutes
Cast: Voices of Vincent Price, Barrie Ingham, Val Bettin, Suzanne Pollatschek, Candy Candido, Eve Brenner, Alan Young, Melissa Manchester, Laurie Main, Shani Wallis
Directors: John Musker, Ron Clements, Burny Mattison, and Dave Michener
Screenplay: Pete Young, Vance Gerry, Steve Hulett, Ron Clements, John Musker, Bruce M. Morris, Matthew O'Callaghan, Burny Mattison, Dave Michener, and Melvin Shaw, based on the book *Basil of Baker Street* by Eve Titus
Animated feature/Mystery
Rated G

Younger kids: VG   Older kids: VG

An excellent latter-day Disney animated feature, *The Great Mouse Detective* has been unfairly overshadowed by the enormous success of the studio's subsequent hits (**The Little Mermaid, Beauty and the Beast,** etc.). Based on Eve Titus' book *Basil of Baker Street,* it transposes the personalities of Sherlock Holmes and his companion Dr. Watson onto mice.

Basil and the faithful Dr. Dawson attempt to locate a kidnapped toy maker who is being held prisoner by evil Professor Ratigan (deliciously voiced by Vincent Price). Ratigan is building a killer robot with which he plans to take over the mouse world. The clues add up and lead the two nemeses to square off inside the clockworks of London's Big Ben.

The film lacks the visual artistry of some of the Disney classics produced before and since, but thrilling chases, enjoyable songs, and good humor combine to make *The Great Mouse Detective* a worthwhile adventure for young and old. It may not be especially memorable; that doesn't mean it isn't a lot of fun.

The film was reissued under the title *The Adventures of The Great Mouse Detective.*

THE GREAT RACE (1965)
Color, 160 minutes
Cast: Jack Lemmon, Tony Curtis, Natalie Wood, Peter Falk, Keenan Wynn, Larry Storch, Dorothy Provine, Arthur O'Connell, Vivian Vance, Ross Martin, George Macready
Director: Blake Edwards
Screenplay: Arthur Ross, based

on a story by Ross and Edwards
Comedy
Unrated
Younger kids: Good   Older kids: VG

This three-hour epic was originally billed as the most expensive (and funniest) comedy ever made. While that's a bit of an overstatement, there is much to enjoy in this boisterous yarn about a New York to Paris auto race in 1908 in which the heroic white-clad Great Leslie (Tony Curtis) and a militant suffragette (Natalie Wood) battle the villainous Professor Fate (Jack Lemmon) and his dim-witted sidekick (Peter Falk). The race covers twenty thousand miles and includes a trip through the wild West, a barroom brawl, rampaging Indians, a sinking iceberg, sword-fighting duels, **a Prisoner of Zenda** parody involving Fate's royal European look-alike, and a massive donnybrook featuring 2,357 pies of all flavors and colors.

Though overlong and over-done, the film is good, silly fun and the broad performances are geared for kids' response. Film-maker Blake Edwards dedicated this movie to "Mr. Laurel and Mr. Hardy," a gracious gesture indeed. Kids who start to squirm during the extended running time might want to try a 20-minute Laurel and Hardy short some time.

GREGORY'S GIRL (1981)
Color, 91 minutes
Cast: Gordon John Sinclair, Dee Hepburn, Chic Murray, Jake D'Arcy, Alex Norton, John Bett, Clare Grogan
Director: Bill Forsyth
Screenplay: Bill Forsyth

Comedy
Rated PG
Younger kids: VG   Older kids: VG

Gregory's Girl is a captivating Scottish film about a gangly teen-ager (Sinclair) who falls for schoolmate Dorothy (Hepburn) even after she takes his position on the school's soccer team. Kids who are used to American teen comedies and their bludgeoning, overemphatic jokes will definitely take a while to warm up to this wonderfully understated study of the pangs of adolescent love, but it is definitely worth the time and trouble.

Director-writer Forsyth's style of filmmaking is loose and casual, with subtle jokes and gags that come out of left field and sometimes farther beyond. (The most famous example is a small boy wandering the school halls in a penguin suit; he never seems to find where he is going, and is never explained.) And Forsyth's affection for all of the characters' feelings and quirks, both young and adult, is refreshingly evident: Gregory's friend Andy, who rattles off useless facts like the speed at which snot comes out of your nose ... Gregory's sister, Madeline, who dispenses worldly advice ... the headmaster who loses himself playing the harmonium.

All are charming, funny, eccentric, silly, clueless—in other words, believable and human. Sometimes the whimsy is spread a bit thick, but it's a small price to pay for an otherwise charming film.

GREMLINS (1984)
Color, 106 minutes
Cast: Zach Galligan, Phoebe
   Cates, Hoyt Axton, Polly
   Holliday, Frances Lee McCain,
   Dick Miller, Glynn Turman,
   Keye Luke, Scott Brady,
   Corey Feldman, Edward
   Andrews, Harry Carey, Jr.,
   Belinda Balaski, Judge
   Reinhold, Chuck Jones, Jackie
   Joseph
Director: Joe Dante
Screenplay: Chris Columbus
Fantasy-Horror/Comedy-drama
Rated PG
Young children: Too
   scary   Older children: OK

Inept inventor Rand Peltzer (Axton)
sends his son Billy (Galligan),
who still lives at home, a box containing a Mogwai, a cute little animal Billy names Gizmo. There
are rules regarding the creature:
Keep it out of sunlight. Keep it
away from water. Never feed it
after midnight. Of course, all
these rules are eventually violated. The water makes more
Mogwais pop out of Gizmo's back,
but they're impish rather than
sweet, and when they eat after midnight, they turn into clawed, reptilian pranksters: Gremlins, led by the
smartest, Stripe. The fast-multi-
plying Gremlins wreak havoc in
Billy's hometown, ranging from
harmless if annoying pranks to
all-out mayhem. Billy and his girlfriend Kate (Cates) have only little Gizmo to help them defeat the
rampaging creatures.
   This is an unusual mixture of
comedy, satire, and out-and-out
horror that some found unpalat-
able but the majority gobbled
down. Advertising for the film implied it was a heartwarming family
comedy like **E.T.**, while director

Dante clearly had something else
in mind. It's studded with movie
in-jokes and is vigorously creative
on its own terms.
   The problem is that the realistically rendered Gremlins are comic
at one moment and gruesome the
next. There is a mean-spiritedness
to their mayhem that (depending
on your point of view) negates
much of the humor here. And of
course, as they become more destructive, the humans in the film
are required to respond in kind:
the scene of Mom attacking the
Gremlins in her kitchen is probably the most famous (and yucky)
scene in the picture.
   Younger children will be disturbed by the Gremlins and the
violence they perpetrate. They
are, in fact, the embodiment of
hedonistic irresponsibility. Older
children may like them *because*
of this.
   A sequel followed six years
later.

**GREMLINS 2: THE NEW
BATCH** (1990)
Color, 106 minutes
Cast: Zach Galligan, Phoebe
   Cates, John Glover, Robert
   Prosky, Robert Picardo,
   Christopher Lee, Haviland
   Morris, Dick Miller, Jackie
   Joseph, Keye Luke, Kathleen
   Freeman, Rick Ducommun,
   Belinda Balaski, Paul Bartel,
   Kenneth Tobey, Henry
   Gibson, Hulk Hogan; voice of
   Tony Randall
Director: Joe Dante
Screenplay: Charlie Haas, based
   on characters created by Chris
   Columbus
Fantasy-Horror/Comedy
Rated PG-13
Young children: Too
   scary   Older children: OK

When Daniel Clamp (Glover), a well-intentioned but clueless multi-billionaire tears down part of Manhattan's Chinatown to build a "smart" skyscraper, little Gizmo the Mogwai is captured by ruthless geneticist Dr. Catheter (Lee). Billy Peltzer (Galligan, Gizmo's friend from the first movie), works in the Clamp Tower and rescues Gizmo from Catheter.

However, while Billy's away, Gizmo is accidentally doused with water and less benign Mogwais pop out of his back, eat after midnight, and turn into a horde of gleefully anti-technology (and anti-people) Gremlins, which overrun the building, threatening to spill out into the streets of New York.

There's very little plot to *Gremlins 2*; instead, once everything is in place, it's a series of wild, cartoon-inspired blackout gags featuring the Gremlins running riot in the gleaming, soulless skyscraper. The cast is game, particularly John Glover, Robert Picardo, and Christopher Lee.

Director Dante's thorough knowledge of and affection for pop culture doesn't stop him from gleefully satirizing it through the grinning, reptilian Gremlins. He good-naturedly trashes everything in sight, including the movie itself. (Many of these in-jokes will go over kids' heads but won't hurt them, either.) And Rick Baker's Gremlins are even more impressive than Chris Walas' in the first movie.

The movie is so clearly a comedy, from Jerry Goldsmith's inspired score to bits with Bugs Bunny and Daffy Duck in the credits at both ends of the film, that only the youngest children are likely to be bothered by it.

Still, those Gremlins are ferocious-looking (and -acting) creatures, and parents should be on the alert. Their menace and violence earned this a PG-13.

THE GREY FOX (1982)
Color, 92 minutes
Cast: Richard Farnsworth, Jackie Burroughs, Wayne Robson, Ken Pogue, Timothy Webber
Director: Phillip Borsos
Screenplay: John Hunter
Drama/Western
Rated PG
Younger kids: OK   Older kids: OK

A unique Western, set at the turn of the 20th century, and based on the true story of Bill Miner, a stagecoach robber known as the Gentleman Bandit who is released from jail after serving thirty-three years. He discovers a world different from the one he had known, and after watching his first-ever movie (Thomas Edison's famous Western film *The Great Train Robbery*), he is inspired to ply his skills in a new way—by robbing trains.

This Western is not a conventional "shoot-'em-up," but it deals with some of the classic themes of Western films: the passing of the frontier and the changing face of the country. Its pacing and subject matter are closer in spirit to an "art" film, and some children (not to mention parents) might have difficulty adjusting to its quiet, reflective tone and to a story that focuses on a character who is past his prime.

But Bill Miner (wonderfully played by Farnsworth) is a man who welcomes risk and adventure, and just because he's mild-mannered doesn't mean he's a wimp. His latter-day criminal career and his romance with an independent-minded female photographer are conveyed in a very light, matter-of-fact way that gives this film its charm. Moreover, director Borsos and cinematographer Frank Tidy give a fresh, elegant look to some standard elements of the Western genre.

GREYSTOKE: THE LEGEND OF TARZAN, LORD OF THE APES (1984)

Color, 129 minutes
Cast: Christopher Lambert, Andie MacDowell, Ian Holm, Ralph Richardson, James Fox, Cheryl Campbell, Ian Charleson, Nigel Davenport
Director: Hugh Hudson
Screenplay: P. H. Vazak and Michael Austin, based on the novel *Tarzan of the Apes* by Edgar Rice Burroughs
Drama/Adventure
Rated PG
Younger kids: OK Older kids: VG

Greystoke is a handsome retelling of the Tarzan legend that bears little resemblance to the movies that most of us have been weaned on. Lord John Clayton and his wife are shipwrecked on an island; both die and their infant son is subsequently raised by a family of apes. He grows, becomes a man (Lambert), and is eventually made leader of the apes. Years later, he is discovered by a Belgian explorer (Holm) and brought back to England, where he is reunited with his grandfather, Lord Clayton, 6th Earl of Greystoke (Richardson).

Children who are used to the straightforward action and adventure usually associated with Tarzan movies may need time to acclimate to this serious-minded examination of the character. The first half of the story—concerned with Tarzan's adjustment to his harsh jungle life—has many tough, savage, violent moments, as Tarzan is humiliated and beaten by other apes and loses his ape mother. But this section is more compelling than the second half of the film, when the action moves to England. There, the emphasis shifts away from dramatic to thematic narrative, and the story concerns itself with issues like Tarzan's struggle with identity, his puzzling status between two types of cultures, and the relative merits and debits of civilization.

This material is not as well thought out, and since every Englishman (except the grandfather, delightfully played by Richardson) is a prig, it's not too hard to see where Tarzan's sympathies (and the filmmakers') lie. Still, it's an admirable attempt to reinvigorate an oft-told tale, with many exciting and memorable moments.

GROUNDHOG DAY (1993)

Color, 103 minutes
Cast: Bill Murray, Andie MacDowell, Chris Elliott, Stephen Tobolowsky, Brian Doyle-Murray, Marita Geraghty, Angela Paton, Rick Ducommun, Rick Overton, Robin Duke
Director: Harold Ramis
Screenplay: Ramis and Danny Rubin, based on a story by Rubin
Comedy
Rated PG
Younger kids: VG Older kids: VG

A delightful story which stars Bill Murray as an arrogant TV weatherman who covers the Groundhog Day ceremony at Punxsutawney, Pennsylvania . . . and finds himself mysteriously reliving the same twenty-four hours of his life over and over and over again. This film actually improves and deepens with each viewing, because it works not only as a very funny comedy but as a fable, with the weatherman eventually learning to use his endless time to improve himself as a person. Murray is the perfect choice to play the cynical weatherman, and his gradual change from heartless cynic to good Samaritan is cleverly, humorously, and believably done.

There is some throwaway violence as Murray's character tries a number of unsuccessful ways to do himself in, but they are treated lightly and—with a word of explanation—shouldn't be too frightening to kids. After watching, you may have Sonny and Cher's "I Got You Babe" stuck in your head for a week.

GULLIVER'S TRAVELS
(1939)
Color, 74 minutes
Cast: Voices of Sam Parker (Gulliver), Jessica Dragonette, Lanny Ross, Pinto Colvig, Jack Mercer, Tedd Pierce
Director: Dave Fleischer
Screenplay: Dan Gordon, Cal Howard, Ted Pierce, I. Sparber, and Edmond Seward, based on the book by Jonathan Swift
Animated musical
Rated G
Younger kids: OK   Older kids: OK

This classic cartoon feature film, while not quite up to Disney standards, will entertain kids of any age. Produced by animation pioneer Max Fleischer during the golden age of Hollywood, *Gulliver's Travels* is less Swift and more *Snow White* in its screen portrayal. (That's because it was intended to compete with Disney's recently produced **Snow White and the Seven Dwarfs**.)

Shipwreck survivor Gulliver washes up in the kingdom of Lilliput, where his giant size becomes an asset to its king in his war against the land of Blefuscu. Kids will love Gabby, Lilliput's town crier, who steals the picture with his neurotic traits and childlike personality.

Impressive, realistic animation of the character of Gulliver wonderfully contrasts the cartoony antics of the Lilliputians. Thankfully a romantic subplot between Princess Glory and Prince David is downplayed in favor of musical sequences and secret-agent slapstick. The songs are mainly upbeat, with "All's Well" and "It's a Hap-hap-happy Day" as standouts.

This will also serve as a lighthearted introduction to a literary classic. Kids who enjoy it may want to see one of the live-action remakes (especially the 1996 version made for television) or even—when they're old enough—read the novel.

GULLIVER'S TRAVELS
(1996)
Color, 178 minutes
Cast: Ted Danson, Mary Steenburgen, James Fox, Thomas Sturridge, Ned Beatty, Geraldine Chaplin, Edward Fox, Alfre Woodard, John Gielgud, Robert Hardy,

Edward Woodward, Kristin Scott Thomas, Edward Petherbridge, Peter O'Toole
Director: Charles Sturridge
Screenplay: Simon Moore, based on the novel by Jonathan Swift
Literary classic/Satire
Unrated
Younger children: OK   Older children: VG

After being shipwrecked, Lemuel Gulliver (Ted Danson) returns from a series of fantastic adventures to find that no one believes him. First he was a giant among the tiny Lilliputians, then microscopic in Brobdingnag. He traveled on to Laputa, where the inhabitants are too smart to be practical, and finally wound up among the gentle and loving horses, the Houyhnhnms, who ride herd on the nasty Yahoos. Although he is deemed mad, his loving wife (Mary Steenburgen) and son see him through to a happy conclusion.

Visually glorious, with terrific special effects, this *Gulliver* (produced as a TV miniseries) has many moments of enchantment, with imaginative ideas throughout. It moves slowly at times, and purists will bemoan the fact that Jonathan Swift's satire is all but lost. The subplot of Gulliver's attempts to prove his sanity may make it confusing and off-putting to some younger viewers. However, there's plenty of adventure and excitement to compensate, and an impressive international cast.

GUNGA DIN (1939)
Black & white, 117 minutes
Cast: Cary Grant, Douglas Fairbanks, Jr., Victor McLaglen, Joan Fontaine, Sam Jaffe, Eduardo Ciannelli, Abner Biberman, Montagu Love, Robert Coote
Director: George Stevens
Screenplay: Joel Sayre and Fred Guiol, from a story by Ben Hecht and Charles MacArthur, based on the poem by Rudyard Kipling
Action-adventure
Unrated
Younger kids: OK   Older kids: VG

Gunga Din is the rip-roaring, slam-bang action-adventure movie *par excellence,* arguably the greatest of its kind ever made. Very loosely based on the Rudyard Kipling poem, the story concerns the exploits of three jaunty British soldiers (Cary Grant, Douglas Fairbanks, Jr., Victor McLaglen) and their brave native water-carrier, Gunga Din (Sam Jaffe), in 19th-century India. Packed with enough action, spectacle, and comedy for a dozen films, this is a tremendously entertaining tour de force that's made with vigor and performed with gusto by a wonderful cast.

If taken seriously, the film's imperialistic attitude and reckless heroics could be accused of glorifying war. It may behoove parents to set this up as a romp that is not to be taken seriously—if kids don't catch on for themselves from the cast members' often shameless mugging. The superbly staged fights and battle scenes and the film's devil-may-care approach have been imitated many times but seldom duplicated. The spirit of *Gunga Din* clearly can be seen in **Raiders of the Lost Ark** and particularly in its sequel, **Indiana Jones and the Temple of Doom**.

GUYS AND DOLLS (1955)
Color, 150 minutes
Cast: Marlon Brando, Frank Sinatra, Jean Simmons, Vivian Blaine, Stubby Kaye, Robert Keith, B. S. Pully, Veda Ann Borg, Sheldon Leonard, Regis Toomey, Johnny Silver, Dan Dayton, George E. Stone
Director: Joseph L. Mankiewicz
Screenplay: Mankiewicz, based on the musical written by Jo Swerling and Abe Burrows based on characters created by Damon Runyon
Musical
Unrated
Young children: OK   Older children: VG

Author-journalist Damon Runyon was fabled for creating larger-than-life characters who were amusingly broad caricatures of 1920s New York gangsters, horse players, showgirls, and Broadway hangers-on. These personalities were high livers and high rollers who acted tough while speaking in a colorful vernacular. They populated the stories Runyon published in 1932 as *Guys and Dolls,* which was the basis of the legendary Broadway musical on which this movie is based.

Younger kids will find some of this too abstract, but older kids, especially those who've become interested in Broadway musicals, will enjoy the parade of characters led by gambler Sky Masterson (Marlon Brando), his crap game–organizing acolyte Nathan Detroit (Frank Sinatra), Nathan's chronically disappointed bride-to-be, nightclub singer Miss Adelaide (Vivian Blaine, re-creating her famous Broadway performance), and Sarah Brown (Jean Simmons), the straight-arrow soul-saver from the neighborhood Mission who's swept off her feet by Sky but also captures his heart in return. Not to mention Nicely-Nicely Johnson, Big Jule, Benny Southstreet, Harry the Horse, Rusty Charlie, Society Max, and Angie the Ox.

Marlon Brando, then coming off his celebrated, Oscar-winning performance in *On the Waterfront,* is more than adequate as hotshot gambler Masterson, while Frank Sinatra and Vivian Blaine are fine as Nathan and Miss Adelaide. Jean Simmons, meanwhile, is perfectly cast as sweet Sarah Brown.

The film is not as buoyant or fast-paced as one would like it to be, but the musical numbers are dynamite. Frank Loesser's score opens with the emblematic "Fugue for Tinhorns" and includes "Luck Be a Lady," "If I Were a Bell," "The Oldest Established," "Adelaide's Lament," and the rousing show-stopper "Sit Down, You're Rocking the Boat," performed by Stubby Kaye (who created the role of Nicely-Nicely Johnson on Broadway).

This may be an instance where kids will best be served by showing them some of the lively musical numbers first; if they respond, they may ask to see the rest of the film as well.

GYPSY (1962)
Color, 149 minutes
Cast: Rosalind Russell, Natalie Wood, Karl Malden, Paul Wallace, Betty Bruce, Parley Baer, Harry Shannon, Suzanne Cupito (Morgan Brittany), Ann Jillian, Harvey Korman
Director: Mervyn LeRoy
Screenplay: Leonard Spigelgass, based on the musical *Gypsy* by Arthur Laurents, based in

turn on *Gypsy, a Memoir* by Gypsy Rose Lee
Musical biography
Unrated
Young children: OK   Older children: VG

Gypsy is a highly entertaining adaptation of a classic Broadway musical based on the true story of Mama Rose, a stage mother supreme who's determined to transform her daughters June and Louise into vaudeville stars in the 1920s. She has guts and determination to spare, as evidenced by the forceful number "Some People" in which she states her goals in no uncertain terms. Circumstance brings Rose and her daughters to a disreputable burlesque theater, where Louise, the quieter of the two girls, winds up going on stage as a stripper—and becoming a star under the name Gypsy Rose Lee.

Rosalind Russell, who made her name as the dynamic star of sharp screen comedies in the 1930s and '40s, is a fine choice to play Rose, the role created on Broadway by brassy Ethel Merman. And willowy Natalie Wood does well as Gypsy, although her singing (like some of Russell's) was dubbed.

Among the memorable Jule Styne and Stephen Sondheim songs are "Let Me Entertain You," "Some People," "Small World," "Everything's Coming Up Roses," and "Together Wherever We Go." *Gypsy* has great dialogue and seedy show-business atmosphere, but what makes it work—and gives it relevance to young viewers especially—is the relationship between a manipulative mother and her daughters. Such songs as "If Mama Was Married" and "Little Lamb" express the feel-

ings of the girls, who've never had a normal childhood—or for that matter, a normal mother!

Despite the fact that Louise strips for a living, the content of *Gypsy* is fairly innocent. The film is long, but youngsters will enjoy the musical numbers and quite likely relate to the youthful characters onscreen.

GYPSY COLT (1954)
Color, 72 minutes
Cast: Donna Corcoran, Ward Bond, Frances Dee, Larry Keating, Lee Van Cleef
Director: Andrew Marton
Screenplay: Martin Berkeley, based on a story by Eric Knight
Animal story/Drama
Unrated
Younger kids: VG   Older kids: VG

This disguised semi-remake of **Lassie Come Home** is a minor but touching children's film that's perfect for young animal lovers; it features some nice scenery and lovely color photography. Child star Donna Corcoran gives a winning performance as a little girl named Meg who owns a beautiful black horse named Gypsy. She rides him to school every morning, and every afternoon, he dutifully trots over to the schoolhouse and waits outside to pick her up. However, when a bad drought affects her farming community, Meg's parents (Ward Bond, Frances Dee) are forced to sell Gypsy to a racing stable some five hundred miles away.

If you remember *Lassie Come Home,* you know what happens next; if not, just reassure your kids that there is a happy ending in sight.

H

HAIR (1979)
Color, 121 minutes
Cast: John Savage, Treat
  Williams, Beverly D'Angelo,
  Annie Golden, Dorsey Wright,
  Don Dacus, Cheryl Barnes,
  Nicholas Ray, Charlotte Rae,
  Miles Chapin, Michael Jeter
Director: Milos Forman
Screenplay: Michael Weller
Musical
Rated PG
Young children: No   Older
  children: VG

Hollywood waited a sensible decade before looking back at the
1960s, in this movie version of the
Rado–Ragni–MacDermot stage
hit of 1967.

More cohesive as a rock movie
than it was as a live musical (although arguably less spontaneous
and energetic), the film version
tells more of a story: young
Claude from Oklahoma comes
close to drowning in New York's
Lower East Side hippie culture, as
he tries to learn everything about
life before facing death in Vietnam.

Lots of songs came out of the
show—"The Age of Aquarius,"
"Let the Sunshine In," "Good
Morning Starshine"—which is the
very definition of pro-drug and
anti-establishment (parents will
want to explain why this is a period piece). It's also just as naked
as the controversial play (parents
may need to explain the differences between boys and girls).

Nevertheless, the movie is recommended as something of a social documentary—albeit with
Twyla Tharp choreography.

HAIRSPRAY (1988)
Color, 96 minutes
Cast: Sonny Bono, Ruth Brown,
  Divine, Colleen Fitzpatrick,
  Michael St. Gerard, Debbie
  Harry, Ricki Lake, Leslie Ann
  Powers, Jerry Stiller, Shawn
  Thompson, Pia Zadora, Ric
  Ocasek
Director: John Waters
Screenplay: John Waters
Comedy
Rated PG
Young children: OK   Older
  children: OK

Shock- 'n' schlockmeister John Waters, of *Pink Flamingos* fame, does
an about-face with this family-
friendly, semi-autobiographical comedy about life in high school in
1962 Baltimore. Crammed with
obscure rock tunes of the times
and peppered with forgotten pop
dances, it's about an *American
Bandstand*-type show on local TV
that's forced to tune in to the new
civil rights and integrate the
dance floor.

Combined with the very real
social commentary is a campy
comic script about overweight
Tracy Turnblad (yes, that's a pre-
diet, pre–talk show Ricki Lake),
who becomes a sensation on *The
Corny Collins Show*, to the dis-
pleasure of her dad (Stiller) and

mom (Divine, who also plays the male station manager).

Well worth it for a PG taste of the dank Waters, who cameos appropriately as a crazy shrink.

HANS CHRISTIAN ANDERSEN (1952)
Color, 120 minutes
Cast: Danny Kaye, Farley Granger, Jeanmaire, Joey Walsh, Philip Tonge, Erik Bruhn, Roland Petit
Director: Charles Vidor
Screenplay: Moss Hart, based on a story by Myles Connolly
Musical
Unrated
Younger children: VG   Older children: VG

Danny Kaye plays the legendary Danish writer of children's stories in this elegant (if imperfect) film about the adventures of Hans Christian Andersen. Never designed to be a genuine biography and bearing little resemblance to the truth, the film strings together a group of charming musical numbers by Frank Loesser with a far-fetched romantic story.

Small children will delight in the musical story numbers, such as "The Inch Worm," "The Ugly Duckling" (which Kaye sings to a small boy whose head has been shaved), and "Thumbelina." There are several ballets featuring French ballerina Jeanmaire, which might not please all the children, but certainly will inspire the youngsters who have been to dance classes.

In his diverse screen career, Kaye could be a rubber-faced clown or a scat-singing hipster. Here he plays the title role with sensitivity, subtlety, and polish. Hans is a cobbler who makes up stories and tells them to the children of his village. When the schoolmaster complains that the children would rather listen to Hans' tales than attend classes, an effort gets underway to throw Hans out of the town. Before they force him away, he travels to Copenhagen and becomes enamored of a beautiful ballerina.

Since the entire production is geared to appeal to children, the production numbers, based on Andersen fairy tales, are lavish and imaginative. And the more dramatic moments in the story are depicted with gentleness so as not to disturb little children.

The songs, more than anything else, make this a family perennial.

HANS CHRISTIAN ANDERSEN'S THUMBELINA
(see **Thumbelina**)

A HARD DAY'S NIGHT (1964)
Black & white, 85 minutes
Cast: The Beatles (John Lennon, Paul McCartney, George Harrison, Ringo Starr), Wilfrid Brambell, Norman Rossington, Victor Spinetti, John Junkin, Anna Quayle, Kenneth Haigh
Director: Richard Lester
Screenplay: Alun Owen
Musical/Comedy
Unrated
Younger children: VG   Older children: VG

In the early 1960s, a mop-topped rock 'n' roll quartet known as The Beatles—John Lennon, Paul McCartney, George Harrison, and Ringo Starr—revolutionized teen culture, style, fashion, and music. Most significantly, their astounding international success conclusively proved that rock 'n' roll was here to stay.

A Hard Day's Night was a low-budget film that was intended to cash in on their enormous popularity, but the filmmakers turned it into something more: an innovative, dazzlingly directed mix of cinema verité and comedy. The slim storyline involves the boys (as themselves) preparing for a London television show, with much of the humor stemming from the antics of Paul's ill-humored and interfering grandfather (Wilfrid Brambell). Along the way, a representative sampling of early Beatles hits are performed, including "Can't Buy Me Love," "I Should Have Known Better," "And I Love Her," "This Boy," "She Loves You," and the title number.

For younger audiences, the film offers an entertaining peek at the melodious madness known as Beatlemania and may help explain the quartet's enormous success. For their elders (who, incredibly in some cases, are now grandparents), *A Hard Day's Night* is a sweet slice of '60s nostalgia.

If your family enjoys this film, you'll also like the Beatles' next movie, **Help!**

HARRIET THE SPY (1996)
Color, 101 minutes
Cast: Michelle Trachtenberg, Rosie O'Donnell, Vanessa Lee Chester, Gregory Smith, J. Smith-Cameron, Robert Joy, Eartha Kitt, Don Francks, Eugene Lipinski
Director: Bronwen Hughes
Screenplay: Douglas Petrie and Theresa Rebeck, based on Greg Taylor and Julie Talen's adaptation of the novel by Louise Fitzhugh
Comedy-drama
Rated PG
Younger kids: OK   Older kids: OK

Harriet's parents are constantly preoccupied, so Harriet (Michelle Trachtenberg) spends most of her time with Gully (Rosie O'Donnell), a nanny and best friend rolled into one. Gully encourages Harriet to keep a journal, to find adventures in her daily life and record her innermost feelings. Harriet's best friends, Sport and Janie, often ask to read the journal, but Harriet refuses and keeps it to herself. One night, Harriet's parents impulsively fire Gully, leaving Harriet to fend for herself. When the class snob gets her hands on Harriet's journal and reads it aloud, including some unflattering and unkind remarks about her best friends, the little girl's life goes to pieces. She is very much alone, and in her despair, takes revenge on everyone who has shunned her—even her former pals.

Youthful fans of Louise Fitzhugh's novel will enjoy seeing it come to life, although this film is slowly paced and, overall, a mixed bag. The cast is fine, but the story has highs and lows, and those lulls get pretty dreary over 100 minutes' time.

The film's greatest value is in its exploration of friendship and its inevitable ups and downs. Kids may well identify with some of the crises in Harriet's relationships and could even learn a few useful things about keeping one's thoughts private.

Rosie O'Donnell is so entertaining as Gully that the film

takes a huge dip when she leaves. Fortunately, she does turn up again later on.

Young kids may be squirming and might not understand all the concepts here; older kids will appreciate *Harriet the Spy* much more.

HARRY AND THE HENDERSONS (1987)
Color, 110 minutes
Cast: John Lithgow, Melinda Dillon, Margaret Langrick, Joshua Rudoy, Kevin Peter Hall, David Suchet, Lainie Kazan, Don Ameche, M. Emmet Walsh
Director: William Dear
Screenplay: William Dear
Comedy/Science fiction
Rated PG
Young children: VG Older children: OK

The Henderson family encounters a huge, hairy Sasquatch (aka "Bigfoot") in the Washington woods; thinking they've killed it, they take it back to their Seattle home, but the Bigfoot, whom they dub Harry, revives. At first, the family and Harry (Kevin Peter Hall) are terrified of each other, but soon they warm to the apelike creature's charming, goofy personality.

Basically a variation on **E.T.**, this movie will delight younger children, who'll adore Harry and who'll best respond to the plentiful slapstick. Older kids may disregard the movie as "kid stuff" but might well find Rick Baker's amazing makeup effects interesting.

However, the film simply goes on too long, and not all the complications that arise are very interesting. For adults, it's all a little too broad, though John Lithgow

and Melinda Dillon are both very good as the parents.

HARVEY (1950)
Black & white, 104 minutes
Cast: James Stewart, Josephine Hull, Peggy Dow, Charles Drake, Cecil Kellaway, Jesse White, Victoria Horne, Wallace Ford
Director: Henry Koster
Screenplay: Mary Chase and Oscar Brodney, based on Chase's play
Comedy
Unrated
Younger kids: Good Older kids: VG

James Stewart is a delight in this wonderful adaptation of the whimsical Broadway hit about Elwood P. Dowd, a gentle boozer whose constant drinking companion is an invisible six-foot rabbit named Harvey—who may or may not be imaginary. Elwood and Harvey become inseparable, much to the chagrin of his dotty socialite sister (Josephine Hull) who wants to have him committed, but when Elwood goes to an asylum for examination, he even manages to make a believer out of the head psychiatrist (Cecil Kellaway).

In a role he was born to play (which he had performed for a while on Broadway, and which he reprised on stage many years later), Stewart is absolutely perfect, exhibiting all the comic warmth and innocence for which he was known and loved. The rest of the cast is excellent, particularly Hull in an Oscar-winning performance and Jesse White as a befuddled asylum attendant.

Behind the laughs, there is a serious philosophical message about escaping from reality and what being "normal" means. At the time *Harvey* was made, drinking—even getting drunk—was acceptable, in life and onscreen. Elwood P. Dowd is not a drunk; he's what used to be called a tippler, but some parents might feel the need to explain this to their kids.

What won't need explaining is the "magic" of Harvey. We never actually see the rabbit, but the illusion is so strong, and our desire to see him so intense, that it almost seems as if he's there, right before our eyes.

THE HARVEY GIRLS (1946)
Color, 101 minutes
Cast: Judy Garland, John Hodiak, Ray Bolger, Angela Lansbury, Preston Foster, Virginia O'Brien, Marjorie Main, Chill Wills, Kenny Baker, Selena Royle, Cyd Charisse
Director: George Sidney
Screenplay: Edmund Beloin, Nathaniel Curtis, Harry Crane, James O'Hanlon, and Samson Raphaelson, based on a story by Eleanore Griffin and William Rankin, from the novel by Samuel Hopkins Adams
Musical
Unrated
Young children: VG Older children: VG

This sprightly musical is set in the Western burg of Sandrock in the 1890s and shows how the town is tamed by the title characters, girl-next-door types who travel west to work as waitresses for a restaurant chain establishing itself along the new Santa Fe Railroad. Along the way there is plenty of drama and passion as sweet Susan Brad-

ley (Judy Garland), who comes to town as a mail-order bride and ends up as one of the Harvey Girls, becomes romantically involved with virile saloon owner Ned Trent (John Hodiak).

It also is fun to see a young Angela Lansbury playing a saloon performer/seductress/villainess.

Kids who only know Judy Garland from **The Wizard of Oz** will enjoy watching her play a different kind of part in this lively, sometimes silly, and innocuous film, which also features Oz's immortal Scarecrow, Ray Bolger.

The film's showcase production number, built around the Academy Award–winning song "On the Atchison, Topeka, and the Santa Fe," is as impressive today as it was upon the film's release, and captures the spirit and spectacle that make these vintage Hollywood musicals so appealing to audiences of all ages.

HATARI! (1962)
Color, 159 minutes
Cast: John Wayne, Elsa Martinelli, Red Buttons, Hardy Kruger, Gerard Blain, Bruce Cabot
Director: Howard Hawks
Screenplay: Leigh Brackett, based on a story by Harry Kurnitz
Action-adventure/Animal story
Unrated
Younger kids: OK Older kids: VG

John Wayne stars as the leader of a group of international big-game catchers in Tanganyika—including two women and four other men—who round up animals to send to zoos around the world. The camera lets us ride along with them as they stalk their prey and take incredible risks.

Director Howard Hawks' mellow and laid-back African travelogue/safari is way too long and spends a lot of time on both comedy relief and the romantic tensions within the group. But the location photography is magnificent, and the action sequences are truly unusual. Older children will appreciate both the camaraderie and the sense of competition within the camp, while younger ones will love the assortment of wild animals on display, particularly the adorable collection of adopted baby elephants (who stomp around to Henry Mancini's catchy theme, "The Baby Elephant Walk").

THE HAUNTED PALACE (1963)
Color, 85 minutes
Cast: Vincent Price, Debra Paget, Lon Chaney, Frank Maxwell, Leo Gordon, Elisha Cook, John Dierkes, Milton Parsons
Director: Roger Corman
Screenplay: Charles Beaumont, from the story "The Case of Charles Dexter Ward" by H. P. Lovecraft
Horror/Melodrama
Unrated
Younger kids: Too creepy   Older kids: OK

Though taking the title from a poem by Edgar Allan Poe, this is really a good adaptation of one of the less outré works by the great American horror writer H. P. Lovecraft and could serve as an introduction to his works for teenagers with an interest in horror fiction. Price plays a dual role, an 18th-century warlock burned at the stake by his New England neighbors and the warlock's descendant. When he moves into his ancestor's home, he is possessed by the dead man's spirit and continues to carry out his evil schemes.

As usual with the films in the Poe series from director Roger Corman, the production values are good, though theatrical, but this time out, the makeup effects are second-rate. Price's performances are always ripe but never hammy, and here he gets to play characters with strongly contrasting personalities. Overall, one of the better films in this series.

THE HAUNTING (1963)
Black & white, 112 minutes
Cast: Julie Harris, Claire Bloom, Richard Johnson, Russ Tamblyn, Lois Maxwell, Rosalie Crutchley
Director: Robert Wise
Screenplay: Nelson Gidding, from the novel *The Haunting of Hill House* by Shirley Jackson
Horror/Drama
Unrated
Younger kids: No   Older kids: OK, with caution

An investigator of haunted houses hires several people who have had psychic episodes to help him in uncovering the secrets of an old New England mansion with a spooky reputation. But none of them really appreciates the power of the supernatural.

One of the best, and scariest, haunted house movies ever made, this film is aimed at adults, not youngsters, but the more mature teenagers of today could well relate to it. As with many horror films, themes of alienation underlie much of the story, and the leading character, perfectly played by Julie Harris, is a classic outsider figure. Though director Wise never uses standard scare techniques, the movie has several distinctly unnerving scenes that can linger in the memory for decades.

HEDD WYN (1992)
Color, 123 minutes
Cast: Huw Garmon, Catrin Fychan, Ceri Cunningham, Llio Silwyn, Grey Evans, Gwen Ellis, Emma Kelly
Director: Paul Taylor
Screenplay: Alan Llwyd
Drama
Unrated
Young children: No   Older children: VG

Hedd Wyn, the first Welsh film ever to earn a Best Foreign Film Academy Award nomination, is a quietly moving and beautifully filmed drama based on the true story of Ellis Evans, whose Welsh name is Hedd Wyn. He comes from a rural farm family, but his interests lie not in tilling soil: Ellis is a talented and compassionate poet. His endeavors are encouraged by his parents and siblings, and he dreams of winning his country's most coveted literary prize.

The time is the 20th century's second decade. World War I is raging not too far from the pastoral Welsh fields where Ellis has come of age. This young man is a life-embracing soul who is horrified by the thought of having to kill another human being. To some—especially those who preach blind, patriotic fervor—Ellis is nothing more than a coward. Inevitably, Ellis finds himself conscripted into the military.

On a universal level, *Hedd Wyn* is a persuasive indictment of war and its utter futility. On a personal level, it is the heartfelt story of one young man and how his life flickers briefly but ever so brightly.

Mature children should find this story both moving and rewarding. It is not meant for younger viewers.

HEIDI (1937).
Black & white, 88 minutes (also available in computer-colored version)
Cast: Shirley Temple, Jean Hersholt, Arthur Treacher, Helen Westley, Pauline Moore, Thomas Beck, Mary Nash, Mady Christians, Sig Rumann, Marcia Mae Jones
Director: Allan Dwan
Screenplay: Walter Ferris and Julien Josephson, based on the novel by Johanna Spyri
Literary classic
Unrated
Young children: VG   Older children: VG

This ageless and beautiful tale of a young girl's loyalty to her beloved grandfather offers just the right mix of melodrama and comedy. As the story unfolds, Heidi is taken by her aunt to live with her crusty old grandfather, an embittered recluse who resides in a cabin in the mountains outside an Alpine village. As the months pass, the youngster and the elderly man grow to love one another and live a life of serenity and joy among their neighbors. Then one day, Heidi is abducted by her greedy aunt and taken to the home of a rich city family, where she is intended to be companion to a crippled girl.

Parents should know that there are scenes of deep emotion in this story, such as when Heidi befriends the disabled girl though she yearns to return to her mountain home, and when the grandfather searches the unfamiliar streets for his missing child. And there are also scenes that are laugh-out-loud delightful, such as when a runaway organ grinder's monkey enters the window of Heidi's adopted city home. This rendering of *Heidi* does take liberties with the book on which it's based, but the appeal of the film is so great that it makes some other more "faithful" versions of the tale seem wanting.

HEIDI'S SONG (1982)
Color, 94 minutes
Cast: Voices of Margery Gray, Lorne Greene, Sammy Davis, Jr., Peter Cullen, Roger DeWitt, Richard Erdman, Fritz Feld
Director: Robert Taylor
Screenplay: Joseph Barbera, Taylor, and Jameson Brewer, based on *Heidi* by Johanna Spyri
Animated feature/Musical
Rated G
Younger kids: OK Older kids: No

The veteran animation team William Hanna and Joseph Barbera (*Tom and Jerry*, *The Flintstones*, etc.) produced this musical cartoon version of the classic *Heidi* tale; the result is sugary sweet but not very exciting.

Heidi is brought to live with her gruff grandfather (Greene) and makes friends with all his pets and animals. The first night she dreams a "Nightmare Ballet," a surreal musical sequence that introduces Heidi to the creatures of the mountain. After becoming friends with goatherd Peter and bonding with Grandfather, Heidi is moved to the city by her Aunt Dete to become a companion to Clara, a young girl who is confined to a wheelchair. Sweet Heidi quickly adapts to her new surroundings and even wins over the cellar rats. The Head Rat (Sammy Davis, Jr.) tries to inspire the others to return to their evil ways with an elaborate musical number, "Ode to a Rat." Peter, along with his animal friends, helps Heidi to return to the mountain and her grandfather with Clara.

Everything about this film seems perfunctory, and it's unlikely to become a family favorite. It's missing a certain spark. There are several live-action versions of the story that are far superior.

HELLO, DOLLY! (1969)
Color, 146 minutes
Cast: Barbra Streisand, Walter Matthau, Michael Crawford, E. J. Peaker, Marianne McAndrew, Tommy Tune, Louis Armstrong
Director: Gene Kelly
Screenplay: Ernest Lehman, based on the musical by Jerry Herman and Michael Stewart, based in turn on the play *The Matchmaker* by Thornton Wilder
Musical
Rated G
Young children: VG Older children: VG

This brash, entertaining musical, based on the long-running Broadway show, takes strength from an energetic cast and a robust score by Jerry Herman. On its surface, the story doesn't sound terribly exciting: Dolly Levi, a widowed Jewish New York City matchmaker, intends to marry a successful grain merchant from Yonkers named Horace Vandergelder. However, it *is* wonderful entertainment, which stars the incomparable Barbra Streisand (in a role usually cast with an older woman) as well as lovable curmudgeon Walter Matthau. The two play scenes that will have the family laughing out loud, especially an elaborate sequence in a restaurant called the Harmonia Gardens, which Dolly enters as a chorus line of welcoming waiters sing her praises in the classic title tune. Although Dolly has arranged for Horace to meet another marriage prospect there, it is clear that she has wedding plans of her own! There also is a comical subplot involving the adventures and subsequent romances of two young clerks in Horace's grain establishment, and this also helps to keep the plot moving at a healthy speed.

This is a stylish and colorful production with fine tunes sung by such top musical performers as Streisand and Tommy Tune. Fans of Michael Crawford (known to a later generation as the star of the musical play *Phantom of the Opera*) will enjoy seeing him as a wiry young man, and even youngsters may recognize the voice (if not the face) of Louis Armstrong, who sings "Hello, Dolly!" with Streisand. (It was his record that made the tune a hit while the show was running on Broadway.)

Although the 146-minute running time may be longer than youngsters are accustomed to, they will probably want to stay and watch the film to its very happy ending.

Hello, Dolly! was based on a (nonmusical) play by Thornton Wilder called *The Matchmaker,* which was filmed in 1958 with Shirley Booth in the leading role.

HELP! (1965)
Color, 90 minutes
Cast: The Beatles (John Lennon, Paul McCartney, George Harrison, Ringo Starr), Leo McKern, Eleanor Bron, Victor Spinetti, Roy Kinnear, John Bluthal, Patrick Cargill, Alfie Bass
Director: Richard Lester
Screenplay: Marc Behm and Charles Wood
Comedy with music
Unrated
Young children: VG Older children: VG

The Beatles' follow-up to **A Hard Day's Night** is completely different in tone, but turned out to be just as great a success.

It's a completely zany, wildly colorful film (which could be described as a live-action cartoon in which Ringo unknowingly finds himself in possession of a red ring that a priest and priestess require in order to perform a human sacrifice). Director Richard Lester led the Fab Four through a myriad of sight gags and clever sequences.

The songs include the title hit, as well as "You're Gonna Lose That Girl," "You've Got to Hide Your Love Away," and "Ticket to Ride."

Kids who've seen *A Hard Day's Night* should certainly make this their next selection.

HERCULES (1959)
Color, 107 minutes
Cast: Steve Reeves, Sylva Koscina, Gianna Maria Canale, Luciana Paluzzi

Director: Pietro Francisci
Screenplay: Pietro Francisci, Ennio de Concini, and Gaio Frattini
Action-adventure/Fantasy
Rated G
Younger kids: OK   Older kids: Good

Fans of the 1990s Hercules TV show may enjoy comparing it to this tacky film, the first of many sword-and-sandal epics that flooded the world's screens throughout the late 1950s and '60s. This Italian import was a big hit when it was released (due to promoter Joseph E. Levine's huge publicity campaign), and it's still pretty entertaining in a cheesy way. Former Mr. America Steve Reeves stars as the mythological muscleman, helping Jason find the Golden Fleece, while performing his legendary twelve labors. Though Levine's hype promised a tantalizing feast of sex and violence ("SEE heroic Hercules rip down the Age of Orgy's palace of lustful pleasure!"—"SEE the powerful Hercules crush the savage apemen that guard the shrine of the Golden Fleece!"), this is actually a fairly tame action fantasy with a comic-strip plot that should capture adolescent imaginations and amuse current Hercules fans.

HERCULES (1997)
Color, 93 minutes
Cast: Voices of Tate Donovan, Susan Egan, James Woods, Danny DeVito, Rip Torn, Samantha Eggar, Bobcat Goldthwait, Matt Frewer, Hal Holbrook, Barbara Barrie; Charlton Heston (narrator)
Directors: John Musker and Ron Clements
Screenplay: Clements, Barry Johnson, Don McEnery, Irene Mecchi, Musker, and Bob Shaw, from a story by Johnson
Animated feature
Rated G
Young children: VG   Older children: VG

When the evil Hades learns that Hercules—the only son of Greek gods Zeus and Hera—is the one thing standing in the way of him taking over control of Mount Olympus, he sends his henchmen, Pain and Panic, to kidnap the baby, make him mortal, and kill him. As it happens, they don't do a thorough job. Not only does Hercules live, but he retains his godlike strength, though he must now live his life as a mortal. While he loves his human parents, he wants to know where he truly belongs, and learns that his destiny is to become a true hero—for when he does, he will rejoin the gods on Mount Olympus. This, however, will take some doing.

Hercules is a lot of fun. You can tell you're going to have a good time from the moment the Muses come to life and begin to sing. The film has been criticized for not having heart and for being too self-aware, which may be true, but it's still a very entertaining movie.

There are some mildly scary moments here and there, including the baby Hercules' fall from grace, the grown-up hero's battle with the fearsome hydra, the gargantuan battle for supremacy on Mount Olympus, and the climax in which we see Hades' whirlpool of lost souls.

But for the most part, children should be wise to the fact that this is a saga, and nothing is to be taken *too* seriously.

One could even say that *Hercules* has educational value, as it does introduce kids to a number of the Greek gods. But mostly it's out for fun.

HERE COMES MR. JORDAN
(1941)
Black & white, 93 minutes
Cast: Robert Montgomery, Evelyn Keyes, Claude Rains, Rita Johnson, Edward Everett Horton, James Gleason, John Emery, Donald MacBride
Director: Alexander Hall
Writer: Sidney Buchman and Seton I. Miller, based on the play *Heaven Can Wait* by Harry Segall
Fantasy/Comedy
Unrated
Younger children: OK, with caution   Older children: VG

Saxophone-playing boxer Joe Pendleton (Robert Montgomery) crashes his small plane and finds himself unexpectedly in heaven. But it's all a mistake made by an overzealous heavenly messenger (Edward Everett Horton). Unfortunately, Joe's body has already been disposed of. To correct this grievous error, the crafty angel Mr. Jordan (Claude Rains) deposits Joe in another body so he can win the championship, which he is destined to do. Joe finds himself inhabiting the body and the life of a recently murdered young millionaire. With the help of his perplexed former manager (James Gleason) and a desperate young woman (Evelyn Keyes), Joe foils plots by the millionaire's avaricious wife and her lover, becomes a better rich man than the fellow he has replaced, and falls in love—all the while preparing to return to the ring.

One of the best fantasies ever made, *Here Comes Mr. Jordan* is a fascinating film for impressionable kids because it deals with the great imponderables of life and death and adds some wrinkles of its own . . . like the notion that a spirit can inhabit more than one body. One of the eeriest scenes occurs near the end of the film, when it's decided to meld the old Joe and the new—and remove his memory of the transition. The scene occurs while Joe is taking a shower, and involves no special effects whatsoever. It's all a matter of the movie's credibility and the viewer's willingness to believe.

Funny, mystical, and endearing, *Here Comes Mr. Jordan* is the kind of film worth introducing your kids to. They just might love it.

The story was remade in 1978 with Warren Beatty as *Heaven Can Wait*.

A HERO AIN'T NOTHIN' BUT A SANDWICH (1978)
Color, 105 minutes
Cast: Cicely Tyson, Paul Winfield, Larry B. Scott, Helen Martin, Glynn Turman, David Groh
Director: Ralph Nelson
Screenplay: Alice Childress, based on her novel
Drama
Rated PG
Younger children: No   Older children: VG

This clear-eyed drama tells the story of Benjamin Johnson, a young African-American growing up in a Los Angeles ghetto, who is thirteen going on middle age. While precocious beyond his years, he still is a child who desperately needs the support and love of his parents. It is no wonder that Benjamin is resentful that his dad abandoned his family and his stepfather-to-be lives with his mother. As a result, the boy becomes insolent and alienated . . . and a junior high school junkie.

A Hero Ain't Nothin' but a Sandwich insightfully examines a number of issues relevant to coming of age in contemporary American society, from the sobering realities of inner-city survival to the detrimental impact media superstars can have on young, impressionable minds.

Producer Robert B. Radnitz carved out a career making meaningful and socially responsible films; this one may strike some kids as being overly preachy, but Larry B. Scott's utterly believable portrayal of Benjamin scores a bull's-eye. A realistic portrayal of urban ghetto life, the film is rated PG for its language and dramatic reality.

HESTER STREET (1975)
Black & white, 92 minutes
Cast: Carol Kane, Steven Keats, Mel Howard, Dorrie Kavanaugh, Doris Roberts, Stephen Strimpell
Director: Joan Micklin Silver
Screenplay: Silver, based on Abraham Cahan's story *Yekl*
Period drama
Rated PG
Young children: No Older children: VG

Hester Street takes place in New York City's Lower East Side immigrant community in 1896, and centers on the relationship between Jake, a Russian Jew who has been in America for three years, and Gitl, his wife who has just arrived in her new homeland. Jake is a braggart and extrovert who speaks fluent English, wears "Yankee" clothing, demands that his son Yossele be called "Joey," and dreams of the day when the boy will be President.

Meanwhile, he constantly and cruelly berates Gitl, a shy and superstitious greenhorn who prefers her Old World garb and would much rather her son be called by his given name. Gitl is adamantly against change at first. But in America, little boys do not wear locks of hair over their ears, Torah scholars have to earn their way just like everyone else, and Gitl must learn to assimilate and find her place within the culture of her adopted country.

Hester Street is remarkable for its period detail and overall atmosphere. At its best, it is a touching portrait (and a pointed feminist statement), as Gitl discovers more about her new country and in so doing gains strength and self-confidence.

Few American films dramatize the turn-of-the-20th-century immigrant experience as well as this one. It should be a springboard for lively conversation with the entire family.

HEY THERE, IT'S YOGI BEAR (1964)
Color, 89 minutes
Cast: Voices of Daws Butler (Yogi Bear), Don Messick, Julie Bennett, Mel Blanc, J. Pat O'Malley, Hal Smith
Directors: William Hanna and Joseph Barbera
Screenplay: Barbera, Warren Foster, and Hanna
Animated feature/Musical
Rated G

Younger kids: OK   Older kids: OK

TV cartoon star Yogi Bear made his movie debut in this lightweight animated musical comedy. The simple story involves Yogi's usual shenanigans in Jellystone Park with pal Boo Boo. Fed up, Ranger Smith ships the necktied bruin to the San Diego Zoo, but Yogi switches places with another bear, remaining at Jellystone as the picnic basket raider known as "The Brown Phantom." His girlfriend Cindy, unaware that Yogi is still in the park, follows him to San Diego, prompting Yogi and Boo Boo to search the country for her. The bears ultimately reunite as captives of a traveling circus; their escape and return to Jellystone provide the action-packed climax.

This Yogi adventure is "smarter than the average" TV episode, featuring six songs, full animation, and clever art direction. Its routine plot may bore older kids, but parents (especially ones who fondly recall the TV cartoons) and younger kids will find much to enjoy.

THE HIDEAWAYS (see From the Mixed-Up Files of Mrs. Basil E. Frankweiler)

HIGH NOON (1952)
Black & white, 84 minutes
Cast: Gary Cooper, Thomas Mitchell, Lloyd Bridges, Katy Jurado, Grace Kelly, Otto Kruger, Lon Chaney, Jr., Henry (Harry) Morgan, Lee Van Cleef, Ian MacDonald, Robert Wilke, Sheb Wooley
Director: Fred Zinnemann
Screenplay: Carl Foreman, based on the story "The Tin Star" by John W. Cunningham

Western/Drama
Unrated
Young children: OK   Older children: VG

Here is one of the great American Westerns, a tense drama that also serves to dramatize the meaning of personal responsibility. Gary Cooper won an Oscar for his performance as Will Kane, a lawman who has tamed a Western town and now is retiring to marry his beloved (Grace Kelly). On his wedding day, word comes that Frank Miller, a vicious varmint he had captured years before, has just won a pardon from jail and is returning to town with the intention of putting a bullet hole through Kane's heart.

No one in town begrudges Kane the opportunity to get away with Amy, his Quaker bride. However, Kane understands that Miller and his gang will return the town to a state of lawlessness and knows that he can never rest easy so long as Miller is on his trail.

The narrative unfolds in real time, encompassing the period from 10:40 A.M. to high noon, from the time of Will's wedding to his inevitable shoot-out with Miller. The echo of Tex Ritter's singing of the ballad "Do Not Forsake Me, Oh My Darlin' " resonates throughout the story.

Fred Zinnemann's direction is masterly, with many memorable images, including a now legendary shot in which the camera pulls back to reveal Will Kane chillingly alone and abandoned by the cowardly townsfolk, striding toward what may be his doom.

Adding a layer of interest to this gripping film is the knowledge that its screenwriter, Carl Foreman, was blacklisted just before the picture's release. Will Kane's dilemma has been widely interpreted as a mirror of the manner in which individuals chose to turn away as their once close friends were subjected to the damnation of the House Un-American Activities Committee and its blacklist.

HIGH SOCIETY (1956)
Color, 107 minutes
Cast: Bing Crosby, Grace Kelly, Frank Sinatra, Celeste Holm, John Lund, Louis Calhern, Louis Armstrong, Sidney Blackmer, Margalo Gilmore
Director: Charles Walters
Screenplay: John Patrick, based on Philip Barry's *The Philadelphia Story*
Musical
Unrated
Young children: OK   Older children: VG

Older children who've had a taste of Broadway and movie musicals, and have shown a liking for this brand of entertainment, should enjoy this slick remake of Philip Barry's sophisticated comedy *The Philadelphia Story,* memorably filmed in 1940 with Katharine Hepburn, Cary Grant, and James Stewart.

Grace Kelly, then on the verge of becoming Monaco's Princess Grace, stars as the patrician Tracy Lord, a wealthy society girl from Newport, Rhode Island, who's about to be married to George Kittredge, a prig who lacks the down-to-earth qualities she really needs in her sheltered life. At this crucial moment, who should show up but her happy-go-lucky ex-husband, C. K. Dexter Haven (Bing Crosby), and a magazine reporter

(Frank Sinatra) who's quickly smitten with the blond beauty.

High Society has personality to spare in its all-star cast, and a wonderful score by Cole Porter, which includes a lively duet for singing icons Crosby and Sinatra, "Well, Did You Evah?" and a sublime romantic ballad, "True Love." The Newport setting allows the movie to incorporate the music of Louis Armstrong, as well, supposedly in town for the Newport Jazz Festival. He kicks off the film with a calypso song that sets the scene, and later scats with Crosby on "Now You Has Jazz."

How well kids will take to this film will depend on their familiarity with both the stars and the conventions of this easygoing Hollywood musical.

A HIGH WIND IN JAMAICA (1965)
Color, 104 minutes
Cast: Anthony Quinn, James Coburn, Deborah Baxter, Dennis Price, Gert Frobe, Lila Kedrova, Martin Amis, Roberta Tovey, Jeffrey Chandler, Karen Flack
Director: Alexander Mackendrick
Screenplay: Stanley Mann, Ronald Harwood, and Denis Cannan, based on the novel by Richard Hughes
Action-adventure
Unrated
Younger kids: OK, with caution   Older kids: VG

While traveling from Jamaica to England in 1870, a boat carrying a group of seven children is attacked by pirates, led by Juan Chavez (Anthony Quinn) and his first mate, Zac (James Coburn).

After the children hide aboard Chavez's ship, he tries to get rid of them, but gradually develops a complex and sympathetic relationship with them, especially with Emily (Baxter), the eldest. His crew, however, fears them as an evil omen, which leads to an ironic and surprising conclusion.

Based on Richard Hughes' acclaimed 1929 best-seller, this is a stylish, exciting and intelligent swashbuckler with zesty and colorful performances, particularly by Quinn. The meaty plot deals with such serious themes as morality and death, which should appeal to adults and older kids, as well as offering lots of traditional buccaneer action for younger viewers.

THE HOBBIT (1977)
Color, 76 minutes
Cast: Voices of Orson Bean, Richard Boone, Hans Conried, John Huston, Otto Preminger, Cyril Ritchard, Paul Frees, Don Messick, Jack DeLeon
Directors: Arthur Rankin, Jr., and Jules Bass
Screenplay: Rankin and Bass, based on the works of J. R. R. Tolkien
Animated feature/Musical
Unrated
Younger kids: OK   Older kids: OK

Originally shown as a TV movie, *The Hobbit* is a faithful animated adaptation of J. R. R. Tolkien's prequel to *The Lord of the Rings*.

The hobbit is Bilbo Baggins, who is hired by wizard Gandalf to rescue a cache of gold stolen from the dwarfs by an evil dragon named Smaug. The journey through Middle Earth is filled with dangerous encounters with trolls, goblins, spiders, eagles, and the like. The lively action is enhanced by sword fights, magical spells, and musical interludes.

Animation quality is far below theatrical feature standards, and visually there is no comparison to Ralph Bakshi's theatrically released **Lord of the Rings,** but the storytelling is fine, and a strong voice cast saves the day. *The Hobbit* won both a Peabody Award and a Christopher Award, and a soundtrack album was released on Disney's Vista Records label.

Small children may not comprehend the story and its fanciful characters, but the film is an enjoyable fantasy adventure for everyone else.

HOCUS POCUS (1993)
Color, 93 minutes
Cast: Bette Midler, Sarah Jessica Parker, Kathy Najimy, Omri Katz, Thora Birch, Vinessa Shaw, Amanda Shepherd, Larry Bagby III, Kathleen Freeman, Penny Marshall, Garry Marshall
Director: Kenny Ortega
Writer: Neil Cuthbert and Mick Garris, from a story by Garris and David Kirschner
Fantasy/Comedy
Rated PG
Younger children: OK, with caution   Older children: OK

This effects-laden fantasy comedy may be too much for younger ones and might give parents a headache, but older kids could enjoy the broomstick ride.

L.A. teenager Max (Omri Katz) and younger sister, Dani (Thora Birch), are having a hard time adjusting to their new life in Salem, Massachusetts. Forced to take his sister trick-or-treating on Halloween night, Max attempts to disprove the legend about local witches by breaking into a haunted mansion with Dani and her classmate Allison (Vinessa Shaw).

The kids accidentally bring three zany witches (Bette Midler, Sarah Jessica Parker, Kathy Najimy) back to life, threatening all the children in the community. (The witches need to suck the life force from children or die forever). A talking black cat—actually a boy trapped under a spell—aids the young trio in defeating the wicked witches.

Super-duper special effects, particularly the talking cat, and a stellar (if strident) cast magically transform the mediocre script into a popcorn movie. But it is awfully intense for young kids, even at the outset: It begins with a flashback to the Salem witch hangings!

HOME ALONE (1990)
Color, 102 minutes
Cast: Macaulay Culkin, Joe Pesci, Daniel Stern, John Heard, Roberts Blossom, Catherine O'Hara, John Candy, Billie Bird, Angela Goethals, Devin Ratray
Director: Chris Columbus
Screenplay: John Hughes
Comedy
Rated PG
Younger kids: OK   Older kids: OK

An 8-year-old boy named Kevin is accidentally left behind by his vacationing family during Christmas and takes it upon himself to defend the homestead against two burglars. A simple idea became an astonishing success and for a very good reason—it's the ultimate in children's wish-fulfillment, executed with super slick energy. Culkin is ideal as the industrious and resourceful hero who comes up with every conceivable type of Rube Goldberg-esque contraption to do battle with the interlopers.

There is considerable violence depicted as Kevin wages his war, and though it is all overscaled and cartoonish, and can't be taken too seriously, it is often unnecessarily rough. (What can you say when Joe Pesci's head actually catches fire? This goes beyond the usual definition of slapstick.)

It's especially difficult to reconcile those harsh moments with the film's sentimental moments, in which Kevin deals with actual feelings of loss and loneliness.

Needless to say, parents should remind younger, more impressionable kids that this kind of stuff does not necessarily happen in real life, nor should it be encouraged. The sequel, **Home Alone 2: Alone in New York,** was a virtual retread of this film; the next sequel didn't even have Macaulay Culkin in it.

A HOME OF OUR OWN (1993)
Color, 103 minutes
Cast: Kathy Bates, Edward Furlong, Soon-Teck Oh, Tony Campisi, Amy Sakasitz, Miles Feulner, Clarissa Lassig, T. J. Lowther, Sarah Schaub
Director: Tony Bill
Screenplay: Patrick Duncan
Drama
Rated PG
Younger children: No   Older children: VG

An inspirational family drama, this has all the right elements to leave you with a tear in your eye.

In 1962, widow Frances Lacey (Kathy Bates), fed up with Los Angeles, packs her six children in a car and heads off looking for a new life. Finding a dilapidated house on the outskirts of tiny Hankston, Idaho, Frances and family make the place their own and try to fit in with the rural community. The day-to-day trials and tribulations of this venture form the core of the story. When tragedy strikes, the town ultimately rallies behind the newcomers.

Though sentimental at times, the film nonetheless presents a realistic portrayal of working-class family life. Bates and Edward Furlong (as eldest son) give solid performances.

Some strong language and occasional violence seem fully in keeping with the tone—and the credibility—of the story. But young kids might find it a bit too dramatic.

HOME OF THE BRAVE
(1949)
Black & white, 88 minutes
Cast: Douglas Dick, Steve Brodie, Jeff Corey, Lloyd Bridges, Frank Lovejoy, James Edwards, Cliff Clark
Director: Mark Robson
Screenplay: Carl Foreman, based on a play by Arthur Laurents
Drama
Unrated
Young children: OK Older children: VG

This penetrating landmark drama chronicles the breakdown of Moss (James Edwards), a black soldier, after he is ignored and maligned by some of his white buddies while patrolling a Japanese-held island during World War II. A psychiatrist tries to help Moss understand his feelings, and with him, comes to realize that the young man's troubles have been caused as much by the racism of his youth as by the abuse he suffered during the mission.

As the soldier recovers, it is noted that he plans to open a bar with a white buddy. The partnership will work, because the men respect each other as equals.

This film was one of a number made in the years following World War II that broke new ground by daring to explore racism, anti-Semitism, and other social ills in American society. (In fact, the play *Home of the Brave* was about a Jewish soldier suffering the wounds of anti-Semitism.)

James Edwards garnered excellent reviews for his work in this film, but his career never took off. There weren't many opportunities for a young, good-looking black actor in Hollywood at this time.

HOMEWARD BOUND: THE INCREDIBLE JOURNEY
(1993)
Color, 84 minutes
Cast: Robert Hays, Kim Greist, Jean Smart, Benj Thall, Veronica Lauren, Kevin Chevalia; voices of Michael J. Fox, Sally Field, Don Ameche
Director: DuWayne Dunham
Screenplay: Caroline Thompson and Linda Woolverton, based on the 1963 film *The Incredible Journey,* from the novel by Sheila Burnford
Adventure/Animal story
Rated G
Younger kids: VG Older kids: VG

After being separated from their masters, an aging golden retriever, a spunky American bulldog, and a spoiled Himalayan cat embark on a perilous journey across the Sierra Nevada mountains—facing bears, mountain lions, porcupines, and raging waterfalls—to be reunited with them.

Disney's anthropomorphic remake of its 1963 film **The Incredible Journey** (which had narration, not talking animals) is self-consciously cute but very well made, and features amusing voice-overs for the animals, performed by Don Ameche as the avuncular retriever, Michael J. Fox as the mischievous bulldog, and Sally Field as the sarcastic feline. Their comic repartee and dialogue are pretty much surefire. As usual, the animals are much more lively and interesting than the one-dimensional humans, but this is a sweet, warm-hearted movie that kids will love. The heart-tugging finale may even bring a tear (of joy) to their eyes.

HOMEWARD BOUND II: LOST IN SAN FRANCISCO (1996)

Color, 88 minutes
Cast: Robert Hays, Kim Greist, Veronica Lauren, Kevin Chevalia, Benj Thall, Michael Rispoli, Max Perlich; voices of Michael J. Fox, Sally Field, Ralph Waite, Sinbad
Director: David R. Ellis
Screenplay: Chris Hauty and Julie Hickson
Adventure
Rated G
Younger kids: Good   Older kids: Good

Chance the bulldog, Sassy the cat, and Shadow the retriever are back for more adventures in this affable, if uninspired, Disney sequel that's bland but wholesome family fare. This time, they're lost at an airport by their owners (who really have to stop being so careless) as they're about to leave for a vacation and have to fend for themselves in the big city. Before the assured happy ending, the trio has various misadventures with some tough street mutts (voiced by Jon Polito and Adam Goldberg) and the friendly leader (Sinbad) of a gang of strays, as well as a pair of bumbling dognappers (Michael Rispoli, Max Perlich).

HONEY, I BLEW UP THE KID (1992)

Color, 89 minutes
Cast: Rick Moranis, Marcia Strassman, Robert Oliveri, Daniel Shalikar, Joshua Shalikar, Lloyd Bridges, John Shea, Keri Russell, Ron Canada, Amy O'Neill, Gregory Sierra, Julia Sweeney, John Paragon, Ken Tobey
Director: Randal Kleiser
Screenplay: Thom Eberhardt, Peter Elbling, and Garry Goodrow
Comedy/Science fiction
Rated PG
Younger children: OK   Older children: OK

Crazy inventor Wayne Szalinski is back, this time with a plan to make things *bigger*; his intention is to grow giant food. But of course, the baby gets in the way and a new adventure starts as the Szalinskis go traipsing around Las Vegas trying to catch up with a runaway, skyscraper-sized infant. While the baby is growing, older brother Nick and his girlfriend are trying to survive the ride from inside baby Adam's pocket!

Not as inventive as the first film, *Honey, I Blew Up the Kid* is still an enjoyable romp and should keep kids entertained throughout the adventure. As in the first film, it's aimed squarely at the family trade, and is fairly innocuous throughout.

HONEY, I SHRUNK THE KIDS (1989)

Color, 86 minutes
Cast: Rick Moranis, Matt Frewer, Marcia Strassman, Kristine Sutherland, Thomas Brown, Jared Rushton, Amy O'Neill, Robert Oliveri
Director: Joe Johnston
Screenplay: Ed Naha and Tom Schulman, based on a story by Stuart Gordon, Brian Yuzna, and Naha
Comedy/Science fiction
Rated PG
Younger children: OK Older children: OK

Oddball inventor Wayne Szalinski (Rick Moranis) designs a machine that will shrink things. His two children and their friends are miniaturized by mistake and inadvertently thrown out with the trash. So begins their adventure in the backyard, traversing dangers that most of us take for granted—grass, bugs, dogs, footsteps, etc.—in their journey back to the house and their correct size.

Humor and thrills dominate this clever science fiction comedy. Smaller children may get scared during some of the dangers, but being a Disney film, it's all fairly benign. Part of the fun is watching the Szalinskis, big and small, solve their problems. As fun as a roller-coaster ride without the upset stomach.

Followed by a sequel, a direct-to-video, and a TV series.

HOOK (1991)

Color, 144 minutes
Cast: Dustin Hoffman, Robin Williams, Julia Roberts, Bob Hoskins, Maggie Smith, Caroline Goodall, Charlie Korsmo, Phil Collins, Arthur Malet, Gwyneth Paltrow
Director: Steven Spielberg
Screenplay: James V. Hart and Malia Scotch Marmo, from a story by Hart and Nick Castle, based on the play *Peter Pan* by J. M. Barrie
Adventure/Fantasy
Rated PG
Younger kids: OK Older kids: OK

There's a dearth of "happy thoughts" in this disappointing Steven Spielberg update of the Peter Pan story. Robin Williams stars as a grown up Peter, who has become a workaholic attorney and has to rediscover his magical youth when his two kids are kidnapped by Captain Hook and taken to Neverland during a trip to London.

The production is physically impressive, but the film has no heart. The Lost Boys are not the kind you would necessarily want to find again (and their occasional crudeness—and language—apparently earned the film its PG rating). The whole production is overblown—not to mention overlong. Spielberg's trademarked sense of wide-eyed wonder seems completely contrived here.

Stick with the wonderful television production of the musical *Peter Pan* starring Mary Martin, or Disney's 1953 cartoon adaptation. Either one is a better bet.

HOOP DREAMS (1994)
Color, 169 minutes
Director: Steve James
Documentary
Rated PG-13
Younger kids: OK, with caution   Older kids: VG

This was intended to be a half-hour short for PBS; it evolved into a three-hour theatrically released documentary that won virtually every critical award to be had. Culled from over 250 hours of footage shot between 1987 and 1991, it chronicles the aspirations of two black youths (Arthur Agee and William Gates) who hope to escape their impoverished lives in Chicago's housing projects by becoming professional basketball stars. The film follows the friends through high school and into their first year of college (along the way meeting ex–NBA star Isaiah Thomas, film director Spike Lee, and college coach Bobby Knight), as they struggle to deal with personal, financial, and family problems and see their dreams turn into sobering realities as basketball becomes more of a job than a game to play.

By placing sports in a social and economic context, the filmmakers dramatically reveal the emotional pressures put on student athletes and also expose the dubious recruiting practices of high schools and colleges. This is a must-see for teens, offering inspiration, education, and heartbreak in equal doses. It also illustrates that life is not like a movie; one could never predict the twists and turns these lives will take during the course of this film.

A frank and unblinking look at inner-city life, *Hoop Dreams* is not kiddie fare.

HOOSIERS (1986)
Color, 114 minutes
Cast: Gene Hackman, Barbara Hershey, Dennis Hopper, Sheb Wooley, Fern Parsons, Brad Doyle, Steve Hollar, Brad Long, David Neidorf
Director: David Anspaugh
Screenplay: Angelo Pizzo
Drama/Sports
Rated PG
Younger kids: OK, with caution   Older kids: VG

A former big-time college basketball coach (played by Hackman) is hired at a small-town Indiana high school in the 1950s. It's his last chance to make good, and while his harsh methods cause concern, he slowly wins the respect of the team, and then the town itself, as they gain self-esteem and head toward the championship.

This is a very formulaic movie with a surefire "underdog" hook. There are few surprises in store, but such fine actors as Hackman, Hopper, and Hershey give it credibility and substance.

The whole film is lovingly burnished in the soft glow of small-town yesteryear Americana. The benefits of hard work, practice, practice, practice, and team spirit are stressed and the coach gets to redeem himself by helping these young men. The most interesting element, in many ways, is the portrait of the town and its almost amusingly fanatical devotion to the high school basketball team.

Everybody—young and old—loves to see an underdog have a shot at the winner's circle; that's why this film works. Some of the story elements, such as Hopper's alcoholism, may be too adult for young children, but older kids will almost certainly respond to this movie.

HOPE AND GLORY (1987)
Color, 113 minutes
Cast: Sarah Miles, David Hayman, Sebastian Rice-Edwards, Derrick O'Connor, Susan Wooldridge, Sammi Davis, Geraldine Muir, Ian Bannen
Director: John Boorman
Screenplay: John Boorman
Comedy-drama/War
Rated PG-13
Younger kids: No   Older kids: VG

John Boorman received Oscar nominations for writing and directing this touching, beautifully crafted film based on his own boyhood experiences in England during World War II. As seen through the eyes of 9-year-old Bill Rohan (Sebastian Rice-Edwards), the war is not a tragedy but an exhilarating adventure filled with great mysteries and excitement. When his father (David Hayman) enlists, Bill's mother (Sarah Miles) is left to care for him and his two sisters (Geraldine Muir, Sammi Davis). He and his friends take to collecting pieces of shrapnel from the numerous air raids and carpet bombings.

Though essentially a lighthearted and affectionate portrait of family life, the film has its share of harrowing moments, particularly when the family has to leave London after their house burns down. The realistically staged bombing attacks are certainly too intense for younger children. On the other hand, older kids will find *Hope and Glory* to be a passport to the past, vividly recreating a special time and place in recent history from a young person's point of view. Language, violence, and some sexual content earn this its PG-13 rating.

HOPPITY GOES TO TOWN (1941) (aka **Mr. Bug Goes to Town**)
Color, 77 minutes
Cast: Voices of Kenny Gardner (Hoppity), Gwen Williams, Jack Mercer, Ted Pierce, Carl Meyer, Stan Freed, Pauline Loth
Director: Dave Fleischer
Original story: Dave Fleischer, Dan Gordon, Ted Pierce, Isadore Sparber
Animated feature/Musical
Rated G
Younger kids: OK   Older kids: OK

Excellent and unfairly overlooked animated feature by the pioneering Max Fleischer studio. (This was its second and final feature-length cartoon, following *Gulliver's Travels.*) The story, about a community of insects looking for a new home, is full of funny ideas, original characters, and lively songs.

Hoppity, an optimistic young grasshopper, returns home to the Lowlands and to his best girl, Honey Bee. Their peace is threatened by rival C. Bagley Beetle, his buzzy henchman, and the human ones who erect a skyscraper on the patch of land the insects call home.

Although some of the film's humor is sophisticated, kids will enjoy the colorful animation and identify with the bug's-eye view of the world. The climactic sequence of the bug society running for their lives on a building under construction is both thrilling and funny. The songs, by Hoagy Carmichael and Frank Loesser, are enjoyable, particularly a night club number, "Katy Did, Katy Didn't."

The film was originally released as *Mr. Bug Goes to Town,* a parody of such popular movies of the time as **Mr. Deeds Goes to Town** and *Mr. Smith Goes to Washington.* After its initial release, however, a distributor decided that having "bug" in a title might be a turn-off to potential audiences and renamed the film (this was decades before the success of **Antz** and **a bug's life**!).

HORROR OF DRACULA
(1958) (aka **Dracula**)
Color, 82 minutes
Cast: Peter Cushing, Christopher Lee, Michael Gough, Melissa Stribling, Carol Marsh, Olga Dickie, John Van Eyssen, Valerie Gaunt, Charles Lloyd Pack, George Woodbridge, Miles Malleson
Director: Terence Fisher
Screenplay: Jimmy Sangster, from the novel by Bram Stoker
Horror/Suspense
Unrated
Young children: Too intense Older children: OK

Bram Stoker's tale of Dracula is efficiently condensed and reshaped here: Van Helsing (Cushing), a scientist dedicated to the eradication of vampires, learns that Count Dracula (Lee), the most dangerous vampire in Europe, is seeking to spread his influence. Van Helsing joins forces with a skeptic (Gough), who becomes convinced of the vampire's deadly intentions when his own wife (Stribling) becomes Dracula's target.

In some ways, this is one of the most significant horror movies ever made. Not only did it cement the reputation of Hammer Films of England as the producer of the best horror films of the period, but it established the fact that *fantasy* horror would be accepted by modern-day audiences. Furthermore, even more than the earlier **The Curse of Frankenstein,** it established Peter Cushing and Christopher Lee as major horror stars, and Terence Fisher as a talented director for the genre.

Cushing's brisk but emotionally involved character is a departure from similar types in earlier films but proved even more durable. His performance here is particularly good: focused, intense, driven, but ultimately warm and caring. Haunted but demonic, Lee became the latter-day personification of Dracula and played the role in a long series of Hammer films.

Horror of Dracula is still exciting stuff, even if it doesn't seem as remarkably inventive as it did in 1958. The pacing is swift, the acting first-rate, and the production values belie their low cost. It is probably the best horror movie of the 1950s, and it is definitely not for younger children.

Contemporary kids might enjoy knowing that the skeptical Arthur is played by the same actor (Michael Gough) who, more than thirty years later, would take on the role of Alfred the Butler in the popular *Batman* movies.

Followed by both **The Brides of Dracula** (featuring Van Helsing as the lead) and **Dracula—Prince of Darkness.**

HORSE FEATHERS (1932)
Black & white, 68 minutes
Cast: Groucho, Harpo, Chico,
  and Zeppo Marx, Thelma
  Todd, David Landau
Director: Norman Z. McLeod
Screenplay: Bert Kalmar, Harry
  Ruby, S. J. Perelman, and Will
  B. Johnstone
Comedy
Unrated
Younger kids: Good Older
  kids: VG

Academia will never be the same
after The Marx Brothers go to
college and Groucho becomes the
president of Huxley College in
this irreverent spoof of 1930s college gridiron movies. During his
inaugural speech, Professor Wagstaff (Groucho) insults the faculty
and bursts into song, then goes to
the local speakeasy (where the
password is *swordfish*) to hire two
professional athletes to play for
the college football team, which
hasn't won a game since 1888. But
Wagstaff mistakenly hires the iceman and bootlegger, Baravelli
(Chico), and his mute assistant
and part-time dog catcher, Pinky
(Harpo). He also falls for Connie,
the college "widow" (Thelma
Todd), with whom his delinquent
son, Frank (Zeppo), has been dal-
lying for the past twelve years.
Unbeknownst to either of them,
however, Connie is in cahoots
with some gamblers who have bet
on Darwin University for the upcoming big game between Darwin
and Huxley.

Like most of the early Marx
Brothers movies, the negligible
plot is merely a framework for
some madcap gags, and this one
has some of their most anarchic
comedy routines. If some of
Groucho's rapid-fire patter goes

over the heads of younger kids,
the pantomime and sight gags of
Harpo will go directly to their
funny bones. The football game
finale is a riot, the one-liners
come fast and furious, and even
the musical interludes are funny,
highlighted by Groucho's uproarious rendition of "I'm Against It"
and the various versions of "Everyone Says I Love You," with
each Marx doing his own interpretation. Groucho serenades the
beautiful Thelma Todd with a guitar while riding in a canoe, Zeppo
sings a straight version, and
Harpo does a harp solo, while
Chico's piano playing prompts
Groucho to stand up and address
the audience, saying "I've got to
stay here, but there's no reason
why you folks shouldn't go out to
the lobby while this blows over."

Some of the humor may be
dated, but it can still produce
solid belly laughs for adults and
kids alike with its mixture of high-
brow puns and lowbrow slapstick.

THE HORSE WHISPERER
(1998)
Color, 164 minutes
Cast: Robert Redford, Kristin
  Scott Thomas, Sam Neill,
  Dianne Wiest, Scarlett
  Johansson, Chris Cooper
Director: Robert Redford
Screenplay: Eric Roth and
  Richard LaGravenese, from
  the novel by Nicholas Evans
Drama/Animal story
PG-13
Young children: No Older
  children: VG

Because of a dreadful riding accident, 13-year-old Grace (Scarlett
Johansson) loses her leg, becoming gravely wounded in body and
soul. Her horse Pilgrim also sur-

vives but is violent and crazed with pain. Grace's mother Annie (Kristin Scott Thomas), a successful, highly driven Manhattan magazine editor, gives up everything in a quest to rescue the girl and her mount from disappearing into their anger. Only one person seems to have the key to everyone's salvation.

It's not Grace's dad but the wise animal trainer Tom Booker (Robert Redford), way out in Montana, who has the power to heal both horses and hearts.

At 60, actor Redford has matured into what director Redford has been waiting for, and this is a perfect part for him. His beautifully photographed movie, shot on location, is about turning tragedy into triumph. Some parts are extremely difficult to watch, especially the terrible accident that sets off the story, but the emotional rewards are plentiful.

Indeed, the movie is even better than Nicholas Evans' 1995 bestseller and improves on the ending of the book a thousandfold.

Some critics and viewers found this film too long and slow, but if you let yourself become enveloped in its story, you'll be happy to go along at the pace Redford intended. The movie is relaxed and deliberate, like its central character, the Horse Whisperer.

The subject matter is too mature and difficult for young kids, but adolescents should find much to savor here.

THE HOUND OF THE BASKERVILLES (1939)
Black & white, 78 minutes
Cast: Richard Greene, Basil Rathbone, Wendy Barrie, Nigel Bruce, Lionel Atwill, John Carradine, Barlowe Borland, Beryl Mercer, Morton Lowry, Ralph Forbes
Director: Sidney Lanfield
Screenplay: Ernest Pascal, from the novel by Sir Arthur Conan Doyle
Horror mystery/Literary classic
Unrated
Young children: Creepy Older children: OK

Ever since a Baskerville ancestor caused the senseless death of a young peasant girl, Baskerville men have been stalked by a living embodiment of retribution, a ghostly hound from hell—or so the legend says. When the latest lord of Baskerville Manor is found dead on the moors nearby, young Sir Henry (Greene) arrives to claim the estate. The family doctor (Atwill) engages the great detective Sherlock Holmes (Rathbone) and his friend Dr. Watson (Bruce) to protect Sir Henry and uncover the secret of the Hound of the Baskervilles.

This was the first time Basil Rathbone played the role that became so much a part of his image, and he was ideally cast, one of the best Holmeses ever. The movie itself is good, but not as entertaining as its follow-up, partly because Doyle's plot requires Holmes to be off-screen much of the time.

Young people who enjoy reading will almost inevitably tackle the wonderful stories by Doyle and will want to see this movie. Conversely, it's a great introduction to Holmes for those who know nothing about the master detective but his name. The somewhat dated film is occasionally scary—but not even as much as an average episode of *Goosebumps*.

259

Followed by *The Adventures of Sherlock Holmes.*

THE HOUND OF THE BASKERVILLES (1959)
Color, 87 minutes (some prints run 84m.)
Cast: Peter Cushing, Andre Morell, Christopher Lee, Marla Landi, David Oxley, Francis De Wolff, Miles Malleson, Ewen Solon, John Le Mesurier
Director: Terence Fisher
Screenplay: Peter Bryan, from the novel by Sir Arthur Conan Doyle
Horror mystery/Literary classic
Unrated
Young children: Intense Older children: OK

Sherlock Holmes (Cushing) and Dr. Watson (Morell) are hired to protect Sir Henry Baskerville (Lee) from the phantom hound that has been stalking members of his family for over a hundred years. Watson accompanies Sir Henry to Baskerville Manor while Holmes watches, hidden away. When he realizes there's more to this than an old legend, Holmes springs into action.

And that describes Cushing's lively, engaging performance as Holmes, too. Nimble, swift, and dynamic, Cushing's Holmes is one of the most exciting ever; the actor makes no concessions to the audience—he simply does not care if we *like* Holmes—and turns in a masterful performance, among the best of his admirable career. Ten years later, his Holmes TV series (never, alas, shown in the U.S.) established him for British audiences as *the* Sherlock Holmes, the way Basil

Rathbone occupied that position for American audiences.

This is a Hammer film and, like most of that studio's product, was made on a modest budget, which occasionally undercuts the film (the hound, for example, is rather dull). At times, the attempt to make it even more of a horror movie shows. But it's a good version of the tale and is suitable for all but the youngest children.

HOUSE ARREST (1996)
Color, 108 minutes
Cast: Jamie Lee Curtis, Kevin Pollak, Jennifer Tilly, Christopher McDonald, Sheila McCarthy, Wallace Shawn, Caroline Aaron, Mooky Arizona, Russel Harper, Jennifer Love Hewitt, Ray Walston
Director: Harry Winer
Screenplay: Michael Hitchcock
Comedy
Rated PG
Younger children: OK Older children: VG

When Grover (Kyle Howard) learns that his parents are planning to separate, he and his little sister stage a party in their basement and try to re-create the mood of their folks' Hawaiian honeymoon. But when Mom and Dad start arguing instead of making up, Grover locks them in and warns that he won't let them out until they stop fighting. When he tells his best friend what he's done and the school bully overhears them, both kids show up at Grover's house with their parents, who are tricked into joining Mom and Dad in the basement—only to become fellow prisoners. Soon Grover's house is overrun with unruly kids upstairs and angry parents in the basement. The kids find themselves bearing a responsibility they never anticipated, while the grown-ups have no choice but to talk things out.

While this may seem like a silly premise, it's played out quite well, from both the grown-ups' and kids' points of view. The problem with *House Arrest* is that it uses up all its story points after about an hour.

Still, kids of all ages are likely to enjoy it, and adolescents will get an extra kick out of seeing future star Jennifer Love Hewitt as the school's most popular girl, whose mom (Jennifer Tilly) refuses to act her age.

The subject of divorce is no laughing matter for some kids, and parents should keep that in mind. There is also some street language—just enough to earn a PG.

of lycanthropy and puzzling over what to do with the Frankenstein Monster (Strange).

This disappointing movie was the last serious film in the long-running Universal horror series, followed as it was by **Abbott and Costello Meet Frankenstein.** Once again, Dracula and the Frankenstein Monster have little to do, and even the Wolf Man ends up cured. Onslow Stevens' doctor with the split personality is therefore the main menace, and though the actor is good in the role, he's no substitute for the real things.

Older kids who enjoy the classic Universal horror movies will insist on seeing this one, too; there's nothing in it to harm those accustomed to horror films, but it will just be an entry on their checklist of Horror Movies I Have Seen.

HOUSE OF DRACULA (1945)

Black & white, 67 minutes
Cast: Onslow Stevens, John Carradine, Lon Chaney, Jr., Glenn Strange, Jane Adams, Martha O'Driscoll, Lionel Atwill, Skelton Knaggs, Ludwig Stossel
Director: Erle C. Kenton
Screenplay: Edward T. Lowe, Jr.
Science fiction/Fantasy horror/ Melodrama
Unrated
Younger kids: Probably too scary   Older kids: OK

Kindly scientist Dr. Edelman (Stevens) runs afoul of Count Dracula (Carradine); a transfusion of the vampire's blood turns Edelman into a Jekyll and Hyde–like killer. When he's normal, Edelman is trying to find a means of curing the Wolf Man (Chaney)

HOUSE OF FRANKENSTEIN (1944)

Black & white, 71 minutes
Cast: Boris Karloff, Lon Chaney, Jr., John Carradine, J. Carrol Naish, Glenn Strange, Anne Gwynne, Elena Verdugo, Peter Coe, Lionel Atwill, George Zucco
Director: Erle C. Kenton
Screenplay: Curt Siodmak and Edward T. Lowe, Jr.
Science fiction/Fantasy horror/ Melodrama
Unrated
Younger kids: Too many scary faces   Older kids: OK

Mad scientist Dr. Niemann (Karloff) escapes from prison and, with the help of a hunchbacked assistant (Naish), takes over a traveling horror show that includes Count Dracula (Carradine). Later, trying to follow in the footsteps of Dr. Frankenstein, he revives the bodies of Larry Talbot, the Wolf Man (Chaney), and the Frankenstein Monster (Strange) himself. Naturally, all this mischief leads to trouble.

This fast-paced, episodic entry in the Universal horror series is a crowded affair and can't find a way to integrate Dracula into the rest of the story, but Carradine is sleek and sinister as the vampire count.

The Wolf Man and the Monster will disturb the youngest kids, but older kids will get a kick out of a movie that crams so many monsters into such a short running time (by today's standards). It's less of a horror movie than a thriller with monsters and probably scared very few people in 1944—but it did entertain them.

Followed by **House of Dracula** (1945).

HOUSE OF USHER (1960)
(aka **The Fall of the House of Usher**)
Color, 79 minutes
Cast: Vincent Price, Mark Damon, Myrna Fahey, Harry Ellerbe
Director: Roger Corman
Screenplay: Richard Matheson, from the story by Edgar Allan Poe
Horror/Literary classic
Unrated
Young children: Of no interest   Older children: OK

In the early 19th century, Philip Winthrop (Damon) arrives at the bleak and eerie House of Usher, to be met by strange, pale Roderick Usher (Price), brother of Philip's fiancée, Madeleine. It's too late, Roderick tells him; Made-

leine has died and already been entombed in the family vault. But Roderick's behavior leads Philip to believe that there may be something far more sinister going on.

When the well-mounted horror movies from England's Hammer Films became major successes in the United States, director Roger Corman and producer James H. Nicholson of American International Pictures became convinced that similar films could be made here. They hired respected horror and science fiction writer Richard Matheson for a screenplay, and turned out this polished, handsome film (shot in CinemaScope) on a reasonable budget. It did very well, leading to a long series of Poe adaptations, many of which were directed by Corman and most of which starred Vincent Price.

This is not the best of the series—most consider **Masque of the Red Death** to be the standout—but it's well made, serious, and, unlike many of the later films, reasonably close to the Poe original.

It's somewhat stately for younger audiences today; the language is earnestly in period, and the story is rather thin. But if your teenagers have become interested in "classic horror," this should be on their viewing list. Younger children will most likely be bored.

HOUSE OF WAX (1953)
Color, 88 minutes
Cast: Vincent Price, Frank Lovejoy, Phyllis Kirk, Carolyn Jones, Paul Picerni, Roy Roberts, Dabbs Greer, Charles Buchinsky (Bronson)
Director: Andre de Toth
Screenplay: Crane Wilbur

Horror/Mystery
Unrated
Younger kids: Too
  intense   Older kids: OK

Horror/Suspense
Unrated
Young children: No   Older
  children: OK

The setting is New York, in the early 20th century. When bodies disappear from the morgue, a young reporter (Kirk) begins to suspect that they're being turned into statues in the wax museum run by kindly, disabled Professor Jarrod (Price). There's also a hideously, if colorfully, deformed phantom roaming the foggy streets.

This vivid, popular movie helped establish Vincent Price as a horror movie star (although he didn't become completely identified with the genre for another five years). It was shot in 3-D, explaining various dimensional "thrills," like paddleballs batted at the camera, which look fairly strange on television.

The makeup on Price is extremely ugly, and we see it a lot; furthermore, there are fires, melting wax statues, threatening guillotines, and other scary stuff, making this too intense for younger kids. It might even still be too much for some older kids, but if yours are already devoted to Freddy Krueger and the like, this is not likely to bother them at all—it might give *you* the creeps, however.

HOUSE ON HAUNTED HILL
(1958)
Black & white, 75 minutes
Cast: Vincent Price, Carol
  Ohmart, Richard Long, Alan
  Marshal, Carolyn Craig, Elisha
  Cook, Jr., Julie Mitchum,
  Leona Anderson, Howard
  Hoffman
Director: William Castle
Screenplay: Robb White

Purring, sardonic Frederick Loren (Price) invites some needy acquaintances to an unusual party at an old house with a reputation for being haunted. He offers to pay $10,000 to anyone who spends the entire night in the house on haunted hill, but before long it appears as though Loren himself might be the target of the spooky activity that follows.

The plot doesn't bear close or even distant examination, being mostly a series of loosely linked weird events. The main appeal of the movie is watching Price and Ohmart trade barbed quips, though there are some genuinely scary scenes.

The film was promoted as being in "Emergo." At a key point in the proceedings—it's blindingly obvious from the movie just when this was—a door opened next to the screen, and a big luminous skeleton drifted on wires out over the audience. Eeeek. This, plus the very clever ad campaign, helped make *House on Haunted Hill* into a hit. Also, more than any other movie, it was responsible for transforming Vincent Price from a suave villain into a horror movie icon.

Even though the movie can be scary at times, it's probably not too strong for any but the very youngest children, provided an adult is around to clutch at the necessary moments. Teenagers will find it more of a comedy than a thriller but are likely to enjoy it anyway.

HOW GREEN WAS MY VALLEY (1941)

Black & white, 118 minutes
Cast: Walter Pidgeon, Maureen O'Hara, Donald Crisp, Anna Lee, Roddy McDowall, John Loder, Sara Allgood, Barry Fitzgerald, Patric Knowles, Rhys Williams, Arthur Shields, Ann Todd
Director: John Ford
Screenplay: Philip Dunne, based on the novel by Richard Llewellyn
Drama
Unrated
Young children: OK   Older children: VG

This deeply felt, Academy Award–winning drama tells the story of Welsh coal miners, centering on the close-knit Morgan family. The scenario focuses on the day-to-day lives of the various clan members as filtered through the perceptions of the youngest of the lot, Huw (Roddy McDowall). The story is held together by the off-screen voice of the grown-up Huw as he remembers his father and brothers, all of whom toil in the mines, and his mother, who is the backbone of the family. Along the way, there is plenty of conflict as the Morgans face a series of travails, beginning with the mining disasters that are an ever-present part of life in a coal mining town.

Older children will relate to the coming-of-age aspect of the story, as Huw is affected by the various characters around him, learns to overcome a disability, fits in at school, faces an intimidating teacher, and finally, decides on the future course of his life.

Despite the high drama and wrenching sadness, the story exudes a sense of nostalgia for times past, as the adult Huw recalls how green his valley once was.

How Green Was My Valley might have been unbearably saccharine, but the film retains its emotional power because of John Ford's loving direction and feel for the material. The acting is consistently first-rate. Donald Crisp won a Best Supporting Actor Oscar for his moving performance as Huw's father, and 14-year-old Roddy McDowall has one of the most memorable roles of his career as the youngster.

The sad parts of the story—relating mostly to a mine cave-in—are too tough for young children to deal with, but older children may warm to the story of this remarkable family unit and its many experiences, both good and bad.

HOW THE WEST WAS WON (1962)

Color, 155 minutes
Cast: Carroll Baker, Henry Fonda, Gregory Peck, John Wayne, James Stewart, Debbie Reynolds, George Peppard, Carolyn Jones, Richard Widmark, Robert Preston, Eli Wallach, Karl Malden; Spencer Tracy (narrator)
Directors: George Marshall, John Ford, and Henry Hathaway
Screenplay: James R. Webb
Western
Rated G
Younger kids: Good   Older kids: VG

A favorite childhood movie of the baby boomer generation, this all-star Western epic filmed in the Cinerama process loses much of its awesome visual impact on TV but otherwise holds up fairly well. It's a rousing example of the kind of old-fashioned blockbuster they just don't make anymore. Three veteran directors were enlisted to handle the multipart frontier stories relating the adventures of a family of Western settlers from the 1830s to the 1880s, beginning with their voyage on the Erie Canal and going on to encompass a Civil War battle, a train robbery, a thrilling white-water rafting sequence, and a thundering buffalo stampede.

It may not be historically accurate, but it's great storytelling, with some wonderful moments along the way. The giant cast reads like a who's who of classic Hollywood.

HUCKLEBERRY FINN (1939)
Black & white, 90 minutes (also shown in computer-colored version)
Cast: Mickey Rooney, Walter Connolly, William Frawley, Rex Ingram, Lynne Carver
Director: Richard Thorpe
Screenplay: Hugo Butler, based on the novel by Mark Twain
Adventure
Unrated
Younger kids: OK   Older kids: VG

A perfectly cast Mickey Rooney gives one of his finest performances as the 19th-century river rat in this classy MGM production that's probably the best film version of Mark Twain's classic novel. After fleeing his abusive father and faking his own death, Huck hightails it to the Mississippi river, where he runs into his slave friend Jim (Rex Ingram) and helps him escape to a free state, unaware that Jim is wanted for his "murder."

Colorful performances, strong atmosphere, and solid storytelling make this a treat for the whole family, and there won't be a dry eye in the house during the poignant finale. While not as "gritty" as later versions of the tale, this has more heart.

THE HUNCHBACK OF NOTRE DAME (1939)
Black & white, 117 minutes
Cast: Charles Laughton, Cedric Hardwicke, Thomas Mitchell, Maureen O'Hara, Edmond O'Brien, Alan Marshal, Walter Hampden, Harry Davenport
Director: William Dieterle
Screenplay: Sonya Levien, based on the novel by Victor Hugo as adapted by Bruno Frank
Historical epic/Literary classic
Unrated
Young children: Too intense   Older children: OK

In 15th-century Paris, there's a deep chasm between the upper and lower classes, but above it all, high in the towers of the cathedral of Notre Dame de Paris, lives Quasimodo (Laughton), the deformed, deaf bell-ringer of Notre Dame. He's deeply devoted to the corrupt Frollo (Hardwicke), the enemy of any kind of progress, who, to his own surprise, develops a powerful lust for Esmeralda (O'Hara), a gypsy dancer. Meanwhile, the earnest young poet Gringoire (O'Brien) takes time out from decrying the evils of the upper classes to fall in love with Esmeralda himself. But the dancer falls in love with Phoebus (Marshal), a handsome captain of the guards. When Frollo orders the uncomprehending but obedient hunchback to kidnap Esmeralda, a chain of events is set into motion that changes their lives forever.

Although Perc Westmore's make-up on Laughton is, to say the least, memorable (you'll have to remember it, since there are no photos), this is far from a horror film. Instead, it's a sweeping, exciting historical epic, with richly drawn characters, excellent production design, and outstanding photography and costumes.

Although the film is one of the best spectacles from Hollywood's golden age, ultimately what everyone remembers is not the sets, not the lavishness of the epic, but Charles Laughton's brilliant, heartbreaking performance as Quasimodo, the hunchback of Notre Dame. The film deviates from the book (in which the hunchback dies) to present one of the most gloriously melancholy endings of Hollywood history, a last shot that everyone in the family will weep over and probably treasure forever.

The sad, sometimes brutal aspects of the story make this unsuitable for younger children.

This famous story was first filmed in 1923 with the great Lon Chaney as Quasimodo, then remade in 1957 with Anthony Quinn, in 1982 (for television) with Anthony Hopkins, and in 1997 (again for television) with Mandy Patinkin. Children will be most familiar with the Disney studio's animated musical, made in 1996.

THE HUNCHBACK OF NOTRE DAME (1996)
Color, 85 minutes
Cast: Voices of Tom Hulce, Demi Moore, Kevin Kline, Tony Jay, Jason Alexander, Heidi Mollenhauer, Paul Kandel, Charles Kimbrough, Mary Wickes, Jane Withers, David Ogden Stiers
Director: Gary Trousdale and Kirk Wise
Screenplay: Tab Murphy, Irene Mecchi, Bob Tzudiker, Noni White, and Jonathan Roberts, from an animation story by Murphy, based on the novel by Victor Hugo
Animated feature
Rated G
Young children: OK, with caution   Older children: VG

Quasimodo, a deformed orphan, has been raised in the belfry of Notre Dame cathedral by his guardian, the evil Frollo. The hunchback's only friends are three gargoyles, Victor, Hugo, and Laverne, who try to lift his spirits, and encourage him to go "out there" into the world of Paris. But when he does, he is ridiculed during the Festival of Fools, and the only person to take pity on him is the dancing gypsy, Esmeralda. In time, the fate of all these characters will be intertwined.

Victor Hugo's famous novel of medieval Paris qualifies as the Disney studio's all-time strangest choice of subject matter for an animated musical, but the result is a bold and striking work. Whether it will appeal to young children is another matter. It is highly emotional and intensely dramatic; the moments of comedy relief (with Quasi's three gargoyle pals) seem completely contrived and out of place here. The music, too, is perfectly suited to the story but not the kind one easily remembers (or hums) afterwards.

Frollo's motivations—particularly in the "Hellfire" sequence, in which he admits to having pas-

266

sionate feelings about Esmeralda—will be difficult to explain to the tiny tots, and the climactic fire and cliffhanging hand-to-hand combat may be too intense for the very young.

Older children, however, should find this both involving and entertaining. If your kids seem genuinely intrigued, they might want to watch a more serious rendition of the same story (like the 1939 Charles Laughton movie)—but you should warn them that the folks at Disney took liberties with the novel, and there will be no comedy relief in other versions of *The Hunchback*.

I

ICE CASTLES (1979)

Color, 109 minutes
Cast: Lynn-Holly Johnson,
  Robby Benson, Colleen
  Dewhurst, Tom Skerritt
Director: Donald Wrye
Screenplay: Wrye and Gary L.
  Baln
Drama/Sports
Rated PG
Young children: OK   Older
  children: VG

A real hankie-soaker, *Ice Castles*
tells the story of a promising
skater who is blinded in an accident but overcomes the odds to
become an Olympic champion.
Real-life skater Johnson is the
fated athlete; she also skates in
the 007 movie *For Your Eyes
Only.*

The rise of an Iowa farm girl to
the rank of world contender is
told in almost *Rocky*-like fashion.
Dewy-eyed Benson is the guy she
meets at the ice rink. He goes into
hockey, while she becomes a fig-
ure-skating competitor to reckon
with. Yet her injury draws the two
closer together, as in the song
"Through the Eyes of Love,"
which was written for this movie.

Despite the schmaltz, the movie
builds satisfyingly toward its inevitable conclusion. Even in the
'90s, this is still a movie young
girls watch over and over. And
why not?

ICEMAN (1984)

Color, 99 minutes
Cast: Timothy Hutton, John
  Lone, Lindsay Crouse, Josef
  Sommer, David Strathairn,
  Philip Akin, Danny Glover,
  Amelia Hall, Richard Monette,
  James Tolkan
Director: Fred Schepisi
Screenplay: Chip Proser and
  John Drimmer
Science fiction/Drama
Rated PG
Young children:
  Marginal   Older children: VG

The perfectly preserved body of a
Neanderthal man (Lone) is discovered in the Arctic; when it is
taken to a research station nearby,
scientists realize that the man can
be brought back to life. Dr. Stanley Shephard (Hutton) makes
friends with the intelligent, lively
Neanderthal man, whom he dubs
"Charlie." While Shephard wants
to treat Charlie as a human being
and to study him for what he can
tell us about the past, cryogenics
expert Dr. Diane Brady (Crouse)
wants to subject him to painful
tests in order to find a way to preserve other people.

This excellent, underrated film
is highlighted by the outstanding
performance of John Lone as a
man who is literally brought back
to life after thousands of years.
(Can you even imagine what that
might be like?) It is intelligent
and moving, a science fiction film

for adults that older children should also respond to.

In other movies, revived cavemen have been played as comic fools (*Encino Man*), tragic if dangerous figures (*Trog*) or all-out menaces (*The Neanderthal Man*). Here, Charlie is a fully realized character who is likely to appeal to children. That is precisely why parents should know that the film does not end happily. Whether your kids are old enough to handle a tragic ending is up to you.

THE IDOLMAKER (1980)
Color, 119 minutes
Cast: Ray Sharkey, Tovah Feldshuh, Peter Gallagher, Paul Land, Joe Pantoliano, Maureen McCormick, Richard Bright, Olympia Dukakis
Director: Taylor Hackford
Screenplay: Edward DiLorenzo
Drama with music
Rated PG
Young children: No Older children: VG

This energetic, fictionalized biography is loosely based on the career of rock 'n' roll promoter Bob Marcucci, who shepherded the careers of teen idols Frankie Avalon and Fabian in the late 1950s.

Vinnie Vaccari is an aggressive dreamer and aspiring songwriter who, through sheer persistence, transforms an obscure saxophonist and a bashful busboy into Tommy Dee and Caesare, rock 'n' roll icons.

The Idolmaker is bursting with intensity and features Ray Sharkey in an energetic performance as Vinnie. It also works as a history lesson on the early years of rock 'n' roll, offering up a graphic portrait of the then burgeoning industry, with its behind-the-

scenes maneuvering and double-dealing. Yet it also trumpets the basic, unbridled appeal of straight-ahead rock 'n' roll, which survives to this day. This is ever so apparent as Tommy Dee sings, Ya got everything I need, wow, wow, wow, and pimply 14-year-olds screech with glee.

The seamier side of show business makes this inappropriate for younger kids.

I KNOW WHY THE CAGED BIRD SINGS (1979)
Color, 100 minutes
Cast: Diahann Carroll, Ruby Dee, Paul Benjamin, Roger E. Mosley, Esther Rolle, Madge Sinclair, Constance Good, Art Evans
Director: Fielder Cook
Screenplay: Leonora Thuna, Ralph B. Woolsey, and Maya Angelou, based on an Angelou autobiography
Drama
Unrated
Young children: VG Older children: VG

The early years of humanist writer-poet Maya Angelou are represented in this heartfelt story of an African-American girl and her brother being raised by their stalwart grandmother in the American South of the Depression era of the 1930s. The family's hardships and joys are dealt with, and particularly the struggles of a gifted child to learn and grow under economic, social, and racial difficulties.

Because Angelou is a notable woman and a role model for all young people (especially those who grow up under troubled conditions), this film serves as an educational resource, a document of humanism and social history . . . as well as providing first-rate entertainment.

First shown on prime-time television, *I Know Why the Caged Bird Sings* is suitable for the entire family.

IMAGINARY CRIMES (1994)
Color, 104 minutes
Cast: Harvey Keitel, Fairuza Balk, Kelly Lynch, Vincent D'Onofrio, Diane Baker, Chris Penn, Amber Benson, Seymour Cassel, Tori Paul
Director: Anthony Drazan
Screenplay: Kristine Johnson and Davia Nelson, based on the novel by Sheila Ballantyne
Drama
Rated PG
Younger children: No   Older children: VG

The story of a dysfunctional family, circa 1962, and a teenage girl's coming-of-age. Sonya (Fairuza Balk), in flashbacks, recalls her chaotic home life with her little sister and ne'er-do-well father (Harvey Keitel) after the death of her mother (Kelly Lynch).

One step ahead of the bill collectors and always prepared with one get-rich-quick scheme or another, father Ray finds himself unprepared to be both father and mother to his children. Encouraged by her English teacher (Vincent D'Onofrio), Sonya falls into writing and literature in order to make sense of home life and find her own voice.

The subject matter is rather harsh for younger children, but adolescents should respond to the family and its trials. Keitel rarely plays sympathetic characters, but he's genuinely likable and believable here as a father who means

well but can't seem to discipline himself—even for the sake of the two girls he loves.

Fine performances distinguish this predictable but well-made film.

IMITATION OF LIFE (1934)
Black & white, 109 minutes
Cast: Claudette Colbert, Warren William, Rochelle Hudson, Louise Beavers, Fredi Washington, Ned Sparks, Alan Hale, Henry Armetta
Director: John M. Stahl
Screenplay: William Hurlbut, based on the novel by Fannie Hurst
Drama
Unrated
Young children: OK   Older children: VG

When a young white widow, Bea, who is struggling to run her late husband's maple syrup business, meets an African-American woman, Delilah, with a mouthwatering family recipe for pancakes, the two join forces and open a pancake restaurant. The business becomes a success, but that's only one facet of the story. Because this film was made in 1934, a black person could not be depicted as the business partner of a white person. As a result, Bea is shown living prosperously in a large house while Delilah, who has been given 20 percent of the profits in the business, stays in the household as a sort of maid to Bea. The story also deals with the women's relationships with their daughters.

In a culture in which segregation and discrimination against minorities was rampant, Delilah's daughter, who is so light-skinned that she appears white, makes up her mind to "pass." It is this significant subplot that gives the story extra punch and made it a controversial movie for its time.

Younger children will need to be informed about race relations during the pre–civil rights era in order to understand the reasons for Delilah's status in the household and the daughter's rebellious move to deny her identity, even if it means rejecting her own loving mother. This is a powerful story of mothers and daughters, which deals frankly with race relations. Because of the mature themes, the film particularly will interest youngsters of adolescent age and up. It was remade in 1959.

IMITATION OF LIFE (1959)
Color, 124 minutes
Cast: Lana Turner, John Gavin, Sandra Dee, Dan O'Herlihy, Susan Kohner, Robert Alda, Juanita Moore, Mahalia Jackson, Troy Donahue, Jack Weston
Director: Douglas Sirk
Screenplay: Allan Scott, based on the novel by Fannie Hurst
Drama
Unrated
Young children: OK   Older children: VG

Even though this film has the same general plot as the 1934 film of Fannie Hurst's novel, the story has been updated and somewhat glamorized. Instead of being in the maple syrup business, Lana Turner plays an aspiring actress, Lora, whose small daughter becomes lost at the beach. When the child is found by Annie, a jobless African-American woman, the two women strike an arrangement by which Annie will be housekeeper and take care of Lora's

child. Annie has a daughter of her own, who happens to be light-skinned.

Although this version is glitzier than the original film, the theme of the daughter's struggle to pass for white is very intense and sincere. It is clear that race relations in the United States had not really changed much by 1959. Both versions of the Hurst book are strong and heartbreaking melodramas, featuring themes of troubled mother-daughter relationships. In addition to examining the struggles between the black mother and the child who wants to "pass," this version also treats the theme of a mother (in this case is the career-minded actress, Lora) who neglects her child. The film will spark plenty of discussion about parental roles and responsibilities, as well as topics related to racial problems.

THE INCREDIBLE JOURNEY (1963)
Color, 80 minutes
Cast: Emile Genest, John Drainie, Tommy Tweed, Sandra Scott
Director: Fletcher Markle
Screenplay: James Algar, based on the book by Sheila Burnford
Adventure/Animal story
Unrated
Younger kids: VG   Older kids: VG

This Disney charmer is the original version of the reportedly true story about three animals who trek home to their owners, remade in 1993 as **Homeward Bound: The Incredible Journey**. Set in Canada, the tale follows a bull terrier, a Siamese cat, and a Labrador retriever as they journey across 250 miles of wilderness to return home after their owners go on a vacation and leave the pets with a friend. The story is essentially the same, but unlike the remake, the animals are not given their own voices; rather, a folksy commentator (Disney veteran Rex Allen) provides narration, and the film is shot in the style of Disney's "True-Life" nature films, giving it a documentary-like feel. The Canadian scenery is beautiful and the animals are hard to resist, making this especially suited for young children.

THE INCREDIBLE MR. LIMPET (1964)
Color, 102 minutes
Cast: Don Knotts, Jack Weston, Carole Cook, Andrew Duggan, Larry Keating, Elizabeth MacRae, Paul Frees
Director: Arthur Lubin
Screenplay: John C. Rose, Jameson Brewer, and Joe DiMona
Live-action/animated feature
Unrated
Younger kids: OK   Older kids: OK

This combination live-action/animation fantasy stars Don Knotts as a bookworm and fish fanatic—rejected for service with a 4F classification—who becomes one of the biggest heroes of World War II.

Falling off a Coney Island pier, Limpet (Knotts) is magically transformed into a fish. Underwater, he meets a grumpy but helpful crustacean (Frees) and a lovely ladyfish (MacRae) who help him maneuver through his new world, a world filled with many dangers. Seeing his duty as an American citizen, Limpet warns the U.S. Navy of Nazi U-boats and helps the Allies win the war.

Although well remembered by those who saw it as children, Limpet isn't a very good movie; it's the sequence of Limpet falling off a pier and being transformed into a fish that would linger in a child's memory. The comedy elements of the film are obvious and exaggerated, but the underwater scenes (handled by the Warner Bros. cartoon department) are attractive and well animated. Jack Weston stands out among the live actors as the befuddled brother-in-law. There are five songs, none of them inspired, by Sammy Fain and Harold Adamson.

Limpet is a squeaky-clean movie, suitable for all ages.

THE INCREDIBLE SHRINKING MAN (1957)
Black & white, 81 minutes
Cast: Grant Williams, Randy Stuart, William Schallert, April Kent, Paul Langton
Director: Jack Arnold
Screenplay: Richard Matheson, from his novel
Science fiction/Suspense
Unrated
Younger kids: May be too intense and cerebral   Older kids: VG

A young husband is accidentally exposed to a radioactive cloud, and he soon begins to shrink. There is nothing he, his wife, or his doctor can do.

A very simple premise is brilliantly explored in this unforgettable movie. Several different stages of the man's progress are dramatized, the most memorable occurring when he's a few inches high and chased by a cat, and later when he's less than an inch in height, trapped in his own basement, and menaced by a spider.

There is no other movie like this, and the sheer novelty of it will catch the imaginations of almost all older kids. The existential nature of the script and the man's eventual acceptance of his fate provide plenty of food for thought. The movie is very well directed, with excellent photography and satisfactory special effects. In a way, the most surprising thing about this film is that it has yet to be seriously remade. (*The Incredible Shrinking Woman,* made years later with Lily Tomlin as a comic "answer" to this well-remembered film, is a badly misfired satirical comedy.)

INDEPENDENCE DAY (1996)

Color, 145 minutes
Cast: Jeff Goldblum, Will Smith, Bill Pullman, Randy Quaid, Vivica A. Fox, Margaret Colin, Judd Hirsch, Mary McDonnell, Brent Spiner, Harvey Fierstein, Robert Loggia, James Rebhorn, Harry Connick, Jr.
Director: Roland Emmerich
Screenplay: Dean Devlin and Emmerich
Science fiction/Action
Rated PG-13
Young children: Too intense   Older children: OK

Giant flying saucers invade the Earth; impervious to Earth's weapons, they go about blowing up the world's cities with impunity. Just when everything seems worst for humanity, the heroes get a bright idea . . .

It's hard to believe that this is only the third English-language movie about a mass alien invasion, but it is. (The others? **War of the Worlds** and **Earth vs. the Flying Saucers. Mars Attacks!** would follow.) However, it feels like a smudged carbon of any number of other movies, because Devlin and Emmerich applied the standard disaster-movie format to the alien-invasion formula. They were cheerfully sanguine about being influenced by movies of the past; they weren't out to make art, after all, but a popcorn movie on a big scale, something to wow audiences, make them cheer for the good guys and hiss the bad ones, and get them to marvel at the swell special effects.

In all this, they've spectacularly succeeded: the movie may require you to park your brains under your seat, but after that, it's the classic E-ticket ride. It doesn't play as well on video as in theaters, and if you loved it at the multiplex, you might be surprised at how many bad lines, improbable coincidences, and sheer stupidities there are.

But kids love this kind of movie and can watch it over and over. It's not well suited for those under 10, with its mass destruction, strong language, and overall intensity, but there's no personal violence to speak of. People die en masse and at a great distance.

INDIANA JONES AND THE LAST CRUSADE (1989)

Color, 127 minutes
Cast: Harrison Ford, Sean Connery, Denholm Elliott, Alison Doody, John Rhys-Davies, Julian Glover, River Phoenix, Alex Hyde-White
Director: Steven Spielberg
Screenplay: Jeffery Boam, based on a story by George Lucas and Menno Meyjes

Action-adventure
Rated PG-13
Younger kids: No   Older kids: VG

Chapter three of the Indiana Jones chronicles is "more of the same," pitting the intrepid professor-explorer (Harrison Ford) against Nazis once again, this time in a quest to find the Holy Grail. The series is given a boost by the classy presence of Sean Connery as Indy's father, an eccentric medievalist who disappears while seeking the Grail. Accompanied by his associate Marcus (Denholm Elliott), Indy goes off in search of his father on an expedition that takes them from the canals of Venice to a German castle to the Middle Eastern desert.

Perhaps in response to the controversy over the terrifying violence in part two, the action is toned down a bit from the first two films, but there are still plenty of exciting set pieces (particularly a prologue featuring River Phoenix as the young Indy), and the story gains an added dimension through the father-son rivalry.

This is not recommended for young kids, but older children who've been fed a diet of action films should have no trouble with this one. Parents might not approve of all the language, however.

INDIANA JONES AND THE TEMPLE OF DOOM (1984)
Color, 118 minutes
Cast: Harrison Ford, Kate Capshaw, Ke Huy Quan, Amrish Puri, Roshan Seth, Dan Aykroyd
Director: Steven Spielberg
Screenplay: Willard Huyck and Gloria Katz, based on a story by George Lucas
Action-adventure
Rated PG
Younger kids: No   Older kids: VG

Steven Spielberg's sequel (actually, a prequel) to his smash hit **Raiders of the Lost Ark** is a ceaseless roller-coaster ride of breakneck action and cliffhanging thrills. It's overdone but enjoyable on a mindless level. This time, the whip-cracking archaeologist (Harrison Ford) finds himself stranded in the Himalayas in 1935 with a feisty singer (Kate Capshaw) and a 12-year-old sidekick named Short Round (Ke Huy Quan). While on the trail of a sacred jewel, he gets mixed up with an evil religious cult that practices human sacrifice and child slavery.

Although pure escapist entertainment, the film sometimes goes too far with its "gross-out" gags and violence, with the bad guys beaten up or killed by the score, a roomful of insects, a scene of eating monkey brains, and in one notorious scene, showing a beating heart being torn from a human chest. The resulting outcry from parents led to the creation of a new rating, the PG-13 classification, designed to indicate that some scenes may be too intense for viewers under 13.

THE INDIAN IN THE CUPBOARD (1995)
Color, 96 minutes
Cast: Hal Scardino, Litefoot, Lindsay Crouse, Richard Jenkins, Rishi Bhat, David Keith, Steve Coogan
Director: Frank Oz
Screenplay: Melissa Mathison,

based on the novel by Lynne Reid Banks
Fantasy
Rated PG
Younger children: OK   Older children: OK

Omri's older brothers give him an unusual present for his ninth birthday: a cupboard for storing toys. His best friend, Patrick, gives him an Indian figure, which fits perfectly inside the cupboard, but while he's sleeping Omri hears a banging sound. When he opens the cupboard door, the figure has come to life—a living, breathing Indian. At first, both are shocked, and Omri seems like a mythic giant to the miniature Indian. In time, they come to trust and depend on one another. Omri tries to keep the Indian's existence a secret, but when he tells Patrick, the boy puts a cowboy figure in the cupboard, and lo and behold, it too springs to life—the Indian's natural enemy.

Lynne Reid Banks' popular children's book was filmed with great care by director Frank Oz (of Muppet and Yoda fame), with a script by Melissa Mathison, who wrote **E.T. The Extra-Terrestrial**. The consensus, from critics and audiences alike, was that this film never quite soared to the heights of *E.T.* in spite of having all the right ingredients.

Still, it's an entertaining tale for younger kids, with a lesson or two along the way about compassion and responsibility. Hal Scardino is very likable as Omri, and recording artist Litefoot is perfectly cast as the Indian, Little Bear.

There is an occasional four-letter word, and there's a scene in which Little Bear is exposed to a scan of the television dial—complete with sexy dancing and violent action—that resulted in this film being given a PG rating.

INHERIT THE WIND (1960)
Black & white, 127 minutes
Cast: Spencer Tracy, Fredric March, Gene Kelly, Florence Eldridge, Dick York, Harry Morgan, Donna Anderson, Elliott Reid, Claude Akins, Noah Beery, Jr., Norman Fell
Director: Stanley Kramer
Screenplay: Nathan E. Douglas (pseud. of Nedrick Young) and Harold Jacob Smith, based on the play by Jerome Lawrence and Robert E. Lee
Drama
Unrated
Younger kids: OK   Older kids: VG

Powerhouse acting by Spencer Tracy and Fredric March sparks this superb adaptation of the play inspired by the famous Scopes "Monkey Trial" in 1925 Tennessee, in which a high school teacher was prosecuted by William Jennings Bryan for teaching Darwin's Theory of Evolution and defended by Clarence Darrow . . . bringing together in one courtroom two of the greatest lawyers and orators of the century.

Although the characters' names have been changed, the facts of the trial are all true, with Tracy and March brilliantly squaring off in a series of riveting encounters that produce dramatic fireworks. Also excellent are Henry Morgan as the wise judge and Gene Kelly, who's surprisingly effective as a cynical reporter modeled on the famous writer-editor H. L. Mencken.

Dealing with religious, scientific, educational, and moral issues, this is an outstanding and thought-provoking film for all but the youngest of children. A 1988 TV-movie remake starred Kirk Douglas and Jason Robards as the legal combatants.

INNERSPACE (1987)
Color, 120 minutes
Cast: Dennis Quaid, Martin Short, Meg Ryan, Kevin McCarthy, Fiona Lewis, Vernon Wells, Robert Picardo, Wendy Schaal, Harold Sylvester, William Schallert, Henry Gibson, John Hora, Kathleen Freeman, Dick Miller, Kenneth Tobey, Joe Flaherty, Andrea Martin
Director: Joe Dante
Screenplay: Jeffrey Boam and Chip Proser
Science fiction/Comedy
Rated PG
Younger kids: Probably too intense   Older kids: OK

Hotdog test pilot Tuck (Dennis Quaid) alienates his fiancée Lydia (Meg Ryan), and volunteers to be miniaturized in a one-man submarine and be injected into a rabbit. But when industrial spies attack, a scientist flees with the syringe that contains Tuck and his sub; while fleeing, the scientist is shot, and injects Tuck into hypochondriacal supermarket clerk Jack (Martin Short). After some setbacks, Tuck is able to communicate with Jack and explains that he has to be re-enlarged soon. Meanwhile, the leaders (Kevin McCarthy, Fiona Lewis) of the industrial spies are after two essential chips, one of which is in Tuck's submarine. So the villains decide to shrink a killer (Vernon

Wells) and send him into Jack to kill Tuck and claim the chip.

This action-comedy variation on **Fantastic Voyage** veers wildly from comedy to action-adventure and back again, but maintains a speedy pace. The characters are broad but appealing, and there are many amazing stunts and plentiful gags. Robert Picardo as an Israeli high-tech spy is particularly funny in his cowboy obsession ("I've got spurs that yingle, yangle, yingle"), while McCarthy makes a colorful villain. This bigstudio movie isn't as distinctive as most of Dante's output, but it's attractive and well made.

Kids with a scientific bent might raise an eyebrow about how teensy little Tuck gets around inside Jack's body so swiftly, and there are other sticking points, too. But the story keeps coming up with new ideas, it's highly visual, and it has an unbeatable "worm turns" theme.

The spy aspect of the film—and the threat the villains pose—are just serious enough to make this too intense for younger children.

THE INNOCENTS (1961)
Black & white, 99 minutes
Cast: Deborah Kerr, Peter Wyngarde, Megs Jenkins, Michael Redgrave, Martin Stephens, Pamela Franklin, Clytie Jessop, Isla Cameron, Eric Woodburn
Director: Jack Clayton
Screenplay: Truman Capote and William Archibald, from Archibald's play of the same title, which was based on Henry James' novella *The Turn of the Screw*
Horror/Literary classic
Unrated

Younger kids: Scary   Older kids: Scary, but okay

Miss Giddens (Kerr) is hired by a wealthy man (Redgrave) to be governess to his young nephew, Miles (Stephens), and niece, Flora (Franklin), at his isolated but beautiful country mansion. However, Miss Giddens soon begins to suspect that the malignant ghosts of the previous governess and her earthy lover are haunting the estate and, especially, preying on the children.

As was clearly (too clearly at times) the intention of director Clayton, the film can be taken as either a ghost story or a tale of repressed sexual obsession, but it definitely works best as a haunting, even poetic ghost story. The shock scenes are so well designed and potent that several take place in the bright daylight of the English countryside without losing impact. The cast, particularly young Martin Stephens, is excellent. The cinematography by Freddie Francis ranks among the best ever done in wide-screen black-and-white, so be sure to seek out a letterboxed version.

Like **The Haunting,** this is one of the greatest haunted house movies, and though it lacks even so much as one drop of blood, it's still too strong to let kids watch it alone. Once they get into the rhythms of the film, the pacing of another time, they'll be mesmerized. This is the kind of experience that turns some kids on to an appreciation of movies as art, while still functioning as a scary movie.

IN SEARCH OF THE CASTAWAYS (1962)
Color, 100 minutes
Cast: Hayley Mills, Maurice Chevalier, George Sanders, Wilfrid Hyde-White, Michael Anderson, Jr.
Director: Robert Stevenson
Screenplay: Lowell S. Hawley, based on the novel *Captain Grant's Children* by Jules Verne
Action-adventure/Fantasy
Unrated
Younger kids: OK   Older kids: Good

Jules Verne's story about the search for a missing 19th-century English explorer gets a fanciful Disney treatment in this highly improbable but entertaining juvenile adventure. Disney discovery Hayley Mills plays the daughter of the explorer, who, along with her brother (Keith Hamilton), a professor (Maurice Chevalier), a boat captain (Wilfrid Hyde-White), and his son (Michael Anderson, Jr.), ventures to South America, Australia, and New Zealand in search of the long-lost Captain Grant.

There's plenty of action, including earthquakes, giant condors, floods, fires, tidal waves, and volcanic mountains, along with romance, comedy, and even a few songs (provided by Chevalier), but the elements don't always mesh. Older viewers in particular may find the clash between the realistic opening and the pure fantasy that follows to be somewhat disconcerting.

IN THE GOOD OLD SUMMERTIME (1949)

Color, 102 minutes
Cast: Judy Garland, Van Johnson, S. Z. Sakall, Spring Byington, Clinton Sundberg, Buster Keaton
Director: Robert Z. Leonard
Screenplay: Samson Raphaelson, Frances Goodrich, Albert Hackett, and Ivan Tors, based on the play *Parfumerie* by Nikolaus Laszlo
Musical
Unrated
Young children: VG   Older children: VG

In the Good Old Summertime is an agreeable remake of *The Shop Around the Corner,* a superb 1940 comedy, which was remade in 1998 with Tom Hanks and Meg Ryan as *You've Got Mail.*

While the settings and specifics are different in each version, the idea remains the same: It is the story of two employees who, while at odds in the workplace, are forging a romantic relationship as pen pals, little dreaming whom they are actually corresponding with! Naturally, as they become increasingly agitated on the job, their letters become warmer and more committed.

Here, the setting is a music store in turn-of-the-20th-century Chicago. Judy Garland and Van Johnson are fine as the unknowing lovers; younger children will be instantly enamored of the jowly, cuddly S. Z. Sakall, cast as their employer. Sakall was a Hungarian-born character comedian who came to Hollywood around 1940 and quickly earned the nickname "Cuddles."

Lastly, if the little girl in the final sequence looks familiar, that is because she is none other than Liza Minnelli, the daughter of Garland and director Vincente Minnelli!

IN THE HEAT OF THE NIGHT (1967)

Color, 109 minutes
Cast: Sidney Poitier, Rod Steiger, Warren Oates, Lee Grant, Scott Wilson, Larry Gates, Beah Richards, Quentin Dean, James Patterson, Anthony James, William Schallert
Director: Norman Jewison
Screenplay: Stirling Silliphant, based on the novel by John Ball
Drama/Mystery
Unrated
Young children: No   Older children: VG

This piercing social drama of murder and racial conflict in the Deep South earned a Best Picture Academy Award. Rod Steiger also won an Oscar for his performance as Bill Gillespie, a redneck Southern sheriff whose small town is shaken by a bizarre murder. At first, his prime suspect is a stranger, Virgil Tibbs (Sidney Poitier). Tibbs comes under suspicion solely because he is an anomaly to the sheriff: a well-dressed black man. Tibbs then reveals himself to be a Philadelphia homicide detective who happened to be in town visiting his mother. Gillespie is resentful, even openly hostile toward this intelligent stranger, but eventually comes to respect Tibbs' professionalism—and to realize his need for expert help in solving the crime at hand.

In the Heat of the Night came to theaters at the height of the civil rights movement. The desegregation of schools and other public institutions had been in the headlines for several years, but the idea of an integrated society was still evolving, especially in the South. While the film works as a solid entertainment, it also telegraphs a potent and relevant message: If someone as set in his ways as Bill Gillespie can regard a black man with respect, greater understanding between the races may well be possible.

The film contains language and situations inappropriate for younger children. It is superior entertainment for older kids and their parents.

INTO THE WEST (1993)
Color, 92 minutes
Cast: Gabriel Byrne, Ellen
   Barkin, Ciaran Fitzgerald,
   Ruaidhri (Rory) Conroy,
   David Kelly, Johnny Murphy,
   Colm Meaney, John
   Kavanagh, Brendan Gleeson,
   Jim Norton
Director: Mike Newell
Screenplay: Jim Sheridan
Adventure/Drama
Rated PG
Young children: No   Older
   children: VG

This appealing, intensely involving tale charts the plight of a pair of scruffy, motherless brothers, 8-year-old Ossie and 12-year-old Tito, who are coming of age in a Dublin slum. Their constantly inebriated father, Papa Riley, is in deep mourning over the death of his wife and emotionally unavailable to the boys. So the entry into their lives of a beautiful, magical white horse, named Tir na nOg (which translated from Gaelic means the Land of Eternal Youth), has extra-special mean-

ing. Tir na nOg, presented to Ossie and Tito by their gypsy granddad, serves as a symbol of what each boy hopes will be a brighter future. And it is no surprise that they refuse to sit passively by when the horse is taken from them.

The boys live in drab surroundings, and much of the drama is directly related to the death of their mother. As such, a melancholy mood pervades the film. This, along with the complex relationship between Papa Riley and his sons, makes the film inappropriate for younger viewers. Older children and their parents, however, will be captivated by this modern-day fable.

INTRUDER IN THE DUST
(1949)
Black & white, 87 minutes
Cast: David Brian, Claude
   Jarman, Jr., Juano Hernandez,
   Porter Hall, Elizabeth
   Patterson
Director: Clarence Brown
Screenplay: Ben Maddow, based
   on a novel by William
   Faulkner
Drama
Unrated
Younger children: No   Older
   children: VG

Intruder in the Dust is one of four films released in 1949—**Pinky, Lost Boundaries,** and **Home of the Brave** are the others—to indict the racial stereotyping and discrimination that then was the norm in American movies, as well as in many sectors of American society. Their production marked a turning point in the way African-Americans were portrayed in Hollywood.

Intruder in the Dust is the story

of a proud, fearless—and innocent—black man who is accused of murder in a small Southern town. Will his lynching be averted by the efforts of the community's few level-headed, truth-seeking whites?

The film is notable for the dignity and uncompromising integrity with which the black man is portrayed. He refuses to condescend to his accusers to avoid being lynched. He would rather die than submit to his tormentors.

And he is beautifully played by a talented but long-forgotten actor named Juano Hernandez.

Anyone who has read William Faulkner's famous novel will want to compare it to this excellent screen adaptation. Older children will find this film fascinating, even inspiring, but its intense drama—and the threat of lynching—make it too strong for younger kids.

INVASION OF THE BODY SNATCHERS (1956)
Black & white, 80 minutes
Cast: Kevin McCarthy, Dana Wynter, Larry Gates, King Donovan, Carolyn Jones
Director: Don Siegel
Screenplay: Daniel Mainwaring, based on the novel by Jack Finney
Science fiction/Suspense
Unrated
Younger kids: Too scary Older kids: VG

A doctor (McCarthy) returns to his hometown to discover people complaining that their relatives aren't really their relatives. He eventually learns that strange seed pods from space are duplicating people, with the duplicates then taking over the originals' lives. (In this version, we never know what happens to the originals, but it can't be good.) The pod duplicates look and act just like the originals, but they have no emotions, and their only drive is to continue the duplication. The doctor finds the number of his allies dwindling night by night.

A classic of its type, with its built-in paranoia so well tuned for the times that some saw it a parable about Communist "witch hunts." Director Siegel considered it an attack on conformity instead. Regardless of subtext, it remains today a terrifying film, dramatizing an irrational but common human fear: no one can be trusted, they're all against me. It's also fast paced, exciting, and very well acted, but the premise is so unnerving that it may upset younger children. Older ones, however, will have fun being scared by this expertly crafted movie.

It has been remade twice, under the same title and as *Body Snatchers.*

INVASION OF THE BODY SNATCHERS (1978)
Color, 115 minutes
Cast: Donald Sutherland, Brooke Adams, Leonard Nimoy, Jeff Goldblum, Veronica Cartwright
Director: Philip Kaufman
Screenplay: W. D. Richter
Science fiction–horror/Suspense
Rated PG
Younger kids: No Older kids: OK

This excellent (if overlong) remake of the 1956 classic sets its story in San Francisco rather than a small town, but otherwise, the plot is much the same as before: people are being taken over by replicas who have no emotions. In some ways, the urban setting somehow makes things even more disturbing.

Again, younger children will find it far too upsetting (when they aren't bored by the grownup stuff). Even older kids may find it unsettling—there's one shot of a dog with a human face that would unsettle *anyone*—and scary at times. Being more contemporary than the 1956 original means that kids can relate to its fears more directly.

Parents may take note of the fact that Kevin McCarthy, the star of the original, has a cameo role; so does that film's director, Don Siegel.

INVISIBLE AGENT (1942)
Black & white, 82 minutes
Cast: Ilona Massey, Jon Hall, Peter Lorre, Sir Cedric Hardwicke, J. Edward Bromberg, Albert Basserman, John Litel, Holmes Herbert, Keye Luke
Director: Edwin L. Marin
Screenplay: Curt Siodmak
Science fiction/Espionage/Thriller
Unrated
Younger kids: OK, with caution   Older kids: OK

Even sci-fi/horror movies went to battle; there are references to World War II in several of the Universal horror movies of the 1940s, but this is the only one in which one of their characters actually fights the Axis. Jon Hall uses the invisibility formula to become the perfect spy in Berlin, but things eventually go awry.

The Invisible Man movies are unique among the Universal horror films; although the titles suggest they're all about the same

individual, it's never the same invisible man twice, not even when Jon Hall played the title role two times. Yet each of the movies, even **Abbott and Costello Meet the Invisible Man,** is carefully linked to the others; there's usually a photo of Claude Rains somewhere.

This one has many great invisibility effects, imaginative and convincing even by today's standards; they were the creation of John P. Fulton. As he parachutes into Germany, Hall becomes invisible and disrobes; later, he covers his face in cold cream to make himself visible enough for Ilona Massey to talk to. He also takes a bubble bath!

All this is great stuff even for very young children, who may never have seen anything like it before, but be warned: this particular entry does include some torture scenes (the invisible spy is caught in a net lined with fishhooks—and remember, he's naked) which might upset younger children.

This was followed by **The Invisible Man's Revenge.**

THE INVISIBLE BOY (1957)
Black & white, 85 minutes
Cast: Richard Eyer, Diane Brewster, Philip Abbott, Harold J. Stone, Robby the Robot
Director: Herman Hoffman
Screenplay: Cyril Hume
Science fiction/Comedy-drama
Unrated
Younger kids: VG   Older kids: Good

A young boy is a disappointment to his computer-scientist father until the day the father allows the youngster to be educated by his invention, a super computer. Now the kid can beat his dad at chess and can reassemble a robot that was evidently brought back from the future. The boy and the robot become inseparable (and for a while, the robot turns the boy invisible, hence the title), but soon the super computer takes control of the robot, with world destruction in mind. . . .

If your kids are used to the slower pacing of some older movies, this one could really delight them, especially the younger ones; older ones might find it corny, but they'll still like Robby the Robot (who, or which, originated in **Forbidden Planet**). Even parents will be amused by the droll satire in the clever script.

THE INVISIBLE MAN (1933)
Black & white, 71 minutes
Cast: Claude Rains, Gloria
  Stuart, William Harrigan,
  Henry Travers, Una
  O'Connor, Forrester Harvey,
  Holmes Herbert, E. E. Clive
Director: James Whale
Screenplay: R. C. Sherriff, from
  the novel by H. G. Wells
Science fiction/Thriller
Unrated
Younger kids: OK   Older kids:
  OK

On a snowy evening, a mysterious stranger, his face completely covered in bandages, takes a room at a pub in a small British town. The locals are very curious about him, until he unwraps himself to reveal—nothing. He's completely invisible and what's more, he's going crazy, changing from a prank-playing if cranky recluse into a full-blown megalomaniac.

This is still the only feature film version of H. G. Wells' famous

novel; it's more melodramatic than the book but otherwise a very fine movie of its type. The characters are ripe and colorful (especially the screaming woman, played with all stops out by Una O'Connor), the frequent humor is sharp and witty, and the special effects are still uncannily convincing. Claude Rains, in his first American film, is outstanding as the Invisible Man; his face isn't seen until the last moments of the movie.

Although the movie is spooky at times, it's not really a horror thriller, but rather a science fiction adventure melodrama, and a good one. Younger kids, who haven't yet developed prejudices against "old-fashioned" movies, might actually enjoy this, but it does depend more on character than special effects.

Another point of interest: The leading lady is the same Gloria Stuart who earned an Oscar nomination sixty-five years later for her performance as Old Rose in *Titanic*.

There were several sequels, beginning with **The Invisible Man Returns.**

THE INVISIBLE MAN RETURNS (1940)
Black & white, 81 minutes
Cast: Vincent Price, Nan Grey,
  John Sutton, Sir Cedric
  Hardwicke, Cecil Kellaway,
  Alan Napier
Director: Joe May
Screenplay: Lester Cole, Joe
  May, and Curt Siodmak.
Science fiction/Melodrama
Unrated
Younger kids: OK, but a little
  scary   Older kids: OK

Price, convicted of murder, is helped by his friend Sutton, who gives him the invisible potion created by Sutton's late brother so he can escape from prison. While the wily local police inspector (Kellaway) tries to find this new invisible man, Price searches for the real killer, with the unwilling help of an opportunistic tramp (Napier).

This sequel doesn't have the sardonic mood of the great James Whale original, but it's an atmospheric, well-directed thriller in its own right. (And, for the record, Claude Rains' photo is on John Sutton's wall, identifying the "original" Invisible Man.) This time out, the Invisible Man is the hero, but just as in the original, he'll go mad unless he's returned to visibility. The special effects are again excellent, and standing sets of a coal mine are used to great effect.

Younger kids won't really be bothered by the film, except intermittently (as when the Invisible Man disrobes), but like all horror movies until the early 1940s, this was made for grownups, so there's not much here to interest littler kids, either. Older kids will enjoy the special effects, the exciting climax, and the near tragedy of the ending.

Followed by **Invisible Agent.**

THE INVISIBLE MAN'S REVENGE (1944)
Black & white, 78 minutes
Cast: Jon Hall, Leon Errol, John Carradine, Alan Curtis, Evelyn Ankers, Gale Sondergaard, Lester Matthews, Halliwell Hobbes
Director: Ford Beebe
Screenplay: Bertram Millhauser
Science fiction/Thriller

Unrated
Young children:
   Marginal   Older children: OK

This time, Jon Hall is Robert Griffin, a madman returned from South Africa; he visits his former partners (Sondergaard, Matthews) and demands a share of their fortune. The demand fails, so he uses John Carradine's formula to become invisible and force the former partners into sharing the loot.

The screenplay shows signs of hasty rewriting, changing the partners from villains to innocent victims, and the invisible man from innocent victim to villain. The plot, in fact, fails to give any good reason for him to become invisible at all. The film is perfunctory but well produced, with excellent special effects by John P. Fulton.

This is a harmless, fairly innocuous film for kids. It even gives the invisible man a comic sidekick in the person of veteran comedian Leon Errol.

I.Q. (1994)
Color, 96 minutes
Cast: Meg Ryan, Tim Robbins, Walter Matthau, Lou Jacobi, Gene Saks, Joseph Maher, Stephen Fry, Tony Shalhoub, Frank Whaley, Charles Durning, Curtis Keene, Alice Playten
Director: Fred Schepisi
Screenplay: Andy Breckman and Michael Leeson
Historical romantic comedy
Rated PG
Younger children: VG   Older children: VG

The setting is Princeton, New Jersey, in the 1950s. Catherine (Meg Ryan) is the niece of Albert Einstein (Walter Matthau), the world's reigning genius. She is a young scientist engaged to a stuffy fellow academic (Stephen Fry). But after she meets Ed (Tim Robbins) at the gas station where he works, her life begins to change. Einstein and his oddball buddies decide Ed is a much better match for Catherine—who's something of an intellectual snob—and connive a way to bring the couple together. In so doing, they convince Ed to fake scientific knowledge about cold fusion in order to win her respect. His rival tries to discredit him with an I.Q. test.

While there is nothing about this comedy aimed specifically at kids, this likable film is so good-hearted, it would be a shame not to share with your family. It's rare to find a modern romance that's chaste, or a comedy that has a realistic foundation; this one, with topical 1950s references and the issue of Communism at stake, provides a minor but valid history lesson that can spark a worthwhile discussion about the period. But most of all, it has charm.

I REMEMBER MAMA (1948)

Black & white, 134 minutes
Cast: Irene Dunne, Barbara Bel Geddes, Oscar Homolka, Philip Dorn, Cedric Hardwicke, Edgar Bergen, Rudy Vallee, Barbara O'Neil, Florence Bates, Ellen Corby
Director: George Stevens
Screenplay: DeWitt Bodeen, based on John Van Druten's play, which was based on Kathryn Forbes' memoirs
Drama
Unrated
Young children: OK Older children: VG

When you have a mama like this one, you are truly blessed! In this heartwarming and often humorous tale of a Norwegian immigrant family in turn-of-the-20th-century San Francisco, the ordinary events of life take on a special meaning because Mama is there to keep the children from being frightened or insecure. The story is told in the form of a reminiscence, narrated by daughter Kathryn, who has become a writer. She relates wonderful stories about her parents and siblings, everyday happenings to which most families can relate. For instance, the little sister has to spend a night at the hospital, and Mama is upset to learn that she is not allowed to stay overnight with her in the ward. The same child's cat becomes ill, and Mama and Papa attempt to deal with the situation. (Parents: this incident should have no adverse effects on the pet lovers in the household.) Then there is the time when the big brother wants to go to high school—a significant decision for an immigrant boy—and Mama and the family must figure out how to budget the money to allow him to continue his studies.

One of the highlights is a clever scene in which Mama arranges a meeting with a famous authoress in order to obtain advice for her daughter, the aspiring writer. The scenario also deals with the death of a beloved uncle in an emotional and realistic scene. Young children may want a parent in the room with them when this scene is being played.

What really makes this movie so wonderful—and memorable—is the character of Mama, beautifully played by Irene Dunne. She doesn't possess particular intelligence, power, or bravery but has uncommon common sense and is driven by the great love she feels for her family. Chances are you'll fall in love with Mama, too.

IRON WILL (1994)
Color, 109 minutes
Cast: Mackenzie Astin, Kevin Spacey, August Schellenberg, David Ogden Stiers, Brian Cox, George Gerdes, John Terry, Penelope Windust, Rex Linn
Director: Charles Haid
Screenplay: John Michael Hayes, Djordje Milicevic, and Jeff Arch
Adventure
Rated PG
Younger kids: OK, with caution   Older kids: VG

A Disney dogsled adventure, *Iron Will* is an action-packed story of bravery and daring.

When his father accidentally drowns, 17-year-old Will Stoneman (Mackenzie Astin), a South Dakota farm boy, enters a sledding race with hopes to save the family home and earn enough to enter college. With the help of farmhand Ned (August Schellenberg), Will trains hard, and with the support of reporter Harry Kingsley (Kevin Spacey), who smells a human interest story in the making, the boy is encouraged to best his rivals.

His real opponent is ruthless Borg Guillarson (George Gerdes), who will do anything to win. Their battles on the race course cause much of the film's tension and excitement. The racing scenes are spectacular and will keep the young ones on the edge of their seats.

Iron Will should please young viewers, though adults who watch with them will find this pretty predictable from start to finish. Very young kids might find this too intense—from the drowning of the dad to the ferocity of the competition.

THE ISLAND AT THE TOP OF THE WORLD (1974)
Color, 93 minutes
Cast: David Hartman, Donald Sinden, Jacques Marin, Mako, David Gwillim, Agneta Eckemyr
Director: Robert Stevenson
Screenplay: John Whedon, based on the novel *The Lost Ones* by Ian Cameron
Adventure/Fantasy
Rated G
Younger kids: OK   Older kids: Good

In 1907, a British explorer (Donald Sinden) whose son has disappeared in the Arctic persuades an American archaeologist (David Hartman) and a Frenchman (Jacques Marin) who has invented an experimental airship to help in his search, and they discover a lost Viking civilization.

Disappointing Disney adaptation of Ian Cameron's Jules Verne–ish novel has some intriguing moments but could have been much better and is let down by dull performances and inconsistent special effects. Still, its abundance of fantastical elements will keep kids entertained.

ISLAND OF LOST SOULS (1932)
Black & white, 70 minutes
Cast: Charles Laughton, Richard Arlen, Leila Hyams, Bela Lugosi, Kathleen Burke,

Arthur Hohl, Stanley Fields,
Tetsu Komai, Hans Steinke
Director: Erle C. Kenton
Screenplay: Waldemar Young,
Philip Wylie, from the novel
The Island of Dr. Moreau by
H. G. Wells
Science fiction–horror/Literary
classic
Unrated
Young children: Too
frightening   Older children:
Maybe

Rescued from a shipwreck, Parker (Arlen) is unwillingly put ashore at the next island, owned by the secretive Dr. Moreau (Laughton). Parker is puzzled by the strangely deformed natives of the island but is attracted to Lota (Burke), an attractive local girl. But we soon learn that Moreau is an unscrupulous scientist using surgery in an attempt to bridge millions of years of civilization and physically *carve* animals into people, but in the jungles of this island of lost souls, the natives are getting restless. . . .

In fact, this seems to be the first movie to use the "natives are getting restless" phrase. When *these* natives finally break loose, it's one of the most horrifying, nightmarish sequences in movie history, an onslaught of twisted, distorted "things," as former wolf Bela Lugosi, the Sayer of the Law, declares.

This is much too strong for younger viewers; in fact, the movie was banned in England for more than twenty years. Even young teens might find some of it rough going. Cinematically, it's dated, and this might prove an obstacle for younger viewers, too, but Laughton is brilliant as the snickering, epicene Moreau, alternately sipping tea and whipping the natives. Children with a historic view of movies (and horror films in particular) will find this a memorable experience.

The novel was remade under its own title twice, once with Burt Lancaster as Moreau (1977) and again in 1996, with Marlon Brando in the lead. It has also been imitated several times, notably in *Terror Is a Man* and *Twilight People*. The Lancaster version is very weak, and the Brando version is genuinely strange. Neither, however, is suitable for younger children, though the Lancaster version is rated PG and the Brando PG-13.

IT CAME FROM BENEATH THE SEA (1955)
Black & white, 80 minutes
Cast: Kenneth Tobey, Faith
Domergue, Donald Curtis, Ian
Keith, Harry Lauter
Director: Robert Gordon
Screenplay: George Worthing
Yates and Hal Smith
Science fiction/Monster
adventure
Unrated
Younger kids: VG   Older kids:
VG

The story could hardly be simpler: a great big octopus is driven from the depths by atomic explosions and begins attacking people along the West Coast, finally ripping down the Golden Gate Bridge in San Francisco before the big cephalopod is destroyed by some grimly purposeful scientists.

Though inexpensive, and with dialogue as corny today as when it was released, this is one of several nearly ideal giant-monster-on-the-loose movies. Like some of the others, it features outstanding special effects by Ray Harryhausen. Though some kids may not like these effects when compared with those in modern movies, they will probably find themselves caught up in the well-told yarn and may eventually accept the effects as absolutely real.

IT CAME FROM OUTER SPACE (1953)
Black & white, 81 minutes
Cast: Richard Carlson, Barbara Rush, Charles Drake, Russell Johnson, Joe Sawyer
Director: Jack Arnold
Screenplay: Harry Essex, from a screen treatment by Ray Bradbury
Science fiction/Suspense
Unrated
Younger kids: VG, if used to scary stuff   Older kids: VG

When what seems to be a meteor crashes into the Arizona desert, an enterprising young astronomer discovers, before it's buried in a landslide, that it's really a spaceship. He can't convince anyone else that aliens have landed, until mysterious events begin happening.

This is not a tale of alien invasion; the spaceship accidentally landed on Earth, and the aliens are just trying to get away. However, there are *good* aliens and *not so good* aliens among them, just as with human beings. The movie has a worthwhile message that's very clearly delivered: don't hate something just because it looks weird.

The film is very striking visually; director Arnold took full advantage of his desert locations and, with this film, established himself as a man who knew his way around science fiction; he made several more films in the genre, all worthwhile, during the 1950s.

This was originally made in 3-D, so there are some intrusive "boo" scenes, which will puzzle youngsters. They'll also be somewhat irked that the aliens are only briefly seen, but the rest of the movie is eerie and scary enough that they'll still enjoy it.

IT HAPPENS EVERY SPRING (1949)
Black & white, 87 minutes
Cast: Ray Milland, Jean Peters, Paul Douglas, Ed Begley, Ted de Corsia, Ray Collins
Director: Lloyd Bacon
Screenplay: Valentine Davies, based on a story by Davies and Shirley W. Smith
Comedy/Sports
Unrated
Younger kids: Good   Older kids: VG

Here's a cute and ingenious comic fantasy about a college chemistry professor (Ray Milland) who, while working on an insect repellent for trees, inadvertently invents a solution that will repel wood from coming in contact with it. Since he's a baseball nut and in need of some extra income so that he can marry his sweetheart (Jean Peters), the good prof soon realizes that his formula will make baseballs avoid being hit by bats. He promptly becomes a major league pitcher, where his doctored balls turn him into a strikeout king and he eventually wins the World Series.

That's all there is to this fanciful story, but it's deftly handled and rich with inventive comic touches, such as the hilarious scenes of baseball players futilely trying to hit the spinning screwballs, and it captures much of the same sense of warmhearted fantasy as screenwriter Valentine Davies' original story for **Miracle on 34th Street.** It's a perfect film for kids.

IT'S A MAD MAD MAD MAD WORLD (1963)

Color, 175 minutes
Cast: Spencer Tracy, Edie Adams, Milton Berle, Sid Caesar, Buddy Hackett, Ethel Merman, Mickey Rooney, Dick Shawn, Dorothy Provine, Phil Silvers, Jonathan Winters, Peter Falk, Jimmy Durante, Terry-Thomas, many many many many others
Director: Stanley Kramer
Screenplay: William and Tania Rose
Comedy
Unrated
Younger kids: Good   Older kids: Good

Producer-director Stanley Kramer, known for such heavy social dramas as **The Defiant Ones** and *Judgment at Nuremberg,* tried to lighten up a little and make the "comedy to end all comedies" with this star-studded, gargantuan production. While the result is certainly the biggest and longest comedy of all time, it's far from the funniest, although it's fondly remembered by those who saw it in their childhood.

The action, motivated by greed and centering on a madcap chase after a $350,000 stash left by a dying crook (Jimmy Durante), features spectacular stunts, car crashes, and slapstick sight gags staged on an enormous scale. A small army of comedians—from Jack Benny, Jerry Lewis, and Buster Keaton to The Three Stooges—guarantees a fair share of laughs, but everything is so overdone, with all of the characters frantically running around and screaming at the top of their lungs for three hours, that it becomes a wearing experience.

Still, kids should enjoy the sheer silliness and overkill of some of the physical comedy, although it will be difficult to get them to sit through the entire movie. What's more, unlike previous generations, they're not likely to be familiar with many of the once-famous cast members.

IT'S A WONDERFUL LIFE (1946)

Black & white, 129 minutes (also available in computer-colored version)
Cast: James Stewart, Donna Reed, Lionel Barrymore, Thomas Mitchell, Henry Travers, Beulah Bondi, Gloria Grahame, Frank Faylen, Ward Bond
Director: Frank Capra
Screenplay: Albert Hackett, Frances Goodrich, and Capra, from the short story "The Greatest Gift" by Philip Van Doren Stern
Fantasy/Drama
Unrated
Young children: OK, with caution   Older children: VG

Largely unheralded on its initial release to theaters, this movie has become a holiday perennial thanks to repeated showings on television. Never intended as merely "a Christmas movie," it has become that because of its unabashed sentiment and its holiday-season finale, which celebrates the best qualities of humanity as the people of Bedford Falls gather around the Bailey family Christmas tree.

It's a Wonderful Life celebrates American values and virtues, but it's no candy-colored piece of fluff. The reason the film has such enormous power to move us is that it follows an ordinary fellow to the very depths of his soul— and the brink of suicide. It is at that point in George Bailey's life that an apprentice angel named Clarence steps in to show him what an important effect he's had on the people around him. He does this in a most unusual and dramatic way, by showing him what his town, his family, his friends would be like if he had never lived.

This kind of fantasy can only work if the filmmakers believe in it—and make us believe, too. That was the genius of director Frank Capra; his film is suffused with sincerity. What's more, there could be no better choice to play George Bailey than James Stewart. Because he is the perfect American everyman, we share his sorrows and frustrations; that is why we also share his unbridled joy when he realizes that his *is* a wonderful life.

It's a Wonderful Life is the kind of film one can watch again and again, and cry in all the same places. Its ultimate message may be too deep for children to appreciate, but its superb storytelling will draw them in. Some of the darker aspects of the tale may put off younger kids or leave them confused. This is probably best reserved for older children.

IT TAKES TWO (1995)
Color, 100 minutes
Cast: Kirstie Alley, Steve Guttenberg, Mary-Kate Olsen, Ashley Olsen, Jane Sibbett, Philip Bosco
Director: Andy Tennant
Screenplay: Deborah Dean Davis
Comedy
Rated PG
Younger children: VG   Older children: OK

Mary-Kate and Ashley Olsen, the popular young twins from television and homevideo, star in this cross between **The Prince and the Pauper** and **The Parent Trap.** Amanda (Mary-Kate) is a tough city kid who's grown up in an orphanage; her look-alike, Alyssa (Ashley), is a rich, pampered child whose widowed father is about to remarry. When the orphan, out in the country for summer camp, chances to meet her twin, they decide to switch places. Out of this adventure comes a scheme to keep Alyssa's father from marrying the mean-spirited woman who's set her trap for him and bring him together with Diane (Kirstie Alley), the goodhearted surrogate mother who's always looked out for Amanda and her fellow orphans.

The Olsen Twins have starred in a number of direct-to-video movies, but this theatrical release is far superior in every way. The adult cast is sincere and appealing, and the kids invest their roles with conviction that encourages us to go along for the ride.

Some mild language earned this otherwise squeaky-clean film a PG rating. Young kids will especially enjoy it, as the good guys triumph, the lovebirds are united, and the villainess gets her just deserts. What more could you ask for?

IVANHOE (1952)
Color, 106 minutes
Cast: Robert Taylor, Elizabeth Taylor, Joan Fontaine, George Sanders, Emlyn Williams, Robert Douglas, Finlay Currie, Felix Aylmer
Director: Richard Thorpe
Screenplay: Noel Langley and Aeneas Mackenzie, based on the novel by Sir Walter Scott
Action-adventure/Literary classic
Unrated
Younger kids: OK   Older kids: VG

Sir Walter Scott's tale of chivalry and romance in medieval England is faithfully brought to the screen in this superb MGM Technicolor production that was filmed on location. Robert Taylor stars as Ivanhoe, the Black Knight who battles the evil Prince John and his henchmen in an attempt to restore Richard Lion-Heart to the throne. The brutal (though not gory) battle scenes are among the most authentic ever filmed, with a plethora of sword fights, jousting tournaments, and the like. The siege of Torquillstone Castle is a truly thrilling sequence, and the final duel between Ivanhoe and the dastardly De Bois-Guilbert (George Sanders) is a scorcher involving axes, maces, and chains.

But this is more than just the usual Hollywood spectacle, as the novel's theme of anti-Semitism is also dealt with honestly—in the person of Ivanhoe's Jewish friend, Rebecca (Elizabeth Taylor), who's discriminated against and put on trial as a witch.

I WALKED WITH A ZOMBIE (1943)
Black & white, 69 minutes
Cast: James Ellison, Frances Dee, Tom Conway, Edith Barrett, James Bell, Christine Gordon, Theresa Harris, Sir Lancelot, Darby Jones
Director: Jacques Tourneur
Screenplay: Ardel Wray, from a screen story by Curt Siodmak and Inez Wallace
Horror/Romantic drama
Unrated
Young children: OK, with caution   Older children: OK

A young woman comes to a Caribbean island to tend to the ailing wife of a wealthy man whose younger brother drinks too much. She begins to suspect that the wife is much more than ill, that in fact she may be a zombie: one of the walking dead.

RKO gave producer Val Lewton this lurid title, and as usual, he turned it into something far better and considerably different from what the title suggests. In fact, the story is very loosely suggested by Charlotte Brontë's *Jane Eyre* (though there are more differences than resemblances) and evokes a similar tone of romantic melancholy. It's also a genuinely frightening horror movie, though the fear is aroused through understatement and atmosphere rathern than sudden shocks. The scene in which the heroine actually does walk with a zombie through the cane fields is both eerie and poetic, and one of the finest sequences in any horror film.

This is one of the best of Lewton's horror film series. It's simply too mature for younger kids, and even older kids raised on a diet of

Hellraiser and *Halloween* movies will find this pretty tame. But other teenagers, particularly those who are fans of Anne Rice novels, could fall in love with this romantic, scary tragedy.

I WANNA HOLD YOUR HAND (1978)
Color, 104 minutes
Cast: Nancy Allen, Bobby DiCicco, Marc McClure, Susan Kendall Newman, Theresa Saldana, Eddie Deezen, Wendie Jo Sperber, Will Jordan
Director: Robert Zemeckis
Screenplay: Zemeckis and Bob Gale
Comedy
Rated PG
Younger kids: OK   Older kids: VG

Robert Zemeckis (**Back to the Future, Forrest Gump**) made his directorial debut with this smart period farce about Beatlemania that was executive-produced by Steven Spielberg. It's February 1964 and The Beatles are making their first visit to the U.S. Desperate to see their idols, a group of teens from New Jersey resort to every trick in the book to sneak into the Plaza Hotel in New York, where the band is staying, then try to crash the Fab Four's first American appearance on the Ed Sullivan TV show (featuring Sullivan impersonator extraordinaire Will Jordan).

This is an amusing piece of nostalgia that captures the look and feel of its period quite nicely, and cleverly gets around not being able to actually show The Beatles by shooting only fleeting glimpses of their backs and feet, etc., while impressionists provide their voices.

It's a little raucous and frenzied, but it's good-natured fun and introduced a flock of fresh talent on both sides of the camera.

Kids, who didn't live through The Beatles' invasion of America, can get a good sense of how things were from this comedy. It's rated PG for language.

I WAS A TEENAGE FRANKENSTEIN (1957)
Black & white, with color scene, 74 minutes
Cast: Whit Bissell, Gary Conway, Phyllis Coates, Robert Burton, George Lynn
Director: Herbert L. Strock
Screenplay: Kenneth Langtry (pseud. of Aben Kandel)
Science fiction/Teenage horror
Unrated
Younger kids: Too gruesome   Older kids: OK for horror fans

Visiting California, the zealous Dr. Frankenstein (Bissell) can't get anyone to believe his theories about returning the dead to life, and experimental subjects are hard to come by. Fortunately, a carload of teenagers is wrecked outside his house, providing him with the necessary body parts. His teenaged creation (Conway), however, behaves much the same as any other Frankenstein Monster. . . .

The script has a few amusing touches, including the often-quoted line, "Speak! I know you have a civil tongue in your head because I sewed it back myself," that indicate that screenwriter Kandel didn't take the movie very seriously. But Strock's clumsy, routine direction flattens everything out: humor, thrills, and performances.

This film cannot really be recommended except for those truly interested in the subject matter. If your younger kids really want to watch it, there are a few scares, mostly the extravagantly ugly makeup on Conway. Older kids are most likely to regard it as quaint and funny, and to scoffingly inquire, "You mean people thought this was *scary*?"

I WAS A TEEN-AGE WEREWOLF (1957)

Black & white, 76 minutes
Cast: Michael Landon, Yvonne Lime, Whit Bissell, Tony Marshall, Dawn Richard, Barney Phillips, Guy Williams
Director: Gene Fowler, Jr.
Screenplay: Ralph Thornton
Science fiction/Teenage horror
Unrated
Younger kids: Too scary Older kids: OK

Troubled teenager Tony (Landon) is sent to see psychiatrist Dr. Brandon (Bissell), who, unfortunately, is a madman trying to throw the human race back to its primitive beginnings (when we were all werewolves). He uses Tony as his experimental subject. Tony then begins turning into a hairy, fanged werewolf, and the hunt is on.

Don't sneer at this movie; despite its silly plot and title, it's well made, well acted, and altogether far better than you'd expect. It's not a classic, but Michael Landon was never ashamed of having been in the film, and he was right to feel that way. It's one of the better teenage-oriented movies of the 1950s, werewolves or no.

Fowler makes a couple of sequences (in the woods and later in a gym) genuinely scary, and Landon's performance as the werewolf is impressively energetic and fierce. Younger kids are likely to be scared (especially if they only know Landon as an angel from TV's *Highway to Heaven*).

J

JACK (1996)
Color, 117 minutes
Cast: Robin Williams, Diane
  Lane, Jennifer Lopez, Bill
  Cosby, Fran Drescher, Adam
  Zolotin, Bruce Kerwin,
  Michael McKean, Don
  Novello
Director: Francis Ford Coppola
Screenplay: James DeMonaco
  and Gary Nadeau
Drama
Rated PG-13
Younger children: No Older
  children: OK

Jack Powell (Robin Williams)
may look like a grown-up, but
he's really just a little boy—a little
boy whose body is aging much
faster than it should. At the age
of 10, he looks like a 40-year-old
man! Sure that no one will understand and that Jack's feelings will
get hurt, his mother (Diane Lane)
hires a tutor (Bill Cosby) to teach
him at home. Like any other
child, though, Jack wants to have
friends his own age. As he ventures into the unknown—and potentially cruel—world of school,
Jack learns to adapt. Although he
is an outcast at first, he soon
makes friends . . . but an aura of
sadness permeates all of Jack's
achievements, because his life is
destined to be short.

Jack is a misfire that was sold,
at the time of its release, as a film
for kids—building on the foundation of Robin Williams' great
popularity with children. It is not,

by any means, a children's film.
(Not with jokes about sex and a
melancholy air about its central
character.) Yet its delicate subject
matter is handled in such a slipshod way that it isn't satisfying for
adults, either.

Kids and adults alike would do
well to simply skip this one.

**JACK AND THE
BEANSTALK** (1952)
Black & white and color, 78
  minutes
Cast: Bud Abbott, Lou Costello,
  Dorothy Ford, Barbara Brown,
  Buddy Baer
Director: Jean Yarbrough
Screenplay: Nat Curtis, based on
  a story by Pat Costello and
  Felix Adler
Comedy/Fantasy
Unrated
Younger kids: Good Older
  kids: Good

Abbott and Costello are less irreverent than usual in this version
of the classic fairy tale that's
aimed squarely at kids. Starting
off in sepiatone (à la **The Wizard
of Oz**), it has babysitters Bud and
Lou falling asleep while reading
the famous story to a child, then
shifts to color as the two stars become part of the fable: buffoonish
Jack (Lou) trades his cow to villainous Dinklepuss (Bud) for five
magic beans. After planting the
beans, which grow overnight into
a giant stalk, Jack climbs up into
the sky and encounters a giant

(Buddy Baer), a talking harp, a hen that lays golden eggs, and rescues a kidnapped prince (James Alexander) and princess (Shaye Cogan).

Though hampered by a low budget, the color segments in giant land have a fairly nice sense of fantasy and contain sufficient lowbrow laughs to keep younger kids amused.

THE JACKIE ROBINSON STORY (1950)

Black & white, 77 minutes
Cast: Jackie Robinson, Ruby Dee, Minor Watson, Louise Beavers, Richard Lane
Director: Alfred E. Green
Screenplay: Lawrence Taylor and Arthur Mann
Biographical drama/Sports
Unrated
Younger kids: VG   Older kids: VG

You never can be too young to learn that, at one time, African-Americans were barred from playing professional baseball. This still timely and surprisingly potent biography charts the life story of Jackie Robinson, the Brooklyn Dodgers great who broke the major league color barrier.

It chronicles his rise from the California sandlots to the athletic fields of UCLA, along with his brief stint in the Negro Leagues. (Baby boomer moms and dads will want to note that the fictional team Robinson plays for is called the Black Panthers!) Eventually, he is signed by the Dodgers' Branch Rickey, plays in the minor leagues in Montreal, and succeeds in Brooklyn.

The Jackie Robinson Story is a valuable and instructive social history; it was also among the first American movies to spotlight race relations and portray blacks in a non-stereotypical manner. Some of its scenes, beginning with one in which a pair of racists taunt Jackie and toss a black cat on the ballfield, are simple, direct, and powerful.

Jackie Robinson effectively plays himself, and it's a treat to watch his athleticism on the field. (And no, just in case any junior football fan should ask, the coscreenwriter is *not* the future New York Giants all-star linebacker!)

JACK THE GIANT KILLER (1962)

Color, 94 minutes
Cast: Kerwin Mathews, Judi Meredith, Torin Thatcher, Walter Burke
Director: Nathan Juran
Screenplay: Orville H. Hampton and Nathan Juran
Action-adventure/Fantasy
Unrated
Younger kids: Good   Older kids: VG

In old Cornwall, while attempting to rescue a beautiful princess (Judi Meredith), Jack the farmer (Kerwin Mathews) has to slay not only a giant, but also ghouls, a sea serpent, a two-headed monster, and a flying dragon, all created by the evil Black Prince Pendragon (Torin Thatcher).

This beguiling Sinbad-like fantasy adventure (reuniting the star and director of **The 7th Voyage of Sinbad**) is a real treat for kids, with Jim Danforth's inventive "Fantascope" special effects, consisting of stop-motion animated puppets that were combined with live action. Though some of the creatures are scary, this is such a pure fairy tale that even younger children won't be frightened.

JAILHOUSE ROCK (1957)

Black & white, 96 minutes
Cast: Elvis Presley, Judy Tyler,
  Vaughn Taylor, Dean Jones,
  Mickey Shaughnessy, Jennifer
  Holden, Anne Neyland
Director: Richard Thorpe
Screenplay: Guy Trosper, based
  on a story by Ned Young
Drama with music
Unrated
Young children: VG   Older
  children: VG

Jailhouse Rock is Elvis Presley's all-time best movie. His hip-shaking, pre-Army charisma, which helped earn him his initial fame, shines through in his role as Vince Everett, a misunderstood young man who is convicted of manslaughter after partaking in a barroom melee. While doing time in the slammer, the fiery-tempered but normally amiable Everett hones his singing and guitar-playing, and eventually goes on to become a surly rock 'n' roll idol.

The songs all are top-notch. They include "Don't Leave Me Now," "Treat Me Nice," and the title number, performed in a flashy dance routine choreographed by Elvis himself. They capture Elvis at his best, before his personality was "blanded out" by Hollywood of the 1960s.

Jailhouse Rock should still intrigue kids today who are curious about the real Elvis—as opposed to the bloated, rhinestone-clad figure who's caricatured so often today.

JAMES AND THE GIANT PEACH (1996)

Color, 80 minutes
Cast: Joanna Lumley, Miriam
  Margolyes, Paul Terry; voices
  of Susan Sarandon, Richard
  Dreyfuss, Jane Leeves, Simon
  Callow, David Thewlis,
  Miriam Margolyes
Director: Henry Selick
Screenplay: Karey Kirkpatrick,
  Jonathan Roberts, and Steve
  Bloom, based on the novel by
  Roald Dahl
Animated feature
Rated PG
Young children: VG, with
  caution   Older children: VG

When 9-year-old James' parents disappear into a mysterious cloud, he is sent to live with his horrible aunts, Spiker and Sponge. James dreams about running away to New York City, because his father always told him that dreams come true there. The boy acquires a bag of magical objects (in reality, crocodile tongues) and accidentally spills them alongside an old peach tree near his aunts' house. Soon a peach appears and grows to be twenty feet across! When James notices a tunnel on the surface of the fruit, he crawls inside and meets its inhabitants: Centipede, Earthworm, Ladybug, Glow-worm, Grasshopper, and Miss Spider. Soon the peach rolls out to sea and sends James and his newfound friends on a grand and glorious adventure, with New York City their destination.

As with all Roald Dahl stories, this one is infused with equal parts imagination and dark humor—some of it too dark for sensitive children, as when James' parents are taken away from him without a tangible explanation. On the other hand, his evil aunts are played as comic-opera villains and can't be taken too seriously.

The eerier aspects of the story are balanced out by the lively sense of fun shared by James (who begins as a live boy, and then becomes an animated creature when he climbs inside the peach) and his insect friends, as colorful a rogues' gallery as ever invented.

Randy Newman's charming songs, and the unusual look of the film, rendered with paper cutouts, stop-motion animation, and computer effects by Henry Selick—the gifted director of Tim Burton's **The Nightmare Before Christmas**—make this film a genuine original. It can't easily be compared to any other movie, animated or live-action. It's unusual, disarming, and an experience of wonder for kids and grown-ups alike.

Parents should be wary, as always, of anything with Roald Dahl's name on it. His strange sensibilities aren't always in alignment with kids or parents—though children seem to have less trouble with his quirky humor than grown-ups do.

JANE EYRE (1944)
Black & white, 96 minutes
Cast: Orson Welles, Joan Fontaine, Margaret O'Brien, Henry Daniell, John Sutton, Agnes Moorehead, Elizabeth Taylor, Peggy Ann Garner, Sara Allgood
Director: Robert Stevenson
Screenplay: Stevenson, Aldous Huxley, and John Houseman, based on the novel by Charlotte Brontë
Drama/Literary classic
Unrated
Young children: No   Older children: VG

The title character of this intense, mostly faithful adaptation of Charlotte Brontë's classic novel is a "solitary little thing," a dreamy orphan who wants people to love and be kind to her. Instead, Jane is forced to survive the most hellish of childhoods, which instills within her a hatred for cruelty and injustice, as well as a determination to go out into the world and make a life for herself.

Jane (Joan Fontaine) secures a position as the governess of Thornfield, an estate owned by Edward Rochester (Orson Welles), who is described on the night of her arrival as a "strange man." Despite this, an attraction grows between Jane and Rochester, and the two are set to marry . . . but there are dark secrets to be revealed.

Some children might find all this remote, but others—particularly older girls who are discovering classic literature—will be intrigued by the story and by Jane's plight. This handsome Hollywood production captures the spirit if not precisely the letter of Brontë's book.

Joan Fontaine is fine as Jane, and Orson Welles offers a delightfully flamboyant performance as Rochester. Of special note is Bernard Herrmann's music score, which adds immeasurably to the film's mood.

Cast in a small but pivotal role in *Jane Eyre*—and not even listed in the credits—is a child actress who was to go on to enjoy a career as one of Hollywood's legendary movie stars. Her name is Elizabeth Taylor.

JASON AND THE ARGONAUTS (1963)
Color, 104 minutes
Cast: Todd Armstrong, Nancy Kovack, Gary Raymond, Laurence Naismith, Niall MacGinnis, Michael Gwynn,

Douglas Wilmer, Honor Blackman, Nigel Green, Jack Gwillim
Director: Don Chaffey
Screenplay: Jan Read and Beverley Cross
Fantasy/Adventure
Unrated
Young children: OK, but scary at times Older children: OK

Zeus (Niall MacGinnis) and Hera (Honor Blackman) are curious about young Jason (Todd Armstrong), son of the King of Thessaly, who was, unknown to Jason, murdered by the king's half-brother, Pelias (Douglas Wilmer). Fearing a prophecy that Jason will kill him, Pelias sends the youth on a quest for the fabled Golden Fleece housed in a cave in the distant land of Colchis. Jason recruits a brave band, including Hercules (Nigel Green), and they set sail for Colchis in the ship *Argos.*

Jason successfully leads his Argonauts through a series of incredible adventures. They're confronted by the colossal bronze statue of Talos, which magically comes to life; they rescue a prophet from marauding harpies and sail unharmed through the clashing rocks . . . and eventually encounter the seven-headed Hydra and an army of sword-wielding skeletons.

Regarded by many as the pinnacle of Ray Harryhausen's career, this was even dubbed the best movie ever made by Tom Hanks, as he helped Ray Bradbury present a special Oscar to the great stop-motion animator. It's not *that* good (it tends toward the ponderous at times), but for the most part, it's a wonderful adventure.

How children today will respond, accustomed as they are to the near-perfect special effects that computers and sheer talent have made possible, is anyone's guess. Ours is that they're likely to have as much fun with the film as their parents did.

JAWS (1975)
Color, 124 minutes
Cast: Richard Dreyfuss, Roy Scheider, Robert Shaw, Lorraine Gary, Murray Hamilton
Director: Steven Spielberg
Screenplay: Peter Benchley, and Carl Gottlieb, based on the novel by Benchley
Action/Horror
Rated PG
Younger kids: No, no, no! Older kids: VG

This electrifying adaptation of Peter Benchley's pulpy bestseller (a kind of *Moby Dick* meets *An Enemy of the People*) about a killer shark on the loose at a New England resort, catapulted an unknown Steven Spielberg into the ranks of directorial superstardom and virtually created the concept of the "summer event" blockbuster.

Roy Scheider stars as Brody, the police chief of fictitious Amity Island, who recommends closing the beaches after a woman is killed in a shark attack. However, the venal mayor (Murray Hamilton) doesn't want to scare away tourists and insists on keeping the beaches open for the Fourth of July holiday weekend after a small shark is caught. But after two more shark attacks, Brody teams up with a hotshot marine biologist (Richard Dreyfuss) and a grizzled old fisherman (Robert

Shaw) to go out on a boat and have a showdown with the creature responsible for the deadly incidents: a twenty-five-foot Great White Shark.

Spielberg tautly manipulates suspense and maintains tension to a degree that would make Hitchcock proud, while handling the lighter moments with equal expertise. Dreyfuss, Scheider, and Shaw are all excellent, but the real star of the movie is the mechanical shark (nicknamed Bruce, after Spielberg's lawyer), which isn't even fully seen until the movie's 80-minute mark. Despite numerous technical problems during the shoot, the shark delivers a truly terrifying "performance," aided immeasurably by John Williams' famous theme music and Verna Fields' razor-sharp editing.

Although initially rated PG, the film would probably receive a PG-13 today, given its intensely frightening shark attack scenes. This is potential nightmare fodder for kids—even older ones. Steven Spielberg did not direct the sequels, and it shows. They're not nearly as good—or as scary.

JETSONS: THE MOVIE (1990)
Color, 81 minutes
Cast: Voices of George O'Hanlon, Mel Blanc, Penny Singleton, Tiffany, Patric Zimmerman, Don Messick, Jean VanderPyl
Directors: William Hanna and Joseph Barbera
Screenplay: Dennis Marks
Animated musical
Rated G
Younger kids: OK   Older kids: No

A mediocre movie adaptation of the animated space-age TV sitcom, *Jetsons: The Movie* will entertain only the youngest of space cadets.

The film begins with the promotion of George Jetson to vice president of Spacely Sprockets. Unfortunately the family must move to deep space and the characters learn to adjust to their new life. George soon gets involved with a sabotage mystery at the factory, while his daughter, Judy, falls in love with rock and roll idol Apollo Blue. (The standout sequence here is a "music video" song number, animated by Kurtz and Friends.) The factory sabotage is caused by a band of cute furry creatures whose continued existence depends on George's help.

The opportunity to make a fun, hip, retro-nostalgic entertainment was wasted in this tired retread of the 1960s TV series. It's a run-of-the-mill story with an ecological message. Older kids and *Jetsons* fans will be disappointed.

JIM THORPE—ALL AMERICAN (1951)
Black & white, 107 minutes
Cast: Burt Lancaster, Charles Bickford, Steve Cochran, Phyllis Thaxter, Dick Wesson, Jack Big Head, Suni Warcloud
Director: Michael Curtiz
Screenplay: Douglas Morrow, Frank Davis, and Everett Freeman, based on the story *Bright Path* by Morrow and Vincent X. Flaherty, based in turn on the biography by Russell J. Birdwell and James Thorpe
Biography/Sports
Unrated
Young children: OK   Older children: VG

Jim Thorpe is one of the 20th century's most notable athletes. After starring on the gridiron at the Carlisle Indian School, he became the first man to win gold medals in both the pentathlon and decathlon at the 1912 Olympics in Stockholm. He also played professional football and baseball. At the Olympics, the King of Sweden placed a wreath on Thorpe's head and proclaimed, "Sir, you are the greatest athlete in the world."

However, the defining event in Thorpe's life was his being stripped of his Olympic medals for the sin of having briefly played semipro baseball prior to his competing. Furthermore, he was banned from participating in all amateur athletics. This penalty seems especially harsh today, when professional athletes like Michael Jordan regularly compete for Olympic gold.

Thorpe's successes and tragedies unfold in this excellent biography, which also deals with its subject's American Indian heritage. In fact, it features a three-dimensional portrait of an American Indian at a time when most celluloid "redskins" were ruined in Westerns and depicted as stereotypical savages who existed solely to attack wagon trains and the U.S. cavalry. Burt Lancaster offers a splendid performance in the title role.

Kids of all ages should know about Jim Thorpe—both his triumphs and his misfortune—and this film is a good place to start.

JINGLE ALL THE WAY
(1996)
Color, 80 minutes
Cast: Arnold Schwarzenegger, Sinbad, Phil Hartman, Rita Wilson, Robert Conrad, James Belushi, Jake Lloyd, Harvey Korman, Laraine Newman
Director: Brian Levant
Screenplay: Randy Kornfield
Comedy
Rated PG
Younger children: OK   Older children: OK

Jamie's dad (Arnold Schwarzenegger) is a neglectful father. All the boy wants for Christmas is a Turbo-Man action figure, so Jamie's mother (Rita Wilson) reminds her husband to get the gift early. But by the time he remembers to make the purchase, he learns—to his dismay—that Turbo-Man is the most sought-after toy in the country. This leads to a frantic search and struggle to get one of the elusive toys in time for Christmas.

Phil Hartman plays a single dad neighbor who's too good to be true, and does everything perfectly—including decorating his house for the holidays. Sinbad is a postman who's just as eager—and just as determined—to find a Turbo-Man for his son as Schwarzenegger.

This contrived holiday comedy would seem to be surefire, but it has two key problems: Arnold Schwarzenegger, for all his abilities, simply isn't funny. And the script is surprisingly mean-spirited.

The competitive postman played by Sinbad turns out to be more than vicious—he's practically psychotic! And as the film runs out of story, it becomes redundant and ever more frantic in tone and pace.

Much of this won't bother kids, but it's bound to irritate their parents. It should also give those parents pause when choosing videos for their children; this film is the equivalent of junk food, offering diversion (through hyperactivity) but no nourishment whatsoever.

With the expected amount of street language and "comic" violence, this film is appropriately rated PG.

JOHNNY TREMAIN (1957)

Color, 80 minutes
Cast: Hal Stalmaster, Luana Patten, Jeff York, Sebastian Cabot, Dick (Richard) Beymer
Director: Robert Stevenson
Screenplay: Tom Blackburn, based on the novel by Esther Forbes
Historical adventure
Unrated
Younger kids: Good   Older kids: Good

Johnny Tremain is a vivid Disney adaptation of Esther Forbes' novel about a young Bostonian boy (Hal Stalmaster) in the 1770s, who gets involved in the Revolutionary War. His adventures include meeting Paul Revere, joining the Sons of Liberty, participating in the Boston Tea Party, and taking part in the fight against the British.

Though partly simplified and fictionalized, this is a colorful and exciting tale that, in the best Disney tradition, entertains while it teaches and brings the past to life, making it an ideal history lesson. The scene in which Johnny injures his hand with molten silver is likely to make a lifelong impression on children.

JOURNEY FOR MARGARET (1942)

Black & white, 81 minutes
Cast: Robert Young, Laraine Day, Fay Bainter, Nigel Bruce, Margaret O'Brien, William Severn
Director: W. S. Van Dyke II
Screenplay: David Hertz and William Ludwig, based on a novel by William L. White
Drama
Unrated
Young children: VG, with caution   Older children: VG

This earnest, three-hanky drama delves into the horrors of World War II from a child's point of view. Robert Young plays an American journalist who is stationed in London during the Blitz. During one particularly close bombing, his pregnant wife is hurt and loses her baby. Later on, Young becomes involved with a private home for war orphans where he becomes attached to two sweet but vulnerable youngsters whose lives have been ravaged by the bombings. The subsequent story deals with love, adoption, and self-sacrifice.

Margaret O'Brien appears in her first major screen role, a tour-de-force interpretation of a little girl whose nervous system has been splintered by the panic of the Blitz. She is extremely winning, as always. (Margaret went on to become one of the top child stars of the 1940s, earning an Academy Award in 1944 as Outstanding Child Actress. She is best remembered as Judy Garland's adorable sister, Tootie, in **Meet Me in St. Louis.**)

Seeing a large home filled with troubled war orphans may be upsetting to very young children;

however, the majority of young people will find this a sincere and engrossing drama. It will also serve as a springboard for conversation about World War II, and the hardships suffered by our allies in England.

THE JOURNEY OF AUGUST KING (1995)
Color, 95 minutes
Cast: Jason Patric, Thandie Newton, Larry Drake, Sam Waterston, Sara-Jane Wylde, Eric Mabius
Director: John Duigan
Screenplay: John Ehle, based on his novel
Drama
Rated PG-13
Young children: No Older children: VG, with caution

Here is an engrossing and poignant film about a simple heroic act and the way two human beings touch each other's lives, if only for a brief time.

The setting is North Carolina in 1815. The title character is a young, widowed farmer (Jason Patric) who has "been waiting his turn most of his life, never doing anything different from one day to the next." The story tells what happens when August comes to the rescue of Annalees Williamsburg (Thandie Newton), a vulnerable 17-year-old slave who has run away from her master, Olaf Singletary (Larry Drake), a hulking man with a brutal temper. By sheltering Annalees, August is not just breaking the law of the land; he is exposing himself to the wrath of Olaf, the "wealthiest man in the mountains."

August acts as he does because it is against his nature to ignore another human being in distress.

Before long, he and Annalees develop a bond with one another (and not—one might add—a sexual relationship).

The Journey of August King is a poetic, richly humanistic film. When August asks Annalees why she ran off, her answer is to the point: "To keep (Olaf) from taking my soul." And the script offers a wonderful definition of love: "A feeling of need for another that's overflowing."

The Journey of August King is about standing up for what you think is right—no matter what the consequences.

Parents should be aware, however, that there is one extremely violent scene, which earned the film a PG-13 rating.

THE JOURNEY OF NATTY GANN (1985)
Color, 100 minutes
Cast: Meredith Salenger, John Cusack, Ray Wise, Lainie Kazan, Scatman Crothers, Barry Miller, Verna Bloom, John Finnegan, Jack Rader
Director: Jeremy Paul Kagan
Screenplay: Jeanne Rosenberg
Adventure
Rated PG
Younger children: OK Older children: VG

Natty Gann is an engrossing story of friendship, love, and survival, set during the Great Depression of the 1930s. Widowed father Saul Gann (Ray Wise) finds a job with a lumber camp in Washington State, necessitating that his daughter stay behind in Chicago. Shortly after he leaves, headstrong young Natty (Meredith Salenger) runs away from her guardian (Lainie Kazan) to join her dad. Her ensuing cross-country journey is filled with excitement and danger.

Riding the rails, hunting for food, surviving the cold become her challenges. Helping her out is a wolf she rescues from hunters and a young hobo (John Cusack), who becomes a good friend.

Kids and parents should enjoy this journey together. There is some peril along the way, which may give the youngest children some anxious moments. You may also have to explain the nature of the Depression, and the need for someone like Natty's father to go in search of work and—however reluctantly—leave her behind.

JOURNEY TO THE CENTER OF THE EARTH (1959)
Color, 132 minutes
Cast: James Mason, Pat Boone, Arlene Dahl, Diane Baker, Thayer David
Director: Henry Levin
Screenplay: Walter Reisch and Charles Brackett, based on the novel by Jules Verne
Adventure/Fantasy
Unrated
Younger kids: Good   Older kids: VG

This adaptation of Jules Verne's classic Victorian fantasy is good old-fashioned fun. James Mason plays the 19th-century Scottish professor who organizes an expedition to explore a secret passageway in Iceland that is said to lead to the center of the earth. During the trip, he and his party have to deal with rival expeditions, endure torrential floods, magnetic storms, volcanic eruptions, and prehistoric monsters, and they discover a forest of giant mushrooms, a cavern of quartz crystals, and the Lost City of Atlantis.

Imaginative sets, lavish use of CinemaScope and Bernard Herrmann's superb score make this an entertaining and lighthearted romp for armchair adventurers. Though modern-day kids may find some of the special effects wanting, the spirit of adventure and fun has survived the years intact.

JUMANJI (1995)
Color, 104 minutes
Cast: Robin Williams, Jonathan Hyde, Kirsten Dunst, Bradley Pierce, Bonnie Hunt, Bebe Neuwirth, David Alan Grier, Patricia Clarkson, Adam Hann-Byrd, Laura Bundy
Director: Joe Johnston
Screenplay: Jonathan Hensleigh, Greg Taylor, and Jim Strain, from the book by Chris Van Allsburg
Fantasy/Comedy/Action
Rated PG
Young children: OK, with caution   Older children: OK

Jumanji, a game buried by two frightened kids in 1869, is dug up a hundred years later by unhappy 12-year-old Alan Parrish (Hann-Byrd). When he plays the game with Sarah (Bundy), a local girl he's sweet on, things go magically awry, and Alan is sucked into the game.

Twenty-six years later, Nora (Neuwirth) moves into the long-unoccupied Parrish mansion with her newly orphaned niece, Judy (Dunst), and nephew, Peter (Pierce); soon, they find the game, too, and by playing it, accidentally free Alan, now a Robinson Crusoe–clad man (Williams).

Reactivating the game causes all hell to break loose, as monkeys, mosquitoes, deadly vines, a lion, and a thundering herd of elephants, rhinoceroses, zebras, and pelicans, as well as other thrills and menaces, erupt out of the Jumanji game. The adults and kids of both time frames have to work together to finish the game and set things right again.

Kids tend to like this elaborate, effects-filled adventure more than adults, who have been known to develop a severe headache from watching it. The effects are hurled in our face without letup—and without much point. And indeed, that's the movie's biggest weakness: it has no point.

Younger kids may find it threatening and a bit too scary; older kids will probably love being jolted this way.

THE JUNGLE BOOK (1942)
Color, 109 minutes
Cast: Sabu, Joseph Calleia, John Qualen, Frank Puglia, Rosemary DeCamp
Director: Zoltan Korda
Screenplay: Laurence Stallings, based on the stories by Rudyard Kipling
Action-adventure
Unrated
Younger kids: Good   Older kids: VG

The Jungle Book is an enchanting and beautifully filmed live-action version of Kipling's stories about a young boy (Sabu) who is reared by wolves in the jungles of India. Children who know the popular 1967 Disney cartoon version of the tale and are familiar with the adventures of Mowgli, Shere Khan the tiger, and Bagheera the panther, will enjoy seeing them all in the flesh, so to speak, along with a whole menagerie of elephants, bears, crocodiles, snakes, and monkeys.

Unlike the cartoon, this film does not have songs, but there is a lovely Miklos Rozsa score that creates theme music for the characters and animals, and adds immeasurably to the film's exotic atmosphere. If this is your kids' first exposure to the young Indian actor Sabu, they might want to see some of his other films, including **The Thief of Bagdad, Elephant Boy,** and **Arabian Nights.**

THE JUNGLE BOOK (1967)
Color, 78 minutes
Cast: Voices of Phil Harris, Sebastian Cabot, Louis Prima, George Sanders, Sterling Holloway, J. Pat O'Malley, Bruce Reitherman, Verna · Felton
Director: Wolfgang Reitherman
Screenplay: Larry Clemmons, Ralph Wright, Ken Anderson, and Vance Gerry, inspired by the Rudyard Kipling *Mowgli* stories
Animated feature
Unrated
Young children: VG   Older children: VG

Rudyard Kipling's stories about the boy raised as a wolf have inspired a number of screen adaptations, beginning with the colorful live-action version starring Sabu in 1942. The animated *Jungle Book* was the last cartoon feature personally produced by Walt Disney and has remained a favorite with kids for more than thirty years, although Mr. Kipling might not recognize his original work.

Mowgli is an Indian boy who was abandoned at birth, discovered by a panther named Bagheera, and raised as a wolf. When he turns 10, it is Bagheera's intention to return him to the human world, especially since the jungle is now threatened by the ferocious tiger Shere Khan. But their journey is continually interrupted, which is fine with Mowgli, who doesn't really want to leave the jungle, the only home he's ever known. He hooks up with happy-go-lucky Baloo the bear, encounters King Louis of the orangutans, and finds unlikely allies in a quartet of vultures who help him when he runs afoul of Shere Khan.

The Jungle Book is much like Baloo: cheerful and lighthearted. It never digs very deep beneath the surface, but kids respond to the colorful characters (voiced by one of the best casts ever assembled at the Disney studio) and their songs, especially Baloo's "The Bare Necessities" (sung by Phil Harris) and King Louis's "I Wanna Be Like You" (featuring the irrepressible Louis Prima).

And if it isn't as heartwarming or profound as other Disney cartoon classics, one can hardly argue with its popularity—or durability.

JUNGLE 2 JUNGLE (1997)
Color, 105 minutes
Cast: Tim Allen, Martin Short, JoBeth Williams, Lolita Davidovich, Sam Huntington, David Ogden Stiers, Bob Dishy, Valerie Mahaffey, LeeLee Sobieski
Director: John Paquin
Screenplay: Bruce A. Evans and Raynold Gideon, based on the film *Un Indien dans la Ville,* written by Herve Palud, Thierry Lhermitte, Igor Aptekman, and Philippe Bruneau de la Salle
Comedy

Rated PG
Younger kids: VG   Older kids: VG

With the long-running success of his TV series *Home Improvement,* Tim Allen has a built-in family audience, which is well served by this entertaining remake of a French comedy hit (briefly released here as *Little Indian, Big City*) about a hard-driven businessman who discovers that his ex-wife (JoBeth Williams)—who now lives in a primitive village on the Amazon—has been raising a son he never even knew about.

The son, Mimi-Siku, accompanies his father back to the urban jungle of New York City, where he's a fish out of water, unaccustomed to the ways of modern civilization. When the boy stays overnight with his dad's business partner (Martin Short) and his family, he and their young daughter are attracted to one another in puppy-love fashion. The two grown-ups find themselves embroiled in a life-and-death crisis with a Russian businessman (David Ogden Stiers), but the boy helps to save the day.

The depiction of modern family and city life is pretty realistic, with just a smattering of PG-rated language, but there's nothing terribly offensive or off-color . . . and just enough wisecracks aimed at adults in the audience to keep them laughing along with the kids. Cat lovers may wince at the treatment of Lolita Davidovich's pampered pet in one comic scene.

Jungle 2 Jungle is excellent family entertainment.

JURASSIC PARK (1993)
Color, 127 minutes
Cast: Sam Neill, Laura Dern,
  Jeff Goldblum, Richard
  Attenborough, Bob Peck,
  Martin Ferrero, B. D. Wong,
  Joseph Mazzello, Ariana
  Richards, Samuel L. Jackson,
  Wayne Knight
Director: Steven Spielberg
Screenplay: Michael Crichton
  and David Koepp, from the
  novel by Crichton
Science fiction/Adventure thriller
Rated PG-13
Young children: Very
  scary   Older children: OK

Billionaire John Hammond (Attenborough) brings paleontologist Alan Grant (Neill), his fiancée and fellow scientist, Ellie Sattler (Dern), and mathematician and chaos theorist Ian Malcolm (Goldblum) to an island off the coast of Costa Rica, hoping to convince them to endorse his new venture, an amusement park. To their astonishment, the park teems with live dinosaurs and other prehistoric creatures cloned from the DNA extracted from dinosaur blood found in mosquitoes preserved in amber: it really is a Jurassic Park (even if most of the dinos we see come from the Cretaceous period). Most of the creatures are harmless, if alarmingly large herbivores, but he's also unwisely cloned the colossal carnivore Tyrannosaurus rex and smaller but more intelligent flesh-eaters called velociraptors.

But not to worry, Hammond assures his fascinated but appalled guests, the park is perfectly safe. Soon everyone in sight is fleeing from dinosaurs, including Hammond's two grandchildren, dinosaur-loving Timmy (Joseph Mazzello) and his slightly older sister, computer hacker Lex (Ariana Richards).

Basically, the plot is a pretext to allow the characters to be chased through lush jungles by fanged behemoths. However, the novel, and the film, too, does raise a question of responsibility: Just because you can bring dinosaurs to life, should you? *Jurassic Park* is at heart a monster movie and a terrific one. The plot line is simplistic and so are some of the characters, but it's good entertainment anyway. Spielberg is so adept at almost everything a director can do that he makes it look easy.

This quickly became the largest-grossing movie in history because it gives audiences exactly what they want, only more so. But its scares are genuine and quite potent; Spielberg wouldn't let his own children (under the age of 10) see it. Many young boys are crazy about dinosaurs, however, so you'll have to make up your own mind by watching the movie yourself before showing it to any young or impressionable child. (This is nightmare fodder, for sure.)

Followed by a sequel, **The Lost World: Jurassic Park.**

K

THE KARATE KID (1984)

Color, 126 minutes

Cast: Ralph Macchio, Noriyuki "Pat" Morita, Elisabeth Shue, Randee Heller, Martin Kove, William Zabka, Chad McQueen

Director: John G. Avildsen

Screenplay: Robert Mark Kamen

Drama/Martial arts

Rated PG

Young children: OK   Older children: VG

In a small California town, the new guy in high school is a bit on the puny side. This makes him the target of tough bike-riding teens, who pick on him mercilessly. What should he do? Turn the other cheek? Or learn how to beat the stuffing out of these bullies?

The answer is the latter, or there'd be no movie. But there's more to karate than hitting people, as young Daniel learns from his martial arts teacher, the often-inscrutable Mr. Miyagi, who's also the handyman in the apartment house where Daniel's family lives.

Just as Obi-wan instructs Luke in The Force, so the devout Mr. M. imparts the wisdom of the East to his protégé . . . although his methods are unorthodox, to say the least.

Much of the movie is about Daniel's training, which not only involves building himself up physically but learning to face his adversaries with mental cunning.

The discipline will carry over into other aspects of his life.

The director is the fellow who made **Rocky,** so expect the same kind of manipulative but visceral fun. The master-pupil relationship is particularly enjoyable here, and kids should have no trouble relating to Daniel and his challenges.

Parents may wish to beware of imitative behavior. And, of course, there is some violence.

It was followed by several sequels, but none as good as this.

KAZAAM (1996)

Color, 93 minutes

Cast: Shaquille O'Neal, Francis Capra, Ally Walker, Marshall Manesh, James Acheson, Fawn Reed, John Costelloe

Director: Paul M. Glaser

Screenplay: Christian Ford and Roger Soffer, from a story by Glaser

Fantasy

Rated PG

Young kids: NG   Older kids: NG

Max (Francis Capra), a latch-key city kid (and brat) fights with bullies at school and is upset with his mother's plans to marry her current boyfriend. Chased by the bullies into an abandoned warehouse, he accidentally hits a battered boom box and unleashes the genie Kazaam (Shaquille O'Neal), who saves him from his predicament. Kazaam insists that Max is his master; he cannot return to his slumber until he grants Max three wishes.

Max doesn't believe him at first, but slowly they become friends. A subplot involves Max's no-good record producer father and some adult bullies who run a nightclub in town and are making pirated recordings of bands that perform there. Max wishes to save his father, who makes it quite clear he wants nothing to do with Max.

Another subplot involves Kazaam rappin' in the club and becoming a huge hit. The evil club owner tries to find out his secret and sends out his pretty assistant to seduce him. When the club owner discovers his powers, he wants Kazaam for his own.

This is one of the most unpleasant "family films" of recent years. It takes place in a gritty, even ugly urban setting, and is peopled with dislikable characters. Its subject matter (aside from the fantasy element of the genie itself) is inappropriate for young children, and the film squanders the presence of its naturally likable star, basketball ace O'Neal.

THE KID (1921)
Black & white, 60 minutes
Cast: Charlie Chaplin, Jackie Coogan, Edna Purviance, Charles Riesner, Lita Grey, Henry Bergman
Director: Charles Chaplin
Screenplay: Charles Chaplin
Comedy/Silent classic
Unrated
Young children: VG   Older children: VG

Charlie Chaplin was accustomed to being the center of attention in his films, but when he met the adorable 5-year-old child performer Jackie Coogan, he decided to write a film in which he would costar with the youngster. This was to be Chaplin's first feature-length film, and it's still a charmer.

Chaplin introduces the film as "a picture with a smile—perhaps a tear." An unwed mother leaves her baby in the backseat of a limousine, hoping that its wealthy owners will care for the child, which she cannot. When the car is stolen, the thieves dump the infant in the alleyway of a slum. Here the child is discovered by The Little Tramp, who through circumstance is forced to take in the child and find a way to raise it. Time passes and we learn that the two have become inseparable, but after five years it is reported to the authorities that the Tramp is not the little boy's father, and a man from the County Orphan Asylum comes to take him away. But he's not going without a fight.

To tell the plot of the film is to do it a great disservice; this is not a film about story but about character and charm. There are winning moments, hilarious gags, a famous dream sequence, and scenes that tug at your heartstrings.

It would be difficult to find a better film to introduce children to the talents of Charlie Chaplin. Chances are they will also want to see more of Jackie Coogan, who became the most popular child actor of the 1920s. His appeal is as evident today as it was way back in 1921.

THE KID FROM LEFT FIELD (1953)
Black & white, 80 minutes
Cast: Dan Dailey, Anne Bancroft, Billy Chapin, Lloyd Bridges, Ray Collins, Richard

Egan, Fess Parker, John Berardino
Director: Harmon Jones
Screenplay: Jack Sher
Drama/Fantasy/Sports
Unrated
Younger kids: VG   Older kids: OK

This sweet, likable baseball film stars Dan Dailey, who the year before portrayed Dizzy Dean in the baseball biography *The Pride of St. Louis*. Here he plays Larry "Pop" Cooper, a widower and washed-up ballplayer whose hot-headedness has resulted in his being thrown out of the sport. He earns his keep and supports his young son Christy by selling peanuts in the stands at home games of the Bisons, a strictly second-division ball club.

Larry's knowledge of the game enables him to understand why the Bisons are so incompetent. His son eventually becomes the Bisons' batboy and begins feeding tips supplied by his dad to the ballplayers. Eventually, this "boy genius" is named the Bisons' new manager, replacing the team's stubborn and manipulative skipper.

The Kid From Left Field is a satisfying entertainment as it plays out the fantasy of a youngster getting to be the boss in an adult world—giving orders to baseball players, no less! It's clean, wholesome entertainment in the vintage Hollywood mold.

It was redone in 1979 as an innocuous made-for-TV movie starring then reigning sitcom stars Gary Coleman and Robert Guillaume.

A KID IN KING ARTHUR'S COURT (1995)

Color, 89 minutes
Cast: Thomas Ian Nicholas, Joss Ackland, Art Malik, Paloma Baeza, Kate Winslet, Ron Moody, Daniel Craig, David Tysall
Director: Michael Gottlieb.
Screenplay: Michael Part and Robert L. Levy, loosely based on Mark Twain's *A Connecticut Yankee in King Arthur's Court*
Fantasy/Comedy
Rated PG
Young kids: VG   Older kids: OK

Awkward young teen Calvin (Thomas Ian Nicholas) is up at bat, about to strike out for his Little League team (The Reseda Knights) when an earthquake hits. The ground cracks open and swallows him whole. He lands in the Middle Ages, atop a black knight stealing something from King Arthur! Calvin was in fact brought to Camelot by Merlin (Ron Moody), now an apparition who has lost his touch for magic.

Hailed as a savior by doddering King Arthur (Joss Ackland), Calvin of Reseda finds a court seat for dinner and is ushered into basic training course for aspiring knights. His knapsack full of tricks—rock 'n' roll via a CD player, makeshift Rollerblades, and a Swiss Army knife—put him at odds with evil Lord Belasco whose true goal is the crown, by hook or by crook. One scheme for Belasco is to wed Arthur's eldest daughter, Princess Sarah (Kate Winslet!), so that he can inherit the throne.

A Kid in King Arthur's Court was released—but not made—by

the Disney company. It's a pleasant and innocuous film for kids that never takes itself too seriously, with scenes of the boy teaching King Arthur to blow bubble gum and such. This may annoy parents who are hoping it will develop into a better, more substantial story, but it isn't likely to bother younger kids.

The old pros in the cast add credibility to the lightweight tale, and there is particular interest—looking back—at seeing young Kate Winslet, before *Titanic* made her a household name.

KIDNAPPED (1960)
Color, 97 minutes
Cast: Peter Finch, James MacArthur, Bernard Lee, Niall MacGinnis, John Laurie, Finlay Currie, Peter O'Toole
Director: Robert Stevenson
Screenplay: Stevenson, based on the novel by Robert Louis Stevenson
Action-adventure/Literary classic
Unrated
Younger kids: OK   Older kids: Good

This Disney version of the Stevenson classic about an 18th-century Scottish lad who's cheated out of his inheritance by a scheming uncle is faithful to its source and handsomely made— but dull. James MacArthur plays young David Balfour who, after his father dies, has his inheritance stolen by his crafty Uncle Ebenezer (John Laurie). Ebenezer then has the boy shanghaied aboard a slave ship, but David escapes with the help of a Scottish loyalist (Peter Finch) who opposes British rule, and the two of them try to regain David's rightful inheritance.

The film features strikingly authentic location photography and a fine cast (which includes a young Peter O'Toole in an early film), yet while the result is creditable, it's somehow not very exciting. The story was also filmed in 1938 (with Freddie Bartholomew), 1948 (with Roddy McDowall), and 1971 (with Michael Caine and an all-star British cast), but as of this writing, none of those versions is available on video. It was remade as a miniseries for cable television in 1995 with Armand Assante.

KIM (1950)
Color, 113 minutes
Cast: Errol Flynn, Dean Stockwell, Paul Lukas, Thomas Gomez, Cecil Kellaway
Director: Victor Saville
Screenplay: Leon Gordon, Helen Deutsch, and Richard Schayer, based on the novel by Rudyard Kipling
Action-adventure/Literary classic
Unrated
Younger kids: OK   Older kids: VG

Kipling's story of an orphan who becomes a spy for the British in 1880s India is a lavish Technicolor spectacle that may be a bit too long and slow for today's hyperactive kids, but has enough action, intrigue, and local flavor (some of it actually shot on location), to keep most older children entertained. Thirteen-year-old Dean Stockwell gives a charming performance as the orphaned son of a British soldier in India who becomes a street urchin and gets involved with a dashing horse dealer/secret agent (a red-bearded Errol Flynn) and a holy lama (Paul Lukas) in an espionage plot involving a Czarist Russian invasion of the Khyber Pass.

Dean Stockwell was one of the more gifted child actors of this period, whose other films include **The Boy With Green Hair,** *The Window*, **Anchors Aweigh,** and *Down to the Sea in Ships*. He had a second career as a young man, then re-emerged yet again in the 1980s and '90s as a seasoned character actor in television and movies.

The classic story was remade for television in 1984 with Peter O'Toole.

THE KING AND I (1956)
Color, 133 minutes
Cast: Deborah Kerr, Yul Brynner, Rita Moreno, Martin Benson, Terry Saunders, Rex Thompson, Carlos Rivas, Patrick Adiarte, Alan Mowbray
Director: Walter Lang
Screenplay: Ernest Lehman, based on the musical by Richard Rodgers and Oscar Hammerstein II, based on the book *Anna and the King of Siam* by Margaret Landon
Musical
Unrated
Young children: VG   Older children: VG

Two of Rodgers and Hammerstein's strongest characters are featured in this superb Broadway musical about a widowed British school teacher and her young son who move to Siam so that she can teach the culture and ways of the Western world to the children and wives of the King. Anna and the King find themselves at odds on several issues, and the story turns on the development of their complex relationship. A romance between the two is suggested, but only with great sensitivity.

Throughout, there is a sense of struggle between peoples of different cultures and races. How we all treat one another is at the heart of this extraordinary musical, summed up in the song "Getting to Know You."

The King has fathered many offspring, who are presented to Anna in stunning royal fashion, with a memorable musical accompaniment called "The March of the Siamese Children." Additionally, the King's various wives are introduced in their living quarters, which essentially is a harem—a place Anna refuses to live.

Then there is the issue of his newest concubine, a "gift" from a neighboring country; she tries to run away with her true love and is punished with a flogging. But for all his appalling behavior and stubbornness, the King is shown to be a man who is constantly refining his philosophy of life—and is worthy of the respect and love he receives.

The most thrilling musical sequence in the film is "Shall We Dance," in which Anna shows him the Western way that men and women dance the waltz. The electric moment in which their hands first touch is as persuasive as any show of affection can be.

Yul Brynner created the role of the King on Broadway, and it became his signature part for the rest of his life.

KING KONG (1933)
Black & white, 100 minutes
Cast: Fay Wray, Robert Armstrong, Bruce Cabot, Frank Reicher, Sam Hardy, Noble Johnson, James Flavin

Directors: Merian C. Cooper and
   Ernest B. Schoedsack
Screenplay: James Creelman and
   Ruth Rose, from an idea by
   Merian C. Cooper and Edgar
   Wallace
Adventure epic/Monster science
   fiction
Unrated
Young children: A
   possibility   Older children:
   VG

Like some people, *King Kong* is
one of the few movies that really
needs no introduction.

For the record, the story is
about a team of moviemakers led
by the energetic Carl Denham
(Armstrong), who's hired homeless Ann Darrow (Wray) to be his
heroine. But the natives of Skull
Island kidnap Ann and tie her to
stakes as an offering for their god,
Kong. When Kong arrives, he
proves to be a colossal ape who,
fascinated by Ann's blonde
beauty, carries her off. Denham
and his men—principally Jack
(Cabot), who's fallen in love with
Ann—follow, battling dinosaurs
and other menaces. Finally, Jack
rescues Ann, and Kong is captured and taken to New York,
where he is put on display at
Madison Square Garden. But
when he thinks Ann is in danger,
he breaks loose and storms
through Manhattan, looking for
her. The climax, of course, takes
place atop the Empire State
Building (which in 1933 was still
shiny and new).

This astonishing, delightful, and
exciting movie is one of the great
wonders of the silver screen, once
seen, never forgotten. Kong has
become one of the greatest icons
of film history and one of the
most beloved characters of fiction

of any sort. Except for the most
fearful, young children will not
only get through the thrills of
King Kong unscathed (as long as
a parent is there to clutch during
the scary stuff), they're likely to
fall in love with the giant, murderous ape. They won't forget the
shots of Kong chomping on slow
natives or casually dropping the
wrong woman in New York, but
they'll forgive him everything, because his passion is so strong, his
courage so great, and his death so
tragically grand.

Kong was really a jointed metal
puppet covered in rubber and fur,
no more than twenty inches tall.
Like the dinosaurs he and our
stalwart heroes battle, Kong was
brought to life through stop-motion animation under the direction of Willis O'Brien. One frame
of film was exposed, O'Brien or
one of the other animators moved
the puppets slightly, and another
frame was shot. When projected
at the standard rate of twenty-
four frames a second, the creatures appear to be moving. (It's
worth emphasizing to kids of
today that this film was made long
before computerized special effects came into existence.)

Although there have been imitations, sequels (*The Son of
Kong*) and remakes (including an
animated musical, *The Mighty
Kong*), *King Kong* is one of a
kind, a breathtaking piece of
moviemaking that remains as
thrilling and delightful as it ever
was. And at the center of it all is
the most fabulous movie monster
of all time, King Kong himself.

KING KONG (1976)
Color, 134 minutes
Cast: Jeff Bridges, Charles
 Grodin, Jessica Lange, John
 Randolph, Rene Auberjonois,
 Julius Harris, Jack O'Halloran,
 Ed Lauter, Joe Piscopo,
 Corbin Bernsen, Rick Baker
Director: John Guillermin
Screenplay: Lorenzo Semple, Jr.
Science fiction/Monster
 adventure
Rated PG
Young children: OK   Older
 children: OK

This remake, produced by Dino
De Laurentiis, basically follows
the story of the original, though it
has a contemporary setting. However, virtually all of the magic and
excitement has been leached out
of the story; the original was notable for its innocence, while this
version is about as innocent as a
career criminal. Bogus ecological
concerns are dragged, kicking and
screaming, into the storyline here;
instead of a dashing filmmaker/
adventurer (Carl Denham in the
1933 movie), the equivalent character is an uncaring exploiter of
natives and the environment. The
movie is almost a textbook example of the wrong approach to updating material from the past.

On the other hand, the story
itself is still compelling, and Bridges gives a good, heartfelt performance. Kong himself is generally
played by makeup maestro Rick
Baker in a suit he designed, although a mechanical version also
turns up briefly.

Younger children are more
likely to enjoy this movie than
older kids (or their parents), because they won't notice the jaded,
cynical elements, but will just see
a story about a giant gorilla who

falls in love with a small blonde—
Jessica Lange, in her movie debut.
(Her shining moment: getting to
call her hairy captor a sexist pig.)

This film did reasonably well at
the box office, but today, when
anyone refers to King Kong, no
one—but *no one*—assumes they're
talking about *this* movie.

There was actually one sequel,
King Kong Lives; though much of
the we're-above-all-this approach
was blessedly gone, the movie itself was pretty dreadful.

KING KONG VS. GODZILLA
(1962)
Color, 91 minutes
Cast: Tadao Takashima, Mie
 Hama, Kenji Sahara, Yu
 Fujiki, Ichiro Arishima, Jun
 Tazaki, Haruo Nakajima,
 Shoichi "Solomon" Hirose
Director: Ishiro Honda
Screenplay: Shinichi Sekizawa
Science fiction/Monster thriller
Unrated
Young children: OK   Older
 children: OK

Godzilla bursts out of the ice that
imprisoned him in **Gigantis, the
Fire Monster** (*Godzilla Raids
Again* in Japan) and heads for
Tokyo. Meanwhile, a giant gorilla
turns up on an island and is
dubbed King Kong, although ob-
viously he's not the "real" Kong.
A showman transports him to
Japan, but he escapes, and soon
Kong and Godzilla are fighting it
out.

Despite a very cheesy-looking
Kong, mediocre special effects,
and a routine story, this was one
of the largest-grossing Godzilla
films ever released and was more
responsible than any other for the
long series of sequels. It is lively,
and if you don't take it seriously,

it's reasonably enjoyable, though not up to the standards of most of the Godzilla films that followed. And it's certainly no rival for the magnificent **King Kong.**

The ideal audience for this, as for many of the Japanese monster movies, is boys, from about 8 to 14. There's nothing in the film that's likely to cause them any anxieties, and it's full of special effects, battling monsters, and exciting action.

Followed by **Godzilla vs. the Thing** (aka *Godzilla vs. Mothra*).

KING OF THE HILL (1993)
Color, 109 minutes
Cast: Jesse Bradford, Jeroen Krabbe, Lisa Eichhorn, Karen Allen, Spalding Gray, Elizabeth McGovern, Joseph Chrest, Adrien Brody, Cameron Boyd, Amber Benson, Kristin Griffith, Remak Ramsay
Director: Steven Soderbergh
Screenplay: Soderbergh, based on the memoir by A. E. Hotchner
Drama
Rated PG-13
Younger kids: No   Older kids: OK, with caution

This marvelous—and unsettling—adaptation of A. E. Hotchner's memoir tells the story of Jesse, a 12-year old boy who lives in a rundown St. Louis hotel during the Great Depression with his brother, his immigrant father and his ailing mother. The boy is separated from his family one by one (his brother is sent to stay with relatives; his mother goes into a sanatorium; his father hits the road as a traveling salesman) until he is forced to fend for himself.

King of the Hill was virtually ignored when originally released, but it is a gem, and perhaps one of the most impressive re-creations of the Depression era ever put on film. The boy's struggle to survive in the hotel while other tenants are gradually ousted because they cannot pay the rent is compellingly and vividly told. At the same time, there is an air of melancholy hanging over the film, and the attendant themes of abandonment and isolation will upset even older children (along with a stark suicide sequence), so parents should be prepared to discuss the Depression and the lengths that people went to stay alive during that time. In one amazing and harrowing sequence, Jesse cuts photographs of food out of a magazine and eats them as if they were real!

Jesse's perseverance and doggedness ultimately see him through, and his triumph over such amazing odds provides the film with a streak of optimism that is honestly earned. However, this is a hard-hitting, adult film that should only be shown to the most mature teenagers.

KING SOLOMON'S MINES (1950)
Color, 102 minutes
Cast: Deborah Kerr, Stewart Granger, Richard Carlson, Hugo Haas, Lowell Gilmore
Directors: Compton Bennett and Andrew Marton
Screenplay: Helen Deutsch, based on the novel by H. Rider Haggard
Action-adventure
Unrated
Younger kids: OK   Older kids: Good

Robert Surtees' Oscar-winning Technicolor location photography of Africa is the main attraction of this exciting film of H. Rider Haggard's popular novel. Stewart Granger plays the rugged adventurer Allan Quatermain, who's searching for the legendary diamond mines of King Solomon while leading prim and proper Englishwoman Elizabeth Curtis (Deborah Kerr) and her brother (Richard Carlson) on a safari to find Elizabeth's missing husband, who was also in pursuit of the fabled treasure.

The outstanding safari footage (which later turned up in many other jungle pictures) of the African veldt and its exotic tribes and animals includes an authentic tribal dance and a thunderous stampede of zebras, giraffes, and other beasts that lasts for several minutes. Although the depiction of Granger's great white hunter character would not be fashionable today and kids will be bored with the film's romantic subplot, they should delight in its adventure elements and vivid shots of elephants, lions, rhinos, crocodiles, and other animals.

KISMET (1955)
Color, 113 minutes
Cast: Howard Keel, Ann Blyth, Dolores Gray, Monty Woolley, Sebastian Cabot, Vic Damone, Jay C. Flippen, Mike Mazurki, Jack Elam, Ted De Corsia, Reiko Sato, Patricia Dunn, Wonci Lui, Ross Bagdasarian
Director: Vincente Minnelli
Screenplay: Charles Lederer and Luther Davis, based on the musical by Lederer, Davis, Robert Wright, and George Forrest, from the play by Edward Knoblock and the musical themes of Alexander Borodin
Musical/Fantasy
Unrated
Young children: VG Older children: VG

This sumptuous film may not be great, but it does offer some beautiful music—including "Stranger in Paradise," "Baubles, Bangles, and Beads," and "Night of My Nights"—within an appealing Arabian Nights–style fantasy.

Kismet is the story of Haaj, a lighthearted, Bagdad-based beggar poet who allegedly has special magical powers. Haaj becomes immersed in a scheme, hatched by a power-mad wazir, that will result in the marriage of a young caliph, who is the wazir's son, to a princess. However, Haaj finds himself in a fix, because his daughter, Marsinah, and the caliph are in love.

You know that all will end on a happy note because Kismet—or Fate—is destined to intervene. *Kismet* was made toward the end of the "golden age of musicals" at MGM, and it is not considered one of the studio's best, but it has attractive performers and settings, and that wonderful score to recommend it.

KISS OF THE VAMPIRE (1963)
Color, 88 minutes
Cast: Clifford Evans, Noel Willman, Edward De Souza, Jennifer Daniel, Barry Warren, Peter Madden
Director: Don Sharp
Screenplay: John Elder (pseud. of Anthony Hinds)
Horror/Suspense
Unrated
Young children: No Older

children: If used to horror movies

Gerald (De Souza) and Marianne (Daniel) are honeymooning in Bavaria when they run afoul of Dr. Ravna (Willman) and his vampire cult. Ravna captures Marianne, so Gerald turns to Professor Zimmer (Evans) for help.

Vivid, exciting Hammer horror. Not part of their Dracula series, this is also one of their sexiest films of the period, most likely making it inappropriate for children under 12. (Actually, they may not know what's going on, since the sex is only implied.) As usual, if older kids are accustomed to horror movies and have developed a taste for blood—stage blood—this is a good film for them.

The Hammer movies were decried at the time for being too bloody, but compared to the horror movies of the 1970s and '80s, they're practically G-rated.

KNIGHTS OF THE ROUND TABLE (1954)
Color, 115 minutes
Cast: Robert Taylor, Ava Gardner, Mel Ferrer, Stanley Baker, Felix Aylmer
Director: Richard Thorpe
Screenplay: Talbot Jennings, Jan Lustig, and Noel Langley, based on *Le Morte D'Arthur* by Sir Thomas Malory
Action-adventure/Historical
Unrated
Younger kids: OK   Older kids: Good

The legendary world of Camelot and King Arthur's court is lavishly brought to life in this MGM spectacular, which was the studio's first CinemaScope produc-

tion. Robert Taylor makes a noble and heroic Lancelot du Lac, whose loyalty to King Arthur (Mel Ferrer) is tested by his love for Queen Guinevere (Ava Gardner at her most beautiful), and who clashes with the scheming Sir Mordred (a glowering Stanley Baker) and Morgan Le Fay (Anne Crawford).

The script is fairly superficial, but the numerous battle scenes filmed on location in England are presented with panache, and the realistic costumes and sets lend the film an aura of authenticity. Kids who are familiar with the Knights of the Round Table tale through such modern movies as **Quest for Camelot** will no doubt grow impatient with the romantic triangle involving Arthur, Guinevere, and Lancelot, but they should enjoy the abundance of rousing sword fights (Lancelot's first meeting with King Arthur is a standout), jousting duels, and exciting, swashbuckling action.

KORCZAK (1990)
Color, 118 minutes
Cast: Wojtek Pszoniak, Ewa Dalkowska, Teresa Budzisz-Krzyzanowska, Piotr Kozlowski, Jan Peszek
Director: Andrzej Wajda
Screenplay: Agnieszka Holland
Biographical drama
Unrated
Young children: No   Older children: VG

This is the tremendously moving real-life story of a truly gentle, remarkable man: Janusz Korczak, a respected doctor, writer, and children's rights advocate who operated a home for Jewish orphans in Warsaw during the 1930s. Korczak's concerns are people and not politics. "I love children," he states, simply and matter-of-factly. "I fight for years for the dignity of children." In his school, he offers his charges a "humanist education."

And then the Nazis invade his homeland. . . .

Given his station in life, Korczak easily could arrange his escape to freedom. But he chooses to remain with his children and do whatever he must to keep his orphanage running and his children alive, even after they all have been imprisoned in the Warsaw ghetto.

Korczak, directed by one of the most skilled filmmakers of his time and written by another great talent who would go on to a notable directing career, tells a universal story of courage and integrity. It can educate and inspire young people, regardless of their religion.

KRAMER VS. KRAMER
(1979)
Color, 104 minutes
Cast: Dustin Hoffman, Meryl Streep, Jane Alexander, Justin Henry, Howard Duff, JoBeth Williams
Director: Robert Benton
Screenplay: Benton, based on the novel by Avery Corman
Drama
Rated PG
Younger kids: No   Older kids: VG

Divorce is a sensitive subject for many children. This Oscar-winning film movingly explores a family relationship and how it brings changes, both good and bad, to a young boy's life. Because the youngster figures so prominently in the story, it's likely that mature children will re-

spond to this film and find many points of reference.

Academy Awards went to Dustin Hoffman and Meryl Streep for their superb performances in this moving film about a father's attempt to raise his 7-year-old son after his wife walks out on them. Hoffman is Ted Kramer, a workaholic advertising executive whose business success has resulted in his neglecting his wife, Joanna (Streep), and their son, Billy (Justin Henry). When the unfulfilled Joanna suddenly walks out on her family and moves to California to "find herself," Ted is forced to care for Billy by himself. He loses his job in the process but develops a loving bond with his son. When Joanna later returns and demands Billy back, a nasty custody battle ensues.

The bare-bones plot is the stuff of many a soap opera, but Robert Benton, who also won Oscars for his intelligent script and sensitive direction, never allows it to become melodramatic or sentimental, and the result is a funny and heartrending look at family life that's one of the best movies of the 1970s.

Many children will respond to the idea of a parent who's too busy to pay attention to them and will enjoy watching Ted Kramer's first bumbling attempts to make breakfast and take care of his son. This film could well be a springboard for lively family conversation about making priorities and choices in a busy world.

The mature subject matter, language, and brief nudity, however, make it inappropriate for younger kids.

KUNDUN (1997)
Color, 134 minutes
Cast: Tenzin Thuthob Tsarong,
  Gyurme Tethong, Jamyang
  Kunga Tenzin
Director: Martin Scorsese
Screenplay: Melissa Mathison
Biography/Drama
Rated PG-13
Younger kids: No Older kids:
  VG

Starring a cast of nonprofessional
Tibetan actors, Martin Scorsese's
visually stunning biography of the
14th Dalai Lama is an intimate,
highly personalized story that unfolds on an epic scale.

The story begins in 1937 Tibet,
where a 2-year-old boy named
Tenzin Gyatso is discovered by a
group of monks who determine
that the child is in fact the 14th
reincarnation of the Buddha,
known as the Dalai Lama, and is
destined to become Tibet's spiritual and political leader. Taken to
live in a monastery, the Dalai
Lama is given training in Buddhist philosophy, including the
central tenet of nonviolence.

Following World War II, he
clashes with Chairman Mao (Robert Lin) after the Communist
leader takes over China, invades
Tibet, and ruthlessly enforces
Marxist ideology. After Chinese
troops begin to massacre innocent
Tibetans and the Dalai Lama is
the target of several assassination
attempts, he reluctantly agrees to
leave the country and flees to
India in 1959. As a postscript
states, he has yet to return.

Although the director of *Taxi
Driver* and *Goodfellas* may not
seem like the ideal person to
make a film about a spiritual

leader, *Kundun* (which is what Tibetans call the Dalai Lama, meaning "Ocean of Wisdom") is not so
much about religion as it is about
the effects of violence (and the
concept of nonviolence) on the
human soul—a subject Scorsese
has dealt with in many of his
pictures.

While eloquently expressing the
Dalai Lama's pacifist beliefs, the
film does not dwell on political or
theological messages but is instead a universal story of love and
compassion. It is also spectacularly beautiful to behold, featuring a lyrical flow of imagery,
including the magnificent desert
panoramas and snow-capped mountains of Tibet (actually filmed in
Morocco), and the mystical journey
to India, which is dazzlingly intercut
with flashbacks and the film's recurring image of the multicolored sand
mandala.

Though the subject matter is
way over the heads of young children, the fact that the story begins
with a child and takes us through
the Dalai Lama's young life—
allowing us to share his point of
view—will draw older, open-
minded children to this fascinating saga.

There are some brief flashes
of violence depicting frightening
bloodshed, which earned the film
a PG-13 rating . . . but any mature
children who are interested in exploring foreign cultures and phi-
losophies should be exposed to
this deeply felt film.

A good companion piece (almost a primer for it) is *Seven
Years in Tibet*, in which Brad Pitt
plays real-life Austrian explorer
Heinrich Harrer, who was befriended by the Dalai Lama during the 1940s.

L

LA BAMBA (1987)
Color, 108 minutes
Cast: Lou Diamond Phillips, Esai
   Morales, Rosana De Soto,
   Elizabeth Pena, Danielle von
   Zerneck, Joe Pantoliano, Rick
   Dees, Marshall Crenshaw,
   Brian Setzer
Director: Luis Valdez
Screenplay: Luis Valdez
Musical biography
PG-13
Young children: OK, with
   caution   Older children: VG

World music history was made
and lost on February 3, 1959,
when the light plane carrying J. P.
Thompson, aka The Big Bopper
(famous for his record of "Chan-
tilly Lace"), Buddy Holly ("Peggy
Sue"), and Ritchie Valens
("Come On, Let's Go") crashed
in an Iowa snowstorm en route to
their next concert.

This excellent film is the flip
side of **The Buddy Holly Story,**
chronicling the rise of one Ricardo Valenzuela, age 19, out of
the San Fernando Valley barrio to
the top of the music charts, where
he became the first Latin rock star
in mainstream America.

While showcasing much of his
music, the accent is firmly on
drama: how Ritchie, the son of a
guitar player, is supported in his
music by his widowed mother (De
Soto) . . . how his half-brother
Bob (Morales) is ripped up by
pride and envy . . . how racial

prejudice both limits and inspires
him.

Full of vitality and energy, and
sparked by Lou Diamond Phillips'
star-making performance in the
leading role, the movie has plenty
of heart but also rough moments
of virulent emotion. It is best
suited to older kids.

La Bamba also marked a Hollywood milestone, being a movie
dealing with Latin Americans,
featuring many Latinos in the
cast, written and directed by a notable Latino filmmaker, which
enjoyed mainstream box-office
success. Certainly Ritchie Valens
would have approved.

LABYRINTH (1986)
Color, 101 minutes
Cast: David Bowie, Jennifer
   Connelly, Toby Froud, Shelley
   Thompson, Christopher
   Malcolm, Natalie Finland,
   Shari Weiser, Rob Mills,
   David Barclay, Karen Prell,
   Frank Oz
Director: Jim Henson
Screenplay: Terry Jones, based
   on a story by Dennis Less and
   Jim Henson
Fantasy
Rated PG
Younger children: VG   Older
   children: VG

When 15-year-old Sarah (Jennifer
Connelly) whispers "I wish the
goblins would come and take you
away" to Toby, her unwanted
toddler stepbrother—they do.

Guilty about his disappearance, Sarah goes after him, and like Dorothy in Oz and Alice in Wonderland, she ventures into a magical land, encountering strange but friendly creatures in her thirteen-hour quest to rescue Toby from the Goblin King (David Bowie).

Produced by George Lucas, written by Monty Python's Terry Jones, and directed by Jim Henson, *Labyrinth* has all the elements of a classic fairy tale or mythic journey. If parents or children notice a resemblance to Oz or Wonderland, or the *Odyssey,* for that matter, it's no accident. This fanciful film, full of original but familiar-seeming creatures (brought to life by Henson's Creature Shop) is a thoroughly satisfying modern-day fable, inventive, often clever, and visually arresting. There's even an M. C. Escher set, based on a poster that hangs in Sarah's bedroom.

LADY AND THE TRAMP
(1955)
Color, 75 minutes
Cast: Voices of Peggy Lee, Barbara Luddy, Larry Roberts, Bill Thompson, Bill Baucon, Stan Freberg, Verna Felton, Alan Feed, George Givot, Dallas McKennon, Lee Millar
Directors: Hamilton Luske, Clyde Geronimi, and Wilfred Jackson
Screenplay: Erdman Penner, Joe Rinaldi, Ralph Wright, and Donald Da Gradi, based on a story by Ward Greene
Animated feature
Rated G
Younger kids: VG   Older kids: VG

The first animated feature made in CinemaScope, *Lady and the Tramp* is also one of Walt Disney's most charming and lovable cartoons, featuring several delightful songs by Peggy Lee and Sonny Burke, including the classics "Bella Notte" and the "Siamese Cat Song."

Set in 1910 New England, the story tells of Jim Dear, a loving husband who gives his wife, Darling, a cocker spaniel named Lady as a Christmas present. Lady's two closest friends in her exclusive neighborhood are Jock, a Scottish terrier, and Trusty, an aging bloodhound who has lost his sense of smell. After Darling has a baby, she and Jim Dear go on vacation, leaving Darling's Aunt Sarah in charge of the house. Aunt Sarah's mischievous Siamese cats, Si and Am, make a shambles of the house and trick Aunt Sarah into thinking Lady is responsible, and she has Lady muzzled. Lady escapes and is chased by a pack of street dogs, but is rescued by Tramp, a carefree mongrel. The two spend a romantic night together, including a spaghetti dinner in the back of Tony's Restaurant, and share several more misadventures before the happy, but peril-fraught, ending.

Despite being considered a fairly lightweight effort in 1955, *Lady and the Tramp* has stood the test of time and has emerged as one of Disney's most pleasing and appealing films. The animation is less stylized and more realistic than usual, featuring soft contours and muted colors, and the widescreen canvas is skillfully utilized and beautifully evokes the small town, turn-of-the-century New England atmosphere. The animal characters are all adorable, but this being a Disney film, there also has to be at least one absolutely terrifying scene to counterbalance the prevailing cuteness, and Tramp's vicious fight with a rat that tries to sneak into the nursery is a doozy. Ironically, most kids seem to love this scene while their parents are the ones covering their eyes.

As in all the best Disney cartoons, there is also a serious subtext, concerning class conflict, and untamed freedom vs. genteel domesticity (or, "the leash and collar set," as Tramp calls it), that's cleverly designed to keep the adults as stimulated as the kids are entertained. Much of the credit for the film's success must go to Peggy Lee, who, in addition to singing some and cowriting all five of the songs, also did the voices for the characters of Peg, Darling, and the nasty Siamese cats. The latter provide the film with one of its most memorable moments, as they slither through the house, terrorizing Lady and singing "We are Siamese, if you ple-e-ease." Another highlight—and for many baby boomers a key childhood memory—is the "Bella Notte" number, where Tramp and Lady have a candlelight dinner and inadvertently kiss as they chew on the same piece of spaghetti.

Lady and the Tramp may lack the razzle-dazzle technique of some of the earlier Disney classics, but in its own short, sweet way, it's nearly perfect.

LADYHAWKE (1985)
Color, 124 minutes
Cast: Matthew Broderick, Rutger Hauer, Michelle Pfeiffer, Leo McKern, John Wood, Ken Hutchison, Alfred Molina
Director: Richard Donner
Screenplay: Edward Kharma, Michael Thomas, Tom Mankiewicz
Comedy/Fantasy/Adventure
Rated PG-13
Younger kids: OK, with caution   Older kids: OK

Ladyhawke is a medieval romance about two lovers, Navarre (Hauer) and Princess Isabeau (Pfeiffer), who are beset by the curse of a jealous bishop: Navarre turns into a wolf at night, while Isabeau becomes a hawk during the day. Enter Philippe (Broderick), a young thief who becomes their ally and helps them in their quest to break the spell.

The settings and cinematography of this movie are magnificent, and Hauer and Pfeiffer are well cast as the doomed lovers, but the direction doesn't make the most of the magical possibilities in this material. (An ear-splitting score from Andrew Powell is also definitely not an asset.)

However, the concept of a man and woman who are unable to connect is compelling, and it is probably an interesting change for kids to watch a film where lovers spend most of the film apart from each other in the physical sense. Broderick, as the rogue who frequently talks to himself in comic asides, is the most problematic element: he isn't really integral to the action, and his funny lines are not in keeping with the overly serious tone which suffuses the rest of the movie. At the same time, he provides a lot of the film's sprightly, entertaining moments and will probably appeal more directly to children than the nominal leads.

The PG-13 rating is for some

violence and vivid scenes of medieval torture.

THE LAND BEFORE TIME
(1988)
Color, 66 minutes
Cast: Voices of Gabriel Damon, Helen Shaver, Pat Hingle, Candice Houston, Judith Barsi, Will Ryan, Burke Barnes
Director: Don Bluth
Screenplay: Stu Krieger
Animated feature
Rated G
Younger kids: OK   Older kids: NG

This prehistoric adventure, about a group of kiddie dinosaurs on a quest, is a favorite among the preschool crowd. Don Bluth provides the lavish settings in this slight story about a baby brontosaurus named Littlefoot, separated from his family after his mother dies, who must find his way to the Great Valley or become extinct. Joining him on his journey are a group of young friends, including Cera, a feminine triceratops, Petrie the pterodactyl, and Ducky, an anatorsaurus. Danger looms in the form of a hungry Tyrannosaurus Rex.

The story is told from a child's point of view and deals with a variety of issues including life, death, and survival. Children over 7 years old will be bored, though some younger ones may be troubled by Littlefoot's tearful inability to accept his mother's death (he even thinks he sees her image in the clouds above). Though barely over an hour, *The Land Before Time* can be slow going at times.

Produced by a pre-**Jurassic Park** Steven Spielberg and George Lucas, the film's popularity has spawned five low-budget direct-to-video sequels: *The Land Before Time II: The Great Valley Adventure* (1994); *III: The Time of Great Giving* (1995); *IV: The Journey Through the Mists* (1997); *V: The Mysterious Island* (1998); *VI: The Secret of Saurus Rock* (1998), as well as a Sing-A-Long video.

LASSIE (1994)
Color, 92 minutes
Cast: Lassie, Helen Slater, Thomas Guiry, Jon Tenney, Brittany Boyd, Frederic Forrest, Richard Farnsworth, Michelle Williams, Charlie Hofheimer
Director: Daniel Petrie
Screenplay: Matthew Jacobs, Gary Ross, and Elizabeth Anderson
Drama/Animal story
Rated PG
Younger kids: VG   Older kids: OK

This update of *Lassie* is a surefire entertainment for young kids and their parents. The plot concerns the Turner family and their move from the big city to the country. Young teenager Matthew is especially upset about changing his skateboarding, MTV-watching lifestyle.

The Turners meet Lassie on the road, the survivor of a car crash, and immediately adopt her. Conflict arises when neighboring sheep rancher Sam Garland (Frederic Forrest) attempts dirty tricks and sabotage to discourage Turner from competing with him. His bullying sons make life even more miserable for Matthew . . . but a budding friendship with a local girl brightens his outlook on life.

Thomas Guiry's believable performance as an alienated teenage boy is right on target, and serves as the centerpiece of this entertaining film. You just know that Lassie is going to win him over, and you also know that somehow, Lassie will find solutions to all the other problems that arise.

With a good cast and beautiful location photography "out in the country," *Lassie* scores as first-rate family entertainment. It's also not as saccharine as the long-running TV series of yore. A few touches of modern life—the kids' misbehavior, some tense moments, some fairly common use of "bad" language—got this a PG rather than G rating.

LASSIE COME HOME (1943)
Color, 90 minutes
Cast: Roddy McDowall, Donald Crisp, Edmund Gwenn, Dame May Whitty, Nigel Bruce, Elsa Lanchester, Elizabeth Taylor
Director: Fred M. Wilcox
Screenplay: Hugo Butler, based on the novel by Eric Knight
Drama/Animal Story
Unrated
Young children: VG   Older children: VG

Lassie, a brave and heroic collie who is heart-tuggingly loyal to her youthful owner, has been the star of numerous feature films (*Lassie, Son of Lassie, The Magic of Lassie, Lassie's Great Adventure*), a cartoon series (*Lassie's Rescue Rangers*), and a long-running television series.

This charming film, based on the original Eric Knight story that introduced the collie into popular culture, is the best of them all. Here, Lassie (played by a male collie named Pal) is the pet of a young Yorkshire lad named Joe

Carraclough (Roddy McDowall). Unfortunately, Joe's family is impoverished, and his parents must sell Lassie to a Duke (Nigel Bruce).

It would be difficult to find a more perfect family film. Young hearts will be warmed and tears will be shed as Lassie undertakes several hazardous journeys and experiences many adventures, in her determination to return to Joe.

While made in Hollywood by MGM, *Lassie Come Home* has a distinct British flair, as all of its primary cast members are English-born. One of them, a beautiful girl cast as Priscilla, the Duke's granddaughter, was a charming young star-to-be named Elizabeth Taylor. Just one year later she would star in another family classic, **National Velvet.**

THE LAST BUTTERFLY
(1991)
Color, 110 minutes
Cast: Tom Courtenay, Brigitte Fossey, Ingrid Held, Freddie Jones, Milan Knazko, Josef Kemer
Director: Karel Kachyna
Screenplay: Ota Hofman, Kachyna, and Marc Princi, based on the novel by Michel Jacot
Drama
Rated PG-13
Young children: No   Older children: VG, with caution

This powerful drama offers proof that Steven Spielberg's **Schindler's List** (1993) is not the only film of the 1990s to deal with the Holocaust in a potent manner.

It is the story of Antoine Moreau, a fabled French mime who, near the end of World War II, is "employed" by the Nazis to mount a single performance of "Hansel and Gretel" for the youngsters confined in Terezin, the notorious "city of Jews." The show is to be observed during an International Red Cross inspection and is intended to distort the reality of life in the camp and display to the world that Jews in concentration camps are treated humanely. Antoine develops a close relationship with the children who become his actors and audience and also comes to realize the sham behind the show.

As one might expect, *The Last Butterfly* is an intense and sobering film, but it offers an especially poignant portrait of the youngest and most innocent victims of Nazi Germany and the Holocaust.

THE LAST EMPEROR (1987)
Color, 160 minutes (also 220m.)
Cast: John Lone, Joan Chen,
Peter O'Toole, Ying
Ruocheng, Victor Wong
Director: Bernardo Bertolucci
Screenplay: Bertolucci and Mark
Peploe, based on the book
From Emperor to Citizen by
Pu Yi
Drama/Biography
Rated PG-13
Younger kids: No   Older kids:
VG

Nine Oscars, including Best Picture and Best Director, went to Bernardo Bertolucci's ravishingly beautiful biography of the last Chinese emperor, Pu Yi, which traces his life from 1908, when he ascended the throne at the age of 3, to his final days working as a gardener during Mao's Cultural Revolution in the 1960s.

Beginning with a scene set in Manchuria in the 1950s where Pu Yi tries to commit suicide before being arrested as a pro-Japanese war criminal by the Communists, the film adroitly jumps back and forth in time, unfurling a series of extraordinary scenes from his life: his meeting as a boy with the Empress Dowager and his pampered upbringing in the palace; lessons with a Scottish tutor (Peter O'Toole); his lonely teenage years; his eviction from the Forbidden City by a hostile warlord; his romantic relationships with his wet nurse and the two wives who are chosen for him; his status as a puppet ruler of Manchuria for the Japanese; his "re-education" at a Communist prison; and after being paroled, his job working in Peking's Botanical Gardens.

Thousands of extras, spectacular locations, and Vittorio Storaro's magnificent, Oscar-winning photography (which includes many scenes actually shot inside the Forbidden City) help to make *The Last Emperor* an epic in the true sense of the word, but it's also a lyrical and intimate portrait of an ordinary man who had greatness thrust upon him, and the extraordinary twists and turns his life took because of it.

Mature kids should be intrigued by the idea of a child born into a situation in which he is treated as something of a god and denied a normal childhood, living as he does in near isolation.

It's fascinating as both art and history, although its violence, brief nudity, and sexual content make it appropriate only for older kids. The film was reissued in 1998 with an additional hour of footage never before seen in the U.S.

THE LAST OF THE MOHICANS (1936)

Black & white, 91 minutes
Cast: Randolph Scott, Binnie
  Barnes, Heather Angel, Hugh
  Buckler, Henry Wilcoxon,
  Bruce Cabot
Director: George B. Seitz
Screenplay: Philip Dunne, John
  Balderston, Paul Perez, and
  Daniel Moore, based on the
  novel by James Fenimore
  Cooper
Historical drama/Action-
  adventure/Literary classic
Unrated
Younger kids: OK   Older kids:
  Good

Randolph Scott is ideally cast as Hawkeye in this action-packed version of James Fenimore Cooper's classic tale of conflict between the British Army and Colonial settlers in upstate New York during the French and Indian Wars. The swiftly told story centers on Hawkeye's perilous trek to a British fort, escorting Col. Munro's two daughters (Binnie Barnes, Heather Angel), and accompanied by Chingachgook (Robert Barrat) and his son Uncas (Philip Reed), while being pursued by the French-allied Hurons, led by the vicious Magua (a snarling Bruce Cabot).

Although the book's plot has been telescoped and Hawkeye's roughneck character softened somewhat to allow for a romance, it remains true to the spirit of the novel and contains vigorous performances and exciting action scenes, particularly the fierce Huron attack on Fort William Henry (which contains scalpings and other brutalities that may frighten younger children). This adaptation was solid enough to serve as the foundation for the even more vivid (and brutal) R-rated remake of 1992 with Daniel Day-Lewis.

THE LAST OF THE MOHICANS (1992)

Color, 122 minutes
Cast: Daniel Day-Lewis,
  Madeleine Stowe, Russell
  Means, Eric Shweig, Jodhi
  May, Steven Waddington, Wes
  Studi, Maurice Roeves, Patrice
  Chereau, Colm Meaney, Pete
  Postlethwaite
Director: Michael Mann
Screenplay: Mann and
  Christopher Crowe, from
  Philip Dunne's 1936 script
  based on the novel by James
  Fenimore Cooper
Historical drama/Action-
  adventure/Literary classic
Rated R
Young children: No   Older
  children: VG, with caution

This modern version of James Fenimore Cooper's classic novel differs from earlier screen versions in interesting and significant ways. For openers, Hawkeye is the primary character, Major Heyward is more of a prig, and Cora falls for Hawkeye, rather than Uncas.

It also mirrors the time in which it was made by explaining the reason for Magua's savagery: the White Man was responsible for the deaths of his loved ones, and he is justifiably seeking revenge

Mohicans is an extremely visceral film—and a beautiful-looking one, as well.

It is included in this book because of its overall quality and integrity of purpose, and because it is based on a genuine literary classic. But it is also rated R, quite appropriately, for the intensity of its violence. This is not to be taken lightly, as the pain and suffering here go far beyond the make-believe of outer space sagas or video game–inspired adventure yarns.

THE LAST STARFIGHTER
(1984)
Color, 100 minutes
Cast: Lance Guest, Robert Preston, Dan O'Herlihy, Catherine Mary Stewart, Kay E. Kuter, Dan Mason, Norman Snow
Screenplay: Jonathan R. Betuel
Science fiction/Space opera
Rated PG
Younger kids: OK, with caution   Older kids: OK

Alex (Guest) is the best video-game player in his trailer park, but doesn't expect this to lead to his being taken into outer space by friendly alien Centauri (Preston). It turns out that the Starfighter video game is, in fact, a recruiting test for *real* spaceship fighter pilots, and Alex's score is the best. He turns down the opportunity to fight for the Ko-Dan Empire against the evil Xur and returns to Earth, where, in the meantime, a robot duplicate has been living his life—none too well. But Xur sends a team of alien warriors to eliminate Alex just the same.

One of many films that tried to capture the appeal of **Star Wars,** this one comes closer than most. There's a sense of playfulness to the movie that makes it entertaining, and it's given a big boost by the charm of veteran actors Robert Preston and Dan O'Herlihy (who plays a lizard man). How-

ever, it's also very lightweight— there's little sense of danger at any time, and it never takes itself very seriously, which makes it fairly trivial fun, even for the kids who like it best.

A LEAGUE OF THEIR OWN
(1992)
Color, 128 minutes
Cast: Tom Hanks, Geena Davis, Madonna, Lori Petty, Jon Lovitz, David Strathairn, Garry Marshall, Megan Cavanagh, Rosie O'Donnell, Renee Coleman, Ann Cusack, Tracy Reiner, Janet Jones, Tea Leoni, Bill Pullman
Director: Penny Marshall
Screenplay: Lowell Ganz and Babaloo Mandel, from a story by Kelly Condaele and Kim Wilson III.
Comedy/Sports
Rated PG
Younger kids: OK   Older kids: VG

During World War II, so many men are called away to fight that a clever entrepreneur gets the idea of launching a women's baseball league. His talent scout finds Dottie (Geena Davis) playing for a local dairy team and signs her up—but she won't go without her kid sister, Kit (Lori Petty). Soon they're part of the Peaches, coached by the eternally frustrated, heavy-drinking Jimmy Dugan (Tom Hanks). Kit blames all of her troubles on Dottie, who seems to be good at everything she does; eventually, Kit gets sent to a rival team, and inevitably the two sisters have to play against each other, in a climactic game at which more than just a baseball score is at stake.

This entertaining movie starts

out in the present day as a group of older women gather at the Baseball Hall of Fame in Cooperstown, New York, to receive belated recognition for their pioneering efforts.

The story that follows is grounded in reality: there were indeed all-female teams during World War II, and they virtually disappeared when the men came home. The rest of the script is fictional and offers many talented performers their chance to shine, including Tom Hanks, who actually gained weight to play the unfulfilled baseball coach.

A League of Their Own is an enjoyable film that also provides a sugar-coated history lesson about society's attitude toward women in the 1940s. It goes on too long, but kids of all ages (especially girls) should find themselves wrapped up in the story and the fate of the characters. There is some mildly raucous humor.

THE LEARNING TREE (1969)
Color, 107 minutes
Cast: Kyle Johnson, Alex Clarke, Estelle Evans, Dana Elcar, Mita Waters, Joel Fluellen, Malcolm Atterbury, Richard Ward, Russell Thorson, Peggy Rea
Director: Gordon Parks
Screenplay: Parks, based on his autobiographical novel
Drama
Rated PG
Young children: OK   Older children: VG

This literate, intensely moving autobiographical drama, lovingly directed by photographer-filmmaker Gordon Parks, tells the story of Newt Winger, a sensitive black adolescent coming of age in rural Kansas during the 1920s.

Newt's mother toils as a domestic in the employ of a judge, while his dad works for a rancher. But the story Parks tells is uniquely Newt's, as the boy mixes with those around him and is exposed to an array of emotions and feelings. He becomes all too aware of brutality and bigotry, and the harsh reality that, however idyllic his surroundings, blacks and whites ultimately remain separate and unequal. All of this is brought home in one potent sequence in which the water in the creek where Newt swims turns red, as it fills with the blood of a black man who has been shot in the back by a racist sheriff.

Parks's story is filled with characters, both black and white, who are compassionate and greedy, angry and loving. They all affect Newt and are certain to mold his character and remain with him for the rest of his life.

The Learning Tree is a small gem of a film: angry, poetic, and deeply felt.

LEAVE IT TO BEAVER (1997)
Color, 88 minutes
Cast: Christopher McDonald, Janine Turner, Cameron Finley, Erik von Detten, Adam Zolotin, Erika Chistensen, Barbara Billingsley, Ken Osmond
Director: Andy Cadiff
Screenplay: Brian Levant and Lon Diamond, based on the television series created by Bob Mosher and Joe Connelly
Comedy
Rated PG
Younger children: VG   Older children: OK

Theodore "Beaver" Cleaver (Cameron Finley) is constantly misunderstood—especially by his Dad (Christopher McDonald). When Beaver wants a new bike, he joins the school football team in an effort to butter up his Dad (who played football when he was in school). It's a disaster from the word go, but he does succeed in getting his bike. He also succeeds in losing it—to a neighborhood wiseguy/bully who steals it right under Beaver's nose. How will Beaver retrieve his bike? How can he square things with his father? And will his big brother Wally get to first base with the girl he's interested in?

This amiable feature film manages to recapture much of the warmth and simple humor associated with the long-running domestic comedy from television's "age of innocence." Young Finley is an excellent choice as Beaver, who has a knack for getting into trouble without even trying, and McDonald is fine as his Dad, who just doesn't get it—until the film's final moments.

There's a dose of slapstick, a subplot about puppy love, and a knowing wink for adults in the audience (cameo appearances from some of the TV series' cast members and the vision of Mom wearing pearls while vacuuming the living room) . . . but for the most part, this is pretty wholesome moviemaking, especially for the 1990s!

Older kids may find it too bland, but younger kids—and nostalgic parents—should enjoy it thoroughly.

LEGEND (1985)

Color, 89 minutes
Cast: Tom Cruise, Mia Sara, Tim Curry, David Bennent, Alice Playten, Billy Barty, Cork Hubbert, Peter O'Farrell, Robert Picardo
Director: Ridley Scott
Screenplay: William Hjortsberg
Fantasy adventure
Rated PG
Young children: No Older children: VG

Adults never seem to get this elaborately produced British fairy tale, but little girls ages 9–11 never get tired of watching it, claim the owners of video stores.

Maybe adults can't quite buy into the idea of Tom Cruise as a long-haired pixie kind of forest guy with fairy friends and goblin enemies. Those who can get past that encounter an enchanting (and expensively mounted) Grimm's Fairy Tale–type parable about how there can be no right without night.

When a mortal girl (Mia Sara) touches the last of the unicorns, it allows the Lord of Darkness (a resonant Tim Curry) to attempt a black coup over the unsuspecting denizens of a sparkling fairyland. Only the Puck-like Jack and his pals can save their heretofore happy way of life.

This elegant but rather simple story wasn't designed as a children's film, but kids have turned out to be its best audience. The Lord of Darkness is a pretty creepy character, however, and will probably frighten the youngest kids.

LEGEND OF THE SPIRIT DOG (1994)

Color, 90 minutes

Cast: Morgan Brittany, David Richards, George Charles, Robert Frier, Jon Paul Nicoll, Marcus Waterman, Martin Balsam; Martin Landau (narrator)

Directors: Michael Spence and Martin Goldman

Screenplay: Rick Fields, Ronald C. Meyer, and Goldman

Outdoor adventure

Rated PG

Young children: OK Older children: VG

A variation on the boy-and-his-dog formula, this rugged wilderness saga with family values pits a boy and his wolf-dog against the elements, as an ancient supernatural evil threatens the very existence of Mother Earth.

The film is somewhat *White Fang*–ish, with an ingenuous hero and a magnificently fuzzy canine. The duo's mission to protect nature from ravage elevates the seemingly pedestrian story to a higher level.

There is some violence but not anything you wouldn't expect from this kind of film.

Actor Martin Landau narrates.

THE LEOPARD SON (1996)

Color, 84 minutes

Cast: the animals of Africa's Serengeti plain

Director: Hugo Van Lawick

Screenplay: Michael Olmert

Documentary

Rated G

Young children: VG, with caution Older children: VG

Like a live-action version of **The Lion King,** the first theatrical feature film from cable TV's The Discovery Channel is a kind of update of Walt Disney's True-Life Adventures. And this one really is true to life.

Director Van Lawick, the ex-husband of famed primatologist Jane Goodall, acquired the remarkably feral feline footage by sitting patiently over a two-year period, photographing the lives of the leopards without ever interfering with them. A harsh beauty emerged, captured totally herein.

The infancy, adolescence, and maturation of a single leopard cub is the ostensible focus, but the sweep of the story encompasses nothing less than the miracle of life itself.

There's death, too. Be prepared to see meal-stalking, meal-eating, and meal-scavenging at its most basic. This is pretty graphic stuff, perhaps too strong for some kids, but that's nature.

Make sure you eat before the movie, and not during.

LIAR LIAR (1997)

Color, 87 minutes

Cast: Jim Carrey, Maura Tierney, Jennifer Tilly, Swoosie Kurtz, Amanda Donohoe, Jason Bernard, Mitchell Ryan, Anne Haney, Justin Cooper, Cary Elwes, Randall "Tex" Cobb, Cheri Oteri

Director: Tom Shadyac

Screenplay: Paul Guay and Steve Mazur

Comedy

Rated PG-13

Young children: No Older children: OK, with caution

Jim Carrey exploded into movie stardom with *Ace Ventura: Pet*

Detective. Since then he's made all kinds of films, but his essential silliness and rubber-faced antics have endeared him to kids—even if his films are not always appropriate for them.

This film has particular resonance for kids, as Carrey plays a divorced attorney whose neglected son makes a birthday wish that comes true. Oh Dad, poor Dad. The wish is that this compulsive, habitual liar must tell the absolute truth for twenty-four hours, no matter what. This magical transformation creates problems with traffic cops, fellow elevator passengers, and would-be bedmates, not to mention his clients and the judge. Imagine the possibilities, and they're all here. (Bob Hope did the same thing in a 1941 movie called *Nothing but the Truth*.)

The fact that Carrey is a neglectful—but still loving—Dad, and that it's his son's wish that triggers the story, gives this film particular kid appeal. Carrey is utterly believable, and even when his character is behaving badly, you like him.

The trouble with *Liar Liar* is that it contains so many crude sex jokes and conversations. Some of this will sail over kids' heads and be of little concern to them. Adolescents, however, will hear more than they ought to about sexual behavior.

Another scene in which Carrey beats himself up in a restroom is brutally off-key.

Still, there's no denying the fact that this film has an enormous attraction for kids and a lot of surefire laughs. But be warned: its PG-13 rating is well earned.

LIES MY FATHER TOLD ME
(1975)
Color, 102 minutes
Cast: Yossi Yadin, Len Birman, Marilyn Lightstone, Jeffrey Lynas, Ted Allan
Director: Jan Kadar
Screenplay: Ted Allan, based on his short story
Drama
Rated PG
Young children: VG   Older children: VG

This pleasant "sleeper" tells the story of David Herman, an impressionable 6-year-old boy growing up in an immigrant neighborhood of Montreal during the 1920s. Although David barely tolerates his insensitive father and loving, if passive, mother, he adores his grandfather (or "zaydeh"), a humble junk dealer who trudges around the city in a horse-drawn cart, haggling with his customers and selling his wares. The old man is stubborn and a bit eccentric, yet he possesses a vivid imagination and fills David's head with explanations of the Talmud and answers to the perennial questions that little children ask their elders. Eventually, the zaydeh dies, and David must learn to accept death as a fact of life.

The characters may be Jewish and live in a specific city during a specific era, but *Lies My Father Told Me* is a timeless and universal story.

It may be a bit sad for younger kids, but if they watch it with their parents it should prove to be a positive and rewarding experience.

LIFE WITH FATHER (1947)
Color, 118 minutes
Cast: Irene Dunne, William
Powell, Elizabeth Taylor,
Edmund Gwenn, ZaSu Pitts,
Jimmy Lydon, Martin Milner
Director: Michael Curtiz
Screenplay: Donald Ogden
Stewart, based on the stage
play by Howard Lindsay and
Russel Crouse, based in turn
on magazine stories by
Clarence Day
Literary classic/Comedy
Unrated
Young children: VG   Older
children: VG

Clarence Day's warm reminis-
cences of growing up with a loving and unorthodox family—all
redheads—including father and
mother and three younger brothers, makes for top-notch family
entertainment. The time is the
turn of the 20th century, and the
place is a large and comfortable
Madison Avenue brownstone in
the New York City of tree-lined
streets and horse-drawn carriages.
The action and the fun are nonstop as the eldest son, Clarence
Jr., experiences the pangs of
puppy love with a teenage visitor
(played by beautiful Elizabeth
Taylor), while his younger brothers focus on baseball, the holy
catechism, and a rather unwhole-
some (!) door-to-door business
scheme.

Meanwhile, in the whirl of their
daily life, Mother Day creatively
balances the household accounts
and Father Day refuses to be bap-
tized—and almost one hundred
years will melt away as the whole
family delights in the Day family's eccentricities.

Based on one of the greatest
hits in Broadway history, this de-

lightful film may also introduce
your family to several outstanding
performers, including William
Powell (who also starred in the
popular *Thin Man* movies as amateur detective Nick Charles),
Irene Dunne (a gifted comedienne and dramatic actress who
starred in such films as *The Awful
Truth*, **Show Boat,** and *Anna and
the King of Siam*), and Edmund
Gwenn (whom some will recognize as Kris Kringle from the original **Miracle on 34th Street**).

LIFE WITH MIKEY (1993)
Color, 94 minutes
Cast: Michael J. Fox, Christina
Vidal, Nathan Lane, Cyndi
Lauper, David Krumholtz,
Barbara Hollerman, David
Huddleston, Victor Garber,
Tony Hendra
Director: James Lapine
Screenplay: Marc Lawrence
Comedy
Rated PG
Younger children: OK, with
caution   Older children: VG

Michael J. Fox stars in this entertaining showbiz comedy as a former child TV star, now a grown-
up talent agent specializing in
kid performers.

In business with his brother Ed
(Nathan Lane), they're tempted
to close their doors for good when
Michael meets up with wayward
youngster Angie Vega (Christina
Vidal) when she tries to pick his
pocket. Angie, a poor street kid
living with her sister, has the attitude and personality to become a
star, or so Michael believes. He
gets her a lucrative cookie commercial and she decides to move
in with him—a move that causes
Michael to reflect upon the direction of his life.

Populated with good actors in both the leading and supporting roles (Cyndi Lauper as their secretary; Ruben Blades as Angie's absent father; David Huddleston as the cookie client), and various child novelty acts, *Life with Mikey* may convince kids to stay out of show business, but they'll enjoy this clever backstage tour.

While the film will entertain kids of all ages, it does contain some strong language and incidents which are not ideally suited to younger eyes and ears.

THE LIGHT IN THE FOREST
(1958)
Color, 93 minutes
Cast: James MacArthur, Carol Lynley, Fess Parker, Wendell Corey, Joanne Dru, Jessica Tandy, Joseph Calleia, John McIntire
Director: Herschel Daugherty
Screenplay: Lawrence E. Watkin, based on the novel by Conrad Richter
Historical adventure
Unrated
Younger kids: OK   Older kids: Good

James MacArthur stars in this live-action Disney film (set in 1764) as a white boy named Johnny Butler who was captured by the Delaware Indians when he was 5 years old and reared as a chieftain's son. When the Indians make peace with the British Colonial forces, they give up all their white captives. Johnny reluctantly returns to his parents, but his strong anti-white feelings make his re-adjustment difficult, and he soon clashes with his Indian-hating uncle (Wendell Corey).

Though modest in scale and not very well known, this is a nice lit-

tle pioneer fable with beautiful scenery and period atmosphere, as well as a progressive approach to the depiction of American Indians and a worthy message for children about prejudice.

LI'L ABNER (1959)
Color, 113 minutes
Cast: Peter Palmer, Leslie Parrish, Stubby Kaye, Julie Newmar, Howard St. John, Stella Stevens, Billie Hayes, Joe E. Marks, Bern Hoffman, Robert Strauss
Director: Melvin Frank
Screenplay: Norman Panama and Frank, based on their Broadway musical inspired by the Al Capp comic strip
Musical/Comedy
Unrated
Young children: VG   Older children: VG

One of the most colorful musicals of the 1950s, *Li'l Abner* is a lively re-creation of the Broadway musical based on Al Capp's famous long-running comic strip. Modern kids may not know about Abner or Mammy and Pappy Yokum, but the characters and their cornpone humor are as likable today as they ever were—and young kids in particular should thoroughly enjoy it.

As the film opens, it's a typical day in Dogpatch, U.S.A. Li'l Abner (Peter Palmer) has been taking a special potion brewed by his mammy. When Dogpatch is earmarked for destruction by the U.S. military, Abner sells the juice in order to keep Dogpatch alive. This makes him and his family rich—and turns him into the most eligible bachelor in the U.S. of A. Daisy Mae (Leslie Parrish) has been in love with Abner since they were small, but she is no match for the high-class woman of Abner's dreams. Her name: Apassionata Von Climax (Stella Stevens), a sexy siren who is in fact a spy for the power hungry General Bullmoose (Howard St. John).

The songs and dances are energetic, the comedy is broad and funny in this overlong but entertaining musical. Stubby Kaye, who stopped the show in Broadway's *Guys and Dolls,* is ideally cast as Marryin' Sam and featured in two of the movie's best numbers, "Jubilation T. Cornpone" and "The Country's in the Very Best of Hands."

There is some sexual humor, but like everything else in the film it is wildly exaggerated.

If your kids really like this movie, they might want to check out the original *Li'l Abner* comic strips, which have been reprinted in book form.

LILI (1953)
Color, 81 minutes
Cast: Leslie Caron, Mel Ferrer, Jean Pierre Aumont, Zsa Zsa Gabor, Kurt Kasznar, Amanda Blake
Director: Charles Walters
Screenplay: Helen Deutsch, based on a story by Paul Gallico
Musical
Unrated
Young children: VG   Older children: VG

This charming musical has delighted audiences for years and can still work its wonders on today's youngsters.

It's the story of a 16-year-old orphan (Leslie Caron) who runs away with a traveling carnival and in her hour of despair is consoled by some puppets in the show. In her naïveté, she never connects the relationship she has with these bright, upbeat characters with the fact that they are manipulated by a man she can't stand (Mel Ferrer). He is moody and self-pitying, and she finds him cruel, but with his puppets she is transported to a magical world all her own.

Lili is not a fairy tale but a story in which imagination and reality clash. The magic is in its title character's ability to believe in those puppets and leave her worldly cares behind. When they sing the song "Hi Lili, Hi Lo," you and your kids may find yourselves wanting to escape to that world with her.

There is harshness in this story, as well, in the fact that the puppeteer is disabled (and miserable) and in the jealousies that swirl throughout the carnival, where Lili has a crush on the handsome magician (Jean Pierre Aumont). There is a climactic sequence in which Lili's emotional conflicts are played out in the form of a ballet; if your kids aren't accustomed to this convention, it may take a bit of explaining.

But this is an MGM musical, from 1953 . . . so never fear. There will be a happy ending.

LILIES OF THE FIELD (1963)
Black & white, 97 minutes
Cast: Sidney Poitier, Lilia Skala, Lisa Mann, Isa Crino, Francesca Jarvis, Pamela Branch, Stanley Adams, Dan Frazer
Director: Ralph Nelson
Screenplay: James Poe, based on the novel by William E. Barrett
Comedy-drama

Unrated
Young children: VG   Older
   children: VG

At the peak of his popularity,
America's first and foremost
African-American star, Sidney
Poitier, became the first black
performer to win an Academy
Award in the category of Best
Actor. This was the film that
earned him that honor.

Lilies of the Field is a sweet and
simple film that recounts what
happens when Homer Smith, an
affable ex-soldier, is persuaded by
a Mother Superior (Lilia Skala) to
build a new church for a group of
nuns, refugees from East Germany who have settled in rural
Arizona.

Simple though it may be, *Lilies
of the Field* remains a charming,
humanistic story—an allegory, if
you will, about how mutual respect and understanding can grow
between people of different races
and cultures, especially when they
join together in a common cause,
united by their faith in God.

LIMELIGHT (1952)
Black & white, 145 minutes
Cast: Charlie Chaplin, Claire
   Bloom, Nigel Bruce, Buster
   Keaton, Sydney Chaplin,
   Norman Lloyd, Marjorie
   Bennett, Wheeler Dryden
Director: Charles Chaplin
Screenplay: Charles Chaplin
Comedy-drama
Unrated
Young children: OK   Older
   children: VG

This sentimental, reflective, and
deeply personal tale stars Chaplin
as Calvero, an aging, dispirited
music hall clown who saves a
young ballerina (Claire Bloom)
from suicide. He becomes her
mentor and, in the process, regains his own self-esteem.

There is less out-and-out comedy in this than in any of
Chaplin's other films, and so it
may not appeal to young children
at all. Older kids, especially those
who have shown an interest in
Chaplin, may become involved in
the melancholy story.

Fans of silent film comedy
(young or old) will enjoy seeing
Chaplin's lone screen appearance
alongside his contemporary Buster
Keaton, as they do a music hall
routine onstage together.

THE LION KING (1994)
Color, 88 minutes
Cast: Voices of Jonathan Taylor
   Thomas, Matthew Broderick,
   James Earl Jones, Jeremy
   Irons, Moira Kelly, Niketa
   Calame, Nathan Lane, Ernie
   Sabella, Robert Guillaume,
   Rowan Atkinson, Madge
   Sinclair, Whoopi Goldberg,
   Cheech Marin, Jim Cummings
Directors: Roger Allers and Rob
   Minkoff
Screenplay: Irene Mecchi,
   Jonathan Roberts, and Linda
   Woolverton
Animated feature/Musical
Rated G
Young children: OK, with
   caution   Older children: VG

The Disney studio's all-time biggest hit, *The Lion King* touches
on universal themes in its surefire story. Simba is the young
heir to his father Mufasa's jungle
throne—a throne coveted by Mufasa's cruel brother, Scar. Scar,
with the help of some seedy hye-
nas, arranges for Simba to be
threatened by a wildebeest stampede; when Mufasa comes to his

rescue, Scar causes his brother's death, then convinces Simba that it was his fault. Horrified, Simba runs off, leaving Scar to take over control of Pride Rock. Simba becomes pals with a couple of carefree jungle characters, Timon and Pumbaa, who convince him to share their "Hakuna Matata" philosophy. But when, as a grownup, he encounters his childhood friend, Nala, she tells him how Pride Rock has been victimized by Scar and urges him to return and take responsibility. But it's the wise monkey, Rafiki, who finally shows Simba the way to come to terms with his past and take control of his future.

The songs, by Elton John and Tim Rice, are expertly woven into the fabric of the story, beginning with the rousing "Circle of Life." And even the potentially mushy love song "Can You Feel the Love Tonight?" is punctuated by the delightfully funny coda, sung by Timon and Pumbaa, in which they predict that their friend is "doomed."

Almost Shakespearean in tone, with more than a few echoes of *Hamlet, The Lion King* veers from high drama to low comedy, covering the entire range of human emotion with its all-animal cast. This is why—like Frank Capra's **It's a Wonderful Life**—it touches people so deeply. If Simba didn't suffer so badly and wrestle with a crisis of conscience and identity, he couldn't take his rightful place at the end of the story—and we wouldn't share his ultimate triumph.

Still, this means that young children must endure a terribly painful sequence in which the mighty Mufasa dies and his loving son is made to feel that he's responsible.

It's a wrenching scene that's meant to be upsetting, and it is.

But as with **Bambi** a generation earlier, this Disney film offers a potent message about the continuity of life, even in the face of tragedy.

THE LION, THE WITCH AND THE WITCH AND THE WARDROBE (1988)
Color, 162 minutes
Cast: Richard Dempsey, Sophie Cook, Jonathan R. Scott, Sophie Wilcox
Director: Marilyn Fox
Screenplay: Alan Seymour, based on the novel by C. S. Lewis
Fantasy/Literary classic
Unrated
Younger children: VG Older children: VG

During World War II, four children are sent to live with a professor in the country for safety. While exploring the house, they find an old wooden wardrobe. When Lucy, the youngest, climbs inside the wardrobe, she finds the enchanted land of Narnia, ruled by the evil White Witch, who has made it forever winter—never Christmas—and who turns her enemies to stone. Soon all four children are in Narnia, where Edmund is enticed by the White Witch and her promise to make him a prince and feed him Turkish delight. With the help of sympathetic inhabitants of the land—including talking beavers, fauns, and other mythical creatures—the children seek the King of the Woods, the magical great lion Aslan, for help in saving Edmund, fighting the evil witch, and returning spring to the frozen land of Narnia.

Although originally written as a Christian allegory in 1950 by Oxford literature professor and theologian C. S. Lewis, *The Lion, the Witch and the Wardrobe* works splendidly as pure fantasy. This faithful version, produced for British T.V., is a superb adaptation combining live action, puppetry, and animation. It is presented in three parts on two videotapes and is well worth the time spent to watch it. Two sequels, *Prince Caspian* and *The Silver Chair,* are also available on video.

THE LITTLE ARK (1972)
Color, 100 minutes
Cast: Theodore Bikel, Philip Frame, Genevieve Ambas, Max Croiset, Johan De Slaa
Director: James B. Clark
Screenplay: Joanna Crawford, based on the novel by Jan de Hartog
Adventure
Rated G
Younger kids: OK   Older kids: Good

The Little Ark is about two World War II orphans—a Dutch boy (Philip Frame) and an Indonesian girl (Genevieve Ambas)—who become separated from their foster parents during a flood in 1953 Holland and are rescued by the captain (Theodore Bikel) of a fishing boat. Together with their four pets (a dog, cat, rabbit, and rooster) they have various adventures with the captain while scouring the country for their parents. (They eventually find their father, but discover their mother has drowned, which, along with the intense flood sequence, may frighten younger kids.)

This is one of many fine family films produced by Robert Radnitz, whose other credits include **Sounder** and **A Hero Ain't Nothin' but a Sandwich**. It was well filmed on location, and even features a cute animated sequence where the captain tells the kids the story of an old Dutch sea legend.

LITTLE BIG LEAGUE (1994)
Color, 119 minutes
Cast: Luke Edwards, Timothy Busfield, John Ashton, Jason Robards, Dennis Farina, Ashley Crow, Kevin Dunn, Billy L. Sullivan, Miles Feulner, Jonathan Silverman
Director: Andrew Scheinman
Screenplay: Gregory K. Pincus and Scheinman
Sports/Comedy
Rated PG
Younger children: NG   Older children: OK

One of the less successful baseball-oriented family films of recent vintage, *Little Big League* seems to have all the right ingredients.

Twelve-year-old Billy is a baseball nut. His beloved grandfather knows this well, and when he passes away, he bequeaths the team he owns—the Minnesota Twins—to the boy! Being owner is one thing, but Billy decides to take on the job of manager—which doesn't sit well with his players. Billy tries to reinstill in them the love he has for the game, but along the way he loses sight of what's important in his own life. His friends are forsaken, and he has to be reminded that he's still a kid with his whole life ahead of him.

Little Big League should have been a cute family film, but it has no energy and runs a deadly two hours long. It has a good premise, a well-cast boy in the leading role, and the always welcome Jason Robards as his grandfather. But it drags on and on and on—like an extra-inning game with no end in sight.

Real-life ball players Ken Griffey, Jr., Randy Johnson, and Wally Joyner appear in the cast.

LITTLE BIG MAN (1970)
Color, 139 minutes (originally 150m.)
Cast: Dustin Hoffman, Faye Dunaway, Martin Balsam, Richard Mulligan, Chief Dan George, Jeff Corey, William Hickey
Director: Arthur Penn
Screenplay: Calder Willingham, based on the novel by Thomas Berger
Western/Drama
Rated PG
Younger kids: No Older kids: VG, with caution

A hip and picaresque epic, this is a stunning film that demythologizes the "winning of the West" and stars Dustin Hoffman as a 121-year-old man named Jack Crabb, who claims to be the sole survivor of Custer's Last Stand. Recalling his frontier days to a young historian, Jack reminisces about how, as an orphan, he was raised by the peaceful Cheyenne tribe (who named him "Little Big Man") under the guidance of their wise leader Old Lodge Skins (Chief Dan George) and then put in the care of a minister's amorous wife (Faye Dunaway).

Later, Jack becomes a medicine show con man, befriends Wild Bill Hickok (Jeff Corey) during a brief and spectacularly unsuccessful career as a gunfighter called the Soda Pop Kid, and rejoins his old Indian tribe and marries, only to see his wife and child slaughtered by General Custer (Richard Mulligan). After Jack tries but fails to assassinate Custer, he becomes a drunkard and a hermit. However, eventually he encounters Custer again and, as an Indian scout, leads the megalomaniac general to his doom at the battle of Little Big Horn.

Both hilarious and heartbreaking, this is an ambitious film in every respect, taking the form of a historical and political parable with allusions to Vietnam and containing some appropriately grisly and horrifying massacre scenes.

Kids who haven't been raised on a steady diet of Westerns (as everyone was who grew up in the 1930s, '40s, '50s, and '60s) will not appreciate how revolutionary this film was considered in 1970—or how it paved the way for further revisionist films to come, including **Dances With Wolves** and *Unforgiven.* Part of its mandate was to redress the way Indians had been portrayed in countless Hollywood films. (One facet of its success is that it turned Chief Dan George into a well-known actor and celebrity for the rest of his life.)

Young viewers also may not appreciate some of the film's satiric tone if they're unfamiliar with the way the historical ground covered here had been treated in scores of earlier books and movies.

But the film is so superbly made and well acted that it can spin its tale effectively even with those caveats.

Its violence, however, is extreme at times, and its sexual content is such that only older children should be allowed to watch it.

LITTLE BOY LOST (1953)

Black & white, 95 minutes
Cast: Bing Crosby, Claude
    Dauphin, Christian Fourcade,
    Nicole Maurey, Gabrielle
    Dorziat
Director: George Seaton
Screenplay: George Seaton,
    based on a story by
    Marghanita Laski
Drama
Unrated
Young children: VG Older
    children: VG

After World War II, an American war correspondent sets out to find the son he has lost. During the war, his French wife had fought with the Resistance in occupied France and subsequently was killed by the Nazis. After the war ends the father locates a boy in a Catholic orphanage in Paris who resembles his son and brings the child back to his apartment, hoping to prove the child is his own. Whether he actually can identify the child as his natural son or not, the fact remains that the boy needs a father and he needs the love of a son.

As such, this is a fine film through which to explore the concept of adoption. The story also can be a springboard for a discussion of such war-related topics as underground resistance movements and the separation or loss of family members. There are some interesting postwar Paris locations, and Bing Crosby sings several entertaining songs to lighten the emotionally charged atmosphere.

LITTLE BUDDHA (1993)

Color, 123 minutes
Cast: Keanu Reeves, Chris Isaak,
    Bridget Fonda, Alex
    Wiesendanger
Director: Bernardo Bertolucci
Screenplay: Rudy Wurlitzer and
    Mark Peploe, based on a story
    by Bertolucci
Drama/Religion
Rated PG
Younger kids: OK Older kids:
    Good

Returning to some of the themes he dealt with in **The Last Emperor,** Bernardo Bertolucci crafted a visually gorgeous but cold and uninspired film that intertwines two stories: the 2,500-year-old legend of the Buddha, Siddhartha (Keanu Reeves), and the search for his reincarnation in modern-day Seattle.

The Siddhartha sequences, which are shown as the 9-year-old boy believed to be the reincarnation of the Dalai Lama reads from a book given him by Buddhist monks, are beautifully shot, like a child's storybook come to life and rich with mystical and exotic beauty, but the modern scenes are drab and emotionally detached (and not helped by the actors' passive performances). Bertolucci is never really able to connect the two in a meaningful way.

It's a sincere attempt to introduce Westerners to the tenets of Buddhism, but it's dramatically inert and the philosophical notions about children and spirituality will be over the heads of most kids. The PG rating was awarded for some disturbing images and the mature subject matter.

THE LITTLE COLONEL
(1935)

Black & white, with a color sequence, 80 minutes (also available in computer-colored version)

Cast: Shirley Temple, Lionel Barrymore, Evelyn Venable, John Lodge, Bill "Bojangles" Robinson, Hattie McDaniel, William Burress, Sidney Blackmer

Director: David Butler

Screenplay: William Conselman, based on the novel *The Little Colonel* by Annie Fellows Johnston

Historical comedy/Melodrama/Musical

Unrated

Young children: VG   Older children: VG

This entertaining story of post–Civil War Kentucky is one of Shirley Temple's most memorable motion pictures. The plot involves a Southern colonel who disowns his daughter when she marries a Northerner. Years pass, and the spirited antics of the old man's granddaughter (played, of course, by Shirley) serve to reunite the family. Also, to keep the story moving, there is a subplot dealing with crooks who try to cheat Shirley's dad of land holdings.

Shirley is surrounded by top-notch character actors such as Lionel Barrymore, who plays her grandfather, and Hattie McDaniel as Mom Beck, the Colonel's cook. Shirley does well in her scenes with veteran stage and screen star Barrymore, as the two play equally stubborn members of a willful family. As the grumpy grandfather pokes little Shirley with his cane, and the youngster retaliates by throwing mud pies at his freshly laundered white suit, the whole family will relish the intergenerational fun!

This is the first film in which Shirley tap-danced with legendary African-American dancer Bill "Bojangles" Robinson. Their sequences together are wonderful, and the natural chemistry between them dissolves any possibility for racial or age-related lines of demarcation. However, because the setting is the post–Civil War South, there are stereotypical presentations of blacks that might need some explanation for younger children. Otherwise, this is a lavishly produced film featuring Shirley at her youthful peak.

LITTLE FUGITIVE (1953)

Black & white, 75 minutes

Cast: Richie Andrusco, Rickie Brewster, Winifred Cushing, Will Lee, Jay Williams

Directors: Ray Ashley, Morris Engel, and Ruth Orkin

Screenplay: Ashley, Engel, and Orkin

Comedy-drama

Unrated

Younger kids: Good   Older kids: VG

The Little Fugitive is a classic early example of New York independent filmmaking, made on a shoestring with a great deal of imagination. The story concerns a 7-year-old Brooklyn boy named Joey (Richie Andrusco), who runs away to Coney Island after his older brother, Lennie (Rickie Brewster), tricks him into believing that he has killed him while playing Cowboys-and-Indians. Joey spends the day stuffing himself with hot dogs, riding on the merry-go-round, playing games and going on pony rides before happily reuniting with Lennie and returning home before their mother even finds out what happened.

It's a simple tale that's beautifully observed, featuring vivid semidocumentary photography of the Coney Island amusement park in which one can practically smell the salt air and popcorn. Though the cast members were nonprofessionals and the filmmakers were former still photographers and journalists, it contains infinitely more truth and genuine charm than Hollywood's usual depictions of childhood. It won an award at the Venice Film Festival, received a Best Screenplay Oscar nomination, and was cited by François Truffaut as a major influence on the French New Wave in general and his landmark film **The Four Hundred Blows** in particular.

It's a film the entire family will enjoy discovering together.

LITTLE GIANTS (1994)
Color, 105 minutes
Cast: Rick Moranis, Ed O'Neill, Shawna Waldron, Mary Ellen Trainor, Matthew McCurley, Susanna Thompson, Brian Haley, Devon Sawa, John Madden, Danny Pritchett
Director: Duwayne Dunham
Screenplay: James Ferguson, Robert Shallcross, Tommy Swerdlow, and Michael Goldberg, based on a story by Ferguson and Shallcross
Sports/Comedy
Rated PG
Younger children: VG Older children: VG

Here's a film whose likability makes up for its predictability. Rick Moranis is well cast as a single father who's always lived in the shadow of his older brother,

a local hero and Heisman Trophy winner (Ed O'Neill). When O'Neill organizes a Pop Warner football team and rejects Moranis' tomboy daughter—even though she's a terrific player—her dad decides to start a rival team and admit all the misfits and outcasts who don't rate a place on his brother's roster.

A typical story of underdogs (of two generations) who come out on top, this movie hits all the right notes and gets its fair share of laughs (even though a disproportionate number come from jokes about bodily functions). There's the novelty value of a girl wanting to play football and the even greater novelty of giving her egotistical uncle a scene in which he shows that he's not a cardboard villain.

Real-life football players Emmitt Smith, Tim Brown, Bruce Brown, and Steve Emtman appear as themselves.

LITTLE MAN TATE (1991)
Color, 99 minutes
Cast: Jodie Foster, Dianne Wiest, Adam Hann-Byrd, Harry Connick, Jr., David Pierce, P. J. Ochlan, Debi Mazar, Celia Weston, Danitra Vance, Josh Mostel, George Plimpton
Director: Jodie Foster
Screenplay: Scott Frank
Drama
Rated PG
Younger kids: VG Older kids: VG

Actress Jodie Foster made an impressive directing debut with this story about Fred Tate, a 7-year-old genius torn between Dede, his single, working-class mother (Foster) and Jane Grierson (Wiest), the director of a school for gifted children, who believes she can help Fred's gifts flower. The screenplay is a bit too pat and schematic in setting up young Fred's conflict and the different personalities of the two women in his life who are battling for his heart and mind. (Dede represents love and emotion; Jane represents intellect and order.)

But the film does succeed in capturing the nature of Fred's isolation. Fred is a special young boy, but his genius is only a dramatic extension of the same inner conflicts that all children have. Parents should be ready to discuss the dilemma that he faces: someone who is profoundly aware of his own intelligence and special abilities yet cannot help but feel awkward, lonely, and different because of them.

As director, Foster treats Fred with sympathy and understanding, and extends the same courtesy to Dede and Jane, who both try to do what they think is best for him but realize that that is not necessarily enough.

THE LITTLE MERMAID
(1989)
Color, 82 minutes
Cast: Voices of Jodi Benson, Pat Carroll, Samuel E. Wright, Buddy Hackett, Kenneth Mars, Christopher Daniel Barnes, Ben Wright
Directors: John Musker and Ron Clements
Screenplay: Musker and Clements
Animated feature/Musical
Rated G
Young children: VG   Older children: VG

Ariel is a teenage mermaid who lives in an undersea kingdom where her father, King Triton, rules with an iron hand. But Ariel longs to be part of the human world. Angered by this, Triton orders his assistant, a crab named Sebastian, to watch out for Ariel and keep her away from human beings. In spite of this, Ariel rescues a prince whose ship runs aground. Eric falls in love with Ariel at first sight but doesn't know that she's a mermaid . . . so the foolish girl strikes a bargain with her father's arch-nemesis, the wily Ursula: she will sacrifice her voice in order to become human.

A clever adaptation of the fable by Hans Christian Andersen, *The Little Mermaid* is a delight, with particular appeal for young girls. Who couldn't (or wouldn't) relate to a youngster with big dreams and an impetuous nature? But not every teen has a cute fish like Flounder for a friend or a Jamaican-voiced crab for a chaperon.

The musical numbers, beginning with Ariel's anthem "Part of Your World," and continuing with Sebastian's "Under the Sea" and love song "Kiss the Girl," are the foundation of this movie, which ushered in a new era of animated moviemaking at the Disney studio.

One song, "Les Poissons," requires a taste for black humor, as a fastidious French chef attempts to dice and cook our friend Sebastian!

Some observers questioned the need for the teenage Ariel to be quite so curvy and show cleavage, to boot, in best Barbie fashion. But the film's enormous success with audiences of all ages seems to have answered that criticism.

340

LITTLE MISS MARKER (1934)

Black & white, 80 minutes
Cast: Shirley Temple, Adolphe Menjou, Dorothy Dell, Charles Bickford, Lynne Overman, Warren Hymer
Director: Alexander Hall
Screenplay: William R. Lipman, Sam Hellman, and Gladys Lehman, based on a story by Damon Runyon
Comedy/Melodrama
Unrated
Young children: VG Older children: VG

Shirley Temple appears in her first starring role, as a child who becomes involved with an uncouth gang of bookies and gamblers who hang around the racetrack. During the course of the film, she is transformed from an innocent tyke into a tough, half-pint version of her adult playmates, who have names like Sorrowful Jones, Sore Toe, Benny the Gouge, and Bangles. (Such characters were distinctively the creation of Broadway columnist Damon Runyon.)

There is a wonderful sequence in which Bangles holds a party in the little girl's honor at which the gang members dress up as knights of King Arthur's court. But there also are some very sad elements to the script. For instance, Little Miss Marker, as the child is dubbed by the bookies, has no mother; her father leaves her in the hands of the gamblers and then he kills himself.

Otherwise, this is a touching story featuring a number of colorful characters. It is a diverting and fanciful yarn that will appeal even to the younger children. It has been remade as *Sorrowful Jones* (1949), with Bob Hope and Lucille Ball, *Forty Pounds of Trouble* (1963), with Tony Curtis, and again as *Little Miss Marker* (1980), with Walter Matthau, but the 1934 original remains the best of them all.

LITTLE NEMO: ADVENTURES IN SLUMBERLAND (1992)

Color, 85 minutes
Cast: Voices of Gabriel Damon, Mickey Rooney, Rene Auberjonois, Danny Mann, Laura Mooney, Bernard Erhard, William E. Martin
Directors: Masami Hata and William Hurtz
Screenplay: Chris Columbus and Richard Outten
Animated feature/Musical
Rated G
Younger kids: OK Older kids: OK

Little Nemo is an elaborate animated fantasy based on Winsor McCay's classic comic strip. Little Nemo, hero of his dream world, Slumberland, accidentally unleashes the evil Nightmare King. Together with his companions, Icarus (his flying squirrel), Professor Genius, and a trickster named Flip, Nemo travels to Nightmare Land to rescue King Morpheus and win the hand of lovely Princess Camille.

The whole movie is a dream, allowing for some wild hallucinatory sequences, imaginative art direction, and wonderful cartoon creations. On the downside, it is a routine "quest" story, with mundane dialogue and forgettable songs (from the Sherman Brothers).

This is a lavish production, but some sensitive, younger kids will be put off by the dark, nightmarish aspects of the story. Parents should be forewarned.

THE LITTLE PRINCE (1974)
Color, 88 minutes
Cast: Richard Kiley, Steven
    Warner, Bob Fosse, Gene
    Wilder, Joss Ackland, Clive
    Revill, Victor Spinetti,
    Graham Crowden, Donna
    McKechnie
Director: Stanley Donen
Screenplay: Alan Jay Lerner,
    based on the book by Antoine
    de Saint-Exupéry
Fantasy/Literary classic
Rated G
Younger children: OK   Older
    children: OK

The little prince (Steven Warner)
journeys from his small planet
and, after several stops on other
minuscule planets, arrives on
earth to make friends with a
downed pilot (Richard Kiley),
who has crash-landed in the
desert.

Although it's a pretty film, *The
Little Prince* has somehow lost the
endearing charm of Antoine de
Saint-Exupéry's cherished classic.
With the exception of Bob Fosse
as the Snake and Gene Wilder as
the Fox, this musical is sluggish
and leaden, and never gets air-
borne. Rather than watch the
film, sit your kids down and read
them the book. It will take less
time than watching this disappointing adaptation, and your
family will get more out of it.

THE LITTLE PRINCESS
(1939)
Color, 91 minutes
Cast: Shirley Temple, Richard
    Greene, Anita Louise, Ian
    Hunter, Cesar Romero, Arthur
    Treacher, Marcia Mae Jones,
    Sybil Jason
Director: Walter Lang
Screenplay: Walter Ferris and

Ethel Hill, based on the novel
    by Frances Hodgson Burnett
Drama/Musical/Literary classic
Unrated
Young children: VG   Older
    children: No

Back in the late 1930s, Shirley
Temple was in line to play Dorothy in **The Wizard of Oz**. When
Judy Garland won the part, her
role in *The Little Princess* became
a consolation prize.

Shirley is cast as a little girl
who's been raised by her loving
father (Ian Hunter); when he goes
off to fight in the Boer War, he
reluctantly leaves her behind at a
boarding school for girls. This
leads to conflict, comedy, and suspense as she crosses paths with a
contemptible villainess, a pair of
young lovers, a sturdy old codger,
and an engaging comic second banana (perfectly played by Arthur
Treacher) who prances and sings
along with Shirley. (Later in the
film she even encounters England's Queen Victoria!)

The Little Princess was filmed
before in 1917, as a silent film
starring Mary Pickford, and brilliantly remade in 1995; this version was tailored to Shirley's
screen persona and may not
please purists who know the Frances Hodgson Burnett book. But
fans of Shirley will likely have a
great time with it; it's one of only
two films she made in Technicolor.

Older kids might prefer the
1995 remake.

A LITTLE PRINCESS (1995)
Color, 97 minutes
Cast: Eleanor Bron, Liam
    Cunningham, Liesel Matthews,
    Rusty Schwimmer, Arthur
    Malet, Vanessa Lee Chester,

Errol Sitahal, Vincent Schiavelli
Director: Alfonso Cuaron
Screenplay: Elizabeth Chandler and Richard LaGravenese, based on the novel by Frances Hodgson Burnett
Drama
Rated G
Young children: VG   Older children: VG

It remains a mystery why this enchanting remake of the Frances Hodgson Burnett classic did not win a bigger audience. Fortunately, its availability on video allows it to be discovered for years to come.

A Little Princess is the story of Sara Crewe (Liesel Matthews), a young and privileged British girl who lives in India with her widowed soldier father. The two are devoted to one another, but their relationship is interrupted when Captain Crewe is called into service at outbreak of World War I. He decides to leave Sara at a New York boarding school with an impeccable reputation. Its headmistress is the imposing Miss Minchin (Eleanor Bron), a classically hissable villainess who is threatened by Sara's likability, keen imagination, and kind heart.

When the child's father is reported killed in battle and funds no longer are available to pay her tuition, Miss Minchin takes revenge by treating Sara as a Cinderella-like slavey. As the story unfolds, Sara comes to realize several hard but important life lessons: Not all people are rich. Not all little girls live like princesses. Not all children have loving parents to protect them.

A Little Princess is storytelling at its best, beautifully realized by

director Alfonso Cuaron and his creative team. (The look of the film is exquisite in every detail.) It is perfect family fare for the young and the young at heart.

While there are some upsetting passages—as when Sara's father is reported dead—the story is told with heart, and there is no real question but that Miss Minchin is going to get her just deserts. The youngest children will need some hand-holding to get through the tougher moments.

THE LITTLE RASCALS (1994)
Color, 72 minutes
Cast: Travis Tedford, Bug Hall, Britanny Ashton Holmes, Kevin Jamal Woods, Zachary Mabry, Ross Elliot Bagley, Sam Saletta, Blake McIver Ewing; guest stars Mel Brooks, Whoopi Goldberg, Daryl Hannah, Reba McEntire, Mary Kate and Ashley Olsen, Raven-Symone, Lea Thompson, Donald Trump, George Wendt
Director: Penelope Spheeris
Writer: Paul Guay and Spheeris
Comedy
Rated G
Younger children: OK   Older children: No

For years, devotees of Hal Roach's wonderful comedy shorts *The Little Rascals* (originally released to theaters as *Our Gang*) dreaded the oft-threatened remakes and TV revivals, knowing that it would be hard, if not impossible, to match the unique quality of the originals.

This feature, then, came as a pleasant surprise to many fans, since it does manage to capture some of the spirit of the original series. It brings back its most familiar and well-loved characters, including Spanky, Alfalfa, Darla, Buckwheat, Porky, Waldo, Butch, and of course Petey, the dog with the ring around his eye. (There's even a brief appearance by schoolteacher Miss Crabtree, played here in a cameo appearance by Daryl Hannah.)

The setting is intended to be Anyplace, U.S.A., and the date Anytime, although it has a modern-day backdrop. The plot is pretty simple: Alfalfa has violated the code of the He-Man Woman Hater's Club by making goo-goo eyes at Darla, which leads to misunderstandings among the Gang. When their beloved clubhouse is destroyed, it becomes necessary to raise money to rebuild it; if one of them can win a go-cart race, they'll be all set.

The main difference between this film and the original series is that this one is *cute* and aimed almost entirely at very young children. The original films were *funny* and meant to be enjoyed by adults as well as kids. Gags here are threadbare or iffy at best; potential jokes are set up but never pay off. What's more, the film has many lulls despite its brief running time.

Most annoying is the occasional interjection of '90s epithets, which seem wholly unnecessary and out of place. Why, in an otherwise squeaky-clean children's film, should one Rascal exclaim, "Bite me!"

Still, in all, for young children, the movie is innocuous and some of the performers—particularly Bug Hall as Alfalfa and Brittany Ashton Holmes as Darla—are genuinely appealing.

If you want to have a really good time with your kids, seek out the original Little Rascals on tape.

A LITTLE ROMANCE (1979)
Color, 108 minutes
Cast: Diane Lane, Thelonious Bernard, Laurence Olivier, Arthur Hill, Sally Kellerman, David Dukes, Broderick Crawford
Director: George Roy Hill
Screenplay: Allan Burns, based on the novel by Patrick Cauvin
Comedy-drama/Romance
Rated PG
Younger children: Probably not   Older children: Yes, with caution

Diane Lane plays a sensitive, lonely, and intelligent American girl who lives with her mother and stepfather in Paris. There she meets a bright young French boy (Thelonious Bernard), whose father is a taxi driver, and they develop an innocent teenage romance. Lane's flighty, pretentious, and much-married mother—currently carrying on with a movie director (David Dukes)—is appalled, mostly because she thinks the boy is common, and tries to break them up. They persevere, but when Lane's kind, quiet stepfather (Arthur Hill) plans to take the family back home to the States, she becomes desperate to find a way to remain with her boyfriend. A shabby, aging con man (Laurence Olivier) has told them that any couple that kisses under the Bridge of Sighs in Venice at sunset is truly in love, so they run away to Venice, to ensure that their love will last forever.

In many ways, *A Little Romance* is a very engaging film, but parents need to be forewarned that this film contains some inappropriate language and sexual references, including a short scene set in the projection booth of a porno house. Diane Lane is luminous; she and Thelonious Bernard play young teenagers at just the age when a romantic myth would have its greatest impact. They make *A Little Romance* totally believable and absolutely charming. Georges Delerue's lyrical music score, which adds to the warmth of the film, won an Academy Award.

Not only does it reveal life in another culture and appeal to the romantic in all of us, but it also shows adults from a kid's-eye view, which is irresistible to most young viewers.

THE LITTLE SHOP OF HORRORS (1960)

Black & white, 70 minutes
Cast: Jonathan Haze, Jackie Joseph, Mel Welles, Dick Miller, Myrtle Vail, Leola Wendorff, Jack Nicholson, John Shaner, Meri Welles, Wally Campo, Jack Warford
Director: Roger Corman
Writer: Charles B. Griffith
Science fiction–horror/Comedy
Unrated
Young children:
  Marginal   Older children: OK

Seymour Krelboined (Haze) and Audrey Fulquard (Joseph) work in the Skid Row flower shop of skinflint Gravis Mushnik (Welles), who is impressed by the weird plant that Seymour has created. The goof keeps it in a coffee can and has named it Audrey Jr., since he's in love with Audrey (Sr.). The plant looks droopy, until one night Seymour accidentally drops blood into its open maw. Audrey Jr. revives, and eventually starts talking, demanding more blood. Eventually, it wants *more* than blood, and the hapless Seymour is reduced to feeding it a series of accidentally killed passersby. But the plant wants even more.

There really had never been a movie like this before, in its blend of horror, comedy, satire, and just plain wackiness. Roger Corman directs in a droll, dry tone that makes writer Charles B. Griffith's vivid lines even more colorful, and the inspired cast rises to the occasion. (One rose even higher: masochistic dental patient Jack Nicholson.)

The Little Shop of Horrors is also something of a legend in the history of low-budget films; it was shot in just two days and three nights!

Even though there's nothing gruesome about the movie, its humor will probably sail over the heads of younger children. Older kids might raise a skeptical eyebrow at the sheer and obvious cheapness of the movie, but if they stick with it, they're likely to love it.

LITTLE SHOP OF HORRORS (1986)

Color, 88 minutes
Cast: Rick Moranis, Ellen Greene, Vincent Gardenia, Steve Martin, Tichina Arnold, Tisha Campbell, Michelle Weeks, James Belushi, John Candy, Christopher Guest, Bill Murray, Miriam Margolyes, Levi Stubbs (voice of Audrey II)
Director: Frank Oz
Screenplay: Howard Ashman, based on his play, from the film written by Charles B.

345

Griffith and directed by Roger Corman
Science fiction–horror/Musical comedy
Rated PG
Young children: No   Older children: OK

Seymour (Moranis), who works in the Skid Row florist shop owned by Mushnick (Gardenia), is hopelessly in love with salesgirl Audrey (Greene). She, however, is devoted to her sadistic biker dentist boyfriend, Orin (Martin). One day, Seymour finds an unusual plant and brings it back to the shop, where it soon becomes a popular attraction. It suddenly withers and seems as if it's about to die when, by accident, Seymour discovers that it thrives on human blood!

Little Shop of Horrors is a most unusual hybrid: a satiric musical comedy horror film! As such, it has elements that will appeal to kids—a tuneful score, colorful production design, a terrific cast with a number of familiar faces. Its satiric moments will probably go over their heads—from the idealized suburban life that Audrey dreams about in her song "Green," to the fact that dental patient Bill Murray actually likes being in pain.

But hovering over all of this is the inescapable fact that Audrey II eats people. And while the film is mostly comic in tone, Audrey's intentions are deadly serious. This might upset or confuse younger kids; it left adult audiences a bit unsettled when the film was first released. It's not that we see the blood; it's that we've been lured into an entertaining world that's dominated by a "Mean Green Mother from Outer Space," to

quote the title of Audrey II's self-defining song.

THE LITTLEST REBEL (1935)
Black & white, 70 minutes
Cast: Shirley Temple, John Boles, Jack Holt, Karen Morley, Bill "Bojangles" Robinson, Guinn "Big Boy" Williams, Willie Best, Frank McGlynn, Sr.
Director: David Butler
Screenplay: Edwin Burke
Historical drama/Musical
Unrated
Young children: VG   Older children: VG

After the popularity of **The Little Colonel,** Shirley starred in this Civil War drama, which shows how war can break up families and destroy homes. Shirley plays a little Southern girl who is so brave that she attempts to save her father from being hanged after he is falsely accused of spying for the Confederacy. She takes her plea directly to President Abraham Lincoln, in an outstanding sequence which blends drama with homespun humor.

The film boasts several entertaining musical numbers featuring traditional songs such as "Polly Wolly Doodle" and "Believe Me If All Those Endearing Young Charms," with Shirley performing duets with legendary African-American tap dancer Bill "Bojangles" Robinson. The script provides Shirley with one of her strongest storylines.

Even so, taking into account the characters of the house slaves, adults should prepare younger members of the family for some stereotypical images of blacks. Also, the script allows for the death of Shirley's mother, a point which—although handled gracefully—still might upset younger children.

LITTLE WOMEN (1933)
Black & white, 115 minutes
Cast: Katharine Hepburn, Joan Bennett, Paul Lukas, Frances Dee, Jean Parker, Edna May Oliver, Douglass Montgomery, Spring Byington
Director: George Cukor
Screenplay: Sarah Y. Mason and Victor Heerman, based on the novel by Louisa May Alcott
Drama/Literary classic
Unrated
Young children: VG   Older children: VG

If family members have seen the 1994 version of Alcott's famous novel so often that they can recite the dialogue, then this early treatment of the beloved story might make for a pleasant surprise. The saga of a Civil War–period New England mother left alone to tend her flock of girls while father fights the good fight was written with a keen edge by Mason and Heerman, who were rewarded with an Academy Award for Best Screenplay of 1933.

Katharine Hepburn's portrayal of Jo, the most energetic and creative of the "little women," is stunning. She plays the part rough-and-tumble, determined, and tomboyish. No modern parent should resist showing this version for fear that its Hollywood creators had reduced this sturdy heroine to sugary femininity. It is a sincere and authentic interpretation of the novel, one that still maintains its charm, strength, and vigor.

Hepburn is matched by a perfect cast of costars.

LITTLE WOMEN (1994)
Color, 118 minutes
Cast: Winona Ryder, Susan Sarandon, Gabriel Byrne, Trini Alvarado, Samantha Mathis, Kirsten Dunst, Claire Danes, Christian Bale, Eric Stoltz, John Neville, Mary Wickes
Director: Gillian Armstrong
Screenplay: Robin Swicord, based on the novel by Louisa May Alcott
Drama/Literary classic
Rated PG
Young children: VG   Older children: VG

If the household has not yet seen this version of Louisa May Alcott's most famous novel, then rush to the video store to rent a copy. The March family has never been more captivating than in this filming of the classic family chronicle. The script is true in almost every way to the original novel, and the sets, props, and costumes beautifully capture Civil War–era New England.

Only in the depiction of Marmee, the mother of the "little women," does the story sometimes seem a bit unbalanced. As she spouts feminist doctrine, the time period feels more like the 1990s than the 1860s. On the other hand, there were free-thinking women even in those seemingly dark ages, and if ever there were a family of one-of-a-kind women, it is the March clan! Although it is too recent a production to be called a family classic, it is safe to predict that the passing of time will award the film this distinction.

The youngest, most impressionable children may have a tough time with the sad passages of the story, especially the death of the beloved Beth.

LOCAL HERO (1983)

Color, 111 minutes
Cast: Burt Lancaster, Peter
  Riegert, Fulton MacKay,
  Denis Lawson, Jenny Seagrove
Director: Bill Forsyth
Screenplay: Bill Forsyth
Comedy
Rated PG
Young children: OK Older
  children: VG

A Houston oil exec has to talk the townspeople of a Scots village into accepting the presence of a new refinery. He thinks it's going to be business as usual, but the locals have a con game of their own in place to fight off the corporate raiders.

A war may be fought by conquering the enemy, but absorbing the enemy accomplishes the same end nonviolently. That's slowly learned not only by the buttoned-down exec (Peter Riegert) but by his lunatic boss (Burt Lancaster, in gruff-but-lovable mode).

One of the best-loved films of the 1980s, *Local Hero* has a quirky charm all its own. It's so low-key and offbeat, however, that it might not communicate with kids who are accustomed to broader, in-your-face comedy. If they see it as a fable, however, they may find themselves succumbing to its delights.

Inoffensive yet insightful, whimsical yet weighty, it's a delightful film for viewers of any age who like to go off the beaten path.

LOGAN'S RUN (1976)

Color, 120 minutes
Cast: Michael York, Richard
  Jordan, Jenny Agutter, Roscoe
  Lee Browne, Farrah Fawcett-
  Majors, Michael Anderson, Jr.,
  Peter Ustinov
Director: Michael Anderson
Screenplay: David Zelag
  Goodman, from the novel by
  William F. Nolan and George
  Clayton Johnson
Science fiction/Thriller
Rated PG
Younger kids: Tense Older
  kids: OK

By the year 2274, war and pollution have wiped out most of the world's population; those remaining live (mildly) hedonistic lives in domed cities. At age 30, however, people turn themselves in for "renewal," only half-aware that they're being killed to maintain a stable population. Many of those who are aware of this flee to join Sanctuary, a supposed underground organization of other "runners." Logan (York), one of the "sandmen" who hunt down runners and kill them, is convinced to pose as a runner to find out more about Sanctuary—but before long, he's really running for his life.

One of the more bizarre manifestations of the "don't trust anyone over 30" slogan of the 1960s, *Logan's Run* is science fiction lite. The pastel designs make it look as if it's taking place in a particularly boring shopping mall (where some of it was shot); the issues are trivial and the action uninvolving. However, it does present one of those self-contained worlds that attracts a lot of youngsters (like *Star Wars*, *Star Trek*, *Babylon 5*, etc.), and the movie was popular enough to spin off a short-lived TV series.

The first half of the film sets up the society, and will be of more interest to brighter kids than the big-chase second half, when their more action-oriented friends might wake up. In general, children are more likely to enjoy this film than their parents and older siblings.

THE LONG, LONG TRAILER
(1954)
Color, 96 minutes
Cast: Lucille Ball, Desi Arnaz, Marjorie Main, Keenan Wynn, Gladys Hurlbut
Director: Vincente Minnelli
Screenplay: Albert Hackett and Frances Goodrich, based on the novel by Clinton Twiss
Comedy
Unrated
Younger kids: VG   Older kids: VG

While their comedy series *I Love Lucy* was one of the top hits on the small screen, Lucille Ball and husband Desi Arnaz took their act to the big screen—in living color—in this amusing slapstick romp. Although they're not playing the Ricardos, their characters are essentially the same, as harried hubby Desi lets dizzy wife Lucy talk him into buying a huge trailer home for a honeymoon on wheels and lives (barely) to regret it. Their scenic tour across the country is filled with one comical catastrophe after another, including a disastrous attempt by Lucy to scramble some eggs while the trailer is tilted, a hilarious encounter with an exasperated traffic cop (Keenan Wynn), and a classic scene where Desi practically destroys his in-laws' house while try-ing to park the humongous trailer in their driveway.

While the film doesn't have the enduring quality of classic *I Love Lucy* episodes, it's consistently funny and the duo's legions of fans—including kids of all ages—will undoubtedly enjoy every minute of it.

LONG JOHN SILVER (1954)
Color, 109 minutes
Cast: Robert Newton, Connie Gilchrist, Kit Taylor, Grant Taylor, Rod Taylor
Director: Byron Haskin
Screenplay: Martin Rackin
Action-adventure/Swashbuckler
Unrated
Younger kids: OK   Older kids: Good

Robert Newton reprised his title role from the 1950 Disney version of **Treasure Island** for this unofficial sequel made by the same director. The plot uses some of the characters from Robert Louis Stevenson's novel but also invents some new ones, as the one-legged buccaneer and young Jim Hawkins (Kit Taylor) plan a return trip to Treasure Island and then battle rival pirate Mendoza (Lloyd Berrell) for the booty.

Attractive Australian locations and a typically overripe performance by Newton make this a fairly entertaining and fast-moving swashbuckler—though not quite as good as the original.

LOOK WHO'S TALKING
(1989)
Color, 93 minutes
Cast: John Travolta, Kirstie Alley, Olympia Dukakis, George Segal, Abe Vigoda, Twink Caplan; voices of Bruce Willis, Joan Rivers

Director: Amy Heckerling
Screenplay: Amy Heckerling
Comedy
Rated PG-13
Young children: No Older
  children: VG

This pleasant romantic comedy tells the story of Mollie (Kirstie Alley), a Manhattan accountant who is involved in an affair with one of her married clients. One day, she discovers she is pregnant. Her loutish boyfriend eventually brushes her off, and Mollie realizes that she must prepare herself for single parenthood. Enter James (John Travolta), a cab driver. He and Mollie "meet cute"—while she is going into labor. James becomes smitten with Mollie and her new baby, who is named Mikey. He tries to woo her by persuading her that he would make a perfect daddy for Mikey.

Much of the appeal of *Look Who's Talking* derives from the clever device of having all of Mikey's thoughts, from before birth through toddlerhood, communicated via the unmistakable voice of Bruce Willis. Kids especially will take to this gimmick. However, the film is inappropriate for the younger kids because much of what Mikey has on his mind is a wee bit risqué. This is unfortunate, because the film is otherwise perfect fare for young children.

Beyond its humor, *Look Who's Talking* offers an interesting view of contemporary relationships. Mollie is a white-collar snob who doesn't view James as a potential romantic partner because he is a lowly cab driver. As the story runs its course, she comes to realize that James is a nice guy—and great father material.

Look Who's Talking was followed by two sequels. The first is *Look Who's Talking Too* (1990), a slapdash, embarrassingly unfunny film that should be avoided. The second is *Look Who's Talking Now* (1993), which would appeal to younger viewers because it introduces a pair of dogs whose thoughts are amusingly voiced by Danny DeVito and Diane Keaton. Unfortunately, *Look Who's Talking Now* also is rated PG-13, for off-color dialogue.

THE LORD OF THE RINGS
(1978)
Color, 131 minutes
Cast: Voices of John Hurt,
  Christopher Guard, William
  Squire, Michael Scholes,
  Anthony Daniels, Simon
  Chandler, Norman Bird.
Director: Ralph Bakshi
Screenplay: Chris Conkling and
  Peter S. Beagle, from the
  novels by J. R. R. Tolkien
Animated feature
Rated PG
Younger kids: OK, with
  caution Older kids: OK

In the mythical realm of Middle Earth, a hobbit named Frodo undertakes a quest to protect a magical ring from the hands of Dark Lord Sauron. Accompanied by wizard Gandalf and assorted warriors, elves, and dwarves, Frodo encounters and overcomes the many forces of evil.

Animation director Ralph Bakshi, who blazed a trail for adult animation with such films as *Fritz the Cat* and *Heavy Traffic,* turned his attention to one of the best-loved fantasy series in all of fiction. This film encompasses two of Tolkien's novels, *The Fellowship of the Ring* and *The Two*

Towers, and does a fair job of bringing them to life.

Animation fans were distressed by the fact that most of the action was rotoscoped—that is, traced from footage of live actors performing these roles. While this makes for amazingly lifelike expressions and movements, it strikes many people as a form of cheating. (Why not simply make a live-action film?) But more damaging is the fact that after more than two hours, the story does not come to an end! A planned sequel never came to pass.

Young children will probably be bored after 20 minutes, while older kids will be disappointed that the film has no ending. Though there are a few moments of inspired magic, *The Lord of the Rings* is a long journey that leads nowhere.

LOST HORIZON (1937)

Black & white, 132 minutes
Cast: Ronald Colman, Jane Wyatt, John Howard, Edward Everett Horton, Margo, Sam Jaffe, H. B. Warner, Isabel Jewell, Thomas Mitchell
Director: Frank Capra
Screenplay: Robert Riskin, based on the novel by James Hilton
Adventure-fantasy/Literary classic
Unrated
Young children: VG Older children: VG

This is an extraordinary, imaginative story of a group of unlikely mates who set off in an airplane to escape a war-torn Asian country and eventually wind up in paradise. When their plane is downed, the group must trek through miles of dangerous snowy terrain before entering the sunshine of the Valley of the Blue Moon at Shangri-La, whose residents live in a setting of unparalleled beauty and experience peace, good health, and long life unheard of in the chaos of the outside world.

As the secrets of Shangri-La unfold, older children will be interested in the story developments and philosophy lessons, while even the youngest members of the audience will be attentive to the hazardous treks through ice and snow, the wonderful fantasy settings, the comedy of Edward Everett Horton, and the youth of Shangri-La at school and at play.

Made at a time when much of the world was at or on the brink of war, its pacifist message was particularly pointed. That aspect of the film seems timeless—even if the barking performance of John Howard, as Ronald Colman's impatient brother, seems strained today.

Shown in edited formats for many years, this film was restored to its original length with a complete soundtrack that is at brief moments accompanied only by still photos of the original action. Rather than treating that as a deterrent to young viewers, it might serve as an educational tool to illustrate the problems that film archivists confront in restoring older films so that we can see them the way they were originally shown to audiences.

LOST IN SPACE (1998)

Color, 130 minutes
Cast: Gary Oldman, William Hurt, Matt LeBlanc, Mimi Rogers, Heather Graham, Lacey Chabert, Jack Johnson, Jared Harris
Director: Stephen Hopkins

Screenplay: Akiva Goldsman
Space opera
Rated PG-13
Young children: No   Older
   children: OK

Though much too scary for tots, this $70 million revamp of the CBS 1965–68 Space Family Robinson is half of a good movie.

Top-billed Oldman plays Dr. Smith, while actorly Hurt and no-nonsense Rogers play the parents with problems between them. Graham and Chabert are somber Judy and grumpy Penny, while newcomer Johnson makes a fine wide-eyed Will, and *Friends'* LeBlanc is the perfect cocky pilot Don West.

Together with hulking Robot (enthusiastically voiced by the series' original Dick Tufeld), they tumble into another galaxy, following a script that's more or less the original pilot plus the first couple of episodes. On a budgetary scale a hundred times greater than original producer Irwin Allen ever dreamed of, this very loud PG-13 theme park ride set in A.D. 2048 has silicon spiders, a hyperspace hurtle through the sun, and a kinda cute new Jim Henson Creature Shop character called Blawp.

However, a long middle act bogs the movie down in "Maybe Father Doesn't Know Best" and gets very tedious. It's a blow from which the film never recovers.

Young people who love outerspace sagas may not mind, but there are so many better films of this genre they could watch, why encourage them to waste more than two hours on this one?

THE LOST WORLD (1925)
Black & white, 65 minutes
Cast: Bessie Love, Lloyd
   Hughes, Lewis Stone, Wallace
   Beery, Arthur Hoyt, Margaret
   McWade, Bull Montana
Director: Harry Hoyt
Screenplay: Marion Fairfax, from
   the novel by Sir Arthur Conan
   Doyle
Adventure/Science fiction
Unrated
Young children: Good   Older
   children: Good

Even after seventy-five years, this remains the only really good film version of Conan Doyle's wonderfully entertaining novel. However, its plot did provide the basic template for almost all other dinosaurs-still-live stories ever since, including **King Kong** and **Jurassic Park**.

The volcanic-tempered Professor Challenger (Wallace Beery) proposes an expedition to South America to investigate whether it is true that dinosaurs still live, a claim based on the notes of a missing explorer. He's accompanied by a newspaperman (Lloyd Hughes), a great white hunter (Lewis Stone), the daughter (Bessie Love) of the missing man, and another skeptical scientist (Arthur Hoyt).

After some travail, the brave little band scales the plateau and discovers that yes, indeed, dinosaurs still live there—and some of them are very hungry. They're also pursued by an ape man (Bull Montana) but manage to return safely to London, taking with them a live brontosaurus, which is not such a good idea.

This lively, entertaining movie is a good introduction both to silent films in general and to the old ways of doing special effects. Younger children, who are rarely critical about this kind of thing, are more likely to have a good time with the movie than more jaded teenagers—but the sheer exuberance of the film (and its remarkable similarity to so many later films) might win them over.

The dinosaurs here—sometimes seen in eye-popping herds—were all rendered by the great Willis O'Brien through the painstaking process of stop-motion animation. Doyle himself was so thrilled by the results that before the film itself was released, he'd occasionally show footage of the dinosaurs to lecture audiences, without explaining that they were actually only a few inches high, moved a frame at a time to achieve a semblance of motion.

THE LOST WORLD: JURASSIC PARK (1997)
Color, 129 minutes
Cast: Jeff Goldblum, Julianne Moore, Pete Postlethwaite, Arliss Howard, Richard Attenborough, Vince Vaughn, Vanessa Lee Chester, Peter Stormare, Harvey Jason, Richard Schiff, Joseph Mazzello, Ariana Richards
Director: Steven Spielberg
Screenplay: David Koepp, from the novel by Michael Crichton
Rated PG-13
Young children: Too scary
  Older children: OK, but scary

Ian Malcolm (Goldblum) hasn't been doing very well since he got back from Jurassic Park, and resents being summoned by John Hammond (Attenborough). The ailing Hammond tells a shocked Malcolm that there is a second island, Isla Sorna, where the dinosaurs were bred before being taken to the Jurassic Park island. Hammond wants Malcolm to join an expedition to Isla Sorna, this time not to exploit the dinosaurs, but to preserve them.

At first, Ian refuses, but when he learns that his girlfriend, paleontologist Sarah Harding (Moore), is already on the island, he joins documentarian Nick Van Owen (Vaughn) and specialist Eddie Carr (Schiff) as they head for the island. They soon find Sarah, who's gleefully photographing a family group of Stegosauruses, and also learn that Kelly (Vanessa Lee Chester), Malcolm's 12-year-old daughter, has stowed away in the van.

Soon, however, a flock of dinosaur catchers hired by Hammond's greedy nephew Ludlow (Howard) arrives; Ian and his group want to keep the living dinosaurs a secret, and a conflict arises between the two groups . . . not to mention the problems that arise between the humans and the carnivorous dinosaurs still roaming the island.

The movie is strung on major action set-pieces, all of which work splendidly, although there's some sag between them. Not everything depends on the dinosaurs: there's a nail-biting sequence involving a van dangling over the side of a cliff. It's a beautifully engineered thrill ride guaranteed to make even the most jaded audiences shriek and giggle with terror and delight. However, it's not as good as **Jurassic Park,** because the plot is so contrived, and there are too many dips between the thrills on this particular rollercoaster.

As with the first film, you'll have to decide if you should show this to your kids, especially if they're crazy about dinosaurs. The thrills are potent, and that's not to be taken lightly.

THE LOVE BUG (1968)
Color, 108 minutes
Cast: Dean Jones, Michele Lee, David Tomlinson, Buddy Hackett, Joe Flynn, Benson Fong, Joe E. Ross, Barry Kelley, Iris Adrian, Andy Granatelli (as himself)
Director: Robert Stevenson
Screenplay: Don Da Gradi and Bill Walsh, based on a story by Gordon Buford
Comedy/Fantasy
Rated G
Younger children: VG   Older children: VG

At the height of the popularity of the Volkswagen Beetle, Disney made *The Love Bug* and its three sequels. Herbie, the Love Bug, is a magical little car with a determined personality; he befriends Jim (Dean Jones), who doesn't realize Herbie's power, and with Jim at the wheel begins winning car races, to the annoyance of the villainous Thorndyke (David Tomlinson).

With a slight but incident-filled story, a colorful hero (the Beetle, that is, not the humans), a likable cast, and plenty of slapstick and special-effects comedy, *The Love Bug* is as surefire as they come. The Disney team responsible for most of the studio's biggest live-action hits was behind this enormous success, and they knew how to please an audience.

The follow-up films are not nearly as good, although they too are peppered with sight gags that younger kids will respond to.

LUCAS (1986)
Color, 100 minutes
Cast: Corey Haim, Kerri Green, Charlie Sheen, Courtney Thorne-Smith, Winona Ryder, Thomas E. Hodges
Director: David Seltzer
Screenplay: David Seltzer
Drama
Rated PG-13
Young children: OK, with caution   Older children: Yes

Precocious but physically under-developed 14-year-old Lucas is so deeply in love with the new girl in town, an older woman named Maggie (she's 16), that he's willing to do anything to get her attention, even to the point of going out for football and getting himself creamed.

Haim is captivating as the love-struck high schooler, whose pluck and heart keep him going against all odds.

The directorial debut for screenwriter Seltzer (**Table for Five,** *Six Weeks*), it's a genuine sleeper with its realistic emotions in all the right places. Anyone who's going through the trials of teendom (or geekdom)—or remembers what it was like—will relate to *Lucas*.

Does the kid get the girl or not? A better question: Is the ending a good one? Yes, and a realistic one, about how things always work out, even if not as anticipated.

Of additional interest today is seeing Winona Ryder in her film debut, as Rina.

Lucas is rated PG-13 for some locker-room sex humor and one emphatic use of a four-letter word.

M

MA AND PA KETTLE AT HOME (1954)

Black & white, 81 minutes
Cast: Marjorie Main, Percy Kilbride, Alan Mowbray, Ross Elliot, Alice Kelley, Brett Halsey, Mary Wickes, Irving Bacon, Emory Parnell, Oliver Blake
Director: Charles Lamont
Screenplay: Kay Lenard
Comedy
Unrated
Young children: VG   Older children: VG

Usually, movies in a series get worse as the years go by. Here's the exception: the sixth and best in the nine-film run of Universal comedies about the down-home Kettles and their brood of children, plus assorted friends, neighbors, and long-lost relatives, all butting heads on a chicken farm in Cape Flattery, Washington.

The exuberant cornball humor is definitely on hand in this hilarious entry, where Ma (gravel-voiced Marjorie Main) and Pa (laconic Percy Kilbride) try hard to impress a visiting East Coast magazine editor (veteran character actor Alan Mowbray) who holds the promise of a college scholarship over a Kettle kid's head. The result is one slapstick gag after another, with a great closing chase that's worth the price of the video rental by itself.

If your family enjoys this entry, you might go back to the origin of the series by watching *The Egg and I,* a cute 1947 comedy in which city folk Claudette Colbert and Fred MacMurray escape to the joys of country life (much like a later couple did in TV's *Green Acres*). It's in this film that Ma and Pa Kettle were introduced; they scored such a hit that they earned their own series. All nine of the films, beginning with *Ma and Pa Kettle* (aka *Further Adventures of Ma and Pa Kettle*), are available on video.

MADELINE (1998)

Color, 90 minutes
Cast: Frances McDormand, Hatty Jones, Nigel Hawthorne, Stephane Audran, Iristian De al Osa
Director: Daisy von Scherler Mayer
Screenplay: Mark Levin and Jennifer Flackett, from a story by Malia Scotch Marmo, Levin, and Flackett, based on the books by Ludwig Bemelmans
Comedy/Adventure
Rated G
Young children: VG   Older children: OK

Anyone who has ever read—or had read to them—the charming *Madeline* books, written and illustrated by Ludwig Bemelmans, will enjoy this sweet film adaptation, which captures both the look and the spirit of the original stories quite well. It was filmed entirely in Paris, where the stories all take place. Newcomer Hatty Jones is an appealing heroine, and Oscar winner Frances McDormand is ideally cast as Miss Clavell, the stern headmistress with a twinkle in her eye.

Elements from several of the books are incorporated with original material to fashion a new story. Madeline has an attack of appendicitis, falls into the River Seine, and discovers a plot to kidnap her new neighbor, Pepito (the son of the Spanish ambassador). But most important, when the owner and benefactor of the girls' school in Paris dies, her husband decides to sell the old house. What will become of the girls . . . and Miss Clavell?

Madeline is an easygoing film designed to amuse and entertain young children; older kids will probably find it too bland.

THE MAGIC SWORD (1962)
Color, 80 minutes
Cast: Gary Lockwood, Basil Rathbone, Estelle Winwood, Anne Helm, Liam Sullivan
Director: Bert I. Gordon
Screenplay: Bernard C. Schoenfeld, based on a story by Bert I. Gordon
Adventure/Fantasy
Unrated
Younger kids: OK Older kids: Good

A juvenile fantasy adventure set in medieval England, *The Magic Sword* concerns a young knight named Sir George (Gary Lockwood), who tries to rescue a beautiful princess (Anne Helm) from the wicked sorcerer Lodac (the incomparably hammy Basil Rathbone). George's stepmother (Estelle Winwood), who's a good witch, provides him with a magic sword, shield, and stallion, as well as six resurrected knights as assistants.

Though hampered by a low budget, the amusing, if unsophisticated (and sometimes genuinely scary) special effects, involving giant ogres, miniaturized people, and a two-headed fire-breathing dragon, should capture the imagination of little boys who are fond of gaudily colored comic-strip sword-and-sorcery tales.

THE MAGNIFICENT AMBERSONS (1942)
Black & white, 88 minutes
Cast: Tim Holt, Joseph Cotten, Dolores Costello, Anne Baxter, Agnes Moorehead, Ray Collins, Richard Bennett, Erskine Sanford
Director: Orson Welles
Screenplay: Orson Welles, based on the novel by Booth Tarkington
Drama/Literary classic
Unrated
Young children: OK Older children: VG

Orson Welles' follow-up project to *Citizen Kane* is in many ways as brilliant, despite the radical re-cutting and reshooting done by RKO executives without Welles' consent. The film centers on a wealthy small-town family that is so cemented in its old-fashioned attitudes that its members shrivel and fail as the world around them becomes modern and mechanized, and their middle-class compatriots flourish. The focus of the drama is George, the fair-haired scion of the Amberson clan. He is a pampered, spoiled-rotten child, and it will be no surprise that he ages into an unpleasant, maladjusted good-for-nothing.

The scenario is as much a character study as it is a parable of the changes in American lifestyles that resulted from the industrial revolution of the early years of the 20th century. There is much fruit for discussion here. What makes this film so outstanding is Welles' unique style of storytelling, which incorporates the best of cinema with radio technique, allowing the plot to be furthered and the characters deepened via narration.

The film is a gem of cinematography and character development, and will especially appeal to young people with a flair for the artistic. The sequence of the horse-driven sleigh ride through the snow is one of the most picturesque and dreamlike moments in film history.

MALCOLM (1986)
Color, 86 minutes
Cast: Colin Friels, John Hargreaves, Lindy Davies, Chris Haywood, Charles "Bud" Tingwell, Beverly Phillips, Judith Stratford
Director: Nadia Tass
Screenplay: David Parker
Comedy
Rated PG-13
Young children: No Older children: VG

This likable slapstick comedy is surefire entertainment. The title character is a shy, none-too-bright young man (Colin Friels) who lives the life of a hermit in his late mother's house. However, Malcolm is possessed with a very special talent: he has the ability to create and construct nifty Rube Goldberg–like contraptions. He uses them to go about the everyday business of retrieving his mail, summoning his pet cockatoo

for feeding, and transporting empty milk bottles to the market. Eventually, Malcolm is drawn into a life of crime, as he uses his oddball genius to plan an elaborate bank robbery with his new tenant, an ex-con.

Kids will be enchanted by the endless toys and gadgets conjured up by Malcolm. However, some of the profanity in its script makes the film unsuitable for children. This is unfortunate, as *Malcolm* otherwise would be ideal fare for kids of all ages.

The film is dedicated to director Nadia Tass's late brother, who was the inspiration for the character of Malcolm.

MALCOLM X (1992)
Color, 201 minutes
Cast: Denzel Washington, Angela Bassett, Albert Hall, Al Freeman, Jr., Delroy Lindo, Spike Lee, Theresa Randle, Kate Vernon, Lonette McKee, Tommy Hollis, Giancarlo Esposito, Craig Wasson, John Ottavino, David Patrick Kelley, Shirley Stoler
Director: Spike Lee
Screenplay: Lee and Arnold Perl, based on the book *The Autobiography of Malcolm X,* as told to Alex Haley
Drama
Rated PG-13
Younger kids: OK, with caution Older kids: VG

Spike Lee's excellent biography follows the controversial black leader's rise from street hustler to national spokesman for the Nation of Islam. This is invaluable as history and first-rate as moviemaking, a complex portrait of a complex man, embodied beautifully by Washington. Parents should be ready to discuss all the facets of Malcolm X's life covered by the film: his loose-living ways as a young man, his time in jail, his conversion to Islam, his advocacy of self-defense for African-Americans, and his later philosophical change upon visiting Mecca.

These concepts might be difficult for younger children to grasp, but Lee presents them in a clear, lucid way that is never stuffy or preachy, and he employs only a few of the visual stylistic flourishes he is famous for. This absorbing film (which, while three hours long, seems to fly by) is an ideal way to introduce children to an important and oft-misunderstood figure in American history, and it's as good an incentive as there is to get them to read *The Autobiography of Malcolm X*.

There are upsetting moments of violence, some strong language, and depiction of drug use (early on), all of which combined to earn this film an appropriate PG-13 rating.

THE MAN CALLED FLINTSTONE (1966)
Color, 87 minutes
Cast: Voices of Alan Reed, Mel Blanc, Jean VanderPyl, Gerry Johnson, Don Messick, Janet Waldo, Harvey Korman, Paul Frees, June Foray
Directors: William Hanna and Joseph Barbera
Screenplay: Harvey Bullock and Ray Allen
Animated musical
Rated G
Younger kids: OK   Older kids: OK

Austin Powers, move over! Fred Flintstone, it turns out, is an exact double of secret agent Rock Slag,

who has been injured on the job. Fred is asked to take his place by helping locate an international spy in Paris. This allows the Flintstones, the Rubbles, and their children to travel the world and seek out adventure in this feature version of the pioneer animated sitcom.

Animation here is a few notches better than the series but certainly no threat to Disney. The 1960s spy-movie craze (launched by the success of James Bond) is the basis for humor here, with seven songs (including one sung by Louis Prima!) to move the story along.

Kids will enjoy this, and parents may derive a few laughs; it's no classic, but it is a pleasant diversion, especially for *Flintstones* fans.

THE MAN FROM SNOWY RIVER (1982)
Color, 115 minutes
Cast: Kirk Douglas, Tom Burlinson, Sigrid Thornton, Jack Thompson, Lorraine Bayly, Tommy Dysart, Bruce Kerr, Terence Donovan
Director: George Miller
Screenplay: John Dixon and Fred Cullen
Western adventure
Rated PG
Young children: OK   Older children: VG

A. B. "Banjo" Patterson's rip-roarin' poem, itself based on age-old Aussie legends, is the skeleton for a script, set in the 1888 outback, about an orphan boy who goes to work taming horses for a wealthy rancher, only to fall for his boss's daughter.

While the sources were founded in heroic feats on the prairie, the movie is purely and simply about horseflesh: rippled, muscular, sweaty, and always on the run. The scenic beauty of the background landscapes provides a suitably broad canvas for the extraordinary horsemanship.

Kirk Douglas, the sole American actor in the cast, has a hoot playing both the cattleman and his one-legged prospector brother, while the young Australian leads are excellent.

This is a rousing, old-fashioned film the whole family can enjoy. It may be hokey and simplistic, but it's tremendously entertaining, too.

Followed by an almost as good sequel, the not unexpectedly titled *Return to Snowy River*.

THE MAN IN THE IRON MASK (1939)

Black & white, 110 minutes
Cast: Louis Hayward, Joan Bennett, Warren William, Joseph Schildkraut, Alan Hale, Walter Kingsford, Marion Martin, Peter Cushing
Director: James Whale
Screenplay: George Bruce, based on the novel by Alexandre Dumas
Swashbuckler-adventure/Literary classic
Unrated
Young children: OK   Older children: VG

Here is a thrilling and full-blooded 17th-century romance/adventure story of sibling rivalry, court intrigue, dank dungeons—in short, all the elements of classic storytelling. Featuring D'Artagnan and his legendary cohorts the Three Musketeers, the action-packed tale revolves around Philippe, a lighthearted chap who is an heir

to the throne of France, a position currently held by his evil identical twin Louis XIV. Threatened by Philippe's sudden appearance in Paris, sadistic Louis throws his brother into the Bastille with a deadly, locked iron mask to hide the young man's all-too-familiar face.

Leonardo DiCaprio fans may be curious to see this exciting early treatment of the classic Dumas tale, but be warned that even in this version, younger children might be frightened by the concept of the locked mask.

THE MAN IN THE IRON MASK (1998)

Color, 117 minutes
Cast: Leonardo DiCaprio, Jeremy Irons, John Malkovich, Gérard Depardieu, Gabriel Byrne, Anne Parillaud, Judith Godreche, Edward Atterton, Peter Sarsgaard
Director: Randall Wallace
Screenplay: Randall Wallace, based on the novel by Alexandre Dumas
Swashbuckler-adventure/Literary classic
Rated PG-13
Young children: No   Older children: VG

A double dose of DiCaprio highlights this literate, entertaining version of the Dumas classic. Leonardo is cast as twin brothers Louis XIV and Philippe, and illustrates why he is no mere pretty-boy teen idol as he offers a fine set of performances. Louis XIV is by far the showier role, and he transforms the character into a thoroughly hissable and believable villain—a young man perfectly willing to let his own brother rot in prison, his face bound inside an iron mask, while he lives to see his tiniest whim obeyed.

DiCaprio is surrounded by a choice cast, headed by Irons, Malkovich, Depardieu, and Byrne as, respectively, Aramis, Athos, Porthos, and D'Artagnan. It is a pleasure seeing Irons playing a heroic character for a change, instead of tiresomely thin and pale, bedraggled men victimized by sexual longing. Depardieu is a hoot as the comically earthy, life-loving Porthos. However, his character is depicted as unabashedly sexually voracious, and in so doing the film takes on an adult sensibility.

In its very first scene, there are several sexual references and scatological humor. That, plus some of the in-your-face (albeit bloodless) violence, makes this inappropriate for some of the younger children.

MAN MADE MONSTER
(1941)
Black & white, 59 minutes
Cast: Lon Chaney, Jr., Lionel Atwill, Anne Nagel, Frank Albertson, Samuel S. Hinds
Director: George Waggner
Screenplay: Joseph West (pseud. of George Waggner), from a story by H. J. Essex, Len Golos, and Sid Schwartz
Science fiction–horror
Unrated
Young children: OK, with caution   Older children: OK

Chaney plays a character strongly suggested by his famous role as Lennie in **Of Mice and Men**; here he is a friendly, not-too-bright carnival performer known for his electrical stunts. Unscrupulous scientist Atwill experiments on

him, subjecting him to increasingly powerful doses of electricity, which finally allow him to completely control Chaney. Lon also now glows—and kills with his electrical touch.

This abruptly short movie (not even an hour long) was the first major horror film to star Lon Chaney, Jr. It was a hit, as was **The Wolf Man** that soon followed, and the actor became even more identified with horror roles than his father had been. Chaney was a limited actor but, when given roles within his range, could deliver oddly touching performances, as here.

The film is reasonably well suited for younger children; Chaney is obviously under the control of the real villain and remains sympathetic throughout the story. He even has a dog that's devoted to him. But children might wonder, as we do, if twenty pages weren't ripped out of the script just before shooting started.

THE MAN WITHOUT A FACE (1993)
Color, 114 minutes
Cast: Mel Gibson, Nick Stahl, Margaret Whitton, Fay Masterson, Richard Masur, Gaby Hoffmann, Geoffrey Lewis, Michael DeLuise, Ethan Phillips, Jean De Baer, Viva
Director: Mel Gibson
Screenplay: Malcolm MacRury, based on the novel by Isabelle Holland
Drama
Rated PG-13
Young children: No   Older children: VG

This involving drama, which marked Mel Gibson's debut behind the camera, is a wonderful film for preteens and adolescents. The setting is a coastal town in Maine, where a relationship develops between Chuck Norstadt, a forlorn youngster who (for good reason) is alienated from his family, and Justin McLeod, a former prep school Latin instructor. McLeod is the title character: half his face and body have been horribly scarred in an automobile accident, and he lives reclusively in an eerie seaside house.

One of the key points of the story is the foolishness of lampooning individuals who are in any way "different." The local children ridicule him, calling him derisive nicknames, and their parents make him the subject of endless gossip. McLeod even is haunted by rumors of child abuse and pedophilia—the "mature subject matter" that earns *The Man Without a Face* a PG-13 rating—and the community comes to view the friendship between man and boy with distrust and cynicism.

But beneath his disfigurement and beyond the harassment, McLeod is a compassionate human being who still has a contribution to make to society. He does that by becoming Chuck's mentor and friend. Meanwhile, Chuck matures as McLeod helps him learn to determine right from wrong and truth from lies, and to make his own decisions.

THE MAN WHO WOULD BE KING (1975)
Color, 129 minutes
Cast: Sean Connery, Michael Caine, Christopher Plummer, Saeed Jaffrey, Shakira Caine
Director: John Huston
Screenplay: John Huston and Gladys Hill, based on the story by Rudyard Kipling
Action-adventure
Rated PG
Younger kids: No Older kids: VG

Sean Connery and Michael Caine give roguishly charming performances as Daniel Dravot and Peachy Carnahan, two crooked ex-British soldiers turned con men who journey to Kafiristan in the 1880s in search of fame and fortune, and set themselves up as kings to the primitive natives who have never seen Europeans before.

This adaptation of Rudyard Kipling's tall tale is an old-fashioned action-adventure in the grand Hollywood manner of **Gunga Din** and **Lives of a Bengal Lancer**. Wryly mixing straight action with a tongue-in-cheek attitude, the story is given an extra dimension by the framing device in which Dravot and Peachy meet Kipling himself (wonderfully played by Christopher Plummer), who was a newspaperman in India at the time, telling him of their extraordinary plan.

Parents who've already weaned their kids on vintage adventure yarns will enjoy sharing this film, one of the last of its kind. The colonialism and superior attitude toward "the natives" is vintage Kipling, and may require some explanation. The story will probably confuse very young children, and in any event the PG-rated violence means it's best suited to older kids.

MAN, WOMAN AND CHILD
(1983)
Color, 99 minutes
Cast: Martin Sheen, Blythe
    Danner, Craig T. Nelson,
    David Hemmings, Nathalie
    Nell, Maureen Anderman,
    Sebastian Dungan, Arlene
    McIntyre
Director: Dick Richards
Screenplay: Erich Segal and
    David Zelag Goodman, based
    on Segal's novel
Drama
Rated PG
Younger children: OK, with
    caution   Older children: VG

Keep the hankies nearby. This
adult family-crisis film is a well-
made soap opera, based on a
book by Erich (*Love Story*) Segal.

The happy home of Bob Beckwith (Martin Sheen), his wife, and
two daughters is interrupted when
Bob learns that a woman he once
had an affair with has been killed
in a car accident. It gets worse:
she has been raising a son—*his*
son—in France. Beckwith con-
fesses to his wife and invites the
boy into their home.

Blythe Danner is excellent as
the wife, Sheila, who is brokenhearted over her husband's un-
faithfulness and resentful toward
the boy.

Some tearjerkers earn their tears
honestly, and this is such a film.
While it deals with an adult situation—the indiscretion of a husband, the resentfulness of a
wife—it paints a picture that older
children should easily relate to.
Its emotions are probably too intense for young viewers.

It's a good, straightforward film
with a story that's presented in
entirely believable fashion. Even

young people can use a good cry
now and then.

MARCH OF THE WOODEN
SOLDIERS (1934) (aka **Babes
in Toyland**)
Black & white, 73 minutes (also
    available in computer-colored
    version)
Cast: Stan Laurel, Oliver Hardy,
    Charlotte Henry, Felix Knight,
    Henry Kleinbach (Brandon),
    Jean Darling, Johnny Downs,
    Florence Roberts, Marie
    Wilson
Directors: Gus Meins and
    Charles R. Rogers
Screenplay: Nick Grinde and
    Frank Butler
Comedy/Fantasy/Musical
Unrated
Young children: VG, with
    caution   Older children: VG

There's no better family introduction to the slow-burn hilarity of
Laurel and Hardy than this
comedy-skewed version of Victor
Herbert's 1903 holiday operetta
Babes in Toyland, which for legal
reasons has been retitled *March
of the Wooden Soldiers*.

It's no secret Herbert wanted to
replicate the success of that same
year's stage version of *The Wizard of Oz*, so he concocted a similar musical fable, with nursery
rhyme characters like Bo-Peep
and Mary Mary Quite Contrary in
the magical kingdom of Toyland.

The scenario expands to include the ample presence of Laurel and Hardy as bumbling
assistants to the short-tempered
Toymaker. In this adaptation of
the story, there's oodles of room
in the story for very funny byplay
between the two, who rent a
room from Mother Peep (the old
woman who lives in a shoe), are

362

friendly with Tom Tom the Piper's Son, and play with an irresistible knick-knack called a pee-wee.

The villainous Barnaby, who has designs on innocent Bo-Peep and threatens to evict Mother Peep from her shoe, is played in the broadest comic-opera fashion, but the climactic attack of the Bogeymen is pretty potent at times, and would certainly scare very young children. On the other hand, it would be a shame for kids to miss the wondrous fantasy of this production, which has Santa Claus as one of its key characters, the Three Little Pigs scampering about, and toy soldiers coming to life . . . all set to Victor Herbert's melodious songs.

Stan and Ollie's comedy is icing on the cake.

THE MARK OF ZORRO
(1940)
Black & white, 93 minutes
Cast: Tyrone Power, Basil Rathbone, Linda Darnell, Gale Sondergaard, Eugene Pallette, J. Edward Bromberg, Montagu Love
Director: Rouben Mamoulian
Screenplay: John Tainter Foote, Garrett Fort, and Bess Meredyth, based on the novel *The Curse of Capistrano* by Johnston McCulley
Swashbuckler/Action-adventure
Unrated
Younger kids: OK   Older kids: VG

Tyrone Power is at his most dashing and romantic in this classic about the adventures of the master swordsman Diego Vega in early 1800s California. When Diego's aristocrat father is deposed and replaced as alcalde by the oppressive Don Luis Quintero (J. Edward Bromberg), with his brutal captain, Esteban Pasquale (Basil Rathbone), Diego springs into action and becomes an avenging masked bandit named Zorro by night, while posing as a foppish dandy by day.

This ranks among the very best Hollywood swashbucklers, zestily performed, beautifully photographed, and featuring an Oscar-nominated score by Alfred Newman. The climactic sword fight between Diego and Pasquale is a doozy that rivals Rathbone's similarly elaborate duel with Errol Flynn in **The Adventures of Robin Hood**. It may still bring a gasp or two from kids who think they've seen it all.

While not as glitzy or as self-conscious as 1998's *The Mask of Zorro* with Antonio Banderas—and a full forty minutes shorter—this exceptionally well made film can still hold its own. There's a good reason that every generation seems to get its own Zorro—the character is irresistible.

MARS ATTACKS! (1996)
Color, 106 minutes
Cast: Jack Nicholson, Glenn Close, Annette Bening, Pierce Brosnan, Danny DeVito, Martin Short, Sarah Jessica Parker, Michael J. Fox, Rod Steiger, Tom Jones, Lukas Haas, Natalie Portman, Jim Brown, Lisa Marie, Sylvia Sidney, Paul Winfield, Pam Grier, Jack Black, Joe Don Baker, Christina Applegate, Jerzy Skolimowski, Barbet Schroeder
Director: Tim Burton
Screenplay: Jonathan Gems, based on the Topps Trading Card series of trading cards
Science fiction/Satiric comedy

Rated PG-13
Young children: No Older
  children: OK

A fleet of flying saucers from
Mars surrounds the Earth and
then, just as the title says, attacks
in this hard-to-describe movie
from Tim Burton. A big cast including major names, such as Jack
Nicholson and Glenn Close as
President Dale and his First Lady,
seem to be having a great time
as the human race scurries about
trying to avoid getting blasted by
the skinny, big-brained, skull-
faced Martians.

This disappointing film treats its
characters as jokes but takes the
Martians seriously—a contradic-
tion that keeps us continually off
guard, so we're never quite sure
when (or whether) to laugh, as
when Secret Service agents hustle
the terrified Dales through the
White House, overrun with Martians, with explosions going off all
around them and bodies being
flung through the air!

The computer-generated Martians, designed in a classic bug-
eyed manner, are fascinating to
watch at first, but we never do
find out why they're attacking.
They're just here to blow us up.
For all we can tell, they're attacking because it's fun.

Young children may not get the
joke (such as it is) at all and could
well be disturbed by the often
graphic violence and some of the
more bizarre touches, such as
what happens to Sarah Jessica
Parker and Pierce Brosnan. Preteens and teenagers might prefer
a straighter but less accomplished
science fiction yarn like **Independence Day.** But if your older children have a warped sense of
humor, this may appeal to them.

MARVIN'S ROOM (1996)
Color, 98 minutes
Cast: Meryl Streep, Diane
  Keaton, Leonardo DiCaprio,
  Gwen Verdon, Robert De
  Niro, Hume Cronyn, Dan
  Hedaya, Hal Scardino, Victor
  Garber, Margo Martindale,
  Cynthia Nixon
Director: Jerry Zaks
Screenplay: Scott McPherson,
  based on his play
Drama
Rated PG-13
Young children: No Older
  children: VG

This extremely moving drama,
based on the acclaimed play by
Scott McPherson, tells the story
of two long-estranged sisters: Bessie (Diane Keaton) has devoted
her adult life to caring for her
flaky aunt (Gwen Verdon) and
her elderly father Marvin (Hume
Cronyn), who has been bedridden
with a stroke for two decades.
Lee (Meryl Streep), Bessie's self-
involved sibling, has been raising
two kids on her own and can't relate to her deeply troubled eldest
son (Leonardo DiCaprio). Lee
and her kids are reunited unexpectedly when Bessie calls with a
health crisis of her own.

Marvin's Room is a touching
and believable drama that explores what it means to care for
another human being during the
best and worst of times. The scenario is crammed with emotion
and, to its great credit, respects all
of the characters in spite of their
imperfections and inconsistencies.

Adolescents may relate best to
the boy, well played by Leonardo
DiCaprio; alienated from his
mother and the world around
him, he finds it easier to talk to
his aunt, and during the course of

the story, he discovers new things about himself. The question is, will he be willing to make a sacrifice to help someone else, when he's lived a life of utter selfishness until now?

Marvin's Room deals with highly emotional issues, but its positive attitude toward caring for loved ones (so movingly expressed by Bessie) has much to impart to young people. There is some strong language here and there, but *Marvin's Room* is a worthwhile film for mature children to watch.

MARY POPPINS (1964)
Color, 140 minutes
Cast: Julie Andrews, Dick Van Dyke, Glynis Johns, David Tomlinson, Ed Wynn, Hermione Baddeley, Karen Dotrice, Matthew Garber, Elsa Lanchester, Arthur Treacher, Reginald Owen, Reta Shaw, Arthur Malet, Jane Darwell
Director: Robert Stevenson
Screenplay: Bill Walsh and Donald Da Gradi, based on the *Mary Poppins* books by P. L. Travers
Musical/Fantasy
Unrated
Young children: VG Older children: VG

Mary Poppins is Walt Disney's masterpiece, one of the best films ever made, and most certainly a family classic.

Julie Andrews earned an Academy Award with her winning performance as the nanny who's practically perfect in every way . . . and who sails into the lives of Jane and Michael Banks in 1910 London. With a flighty mother and a fussbudget of a father, the Banks children have

worn out a series of nannies, but this one is different: She works magic, takes them on incredible journeys, and introduces them to Bert, an equally magical fellow who is at one moment a chimney sweep, another a sidewalk chalk artist. Eventually, Mary's presence has its effect on Mr. and Mrs. Banks, who join their children in a triumphant show of togetherness while flying a kite.

Words can't do justice to this supercalifragilisticexpialadocious movie. It's brimming with imagination, flights of fancy, and wonderful songs (by the Sherman Brothers, who won an Oscar for "Chim Chim Cheree"). The lessons learned are, in best Poppins tradition, sugar-coated, and the film is the kind one can watch over and over again.

Word has it that the eccentric author of the original Poppins stories, P. L. Travers, didn't like this film. She must be the only one who felt that way.

MASK (1985)
Color, 120 minutes
Cast: Cher, Sam Elliott, Eric Stoltz, Estelle Getty, Richard Dysart, Laura Dern, Harry Carey, Jr., Lawrence Monoson, Marsha Warfield, Barry Tubb, Andrew Robinson
Director: Peter Bogdanovich
Screenplay: Anna Hamilton Phelan
Drama
Rated PG-13
Younger kids: OK, with caution Older kids: VG

Mask tells a moving story based on the life of Rocky Dennis (Eric Stoltz), a teenager who was afflicted with a rare disease, craniodiaphyseal dysplasia, that disfigured his face. He tries to live a normal life with his mother Rusty (Cher), who is fiercely loyal to him but hangs out with bikers and is rather irresponsible when it comes to her own life. Rocky's appearance could be off-putting at first to younger children, but his sweet, considerate nature is abundantly clear from the start, and Eric Stoltz makes the character into a likable, regular teenager—one with everyday dreams and hobbies, who treats everyone the way he would like to be treated.

The somewhat saccharine elements of the story—Rocky's too good-to-be-true attitude and the bikers who all come across as wonderful folks who are best buds with Rocky—is balanced by the portrait of Rusty, a woman who "sleeps around" and frequently spirals into booze and drugs. The discrepancy between her behavior and Rocky's upstanding virtues provides the story with some interesting and unsettling ambiguities. Like **The Elephant Man**, another film about a sweet-souled person trapped behind a distorted face, *Mask* does not exploit Rocky's state, and the message of inner beauty will be appreciated by parents and children alike.

Rusty's unusual lifestyle leads this film into PG-13 territory, but there is nothing exploitative in the film.

THE MASK (1994)
Color, 101 minutes
Cast: Jim Carrey, Cameron Diaz, Peter Riegert, Peter Greene, Amy Yasbeck, Richard Jeni, Orestes Matacena, Timothy Bagley, Nancy Fish, Ben Stein
Director: Charles Russell
Screenplay: Mike Werb, based on the comic book created by Mike Richardson
Comedy/Fantasy
Rated PG-13
Younger kids: OK, with caution   Older kids: VG

Mild-mannered bank clerk Stanley Ipkiss (Carrey) stumbles upon an ancient wooden mask that transforms him into a green-faced hellion who is able to alter his physical form and give free rein to his wildest impulses.

As a movie, this is no great shakes, with a nonexistent plot and uninteresting supporting characters. (The exceptions are Diaz as a sexy singer and a Jack Russell terrier named Max who steals several scenes.) But as a vehicle for Carrey's manic, over-the-top brand of humor, it hits the spot, with some terrific set pieces—memorably, a sequence when the green-faced crazy inspires a bunch of police to dance as he sings Desi Arnaz's signature song, "Cuban Pete."

There are also amazing computer-generated effects which turn Ipkiss' wild alter ego into a living Tex Avery cartoon, and seem a natural extension of Carrey's seemingly rubber-limbed body.

Parents should note that some of the mayhem is a bit rough, surprisingly dark, and mean-spirited for such a throwaway film (hence the PG-13), but kids who are fans of Carrey (and the cartoon series based on the film) will probably not care too much.

THE MASQUE OF THE RED DEATH (1964)
Color, 90 minutes
Cast: Vincent Price, Hazel Court, Jane Asher, David

Weston, Patrick Magee, Nigel
Green, Skip Martin
Director: Roger Corman
Screenplay: Charles Beaumont
and R. Wright Campbell, from
the story by Edgar Allan Poe
Horror/Literary classic
Unrated
Younger kids: No   Older kids:
OK

The finest of Roger Corman's Poe
movies, this was shot in England,
where dollars went a bit further at
the time, so the film is particularly
lavish in terms of sets, costuming,
and design. It even follows the
Poe story reasonably closely, as
the wicked Prince Prospero (Price,
of course) holds an elaborate
masque while plague sweeps the
countryside beyond his castle
walls.

At times the movie slips into
the conventional, and sometimes
Corman tries too hard for "artistic" effects, but overall, this is one
of the best American horror movies of its period. Whether kids of
today will relate to it is another
matter.

MATILDA (1996)
Color, 93 minutes
Cast: Danny DeVito, Rhea
Perlman, Embeth Davidtz,
Pam Ferris, Mara Wilson, Paul
Reubens, Tracey Walter,
Kiami Davael, Jon Lovitz
Director: Danny DeVito
Screenplay: Nicholas Kazan and
Robin Swicord, based on the
novel by Roald Dahl
Comedy-drama/Fantasy
Rated PG
Younger kids: OK, with
caution   Older kids: OK

Matilda is a dark fairy tale of a
movie, based on the popular chil-

dren's novel by Roald Dahl. The
story concerns little Matilda
Wormwood (Mara Wilson), a special girl in two ways. Unlike her
trashy, loutish parents (Danny
DeVito and Rhea Perlman), she
is highly intelligent and caring . . .
and she happens to have telekinetic powers. Her home life is
miserable, and school isn't much
better: her principal (Pam Ferris)
is a hellish woman who throws
disobedient children out the window! Matilda finds a friend and
soul mate in Miss Honey (Embeth
Davidtz), and together they combat the ignorance and evil all
around them.

Roald Dahl's jet-black sense of
humor is an acquired taste for
some adults, though kids seem to
understand his twisted approach
right away. The characters here
are patently unreal, so when the
witchlike principal swings a
schoolgirl in circles by her pig-
tails, we're not supposed to take
it seriously.

Kids will enjoy the over-the-top
approach and relate to the "us"
(kids) versus "them" (grownups)
point of view; parents may find it
all a little too much. Young Mara
Wilson is a gem, and she radiates
charm and goodness on-screen.

The youngest children may not
"get" the comic exaggeration in
Matilda and could be frightened
by the hideous characters and
their equally hideous deeds . . .
but on the other hand, they might
take great delight in seeing these
monstrous people get their
comeuppance.

MATINEE (1993)
Color, 98 minutes
Cast: John Goodman, Cathy
Moriarty, Simon Fenton, Omri
Katz, Lisa Jakub, Kellie

Martin, Jesse Lee, Lucinda Jenney, Robert Picardo, Jesse White, Dick Miller, John Sayles, David Clennon, Belinda Balaski, Archie Hahn, Luke Halpin, Robert Cornthwaite, Kevin McCarthy, William Schallert
Director: Joe Dante
Screenplay: Charles S. Haas, from a screen story by Haas and Jerico Stone
Period comedy-drama
Rated PG
Young children: OK Older children: VG

In 1962, 15-year-old Gene Loomis (Fenton) and his younger brother, Dennis (Lee), have just moved to Key West with their mother (Jenney); Gene's father, who's in the Navy, has gone to sea on an emergency basis, which we soon learn is part of the blockade thrown around Cuba to prevent Khrushchev from shipping more missiles to Castro—the Cuban Missile Crisis.

Gene is a quiet, lonely boy, in love with monster movies and science fiction, and this helps him make a new friend in local teenager Stan (Katz), for Gene knows everything about Lawrence Woolsey (Goodman), the horror movie producer-director who's debuting his newest film, *Mant!,* at the local theatre.

Matinee is a wistful, funny, and nostalgic look at youth, exploitation movies, and Key West. You can easily accuse the film of having too many characters and at least two climaxes too many, but Charlie Haas' script and Dante's direction have a tenderness and clear-eyed nostalgia for these lost times, which make up for the movie's occasional lapses.

Woolsey is largely based on the late, great William Castle, master of showmanship. Like Castle's, Woolsey's movies are driven by their gimmicks, and *Mant!* is laden with them: seat buzzers, thunderous rumbles, sparks, clouds of dust, etc. Goodman understands this guy down to his cheap socks and seems to be having a fine time in the role. There's one wonderful sequence in which Woolsey explains to a wide-eyed Gene just why people love scary movies so; it's a magical moment and one of the most heartfelt and moving paeans to cheap thrills ever.

Matinee is really aimed at adults who feel nostalgic for this period—and for a kind of movie experience that doesn't exist anymore—but kids who enjoy the shlocky films of today might find some connection here, in the context of a charming and enjoyable comedy.

MAX DUGAN RETURNS
(1983)
Color, 98 minutes
Cast: Marsha Mason, Jason Robards, Donald Sutherland, Matthew Broderick, Dody Goodman, Charlie Lau, Kiefer Sutherland
Director: Herbert Ross
Screenplay: Neil Simon
Comedy
Rated PG
Younger kids: OK Older kids: VG

Matthew Broderick makes his screen debut (and, along with his fellow cast members, offers a winning performance) in this funny Neil Simon–scripted comedy as Michael McPhee, a fatherless 15-year-old who loves playing baseball. Only trouble is, once he has a bat in his hands he is embarrassingly inept.

Michael's life changes with the appearance of Max Dugan (Jason Robards), his dying grandfather. Max abandoned Michael's mother Nora (Marsha Mason) when she was a child, so Mom is naturally suspicious when Max arrives on the scene and attempts to play the role of perfect father/grandfather. Unable to communicate his feelings effectively to his suspicious daughter, he attempts to buy his way into Nora's and Michael's hearts. And he does it in a big way. Max also hires Charlie Lau, the real-life former major leaguer who became an expert batting coach, to teach young Michael the ins and outs of successfully swinging a stick.

While no comedy classic, *Max Dugan Returns* is ingratiating and highly entertaining, particularly as Max begins lavishing oddball gifts on his daughter and grandson in a grandstand play for their affection.

Max's dubious morality may have helped earn this a PG, but on the whole, it's good family fare.

McHALE'S NAVY (1997)
Color, 108 minutes
Cast: Tom Arnold, Tim Curry, Dean Stockwell, David Alan Grier, Debra Messing, Ernest Borgnine, Tommy Chong, Bruce Campbell, French Stewart, Brian Haley
Director: Bryan Spicer
Screenplay: Peter Crabbe, based on a story by Crabbe and Andy Rose, based in turn on the television series
Comedy/Adventure
Rated PG

Younger kids: OK   Older kids: OK

This simple, formulaic comedy is aimed squarely at juvenile audiences, with Tom Arnold as the wheeler-dealer of the Pacific Islands who's called back to active Navy duty to do battle with a terrorist mastermind (Curry, in a performance that, like the film itself, is anything but subtle). McHale has never played by the rules before, and while he runs afoul of an incompetent Captain (Dean Stockwell), it's his freewheeling way of doing things that gets the job done.

This film bears little relation to the popular 1960s TV series from which it takes its title, except for the general notion of a naval officer who runs his own operation in the Pacific. (The original show spawned two slapstick feature films in the 1960s, *McHale's Navy* and *McHale's Navy Joins the Air Force.*) The only true reminder of the earlier show is the presence of its star, Ernest Borgnine, in a supporting role.

Most of the chicanery is mild, and the villainy is comic-opera style and not terribly threatening. The sailors' sexist attitudes might be troubling to some girls, but the female lieutenant in the film (Debra Messing) turns out to be one of the most capable officers on hand.

The language is fairly mild by '90s standards, if not quite squeaky clean. The same can be said for the violence. This is the kind of easy-to-take movie that will amuse kids in the 10- to 12-year-old range—and probably disappear from their memory as soon as it's over.

MEET ME IN ST. LOUIS
(1944)

Color, 113 minutes

Cast: Judy Garland, Margaret O'Brien, Lucille Bremer, Tom Drake, Mary Astor, Leon Ames, Marjorie Main, June Lockhart, Harry Davenport, Henry H. Daniels, Jr., Joan Carroll, Hugh Marlowe, Robert Sully, Chill Wills

Director: Vincente Minnelli

Screenplay: Irving Brecher and Fred F. Finkelhoffe, based on the stories published in *The New Yorker* and a subsequent book by Sally Benson

Musical

Unrated

Young children: VG   Older children: VG

When this all-time classic musical came to movie theaters, United States involvement in World War II was nearing the start of its fourth year. Americans were wearying of war and yearning for a simpler time, one in which problems did not seem as complex and armed conflict had not separated families. *Meet Me in St. Louis* captures this longing and, decades later, it remains one of the finest MGM musicals.

The film is simple, warm, and eloquent. The time is 1903, the year of the St. Louis World's Fair, and the scenario charts the various incidents in the lives of members of the all-American Smith clan—three generations under one roof. Their dilemmas range from arguing over the proper seasoning for soup to playing hard-to-get for a lovesick boyfriend to approaching the scariest house on the block on Halloween.

Judy Garland, playing lovesick Esther Smith, performs one memorable number after another, including "The Trolley Song," "The Boy Next Door," and the incomparable "Have Yourself a Merry Little Christmas." The latter beautifully captures the sense of separation between loved ones at holiday time that was very much a part of people's lives in 1944.

The film also showcases the talents of a pint-sized scene stealer named Margaret O'Brien, cast as impish kid sister Tootie. For her ebullient performance, the 7-year-old actress won a special Academy Award as the year's top child performer. Youngsters who are O'Brien's age should be captivated by her presence and her character's mischievous antics.

Every family deserves to share the adventures of the Smith household; this is one of the best musicals of all time.

MELODY TIME (1948)

Color, 75 minutes

Cast: Roy Rogers and the Sons of the Pioneers, Bobby Driscoll, Luana Patten, Ethel Smith, voices of The Andrews Sisters, Dennis Day, Dinah Shore, Buddy Clark, Fred Waring and His Pennsylvanians, Frances Langford, Freddy Martin and His Orchestra, featuring Jack Fina

Directors: Clyde Geromini, Wilfred Jackson, Hamilton Luske, and Jack Kinney

Screenplay: Winston Hibler, Harry Reeves, Ken Anderson, Erdman Penner, Homer Brightman, Ted Sears, Joe Rinaldi, Art Scott, Bob Moore, Bill Cottree, Jesse Marsh, and John Walbridge; "Little Toot" based on the book by Hardie Gramatky

Animated feature
Unrated
Young children: VG Older
 children: VG

Melody Time is one of several animated features Walt Disney produced in the 1940s consisting of multiple segments strung together. These films naturally don't have the heart, or the impact, of great fairy tales or fables like **Cinderella** or **Pinocchio**. But they do offer a lot of entertainment value, as well as the possibility of watching them in segments—thanks to home video.

Among the highlights in *Melody Time*: a glorious musical tale of folk hero Johnny Appleseed, sung and told by Dennis Day (of *The Jack Benny Show*). This is Disney storytelling at its best, with delightful songs and real depth of feeling.

"Little Toot" is a charming musical segment based on the famous children's book by Hardie Gramatky about a tiny tugboat trying to make good. Young kids should especially like this one.

"Pecos Bill" is a great American tall tale, done to perfection, and introduced on camera by the well-loved cowboy star Roy Rogers, with his horse, Trigger, and his musical companions, The Sons of the Pioneers. (Only complaint: the Disney company decided to digitally remove Pecos Bill's cigarette from the 1998 home video release of *Melody Time*, so as not to corrupt youngsters. This strikes us as political correctness gone berserk.)

Other musical novelties include "Bumble Boogie," a fun, up-tempo visualization of a pop music rendition of "The Flight of the Bumblebee," and "Blame It on the Samba," which recalls **The Three Caballeros** as it reunites Donald Duck and Joe Carioca, who cavort with real-life organist Ethel Smith.

There are some lulls here and there, and today's kids might not have the patience for a reverent moment like "Trees," a musical setting of Joyce Kilmer's poetic favorite. If they do, good for them. If not, there's always the fast-forward button.

MEN IN BLACK (1997)
Color, 99 minutes
Cast: Tommy Lee Jones, Will
 Smith, Linda Fiorentino, Rip
 Torn, Vincent D'Onofrio,
 Tony Shalhoub
Director: Barry Sonnenfeld
Screenplay: Ed Solomon, based
 on the Malibu comic by
 Lowell Cunningham
Comedy/Science fiction
Rated PG-13
Younger kids: VG, with
 caution Older kids: VG

A young New York cop (Will Smith) becomes part of an elite, top-secret government agency whose job is to monitor aliens (outer space, not illegal) in the United States. The assignment for him and his partner (Tommy Lee Jones): to prevent an intergalactic terrorist from destroying the Earth. Or something like that.

This is a fast-paced, highly entertaining diversion which is solidly anchored by the byplay between hip recruit Smith and all-business Jones, who reacts to the most amazing creatures and situations with total Jack Webb–like impassivity.

All kids will delight over the gallery of bizarre creatures, while adults will appreciate the overriding joke of aliens not only hiding among us on Earth, but fitting right in. There is violence and gore, but it is all conceived and executed with wit and cartoonlike flair. The scarier scenes involving aliens and alien transformations are not so much intense as they are amusingly gross.

Classic scene: Jones interrogates an alien in the body of a pug dog.

The strong language, potentially frightening images, and over-the-top violence understandably earned this a PG-13 rating, but the cartoonish tone of the film makes it palatable to all but the youngest kids.

MERMAIDS (1990)
Color, 110 minutes
Cast: Cher, Bob Hoskins, Winona Ryder, Michael Schoeffling, Christina Ricci, Caroline McWilliams, Jan Miner, Betsey Townsend
Director: Richard Benjamin
Screenplay: June Roberts, based on the novel by Patty Dann
Comedy-drama
Rated PG-13
Young children: No Older children: OK

An unusual coming-of-age story that will appeal to older girls and women, *Mermaids* stars a well-cast Cher as the outrageous Mrs. Flax, a free-spirited mother of two, who has just moved to the small town of East Port, Massachusetts, in the early 1960s. Her teenage daughter, Charlotte (Winona Ryder), finds her mother's sexual escapades embarrassing, especially as she is dealing with her own budding sexuality. (During the course of the story, she falls in love with the handsome

groundskeeper of a nearby convent.) Younger sister, Kate (Christina Ricci), is obsessed with learning how to swim. And both daughters are not quite sure what to make of their mom's new boyfriend (Bob Hoskins), a nice man who works at the town shoe store.

This entertaining chronicle of an unconventional family encompasses comedy, sexual awakening, and melodrama. The younger daughter's climactic adventure as a would-be swimmer provides moments that might be too tense for the youngest viewers. Discussions of sexual matters and the teenager's behavior earn this an appropriate PG-13 rating in any case.

Parents (or in some cases, grandparents) might compare notes with kids about the re-creation of a real-life event in the course of the story: the shocked reaction to the assassination of President John F. Kennedy.

Mermaids is an unusual but satisfying film that should particularly appeal to older children.

MICHAEL (1996)
Color, 105 minutes
Cast: John Travolta, Andie MacDowell, William Hurt, Robert Pastorelli, Bob Hoskins, Jean Stapleton, Teri Garr, Joey Lauren Adams
Director: Nora Ephron
Screenplay: Nora Ephron and Delia Ephron
Comedy/Fantasy
Rated PG
Young children: OK Older children: VG

What would you do if an angel landed in your backyard? What would your family do? Your friends and neighbors? What would you say at school? What if the church called? What if the media found out?

All these questions and more are answered in an original screen comedy about a heavenly spirit who's way down-to-earth.

Crawling with charisma, Travolta once again proves himself a skillful actor with major movie star charm. As an archangel on a final visit to Earth, this nearly fallen fellow eagerly pursues his unholy vices of wine, women, and song ("Chain of Fools"), taking time out every now and then to work a few miracles in the lives of the astonished Iowa townsfolk around him. Meanwhile, some cynical reporters fall under his spell.

Although this jokey movie misses the chance to explore its potential, it's nevertheless genteel, unpredictable, and risqué without being vulgar, witty without being nasty, and sweet without being sugary. It does take its time getting where it's going, which may not please the younger, squirmier members of your family, but they'll have a good time just the same.

MICROCOSMOS (1996)
Color, 77 minutes
Cast: Lots of bugs; Kristin Scott Thomas (narrator)
Directors: Claude Nuridsany and Marie Perennou
Nature
Rated G
Younger children: VG Older children: VG

A dragonfly soars, a ladybug has trouble taking off, snails kiss, larvae hatch, and beetles engage in battle. It's real life on a miniature scale, an entire universe compressed into one small French meadow. Think you hate bugs? Think again. These bugs are just plain beautiful.

There's no plot, almost no words, and yet *Microcosmos* is one of the most enthralling and beautiful films in recent memory. Photographed with an amazing camera, the insects go about their business while filmmakers Claude Nuridsany and Marie Perennou allow us the great pleasure of peeking into their world and their lives. Music, an occasional comment, and sound effects help tell this "story" and should keep the whole family riveted to the screen. Even if you think you hate bugs.

A MIDNIGHT CLEAR (1992)
Color, 107 minutes
Cast: Peter Berg, Kevin Dillon, Arye Gross, Ethan Hawke, Gary Sinise, Frank Whaley, John C. McGinley, Larry Joshua, Curt Lowens
Director: Keith Gordon
Screenplay: Gordon, from a novel by William Wharton
Drama/War
Rated R
Young children: No Older children: VG, with caution

This haunting antiwar drama is set at the end of World War II, in the Ardennes Forest near the French-German border. The scenario follows some young Americans in an army intelligence and reconnaissance squad after they are ordered to take an abandoned mansion and report on enemy activity. The oldest G.I. in the group (who is nicknamed Mother) is all of 26; at the outset he goes berserk, which is a perfectly logical reaction to his plight. This sets the story in motion.

A Midnight Clear is anything but a gung-ho drama portraying war as a rite of passage in which inexperienced boys are transformed into macho men and heroes. Instead, it is filled with moments of eloquence and irony, reflecting a sober and distinct antiwar point of view.

Parents might want to watch this with their older children, particularly if the subject of war has already come up in the family. They should know that this film is rated R, however, for its language, violence, and a scene of sensuality.

THE MIGHTY DUCKS (1992)
Color, 100 minutes
Cast: Emilio Estevez, Joss Ackland, Lane Smith, Heidi Kling, Josef Sommer, Joshua Jackson, Elden Ratliff, Shaun Weiss, M. C. Gainey, Matt Doherty, Brandon Adams, J. D. Daniels, Aaron Schwartz
Director: Stephen Herek
Screenplay: Steven Brill and Brian Hohlfield
Comedy/Sports
Rated PG
Younger children: VG   Older children: VG

Gordon Bombay (Emilio Estevez) is a hotshot lawyer who, years ago, was a professional hockey star. When he's brought up on an ethics charge, the judge sentences him to perform community service by coaching a ragtag peewee hockey team. He's as reluctant to work with them as they are to have him, but his onetime mentor reminds him that someone gave him a chance long ago, and he should do the same. Meanwhile, young Charlie (Joshua Jackson) convinces his teammates that Gordon might be able to help them. Newly motivated, the coach and his team start working together in earnest.

There are no surprises in *The Mighty Ducks,* but there's always something satisfying about watching underdogs rise to the top and seeing a group of misfits turn into a genuine team. That's the appeal of this likable, well-cast film.

There is, inevitably, some modern-day language and behavior worthy of a PG rating.

The Disney studio made two redundant sequels to this hit movie: *D2: The Mighty Ducks,* which halfheartedly repeats the first movie's formula, and *D3: The Mighty Ducks,* which follows the teammates to college. The company also decided to pursue hockey in real life by launching a professional NHL team in Anaheim, California, and calling them the Mighty Ducks.

MIGHTY JOE YOUNG (1949)
Black & white, 94 minutes
Cast: Terry Moore, Ben Johnson, Robert Armstrong, Frank McHugh, Mr. Joseph Young
Director: Ernest B. Schoedsack
Screenplay: Ruth Rose, based on a story by Schoedsack
Action-adventure/Fantasy
Unrated
Younger kids: OK   Older kids: VG

From the creators of **King Kong** comes a kinder and gentler update about a baby gorilla, Joe, raised as a pet by a young girl in Africa, who grows to gigantic size but remains obedient to his mistress, Jill (Terry Moore). When

Joe (Mr. Joseph Young) is discovered by a nightclub impresario (Robert Armstrong), the showman brings Joe and Jill to Hollywood to perform in a show. After being provoked into going on a rampage, Joe is hunted down by the police, but all ends happily when he saves a child from a burning orphanage.

Though the film is much campier and sillier than *King Kong,* the Oscar-winning special effects by Willis O'Brien and Ray Harryhausen are super, and the light-hearted, comical tone (as well as Joe's relationship to Jill) makes this better suited for young children than the horrific *Kong.* The film was remade in 1998.

MIRACLE ON 34TH STREET (1947)

Black & white, 96 minutes (also available in computer-colored version)
Cast: Maureen O'Hara, John Payne, Edmund Gwenn, Gene Lockhart, Natalie Wood, Porter Hall, William Frawley, Thelma Ritter
Director: George Seaton
Screenplay: Seaton, from a story by Valentine Davies
Comedy/Fantasy
Unrated
Young children: VG Older children: VG

This holiday classic tells the story of a kindly, good-hearted man who calls himself Kris Kringle (Edmund Gwenn) and who, by sheer chance, comes to work as Santa Claus at Macy's department store in New York City. The woman who hires him, Doris Walker (Maureen O'Hara), is pleasant but businesslike—and she is raising her daughter, Susan

(Natalie Wood), to be much the same. Susan doesn't believe in Santa . . . but Kris has a magical way about him, and the child begins to question her own beliefs. Meanwhile, a friendly next door neighbor (John Payne) is trying to get her mother to melt her icy facade.

At first, Kris is a great success, but circumstances work against him and he winds up on trial, having to prove in a court of law that he is the one and only, bona fide Santa Claus.

This is one of Hollywood's all-time best fantasies, in part because it's played with such conviction—especially by character actor Edmund Gwenn, who's absolutely believable as Kris Kringle—and in part because the movie deliberately leaves some questions unanswered, inviting us to believe, too.

The pacing may be a tad slow for today's youngsters, but the warmth of the performances should win them over. And the film is twenty minutes shorter than its hot-and-cold remake from 1994.

MIRACLE ON 34TH STREET (1994)

Color, 114 minutes
Cast: Richard Attenborough, Elizabeth Perkins, Dylan McDermott, Mara Wilson, Robert Prosky, J. T. Walsh, James Remar, Jane Leeves, Simon Jones, William Windom
Director: Les Mayfield
Screenplay: John Hughes
Comedy/Fantasy
Rated G
Younger children: OK Older children: OK

Richard Attenborough is ideally cast as Kris Kringle in this remake of the 1947 Hollywood classic, and Mara Wilson is adorable (as always) as the little girl who's been raised not to believe in Santa Claus . . . until she encounters Kris. Elizabeth Perkins is good as Wilson's businesslike mother, and Dylan McDermott is charming as the man who takes a romantic interest in her—and a friendly interest in the fate of Kris Kringle.

Unfortunately, this well-meaning remake hits a few snags along the way. Mara Wilson is offscreen for a lengthy chunk midway through the film, when adults take over and Kris is thought to be insane. This is a fairly bleak stretch of film and is likely to make younger kids lose interest.

The climactic trial becomes so complicated that it may be hard even for an adult to explain exactly what is going on.

And worst of all, when Kris is taunted by the drunken former Santa, he's called at least one epithet that has no place in a G-rated movie. (There is nothing else objectionable in the film.)

As remakes go, *Miracle on 34th Street* isn't bad, but it should have been better. And it certainly should have been shorter; it's difficult for little kids to sit still for a 114-minute movie. The original was only 96 minutes long.

THE MIRACLE WORKER
(1962)
Black & white, 107 minutes
Cast: Anne Bancroft, Patty Duke, Victor Jory, Inga Swenson, Andrew Prine, Beah Richards, Kathleen Comegys
Director: Arthur Penn
Screenplay: William Gibson, based on his play
Biographical drama

Unrated
Young children: OK   Older children: VG

For young people who spend so much time learning, this film will prove to be an opportunity to examine a very unusual and special pupil-teacher relationship that began in 1887. The student is 7-year-old Helen Keller, who is both deaf and blind. Her teacher is Annie Sullivan, who moves in with Helen and her family in order to teach the child a language based upon the sense of touch. Seeing that Helen's development is being stifled by her dependency upon her doting mother and overbearing father, Annie pleads to remove the child from their influence for two weeks.

The initial results are petrifying, with Helen hysterically biting and clawing like a frightened, captured animal. The savagery of young Helen at this point in the story could be upsetting to younger children, who may not clearly understand Helen's disabilities.

This is a forceful drama about the extraordinary Helen Keller, who became one of the most remarkable achievers of the 20th century, and serves as a testimonial to the work of determined teachers.

It is also an exceptionally well made film, based on a television play that went on to become a great success on Broadway. In a rare move for Hollywood, the stage stars were enlisted to appear in the film, and both Anne Bancroft and Patty Duke went on to win Academy Awards for their outstanding performances. *The Miracle Worker* was remade for television in 1979, with Patty Duke in the role of Annie Sullivan.

MISTY (1961)
Color, 93 minutes
Cast: David Ladd, Arthur O'Connell, Pam Smith, Anne Seymour, Duke Farley, and the people of Chincoteague, Virginia
Director: James B. Clark
Screenplay: Ted Sherdeman, based on the novel *Misty of Chincoteague* by Marguerite Henry
Animal story/Drama
Unrated
Younger children: VG   Older children: VG

After two orphaned children (David Ladd and Pam Smith) have gone to live on their grandparents' farm in Chincoteague, Virginia, they decide to raise $100 to buy a wild mare called the Phantom. In four months, they "gentle" six ponies for their grandfather to sell and do odd jobs for the townspeople, eventually raising the money they need. Finally, the big moment comes. It's Pony-Penning Day, the day when the residents go to the island of Assateague to round up wild horses—descendants of those stranded on the island when a Spanish galleon was shipwrecked in the 16th century—swim them across to town, and sell them. When the children eagerly present their hard-earned money to the local fire chief, however, they tearfully discover that someone else has bought not only the horse they want but her foal, Misty, as well.

This sweet-spirited movie is ideal for children who love horses and nature: no car chases, violence, sex, or bad language here;

just some delicate moral lessons about hard work and what ownership and responsibility really mean. It's not in the same class with the great films about horses and children (**National Velvet, Black Beauty**), but it's still pleasing.

Misty was filmed in the lovely natural setting of Chincoteague, Virginia, which still holds the annual Pony-Penning Day.

MODERN TIMES (1936)
Black & white, 89 minutes
Cast: Charlie Chaplin, Paulette Goddard, Henry Bergman, Chester Conklin, Stanley J. Sanford, Hank Mann
Director: Charles Chaplin
Screenplay: Charles Chaplin
Comedy/Satire/Silent classic
Unrated
Young children: VG   Older children: VG

Modern Times is Chaplin's exquisite, final silent comedy (except for special background sounds and a gibberish song), as well as the last film in which he played The Little Tramp. It was made almost a decade after the silent cinema had been put to sleep, but it "spoke" as clearly to audiences of 1936 as it does today.

In *Modern Times,* Chaplin keenly satirizes the machine age as the character struggles to survive in a most dehumanizing modern era. Among its many classic images: the Tramp trying to keep up with his rapid-paced job along an assembly line, becoming helplessly and hilariously caught inside a giant factory mechanism, riding blissfully along among the gears and pulleys . . . and being chosen to demonstrate an automatic eating machine!

For once, the Tramp is given a female counterpart (played by Paulette Goddard); she is a delightful partner. The film's eloquent final shot, in which they both walk off into the sunset, is one of the most famous in film history.

Modern Times has so many wonderful, funny moments that anyone can (and will) enjoy it. Some of the more specific points—about the lack of jobs during the Depression, the idea that Charlie picking up a red flag means he's mistaken for a Communist—may require some explanation.

THE MONEY PIT (1986)
Color, 91 minutes
Cast: Tom Hanks, Shelley Long, Alexander Godunov, Maureen Stapleton, Joe Mantegna, Philip Bosco, Josh Mostel
Director: Richard Benjamin
Screenplay: David Giler
Comedy
Rated PG
Young children: OK   Older children: VG

A yuppie couple moves into a big beautiful house on Long Island but soon find it's something short of paradise. Everything that still works in the house breaks quickly; everything that doesn't work will cost a fortune to fix. Hence the title.

Incompetent contractors, inferior building supplies, uncaring construction workers, escalating accidents and injuries, and a checking account rapidly descending into overdraft are the hurdles facing Walter (Tom Hanks) and Anna (Shelley Long) as they watch their dream house turn into a nightmare.

Like a slapstick tragedy, the situation gets worse and worse. People who rent their homes will find this movie funny. People who own will see it as a documentary.

Kids will like it because so much of it is based on physical comedy (although it can't hold a candle to similar outings from the silent-movie era—try finding a copy of Buster Keaton's short subject *One Week* for the best comedy ever made about building a house). The sheer likability of its well-matched stars also goes a long, long way.

MONKEY TROUBLE (1994)
Color, 95 minutes
Cast: Thora Birch, Harvey Keitel, Mimi Rogers, Christopher McDonald, Finster
Director: Franco Amurri
Screenplay: Amurri and Stu Krieger
Comedy/Animal story
Rated PG
Younger children: VG   Older children: VG

This animal comedy will be a hit with younger kids and their parents. Thora Birch stars as Eva, a little girl desperate for a pet. When she meets a monkey in the park, it transforms her into a model child—as a cover to conceal the pet from her parents. Meanwhile, Shorty (Harvey Keitel), a con artist gypsy, tries to retrieve his lost monkey, who's been trained as an expert pickpocket.

With comedy chases all over Venice Beach, zany monkey high jinks, and a good cast, including the talented young actress Thora Birch, *Monkey Trouble* is a fun family film.

There's one menacing moment

that earns the film a PG; if parents are watching along with their younger kids, and can reassure them that everything will be OK, it shouldn't be a problem.

THE MONSTER SQUAD
(1987)
Color, 82 minutes
Cast: Andre Gower, Robby Kiger, Stephen Macht, Duncan Regehr, Tom Noonan, Brent Chalem, Ryan Lambert, Ashley Bank, Mary Ellen Trainor, Leonardo Cimino
Director: Fred Dekker
Screenplay: Shane Black and Dekker
Science fiction–horror/Comedy
Rated PG-13
Young children: Marginal   Older children: OK

Led by Sean (Gower), several junior high boys form a Monster Club, dedicated to the love of monster movies. When Count Dracula (Regehr), seeking ultimate power, arrives in their hometown accompanied by the Wolf Man, a living Mummy, the Gill-Man (from a nearby swamp), and a gentle-natured Frankenstein Monster (Noonan), only the boys stand between these monsters and the end of the world as we know it. Armed with knowledge obtained from a Scary German Guy, they decide to take on these famous monsters of filmland.

A great idea is given unfortunately lackluster treatment. Every little boy who loves monster movies has wondered what he'd do if confronted with the real thing, and that's what happens to the Monster Club here.

Because Universal chose not to make this film, director-cowriter Dekker had to employ ersatz versions of the monsters, instead of "the real thing" as established in Universal's movies. The plotting tends to be a little crowded and slapdash, but the movie is made with love and knowledge of the old movies, which will make it perfect for any young people who've gotten hooked on this classic film genre.

It's a little intense for younger kids, though not really scary, and the definition of "virgin" does figure into the plot.

THE MONSTER THAT CHALLENGED THE WORLD
(1957)
Black & white, 83 minutes
Cast: Tim Holt, Hans Conried, Audrey Dalton, Casey Adams
Director: Arnold Laven
Screenplay: Pat Fielder, based on a story by Albert Duncan
Science fiction/Monster suspense
Unrated
Younger kids: Probably too scary   Older kids: Good

Another well-made if low-budget monster-on-the-loose thriller from the 1950s, this features giant caterpillarlike snails that awaken in the Salton Sea and begin devouring hapless swimmers, boaters, and whomever else they can catch. The movie makes good, eerie use of an extensive irrigation-canal system in the area.

The monsters are particularly well done, being full-sized mechanical props (really, just one that gets a heavy workout) rather than photographically enlarged creatures or animated entities. Boys around 10–12 are likely to find the creatures very cool and may end up adopting them as personal totems.

Younger children will be disturbed by the monsters' blank-eyed stare and upset by the scene near the end in which the last of the creatures bites its way through a door, trying to reach a mother and her young daughter.

MONTY PYTHON AND THE HOLY GRAIL (1974)
Color, 90 minutes
Cast: Graham Chapman, John Cleese, Terry Gilliam, Eric Idle, Terry Jones, Michael Palin, Neil Innes, Connie Booth, Carol Cleveland, Bee Duffell, John Young, Rita Davies, Sally Kinghorn, Avril Stewart
Directors: Terry Gilliam and Terry Jones
Screenplay: Graham Chapman, Terry Jones, Terry Gilliam, Michael Palin, Eric Idle, and John Cleese
Comedy
Rated PG
Younger children: No Older children: It all depends

Britain's Monty Python troupe offers its unique take on Arthurian legend. King Arthur (Graham Chapman) and his knights set out to search for the Holy Grail. Along the way, they meet the Black Knight (John Cleese), who is dismembered by Arthur; Sir Lancelot (John Cleese again) slays guests at a wedding party; and eventually all ends with a big, bloody battle interrupted by modern-day policemen.

There's lots of typical Python humor about killer rabbits, the Holy Hand Grenade, etc. which is sure to delight fans, but *Monty Python and the Holy Grail* could easily frighten and disturb many children. It's very gory, and the humor often depends on gruesomeness.

On the other hand, boys who revel in "gross-out" comedy may be attracted to this film, and at least there is wit to go along with the gore.

MOTHRA (1961)
Color, 101 minutes
Cast: Franky Sakai, Hiroshi Koizumi, Ken Uehara, Kyoko Kagawa, Yumi Ito, Emi Ito
Director: Ishiro Honda
Screenplay: Shinichi Sekizawa
Monster/Science fiction
Unrated
Younger kids: Good Older kids: Good

On an island used for atomic tests, a greedy businessman captures tiny twin girls (the Ito sisters) and takes them back to Tokyo as a stage attraction. However, the girls' singing wafts back to the island, where a giant egg soon hatches, revealing a colossal caterpillar. It has only one mission: to rescue the girls—and it crawls over everything in its path. Finally, it cocoons itself on the wreckage of Tokyo Tower; when the cocoon opens, a colossal moth emerges, still intent on rescuing the girls, who have by now been taken to another country (a thinly disguised United States).

Unlike American giant-bug movies, the Japanese *Mothra* is closer to a fairy tale than a horror movie, with the imprisoned princesses being rescued by a magical, unstoppable force. This is also a remarkably beautiful movie (especially if seen in the letterbox format), and was a very lavish production by Japanese standards.

It's almost the ideal monster movie for children: the monster isn't bad, just set on saving the tiny twins. There's a lot of colorful destruction, the bad guy gets his just deserts (but not from Mothra), and at the climax, the girls and Mothra fly off into the sunset. Older kids will prefer the more vigorous Godzilla movies, but little kids could well be enchanted by this unusual film.

Mothra returned in other movies.

MOUSE HUNT (1997)
Color, 97 minutes
Cast: Nathan Lane, Lee Evans, Vicki Lewis, Maury Chaykin, Eric Christmas, Michael Jeter, Debra Christofferson, Camilla Soeberg, William Hickey, Christopher Walken
Director: Gore Verbinski
Screenplay: Adam Rifkin
Comedy
Rated PG
Younger kids: OK, with caution   Older kids: OK

Two hapless brothers inherit a creaky old house—and in it, a small but crafty rodent who seems to defy extermination.

This unusual combination of slapstick and black comedy works surprisingly well, with Nathan Lane and Lee Evans as an ideal Laurel and Hardy–ish duo. (Lane even does Ollie's tie-twiddle when he's flirting with some women.) But Laurel and Hardy, and The Three Stooges for that matter, accomplished what they had to do in 20-minute shorts, while this film goes on so long it becomes exhausting.

Kids will like its energy and slapstick gusto . . . but little ones may be put off by some of the darker moments, including a visit to an animal pound where there are sidelong references to cats being gassed, etc. And sensitive parents might wince at lines like "rat bastard" and "see you in hell." There are some other moments in the climactic scene that would be considered risqué were they not handled so broadly. Welcome to the '90s.

MR. BUG GOES TO TOWN
(see **Hoppity Goes to Town**)

MR. DEEDS GOES TO TOWN (1936)
Black & white, 115 minutes
Cast: Gary Cooper, Jean Arthur, George Bancroft, Lionel Stander, Douglass Dumbrille, Mayo Methot, Raymond Walburn
Director: Frank Capra
Screenplay: Robert Riskin, based on the story "Opera Hat" by Clarence Budington Kelland
Comedy
Unrated
Younger kids: Good   Older kids: VG

Frank Capra won his second Best Director Oscar for this classic comic fable, a prime example of the kind of populist, root-for-the-little-guy story that the filmmaker later labeled "Capra corn." Gary Cooper stars as Longfellow Deeds, a tuba-playing poet who lives in a small town in Vermont. When Deeds' rich uncle dies and leaves him $20 million, Deeds is whisked off to New York City, where the innocent rube quickly falls prey to the local cynics and swindlers. Deeds falls for a pretty reporter (Jean Arthur) posing as a homeless woman, unaware that she then writes a series of mocking newspaper articles about him in which he is ridiculed as "The

Cinderella Man." When Deeds gets fed up with the back-stabbing and the burden of being rich, he decides to give away his entire fortune to the poor, but his uncle's scheming lawyer (Douglass Dumbrille) and some greedy cousins accuse him of being insane and have him committed, leading to a courtroom showdown.

Although not necessarily a kid's movie and inevitably dated in some respects, this remains a charming and very funny film dealing with the timeless themes of money, love, and trust. Capra keeps the pace moving at lightning speed, and the performances are all a joy, with Cooper superb in his quintessential role of a sincere and unsophisticated country boy who's not as dumb as he looks. There are several hilarious scenes, such as when Deeds goes out for a night on the town and ends up getting drunk, and feeds donuts to a police horse while wearing only his underwear. The riotous courtroom finale is an all-time classic sequence that helped introduce the word "pixilated" into common usage and cleverly illustrates how everyone is just a little bit crazy in their own way.

Frank Capra made movies that touched people's hearts and sent them out of the theater feeling wonderful. That's a feeling today's kids deserve to share.

MR. HOLLAND'S OPUS
(1995)
Color, 142 minutes
Cast: Richard Dreyfuss, Glenne Headly, Jay Thomas, Olympia Dukakis, William H. Macy, Alicia Witt, Jean Louisa Kelly, John Renner, Anthony Natale
Director: Stephen Herek
Screenplay: Patrick Sheane Duncan
Drama
Rated PG
Young children: OK, with caution   Older children: VG

Mr. Holland (Richard Dreyfuss) is a young composer who takes a job as a high school music teacher in the 1960s; he sees this as a stopgap, a way to make a living while he finishes writing a concerto. At first he's discouraged by his students' lack of motivation to learn about music, but the first day he finds a way to reach them—by playing rock 'n' roll—he starts to appreciate the rewards of being a teacher. Over the years, he becomes more dedicated to his students, especially the ones who need special help. When he and his wife learn, quite by chance, that their infant son is deaf, he retreats even further into his work. Years later, confronted by his wife, he finds a way to communicate with his son, Cole, through the medium he loves best, his music. But this triumph is eclipsed by the sad news that his school system is cutting back its music program.

This tearjerker may remind older viewers of other films about dedicated schoolteachers (**Goodbye, Mr. Chips** or **To Sir, With Love,** to name two), but it manages to dodge the "been there, seen that" curse with good writing, some very moving vignettes, and fine performances . . . not to mention excellent period detail as it moves from the 1960s to the 1990s.

One could hardly find a better tribute to the teaching profession or a more honest dramatization of the dilemma faced by a man who puts more effort into his job than his home.

The main problem in recommending *Mr. Holland's Opus* to children is that it's so long—too long for anyone to sit through without squirming a bit. (The subplot about staging a Gershwin musical seems very much tacked on.) But kids and adults alike will relate to the ups and downs of school life, and have a lump in their throats as Mr. Holland's career comes to a fitting conclusion.

There is some mild use of language and the implication of the teacher becoming interested in one of his female students.

MR. MOM (1983)
Color, 91 minutes
Cast: Michael Keaton, Teri Garr, Martin Mull, Ann Jillian, Christopher Lloyd
Director: Stan Dragoti
Screenplay: John Hughes
Comedy
Rated PG
Younger kids: OK   Older kids: Good

With his wry, laid-back charm, Michael Keaton singlehandedly made this fluffy domestic farce seem much funnier than it is and helped turn it into a surprise box-office hit, despite being trashed by critics as little more than a big screen sitcom. Keaton plays Jack Butler, a laid-off auto engineer who swaps roles with his wife,

Caroline (Teri Garr), and becomes a homemaker after she gets a job at an ad agency.

While Jack becomes addicted to daytime soaps and has to deal with dirty diapers, uncooperative appliances, and a seductive neighbor (Ann Jillian), Caroline moves up the corporate ladder and has to fend off the advances of her lecherous boss (Martin Mull). John Hughes' script is utterly predictable and formulaic (recalling a situation mined before by every vintage situation comedy from *I Love Lucy* onward), but the movie is nevertheless lightweight fun whose very familiarity is its most appealing attribute.

Keaton generates some undeniable laughs in the slapstick scenes involving his three children, which kids should find most amusing. Aside from some mild language that earned it a PG, it's all pretty innocuous.

Kids might enjoy asking themselves whether or not their parents could switch roles successfully.

MRS. DOUBTFIRE (1993)
Color, 125 minutes
Cast: Robin Williams, Sally Field, Pierce Brosnan, Harvey Fierstein, Polly Holliday, Lisa Jakub, Matthew Lawrence, Mara Wilson, Robert Prosky
Director: Chris Columbus
Screenplay: Randi Mayem Singer and Leslie Dixon, based on the book *Alias Madame Doubtfire* by Anne Fine
Comedy
Rated PG-13
Young children: OK   Older children: VG

An irresponsible father (Robin Williams) is crushed when his wife (Sally Field) divorces him and he's forbidden from seeing his three children except on weekends. Determined to spend more time with them, he prevails on his brother (Harvey Fierstein), a makeup artist, to transform him into a woman so that he can apply for a job as family housekeeper. In the guise of Mrs. Doubtfire, an eccentric Scotswoman, he becomes a much-loved fixture in the household; both his kids and his ex-wife start to rely on him as friend and confidante. This is quite a feat, as Daniel holds down a "day job" at a local TV station. Trouble arises when the wife invites Mrs. Doubtfire to a birthday dinner hosted by her new boyfriend (Pierce Brosnan) at the same time and place where his boss wants to hear his ideas about a new TV show—which could change the course of his career.

Kids love *Mrs. Doubtfire,* and it's easy to see why. Robin Williams has never been more likable, and his character—a father who cares more about his kids than anything else in his life—is irresistible. As Mrs. Doubtfire he is downright hilarious.

The story touches on very real issues of parental responsibility and sexual identity—that and some of Williams' sexually oriented jokes and asides won this film a PG-13—but the serious themes are never made fun of and dovetail seamlessly into the movie's farcical moments.

Some of those jokes may raise parents' eyebrows, but may just as easily go over the heads of younger kids. On the whole, *Mrs. Doubtfire* is a surefire audience-pleaser for the entire family.

MRS. SANTA CLAUS (1996)
Color, 100 minutes
Cast: Angela Lansbury, Charles Durning, Michael Jeter, Terrence Mann, David Norona, Debra Wiseman
Director: Terry Hughes
Screenplay: Mark Saltzman
Musical fantasy
Unrated
Young children: VG Older children: VG

This savory Hallmark Hall of Fame holiday musical features Angela Lansbury in a tailor-made role, with tuneful songs written by Jerry Herman (with whom she worked on Broadway years ago in *Mame*), and offers much food for thought in its message that Christmas is a special time of year—but only if you love and are loved.

The year is 1910. Christmas Eve is fast approaching, and Mrs. Claus has concocted a new itinerary that surely will help to expedite Santa's around-the-world duties. Her husband is too immersed in his work to pay her mind, so Mrs. Claus hitches up the old sleigh and sets out to test the route. She is forced to land in New York City and winds up living there for a spell. She quickly ingratiates herself into the stream of life in the city's Lower East Side melting pot. Taking the name Mrs. North, she plays cupid, goes up against a greedy toy manufacturer, and even joins in a women's suffrage rally. All the while, Mrs. C. remains fully aware that she somehow must get back to the North Pole before Christmas Eve.

Mrs. Santa Claus is a top-notch vehicle for its seventysomething star, who sings and dances and clowns. The result is a happy musical entertainment for every member of the family that deserves to be a holiday perennial.

MUCH ADO ABOUT NOTHING (1993)
Color, 111 minutes
Cast: Kenneth Branagh, Emma Thompson, Michael Keaton, Robert Sean Leonard, Keanu Reeves, Denzel Washington, Richard Briers, Kate Beckinsale, Brian Blessed, Richard Clifford, Ben Elton, Gerard Horan, Phyllida Law, Imelda Staunton, Jimmy Yuill
Director: Kenneth Branagh
Screenplay: Branagh, based on the play by William Shakespeare
Comedy/Literary classic
Rated PG-13
Younger kids: No   Older kids: VG

After exploring the dark, brooding side of Shakespeare's *Henry V,* Kenneth Branagh made this sunny adaptation of his romantic comedy about love and the attendant tests that two couples must go through to find it: young, passionate Hero and Claudio; and the headstrong, bickering Beatrice and Benedick. Very few of the films based on Shakespeare's plays have clicked with younger audiences, but this merry romp is one of the most accessible versions imaginable of a delightful play and ideal if you're interested in introducing your children to the great Bard's work.

Branagh directs with a very light hand and the playful spirit is infectious. The big-name American actors like Keanu Reeves and Denzel Washington are also an undeniable draw for kids, although acting-wise, they do not

fare as well as their British counterparts. (Michael Keaton is a hoot as Dogberry, however.) All of the players are charming, and this, coupled with the high spirits of romance, compensates for what children might miss from line to line in the dialogue.

One sexy scene earned this film a PG-13 rating. It, too, adds to the contemporary flavor of the production, but you may prefer that your children see a more chaste approach to Shakespeare.

MULAN (1998)
Color, 88 minutes
Cast: Voices of Ming-Na Wen, Lea Salonga, Eddie Murphy, B. D. Wong, Donny Osmond, Harvey Fierstein, Miguel Ferrer, Miriam Margolyes, June Foray, James Shigeta, George Takei
Directors: Barry Cook and Tony Bancroft
Screenplay: Rita Hsiao, Christopher Sanders, Philip LaZebnik, Raymond Singer, and Eugenia Bostwick-Singer, from a story by Robert D. San Souci
Animated feature
Rated G
Young children: VG   Older children: VG

In ancient China, a young girl who doesn't seem to fit in and fails miserably at upholding family honor makes a bold move. When her aged father is called upon to join the Emperor's Army, she secretly cuts her hair, takes his armor and sword, and runs off to join the other new recruits in his place. After a rocky start, she proves herself a brave and daring soldier, especially in combat with the dreaded Huns. But when her identity is revealed, she finds she has to prove herself all over again.

Mulan is based on a story that is part of Chinese lore, known to every man, woman, and child. . . . and no wonder. It is a great story of sacrifice, love, bravery, and honor. Girls will especially enjoy it, as Mulan rejects the life that has been set out for her and makes a shambles of her "audition" for the village matchmaker. But boys will also enjoy the way Mulan stands up to the rigors of army training and does her best to be one of "the boys."

Eddie Murphy enters the picture as the voice of Mushu, a pipsqueak dragon who becomes Mulan's Jiminy Cricket—that is to say, her companion, conscience, and commentator. His dialogue is often uproariously funny, and it's unlikely that kids will feel—as some adults do—that it undercuts the drama of the story.

The battle scenes are not gory, but they are intense at times, and there is a frightening moment when the soldiers come upon a burnt-out village, and even find the charred remains of a little girl's doll. This should be of concern only to the youngest members of the audience.

Mulan is a very entertaining film that may introduce children to an unfamiliar culture . . . and teach some valuable lessons about family honor.

THE MUMMY (1932)

Black & white, 72 minutes
Cast: Boris Karloff, Zita Johann, David Manners, Arthur Byron, Edward Van Sloan, Bramwell Fletcher, Noble Johnson
Director: Karl Freund
Screenplay: John L. Balderston, from a story by Nina Wilcox Putnam and Richard Schayer
Fantasy horror/Romance
Unrated
Young children: Too slow   Older children: OK

Egypt, 1921. The archaeological expedition of Sir Joseph Whemple (Byron) discovers the tomb of Imhotep, a high priest of ancient Egypt who, unaccountably, was buried alive, along with the Scroll of Thoth. When alone, a curious assistant reads the scroll aloud, and Imhotep (Karloff) returns to life, claims the scroll, and goes "for a little walk." Eleven years later, Whemple's son David (Manners), with the help of the mysterious Egyptian Ardath Bey (also Karloff), finds the tomb of Princess Ankh-es-enamon. Ardath Bey turns out to be Imhotep himself; he was buried alive when he tried to use the scroll to bring his beloved Ankhes-en-amon back to life. Now convinced that Helen Grosvenor (Johann) is the reincarnation of Ankhes-en-amon, Imhotep is determined to prove to her they were destined to be together.

Although slow moving and dated, *The Mummy* retains some of its original power, thanks partly to Karloff's careful performance (Ardath Bey moves as though he's brittle), and partly to the excellent makeup by Jack P. Pierce. There's little in the film, apart from Imhotep's revival and his final fate, to bother younger children; teenagers are likely to be put off by the archaic feel of the movie, but the more romantic might be caught up by the story. This is one of a handful of horror films that could well appeal more to teenage girls than boys.

No sequels followed, but Universal did create a series about another mummy, starting with **The Mummy's Hand** in 1940.

THE MUMMY (1959)
Color, 86 minutes
Cast: Peter Cushing, Christopher Lee, Yvonne Furneaux, Eddie Byrne, Felix Aylmer, Raymond Huntley, George Pastell, Michael Ripper, George Woodbridge
Director: Terence Fisher
Screenplay: Jimmy Sangster
Horror/Suspense
Unrated
Young children: Scary   Older children: OK

Years after the Banning expedition found the tomb of the Princess Ananka and something mysterious happened that drove one of them insane, a devoted priest of the god Karnak (Pastell) commands the living mummy Kharis (Lee) to kill the surviving members of that expedition. Stephen Banning (Cushing) eventually realizes what's going on but may be helpless to stop the power of the mummy.

A lively, colorful Hammer horror movie, one of the best of their early period, this is partly a remake of **The Mummy's Hand**. The towering Christopher Lee, who here looks like he's seven feet tall, spends most of the film in a very uncomfortable-looking mummy mask, but still gives one of his finest performances in a horror movie, acting through body movement and gesture alone. He's matched by the rest of the fine cast, and Hammer's impeccable, if low-budget, production values give the movie a polished look.

Although it is a horror movie, the more venturesome younger children could find this a treat; still, the presence of at least one parent is highly advisable. Teenagers who love horror movies already will find this one somewhat old-fashioned but still entertaining.

No sequels followed, but Hammer did a few other mummy movies.

THE MUMMY'S CURSE (1944)
Black & white, 62 minutes
Cast: Lon Chaney (Jr.), Peter Coe, Virginia Christine, Kay Harding, Dennis Moore, Martin Kosleck, Kurt Katch, Addison Richards, Holmes Herbert
Director: Leslie Goodwins
Screenplay: Bernard Schubert, from a story by Leon Abrams and Dwight V. Babcock
Horror/Suspense
Unrated
Young children: Marginal   Older children: OK

Kharis (Chaney), the living mummy, and the nearly mummified Princess Ananka/Amina (Christine) emerge from the mud of a Louisiana swamp, and soon mystical forces drive Kharis to kill again.

This is the strangest of the 1940s Universal mummy movies. Not only has the locale inexplicably shifted from New England to Louisiana, but the Mummy now has super strength, demonstrated in the crashing, dusty finale. There are some interesting lines, and the story has an oddly tragic, predestined mood. It's still just a low-budget thriller, but definitely better than the previous film in the series, **The Mummy's Ghost**.

Again, and finally (this being the last of the Kharis movies), if younger kids find the mummy himself scary, but want to watch the movie anyway, the presence of a parent close at hand will get all but the most easily disturbed through the film.

THE MUMMY'S HAND (1940)
Black & white, 67 minutes
Cast: Dick Foran, Peggy Moran, Wallace Ford, Eduardo Ciannelli, George Zucco, Cecil Kellaway, Charles Trowbridge, Tom Tyler
Director: Christy Cabanne
Screenplay: Griffin Jay and Maxwell Shane
Horror adventure/Thriller
Unrated
Young children: Scary Older children: OK

In Egypt, dashing, adventurous archaeologist Steve Banning (Foran) and his buddy Babe Jenson (Ford) convince stage magician Solvani (Kellaway) and his daughter, Marta (Moran), to finance their expedition to the Valley of the Jackals to look for the tomb of the Princess Ananka. Egyptian Andoheb (Zucco) tries to block their progress, and he has the muscle to back him up: the still-living mummy of Kharis (Tyler), buried alive for having dared to love the Princess Ananka in ancient Egypt.

This lively little movie is more adventure than horror thriller; the mummy's attacks are brief and staged for suspense rather than shock. Young children today see scarier things on Saturday morning cartoons than they're likely to find in *The Mummy's Hand,* but it's good-natured fun with broad, likable characters. The chances are that kids from around 8 to 12

are the best audience for this movie today.

It turned out to be unexpectedly successful and spun off a series of its own; the next in the series is **The Mummy's Tomb**.

THE MUMMY'S GHOST (1944)
Black & white, 61 minutes
Cast: Lon Chaney (Jr.), John Carradine, Robert Lowery, Ramsay Ames, Barton MacLane, George Zucco, Frank Reicher, Harry Shannon
Director: Reginald Le Borg
Screenplay: Griffin Jay, Henry Sucher, and Brenda Weisberg
Horror/Suspense
Unrated
Young children: Marginal Older children: OK

Now being controlled by Yousef Bey (Carradine), another priest of Karnak, Kharis (Chaney), the living mummy, is still at large in New England, intent on destroying all those who had profaned the tomb of the Princess Ananka. Yousef Bey's plans are complicated when the spirit of Ananka herself inhabits the body of a beautiful young woman (Ames) at a local college.

Until the haunting (and unexpected) ending, this is the weakest of the Universal mummy movies, plodding through its weary paces with no enthusiasm and little conviction. Chaney still gives a surprisingly strong performance, considering his face is never visible and he has no lines.

Younger children might be disturbed by Kharis—either his look or the shots of him shambling through the night—but otherwise, by today's standards, this is pretty tame.

Followed by **The Mummy's Curse**.

THE MUMMY'S TOMB (1942)
Black & white, 71 minutes
Cast: Lon Chaney (Jr.), Dick Foran, John Hubbard, Elyse Knox, George Zucco, Wallace Ford, Turhan Bey, Virginia Brissac, Cliff Clarke, Frank Reicher
Director: Harold Young
Screenplay: Griffin Jay and Henry Sucher, from a story by Neil P. Varnick
Horror/Sequel
Unrated
Young children: Scary at times   Older children: OK

Using a solution of mystical tana leaves, Mehemet (Bey), priest of Karnak, uses the living mummy Kharis (Chaney), now at large in New England, in a plan to destroy all those who had profaned the tomb of the Princess Ananka—and all their families as well. Kharis kills two men (Foran and Ford) who had found the tomb (in **The Mummy's Hand**) and then starts in on their families, but the sinister agenda is derailed when Mehemet becomes obsessed with a local woman (Knox).

This brisk, efficient thriller has some very eerie scenes of Chaney lurching through the night in search of his victims, who never seem to be able to outrun the shambling mummy. It's a routine studio film in most ways, but done with tidy professionalism.

More sensitive younger children may still be scared by Chaney in his convincing wrappings and well-designed mask, but older kids are likely to want to watch a more recent horror movie. Still, there will be some who will be caught up by the sheer strangeness of a living mummy and affected by Chaney's performance.

This was followed by **The Mummy's Ghost**.

THE MUPPET CHRISTMAS CAROL (1992)
Color, 120 minutes
Cast: Michael Caine; voices of Dave Goelz, Steve Whitmire, Jerry Nelson, Frank Oz
Director: Brian Henson
Screenplay: Jerry Juhl, based on the novel by Charles Dickens
Comedy-drama/Literary classic
Rated G
Younger children: VG   Older children: VG

It would be difficult to find a more colorful or entertaining variation on Charles Dickens' Christmas classic than this Muppet movie. It's true to Dickens and faithful to his message. Michael Caine is excellent as Ebenezer Scrooge, who learns (the hard way) the lessons of humility and generosity.

Most of the other cast members, however, are Muppets, including such old favorites as Kermit, Miss Piggy, Fozzie Bear, et al., and they bring their unique sense of humor (and even irreverence) to the proceedings.

To pull this off without undermining the seriousness of Dickens' story is no small feat. But that's exactly what the Muppet team accomplishes in this delightful movie.

It's perfect family viewing, although, as with every version of *A Christmas Carol,* there are eerie elements to the story that might be off-putting or even upsetting to very young children.

THE MUPPET MOVIE (1979)
Color, 94 minutes
Cast: Kermit the Frog, Miss
    Piggy, Fozzie Bear, Gonzo, et
    al. (voices of Jim Henson,
    Frank Oz, Jerry Nelson,
    Richard Hunt, Dave Goelz),
    Charles Durning, Austin
    Pendleton, guest stars aplenty
Director: James Frawley
Screenplay: Jerry Juhl and Jack
    Burns
Comedy
Rated G
Younger kids: VG   Older kids:
    VG

This is the story of Kermit the
Frog, Fozzie Bear, Miss Piggy,
and the rest of the Muppet gang,
their rise from obscurity to fame,
fortune and . . . this movie. The
first Muppet feature film is a gentle parody of show business biographies, which is just an excuse
to bring all of Jim Henson's wonderful creations to the screen.

Kids used to computer animated wonders and razzle-dazzle
special effects may scoff, but it all
works because each Muppet is
such a distinct, colorful character,
representing the entire spectrum
of show business history: earnest
straight man Kermit; flighty diva
Miss Piggy; vaudeville comic Fozzie Bear; hip, seen-it-all pianist
Rowlf the Dog; crazed, brain-
blasted rock super id Animal; and
so on. As a result, their individual
stories and dreams seem absolutely "real," and they're a whole
lot more interesting than most of
the humans onscreen (particularly
the incessant "guest cameos"
by the likes of Bob Hope, Richard Pryor, Dom DeLuise, Mel
Brooks, Steve Martin, and many
others).

Parents will take the message of
the Muppets' following a dream
(expressed in the movie's theme
song, "The Rainbow Connection") to heart, but what counts is
how entertaining these little col-
lections of felt, strings, and wires
remain after all these years.

**MUPPET TREASURE
ISLAND** (1996)
Color, 99 minutes
Cast: Tim Curry, Kevin Bishop,
    Billy Connolly, Jennifer
    Saunders; voices of Steve
    Whitmire, Frank Oz, Dave
    Goelz
Director: Brian Henson
Screenplay: Jerry Juhl, Kirk R.
    Thatcher, and James V. Hart,
    based on the novel by Robert
    Louis Stevenson
Adventure/Comedy
Rated G
Younger children: VG   Older
    children: VG

As they did in **The Muppet
Christmas Carol**, the Jim Henson
puppet troupe puts its own spin
on another classic story, Robert
Louis Stevenson's *Treasure Island,* with Kermit as Captain
Smollett and Miss Piggy as Benja-
mina Gunn. There are a handful
of live performers who interact
with the Muppets, notably Tim
Curry as the scurrilous Long
John Silver.

This is not one of the Muppets'
best outings; it doesn't flow as effortlessly as *Christmas Carol* did
and seems more strained. Furthermore, the usually flamboyant Tim
Curry is actually rather subdued
in a part that normally calls for
all stops out.

Still, second-best Muppet material is better than many others'
finest efforts, and the film has
some funny material and enter-

taining moments. And, where very young children are concerned, it's a bloodless way to be introduced to one of literature's most full-blooded stories.

THE MUSIC MAN (1962)
Color, 151 minutes
Cast: Robert Preston, Shirley Jones, Buddy Hackett, Hermione Gingold, Paul Ford, Pert Kelton, Susan Luckey, Ronny Howard, Mary Wickes, Charles Lane, The Buffalo Bills
Director: Morton DaCosta
Screenplay: Marion Hargrove, based on the musical by Meredith Willson and Franklin Lacey
Musical
Unrated
Young children: VG Older children: VG

In this brassy, all-American musical, Robert Preston re-creates his bouncy, energetic stage performance as "Professor" Harold Hill, the title character who dreams of a band with "76 Trombones."

The Music Man tells the story of a slick, know-it-all con artist who schemes to hustle money from the good citizens of River City, Iowa, in the summer of 1912. He will persuade them that their community is on the fast track to ruin because of the existence of a pool hall in their midst. Hill, of course, has the perfect antidote: organize a marching band, to be comprised of the town's schoolboys. He will happily teach each kid how to play a musical instrument. Hill is planning to filch the money that is forked out to purchase instruments and uniforms. But romance and redemption come his way in the person of Marian Paroo (Shir-

ley Jones), the shy town librarian and piano teacher.

Younger kids will especially take to *The Music Man* because Harold Hill is such a colorful character, and children their own age have such a key role in the proceedings. Fans of *The Andy Griffith Show*, *Happy Days*, and **American Graffiti** will especially enjoy seeing a very young Ronny Howard, cast as Winthrop Paroo, Marian's kid brother with an adorable lisp. Youngsters will be fascinated to learn that this little boy grew up to direct **Splash, Cocoon, Parenthood,** and **Apollo 13**.

MUTINY ON THE BOUNTY (1935)
Black & white, 132 minutes
Cast: Charles Laughton, Clark Gable, Franchot Tone, Herbert Mundin, Eddie Quillan, Dudley Digges, Donald Crisp, Movita, Henry Stephenson, Spring Byington
Director: Frank Lloyd
Screenplay: Talbot Jennings, Jules Furthman, and Carey Wilson, based on the novels *Mutiny on the Bounty* and *Men Against the Sea* by Charles Nordhoff and James Norman Hall
Action-adventure
Unrated
Younger kids: No Older kids: VG

One of the great seafaring adventure movies, *Mutiny on the Bounty* won an Oscar for Best Picture and remains the best of many versions about the real-life 1787 mutiny aboard the English ship H.M.S. *Bounty* (including the lavish but unexciting 1962 remake starring Marlon Brando, and the revisionist Mel Gibson–

Anthony Hopkins 1984 film called *The Bounty,* in which Captain Bligh was seen as less villainous).

The story involves the *Bounty*'s voyage from England to Tahiti to collect breadfruit trees and import them to slave camps in the West Indies. Once at sea, the ship's lieutenant, Fletcher Christian (Clark Gable), clashes with the tyrannical Captain Bligh (Charles Laughton) over the latter's brutal and sometimes deadly punishment of the crew for minor offenses. Following an idyllic respite in Tahiti, during which Christian has an affair with a beautiful native, the ship embarks on its journey home, but Bligh's sadistic punishments continue and Christian leads the crew in a mutiny. He sails the ship back to Tahiti, casting Bligh and his allies out to sea, but the determined captain plots to get revenge.

This grand-scale MGM production is distinguished not only by its epic sweep and scope (costing over $2 million in mid-'30s money), but also by the caliber of its performances, highlighted by Laughton's extraordinarily chilling portrayal of Bligh (even if history says that this is an exaggeration). Featuring second-unit footage filmed in Tahiti and on Pitcairn Island, the movie contains several unforgettable scenes that are definitely too intense for young kids, including the mutiny itself and Bligh's vicious punishments, in which sailors are flogged, keel-hauled, and even tied to a masthead during a storm.

MY ÁNTONIA (1995)
Color, 100 minutes
Cast: Jason Robards, Eva Marie Saint, Neil Patrick Harris, Elina Lowensohn, Anne Tremko, Travis Fine, Jan Triska
Director: Joseph Sargent
Screenplay: Victoria Riskin, based on the novel by Willa Cather
Drama/Literary classic
Rated PG
Young children: OK, with caution   Older children: VG

Willa Cather's sensitive novel tells the story of a Bohemian immigrant family who move westward to rural Nebraska in the 1890s. There, the teenage daughter Ántonia is befriended by the grandson of one of the local farm families, and a special bond develops between the two young people, which continues long into adulthood.

This is a realistic story of pioneer people and, as such, it includes scenes of death and hardship. Also, Ántonia has a romance and winds up deceived and with child. The film is true to the novel, and while the life it depicts is harsh at times, it doesn't dwell on the pain of life's struggles and defeats. Instead, it celebrates the beauty of the prairie and its vast fields of grain, along with the deep and unending friendship of a man and woman.

MY BODYGUARD (1980)
Color, 96 minutes
Cast: Chris Makepeace, Adam Baldwin, Martin Mull, Ruth Gordon, Matt Dillon, John Houseman, Joan Cusack, Craig Richard Nelson
Director: Tony Bill

Screenplay: Alan Ormsby
Comedy-drama
Rated PG
Younger kids: OK   Older kids:
  OK

A smart, shy transfer student, Clifford (Makepeace) runs afoul of local bullies at his new public school, so he hires loner Ricky Linderman (Baldwin), another student at the school, as his bodyguard. This movie nicely captures some of the fears and pressures of high school and teen life, and the young actors underplay in a style that is very much in keeping with the naturalistic tone. (The few adults present, like Clifford's busy hotel manager father and eccentric grandmother, are kept to the periphery of the action, but they are at least amusingly sketched and not standard dunderheads.)

The "revelation" of Ricky's dark secret—he accidentally killed his brother years earlier—serves to bring Clifford and Ricky closer together as friends, but it's a bit heavy for such a "little" film. Kids can certainly relate to Clifford's attempts to find his way in a strange new place. Parents may not appreciate the final scenes, which encourage kids to resolve their problems with violence . . . but at least they use fists and not guns.

MY FAIR LADY (1964)
Color, 170 minutes
Cast: Rex Harrison, Audrey
  Hepburn, Stanley Holloway,
  Wilfrid Hyde-White, Gladys
  Cooper, Jeremy Brett,
  Theodore Bikel, Mona
  Washbourne
Director: George Cukor
Screenplay: Alan Jay Lerner,
  based on the musical by
Lerner and Frederick Loewe,
  from the play *Pygmalion* by
  George Bernard Shaw
Musical
Unrated
Young children: VG   Older
  children: VG

This consummate Broadway musical turned Academy Award–winning spectacular remains a must-see for the entire family. Rex Harrison re-creates his stage role as Henry Higgins, a pompous phonetics professor who brags to his pal Colonel Pickering (Wilfrid Hyde-White) that he can transform ill-kempt Cockney flower girl Eliza Doolittle into a lady in three months flat. In fact, he will do such a fine job that he will be able to pawn her off as a duchess.

Audrey Hepburn is resplendent as Eliza. (She was cast because the Hollywood "suits" felt that Julie Andrews, who originated the role, was not a big enough movie name. So Andrews instead found herself playing the title role in **Mary Poppins**—and winning a Best Actress Oscar the same year that *My Fair Lady* won as Best Picture.)

Just about every song composed by Alan Jay Lerner and Frederick Loewe for *My Fair Lady* has become a standard. They are either rousing and fun ("Wouldn't It Be Loverly?" "With a Little Bit of Luck," "The Rain in Spain," "Get Me to the Church on Time"), filled with romance and longing ("On the Street Where You Live," "I Could Have Danced All Night"), or perfectly capture the essence of enduring love ("I've Grown Accustomed to Her Face").

The movie may be long for the youngest kids and might be split into two evenings' viewing. But with the magnetic performance of Rex Harrison as the centerpiece, the literate lyrics of Alan Jay Lerner as brainteasers, and Cecil Beaton's incredible costume designs and sets as window dressing, *My Fair Lady* is a treat every family should share.

MY FATHER, THE HERO
(1994)
Color, 90 minutes
Cast: Gérard Depardieu, Katherine Heigl, Dalton James, Lauren Hutton, Faith Prince, Stephen Tobolowsky
Director: Steve Miner
Screenplay: Francis Veber, Charlie Peeters, based on the movie *Mon Père, Ce Héros* by Gerard Lauzier
Comedy
Rated PG
Young kids: OK Older kids: VG

Nicole (Katherine Heigl) lives with her mom in New York City but agrees to spend some vacation time with her busy European father (Gérard Depardieu) at a tropical resort. When she meets the boy of her dreams, she doesn't want to admit that she's traveling with her dad, so she claims instead that he's her lover . . . a lie that mushrooms beyond her expectations. Her father is unaware of this deception and doesn't understand why a growing number of people at the resort begin to question and shun him.

What could have been strained or smutty turns out to be a delightful comic farce, thanks to the spirited performance of Gerard Depardieu, France's most popular star. His reactions to the growing predicaments his daughter creates for him are somehow believable—and often hilarious.

Depardieu was certainly familiar with the role: he played it once before in the French movie on which this was based.

There are some jokes that will go over young children's heads (and just as well), regarding affairs of the heart and the unsuitability of an older man pairing off with a teenage girl. That aside, this is a highly entertaining comedy the whole family can enjoy.

MY FRIEND FLICKA (1943)
Color, 89 minutes
Cast: Roddy McDowall, Preston Foster, Rita Johnson, Jeff Corey, James Bell
Director: Harold Schuster
Screenplay: Lillie Hayward and Francis Edwards Faragoh, based on the novel by Mary O'Hara
Drama/Animal story
Unrated
Younger kids: VG Older kids: VG

Mary O'Hara's classic novel about a boy and his beloved horse became one of the best children's films ever, featuring adorable animal footage and breathtaking photography of the Rockies, all in blazing Technicolor. The talented young Roddy McDowall stars as Ken, the son of a horse rancher, who can't seem to stay out of trouble and desperately wants a colt of his own. Hoping to give the boy a sense of discipline, his father (Preston Foster) agrees to give him a horse, but Ken picks a wild filly whose mother is "loco."

Ken tries to tame Flicka, as he names it, nurses it back to health after it's injured, and becomes great friends with his fellow "misfit," but then has to deal with several crises, including Flicka getting a serious fever and his father's decision to shoot the horse to put it out of its misery. All ends happily, of course, and Ken gets a valuable lesson about responsibility and gains emotional maturity, while Dad learns about love, patience, and hope. This is a lovely and sentimental piece of Americana that's perfect for all kids, as is its 1945 sequel, **Thunderhead, Son of Flicka.**

MY GIRL (1991)
Color, 102 minutes
Cast: Dan Aykroyd, Jamie Lee Curtis, Macaulay Culkin, Anna Chlumsky, Richard Masur, Griffin Dunne, Ann Nelson, Peter Michael Goetz
Director: Howard Zieff
Screenplay: Laurice Elehwany
Comedy-drama
Rated PG
Younger children: No Older children: VG

Eleven-and-a-half-year-old Veda Sultenfus (Anna Chlumsky) lives with her father (Dan Aykroyd) in a combination house and mortuary, where he prepares bodies for funeral services. Veda misses her mother terribly and believes that she caused her death; as a result of this and the environment in which she's been raised, she's obsessed with death and pays regular visits to her family doctor, certain that she's about to pass away.

Veda's only real friend is Thomas J. (Macaulay Culkin), who like her is a misfit. A budding writer, Veda has a crush on her schoolteacher (Griffin Dunne), who's conducting a creative writing class for adults—but allows her to attend. Meanwhile, her father's newest employee, a vivacious makeup artist (Jamie Lee Curtis) brings new life to their household . . . but Veda begins to realize that she's not the only woman in her father's life.

My Girl is a bittersweet slice of life about a precocious youngster. The movie tends to wander all over the place, but has many touching scenes and sincere performances from its first-rate cast. It's certain to strike a responsive chord with sensitive adolescents, but it also deals with serious, even somber subject matter that puts it out of reach for younger children. The fact that the character played by Macaulay Culkin meets an unhappy fate will be particularly upsetting (as it is for the characters on screen).

My Girl is excellent fare for preteens but shouldn't be shared with their younger siblings.

MY GIRL 2 (1994)
Color, 99 minutes
Cast: Dan Aykroyd, Jamie Lee Curtis, Anna Chlumsky, Austin O'Brien, Richard Masur, Christine Ebersole, John David Souther, Angeline Ball, Aubrey Morris, Gerrit Graham, Ben Stein
Director: Howard Zieff
Screenplay: Janet Kovalcik
Comedy-drama
Rated PG
Younger children: OK Older children: OK

Veda (Anna Chlumsky) receives a challenging school assignment: to write an essay about a person she's never met who has achieved something important in life. She decides to make the subject her mother, who died giving birth to her. To do this, Veda travels to Los Angeles, where she can stay with her Uncle Phil (Richard Masur) and his girlfriend, Rose (Christine Ebersole), while she tries to find people who knew her mom. This leads her on an adventurous trail, in the company of Rose's son, Nick (Austin O'Brien).

My Girl 2 is a pleasant sequel that captures much of the quality of the original film. This time, Veda finds herself with a budding boyfriend—although that isn't part of her plan—and gets to see her own mother for the first time in vintage home movies.

While this film isn't as morbid as the original—which had death as a constant presence—it does again have a bittersweet quality that makes it more appropriate for older children than younger ones. There is a smattering of bad language.

MY LIFE AS A DOG (1985)
Color, 101 minutes
Cast: Anton Glanzelius, Tomas von Bromssen, Amki Liden, Melinda Kinnaman, Kicki Rundgren, Ingmar Carlsson
Director: Lasse Hallstrom
Screenplay: Hallstrom, Reidar Jonsson, Brasse Brannstrom, and Per Berglund, based on the novel by Reidar Jonsson
Comedy-drama
Unrated
Younger kids: OK, with caution   Older kids: VG

This touching Swedish film (based on an autobiographical novel) tells the story of Ingemar, a 12-year-old boy who is sent to live with relatives in rural Sweden during the 1950s while his ailing

mother rests. In the village, he encounters an assortment of eccentric characters, makes friends with a young girl who pretends she is a boy, and deals with the deaths of his mother and his dog.

The story is filled with funny incidents, but there is also real sadness at its core, and the film often treads a delicate line between humor and tragedy. Children and adults, though, will find young Ingemar—remarkably portrayed by Glanzelius—an unusual and indomitable hero. Though he is thrown into a strange new environment and must cope with a bewildering variety of conflicting emotions, he is optimistic, clever, and imaginative. He may not always understand what is going on around him, but he jumps in with eyes wide open, ready to learn. (When he learns his dog has been put to sleep, Ingemar imitates a dog.)

This hero's willingness to embrace the unknowable allows the film to avoid any pitfalls of oversentimentality or maudlin excess, and makes it an absorbing experience for children and adults alike. The youngest viewers will find some of the story too sad to enjoy.

Years after this film was made, it was adapted as a series for cable television.

MY NEIGHBOR TOTORO (1988)
Color, 87 minutes
Cast: Voices of Lisa Michaelson, Cheryl Chase, Greg Snegoff, Alexandra Kenworthy, Natalie Core, Kenneth Hartman
Director: Hayao Miyazaki
Screenplay: Hayao Miyazaki
Animated feature
Rated G

Young kids: OK   Older kids: OK

My Neighbor Totoro is a charming original fable by Japan's master animator Hayao Miyazaki.

Two young sisters move to the country with their father while their mother recuperates from an illness at the hospital. The girls discover a fantasy creature living in the woods near their home, whom they name Totoro; he helps them overcome their fear of their new surroundings and deal with the fate of their mother.

This is a gentle tale, enhanced by beautiful artwork, combining fantastic characters with moments of touching realism. The story takes place in rural Japan, leading to a few moments parents may want to note. A brief sequence when father and the girls bathe together is handled in good taste; children may want to know more about the architecture of the girls' home and their unfamiliar school uniforms.

Young kids, particularly girls, will identify with the lead characters and boys may go for the fantasy action.

MY SCIENCE PROJECT

(1985)
Color, 94 minutes
Cast: John Stockwell, Danielle von Zerneck, Fisher Stevens, Rafael Sbarge, Richard Masur, Barry Corbin, Ann Wedgeworth, Dennis Hopper
Director: Jonathan R. Betuel
Screenplay: Jonathan R. Betuel
Science fiction/Comedy/ Adventure
Rated PG
Young children: Marginal   Older children: OK

When his teacher, Bob Roberts (Hopper), orders high school student Mike (Stockwell) to come up with a science project right away or flunk out *and* he's dumped by his girlfriend, despondent Mike takes scientifically inclined Ellie (von Zerneck) to an abandoned Air Force base to look for something, anything, to use as his project. He happens upon an interesting-looking gadget which we know (but he doesn't) came from a flying saucer that President Eisenhower ordered be kept a secret back in 1957. The device turns out to be very dangerous: it creates whirlwinds in time so that people and creatures from the past and present converge upon the high school.

Some of the ideas in the movie are ingenious, but the overall film is tasteless—and worthless, except for Dennis Hopper's enthusiastic performance as a hippie turned teacher.

There are menaces aplenty, including a dinosaur, which might make the film rough sledding for younger kids.

MY SISTER EILEEN (1955)

Color, 108 minutes
Cast: Betty Garrett, Janet Leigh, Jack Lemmon, Kurt Kasznar, Richard (Dick) York, Horace McMahon, Robert (Bob) Fosse, Lucy Marlow, Tommy Rall, Barbara Brown, Henry Slate, Hal March, Richard Deacon, Queenie Smith
Director: Richard Quine
Screenplay: Blake Edwards and Quine, based on the play by Joseph Fields and Jerome Chodorov adapted from stories by Ruth McKenney
Musical
Unrated

Young children: VG   Older children: VG

Back in the 1930s, Ohio native Ruth McKenney wrote a series of semi-autobiographical stories published in *The New Yorker,* in which she charted her experiences with her sister, Eileen, when the pair came to New York in search of success. Ruth was a would-be writer, Eileen a hopeful actress, and the sisters settled into a shabby basement apartment in Greenwich Village. McKenney's stories were the basis of a popular romantic comedy that premiered on Broadway in 1940 and were adapted as a movie two years later. The property eventually was developed into two separate musicals: *Wonderful Town,* which became a hit on the Great White Way in 1953, and this agreeable musical made directly for the screen.

Here, Ruth and Eileen Sherwood are nicely played by Betty Garrett, in a rare leading role, and Janet Leigh, whom younger audience members may know as the mother of Jamie Lee Curtis. Their young leading man is Jack Lemmon, who even gets to sing in his role as Bob Baker, a publisher who romances Ruth. Legendary choreographer-director Bob Fosse plays soda jerk Frank Lippincott and marked this as his first movie musical as sole choreographer.

My Sister Eileen doesn't have a reputation as a great movie musical, but it's an extremely pleasant and enjoyable one, with a handful of talented, likable performers in the leading roles.

The view of New York in general, and Greenwich Village in particular, may seem quaint.

However, *My Sister Eileen*—like so many other musicals of decades past—is a depiction of a much simpler age.

MYSTERIOUS ISLAND (1961)
Color, 101 minutes
Cast: Michael Craig, Joan Greenwood, Herbert Lom, Gary Merrill, Michael Callan, Percy Herbert, Beth Rogan, Dan Jackson
Director: Cy Endfield
Screenplay: John Prebble, Daniel Ullman, and Crane Wilbur, from the novel by Jules Verne
Science fiction/Adventure
Unrated
Younger kids: Okay, but scary   Older kids: OK

During the Civil War, some Union soldiers use a balloon to escape from a Confederate prisoner of war camp, with a Rebel soldier along as well. A storm carries them to sea, where they crash-land on an island. Two women castaways join them, and together, they try to find a way to survive. They encounter giant animals of various types, including a huge crab, a large flightless bird, and colossal bees . . . but there's also a mysterious benefactor somewhere about, who leaves them necessary items. He turns out to be none other than Captain Nemo, the central character from **20,000 Leagues Under the Sea,** here played by Herbert Lom. (This isn't Hollywood at work; the Jules Verne novel on which *Mysterious Island* is based was indeed a sequel to his novel *20,000 Leagues Under the Sea.*)

The brilliant stop-motion animation of Ray Harryhausen enlivens this otherwise plodding adventure. The feeling that the story has been warped somewhat to appeal to audiences in 1961 pervades the whole movie, which dates it to a degree. But the effects are excellent, and the thunderous score by Bernard Herrmann, though not one of his very best, is exciting and dramatic in ways the film itself sometimes isn't.

Younger kids are more likely to enjoy this movie than older kids, who might scoff at the "old-fashioned" special effects. It's a little scary at times, as when two people are walled up by a giant bee, but the scares are over with quickly. Like almost all of the films Harryhausen worked on, this is good rainy-afternoon entertainment.

MYSTERY OF THE WAX MUSEUM (1933)
Color, 77 minutes
Cast: Lionel Atwill, Fay Wray, Glenda Farrell, Frank McHugh, Allen Vincent, Gavin Gordon, Edwin Maxwell, Holmes Herbert, Arthur Edmund Carewe
Director: Michael Curtiz
Screenplay: Don Mullaly and Carl Erickson, from a story by Charles S. Belden
Horror/Suspense
Unrated
Young children: Boring but scary   Older children: OK

After his beloved London wax museum is destroyed by fire, Mr. Igor (Atwill) opens another in New York twelve years later. The body of a young woman disappears from the morgue, and when her roommate Charlotte (Wray) and wisecracking reporter Florence (Farrell) visit Igor's new museum, Florence is surprised to notice that one of the wax statues strongly resembles the missing corpse. The hideous, cloaked figure we saw steal the body turns up again, pursuing Charlotte.

One of the last features made in Technicolor's original "two-strip" process (only two primary hues were available), this stylish thriller was thought to be a lost film for many years, but is now widely available. Like its companion piece, **Doctor X,** this is a curiosity for horror movie fans and those interested in the history of color films.

Nonetheless, at times, it is still effective as a horror movie, partly thanks to Atwill's skillful playing, making Igor both frightening and pitiable. Curiously, the lack of a musical score heightens the climax, which is more like that of an action thriller than a horror shocker. The makeup is horrifying, perhaps too much so for younger children, and the wax statues melting in the fire is peculiarly gruesome in its own odd way.

Remade as **House of Wax.**

N

NAMU, THE KILLER WHALE (1966)

Color, 88 minutes
Cast: Robert Lansing, John Anderson, Lee Meriwether, Richard Erdman, Robin Mattson
Director: Laslo Benedek
Screenplay: Arthur Weiss
Animal adventure
Unrated
Young children: VG   Older children: VG

Distinguished from other animal movies in that it's based on a true story, this wildlife adventure concerns a marine biologist who captures and trains a killer whale.

Shot on location in Washington State's Puget Sound, where the real Namu lived, the twenty-five-foot aquatic mammal is snared in a British Columbia cove, then transferred to Seattle, where it becomes the star attraction in a Marineland-type water zoo. The local fishermen want it killed because it devours their salmon. But common sense prevails, and the animal is saved.

It's like a giant version of **Flipper** (which was also an Ivan Tors production) . . . or if you prefer, a forerunner to **Free Willy**.

On video as *Namu, My Best Friend*, a much more child-friendly title.

THE NASTY GIRL (1990)

Color and black & white, 92 minutes
Cast: Lena Stolze, Monika Baumgartner, Michael Gahr, Fred Stillkrauth, Elisabeth Bertram, Robert Giggenbach
Director: Michael Verhoeven
Screenplay: Michael Verhoeven
Drama/Satire
Rated PG-13
Young children: No   Older children: VG, with caution

Given the disturbing rise of neo-Nazism in Europe, *The Nasty Girl* takes on extra special meaning. It is a biting, seriocomic chronicle of Sonja Rosenberger, a young woman who lives in a small Bavarian town and enters a nationally sponsored essay contest on the subject "My Hometown During the Third Reich." Her mother tells her, "Just write about the positive things," but instead, she begins an unyielding search for the truth. She will not accept the fiction, perpetuated by her elders, that every German resisted Nazi ideology during the rule of Adolph Hitler.

The Nasty Girl is based on a true story; Sonja is the alter ego of Anna Rosmus, who actually investigated the history of her own community. As indicated in its prologue, the film is "relevant to all towns in Germany" in that so many of today's respected elder citizens were yesterday's Nazis.

A sobering story of hypocrisy

and historical revisionism, this film may strike a responsive chord in adolescent viewers who recognize the problems of digging for the truth in their own lives. It is rated PG-13 and is not suitable for younger children.

Lena Stolze, who plays the heroine, also appears in writer-director Verhoeven's 1983 drama, *The White Rose,* the based-on-fact story of a group of heroic Munich students who, in 1942, initiated an anti-Nazi rebellion.

NATIONAL LAMPOON'S CHRISTMAS VACATION
(1989)
Color, 97 minutes
Cast: Chevy Chase, Beverly D'Angelo, Randy Quaid, Diane Ladd, John Randolph, E. G. Marshall, Doris Roberts, Julia Louis-Dreyfus, Mae Questel, William Hickey, Juliette Lewis, Brian Doyle-Murray, Nicholas Guest, Miriam Flynn
Director: Jeremiah S. Chechik
Screenplay: John Hughes
Comedy
Rated PG-13
Younger kids: No Older kids: Good

This third entry in the *Vacation* series is typical John Hughes family fare—which means you can expect lots of raunchy language, tasteless gags involving senior citizens and animals (such as an electrocuted cat), and a general mocking of its obnoxious characters—yet this also has some genuinely funny and, yes, even warmhearted moments.

Chevy Chase is in good pratfall form as Clark Griswold, the goofily hapless paterfamilias whose one desire is to have an old-fash-

ioned Yuletide at home with his family. Unfortunately, whatever can go wrong for Clark, does, including trying to stuff an oversized Christmas tree in his living room, causing a power outage by stapling twenty-five thousand bulbs to his roof, enduring the unwelcome arrival of his redneck cousin, Eddie (Randy Quaid), and his brood, and having a SWAT team drop in for Christmas dinner after Eddie takes his boss hostage for not giving him a holiday bonus.

The crude humor makes this one definitely for teens only, but it's generally good-natured and one of the better *Vacation* films.

NATIONAL LAMPOON'S EUROPEAN VACATION
(1985)
Color, 94 minutes
Cast: Chevy Chase, Beverly D'Angelo, Jason Lively, Dana Hill, Eric Idle, Victor Lanoux
Director: Amy Heckerling
Screenplay: John Hughes and Robert Klane
Comedy
Rated PG-13
Younger kids: No Older kids: OK, with caution

In this first sequel to **National Lampoon's Vacation**, the bumbling Griswald family—Clark (Chevy Chase), Ellen (Beverly D'Angelo), daughter Audrey (Dana Hill), and son Rusty (Jason Lively)—appear on a TV game show and win a trip to Europe. In England, klutzy Clark immediately drives into some people (including Eric Idle, who reappears throughout the story) and crashes into the ancient Stonehenge, while his homesick kids stew over not being able to watch MTV. In

France, they all don berets and are ridiculed by the arrogant Parisians; Clark puts on lederhosen and causes a riot at a beer festival in Germany; and in Italy, they get mixed up in a robbery and kidnapping.

Although this frenetic, whirlwind tour offers a few chuckles by putting these stereotypical Ugly Americans into the sophisticated Old World milieu, it's generally a slipshod, simpleminded affair that lays on the slapstick gags with a heavy hand.

There's also a fair degree of nudity and profanity for a so-called family film, and the level of humor is pretty crude, exemplified in the character of the sexually obsessed Rusty, and even a scene where the lecherous game show host lasciviously kisses Audrey. A good measure of the film's overall sloppiness is the fact that the family's name is spelled Griswald here, but in all of the other *Vacation* movies it's Griswold.

NATIONAL VELVET (1944)
Color, 125 minutes
Cast: Mickey Rooney, Donald Crisp, Elizabeth Taylor, Anne Revere, Angela Lansbury, Jackie "Butch" Jenkins, Juanita Quigley, Arthur Treacher, Reginald Owen, Terry Kilburn, Alec Craig, Arthur Shields
Director: Clarence Brown
Screenplay: Theodore Reeves and Helen Deutsch, based on the novel by Enid Bagnold
Drama/Animal story
Unrated
Young children: VG   Older children: VG

Pre-adolescent girls will take to this timeless tale of a youngster and her all-encompassing love for a horse.

Twelve-year-old, violet-eyed Elizabeth Taylor won motion picture stardom in the role of Velvet Brown, the youngest of three sisters in an amiable family that lives in a small seaside village in England. Like many preteen girls who have yet to discover boys, Velvet is a dreamy child who is obsessed with horses. In fact, she's determined to have her horse entered in Britain's fabled Grand National Steeplechase and sets out to do so with the help of Mi Taylor (Mickey Rooney), a former jockey who is drifting through her town.

National Velvet remains one of the all-time great family films, filled with suspense and surprises, as well as drama, warmth, humor, and excitement, as young Velvet seeks to realize her dream.

Like all great children's stories, this one doesn't talk down to kids and offers a clear-eyed but sympathetic look at both children and their parents. The scene in which Velvet's mother (Anne Revere) talks about her own youthful ambitions is one of the most touching in the entire film.

It was followed thirty-four years later by an entertaining sequel, *International Velvet*. Here, Velvet is a grown-up, and the spotlight is on her niece (played by Tatum O'Neal), who desires to become an Olympic horsewoman.

THE NAVIGATOR (1924)
Black & white, 69 minutes
Cast: Buster Keaton, Kathryn McGuire, Frederick Vroom
Directors: Buster Keaton and Donald Crisp

Screenplay: Clyde Bruckman,
Joseph Mitchell, and Jean
Havez
Comedy/Silent classic
Unrated
Young children: VG   Older
children: VG

This was the first of Buster Keaton's feature comedies to win mass popularity, and earned him his niche as an important screen star. Buster plays Rollo Treadway, an overindulged rich man's son who finds himself on board a large abandoned ship that has been cast out to sea. Rollo's lone fellow "passenger" is Betsy O'Brien, his estranged girlfriend, who (in spite of everything) he is determined to marry.

The Navigator is a quiet film that, like some of Keaton's others, only really comes to life with an audience. Nevertheless, it has many wonderful comic routines. These involve the manner in which Rollo and Betsy come to realize they both are on board, followed by their adventures on the vessel—trying to make do when everything is designed for a huge number of passengers—and later, on an island whose residents are cannibals!

NEVER CRY WOLF (1983)
Color, 105 minutes
Cast: Charles Martin Smith,
Brian Dennehy, Zachary
Ittimangnaq, Samson Jorah
Director: Carroll Ballard
Screenplay: Curtis Hanson, Sam
Hamm, and Richard Kletter,
based on the novel by Farley
Mowat
Drama/Animal story
Rated PG
Younger kids: VG   Older kids:
VG

Tyler (Smith), a young Canadian biologist, spends a year in the Arctic North to study the behavior of wolves that are destroying herds of caribou. As he gets to know his subjects, the biologist learns that the wolves are not the cause of the disappearing caribou at all and that hunters may be the culprits. Directed by the same man who helmed *The Black Stallion,* this is—not surprisingly—a magnificent-looking and -sounding film, which captures the beauty and starkness of nature as few films have. Children should have no trouble responding to Tyler as he grows to respect and understand the wolves, and adjusts to his surroundings with the help of two friendly Eskimos.

Parents, in turn, should be ready to discuss the question of man's own encroachment on the natural order of things. Though there is virtually nothing objectionable here, parents might want to note the sequence where Tyler marks his territory by urinating in the same manner as the wolves he is studying. (Unlike the wolves, it takes him twenty-seven cups of tea to do it.)

THE NEVERENDING STORY
(1984)
Color, 92 minutes
Cast: Barret Oliver, Gerald
McRaney, Thomas Hill, Deep
Roy, Tilo Pruckner, Moses
Gunn, Noah Hathaway,
Sydney Bromley, Patricia
Hayes, Tami Stronach
Director: Wolfgang Petersen
Screenplay: Petersen and
Herman Weigel, from the
novel by Michael Ende
Fantasy/Adventure
Rated PG

Young children: OK   Older children: OK

Motherless Bastien (Oliver), a boy living in New York, takes refuge from his unhappy life by reading a book called *The Never-Ending Story,* and we see what he reads: The magical world of Fantasia is threatened by the advance of Nothing, which will eventually wipe out everything. The nameless princess (Stronach) reveals that only young Atreyu (Hathaway) can save Fantasia, but he needs a human being to help him.

Wolfgang Petersen directs this elaborate fantasy with conviction and style, using special effects techniques and a general approach very different from similar American movies. (This is German but was shot in English.) There are no winks to the audience and no contemporary references. It's a full-bodied, beautifully made children's adventure film, with a strong message: Read more books.

The production design is reminiscent of an ornate European illustrated children's book; this helps give the film a sense of wonder and visual beauty quite unlike most American special-effects movies. This means that American kids might not take to the film at first, but the story, filled as it is with creatures both weird and beautiful, is likely to sweep them up.

This was followed by two sequels, one made for theaters and one for video, as well as a TV series.

THE NEVERENDING STORY II: THE NEXT CHAPTER
(1991)
Color, 89 minutes
Cast: Jonathan Brandis, Kenny Morrison, Clarissa Burt, Alexandra Johnes, Martin Umbach, John Wesley Shipp, Helena Michell
Director: George Miller
Screenplay: Karin Howard, from the novel by Michael Ende
Fantasy adventure
Rated PG
Younger children: OK   Older children: OK

Bastien (Jonathan Brandis), several years older, is still grieving over the death of his mother and having trouble with his father. His only escape is the magic book that takes him to Fantasia to fight the Nothingness and the evil sorceress Xayide, who steals his memories every time he makes a wish. He's helped by his old friends, including Atreyu (Kenny Morrison), and is psychically supported by his father reading the book at home.

We know right from the beginning how it's all going to end; even individual scenes and characters' behavior can be predicted. And by golly, we're right.

Although the sets and special effects are still visually appealing and the moral about reading remains, the whole film—script, direction, acting—is a sorry imitation of its predecessor. Anyone who has seen the first film is bound to be disappointed.

There was a second nondescript sequel released direct to video.

THE NEW LAND (see **The Emigrants**)

A NIGHT AT THE OPERA
(1935)
Black & white, 101 minutes
Cast: Groucho, Harpo, and Chico Marx, Allan Jones, Kitty Carlisle, Walter Woolf King, Sigfried Rumann,

Margaret Dumont, Robert Emmett O'Connor
Director: Sam Wood
Screenplay: George S. Kaufman and Morrie Ryskind, from a story by James Kevin McGuinness
Comedy
Unrated
Young kids: OK   Older kids: VG

For many people, this is the perfect Marx Brothers movie, and certainly it is the perfect way to introduce kids to the madness of the Marxes, in the context of a well-told story.

The scheming Groucho has set his sights on wealthy Mrs. Claypool (Margaret Dumont), who's being wooed by an opera impresario. Harpo has just been fired by his temperamental boss, an egotistical opera singer (Walter Woolf King). Somehow, Groucho, Harpo, and Chico are brought together, and share a tiny cabin on an ocean liner that brings the entire opera troupe—including their friend, an aspiring singer (Allan Jones)—to New York. There, they scheme to get their pal hired by the Cosmopolitan Opera troupe and wreck his rival's debut performance.

No one ever made a funnier movie than *A Night at the Opera,* and the beauty of the film is that it can be enjoyed by young and old alike. Groucho's repartee has a more adult appeal, but he can be silly, too, and the pantomime of Harpo is irresistibly appealing to kids . . . just as Chico's trigger-finger piano playing is shown to be in one memorable scene.

The stateroom scene, in which one person after another tries to crowd into an itty-bitty space, is justifiably famous, but it's just one of many great routines sprinkled throughout the film.

Yes, there is a romantic subplot, and a handful of songs, but they are so well integrated into the story that you never mind; there is never a feeling of the music interrupting or slowing down the comedy.

The Marx Brothers performed this screenplay as a theatrical vehicle in a number of cities, to refine the material and see just where the laughs would come. The result is a film that's pretty well surefire—even after all these years.

THE NIGHTMARE BEFORE CHRISTMAS (1993) (aka **Tim Burton's The Nightmare Before Christmas**)

Color, 75 minutes
Cast: Voices of Danny Elfman, Chris Sarandon, Catherine O'Hara, William Hickey, Glenn Shadix, Paul Reubens, Ken Page, Ed Ivory
Director: Henry Selick
Screenplay: Caroline Thompson, adaptation by Michael McDowell, based on a story and characters by Tim Burton
Animated musical fantasy
Rated PG
Young children: OK, with caution   Older children: VG

This ingenious and entertaining fantasy, designed by Tim Burton, transports viewers to a strange community called Halloween Town where the populace is unique and quite grotesque: The residents range from a sharp-toothed monster who lives under a bed to skeletons, mummies, ghouls, and a chap with a tear-away face. There is a young woman who keeps removing her limbs, and there's a nutty scientist who can open his skull to scratch his brain! One of the more prominent citizens is a bony character named Jack Skellington, the Pumpkin King, who accidentally discovers the joys of Christmas and decides to have Halloween Town take over the management of that holiday. To accomplish that goal, all the eerie creatures start manufacturing toys and tree decorations in preparation for the big holiday. To assure the success of his plan, Jack even has Santa Claus captured and held prisoner by a boogey man named Mr. Oogie Boogie while he delivers some of the oddest and most disgusting holiday gifts imaginable to unsuspecting kiddies.

The Nightmare Before Christmas presents the strangest "spin" on the holiday season ever put on film—but the results are delightful, and the music score (written and largely sung by Danny Elfman) is terrific. Even with its array of oddities, the film has many sweet, gentle moments and genuinely likable characters. It's fast paced, imaginative, and loads of fun, at least for the older children in the family. For the very young, this movie could result in real nightmares. Seeing Santa being tortured at the hands of a huge boogeyman might be too cruel and powerful an image for them. And if your kids blanched at seeing the discombobulated playthings in the "mean boy's" room in **Toy Story,** they'll cringe in terror at the sight of Halloween Town's bizarre population.

NIKKI, WILD DOG OF THE NORTH (1961)
Color, 74 minutes
Cast: Don Haldane, Jean Coutu, Emile Genest, Uriel Luft, Robert Rivard
Director: Jack Couffer
Screenplay: Winston Hibler and Ralph Wright, based on a novel by James Oliver Curwood
Adventure/Animal story
Unrated
Younger kids: Good   Older kids: VG

Nikki is a Canadian wolf dog who gets separated from his owner, trapper Andre Dupas (Jean Coutu), along with a bear cub who—after a difficult beginning—becomes his friend. Nikki is later captured by a nasty trapper named LeBeau (Emile Genest), who trains him to be a vicious fighter dog, despite the outlawing of dogfights. When the new factor tries to stop a pit fight, LeBeau pushes him into the pit and orders Nikki to attack him, but Nikki recognizes the factor as his old owner, Dupas, and after a fight in which LeBeau is killed, master and dog are happily reunited.

This is an entertaining hybrid of Disney's "True-Life" nature documentary films with a fictional story, which will delight children with its outstanding animal footage and stunning photography of the Canadian Rockies. Still, in all, the fight between LeBeau and Dupas is surprisingly brutal, and some children might find it upsetting.

NORMA RAE (1979)
Color, 113 minutes
Cast: Sally Field, Ron Leibman,
  Beau Bridges, Pat Hingle,
  Barbara Baxley, Gail
  Strickland
Director: Martin Ritt
Screenplay: Irving Ravetch and
  Harriet Frank, Jr.
Drama
Rated PG
Young children: No Older
  children: VG

Sally Field won her spurs as a
movie star and earned a well-de-
served Best Actress Academy
Award for her trenchant portrayal
of a real-life heroine: Norma Rae,
a poor, uneducated small-town
Southern textile worker. During
the course of the story, Norma
Rae is gradually won over to the
idea of organizing a labor union
in her factory by Reuben (Ron
Leibman), an intense and earnest
labor organizer from New York.

It is a pleasure to watch Field
as her character blossoms before
our eyes and is transformed from
a passive drone to a fiery and self-
assured leader who exerts her will
and takes control of her life. In
this regard, her character serves
as a role model for all children.
And it is a pleasure to watch
Norma Rae interact with Reuben,
a New Yorker and a Jew who is
as alien to her as if he had just
emerged from a spaceship.

Director Martin Ritt and screenwriters Irving Ravetch and Harriet
Frank, Jr., treat their working-
class characters with respect and
not a hint of condescension. It's
also refreshing that while Norma
Rae and Reuben become close
and develop a shared affection
and admiration, they do not fall
into each other's arms (or into

bed) in typical, clichéd Hollywood fashion.

This is a superior film that parents and older children will enjoy
together. There is, however, some
rough language and dramatic tension that puts it out of reach for
younger kids.

NORTH (1994)
Color, 87 minutes
Cast: Elijah Wood, Jason
  Alexander, Julia Louis-
  Dreyfus, Bruce Willis, Jon
  Lovitz, Alan Arkin, Mathew
  McCurley, Dan Aykroyd,
  Reba McEntire, Kathy Bates,
  Graham Greene, Kelly
  McGillis, Alexander Godunov,
  John Ritter, Faith Ford, Alan
  Arkin
Director: Rob Reiner
Screenplay: Alan Zweibel and
  Andrew Scheinman, based on
  a novel by Zweibel
Comedy-fantasy/Satire
Rated PG
Younger children: No Older
  children: No

North earned its reputation as one
of Hollywood's biggest misfires. A
wrongheaded parable, it will confuse or annoy children and parents alike.

Elijah Wood plays North, an
11-year-old boy who "divorces"
himself from his parents and goes
on a worldwide quest to find an
ideal mother and father. This includes visits with Ma and Pa Tex
(Reba McEntire and Dan Aykroyd), Alaskan Mom and Dad
(Kathy Bates and Graham
Greene), Amish Ma and Pa
(Kelly McGillis and Alexander
Godunov) and an "Ozzie and
Harriet" all-American couple
(John Ritter and Faith Ford),
among others.

An unnecessary subplot involves North's school chum, who leads a children's revolution based on North's precedent-setting divorce action.

The tone of the film suggests a fable, but it never delivers the goods . . . right up to the very predictable (and unemotional) finale. Awkward, heavy-handed, and utterly without charm, *North* is, simply put, a dud.

NORTHWEST PASSAGE [BOOK 1—ROGERS' RANGERS] (1940)
Color, 125 minutes
Cast: Spencer Tracy, Robert Young, Walter Brennan, Ruth Hussey, Nat Pendleton, Robert Barrat, Addison Richards
Director: King Vidor
Screenplay: Laurence Stallings and Talbot Jennings, based on the novel by Kenneth Roberts
Action-adventure
Unrated
Younger kids: NG   Older kids: VG

Spencer Tracy gives a powerful performance in this superb film about the adventures of the 18th-century American explorer and Indian fighter Major Robert Rogers. Originally planned as a two-part epic (the second was never made), this part focuses on the story of a mapmaker (Robert Young) and his friend (Walter Brennan) who join Rogers' troop of Rangers on a perilous mission to wipe out a tribe of bloodthirsty Indians, who have been staging violent attacks in the Ohio Valley and western New York with the encouragement of the French. After completing their mission, Rogers prepares to embark on an even more dangerous one: to march through uncharted territory and find a passage that will lead to the Pacific and the Orient.

This is no schoolbook history lesson filled with cardboard characters, but a passionate, potent and visually stunning depiction of the rigors and hardships of frontier life—one of the best ever made by Hollywood. It's also quite fierce and violent at times, making it inappropriate for young viewers.

NOTHING BUT A MAN (1964)
Black & white, 92 minutes
Cast: Ivan Dixon, Abbey Lincoln, Julius Harris, Gloria Foster, Martin Priest, Leonard Parker, Yaphet Kotto, Stanley Greene, Esther Rolle, Moses Gunn.
Director: Michael Roemer
Screenplay: Roemer and Robert Malcolm Young
Drama
Unrated
Young children: No · Older children: VG

This quietly persuasive independent production was one of the first American films to present blacks in their own society, and not in relation to whites. Set in rural Alabama, it tells the story of Duff, a young railroad worker who marries Josie, a preacher's daughter. The focus is on Duff's emotional struggles and uncertainties, and his need to affirm his own sense of self-worth.

Duff and Josie are portrayed with sincerity and believability. The characters' conflicts and the issues raised within the story make *Nothing but a Man* as timely and affecting today as it was in 1964. The central characters are not symbolic heroes; they're just ordinary people trying to get on with their lives.

At a time when some Americans believe in separatism, it might also be noted that this film—one of the most honest and poignant portrayals of blacks in our society—was written and directed by whites.

NOW AND FOREVER (1934)

Black & white, 81 minutes (also available in computer-colored version)

Cast: Shirley Temple, Gary Cooper, Carole Lombard, Sir Guy Standing, Charlotte Granville, Gilbert Emery, Henry Kolker

Director: Henry Hathaway

Screenplay: Vincent Lawrence and Sylvia Thalberg, based on the story "Honor Bright" by Jack Kirkland and Melville Baker

Drama

Unrated

Young children: OK   Older children: VG

In an early co-starring role, Shirley Temple plays opposite two Hollywood legends, Gary Cooper and Carole Lombard. Her parents are estranged; she lives with her mother in a conservative Connecticut home, while her father is a somewhat reformed international thief. When her mother dies, she joins her father and his lady love. The plot deals with the father's efforts to go straight and his attempts to respect his child's "honor bright" system. Eventually, however, the father resumes his criminal lifestyle and even involves his little daughter in his misconduct.

Because this drama is primarily a love story focusing on Cooper and Lombard and not specifically about the little girl, it will interest adolescents and adults more than the youngsters. It is not a Shirley Temple movie in the accepted sense of that term and was made just before the curly-haired moppet became a superstar. Even so, she outshines leading lady Lombard (who was just on the verge of real stardom herself), and her scenes with Cooper are a delight. The story is predictable from an adult point of view but worth seeing for the winning personalities of its stars.

NOW AND THEN (1995)

Color, 96 minutes

Cast: Christina Ricci, Thora Birch, Gaby Hoffmann, Ashleigh Aston Moore, Demi Moore, Rosie O'Donnell, Rita Wilson, Melanie Griffith, Bonnie Hunt

Director: Lesli Linka Glatter

Screenplay: I. Marlene King

Comedy-drama

Rated PG-13

Younger children: OK, with caution   Older children: OK

A formulaic comedy-drama about four female teens coming of age in 1970, this story is told in flashback, as the friends share secrets and misadventures during summer vacation in their hometown of Shelby, Indiana.

Seances, summer romance, a first kiss: these are some of the highpoints of their time together, during what will be the last summer of their childhood, along with the mystery surrounding the unsolved murder of "Dear Johnny," a boy buried in the local cemetery.

The four girls, played by Gaby

Hoffmann, Thora Birch, Christina Ricci, and Ashleigh Aston Moore, are appealing and smart. Their 1995 counterparts, Demi Moore, Rosie O'Donnell, Rita Wilson, and Melanie Griffith, make the best of their brief moments throughout the film.

NO WAY OUT (1950)
Black & white, 106 minutes
Cast: Richard Widmark, Linda Darnell, Stephen McNally, Sidney Poitier, Mildred Joanne Smith, Harry Bellaver, Stanley Ridges, Dots Johnson, Amanda Randolph, Ruby Dee, Ossie Davis
Director: Joseph L. Mankiewicz
Screenplay: Mankiewicz and Lesser Samuels
Drama
Unrated
Young children: No Older children: VG

This early racial drama—released the same year Joseph L. Mankiewicz won Oscars for directing and writing *All About Eve*—offers a stinging portrait of bigotry in America. It also features star-to-be Sidney Poitier in his screen debut, as a young medical intern who is derided by a white, racist hoodlum. As the story evolves, he must prove that he did not allow the thug's brother to die while under his care.

While many landmark social dramas of this period have dated badly, this one still cuts pretty deep, in part because of Richard Widmark's chilling portrayal of the bigot, as frightening a character as any ever seen in a Hollywood movie. The determination of the young black doctor to care for him—in spite of his steady stream of insults—is equally compelling. He refuses to sink to the racist's level; he feels duty-bound to do his job, no more, no less.

While *No Way Out* remains a cogent drama, it is of more than passing interest on historical terms. Back in 1950, simply casting a black actor as a physician in a major Hollywood feature was news; until then most blacks were only portrayed as servants. As the character's wife observes, "We've been a long time getting here. We're tired but we're here, honey. We can be happy. We've got a right to be."

This is still a tough, occasionally violent movie, but older children will find its central issues still relevant.

THE NUTTY PROFESSOR (1963)
Color, 107 minutes
Cast: Jerry Lewis, Stella Stevens, Del Moore, Kathleen Freeman, Med Flory
Director: Jerry Lewis
Screenplay: Lewis and Bill Richmond, based on a story by Lewis
Comedy
Unrated
Younger kids: Good Older kids: Good

Before Eddie Murphy revived his career with a 1996 remake, Jerry Lewis had one of his biggest hits as the star, director, and cowriter of this comic variation of *Dr. Jekyll and Mr. Hyde*. In his most famous role, Lewis plays super nerd Julius Kelp, an accident-prone chemistry professor with buck teeth and glasses who concocts a potion that transforms him into a super-cool singer named Buddy Love and, in that guise, tries to woo one of his beautiful students (Stella Stevens) but has to deal with the formula wearing off.

This is one of Lewis' better solo films. He's hilarious as the bespectacled, chipmunklike Kelp, while his swaggering impersonation of the smarmy Buddy Love has prompted some to believe that it's a satire of Lewis' former partner Dean Martin, although it also contains a lot of Jerry's own real-life "showbiz" persona. Lewis' direction is also very good, accentuating the laughs with plenty of gags in which he becomes a human cartoon and gets flattened by doors and barbells, etc., which are reminiscent of the films he made with his mentor, Frank Tashlin.

Kids who like Jerry will like this, although the film's maudlin attempt to wrap up its story with a "moral" is a bit hard to take. Young fans may prefer the older, goofier Jerry Lewis comedies as a result.

O

THE ODYSSEY (1995)

Color, 165 minutes

Cast: Armand Assante, Greta Scacchi, Geraldine Chaplin, Eric Roberts, Bernadette Peters, Isabella Rossellini, Irene Papas, Vanessa Williams, Christopher Lee

Director: Andrei Konchalovsky

Screenplay: Konchalovsky and Chris Solimine, from the epic poem by Homer

Epic drama

Rated PG-13

Young children: OK   Older children: VG

Little did the ancient Greek poet Homer know that his epic poem, written circa 800 B.C., would be a lasting effort read through the ages . . . or that it would become an opulent television miniseries with an all-star cast!

This extravaganza retells the saga of Odysseus (aka Ulysses) and his twenty-year struggle to return to his native Ithaca from the Trojan War.

Far better than the only other cinematic version of the tale, the botched 1955 Italian job with Kirk Douglas, this long movie takes the time to explore the character of Odysseus as he sails the Mediterranean trying to get home.

All the familiar figures of the legend are here: Scacchi as the ever-faithful Penelope, Williams as the seductive Calypso, Rossellini as the goddess Athena, the sinister cyclops, the sea monsters Scylla and Charybdis, the enchantments of Circe (Peters) . . . all rendered with eye-popping computer animation effects.

Some of the material is a bit mature for youngsters, but some of it is rousing movie-style adventure.

Western literature begins with Homer. The old stories are the best ones.

OF MICE AND MEN (1939)

Black & white, 107 minutes

Cast: Burgess Meredith, Lon Chaney, Jr., Betty Field, Charles Bickford, Roman Bohnen, Bob Steele, Noah Beery, Jr.

Director: Lewis Milestone

Screenplay: Eugene Solow, based on the novel by John Steinbeck

Drama

Unrated

Young children: No   Older children: VG

This searing drama, based on John Steinbeck's timeless novel, details the friendship of the physically imposing but feeble-minded Lennie (Lon Chaney, Jr.) and his loyal guardian/pal, George (Burgess Meredith). Homeless drifters in Depression-era California, they hire on to work at a ranch. As they dream of one day owning their own small homestead, they contend with their boss' sadistically evil son, Curley (Bob Steele), and his attractive but discontented wife (Betty Field).

The focal point of the story is the warmth and loyalty shared by the kindhearted, protective George and the childlike Lennie, whose innocence does not insulate him from an unfriendly, often hateful world.

Lon Chaney, Jr., who was most famous for horror films, gives the best performance of his career as Lennie. Indeed, in his own way Lennie is like the Frankenstein monster, a gentle but ill-fated creature who knows neither his own strength nor right from wrong.

The story told in *Of Mice and Men* is too harsh and unconventional for younger children; Lennie's habit of squishing animals by literally loving them to death, the sexual behavior of Curley's wife, and the heartrending climax could be confusing and certainly upsetting. But this haunting, deceptively simple, emotionally complex morality play is ideal viewing for older kids.

OF MICE AND MEN (1992)
Color, 110 minutes
Cast: John Malkovich, Gary Sinise, Alexis Arquette, Sherilyn Fenn, Joe Morton, Richard Riehle, Casey Siemaszko, John Terry, Ray Walston, Noble Willingham.
Director: Gary Sinise
Screenplay: Horton Foote, based on the novel by John Steinbeck
Drama
Rated PG-13
Young children: No   Older children: VG, with caution

Remakes of classic films are generally serviceable at best and downright dreadful at worst. This solid reworking of the Steinbeck story is a refreshing exception: well acted and scripted, and just as moving as the original.

John Malkovich plays the feeble-minded Lennie, and Gary Sinise is his loyal friend, George. Once again, these drifters find themselves working on a ranch where frustrated and in some cases mean-spirited people change the course of their lives. And while the setting remains the 1930s, during the Great Depression, there is a potent subtext relating the story to the homeless in contemporary America, luckless individuals subsisting in their own Great Depression.

As with the 1939 version, this is too tough a story for young, impressionable kids; even older children may have a hard time with some of the scenes, especially in this version, which is more explicit (both in terms of sex and violence) than the earlier film.

A third version of the story is also available on video, a workmanlike TV production that aired in 1981, with Robert Blake as George and Randy Quaid as Lennie.

OH, GOD! (1977)
Color, 104 minutes
Cast: George Burns, John Denver, Teri Garr, Paul Sorvino, George Furth, Ralph Bellamy, Barnard Hughes, David Ogden Stiers
Director: Carl Reiner
Screenplay: Larry Gelbart, from the book by Avery Corman
Comedy
Rated PG
Younger kids: OK   Older kids: VG

Kids should enjoy this gentle comic fable in which supermarket assistant manager Denver is chosen by God to spread the message that He is still alive and watching over humanity. A throwback of sorts to the quieter fantasy comedies of Hollywood's "golden age," this entertaining film is a nice examination of faith, and while not terribly deep, it *is* funny, with some thoughtful comments on the state of today's world.

Denver is a good choice as the shy, modern-day Moses, and Burns is as ideal a Supreme Being as anyone could wish for: charming, understanding, easygoing, raffish, and quick with a miracle and a one-liner. (Wondering why he was asked to play God, show business veteran Burns noted that he was the closest one to His age and that "since Moses wasn't around, I suppose I was next in line.")

There are some mildly tart observations about organized religious figures (who attempt to manipulate and exploit Denver), but unless one is offended by the idea of God appearing in the guise of George Burns in a golfing hat and plaid shirt, there is little that could possibly offend. The sequels, *Oh God! Book II* and *Oh God! You Devil*, were, shall we say, not as divinely inspired.

OKLAHOMA! (1955)
Color, 145 minutes
Cast: Gordon MacRae, Shirley Jones, Charlotte Greenwood, Rod Steiger, Gloria Grahame, Eddie Albert, James Whitmore, Gene Nelson, Barbara Lawrence, Jay C. Flippen, Roy Barcroft, James Mitchell, Bambi Linn
Director: Fred Zinnemann
Screenplay: Sonya Levien and William Ludwig, adapted from the musical by Richard Rodgers and Oscar Hammerstein II based on Lynn Riggs' dramatic play *Green Grow the Lilacs*
Musical
Unrated
Young children: VG   Older children: VG

Here is a richly rewarding and beautifully expanded screen adaptation of one of Broadway's most fabled and influential musicals. The performances all are letter-perfect. The settings are magnificent. The music, including "Oh, What a Beautiful Mornin'," "The Surrey With the Fringe on Top," "I Cain't Say No," "People Will Say We're in Love," and the title tune, is timeless. And the story is nothing less than compelling

Oklahoma! is set in the Oklahoma Territory. It is the tale of a cowboy named Curly (Gordon MacRae) and Laurey (Shirley Jones), the sweet young girl he woos. They are surrounded by a gallery of memorable supporting characters, beginning with the ever-commiserating Aunt Eller (Charlotte Greenwood), easy-to-please Ado-Annie (Gloria Grahame), and rangy cowhand Will Parker (Gene Nelson). It would be difficult to find a better cast— or a more glorious pair of voices than those of MacRae and Jones. (A younger generation got to know Shirley Jones better as the mom on television's *The Partridge Family*. This was her screen debut.)

The very youngest family members may be put off by the personality and actions of Jud Fry (Rod Steiger), a farmhand who is the story's darkly sinister and deeply troubled villain.

One of the film's many high-lights is the exquisitely beautiful "Out of My Dreams" ballet, in which dancers James Mitchell and Bambi Linn impersonate the characters of Curly and Laurey.

By the way, *Oklahoma!* was shot in two separate versions, employing different "takes" with the performers, one using the Todd-AO process—this was the print originally projected in movie theaters—and the other in CinemaScope. However, the CinemaScope version is the one that has been broadcast on television and released to video. But in 1994, the Todd-AO print was made available on laser disc—and it is fascinating to compare the two.

THE OLD MAN AND THE SEA (1958)
Color, 86 minutes
Cast: Spencer Tracy, Felipe Pazos, Harry Bellaver
Director: John Sturges
Screenplay: Peter Viertel, based on the novella by Ernest Hemingway
Adventure/Literary classic
Unrated
Young children: OK   Older children: VG

Ernest Hemingway himself is re-ported to have approved of this adaptation of his classic fish tale, which is a beautifully drawn parable of man's struggle against the challenges of nature and life. Spencer Tracy offers a tour-de-force performance as an elderly Cuban fisherman who is determined to hook a gigantic marlin and then bring it into port. The unusual scenario spends much of its time focusing on the old man seated in his small boat, alone with his thoughts and memories,

and the result is a powerful lesson in human endurance and will-power. There is a subplot, involving a young boy who loves and believes in the old man, which will make this film particularly likable for youngsters.

Sequences showing sharks attacking a dead fish may not be for the whole family, but they resemble a straightforward wildlife special more than a horrific scene from **Jaws.** Because the scenario focuses on the fisherman and his singular quest, rather than telling a more varied traditional story, some family members may lose patience with the lack of plot, while others—especially fishing enthusiasts—will be riveted. Modern-day kids may also look askance at some of the substandard process-screen shots which show Tracy in his seagoing environment.

OLD YELLER (1958)
Color, 83 minutes
Cast: Dorothy McGuire, Fess Parker, Tommy Kirk, Kevin Corcoran, Jeff York, Beverly Washburn, Chuck Connors
Director: Robert Stevenson
Screenplay: Fred Gipson and William Tunberg, based on the novel by Gipson
Family drama/Animal story
Rated G
Younger kids: Good, with caution   Older kids: VG

Old Yeller is a sentimental Disney favorite that has entered the national consciousness as perhaps the ultimate boy-and-his-dog story . . . and the one movie that has reduced every viewer to tears. Moppet star Kevin Corcoran plays Arliss, a lonely little boy in 1869 Texas who lives on a farm with his teenage brother, Travis (Tommy Kirk), his mother, Katie (Dorothy McGuire), and his father, Jim (Fess Parker). When Jim has to leave for three months to go on a cattle drive, Travis becomes the head of the household and Arliss adopts a lop-eared yellow mutt who wanders onto the farm. Travis considers the dog a no-account "eggsucker," but Yeller wins the whole family over by proving to be a fine watchdog and protector. Before the happy ending, however, there is tragedy and heartbreak.

This is a poignant frontier saga with something for everyone: delightful animals and wildlife footage for kids (Travis is a walking zoo whose pants are stuffed with frogs, snakes, and lizards), a lesson about maturity, courage, and loss for teens, and a warm romance between Katie and Jim for adults. Some of the situations, such as a ferocious fight between the dog and some wild pigs, the subsequent incidence of rabies, and Yeller's ultimate fate might be too intense for younger children, but these events add a note of realism and honesty to the story that keeps it from becoming saccharine.

The loss of any pet is upsetting, but like all the best Disney films, this one stresses the continuity of life and the importance of being able to move on. Still, parents shouldn't let their young ones see this film without being at their side . . . with tissues handy.

OLIVER! (1968)
Color, 153 minutes
Cast: Ron Moody, Shani Wallis, Oliver Reed, Harry Secombe, Mark Lester, Jack Wild, Hugh Griffith, Joseph O'Conor, Peggy Mount, Leonard Rossiter, James Hayter
Director: Carol Reed
Screenplay: Vernon Harris, based on the musical play by Lionel Bart, from the novel *Oliver Twist* by Charles Dickens
Musical
Rated G
Young children: VG, with caution   Older children: VG

Oliver!, which won a Best Picture Oscar, is the adaptation of Lionel Bart's stage musical based on the venerable Charles Dickens tale about orphaned Oliver Twist in 19th-century London. The film won a bundle of other Academy Awards, including Best Director, Art Direction, Scoring, and a special statuette for choreographer Onna White, who created some of the best dance numbers ever put on film, notably "Who Will Buy?"

Onscreen as onstage, all of Dickens' characters come colorfully alive, from innocent Oliver to the crafty Fagin, the good-hearted Nancy, and the cruel Bill Sikes. What's more, the wonderful songs seem to grow naturally out of the story—as when Oliver and his fellow orphans sing out for "Food, Glorious Food." When Oliver joins the ranks of Fagin's young pickpockets, The Artful Dodger helps welcome him by leading the group in singing "Consider Yourself."

Just because this is a G-rated musical doesn't mean it ignores the darker aspects of Dickens' story, however. (In today's sensitive society, the film would probably warrant a PG.) Nancy's relationship with the brutal Bill Sykes is discreet but clear, which may cause children to wonder why she puts up with his physical abuse. And Sykes' eventual fate is not the stuff of normal "happy" musical movies.

But that's what gives *Oliver!* its substance. Life is not peaches and cream for the lower classes in London, but the smart ones learn how to get along just the same.

OLIVER & COMPANY (1988)
Color, 72 minutes
Cast: Voices of Joey Lawrence, Billy Joel, Cheech Marin, Richard Mulligan, Roscoe Lee Browne, Sheryl Lee Ralph, Dom DeLuise, Robert Loggia, Bette Midler
Directors: George Scribner
Screenplay: Jim Cox, Timothy J. Disney, and James Mangold, from a story by Vance Gerry, Mike Gabriel, Roger Allers, Joe Ranft, Gary Trousdale, Jim Mitchell, Kevin Lima, Chris Bailey, Michael Cedeno, Kirk Wise, Pete Young, Dave Michener, and Leon Joosen, inspired by Charles Dickens' *Oliver Twist*
Animated feature/Musical
Rated G
Younger kids: OK   Older kids: VG

Perhaps the Disney studio's grittiest cartoon (both in subject matter and setting), this modern version of Charles Dickens' *Oliver Twist* set in an all-too-believable New York City features a cast comprised of dogs and cats.

Young Oliver is a stray kitten who hooks up with savvy street mutt Dodger (the voice of Billy Joel) and his pack of canine scavengers. Fagin (Dom DeLuise) is a hapless homeless human who owes big money to evil gangster Sykes (Robert Loggia). When Oliver is adopted by a lonely little rich girl named Jenny, Dodger and his gang attempt a "rescue"—aided by Georgette (Bette Midler), the family's pampered pooch, who is only to happy to let Oliver return to the streets. Fagin sees an opportunity to pay Sykes by holding the kitten for ransom, but Sykes prefers the larger financial possibilities of kidnapping little Jenny himself.

This picture was made right before Disney animation "got its groove back," so the artwork is a bit flat and sketchy, with an early use of computer animation to create some of the cars and cityscapes. But the story, acting, and music more than make up for it.

The voice work is excellent. Billy Joel has the film's best song, "Why Should I Worry?" and Bette Midler has a funny showcase piece, "Perfect Isn't Easy." But it's Cheech Marin who steals the show as a feisty, hyperactive little Chihuahua.

Some of the villainy is threatening indeed, and the bad guy has a couple of truly menacing dogs who might scare little kids (and rightly so). But on the whole, *Oliver & Company* is a cheerful piece of entertainment that most kids will enjoy.

OLIVER TWIST (1948)
Black & white, 105 minutes
Cast: Robert Newton, Alec Guinness, Kay Walsh, Francis L. Sullivan, Henry Stephenson, Mary Clare, John Howard

Davies, Josephine Stuart, Henry Edwards, Ralph Truman, Anthony Newley
Director: David Lean
Screenplay: Lean and Stanley Haynes, based on the novel by Charles Dickens
Drama/Literary classic
Unrated
Young children: VG   Older children: VG

Oliver Twist, the 1838 Charles Dickens novel about a mistreated London orphan who becomes involved with the devilish Fagin and his gang of street urchins, has long been a popular celluloid property. By far the best nonmusical mounting of the property is this British-made feature, superbly directed and cowritten by David Lean, who brought Dickens's *Great Expectations* to the screen just two years earlier.

It is beautifully acted, with the always brilliant Alec Guinness as Fagin and a very young Anthony Newley as The Artful Dodger, one of Fagin's street boys. (Upon the film's release, the depiction of Fagin was denounced as anti-Semitic because of the character's stereotypical Jewish mannerisms and the size of his nose. This is still a subject of some debate.)

There is nothing cheerful or pretty about this version of *Oliver.* Street life in London of the early 1800s was harsh—which is why the contrast between Oliver's life as a would-be pickpocket and the privileged existence he attains is so great. Fagin is more a villain than a rogue, as he was in the later musical *Oliver!,* and Bill Sykes is fearsome indeed.

Children who are accustomed to lighter treatments of this story should know that this one is much more serious—though not without its moments of warmth and humor. It is, by any standards, a great film.

ONE FINE DAY (1997)
Color, 108 minutes
Cast: Michelle Pfeiffer, George Clooney, Mae Whitman, Alex D. Linz, Charles Durning, Jon Robin Baitz, Ellen Greene, Joe Grifasi, Anna Maria Horsford, Holland Taylor
Director: Michael Hoffman
Screenplay: Terrell Seltzer and Ellen Simon
Comedy
Rated PG
Young children: VG   Older children: VG

Here is one of those rare Hollywood movies of the 1990s that can actually be called "nice." While not aimed specifically at children, it's the kind of film that parents and kids can enjoy together—because it speaks to both age groups equally well.

One Fine Day is the story of two single working parents who live in Manhattan. When the very conscientious Michelle Pfeiffer and the casually irresponsible George Clooney fail to get their respective children to the pier in time for a floating field trip, they have to find a way to attend to pressing business matters and take care of their kids at the same time. Although they keep rubbing each other the wrong way, they agree to take turns watching the kids in order to make their complicated schedules work, for one very hectic day.

Kids may not fully appreciate the parental worries and business-related problems each grown-up has to face, but the film's breathless pace, and ever-changing location, should keep them interested all the way . . . especially when the children are involved in the action. (Each parent, in turns, manages to lose the kids for a short spell.)

Some mild language and several sexual references occur, but nothing shocking in a modern-day context and nothing that isn't overriden by the film's general sense of goodwill.

ONE HUNDRED AND ONE DALMATIANS (1961)

Color, 79 minutes
Cast: Voices of Rod Taylor, Lisa Davis, Cate Bauer, Ben Wright, Fred Warlock, J. Pat O'Malley, Betty Lou Gerson
Directors: Wolfgang Reitherman, Hamilton Luske, and Clyde Geronimi
Screenplay: Bill Peet, based on the book *The Hundred and One Dalmatians* by Dodie Smith
Animated feature
Unrated
Young children: VG Older children: VG

Walt Disney struck pay dirt with a deceptively simple story about a man and woman who fall in love—with a little help from their dogs—and raise a family of dalmatians, only to fall prey to the evil schemes of a so-called friend named Cruella De Vil.

What makes *One Hundred and One Dalmatians* so good is the way it leaves the human world behind at one point and takes the animals' point of view. Not only do we get to know Pongo and Perdita, the dalmatian parents, but we see them as part of the larger animal community. It is that

community which helps to organize a rescue effort, and it engages us as an audience completely. (And it is precisely that element that was missing from the live-action remake.)

The other memorable ingredient of *Dalmatians* is its incredible, larger-than-life villainess, Cruella De Vil. She is one of Disney's great creations, an absolutely awful woman who is a complete caricature—yet strangely believable.

One Hundred and One Dalmatians has comedy, adventure, and suspense—but nothing too strong for young children. It's a delight for all ages.

101 DALMATIANS (1996)

Color, 103 minutes
Cast: Glenn Close, Jeff Daniels, Joely Richardson, Joan Plowright, Hugh Laurie, Mark Williams, John Shrapnel
Director: Stephen Herek
Screenplay: John Hughes, based on the novel by Dodie Smith
Comedy/Animal story
Rated G
Young kids: OK Older kids: OK

A chance meeting between Roger, an American game inventor (Jeff Daniels), and Anita, a British fashion designer (Joely Richardson), is propelled even further by the mutual affection of their dalmatians, Pongo and Perdita. Soon they are one big happy family. But Anita's boss, Cruella DeVil, begins to take an unnatural interest in the new dalmatian puppies. . . .

Although Glenn Close gives a strikingly flamboyant performance as villainous Cruella, there seems no point to having made a live-action version of the much-loved Walt Disney animated feature.

In spite of computer-generated special effects, it's not possible to give many of the spotted dogs their own personalities (certainly not without voices), so the emphasis in this film is on the human beings, who quickly become tiresome. And one of the cartoon movie's best story points—the twilight bark, which warns everyone in the canine kingdom of what is going on—isn't used in this remake.

What we get instead is another retread of screenwriter John Hughes' trademarked slapstick violence, as Cruella's lamebrained henchmen attempt to guard and then recapture the dalmatians. Even kids seem to like the cartoon version better—because more time is spent with the dogs and less with humans.

ONE HUNDRED MEN AND A GIRL (1937)
Black & white, 84 minutes
Cast: Deanna Durbin, Adolphe Menjou, Alice Brady, Eugene Pallette, Mischa Auer, Billy Gilbert, Alma Kruger, Jack Smart, Jed Prouty, Leopold Stokowski
Director: Henry Koster
Screenplay: Bruce Manning, Charles Kenyon, and James Mulhauser
Musical
Unrated
Young children: VG Older children: VG

This delightful musical served to solidify the stardom of sweet 16-year-old Deanna Durbin, whose astounding celluloid success helped to save Universal Pictures from bankruptcy. Under the tutelage of producer Joe Pasternak and director Henry Koster, the perky young actress with the beautiful soprano voice blossomed onscreen.

Kids and adults alike might find this movie old-fashioned, but it's also surefire entertainment, a story of underdogs and of a determined girl who makes good against all odds. Durbin is a delight, but she's surrounded here with a peerless cast of old pros who make the most of every comic moment.

Deanna plays Patsy Cardwell, who schemes to find employment for her jobless trombonist father (Adolphe Menjou) and his musician pals. (The title refers to the one-hundred-member orchestra Patsy ends up establishing for them.) Along the way, this spunky heroine connives to convince the renowned Leopold Stokowski to lead the orchestra. Stokowski then was the head of the Philadelphia Symphony Orchestra, and was one of America's reigning conductors.

Given its scenario, most of the music in the film is of a classical or operatic nature. There are compositions by Berlioz, Liszt, Mozart, Tchaikovsky, Wagner, Verdi, and others, and *One Hundred Men and a Girl* thus serves as a fine introduction to the joys of classical music and opera. Meanwhile, preteen girls should relate to Durbin because of her character's vitality and the way she thrives in an adult world.

Indeed, a year after the release of *One Hundred Men and a Girl,* Durbin and Mickey Rooney were given special Academy Awards for "bringing to the screen the spirit and personification of youth."

ONE MAGIC CHRISTMAS
(1985)
Color, 88 minutes
Cast: Mary Steenburgen, Gary
  Basaraba, Harry Dean
  Stanton, Arthur Hill, Elizabeth
  Harnois, Robbie Magwood,
  Michelle Meyrink, Elias
  Koteas, Jan Rubes, Sarah
  Polley, Graham Jarvis
Director: Phillip Borsos
Screenplay: Thomas Meehan,
  from a story by Meehan,
  Borsos, and Barry Healey
Christmas/Fantasy
Rated G
Younger children: OK, with
  caution   Older children: OK

An attempt to rekindle some of
the feeling of Frank Capra's classic **It's a Wonderful Life,** this entertaining film starts out in a very
downbeat manner. A depressed
mother (Mary Steenburgen), trying to support her two children, is
heading for a terrible Christmas.
Just when things look worst, a
guardian angel (Harry Dean Stanton) appears and restores her
faith in the spirit of the holiday.
  Midway through the film the
tone shifts from grim reality to
whimsical fantasy—and not a moment too soon! Excellent performances keep this afloat, with
Arthur Hill as Grandpa and Jan
Rubes as Santa Claus. Adorable
Elizabeth Harnois as the young
daughter practically steals the
show. As for Harry Dean Stanton,
adults will recognize what a startling change of pace it is to cast
him as a guardian angel; for kids,
it may not matter, but his stark-
looking face is not the kind you'd
automatically think of for this
part.
  Although rated G, and offering
fantasy and wish-fulfillment ingre-

dients that are bound to appeal to
kids, *One Magic Christmas* paints
a bleak picture of contemporary
working-class life. Some children—and parents—might find
this off-putting, to say the least.

ONE ON ONE (1977)
Color, 98 minutes
Cast: Robby Benson, Annette
  O'Toole, G. D. Spradlin, Gail
  Strickland, Melanie Griffith,
  James G. Richardson, Hector
  Morales
Director: Lamont Johnson
Screenplay: Robby Benson and
  Jerry Segal
Drama/Sports
Rated PG
Young children: VG   Older
  children: VG

In recent years, basketball films
have been arriving on movie
screens with as much frequency as
a Chicago Bulls championship.
Unfortunately, most of them have
been virtual airballs.
  This earnest drama, which
dates from the time when Michael
Jordan was a mere schoolboy, is
one of the better basketball movies. It tells the story of Henry
Steele (played by Robby Benson,
who co-authored the screenplay
with his father, Jerry Segal), a
high school hoop sensation who
heads off to college. Henry is
naive, a purist who rebels at the
crass commercialization of college
athletics. Meanwhile, he must
contend with his sadistic coach,
who sets out to humiliate him and
bounce him from the squad.
  While on many levels the story
told in *One on One* is predictable,
the film is nicely done and will be
of special interest to sports-
minded youngsters. Some strong

language and rough behavior earn this a PG.

ON GOLDEN POND (1981)
Color, 109 minutes
Cast: Henry Fonda, Katharine Hepburn, Jane Fonda, Doug McKeon, Dabney Coleman, William Lanteau
Director: Mark Rydell
Screenplay: Ernest Thompson, from his play
Comedy-drama
Rated PG
Younger kids: Good Older kids: Good

Here is a sentimental story about cantankerous, death-obsessed Norman Thayer (Henry Fonda) and his loving wife, Ethel (Hepburn), an elderly couple who spend each summer in a New England cottage overlooking beautiful Golden Pond. Daughter Chelsea (Jane Fonda), who's always felt emotionally distant from Norman, arrives with her new fiancé, Bill (Coleman); the two then take off for Europe, leaving Bill's 13-year-old son, Billy (McKeon), to stay with Norman and Ethel. When Chelsea returns, she discovers Norman and Billy have bonded, and the stage is set for her to finally come to terms with her father.

This is a manipulative film, to be sure, that spells out its themes and conflicts in big block letters; it has plenty of shots of golden sunsets and a treacly music score. But that can't alter the fact that it is highly entertaining and manages to touch on serious issues that are relevant to kids and their parents, mainly the pain and fear of growing old, and the importance of communication between all generations.

It is also interesting in terms of film history, for *On Golden Pond* brought together the dream trio of Jane Fonda, her legendary father, Henry (in his last screen appearance), and the indomitable Katharine Hepburn. Fonda and Hepburn had never appeared together in a film before this, but they make a perfect onscreen couple, giving substance and texture to their roles. For kids unaware of Fonda and Hepburn's screen pasts, it will be an education to watch these acting legends of the "old" school; for those who grew up with them, it is edifying to see them still so unerringly true to their craft.

ON THE TOWN (1949)
Color, 98 minutes
Cast: Gene Kelly, Frank Sinatra, Jules Munshin, Ann Miller, Vera-Ellen, Betty Garrett, Alice Pearce
Directors: Gene Kelly and Stanley Donen
Screenplay: Betty Comden and Adolph Green, based on their Broadway show
Musical
Unrated
Young children: OK Older children: VG

This buoyant musical has one of the best opening sequences in all of Hollywood history: three energetic sailors bursting forth from their ship as they get ready to enjoy 24 hours in "New York, New York." The energy and sheer likability of Gene Kelly, Frank Sinatra, and Jules Munshin make it difficult to resist this number and get involved in the film.

The movie as a whole can't live up to that opening musical number, but it's still fun to watch, especially for kids who've already logged some time with vintage Hollywood musicals. The women are a diverse and interesting trio: dancer Vera-Ellen, who comes to Gene Kelly's attention as a subway beauty queen known as Miss Turnstiles; paleontologist Ann Miller, who meets the sailors at the Museum of Natural History; and cabdriver Betty Garrett, who's not at all shy about inviting Frank Sinatra "up to my place."

The storyline sags, but the songs and dances are great fun.

OPERATION DUMBO DROP
(1995)
Color, 107 minutes
Cast: Danny Glover, Ray Liotta, Denis Leary, Doug E. Doug, Corin Nemec, Dinh Thien Le, Tcheky Karyo
Director: Simon Wincer
Screenplay: Gene Quintano and Jim Kouf, based on a story by Jim Morris
Adventure/Animal story
Rated PG
Younger children: No   Older children: OK

In the midst of Vietnam in 1968, with American soldiers doing their best to survive jungle warfare, a squadron is assigned to locate an elephant and transport him over two hundred miles of rugged terrain to a village that simply cannot exist without him. It seems that the elephant is a kind of sacred totem to these Vietnamese villagers; when their existing pachyderm is killed because of information leaked by a straight-arrow U.S. officer (Ray Liotta) who's new to the territory, the man he's been sent to replace (Danny Glover) insists he make good on a new elephant, despite the odds and the logistics.

Based on a true incident, *Operation Dumbo Drop* is a film that isn't destined to please anybody entirely. The story itself is interesting enough, but because this is a PG-rated Disney film, the war is treated in an almost make-believe manner. (For one thing, none of the hard-bitten soldiers here ever swear!)

For kids, the climactic scene of an elephant being dropped by helicopter could be genuinely upsetting—even though the shot was achieved through special effects. For everybody, the film has surprisingly little energy or pizzazz until the finale.

OUR HOSPITALITY (1923)
Black & white, 74 minutes
Cast: Buster Keaton, Natalie Talmadge, Buster Keaton, Jr., Joseph Keaton, Kitty Bradbury, Joe Roberts
Directors: Buster Keaton and John Blystone
Screenplay: Clyde Bruckman, Joseph Mitchell, and Jean Havez
Comedy/Silent classic
Unrated
Younger children: VG   Older children: VG

This outstanding comedy is one of Buster's very best. The setting is the pre–Civil War South, and Keaton plays Willie McKay, a young fellow who heads from New York to the small Southern town of Rockville to claim a family inheritance. Willie imagines an idealized antebellum environment of stately columned mansions and mint julep–style hospitality. Instead, he finds himself in the midst of a long-running Hatfield and McCoy–like feud with the rival Canfield clan. Further complications arise when Willie falls in love with Virginia Canfield (played by Natalie Talmadge, who was to become Keaton's real-life spouse).

Most Keaton features end with a rousing, extended comedy sequence. In *Our Hospitality,* it is an especially hair-raising one that involves Willie's derring-do as he attempts to save damsel-in-distress Virginia, who is about to be sent to her death over a waterfall. As always, Buster's acrobatic stunt work leaves the viewer breathless, even after all these years.

But like all the best silent comedies, this one works so well because it's built on the foundation of a really good story. Parents may have to explain the nature of backwoods feuds to kids, but after that, everyone should have a good time watching *Our Hospitality.*

OUR LITTLE GIRL (1935)

Black & white, 63 minutes (also available in computer-colored version)
Cast: Shirley Temple, Rosemary Ames, Joel McCrea, Lyle Talbot, Erin O'Brien-Moore, J. Farrell MacDonald, Rita Owin
Director: John Robertson
Screenplay: Stephen Avery and Allen Rivkin, based on the story "Heaven's Gate" by Florence Leighton Pfalzgraf
Drama
Unrated
Younger children: VG   Older children: VG

In this early starring role, young Shirley Temple appears as the lovable, cuddly, and super-bright offspring of a couple on the brink of divorce. As she dreams of a picnic with her parents to commemorate their romantic first meeting, their marriage is dissolving. Her doctor dad spends all his time with a female assistant at his office, and her mom is distracted by a handsome playboy who has just returned from Europe.

The film is a teary soap opera at heart. As such, it ordinarily would appeal primarily to adults. However, a fair amount of time is spent showing the results of the marital split on the child. For this reason, it might interest even the younger children and lead to some thought-provoking conversation with your family.

OUR RELATIONS (1936)

Black & white, 65 minutes
Cast: Stan Laurel, Oliver Hardy, Sidney Toler, Alan Hale, Daphne Pollard, Betty Healy, Iris Adrian, Lona Andre, James Finlayson, Arthur Housman, Charles D. Hall
Director: Harry Lachman
Screenplay: Richard Connell, Felix Adler, Charles Rogers, and Jack Jevne, based on the short story "The Money Box" by William Jacobs
Comedy
Unrated
Younger children: OK   Older children: OK

Laurel and Hardy play two sets of separated twins: a couple of sailors on leave with a diamond ring in hand and two henpecked husbands. Of course, mix-ups ensue. The wives (Daphne Pollard and Betty Healy) think their husbands are cheating on them when they see the sailors with some girls they've just met. The diamond ring disappears, and gangsters enter the picture demanding its return.

There's more plot than usual in this Laurel and Hardy comedy, but then, there are two Laurel and Hardys. It's fun to see Stan and Ollie in a different guise than usual, though ultimately Alf and Bert are not much smarter than the fellows we already know and love.

Kids who are already fans of the duo will enjoy this outing because it's different from the norm.

OUR TOWN (1940)
Black & white, 89 minutes
Cast: William Holden, Martha Scott, Fay Bainter, Beulah Bondi, Thomas Mitchell, Guy Kibbee, Stuart Erwin, Frank Craven
Director: Sam Wood
Screenplay: Thornton Wilder, Frank Craven, and Harry Chandlee, based on the play by Wilder
Drama/Literary classic
Unrated
Younger children: OK   Older children: VG

Thornton Wilder won a Pulitzer prize for his artful, broad-stroked play about small-town New Hampshire life in 1901, 1904, and 1913. Through a series of vignettes, some comical and others deeply heartfelt, the story of two families, the Gibbs and the Webbs, is unfurled. There are the everyday moments showing the family breakfast, high school athletics, a sweet-sixteen birthday, as well as scenes depicting neighborliness, romance, and the enduring and sometimes painful experiences of marriage and family, childbirth and death.

Because a good deal of the action focuses on the younger generation going through emotions and activities that are timeless, this film communicates well to adolescents. Those familiar with the play will note that the film does away with the tragic ending. Even so, the stark cemetery scenes are emotional and may provoke questions from, or fear in, youngsters.

THE OUTSIDE CHANCE OF MAXIMILIAN GLICK (1988)
Color, 96 minutes
Cast: Saul Rubinek, Jan Rubes, Noam Zylberman, Susan Douglas Rubes, Fairuza Balk, Cathryn Balk, Nigel Bennett, Sharon Corder
Director: Allan A. Goldstein
Screenplay: Phil Savath, based on a novel by Morley Torgov
Comedy-drama
Rated G
Young children: OK   Older children: VG

This touching, keenly observed Canadian-made comedy/drama/coming-of-age story is perfect fare for older children, who need not be Jewish in order to relate to its title character, a 12-year-old Jewish boy growing up in rural Manitoba in the early 1960s. As he prepares for his bar mitzvah, young Max becomes smitten with Celia, a pretty non-Jew with whom he studies piano. As a result, Max finds that he is conflicted by his desire to be his own person and his duty to his family.

Playing a key role in the story is the town's new rabbi, a likably eccentric cleric who stresses to Max the importance of making his own decisions.

The Outside Chance of Maximilian Glick is perfect fare for preteens who are beginning to wonder about the world that exists beyond their home and community.

THE OUTSIDERS (1983)
Color, 91 minutes
Cast: C. Thomas Howell, Matt Dillon, Ralph Macchio, Patrick Swayze, Rob Lowe, Diane Lane, Emilio Estevez, Tom Cruise, Leif Garrett
Director: Francis Ford Coppola
Screenplay: Kathleen Knutsen Rowell, from the novel by S. E. Hinton
Drama
Rated PG
Younger kids: No   Older kids: VG

The first of Francis Ford Coppola's two adaptations of S. E. Hinton's popular teen novels about disaffected youth (the other was *Rumblefish*) is an unusual and well-made tale of sensitive juvenile delinquents that's directed in the manner of an art film version of **Rebel Without a Cause** and is a stylistic homage to **Gone With the Wind.**

Matt Dillon, who at the time was the only "name" in a cast filled with future stars, plays a member of the Greasers, a tough gang from the wrong side of the tracks whose rivalry with the well-off Socs gang leads to tragedy in 1966 Oklahoma. Coppola's stylistic touches, including blazing sunset backdrops à la *GWTW* (which C. Thomas' Howell's character is seen reading throughout), a lush symphonic score, and having the characters discuss Robert Frost poems, are at odds with the gritty story, but create a sense of mythic grandeur.

The result is overblown but oddly affecting, and a dramatic change from realstic interpretations of teen angst seen in so many other movies and TV shows. Some of the language and the gang fights are too rough for younger kids, but teens should enjoy it, particularly since its cast reads like a veritable who's who of Brat Packers, including a very young Tom Cruise.

P

THE PAGEMASTER (1994)

Color, 75 minutes

Cast: Voices of Macaulay Culkin, Christopher Lloyd, Whoopi Goldberg, Patrick Stewart, Frank Welker, Leonard Nimoy

Directors: Joe Johnston (live-action) and Maurice Hunt (animation)

Screenplay: David Casci, David Kirschner, and Ernie Contreras

Live-action/animated feature

Rated G

Younger kids: OK   Older kids: NG

Brimming with good intentions, this misguided movie is one of the weakest family films ever made.

A nerdy, frightened-by-his-own-shadow little kid (Macaulay Culkin), sent on an errand by his father, freaks out during a thunderstorm and seeks refuge in a public library. There, he is transformed into an animated character (the film's best sequence) and spends the rest of the story trying to get out of the cartoon—and the library. He meets up with three of the worst-designed cartoon characters we've ever seen: books come-to-life as Horror (voice of Frank Welker), Fantasy (voice of Whoopi Goldberg), and Adventure (voice of Patrick Stewart). They draw their young friend into the sagas of *Moby Dick*, *Treasure Island*, and *Dr. Jekyll and Mr. Hyde*.

The Pagemaster is supposed to encourage kids to read by underscoring the fact that the greatest adventures in the world are contained in the pages of a book. However, the only thing that might inspire reading is the desire to turn off the video machine that's running this dreary film.

PAINT YOUR WAGON (1969)

Color, 166 minutes

Cast: Lee Marvin, Jean Seberg, Clint Eastwood, Harve Presnell, Ray Walston, Tom Ligon, Alan Dexter, William O'Connell, Ben Baker, Alan Baxter, Paula Trueman, Robert Easton, The Nitty Gritty Dirt Band

Director: Joshua Logan

Screenplay: Alan Jay Lerner; adaptation by Paddy Chayefsky, based on the musical by Lerner and Frederick Loewe

Musical

Rated M

Young children: No   Older children: VG

What makes this solid filming of the Lerner and Loewe Broadway hit so interesting is that its three leads are nonmusical performers. If you ever longed to hear Clint Eastwood singing, here is your opportunity.

The story unfolds in No Name City, California, in the 1840s—the time of the fabled California gold rush—and involves a pair of prospectors, Ben Rumson (Lee Mar-

427

vin) and Pardner (Eastwood). These two have a most unusual marital arrangement. They share the same wife, Elizabeth (Jean Seberg), who has come to love them both. Elizabeth originally was one of several spouses of a Mormon and was sold to the highest bidder—Rumson—in an auction.

Add to this the presence of French prostitutes and a subplot involving a shy young man's sexual initiation, and *Paint Your Wagon* clearly is unsuitable for younger viewers. But its witty script and songs should attract older children, along with the spectacular scenery and staging.

Older kids should be enamored of Ben Rumson, a character who cherishes his freedom and individuality; he's a product of the unsettled West, a man who never could thrive in a "civilized" society.

THE PAJAMA GAME (1957)
Color, 101 minutes
Cast: Doris Day, John Raitt, Carol Haney, Eddie Foy, Jr., Barbara Nichols, Reta Shaw, Thelma Pelish, Jack Straw, Ralph Dunn, Owen Martin
Directors: George Abbott and Stanley Donen
Screenplay: Abbott and Richard Bissell, from the musical by Abbott, Bissell, Richard Adler, and Jerry Ross, based on Bissell's novel *7½ Cents*
Musical
Unrated
Young children: VG Older children: VG

This effervescent musical is crammed with charm and spirit, and is a sure ticket to an entertaining 101 minutes.

Doris Day is tops as Babe, a pajama factory worker and the leader of her shop's grievance committee. To Babe's consternation, she finds herself becoming romantically entangled with Sid (John Raitt), the factory's new foreman, who is her chief adversary at the bargaining table.

One wouldn't think that labor-management relations would be the foundation for a great musical, but it gives this one credibility and relevance beyond that of most such films. (It's a sad comment that the factory town depicted in *The Pajama Game* is now pretty much a thing of the past in America.)

Virile Broadway musical star John Raitt, who always seemed to be losing the roles he created on stage to Gordon MacRae, finally gets to play one here, and he's excellent. Raitt and Day are supported by a handpicked cast, including several veterans of the Broadway play like Eddie Foy, Jr., and dancer Carole Haney, who sizzles in the celebrated "Steam Heat" number, choreographed by the great Bob Fosse.

The Pajama Game is marked by tremendous exuberance, which hasn't dimmed one bit over the years.

PAPER MOON (1973)
Black & white, 102 minutes
Cast: Ryan O'Neal, Tatum O'Neal, Madeline Kahn, John Hillerman, Randy Quaid
Director: Peter Bogdanovich
Screenplay: Alvin Sargent, based on the novel *Addie Pray* by Joe David Brown
Comedy
Rated PG
Younger kids: Good Older kids: VG

Making her film debut, ten-year-old Tatum O'Neal won an Oscar for her delightful performance as a precocious orphan named Addie in this charming tale about a pair of Depression-era con artists. Tatum's father Ryan O'Neal plays slick con man Moses Pray, who's traveling through the Midwest, fleecing widows by selling them Bibles supposedly ordered by their late husbands. When Addie convinces Moses that he may actually be her father, he reluctantly takes her along with him on his scams, and she proves to be even more adept and resourceful than he is.

This is a terrific movie, wonderfully acted by both O'Neals, whose comic chemistry is perfect, with young Tatum a riot as the smoking, swearing Addie. Kids should especially enjoy her ability to act dumb, smart, or whiny as the con game occasion demands. The supporting cast is also a joy, particularly Madeline Kahn as one of Moses' floozies and John Hillerman in a dual role as a bootlegger and his sheriff brother. Peter Bogdanovich's lyrical direction and the beautiful black-and-white photography of the Kansas and Missouri locations evoke the bleak mid-'30s atmosphere impeccably and the entire film takes on a poetic tone that transcends mere nostalgia.

There is some "cussing" but nothing too drastic.

PARENTHOOD (1989)
Color, 124 minutes
Cast: Steve Martin, Mary Steenburgen, Dianne Wiest, Jason Robards, Rick Moranis, Tom Hulce, Martha Plimpton, Keanu Reeves, Harley Kozak
Director: Ron Howard
Screenplay: Lowell Ganz and Babaloo Mandel, from a story by Howard, Ganz, and Mandel
Comedy
Rated PG-13
Younger children: OK, with caution   Older children: VG

The patriarch (Jason Robards) of four grown children is reunited with his progeny, each of whom has become a dysfunctional parent in one way or another. Gil (Steve Martin) will do anything to bring his 8-year-old son out of his emotional hidey-hole. Helen (Dianne Wiest) is a now single mother trying to raise two rebellious teens. Yuppie Nathan (Rick Moranis) forces advanced learning onto a 3-year-old who doesn't want to be precocious. And prodigal son Larry (Tom Hulce) returns with a half-black child and a fistful of gambling debts. Frank oversees it all, with an air of wistful regret.

Parents aren't necessarily grown-ups, the movie asserts, and it's proven absolutely true by a terrific cast in this immensely likable ensemble piece about changing generational attitudes. Usually funny, occasionally dramatic, generally evasive of artificial sweeteners, and with estimable performances from all (particularly Martin and Oscar-nominated Wiest), this is a fairly realistic look at middle-class American life in the 1980s. Best of all, it treats everyone, young and old, with understanding.

As such, there is some material (and language) not suited for young kids. Although children figure prominently in the story, the film is told from an adult point of view. Teens, however, will certainly recognize themselves, and perhaps their own parents, onscreen.

THE PARENT TRAP (1961)
Color, 124 minutes
Cast: Hayley Mills, Maureen O'Hara, Brian Keith, Joanna Barnes, Charlie Ruggles, Una Merkel, Leo G. Carroll, Cathleen Nesbitt
Director: David Swift
Screenplay: Swift, based on the book *Das Doppelte Lottchen* by Erich Kastner
Comedy/Family story
Unrated
Younger children: VG Older children: VG

Having made Hayley Mills a star in **Pollyanna,** Walt Disney reasoned that the only thing better than one Hayley would be two. The result is this delightful comedy about identical twins—Sharon and Susan—who've never met before and aren't even aware of each other's existence because one has been raised by her mother (Maureen O'Hara) and the other by her father (Brian Keith), a continent away from each other. After a rocky start at summer camp, the two become friends, and conspire to bring their long-estranged parents back together by switching places . . . and scaring off their dad's snooty new fiancée.

The Parent Trap is great fun from start to finish, and Hayley Mills is a delight, especially when she—two times over—sings "Let's Get Together (Yeah Yeah Yeah)."

Contemporary kids have a new *Parent Trap* to enjoy, but if they're curious to see another version of the same story, or if they've discovered Hayley Mills

in other Disney movies, they won't be disappointed with this "older" rendition.

THE PARENT TRAP (1998)
Color, 127 minutes
Cast: Lindsay Lohan, Dennis Quaid, Natasha Richardson, Elaine Hendrix, Lisa Ann Walter, Simon Kunz, Polly Holliday, Maggie Wheeler, Ronnie Stevens
Director: Nancy Myers
Screenplay: David Swift, Myers, and Charles Shyer, based on the book *Das Doppelte Lottchen* by Erich Kastner
Comedy/Family story
Rated PG
Younger children: VG Older children: VG

One wouldn't have thought it possible for 1990s Hollywood to recapture the charm of the 1960s Disney hit *The Parent Trap*—but they did. Newcomer Lindsay Lohan is delightful as the twins who've never met before—who don't even know the other exists, one having been raised by her mother in London, the other by her father on his vineyard property in the Napa Valley of California. Once they meet each other at summer camp and realize who they are, they conspire to change places in order to meet the parents they've never known and try to bring them back together.

The new *Parent Trap* is fresh, up-to-date, but true to the original. (In fact, Joanna Barnes, who played "the other woman" in the Hayley Mills version, appears here as the mother of Elaine Hendrix, the woman who's trying to marry Dennis Quaid.)

A PATCH OF BLUE (1965)
Black & white, 105 minutes
Cast: Sidney Poitier, Elizabeth
   Hartman, Shelley Winters,
   Wallace Ford, Ivan Dixon,
   John Qualen, Elisabeth Fraser
Director: Guy Green
Screenplay: Green, based on
   Elizabeth Kata's story "Be
   Ready With Bells and Drums"
Drama
Unrated
Younger children: No   Older
   children: VG

This sensitive, well-acted drama
tells the story of Selina D'Arcey,
an 18-year-old who was blinded
many years ago by her mother, a
prostitute. She now lives in a
dreary tenement with her mother
and alcoholic grandfather. Future
prospects are gloomy for Selina,
who has never gone to school or
socialized with others her own
age. Furthermore, her mother is
intent on opening a whorehouse
and featuring Selina as its main
attraction. At the core of the
story is Selina's evolving friendship with Gordon Ralfe, a young
black man who becomes her
savior.

   The point of *A Patch of Blue* is
that Selina's lack of sight has
made her blind to everyday prejudice. Because she is blind, she is
oblivious to the fact that Gordon
is black. All she sees, in essence,
is his soul. He is kind to her, and
understanding of her, and that is
all that matters.

   The nature of the story and its
characters (particularly the slat-
ternly mother) makes this inappropriate for younger viewers.
Older children should enjoy it
with their parents, who might also
explain that it was made during
the breakthrough years of the

1960s when the civil rights movement changed many people's attitudes toward race in this country.
Sidney Poitier was the first great
black movie star, and this was one
of his many successes (although it
was Shelley Winters who walked
away with an Oscar for her performance as Hartman's cruel
mother).

THE PATHFINDER (1994)
Color, 104 minutes
Cast: Kevin Dillon, Graham
   Greene, Russell Means, Stacy
   Keach, Laurie Holden,
   Stephen Russell, Jaimz
   Woolvett
Director: Donald Shebib
Screenplay: James Mitchell
   Miller and Thomas W. Lynch
Historical drama/Action-
   adventure/Literary classic
Rated PG-13
Young children: OK, with
   caution   Older children: VG

Parents who feel 1992's R-rated
The Last of the Mohicans is too
violent for their children may
want to suggest the less bloody
but nonetheless faithful adaptation of the second in James Fenimore Cooper's Leatherstocking
trilogy.

   Cooper (1789–1851) wrote historical novels about the American
frontier, incorporating the pioneer spirit in the improbably
named Natty Bumppo. The life-
and-death struggle of the Mohi-
can tribe during the French and
Indian Wars is again the basis of
this story, written in 1840, which
concludes in 1841's *The Deer-
slayer* (never adequately filmed,
so it's absent from this guide).

   In this heroic romance Natty,
his foster father, Chingachgook,
and winsome Mabel Dunham

seek to save a British military fort from capture.

PATHS OF GLORY (1957)
Black & white, 86 minutes
Cast: Kirk Douglas, Ralph Meeker, Adolphe Menjou, George Macready, Wayne Morris, Richard Anderson, Timothy Carey, Joseph Turkel
Director: Stanley Kubrick
Screenplay: Kubrick, Calder Willingham, and Jim Thompson, based on the novel by Humphrey Cobb
Drama/War
Unrated
Young children: No   Older children: VG

This early film by legendary director Stanley Kubrick is one of the all-time great antiwar films: a literate, intense, profoundly moving drama about the stupidity of war and the reckless abuse of power. It is set during World War I and tells the story of a French general who orders his men out on a futile mission. To save face after its failure, he decrees that three arbitrarily selected soldiers—Corporal Paris, Private Ferol, and Private Arnaud—will be tried and executed for cowardice. At the core of the drama is Colonel Dax (Kirk Douglas), the officer ordered to lead the mission, who serves as the story's conscience and defends the men at their trial.

Decades after its release, *Paths of Glory* remains a shattering study of the insanity of war—and of the misuse of authority, which oftentimes is allowed to fester not only in the military but at all levels of society.

In its day, this film was considered as potent as *Saving Private Ryan,* with grim scenes in the trenches and frightening moments on the battlefield. It still packs a wallop and is much too intense for younger kids, but it could well make a lasting impression on older children.

PAULIE (1998)
Color, 91 minutes
Cast: Gena Rowlands, Tony Shalhoub, Cheech Marin, Bruce Davison, Jay Mohr, Trini Alvarado, Buddy Hackett, Hallie Kate Eisenberg, Matt Craven, Bill Cobbs, Tia Texada
Director: John Roberts
Screenplay: Laurie Craig
Animal story/Comedy/Adventure
Rated PG
Young kids: VG   Older kids: VG

A refreshing family film that isn't stupid or condescending, and dodges cheap jokes at every turn . . . yet still provides colorful, intelligent, even enlightening entertainment. Paulie is a parrot, now perched in a dungeonlike room at a scientific institute. A lonely Russian immigrant who's just taken a janitorial job there is curious about the bird and befriends Paulie, persuading him to tell what brought him to this sorry spot. "It's a long story," says Paulie. "I'm Russian," says the janitor, "I like long stories." Thus begins Paulie's saga, from babyhood (in the care of an adoring little girl) through a series of owners, always with the goal of finding the girl from whom he was separated so early on.

Paulie is a story that touches on many facets of life and embraces many kinds of people, both good and bad. The PG rating probably covers the fact that not everyone in the film is as savory as the cute little girl (Hallie Kate Eisenberg), and there are a couple of cusswords here and there.

THE PEBBLE AND THE PENGUIN (1995)
Color, 74 minutes
Cast: Voices of Martin Short, James Belushi, Annie Golden, Tim Curry, Shani Wallis
No director credited
Screenplay: Rachel Koretsky and Steve Whitestone
Animated feature/Musical
Rated G
Younger kids: OK   Older kids: NG

Another Don Bluth production with superior production values, passable songs, and a story aimed exclusively at the 6-year-old crowd. Hubie the penguin falls in love with lovely Marina, but in order to secure his mate, according to penguin tradition, must drop a pebble at her feet. An evil penguin named Drake also covets Marina and has Hubie swept out to sea. Hubie's trek home with comic companion Rocko provides the alternating dramatic adventures and musical numbers that make up the bulk of the film's running time.

Dangers include killer whales and human fishermen with underwater chase sequences that are quite effective. Songs by Barry Manilow and Bruce Sussman are momentarily fun but forgettable. Jim Belushi, Martin Short, and Tim Curry give it their all, but—at least from a grownup's perspective—the story just isn't worth it.

PEE-WEE'S BIG ADVENTURE (1985)
Color, 90 minutes
Cast: Pee-wee Herman (Paul Reubens), Elizabeth Daily, Mark Holton, Diane Salinger, Tony Bill, Cassandra Peterson, James Brolin, Morgan Fairchild, Jan Hooks, Phil Hartman
Director: Tim Burton
Screenplay: Phil Hartman, Paul Reubens, and Michael Varhol
Comedy/Fantasy
Rated PG
Younger kids: VG   Older kids: VG

Perpetual adolescent Pee-wee Herman, neatly coiffured and always impeccable in his grey suit and red bow tie, goes on a cross-country search when his beloved bicycle is stolen. Tim Burton—later of **Batman** and **Edward Scissorhands** fame—made his directing debut here, and his unique, cartoon-inspired visual style found a perfect match in Pee-wee's kitschy, cartoonlike world, which is set in the present day but seems more like some retro '50s time warp.

There are a number of surprising, original moments—from Pee-wee surrounded by animals to a wonderful tour of the Alamo—but, of course, the film's success pretty much depends on how much you like Pee-wee himself. Some love him, some hate him, and others shake their heads because they don't "get" him. Yet he is an original comic creation: childish but strangely endearing, taking delight in the smallest things life has to offer and never so likable as when he is determined to overcome an obstacle (particularly when he charms a bar full of biker toughs by dancing on his heels).

At the very least, this is a hero who is true to himself, always keeps his promises to friends, and will even risk his life to rescue icky snakes from a fire. Kids who enjoyed Herman's adventures on *Pee-wee's Playhouse* have a head start, but there is plenty here to amuse everyone.

PELLE THE CONQUEROR
(1988)
Color, 150 minutes
Cast: Max von Sydow, Pelle Hvenegaard, Erik Paaske, Kristina Tornqvist, Morten Jorgensen
Director: Bille August
Screenplay: August, from the novel by Martin Andersen Nexo
Drama
Rated PG-13
Younger kids: OK   Older kids: OK

In the 19th century, Lasse, an old widower, and his young son, Pelle, sail from Sweden to Denmark in search of a better life; they find themselves on a rural estate and endure great hardships as they try to survive.

Based on the first of a four-volume novel by Nexo (regarded as a classic in Denmark), this is a stark and often unsettling film. Though there is only a little in the way of physical violence (Pelle getting a whipping from a trainee at the rural estate, and a friend of Pelle's who becomes brain-damaged after a fight), it is the harshness of life on the farm, both physically and psychologically, that presents a constant challenge to Pelle. The numerous indignities and cruelties that he and his father suffer may be difficult for smaller children to take. Also, the relationship between father and son is heartbreaking, with the well-meaning but weak Lasse—especially as played by von Sydow, in a magnificent performance—aware of how little he can provide for Pelle, and Pelle always searching for a way out. In the end, it is Pelle's perseverance and determination to find that escape that carries him through and provides the film with an underpinning of hope.

There are few Hollywood happy moments here—just a gripping tale of survival and small triumphs in the most desperate of circumstances.

PEOPLE WILL TALK (1951)
Black & white, 100 minutes
Cast: Cary Grant, Jeanne Crain, Finlay Currie, Walter Slezak, Hume Cronyn, Sidney Blackmer, Basil Ruysdael, Katherine Locke, Margaret Hamilton
Director: Joseph L. Mankiewicz
Screenplay: Mankiewicz, based on the play *Dr. Praetorious* by Curt Goetz
Drama/Satire
Unrated
Young children: No Older children: VG

People Will Talk is not as well-remembered as some of writer-director Joseph L. Mankiewicz's other films, including *All About Eve* and *A Letter to Three Wives,* but it's a unique and offbeat mixture of high drama, mature wit, and keen observations on the human condition.

It is the story of Dr. Noah Praetorious (Cary Grant at his most winning), the head of a medical clinic affiliated with a large and prestigious university. Praetorious runs his clinic his way, and his no-nonsense approach is unusual and refreshing. He believes that "patients are sick people, not inmates," and that the practice of medicine primarily involves human beings, not pills and scalpels.

A man like Praetorious naturally has enemies who are intimidated by his "radical" way of thinking. One such person is the small-minded Professor Elwell, who commences an investigation into Praetorious' background in an effort to discredit him.

(Back in 1951, the House Un-American Activities Committee was making headlines by harassing Hollywood professionals in a manner similar to the way in which Elwell badgers Praetorious.)

If your older kids are open-minded and enjoy stories with rich, unpredictable characters, they may enjoy *People Will Talk* as much as you do. Mankiewicz's script is precision-perfect, and his film may be described in a word: *intelligent.*

PERSUASION (1995)
Color, 107 minutes
Cast: Amanda Root, Ciaran Hinds, Susan Fleetwood, Corin Redgrave, Fiona Shaw, John Woodvine, Phoebe Nicholls, Samuel West, Sophie Thompson, Judy Cornwell
Director: Roger Michell
Screenplay: Nick Dear, based on the novel by Jane Austen
Drama/Literary classic
Rated PG
Young children: No Older children: VG

Persuasion is based on Jane Austen's last completed novel, which she penned in 1816. It may lack some of the spirit and energy (not to mention star power) of **Sense and Sensibility** and **Emma,** two other Austen adaptations released to theaters in the mid 1990s, but it is certainly their equal as a film.

The setting is early-19th-century provincial England, and the heroine is Anne Elliot (Amanda Root). The story picks up with the return of Captain Frederick Wentworth, a naval officer whose offer of marriage Anne had spurned eight years earlier. At the time, Anne was just 19 years old and a child of the upper class, while Wentworth was "a man who had nothing but himself to recommend him—spirit and brilliance, to be sure, but no fortune, no connections." Anne had been persuaded by a family friend to reject Wentworth because it is "entirely prudent" for a woman of wealth to rebuff a man of insufficient means. (In 19th-century England, as today, in some circles money and contacts, not rather passion and love, were reason enough to enter into a marriage.)

Now that Wentworth is back on the scene, what will Anne do? What of the Captain? To add to the complications, Anne's aristocratic father has become financially strapped, while Wentworth is newly wealthy.

Persuasion reveals the depth of emotions that exist beneath the superficial propriety of upper-class English society and how important it was to put on "a good face." Austen is also concerned with the women's frustration over their status as second-class citizens who lack the opportunity to fulfill their dreams.

Persuasion is a literate, civilized film. But it is also quiet in tone and slow of pace. Younger children will be bored to tears. Only mature children who have discovered the joys of Jane Austen will have the patience to get into the film's subtle rhythms—and share in its many pleasures.

PETER PAN (1953)
Color, 76 minutes
Cast: Voices of Bobby Driscoll, Kathryn Beaumont, Hans Conried, Bill Thompson, Heather Angel, Paul Collins, Tommy Luske, Candy Candido, Tom Conway
Directors: Hamilton Luske, Clyde Geronimi, and Wilfred Jackson
Screenplay: Ted Sears, Bill Peet, Joe Rinaldi, Erdman Penner, Winston Hibler, Milt Banta, and Ralph Wright, from the play by Sir James M. Barrie
Animated feature
Unrated
Young children: VG Older children: VG

James Barrie's *Peter Pan* is a story of timeless appeal, as has been proven from its many incarnations on stage, screen, and television. (The Broadway musical of the 1950s starring Mary Martin and Cyril Ritchard holds a special place in the hearts of an entire generation, because it was broadcast on television and, thankfully, preserved on video.)

The Walt Disney cartoon version may not be the greatest rendition of the story ever realized, but it's highly entertaining and is sure to please children of all ages. It's stylishly designed, briskly ani-

mated, and full of humor and tuneful songs.

Because this is a cartoon, Peter is a "real" boy, contradicting the age-old theatrical tradition in which he's played by a young woman. (Persistent stories that Tinker Bell was fashioned after Marilyn Monroe are false, however; Monroe was barely known at the time this film was being prepared.)

Everything else about this *Peter Pan* is fairly traditional: Peter appears in the Darling children's bedroom as Wendy is about to take the first, fateful step toward adulthood. Instead, Peter whisks her (and her brothers) off to Neverland, where she will never grow up—and where she can continue to tell stories to Peter and his Lost Boys. Getting there is easy: by thinking happy thoughts and adding some pixie dust, the children take flight and soar over the nighttime London sky.

Children won't get to clap to save Tinker Bell, but they'll be too busy enjoying the colorful antics of Peter, Captain Hook, Mr. Smee, and all the other characters in Neverland to be concerned about what isn't here.

Some parents may not approve of the depiction of Indians, as in the song "What Makes the Red Man Red," but if the film doesn't bend over backward to be enlightened, its good spirits make up for that.

Put simply, *Peter Pan* is great fun. We could all use some pixie dust now and then.

PETER RABBIT AND TALES OF BEATRIX POTTER (1971)
Color, 90 minutes
Cast: Frederick Ashton, Alexander Grant, Michael Coleman, Brenda Last, Ann

Howard, Robert Mead, Lesley
Collier, Sally Ashby, Carole
Ainsworth, Avril Bergen, the
Royal Ballet
Director: Reginald Mills
Screenplay: Richard Goodwin
and Christine Edzard
Ballet/Fantasy
Rated G
Young children: VG   Older
children: VG

That's the highly regarded British
choreographer Sir Frederick Ashton skipping all around and having a merry old time playing Mrs.
Tiggy-Winkle, the dear hedgehog made famous by Victorian
children's author Beatrix Potter
(1866–1943).

Her tales of Peter Rabbit began
as a series of stories sent to a sick
child. Though childless herself,
Potter created twenty-three books
about happy animals in the domain of childhood.

Oodles of charm suffuse this
winning adaptation, featuring five
Potter stories told through dance
alone. There's Mrs. Tittlemouse
and Johnny Townmouse waltzing;
Jemima Puddle-Duck saved from
the clutches of Mr. Fox; a piggy
pas de deux; the frog Jeremy
Fisher gone a-fishin'; and a dollhouse duet, among other treats.

Hate ballet? Hate cute animals? Hate the English? Too bad.
They're all here, and they're all
beguiling.

PETE'S DRAGON (1977)
Color, 134 minutes
Cast: Helen Reddy, Jim Dale,
Mickey Rooney, Red Buttons,
Shelley Winters, Sean
Marshall, Jeff Conaway, Jim
Backus
Director: Don Chaffey

Screenplay: Malcolm
Marmorstein
Live-action/Animated musical
Rated G
Younger kids: OK   Older kids:
OK

The Disney studio made several
attempts to re-create the appeal—
and success—of **Mary Poppins.**
This was one of their least successful endeavors, though it may
please kids.

Runaway orphan Pete (Sean
Marshall) and his (mainly) invisible dragon pal Elliot wind up in
a New England coastal town, pursued by evil backwoods guardians
(Shelley Winters and her clan),
who want the boy for slave labor,
and con men (Dale and Buttons),
who want to exploit his remarkable dragon.

Town drunk (Rooney) and
his lighthouse-keeping daughter
(Reddy) befriend the boy, clean
him up, and send him to school.
Townspeople's reactions to the invisible dragon's high jinks account
for most of the comedy here; numerous song and dance numbers
pad the otherwise slim story.

Even kids may find the story familiar and derivative; there's
nothing memorable about the
music, either, although pop singer
Reddy's rendition of "Candle on
the Water" is pleasant. The animated Elliot, directed by Don
Bluth, easily steals the show.

The villainy here is all buffoonish, and there's nothing objectionable for younger kids. Adults,
however, may be bored silly.

THE PHANTOM (1996)
Color, 105 minutes
Cast: Billy Zane, Kristy
Swanson, Treat Williams,
Catherine Zeta-Jones, James

Remar, Cary-Hiroyuki
Tagawa, Casey Siemaszko,
Samantha Eggar, Patrick
McGoohan
Director: Simon Wincer
Screenplay: Jeffrey Boam, based
on characters created by Lee
Falk
Action-adventure
Rated PG
Younger children: OK Older
children: OK

Set in the 1930s, this comic book-
styled adventure (based on Lee
Falk's popular comic strip character) may be too old-fashioned for
some kids, but adults may enjoy
reliving memories of the Saturday
matinee serials of the era. Billy
Zane plays The Phantom, "The
Ghost Who Walks," protector of
the jungle and its inhabitants
(both animal and human).

The Phantom battles master
criminal Xander Drax (a flamboyant performance by Treat Williams), who is trying to acquire
the legendary Skulls of Touganda,
which when united can produce a
weapon of enormous power.

A series of spectacular cliffhang-
ers, a trip to art deco New York
City, and a special effects–laden climax are among the highlights. Action set pieces (with no blood) and
tongue-in-cheek dialogue make this
strictly a kid-level movie.

Bona fide serial fans may wish
that one of the old Republic Pictures directors or stuntmen had
had a hand in this picture, which
lacks the energy and oomph of
those breakneck-paced chapter
plays. Zane, however, has just the
right look and attitude for a serial hero.

THE PHANTOM OF THE OPERA (1925)

Black & white, with color scene,
93 minutes
Cast: Lon Chaney, Mary Philbin,
Norman Kerry, Arthur
Edmund Carewe, Gibson
Gowland, John St. Polis, Snitz
Edwards, Mary Fabian
Director: Rupert Julian
Screenplay: Raymond L. Shrock
and Elliott J. Clawson, from
the novel by Gaston Leroux
Horror/Romantic melodrama
Unrated
Young children: Too
intense Older children: OK

In the late 19th century, the man-
agers of the Paris Opera House
have reached an uneasy truce
with an eerie, unseen stranger
who lives somewhere in the re-
cesses of the vast building, and
who is known only as the Opera
Phantom. He demands they keep
one deluxe audience viewing box
free for his personal use and
doesn't hesitate to resort to murder to achieve his ends. He's a
brilliant expert on opera himself,
and when he hears the voice of
young singer Christine Daae, he
decides that she should be the
prima donna; he begins to secretly
train her—and more deaths follow when his plans are thwarted.

One of the most elaborate films
of its type ever made, *Phantom of
the Opera* was a major success in
1925, thanks in part to Chaney's
full-bodied, powerful performance
and his sheer genius at makeup.
Only this version of the story follows the description of the Phantom as given in Leroux's novel:
with relatively few appliances, Chaney turned his head into a living
skull.

The famous unmasking scene—

in which a curious Christine insists on ripping off the mask while the Phantom serenades her at his organ—is still a stunner, and his pale, grinning face is both disturbing and mesmerizing.

That one scene might disturb very young children, but the rest of the film is likely to bore them. Teenagers, particularly those already familiar with the Andrew Lloyd Webber musical based on the Leroux novel, may be drawn to this film. It's still by far the best movie version, and might be a good introduction to the art of the silent movie for hesitant kids.

PHANTOM OF THE OPERA
(1943)
Color, 92 minutes
Cast: Nelson Eddy, Susanna Foster, Claude Rains, Edgar Barrier, Leo Carrillo, Jane Farrar, J. Edward Bromberg, Fritz Feld, Frank Puglia, Steven Geray, Hume Cronyn, Fritz Leiber (Sr.).
Director: Arthur Lubin
Screenplay: Samuel Hoffenstein and Eric Taylor, from the novel by Gaston Leroux
Romantic melodrama/Horror
Unrated
Young children: OK   Older children: OK

A mysterious, masked Phantom (Rains) haunts the Paris Opera House; he takes a fancy to a young soprano (Foster) and begins trying to help her career. But he also has a program of revenge: he was a violinist with the opera who had ambitions of being a composer, but when his music was stolen and he tried to get it back, acid was thrown in his face. (Opera star Eddy and police inspector Barrier are romantic rivals for Foster.)

Far more opera than Phantom, this version of Leroux's novel is very tame; the Phantom is only briefly unmasked at the climax, and the makeup is pretty ordinary—just a big scar. There's not a trace of the romantic obsession of the novel or the original film (or of Webber's subsequent musical, for that matter); there are very few "scary" scenes; and there's a lot of opera singing. It is a handsome production, shot on some of the same sets as the Chaney version (which still stand today at Universal studios), and Rains is excellent, but he isn't on-screen enough.

There's virtually nothing in the film to offend even the youngest children—or much to interest them, either. It's just a nice old movie with a few shots of a small, masked man running about in darkened hallways.

THE PHANTOM OF THE OPERA (1962)
Color, 84 minutes
Cast: Herbert Lom, Heather Sears, Thorley Walters, Edward De Souza, Michael Gough, Miles Malleson, Ian Wilson, Michael Ripper, Patrick Troughton
Director: Terence Fisher
Screenplay: John Elder (pseud. of Anthony Hinds), from the novel by Gaston Leroux
Romantic melodrama/Horror
Unrated
Younger kids: A little too scary   Older kids: OK

Hammer's take on the often-filmed tale is one of their tamer offerings, with a non-menacing Phantom (Lom)—he has an assistant to do his dirty work—and a lot more opera than opera ghost. The story is closer to that of the 1943 version than to the silent film or the novel, with a scarred musician lurking in the catacombs beneath the London (not Paris this time) opera house.

Only intermittently entertaining, this is lesser Hammer; the opera (written for the movie) is dull and the cast mostly uninteresting, but director Fisher still has a fine eye for design and composition.

If your kids have heard about this famous story, have them try either the silent film with Lon Chaney, from 1925, or the remake with Claude Rains, from 1943.

PHANTOM OF THE PARADISE (1974)
Color, 92 minutes
Cast: William Finley, Paul Williams, Jessica Harper, George Memmoli, Gerrit Graham, Jeffrey Comanor, Archie Hahn, Harold Oblong
Director: Brian De Palma
Screenplay: Brian De Palma
Rock 'n' roll–horror/Comedy-drama
Rated PG
Young children: A bit rough   Older children: OK

Searching for the right music to inaugurate his new theater, The Paradise, corrupt music entrepreneur Swan (Paul Williams) steals a rock opera of *Faust* from naive, obsessed composer Winslow Leach (Finley), who is then arrested on phony drug charges and tossed into prison. When he learns that Swan has stolen his music, Winslow escapes from prison, but in trying to destroy the records, his face is maimed. Wearing a mask, he begins haunting The Paradise

and becomes convinced that young singer Phoenix (Harper) is the only person who can do his music justice. So Winslow, now the Phantom, tries to force his will on Swan.

Neither spoofy nor straight, drama or comedy, musical or horror film, *Phantom of the Paradise* contains all these elements and so is very difficult to define. Like Popeye, it is what it is: a fascinating, wildly entertaining, one-of-a-kind movie that gradually became a cult favorite. It's unique in the career of the erratic but occasionally brilliant Brian De Palma and, in an odd way, seems more heartfelt than most of his movies. The songs, written and mostly performed by Paul Williams, are often outstanding, and the cast is excellent down to the smallest roles. As a result, those who love this movie, love it hard.

Whether your kids will embrace it is a good question. William Finley's performance is intense and passionate enough that kids could easily identify with him and, as a result, find the movie disturbing. Though occasionally very funny, *Phantom* takes its story very seriously indeed. But if kids get caught up in the movie's bumpy rhythms, this could become a favorite.

PHANTOM OF THE RUE MORGUE (1954)
Color, 84 minutes
Cast: Claude Dauphin, Karl Malden, Steve Forrest, Patricia Medina, Anthony Caruso, Rolfe Sedan, Paul Richards, Allyn Ann McLerie, Charles Gemora, Merv Griffin
Director: Roy Del Ruth
Screenplay: Harold Medford and James R. Webb, from the

story "Murders in the Rue Morgue" by Edgar Allan Poe
Horror/Melodrama
Unrated
Younger kids: No   Older kids: OK

In 19th-century Paris, a strange, powerful killer stalks the streets, including Rue Morgue, murdering unsuspecting women. As in the original Poe story, the killer turns out to be an ape, played by Charles Gemora in a particularly good gorilla suit, and this convincing costume turns out to be the best thing about this uneven movie.

This was intended as a follow-up to **House of Wax,** and was also filmed in 3-D, but where Vincent Price's ripe performance fit the character and the film, here Karl Malden's simply does not. The film is handsomely produced and well photographed, and occasionally frightening as well, but over-all, it's really just a footnote to horror movie history. Of course, if your teenager is heavily into horror movie history, footnotes are important, too. . . .

THE PHANTOM TOLLBOOTH (1970)
Color, 90 minutes
Cast: Voices of Butch Patrick, Mel Blanc, Daws Butler, Candy Candido, Hans Conried, June Foray, Les Tremayne, Shep Menken
Directors: Chuck Jones, Abe Levitow, and David Monahan
Screenplay: Chuck Jones and Sam Rosen, based on the book by Norton Juster
Live-action/Animated musical feature
Rated G

Younger kids: No   Older kids: OK

Chuck Jones is responsible for some of the greatest—and funniest—cartoons of all time, including scores of Looney Tunes with Bugs Bunny, Daffy Duck, and the Road Runner. But this serious-minded, educational animated feature can only be described as tedious.

The story begins in live action. Milo (Butch Patrick, best remembered as Eddie on *The Munsters* TV series) is a totally bored 12-year-old who one day finds a tollbooth and large toy car in his room. Driving through the toll transforms him (and the film) into animated form and plunges Milo into a strange universe where letters and numbers are at war.

Based on a well-regarded book by Norton Juster (who also wrote *The Dot and the Line,* which Chuck Jones turned into an Oscar-winning short subject), and well designed and animated, this movie's sophisticated, didactic script will cause most kids to snore. In fact, it's liable to be of greater interest to adults—and animation buffs—than to kids of any age.

PHAR LAP (1983)
Color, 107 minutes
Cast: Tom Burlinson, Ron Leibman, Martin Vaughan, Judy Morris, Celia De Burgh, Richard Morgan, Robert Grubb, Georgia Carr, James Steele
Director: Simon Wincer
Screenplay: David Williamson, based on the book *The Phar Lap Story* by Michael Wilkinson
True-life drama/Animal story

Rated PG
Younger children: OK, with
caution   Older children: VG

This true story of an ill-fated
champion racehorse, born in New
Zealand but raised in Australia,
named Phar Lap, is excellent family fare set in the 1920s and early
1930s: Phar Lap, despite his thoroughbred heritage, is a stubborn
racer at first, but a loving relationship develops between the horse
and stableboy Tommy (Tom Burlinson). His winning ways bring
the horse to the U.S., where trouble follows by way of some
shady characters.

The photography and period
costuming are superb, but it's the
racing scenes that really stand
out. The performances by Ron
Leibman (as the horse's owner)
and Martin Vaughan (as his tough
trainer) are first-rate.

In Australia, the story of Phar
Lap is part of national lore.
American kids should find his
story fascinating—so long as they
know up front that Phar Lap
doesn't survive. The film downplays this part of the Phar Lap
saga and concentrates instead on
his incredible achievements, but
there's no avoiding the sadness of
his untimely demise. (As in real
life, the film offers no answer to
the mystery of his death.)

PINOCCHIO (1940)
Color, 88 minutes
Cast: Voices of Dickie Jones,
    Cliff Edwards, Christian Rub,
    Walter Catlett, Frankie Darro,
    Evelyn Venable, Charles
    Judels
Director: Ben Sharpsteen and
    Hamilton Luske
Screenplay: Ted Sears, Otto
    Englander, Webb Smith,

William Cottrell, Joseph Sabo,
    Erdman Penner, and Aurelius
    Battaglia, from the stories by
    Carlo Collodi
Animated feature
Unrated
Young children: VG, with
    caution   Older children: VG

Walt Disney's second animated
feature film, *Pinocchio,* is much
more sophisticated than its predecessor, **Snow White and the Seven
Dwarfs,** and it offers a more complex emotional experience for
viewers of all ages.

Geppetto is a lonely woodcutter who creates a boy out of wood
and wishes that he were real. Because Geppetto is such a good-
hearted soul, the Blue Fairy
brings little Pinocchio to life, but
because he is still a wooden-head,
she assigns Jiminy Cricket to be
his official conscience and teach
him right from wrong. Pinocchio
is easily led off the straight-and-
narrow path, however, and when
J. Worthington Foulfellow and his
cohort, Gideon, lead him away
from school with tales of "an
actor's life," he swallows their
bait and becomes the prisoner of
traveling showman Stromboli.

The Blue Fairy decides to give
him a second chance—even
though he lies to her at first—but
he falls prey to the spirit of fun
and adventure once more and
winds up on Pleasure Island,
where he falls under the influence
of a pool-playing wiseguy named
Lampwick. After watching his
friend be transformed into a jackass by Stromboli, Pinocchio finally
realizes the danger he's in and
manages to escape. But there is
no one waiting for him at home;
Geppetto has taken off to sea in
search of his wooden son. Before

long, they're both in the belly of the giant whale, Monstro, where Pinocchio must prove his mettle and earn the right to become a real, live boy.

There is so much to enjoy in *Pinocchio*—so many amazing sights and sounds, such wonderful music, such colorful characters—that young children may not fully appreciate some of the film's darker facets. That's just as well. As kids get older and they understand the evil nature of Stromboli, the terror of Lampwick turning into a jackass, or the very real threat of being separated from Geppetto forever, *Pinocchio* can be come deeply troubling.

As with all the classic Disney fables, however, these disturbing moments are there for a reason—to give children a genuine catharsis, to steer them through troubled waters (no pun intended) to safety, with a genuine and well-earned happy ending.

Parents should be aware of this emotional roller coaster and watch *Pinocchio* with their kids to reassure them during the rockier moments. Chances are they'll thank you for sharing such a rich experience.

PIPPI LONGSTOCKING (1997)
Color, 75 minutes
Cast: Voices of Melissa Altro, Catherine O'Hara, Dave Thomas, Carole Pope, Gordon Pinsent
Director: Clive Smith
Screenplay: Clive Smith, Ken Sobol, and Frank Nissen, based on the books by Astrid Lindgren
Animated feature/Musical
Rated G
Younger kids: OK   Older kids: NG

This animated feature based on popular series of books about the strongest girl in the world comes off as a weak kid's time-killer. Pippi's character design and annoying, high-pitched voice do nothing to endear her personality to us.

A storm separates Pippi from her sea captain father and she remains home alone to guard dad's precious gold coins. Pippi engages in all sorts of eccentric fun with the kids next door, Tommy and Annika, her mangy horse, and a manic monkey. When two bumbling crooks plot to steal her gold . . . well, you can see where this is going.

Awkward Broadway-style musical numbers break whatever "reality" the story had going for it. Kids have certainly identified with Pippi's literary adventures for years; it's too bad this offering (from renowned Canadian studio Nelvana) is so bland. A letdown.

THE PIRATE (1948)
Color, 102 minutes
Cast: Gene Kelly, Judy Garland, Walter Slezak, Gladys Cooper, Reginald Owen, George Zucco, The Nicholas Brothers, Lester Allen
Director: Vincente Minnelli
Screenplay: Albert Hackett and Frances Goodrich, based on a play by S. N. Behrman
Musical
Unrated
Young children: VG   Older children: VG

The plot of this light, colorful, and lively musical will be sufficient enough to intrigue young viewers. Judy Garland stars as Manuela, a dreamy, sheltered maiden on a Caribbean island who's always fantasized about a dashing and fabled pirate. She is about to become the bride in an arranged marriage, but when she comes upon a company of wandering performers, she not only finds them magical and liberating but becomes convinced that their leading clown, Serafin (Gene Kelly), is actually the pirate of her dreams.

Kelly offers an energized performance, and his acrobatic dancing is what makes *The Pirate* a treat for children. He shines in a fire dance, surrounded by pirates and a burning ship, and alongside the incomparable Nicholas Brothers, Harold and Fayard, in the eye-popping "Be a Clown" routine.

THE PIT AND THE PENDULUM (1961)
Color, 85 minutes
Cast: Vincent Price, John Kerr, Barbara Steele, Luana Anders, Antony Carbone
Director: Roger Corman
Screenplay: Richard Matheson, from the story by Edgar Allan Poe
Period horror/Melodrama
Unrated
Younger kids: Probably OK   Older kids: OK

The success of **House of Usher** led Roger Corman and American-International Pictures to launch a series of relatively lavish horror movies based, usually very distantly, on stories by Edgar Allan Poe; all but one in the series starred Vincent Price. This was the second and is at once the liveliest and the most absurd, with Price giving what may be the most flamboyant performance of his career. Depending on your taste, this is either a very good or a very bad thing.

Screenwriter Matheson essentially grafted the plot of *Gaslight* onto the newly established Poe format. Here, Price is convinced that his wife (Steele) has come back from the grave; in fact, she's really alive, trying to drive him mad with the help of her lover (Carbone). Unfortunately, it works all too well, and he becomes convinced he's his own father, a master torturer of the Spanish Inquisition . . .

Not a true horror movie, this is instead a somewhat ponderous but handsomely photographed period thriller, climaxing with the promised pit and pendulum torture sequence, the strongest stuff in the film.

PLACES IN THE HEART (1984)
Color, 102 minutes
Cast: Sally Field, Lindsay Crouse, Ed Harris, Amy Madigan, John Malkovich, Danny Glover, Terry O'Quinn, Bert Remsen, Ray Baker
Director: Robert Benton
Screenplay: Robert Benton
Drama
Rated PG
Younger kids: OK   Older kids: VG

In 1930s Waxahachie, Texas, housewife Edna Spalding (Field) becomes a widow when her sheriff husband is suddenly killed; she is forced to take on a boarder and become a cotton farmer in order to save her house and family. Small-town life in the Depression era is lovingly re-created in *Places in the Heart*. In addition to Edna's trials and tribulations, there is a subplot involving her sister, whose husband is having an affair with a local schoolteacher, but the story mainly focuses on the triumph of Edna in the face of tremendous odds. It is a celebration of the land and the family unit.

The harsh realities of the Depression are not ignored, and there are rough moments throughout the film—a KKK ambush, the onslaught of a tornado, and the sequences where Edna toils at picking cotton with workers in the field. But Edna's indomitability and pluck see her through each obstacle. The result is a very warm, old-fashioned film that is very inviting but more than a little manipulative. (The most startling moment comes toward the beginning, when Edna's husband is swiftly and accidentally shot by a drunk young boy.) However, you can't help but root for the characters, and the cast is exceptional.

PLANET OF THE APES
(1968)
Color, 112 minutes
Cast: Charlton Heston, Roddy McDowall, Kim Hunter, Maurice Evans, James Whitmore, James Daly, Linda Harrison
Director: Franklin J. Schaffner
Screenplay: Michael Wilson and Rod Serling, from the novel by Pierre Boulle
Science fiction/Satiric adventure
Rated G
Young children: OK Older children: OK

A spaceship with American astronauts undergoes a mishap and crashes on a strange planet. The three survivors are attacked by armed gorillas on horseback, who are rounding up mute human beings, who barely sustain themselves by foraging; ultimately, only one man, Taylor (Heston), survives. His ability to speak shocks the apes, who regard human beings as inferior creatures. In the civilization of the apes, gorillas are the "muscle," orangutans the intellectual ruling elite, and chimpanzees the scientists. Two chimps, Cornelius (McDowall) and his fiancée Dr. Zira (Hunter) befriend Taylor, but he's regarded as a threat by ape leader Zaius (Evans), who knows more about the past of his world than he lets on.

This was never a deft satire, and as science fiction it leaves something to be desired, but as an exotic adventure movie, it's exciting, well produced, and entertaining; Schaffner's direction is nothing less than brilliant. Technically, the makeup effects have been surpassed since 1968, but the actors *in* these makeups knew how to use them, and the characters are well drawn, so they're still oddly convincing. Heston is properly granitic, in contrast to the more natural (and excellent) work by Hunter, McDowall, and particularly, Evans.

Older children might find the movie unintentionally funny some of the time (especially after its skewering on an episode of *The Simpsons*), but it's so beautifully made, they're likely to be drawn into the adventure anyway. Younger kids will have a fine time, if you prepare them beforehand for the brief moments of violence.

This smash hit spawned a number of sequels and a short-lived television series. The first sequel was **Beneath the Planet of the Apes,** much inferior to this one.

PLEASE DON'T EAT THE DAISIES (1960)

Color, 111 minutes
Cast: Doris Day, David Niven, Janis Paige, Spring Byington, Richard Haydn, Jack Weston, Patsy Kelly
Director: Charles Walters
Screenplay: Isobel Lennart, based on the stories by Jean Kerr
Comedy
Unrated
Younger kids: Good Older kids: VG

Here's a charming, if old-fashioned family comedy about what happens when stuffy professor Larry Mackay (David Niven) becomes a theater critic and moves his wife, Kate (Doris Day), their four boisterous boys, one mother-in-law (Spring Byington), a wisecracking maid (Patsy Kelly), and an extremely large sheepdog named Hobo to a dilapidated country house. While Kate plays the dutiful homemaker and tries to get the house in shape, Larry incurs the wrath of his best friend (Richard Haydn) after panning his play and is slapped by the show's star (a very funny Janis Paige), but later finds himself being pursued by the sexy vamp.

Based on the book by Jean Kerr, wife of Walter Kerr, then drama critic for the *New York Herald Tribune,* the episodic plot is little more than a string of amusing incidents on the theme of suburban domesticity, but Niven, Day, and Co. wring every last laugh and bit of warmth out of them, the kids are cute, and Hobo steals every scene he's in. The whole film is as warm and pleasant as can be, and later inspired a TV sitcom.

POCAHONTAS (1995)

Color, 82 minutes
Cast: Voices of Irene Bedard, Judy Kuhn, Mel Gibson, David Ogden Stiers, John Kassir, Russell Means, Christian Bale, Linda Hunt, Billy Connolly
Directors: Mike Gabriel and Eric Goldberg
Screenplay: Carl Binder, Susannah Grant, and Philip LaZebnik
Animated musical
Rated G
Young children: OK Older children: VG

An unusually serious Disney cartoon feature, *Pocahontas* plays with the facts of history but presents a likable and empathetic heroine. She is a great Indian chief's daughter, who defies his orders and her tribe by falling in love with a white man, Captain John Smith, who has arrived in America as part of a plundering party from England in search of gold. As they fall in love, she manages to teach him about her people's respect for the land and its riches—but their relationship is as threatening to the British newcomers as it is to Pocahontas' tribe.

As usual, the Disney team knows how to lighten a story for the benefit of the youngest members of the audience, and Pocahontas' little animal friends, Meeko, a raccoon, and Flit, a hummingbird, provide welcome and often hilarious comedy relief. Even the villain, a hollow character named Ratcliffe, has a comic counterpart in his pampered dog.

Pocahontas benefits from good, solid storytelling and a pair of wonderfully expressive songs for its main character, the Oscar-winning "Colors of the Wind" and "Just Around the Riverbend," both beautifully sung by Judy Kuhn.

POLLYANNA (1960)
Color, 134 minutes
Cast: Hayley Mills, Jane Wyman, Richard Egan, Karl Malden, Nancy Olson, Adolphe Menjou, Donald Crisp, Agnes Moorehead, Kevin Corcoran, James Drury
Director: David Swift
Screenplay: Swift, based on the novel by Eleanor H. Porter
Drama-comedy
Unrated
Young children: VG Older children: VG

Pollyanna is a warmhearted story of the character who comes to be known as "the glad girl," an eternal optimist who has a remarkable effect on everyone around her, from an austere aunt to a timid preacher.

Pollyanna is one of the best live-action films Walt Disney ever produced, and it introduced America to his latest discovery, the wonderful British child actress Hayley Mills.

Because the film is set in period (1912) and is so well made (intelligently written and beautifully acted by a strong and diverse cast), it doesn't date a bit. It still works its magic today as effectively as it did in 1960.

Pollyanna is an orphan who comes to live with her Aunt Polly, a stern, wealthy woman who dominates the town of Harrington. From the moment she arrives, Pollyanna starts upsetting the normal order of things—in her aunt's household and with some of the town's colorful characters (the ineffectual Reverend Ford, the hermitlike Mr. Pendergast, and Mrs. Snow, a cranky hypochondriac, played by Agnes Moorehead, whom some kids will recognize as Endora from *Bewitched*)—simply by seeing the bright side of life, in what she calls "the glad game." A crisis puts Pollyanna's optimism to the ultimate test but enables her to learn how deeply she has affected all the citizens of Harrington—even her Aunt Polly.

Pollyanna is a lovely film in every respect; one could barely find a better one for families to share together.

POOR LITTLE RICH GIRL (1936)
Black & white, 72 minutes (also available in a computer-colored version)
Cast: Shirley Temple, Alice Faye, Gloria Stuart, Jack Haley, Michael Whalen, Sarah Haden, Jane Darwell, Claude Gillingwater, Paul Stanton, Henry Armetta
Director: Irving Cummings
Screenplay: Sam Hellman, Gladys Lehman, and Harry Tugend, based on stories by Eleanor Gates and Ralph Spence
Comedy/Drama/Musical
Unrated
Young children: VG Older children: VG

This lively story provides Shirley Temple with one of her most entertaining vehicles—for grownups as well as kids. As the yarn begins, she is the daughter of a wealthy soap manufacturer. With her widowed father distracted by his business, she is raised by a strict, overprotective spinster who

447

sends her to bed when she sneezes more than a couple times in a row. Due to a set of remarkable circumstances, the child is left alone one day, and temporarily takes a new identity. She eventually becomes part of a husband-and-wife musical act, portrayed with gusto by two wonderful rising screen talents of the time, Alice Faye and Jack Haley (whom everyone will know as the Tin Woodsman in **The Wizard of Oz**). The threesome performs top-notch musical numbers with sparkling results, especially the rousing "I Like a Military Man."

The film will enthrall youngsters, and not only because it's entertaining. It also allows a child who is restricted by an overbearing adult to flee her surroundings and enter a fantasy world populated by more sympathetic grown-ups.

POLTERGEIST (1982)
Color, 114 minutes
Cast: Craig T. Nelson, JoBeth Williams, Beatrice Straight, Dominique Dunne, Oliver Robins, Heather O'Rourke, Zelda Rubinstein, James Karen
Director: Tobe Hooper
Screenplay: Steven Spielberg, Michael Grais, and Mark Victor
Horror
Rated PG
Young children: No Older children: OK

The Freeling family, having just moved into a nice new housing subdivision, can't understand why their home is the target of increasingly malevolent pranks. Maybe the place is haunted. Big time. By more than one ghost. And they're mad. Mad enough to kidnap the Freelings' little girl Carol Ann, sucking her through the TV screen into the Other Side.

Call the ghostbusters! But even professional exorcists turn tail and run from the big and the terrifying. If it weren't a movie, you would too.

The scariest PG movie ever (it should have been a PG-13, but that rating didn't exist at the time), it's crammed with shocks, clever special effects, and escalating fear, with one climax after another.

Best seen in widescreen (you can get a letterboxed tape), it can be deceptively sunny and funny, like the first calm climb on a roller coaster. Then gravity kicks in and your heart's in your throat for the rest of the ride.

Startling stuff, but not half so much as when the parents smoke marijuana in their bedroom. Kids will ask why.

THE POWER (1968)
Color, 109 minutes
Cast: George Hamilton, Suzanne Pleshette, Michael Rennie, Richard Carlson, Arthur O'Connell, Nehemiah Persoff
Director: Byron Haskin
Screenplay: John Gay, from the novel by Frank M. Robinson
Science fiction/Pursuit suspense
Unrated
Younger kids: Of little interest Older kids: Good

A team of scientists discovers that one among them secretly has superpowers of mind control and telekinesis, and is not at all a nice person: the scientists begin to be killed off, one by one, as Hamilton and Pleshette try to discover who has the deadly power.

If adults can get past the idea of George Hamilton as the two-fisted hero, they're likely to have fun with this underrated George Pal production. It's a little pokey here and there, and tends to be repetitious, but it's imaginative, with an exceptionally good score. Kids, who don't know George Hamilton from Alexander Hamilton, will probably be engrossed by the mystery, though the ending may confuse them. Younger kids will be bored.

PRANCER (1989)
Color, 103 minutes
Cast: Sam Elliott, Rebecca Harrell, Cloris Leachman, Rutanya Alda, John Joseph Duda, Abe Vigoda, Michael Constantine, Ariana Richards, Mark Rolston, Johnny Galecki, Walter Charles
Director: John Hancock
Screenplay: Greg Taylor
Christmas/Drama/Animal story
Rated G
Younger children: VG Older children: Good

Here is a heartwarming Christmas-themed story of a little girl who nurses a reindeer back to health. Nine-year-old Jessica (Rebecca Harrell) secretly befriends a wounded reindeer, believing it to be one of Santa Claus' team, under the nose of her father (Sam Elliott), a failing farmer.

Jessica's belief in Prancer spreads to the local townspeople, including a helpful doctor (Abe Vigoda) and a newsman who reports the story in the paper. When Dad discovers the animal, he sells it to a local merchant for a promotional stunt. Jessica's attempt to free Prancer leads her to injury in a fall from a tree. Recov-

ering at home, she begins to lose faith in Prancer, who remains at her side rather than rejoin Santa, as she had hoped he would.

It would be Scrooge-like to give away the ending of this story, but suffice it to say that there is a lovely, even tearful, finale that in the spirit of the best Christmas tales, confirms the little girl's faith and softens her hard-hearted father at the same time.

This is good family entertainment for all ages, with just enough story twists to keep the youngest children attentive. Eight-year-old Rebecca Harrell is a charmer.

THE PREMATURE BURIAL (1962)
Color, 81 minutes
Cast: Ray Milland, Hazel Court, Richard Ney, Heather Angel, Alan Napier, John Dierkes, Dick Miller
Director: Roger Corman
Screenplay: Charles Beaumont and Ray Russell, suggested by the essay by Edgar Allan Poe
Period horror/Mystery
Unrated
Younger kids: Probably not Older kids: OK

Underplotted and ponderous, this is one of the weaker entries in the Roger Corman Poe series and recycles a plot element from **The Pit and the Pendulum.** Milland is afraid that he has inherited his father's catalepsy, and fears that he will be buried alive; he constructs a tomb with an assortment of escape devices and grows increasingly morbid, until his fiancée (Court) convinces him to give up his fearful ways—but that's when things get really sticky.

Milland is fine, as are Court

and Heather Angel, but the film seems almost as confining as the coffins that Milland so fears.

There's little here to disturb children except for a nightmare sequence—and of course the whole concept of being buried alive. At the same time, there will be little to interest them.

PRIDE AND PREJUDICE
(1940)
Black & white, 118 minutes
Cast: Laurence Olivier, Greer Garson, Edna May Oliver, Edmund Gwenn, Frieda Inescort, Mary Boland, Maureen O'Sullivan, Karen Morley, Heather Angel, Melville Cooper, E. E. Clive, Ann Rutherford, Marsha Hunt
Director: Robert Z. Leonard
Screenplay: Aldous Huxley and Jane Murfin, based on the novel by Jane Austen
Comedy-drama/Literary classic
Unrated
Young children: OK   Older children: VG

Jane Austen's celebrated comedy of manners in early-19th-century England comes to the screen in a near flawless adaptation. It is the story of the Bennets, a quintet of unmarried siblings who reside in a rural village. The story is set into motion with the arrival of Charles Bingley and Darcy, two wealthy bachelors. The mother of the young women is particularly interested in this development; she is well aware that unless a male inheritor is produced—and soon—she will forfeit the family farm to her husband's cousin.

Elizabeth (Greer Garson), the eldest of the Bennets, is a bright and free-thinking young woman who will have none of her moth-er's machinations. What's more, she is less than overwhelmed by Darcy (Laurence Olivier), whom she discovers to be scornful and overbearing.

This flavorful film not only is ideal fare for adolescents, but remains one of the best Hollywood versions of a distinctly British story. Laurence Olivier is a perfect choice to play Darcy, while classy Greer Garson exudes just the right bit of spunk as Elizabeth.

THE PRIDE OF THE YANKEES (1942)
Black & white, 127 minutes
Cast: Gary Cooper, Teresa Wright, Walter Brennan, Dan Duryea, Babe Ruth, Elsa Janssen, Ludwig Stossel, Virginia Gilmore, Bill Dickey
Director: Sam Wood
Screenplay: Jo Swerling and Herman J. Mankiewicz, based on a story by Paul Gallico
Biography/Sports
Unrated
Younger children: OK   Older children: VG

As a young man Lou Gehrig (Gary Cooper) gives up a career as an engineer to play baseball, to the dismay of his mother. But soon he is one of the greats, playing for the New York Yankees alongside Babe Ruth (played by the Sultan of Swat himself). His well-intentioned mother not only disapproves of him as a ball player, she doesn't care much for the girl he marries (Teresa Wright) either, but eventually she comes around. After an extraordinary career, Gehrig finds himself ill and unable to play. He retires from the game, giving one of the most moving farewell speeches of all time.

Pride of the Yankees is less about baseball than it is about heart. If kids are looking for sports action, this isn't the film for them; there aren't many ball-playing scenes here. If, however, they want to know what it takes to be a champion, what it means to show grace under pressure, and if perhaps they need to learn that nice guys can finish first, then this biography is a must-see.

True baseball fans will also enjoy seeing the immortal Babe Ruth, a real-life teammate of Gehrig's, playing himself in several scenes, with great gusto and appeal.

THE PRIME OF MISS JEAN BRODIE (1969)
Color, 116 minutes
Cast: Maggie Smith, Robert Stephens, Pamela Franklin, Gordon Jackson, Celia Johnson, Diane Grayson, Jane Carr, Shirley Steedman
Director: Ronald Neame
Screenplay: Jay Presson Allen, based on her stage adaptation of the novel by Muriel Spark
Drama
Rated PG
Young children: No   Older children: VG

Most movies about schoolteachers depict their central characters as uncelebrated, underpaid, and overworked heroes and heroines, dedicated to inspiring the young minds in their care.

One unforgettable exception is Jean Brodie, an educator who is superficially supportive of her charges yet who, ultimately, is as dangerous and destructive as any overt villain. Miss Brodie (Maggie Smith, in a superlative Oscar-winning performance) teaches at the exclusive, conservative Marcia Blaine School for Girls in 1932 Edinburgh. She is an elitist and romantic whose passions are music, art, and Mussolini. The autocracy at the core of her character manifests itself as Miss Brodie recruits a coterie of students, the "crème de la crème" whom she dubs the "Brodie Set." Miss Brodie's unnatural influence on her girls leads to unexpected, even tragic, consequences.

The Prime of Miss Jean Brodie is an extraordinary character study that has not lost any of its potency or relevance, and is certain to be savored by more discerning older children. Its mature situations (and brief nudity) make it unsuitable for young viewers.

THE PRINCE AND THE PAUPER (1937)
Black & white, 120 minutes
Cast: Errol Flynn, Billy and Bobby Mauch, Claude Rains, Alan Hale, Montagu Love, Henry Stephenson, Barton MacLane
Director: William Keighley
Screenplay: Laird Doyle, based on the novel by Mark Twain
Adventure
Unrated
Younger kids: OK   Older kids: VG

This is the best film version of Mark Twain's delightful (and much imitated) story about two look-alike boys in 16th-century England—Prince Edward and an abused street urchin—who decide to trade places. The lark goes well for a while, until an enemy (Claude Rains) of King Henry's discovers the truth. He conspires to kill Edward and replace him with the beggar boy, as part of his scheme to seize the throne, but a soldier of fortune (Errol Flynn) befriends the real prince and comes to his rescue for a rousing nick-of-time finale.

Flynn is his usual lighthearted self and adds a note of swash-buckling to the tale, but he's actually upstaged by the boys, who are played with puckish charm by real-life twins Bobby and Billy Mauch. (Think what that must have saved in special-effects bills!) Like Flynn's **The Adventures of Robin Hood,** made by many of the same hands, this film is sparked by a rousing musical score by the great Erich Wolfgang Korngold.

THE PRINCESS BRIDE (1987)
Color, 98 minutes
Cast: Cary Elwes, Mandy Patinkin, Chris Sarandon, Christopher Guest, Wallace Shawn, Andre the Giant, Fred Savage, Robin Wright, Peter Falk, Peter Cook, Billy Crystal, Carol Kane, Mel Smith
Director: Rob Reiner
Screenplay: William Goldman, based on his novel
Fantasy/Romance/Comedy
Rated PG
Younger children: OK Older children: VG

When young Charlie is sick in bed, his grandfather (Peter Falk) comes to read him a story; at first the boy is bored and fears that this will be a mushy, old-fashioned tale . . . but soon he's hooked. The story tells of Princess Buttercup (Robin Wright), who falls in love with Wesley (Carey Elwes), a stableboy; he goes off to better himself so that he will be worthy of her but never

comes back. Instead, she is carried off by the evil Prince Humperdinck (Chris Sarandon), who plans to make her his bride.

When Wesley comes back into her life, the adventure really begins, and we meet a gallery of colorful characters, including Inigo Montoya (Mandy Patinkin), who lives his life only to avenge his father, the crafty Vizzini (Wallace Shawn) and his hulking henchman, Fezzik (Andre the Giant), and of course, Miracle Max (Billy Crystal). The colorful story is serpentine and full of surprises.

The Princess Bride wants to be a little bit of everything: comedy, fairy tale, spoof, old-fashioned swashbuckler, romance. As a result, it's a bit lopsided at times, but its ingredients are strong enough to make up for some shortcomings.

There is some violence, fairly muted, and the villains' lascivious feelings for Princess Buttercup are far from subtle. But on the whole this film is suitable for all but the youngest kids—who may find its story (and constant shift of tone) utterly confusing. Adolescents tend to love it.

PRINCESS CARABOO (1994)
Color, 96 minutes
Cast: Phoebe Cates, Jim Broadbent, Wendy Hughes, Kevin Kline, John Lithgow, Stephen Rea, Peter Eyre, Jacqueline Pearce
Director: Michael Austin
Screenplay: Michael Austin
Comedy-drama
Rated PG
Younger kids: VG Older kids: VG

This neglected little charmer—based on a true story!—stars

Phoebe Cates as a mysterious young woman who appears in Bristol, England, circa 1817, and manages to convince everyone that she is a princess from a faraway South Sea island. The story is told with a gentle, lighter-than-air touch and plays like an extended fairy tale, ideal for children. However, there is also some neat social satire thrown in for added weight, as the young woman is taken in by a British couple and becomes a darling of society, winning over skeptics with the greatest of ease.

The cast is delightful, particularly John Lithgow as a stuffy Oxford professor who at first is convinced that the woman is a fraud, but is soon love-struck and reduced to tears by the "princess." Cates is so winning that you (like the characters in the film) forget to question whether or not she is pulling a scam and simply want her to be a princess.

Princess Caraboo is a delight for the entire family.

PRINCE VALIANT (1954)
Color, 100 minutes
Cast: Robert Wagner, James Mason, Janet Leigh, Debra Paget, Sterling Hayden, Victor McLaglen, Donald Crisp, Brian Aherne
Director: Henry Hathaway
Screenplay: Dudley Nichols, based on the comic strip by Harold Foster
Swashbuckler/Action-adventure
Unrated
Younger kids: Good Older kids: Good

Robert Wagner sports a rather silly-looking black pageboy wig in order to look like Hal Foster's popular comic strip hero in this cheerfully entertaining, cartoonish costumer about Arthurian knights. The plot entails Prince Valiant coming to Camelot to get help for his father (Donald Crisp), an exiled Viking king. There, Valiant is made squire to Sir Gawain (Sterling Hayden), falls in love with Princess Aleta (Janet Leigh), and battles the villainous Sir Brack (James Mason), who's actually the Black Knight.

This juvenile nonsense has no pretensions to historical accuracy, but it's filled with jousts and sword fights, and can be quite enjoyable if you're a 10-year-old— or can manage to think like one.

THE PRISONER OF ZENDA (1937)
Black & white, 101 minutes
Cast: Ronald Colman, Madeleine Carroll, Douglas Fairbanks, Jr., Mary Astor, C. Aubrey Smith, Raymond Massey, David Niven, Montagu Love, Alexander D'Arcy
Director: John Cromwell
Screenplay: John Balderston, Wells Root, and Donald Ogden Stewart, based on the novel by Anthony Hope and the play by Edward Rose
Swashbuckler adventure/Literary classic
Unrated
Young children: VG Older children: VG

Here is one of the all-time great Ruritanian romance-adventure stories, with genteel Ronald Colman playing two roles: Major Rudolf Rassendyll, an Englishman who arrives in a mythical Balkan country to hunt game but is swept up in a thrilling and life-threatening court intrigue that involves posing as his own distant but identical cousin, the irresponsible, hard-drinking Prince Rudolf. When it comes to movie villains, it's hard to beat the performance of Raymond Massey as Black Michael, the prince's wicked half-brother . . . or the seemingly cavalier Rupert of Hentzau, played with great flair by Douglas Fairbanks, Jr., who shows his true stripes in a long, climactic duel with Colman in which the clanks of swords are punctuated by witty lines of dialogue.

Producer David O. Selznick spared nothing in presenting a lavish, breathtaking fantasy world, including lush royal palaces, the pomp and circumstance of a coronation and a royal ball, as well as duels by expert swordsmen and sinister hideouts like the dungeon of Zenda castle. The 1952 remake (which followed this version scene-for-scene) is also quite good, but if you only want to sample one of the two, this is the smart choice.

As with so many adventure classics, the girls in the family may be bothered by the fact that the women in the story stand by and look pretty while the men experience the escapades.

THE PRISONER OF ZENDA (1952)
Color, 101 minutes
Cast: Stewart Granger, Deborah Kerr, Jane Greer, Louis Calhern, Lewis Stone, James Mason, Robert Douglas, Robert Coote
Director: Richard Thorpe
Screenplay: John Balderston, Wells Root, and Noel Langley, based on the novel by Anthony Hope and the play by Edward Rose
Swashbuckler adventure/Literary classic
Unrated

Young children: VG   Older children: VG

The most obvious difference between the 1937 film of the classic Ruritanian adventure and this subsequent screen version is that this was shot in amazingly vivid Technicolor. Both films tell the thrilling story of an Englishman who comes to a Balkan country for a hunting trip only to be drawn into a fascinating and possibly fatal court intrigue.

The two films have similar screenplays, and both are expensively and tastefully presented. Either film is highly recommended for the entire family. However, the cast of this film, with the exception of James Mason (cast as the villainous Rupert of Hentzau), appears a bit wooden when compared with Ronald Colman and Raymond Massey in the roles of consummate hero and villain in the earlier treatment.

Of course, if possible, try to see both versions and then make your own decision!

PROJECT X (1987)
Color, 108 minutes
Cast: Matthew Broderick, Helen Hunt, Bill Sadler, Johnny Ray, Jonathan Stark, Robin Gammell, Stephen Lang, Dick Miller, Willie, Okko, Karanja, Lulu
Director: Jonathan Kaplan
Screenplay: Stanley Weiser
Science thriller/Suspense
Rated PG
Young children: Too intense   Older children: OK

A young chimpanzee is captured in Africa and taken to the United States, where Teri McDonald

(Hunt), a researcher, is very kind to him and teaches him sign language. However, lack of funds separates them, and the chimp, Virgil, ends up as one of the experimental subjects in a project studying the abilities of pilots to perform under stress. Airman Jimmy (Broderick) is assigned to take care of the chimps and enjoys working with them. He's surprised when Virgil "talks" to him through sign language, but can't convince coldhearted Dr. Carroll (Sadler) that this is really happening. Jimmy is disturbed when he learns that previous people in his job have suffered emotional problems—and then he learns what's really going on in Carroll's lab.

Smoothly made and entertaining, *Project X* takes its story seriously and doesn't anthropomorphize the chimpanzees any more than the plot requires, though the story is resolved in such a conventional manner that the end result is not terribly satisfying.

Nonetheless, animal-loving kids will enjoy the film because the chimps are endearing and entertaining just being themselves. Few kids have seen enough movies to recognize clichés when they see them, so this movie may seem fresh to them.

However, the scenes in which the chimps are exposed to radiation will be upsetting, especially to younger children.

Q

QUATERMASS AND THE PIT (1968) (aka Five Million Years to Earth)
Color, 98 minutes
Cast: Andrew Keir, Barbara
    Shelley, James Donald, Julian
    Glover, Duncan Lamont
Director: Roy Ward Baker
Screenplay: Nigel Kneale, based
    on his teleplay
Science fiction/Suspense
Unrated
Young children: Won't get
    it Older children: VG

While excavating for a London subway extension, a crew finds unusual skeletons of apelike creatures, then what is first assumed to be an unexploded bomb from World War II. However, further investigation reveals that it has been buried for five million years—and came from Mars. More revelations occur as a team of scientists continues investigating the mysterious object, but then eerie and dangerous events begin to happen, culminating in a threat to the entire world.

If older kids can get past the crucial but unexciting first twenty minutes of the film, they're likely to be as absorbed by the deepening mystery as you will be. This is one of the most intelligent science fiction movies ever made, with a challenging and imaginative premise, and a haunting conclusion—though the deeply religious may find it objectionable. (It shares some important themes with **2001:** A Space Odyssey, coincidentally released the same year.) The cast is fine, and while the special effects are just adequate, the content is what counts.

It's the third, and best, in the series of movies about rocket scientist Bernard Quatermass, created in a television play by Nigel Kneale, and played here by Andrew Keir. The fourth and last, *The Quatermass Conclusion,* is a well-intentioned but lesser effort.

QUATERMASS II (1957) (aka Enemy From Space)
Black & white, 84 minutes
Cast: Brian Donlevy, John
    Longden, William Franklyn,
    Tom Chatto, Percy Herbert,
    Sidney James, Bryan Forbes,
    Vera Day, John Van Eyssen
Director: Val Guest
Screenplay: Nigel Kneale and
    Guest, from Kneale's teleplay
Science fiction/Suspense
Unrated
Younger kids: No Older kids:
    OK

In this sequel to **The Quatermass Xperiment/The Creeping Unknown,** Professor Quatermass (Donlevy) is angry when his plans for a Moon colony are quashed and then stunned to discover that one has been built on Earth. He also learns that aliens are taking over people as part of a plan to alter the Earth to suit them, and they have already infiltrated the British government.

Suspenseful, realistic, and very taut, *Quatermass II* is the very model of an inexpensive science fiction movie of the 1950s, nearly a classic of its type. The climax is marred by some fairly ridiculous-looking giant monsters, but they're not around long, and the focus of the movie definitely lies elsewhere.

The dry, documentarylike tone of the movie and a minimum of "bad laughs" make the film pretty much timeless. Even kids weaned on today's lavish sci-fi movies are likely to find themselves caught up in this well-told story.

THE QUATERMASS XPERIMENT (1956) (aka **The Creeping Unknown**)

Black & white, 82 minutes
Cast: Brian Donlevy, Margia Dean, Jack Warner, Richard Wordsworth
Director: Val Guest
Screenplay: Richard Landau and Guest, from the teleplay *The Quatermass Experiment* by Nigel Kneale
Science fiction–horror/Monster
Unrated
Younger kids: No   Older kids: VG

The first rocketship, designed by Professor Quatermass (Donlevy), crash-lands in England; three of the four men aboard have vanished, and the fourth (Wordsworth) is acting very strangely. It turns out he's been invaded by an alien life form and is slowly evolving into something that's not remotely human.

This was based on a phenomenally popular BBC TV serial written by Nigel Kneale, and was an early production of Hammer Films, later known for their high-quality horror films. It's a tense, scary movie, unusual in the strong sympathy it builds for the hapless Wordsworth (who gives an excellent performance). Director Guest increases the pace and the suspense as the film heads for its climax in Westminster Abbey.

The film's approach takes it out of the "kiddie" domain, but older kids (especially science ficiton fans) should like it.

QUEST FOR CAMELOT (1998)

Color, 85 minutes
Cast: Voices of Jessalyn Gilsig, Cary Elwes, Gary Oldman, Eric Idle, Don Rickles, Jane Seymour, Pierce Brosnan, Bronson Pinchot, Sir John Gielgud, Gabriel Byrne
Director: Frederick Du Chau
Screenplay: Kirk De Maicco and William Schifrin
Animated feature/Musical
Rated G
Younger kids: OK, with caution   Older kids: OK

This medieval musical has its moments, but is ultimately a grade-B animated adventure. An ousted knight, Ruber, plots to steal the legendary sword Excalibur, which gave King Arthur his power and united the noble knights of the Round Table. When his griffin accidentally drops it in the forest, Ruber begins an all-out search. Enter Kayley, brave daughter of one of the (now-deceased) knights, who sneaks away from Ruber's invaders and begins a quest to find the sword. Detouring through a forbidden forest, she encounters Garrett, a blind warrior, who befriends her. They are joined by Devon and Cornwall, a wise-cracking two-headed dragon. This crew makes its way through numerous cliffhanging sequences to rescue the sword and save Camelot.

Very young viewers may find this too dark and intense, but older girls should like and identify with the plucky Kayley (whose father is murdered early on). The danger and menace are just credible enough to draw kids into the story. *Quest for Camelot* has the usual problems of a Disney knock-off animated feature: blending musical numbers, sidekick zaniness, and dramatic action into one cohesive whole. Art direction and character animation are standard, while a computer-generated three-dimensional Ogre looks completely out of place. The songs by David Foster and Carole Bayer Sager are forgettable.

QUIGLEY DOWN UNDER
(1990)
Color, 119 minutes
Cast: Tom Selleck, Laura San Giacomo, Alan Rickman
Director: Simon Wincer
Screenplay: John Hill
Western
Rated PG-13
Young children: No   Older children: VG

So many mediocre Westerns have come along in recent years that it's a wonder the genre has survived at all. This is one of the best, a perfect coupling of contemporary sensibilities and traditional Western moviemaking. It might even get your kids interested in watching this kind of movie!

Australian land baron Alan Rickman imports hired American gun Tom Selleck to "protect" his property. When the sharpshooter discovers that *protection* means murdering the land's aborigines, he turns against his vile employer to the point where only one of them is going to live through the movie.

Which one? That would be telling. The grit of the movie is in the cat and mouse game the two play while stalking each other. To use another animal analogy, Selleck is the fish out of water, Rickman the experienced fisherman.

Guns are fired repeatedly in this rough (but not overly violent) outdoor drama, with Laura San Giacomo as a feebleminded woman in need of Selleck's protection. With a good cast, outstanding scenery, and an unusual location, *Quigley Down Under* is a winner, best suited to older children and their parents.

quences: their initial encounter with the Camel with the Wrinkled Knees (in which he sings "Blue") and their capture by the Greedy, a morphing muck of candy.

Brief live-action footage features director Williams' daughter, Claire, as the toys' owner. The Broadway-style score by Joe Raposo (*Sesame Street*) contains too many songs, and the overall feel of the film is melancholy, but the colorful characters may entertain younger kids who don't demand nonstop action.

RAIDERS OF THE LOST ARK (1981)
Color, 115 minutes
Cast: Harrison Ford, Karen Allen, Paul Freeman, Ronald Lacey, John Rhys-Davies, Denholm Elliott, Wolf Kahler
Director: Steven Spielberg
Screenplay: Lawrence Kasdan, based on a story by George Lucas and Philip Kaufman
Action-adventure
Rated PG
Younger kids: No Older kids: VG

The first—and best—of Steven Spielberg and George Lucas' *Indiana Jones* trilogy is a Saturday matinee B movie writ large, which pays tongue-in-cheek homage to the cliff-hanging serials of yesteryear. Harrison Ford (in a role originally offered to Tom Selleck) stars as an archaeologist university professor whose only fear is snakes—(of which there are six thousand in the film). He trades in his glasses and bow tie for a bullwhip and leather jacket after being recruited by the U.S. government in 1936 to find the lost Ark of the Covenant before the

Nazis can get their hands on it and harness its awesome power.

Filled with nonstop thrills and hyperkinetic action, death-defying stunts and eye-popping special effects, the comic strip–style violence (including melting flesh and grisly corpses) is definitely too intense and frightening for younger children, but the movie is perfect escapist entertainment for teens, especially boys, and Harrison Ford is a perfect hero.

RAISING ARIZONA (1987)
Color, 92 minutes
Cast: Nicolas Cage, Holly Hunter, Trey Wilson, John Goodman, William Forsythe, Sam McMurray, Frances McDormand, Randall (Tex) Cobb, M. Emmet Walsh
Director: Joel Coen
Screenplay: Ethan and Joel Coen
Comedy
Rated PG-13
Younger kids: OK, with caution Older kids: VG

Raising Arizona is a dizzy, off-center comedy about a mismatched couple, H. I. ("Hi") McDonnough (Cage), a convenience store robber, and Edwina (Hunter), a former police officer who desperately want a baby. Unfortunately, she can't have one, so the couple decide to steal one of the new quintuplets from the home of unpainted furniture magnate Nathan Arizona, Jr. They encounter a few complications along the way, including some escaped cons and a seemingly hell-spawned bounty-hunting biker.

The Coen Brothers are renowned for their odd, unique slant on film conventions in such films as *Miller's Crossing*, *Barton Fink*, and *Fargo*, and this twisted sort of screwball comedy is no exception. There is an off-kilter sweetness underneath all of the craziness, but the tone is also ironic as only the Coens can make it, and the subtle tweaking of the joys of family and the demands of the American Dream is not every moviegoer's cup of tea. The humor may escape some viewers altogether—or be misunderstood. But older kids with a sense of the bizarre could catch on fast and have a great time. The chases are beautifully choreographed and edited with Road Runner–cartoon precision, and greatly abetted by cinematographer (and later director) Barry Sonnenfeld's patented "wacky cam," which can track bikers and crawling babies with equal abandon.

The violence, however cartoonish, and sensitive subject matter (kidnapping a baby), make this inappropriate for young ones.

A RAISIN IN THE SUN (1961)
Black & white, 128 minutes
Cast: Sidney Poitier, Claudia
    McNeil, Ruby Dee, Diana
    Sands, Ivan Dixon, John
    Fiedler, Louis Gossett
Director: Daniel Petrie
Screenplay: Lorraine Hansberry,
    based on her play
Drama
Unrated
Young children: OK Older
    children: VG

A Raisin in the Sun is a potent allegory that reflects the hopes and dreams of black America at a pivotal point in the then evolving civil rights movement. It is the story of one African-American family, the Youngers, who reside in an overcrowded apartment on Chicago's South Side. Lena

Younger, the family matriarch (Claudia McNeil), receives a $10,000 insurance policy left her by her late husband. She wishes to use the money as a down payment on a house in the suburbs and to further the education of her daughter, Beneatha. Her son, Walter Lee (Sidney Poitier), however, is intent on purchasing a liquor store, which will allow him to leave his job as the chauffeur of a moneyed white man.

This hard-hitting drama explores the anxiety within the Younger family, whose members have been living lives of quiet hopelessness. It also reflects on the matriarchal structure in many black families and examines the emasculation of the black man by an antagonistic white society.

Young viewers today might see this as a kind of time capsule, but it still has great dramatic power—thanks to Hansberry's writing and an exceptional cast. It's also a reminder of a time when a film could deal with the black experience in America with honesty and candor.

A RAT'S TALE (1997)
Color, 89 minutes
Cast: Beverly D'Angelo, Jerry
    Stiller, Josef Ostendorf,
    Lauren Hutton
Director: Michael F. Huse
Screenplay: Werner Morgenrath
    and Peter Scheerbaum, based
    on the book by Tor Seidler
Children's fantasy
Rated G
Young children: VG Older
    children: OK

Montague Mad-Rat, a wharf rat, and Isabella Noble-Rat, an uptown girl, are the Romeo and Juliet heroes who take on Rat

Rescue's latest mission: find more magical aloe vera to make a vaccine against the exterminator's toxins. Three magical seashells hold the key to saving the Democ-rat-cy from decimation, and a kindly sewer gator dispenses advice on the journey.

No, this isn't another sequel to **The Rescuers,** and these aren't cuddly cartoon characters. Astonishingly, they're low-tech, old-fashioned marionettes, strings and all, wielded by Germany's Augsburger Puppenkiste ensemble in an adaptation of Tor Seidler's novel (a Library of Congress Children's Book of the Year).

Shot largely on location in Manhattan, the sequences with live actors are a bit over the top and not convincingly directed. Underground, though, the scraggly, rather unattractive rodents are strangely compelling in their own medieval way.

Young children, once they get past the unfamiliarity of the medium, may find themselves hooked. Older kids may feel they're past this kind of entertainment.

The best thing is there are no dumb songs.

THE RAVEN (1963)
Color, 86 minutes
Cast: Vincent Price, Boris Karloff, Peter Lorre, Hazel Court, Olive Sturges, Jack Nicholson
Director: Roger Corman
Screenplay: Richard Matheson, suggested by the poem by Edgar Allan Poe
Comedy horror
Unrated
Younger kids: Probably harmless Older kids: Likewise

Reclusive sorcerer Price restores a raven to human form, only to discover it's Lorre, a cranky and inept magician who reveals that Price's wife, the supposedly late Lenore (Court), is living with master magician Karloff.

This is one to save for when your kids have seen a few of the other entries in Roger Corman's Edgar Allan Poe series, such as **House of Usher, Pit and the Pendulum,** and **Tales of Terror,** because it's actually a spoof of those movies, and a funny one. The pacing is erratic, and the heavily "funny" score is a handicap, but it's well produced and very entertaining.

The cast, a sort of summit meeting of great stars associated with horror and the macabre, is having a fine time, and that makes it fun for the audience. Peter Lorre is particularly funny as the half-man half-raven. Youngsters who like Jack Nicholson will be delighted and startled by his role here, as Lorre's thick-witted son. And the movie can serve as either an introduction to, or a reminder of, the work of Boris Karloff and Vincent Price.

Kids who have never seen the Corman Poe movies will probably be amused, but it will appeal more to "veterans."

REAL GENIUS (1985)
Color, 106 minutes
Cast: Val Kilmer, Gabe Jarret, Michelle Meyrink, William Atherton, Patti D'Arbanville, Robert Prescott, Louis Giambalvo, Jonathan Gries, Ed Lauter, Severn Darden, Dean Devlin
Director: Martha Coolidge
Screenplay: Neal Israel, Pat Proft, and Peter Torokvei.

Comedy
Rated PG
Young children:
  Marginal   Older children: OK

Fifteen-year-old Mitch (Jarret) is recruited by Professor Hathaway (Atherton) to join other precocious geniuses in a "think tank" at an aging California college that has come to specialize in advanced science. Mitch becomes good friends with school prankster Chris (Kilmer) and others at the college; they go into action when they learn that Hathaway has been using their skills for military research.

The best and most serious of the three 1985 kids-and-science movies (the others being **Weird Science** and **My Science Project**), this starts out as a satire and winds up as an all-too-conventional teen revenge comedy, with characters like Professor Hathaway portrayed as caricatures, not real people. There is some emphasis on worrying about sex but very little activity in that regard. Incidentally, some of the scientific gags in this movie were inspired by the real-life pranks of students at CalTech.

Younger children will find little here to interest them. Teenagers, especially those who have a scientific bent themselves, will be more likely to have fun with it, even though it runs out of steam before its popcorn-filled climax.

REBECCA OF SUNNYBROOK FARM (1938)
Black & white, 80 minutes (also available in computer-colored version)
Cast: Shirley Temple, Randolph Scott, Jack Haley, Gloria Stuart, Phyllis Brooks, Helen Westley, Slim Summerville, Bill "Bojangles" Robinson, J. Edward Bromberg, Alan Dinehart, Dixie Dunbar, William Demarest
Director: Allan Dwan
Screenplay: Karl Tunberg and Don Ettlinger, suggested by the novel by Kate Douglas Wiggin
Comedy/Musical
Unrated
Young children: VG   Older children: VG

This fine vehicle for Shirley Temple opens with a company auditioning tots to become "Little Miss America" as part of a nationwide advertising campaign to promote a new radio show. Shirley's tryout is so impressive that she is chosen. Through a misunderstanding, however, the child believes that she has lost the opportunity. Since she and her father have no more money and are evicted from their home, her dad makes arrangements for her to live with her stern but loving aunt (who hates show business) at Sunnybrook Farm in upstate New York. While the advertising men search for their new little star, Shirley chases piglets, feeds the chickens, and has a delightful time.

While the fact that radio predated television as the public's favorite leisure time activity might have to be explained to the young children, the rest of the story is easily enjoyed by the whole family. This film bears little relation to the Kate Douglas Wiggin novel of the same name (which was filmed before, in the silent era with Mary Pickford) but stands on its own as an entertaining vehicle for Shirley.

REBEL WITHOUT A CAUSE
(1955)
Color, 111 minutes
Cast: James Dean, Natalie
    Wood, Sal Mineo, Corey
    Allen, Jim Backus, Ann
    Doran, William Hopper,
    Rochelle Hudson, Dennis
    Hopper
Director: Nicholas Ray
Screenplay: Stewart Stern, based
    on a story by Ray
Drama
Unrated
Younger kids: OK   Older kids:
    VG

James Dean's legendary status as
a teen icon was established for
eternity with this seminal juvenile
delinquency drama, which was released one month after he was
killed in a car crash at the age of
24. Dean is sensational as Jim
Stark, a sensitive kid with family
troubles who moves to a new
town and immediately falls afoul
of the local gang of toughs (which
includes a baby-faced Dennis
Hopper). Following a knife fight
in L.A.'s Griffith Park and the
classic "chickie-run" scene, in
which Jim and the gang leader,
Buzz (Corey Allen), race their
cars towards the edge of a cliff,
Jim and Buzz's girl, Judy (Natalie
Wood), fall in love and form a
short-lived happy family with
Plato (Sal Mineo), another troubled teen.

This is a poignant and powerful
portrait of alienated youth. It was
the first movie to accurately deal
with the "generation gap" and depict teens as real people with real
problems. Nicholas Ray's superb
direction utilizes dynamic widescreen compositions and symbolic
use of color to reveal the cracks
in the 1950s middle-class "good

life." He also elicits fine performances from his entire cast, including 16-year-old Natalie Wood
in her first adult role. Though inevitably dated in some respects,
the film's theme of misunderstood
and disaffected youth searching
for love in a cold universe is timeless, and it still has the ability to
make an emotional connection
with kids. It should be essential
viewing for teenagers.

THE RED PONY (1949)
Color, 89 minutes
Cast: Myrna Loy, Robert
    Mitchum, Peter Miles, Louis
    Calhern, Shepperd Strudwick,
    Margaret Hamilton, Patty
    King, Jackie Jackson, Beau
    Bridges
Director: Lewis Milestone
Screenplay: John Steinbeck,
    based on his novella
Drama/Animal story
Unrated
Young children: VG   Older
    children: VG

Here is another potent drama that
spotlights a youngster's undying
devotion to a pet—in this case, a
horse—and how that relationship
forces the child to mature. The
child in question is young Tom
Tilfin, whose father, Fred, a former schoolteacher, now owns a
ranch. But Fred hasn't been accepted into the ranching community, and even his son seems to
idolize virile ranch hand Billy
Buck more than he does his own
father.

These scenes are told from a
grown-up point of view and may
not interest kids, but the depiction of ranch life and the scenes
featuring Tom and his beloved
pony will enthrall most kids.
The Red Pony has an unusually

fine cast and was obviously made with great care. Novelist John Steinbeck adapted his own story for the screen, and the great American composer Aaron Copland provided the music.

It is important for parents to know, however, that the pony dies during the course of the story, and children will naturally be upset by this.

THE RED SHOES (1948)
Color, 133 minutes
Cast: Anton Walbrook, Moira Shearer, Marius Goring, Robert Helpmann, Leonide Massine, Albert Basserman, Ludmilla Tcherina, Esmond Knight
Directors: Michael Powell and Emeric Pressburger
Screenplay: Powell and Pressburger, based on a story by Hans Christian Andersen, with additional dialogue by Keith Winter
Ballet/Musical drama
Unrated
Young children: No   Older children: VG

This classic film is to ballet what *Stagecoach* and *The Maltese Falcon* are to the Hollywood Western and whodunit. The scenario artfully combines romantic drama with dance as it tells the story of a young ballerina, Victoria Page (Moira Shearer), who is forced to choose between her love for Julian Craster (Marius Goring), a talented composer, and her desire to attain greatness under the tutelage of the impresario Boris Lermontov (Anton Walbrook). According to Lermontov, a dancer who relies on the comforts of human love never will be a great artist. Yet Victoria falls for Julian, resulting in assorted complications.

The Red Shoes is memorable for the detail of its characterizations and its depiction of the ballet world. At the core of its story is the tough, uncompromising Lermontov and the manner in which he attempts to control Victoria and Julian. Its climax is the twenty-minute-long title ballet, based on Hans Christian Andersen's fable of a little girl enchanted by her red dancing shoes.

Younger kids may find some of the film confusing, even off-putting at times, but there is a fascination here, as well, and an almost mystical blending of the onstage and offstage stories.

Victoria's conflict may be emotionally wrenching, but today as in 1948, *The Red Shoes* is potent enough to encourage starry-eyed young girls to fantasize that they, too, can be great ballerinas. It's long been a favorite of dance aficionados young and old.

THE REIVERS (1969)
Color, 107 minutes
Cast: Steve McQueen, Sharon Farrell, Will Geer, Michael Constantine, Rupert Crosse, Mitch Vogel, Lonny Chapman, Juano Hernandez, Clifton James, Ruth White, Dub Taylor, Allyn Ann McLerie, Diane Ladd, Ellen Geer; Burgess Meredith (narrator)
Director: Mark Rydell
Screenplay: Irving Ravetch and Harriet Frank, Jr., based on the novel *The Reivers, a Reminiscence* by William Faulkner
Adventure
Rated M
Young children: No   Older children: VG

This striking, charming slice of Americana tells the story of Lucius McCaslin, an 11-year-old boy growing up in 1905 Mississippi. Lucius will have the experience of his young life when he takes off on a wild automobile adventure in the company of a pair of roguish adults. The first is outgoing, fearless Boon Hogganbeck (Steve McQueen), the McCaslin family handyman. The other is a fascinating character: Ned (Rupert Crosse), an African-American who is comically cheerful yet also pointedly sarcastic, which is more than appropriate, given that he is a Negro in the Jim Crow South.

The Reivers is a wild and woolly coming-of-age yarn. Lucius is fated to encounter much that is foreign to most 11-year-olds. A chunk of the story is set in a brothel and has the boy defending the honor of a prostitute. For this reason, the film is not recommended for children younger than Lucius.

The Reivers offers more than just a rollicking good time, as it is also a vivid portrayal of race relations at a time when Southern justice was unequal justice and the manner in which it was meted out depended upon the color of one's skin.

THE RESCUERS (1977)
Color, 76 minutes
Cast: Voices of Bob Newhart, Eva Gabor, Geraldine Page, Joe Flynn, Jeanette Nolan, Pat Buttram, Jim Jordan, Michelle Stacy
Directors: Wolfgang Reitherman, John Lounsbery, Art Stevens
Screenplay: Larry Clemmons, Ken Anderson, Vance Gerry, David Michener, Burny Mattinson, Frank Thomas, Fred Lucky, Ted Berman, and Dick Sebast, suggested by *The Rescuers* and *Miss Bianca* by Margery Sharp
Animated feature
Rated G
Younger kids: VG   Older kids: VG

This clever Disney animated feature introduces two winning personalities: timid Bernard (Newhart) and headstrong Miss Bianca (Gabor), two mice of the Rescue Aid Society. Located beneath the United Nations building in New York, this organization rescues children in trouble throughout the world.

Bernard and Bianca fly to the Louisiana swamps (courtesy of a dizzy albatross named Orville) to find Penny, a little orphan held captive by the power-mad Madame Medusa (Page). Medusa needs the child to locate a diamond, which is caught in a tight place.

A bit slower paced than usual Disney features, this offers great fun built on the foundation of a solid story. Bernard and Bianca are very likable characters, but as often happens they are outshone by such colorful supporting players as the aforementioned Orville, a dragonfly named Evinrude, etc.

Young children may be concerned about Penny's predicament, but this being a Disney cartoon, you can reassure them that everything will turn out all right. Followed by a sequel, **The Rescuers Down Under** (1990).

THE RESCUERS DOWN UNDER (1990)

Color, 74 minutes
Cast: Voices of Bob Newhart, Eva Gabor, John Candy, Tristan Rogers, Adam Ryen, George C. Scott, Wayne Robson, Bernard Fox, Billy Barty
Directors: Hendel Butoy and Mike Gabriel
Screenplay: Jim Cox, Karey Kirkpatrick, Byron Simpson, and Joe Ranft, suggested by characters created by Margery Sharp
Animated feature
Rated G
Young children: VG   Older children: VG

For years, the Disney studio resisted the idea of sequels, but in 1990 they cooked up an entertaining follow-up to the 1977 film about Bernard and Bianca, the intrepid mice of the Rescue Aid Society who, this time, journey to Australia to help a boy in trouble.

The boy is concerned about the fate of a magnificent eagle named Marahute, who has fallen prey to the evil Percival McLeach. Bernard and Bianca are joined in their adventure by an Aussie mouse named Jake and a lizard known as Frank.

There's more plot than usual—and more than necessary—in this straightforward story, but the charm of the characters, and the excellence of the staging and animation more than make up for it. Orville, the hilarious albatross/one-man airline from *The Rescuers*, is replaced here by his brother, Wilbur, voiced by the talented comic actor John Candy.

There are several genuinely exciting, suspenseful scenes but nothing too grim for young viewers so long as their parents are nearby.

RETURN FROM WITCH MOUNTAIN (1978)

Color, 93 minutes
Cast: Bette Davis, Christopher Lee, Kim Richards, Ike Eisenmann, Jack Soo, Anthony James, Richard Bakalyan, Ward Costello, Brad Savage
Director: John Hough
Screenplay: Malcolm Marmorstein
Science fiction
Rated G
Younger children: VG   Older children: OK

This entertaining sequel to **Escape to Witch Mountain** (1975) benefits from the casting of Christopher Lee and Bette Davis as a villainous team out to rule the world. Two children (Kim Richards, Ike Eisenmann), having discovered their true identities at the conclusion of the first film, return to Earth for summer vacation. Their telekinetic powers are witnessed by Victor (Lee) and Letha (Davis), who quickly see how this can benefit their evil plans. They kidnap the boy and brainwash him into doing their bidding. The girl and a ragtag group of L.A. street kids track down the bad guys before they can complete their blackmail plans.

The film is filled with floating objects and animal antics (provided by a spunky goat who joins the rescue). Kids will enjoy the adventure and the young characters' super powers. As with the first film, this is Disney-sanctioned family fare for all ages.

RETURN OF THE JEDI (1983)
Color, 131 minutes
Cast: Mark Hamill, Harrison
  Ford, Carrie Fisher, Billy Dee
  Williams, Anthony Daniels,
  Peter Mayhew, Sebastian
  Shaw, Ian McDiarmid, David
  Prowse, Alec Guinness, Kenny
  Baker, Denis Lawson,
  Warwick Davis; voices of
  James Earl Jones, Frank Oz
Director: Richard Marquand
Screenplay: Lawrence Kasdan
  and George Lucas, based on a
  story by Lucas
Science fiction/Adventure
Rated PG
Younger kids: VG   Older kids:
  VG

The third installment of the **Star
Wars** saga (or technically speaking, Episode Six) finds Luke Skywalker and the Rebellion facing
challenges from Darth Vader, the
evil Empire, and a brand new
Death Star. *Return of the Jedi* answers all of the questions left
hanging in **The Empire Strikes
Back,** however it is not quite up
to the level of *Star Wars* or *The
Empire Strikes Back* in terms of
character development or surprises in the story. It still delivers
almost everything you could ask
for in an adventure saga, however: a galaxy's worth of imaginative alien creatures, stunning
special effects, and most of all, a
sense of fun inspired by the best
of the classic Saturday matinees
and serials from the 1930s and
'40s.

The cuddly, teddy bear–like
Ewoks might be a tad too childish
for some, but they give the whole
venture an innocence that contrasts nicely with the mechanical
marvels surrounding them and
sets this apart from most other at-

tempts to duplicate the *Star Wars*
formula for success.

There is the usual amount of
action-violence, with shooting and
explosions, but no blood.

RETURN TO OZ (1985)
Color, 110 minutes
Cast: Fairuza Balk, Nicol
  Williamson, Jean Marsh, Piper
  Laurie, Matt Clark, Michael
  Sundin, Tim Rose, Sophie
  Ward
Director: Walter Murch
Screenplay: Murch and Gill
  Dennis, based on books by L.
  Frank Baum
Fantasy
Rated PG
Younger children: No   Older
  children: OK

After her adventures in Oz, Dorothy (Fairuza Balk) isn't happy
back in Kansas. Aunt Em and
Uncle Henry (Piper Laurie, Matt
Clark) think she has emotional
problems, so they take her to a
clinic where she is given shock
treatments. Dorothy and her
chicken Billina finally get to Oz
again, but this time, it's a dark Oz
in trouble, with the wicked
Mombi (Jean Marsh, who also
plays the nurse) in charge. She
changes her heads as others
change their clothes. Dorothy's
friends the Scarecrow, Tin
Woodsman, and Lion have been
turned to stone, and the Emerald
City and Yellow Brick Road are
in ruins, beset by evil and scary
creatures, including the Nome
King (Nicol Williamson, who also
plays the sanitarium doctor). Dorothy must restore Oz to its previous glory.

To the millions of people,
young and old, who love and
cherish **The Wizard Of Oz,** this

sequel, produced by the Disney studio, will come as a shock—and more than likely an unpleasant one. It's hard to picture a story about Oz being so completely bleak and downbeat.

The film does have some imaginative moments. There are many colorful characters and some terrific scenes in which rock faces come to life (courtesy of Will Vinton's Claymation studio). The final showdown with the Nome King is also impressive.

But the overall feeling of the film is cold; there are no characters to warm up to. On anybody's terms, this film would be a letdown; as a sequel to one of the best-loved movies of all time, it's a near disaster.

REVENGE OF FRANKENSTEIN (1958)
Color, 94 minutes
Cast: Peter Cushing, Michael Gwynn, Francis Matthews, Eunice Gayson, Richard Wordsworth, Oscar Quitak, Charles Lloyd Pack, George Woodbridge, Michael Ripper, Lionel Jeffries
Director: Terence Fisher
Screenplay: Jimmy Sangster
Science fiction–horror/Sequel
Unrated
Young children: No   Older children: OK

Saved from the execution he faced at the end of **The Curse of Frankenstein,** ruthless scientist Victor Frankenstein goes to another city where he becomes a popular society doctor and works in a hospital for the poor, where he uses hapless patients as unwitting donors for a new Creature he's piecing together. He's assisted by a deformed man (Qui-

tak), who wants his brain placed in the new body (Gwynn), and also by an ambitious young doctor (Matthews). The operation goes very well—at first. . . .

This sequel is better than the original: the plot is fresher, the production values sharper, and Cushing's steely, controlled performance even more interesting. The idea that the Creature, played very well by Michael Gwynn, is, at first, a perfect realization of Frankenstein's goals, is a novelty for one of these movies. This Hammer movie is one of their best overall: good entertainment even for adults partial to this kind of thing. It also has a very neat twist at the end, which, unfortunately, was ignored in later entries in the series.

However, be cautioned: it's pretty strong stuff, with gory operations and violent fights; young children probably would find it more than they can take. Horror-loving teenagers are likely to enjoy it.

This was followed by **Evil of Frankenstein.**

REVENGE OF THE CREATURE (1955)
Black & white, 82 minutes
Cast: John Agar, Lori Nelson, John Bromfield, Nestor Paiva, Grandon Rhodes, Dave Willock, Brett Halsey, Ricou Browning, Clint Eastwood
Director: Jack Arnold
Screenplay: Martin Berkeley
Monster/Science fiction
Unrated
Younger kids: OK   Older kids: Good

In this sequel to **Creature From the Black Lagoon,** the Gill-Man is found alive in the Black Lagoon and taken to an oceanarium in Florida. He hangs around there a while, long enough to develop a fixation on Lori Nelson, then escapes into the mangrove tidal pools.

In the first film, we were the intruders into the Creature's domain; in the sequel, he's dragged into ours, and the change doesn't do anyone much good. Children are not likely to notice this; in fact, they may prefer this to the first film, because there's less scary stuff in the background. There is also, however, less of the Creature.

Like the first film, this was also shot in 3-D.

By the way, that's an incredibly young Clint Eastwood as a laboratory technician in an early scene.

Followed by **The Creature Walks Among Us.**

RHUBARB (1951)
Black & white, 94 minutes
Cast: Ray Milland, Jan Sterling, Gene Lockhart, Elsie Holmes, Taylor Holmes, William Frawley, Willard Waterman, Strother Martin, Leonard Nimoy
Director: Arthur Lubin
Screenplay: Dorothy Reid and Frances Cockrell, based on the novel by H. Allen Smith
Comedy/Fantasy/Sports
Unrated
Younger kids: VG   Older kids: VG

If the likes of Marge Schott, Jerry Reinsdorf, and George Steinbrenner can own major league baseball teams, why can't a cat? That is precisely what happens in this zany slapstick comedy about Thaddeus J. Banner (Gene Lockhart),

an eccentric millionaire. One of his possessions is a major league ballclub, the Brooklyn Loons. Upon his death the team is willed to a new owner: Banner's best friend in the world, Rhubarb, a spunky former alley cat.

Eric Yeager (Ray Milland), the Loons' press agent, is entrusted with the care and feeding of the feline, a responsibility he is not too keen on if only because his fiancée (Jan Sterling) seems to be allergic to Rhubarb! Nonetheless, the cat goes on to have a positive effect on the Loons, with complications arising when Banner's self-centered daughter attempts to wrest away ownership of the club.

This innocuous, old-fashioned comedy should please kids of all ages. The comic highlight is a goofy sequence involving Rhubarb's on-field antics with a rival team's mascot—a dog!

Star Trek buffs will get a kick out of the presence of a very young Leonard Nimoy in a small role as a ballplayer.

If your kids really enjoy this film, the popular book on which it was based, by noted humorist H. Allen Smith, is still on library shelves and easily found in used bookstores.

RI¢HIE RI¢H (1994)
Color, 94 minutes
Cast: Macaulay Culkin, John Larroquette, Edward Herrmann, Christine Ebersole, Jonathan Hyde, Michael McShane, Stephi Lineburg, Chelcie Ross
Director: Donald Petrie
Screenplay: Tom S. Parker and Jim Jennewein, from a story by Neil Tolkin based on the Harvey Comics characters
Comedy

Rated PG
Younger children: VG Older
  children: VG

Generations of comic-book fans need no introduction to Richie Rich, the world's richest boy. One wouldn't think such a wildly exaggerated premise would work as a live-action movie, but it does, with Macaulay Culkin as the kid who has everything—except friends. After establishing just how rich Richie is—he has his own private McDonald's in the family mansion—the straightforward plot unfolds.

During one of Richie's parents' trips away from home, villainous Lawrence Van Dough (John Larroquette) devises a way to drain all of Mr. Rich's billions out of his accounts. He also plots to have Richie's parents killed in a plane "accident," but they manage to survive. Alone on a life raft, they're unable to contact Richie to tell him they're all right. Meanwhile, it's up to Richie, his loyal manservant, Cadbury, and some newly found friends (from a "normal" school in town) to defeat the bad guys who have taken over the Rich household.

Richie Rich is a rare example of a kid-oriented comedy that isn't stupid, doesn't rely on cheap jokes, and won't bore parents to tears. It's a benign, entertaining film with some good gags and likable characters. (Even Richie's parents, who are spoiled rich people, genuinely love their son.) The villainy is buffoonish, the peril facing Richie's parents is dispensed with quickly, and the final battle for the Rich mansion uses slapstick more than violence.

RICH KIDS (1979)
Color, 96 minutes
Cast: Trini Alvarado, Jeremy Levy, Kathryn Walker, John Lithgow, Terry Kiser, David Selby, Roberta Maxwell, Paul Dooley, Diane Stilwell, Dianne Kirksey, Irene Worth, Olympia Dukakis, Jill Eikenberry
Director: Robert M. Young
Screenplay: Judith Ross
Comedy-drama
Rated PG
Younger children: OK Older
  children: OK

Divorce, from the point of view of two upscale New York City preteens, is the subject of *Rich Kids*, a lightweight but likable comedy.

Twelve-year-old Franny (Trini Alvarado) knows her parents (John Lithgow, Kathryn Walker) are going to divorce, but they aren't ready to tell her. She seeks advice from Jamie (Jeremy Levy), a classmate with divorced parents (Roberta Maxwell, Terry Kiser) who's seen it all. Through the eyes of the two kids, we observe the often absurd behavior of their parents, respective lawyers, friends and lovers, while a puppy-love romance blooms between the youngsters.

The acting is exceptional by both generations, and director Robert M. Young and screenwriter Judith Ross have captured a unique look at contemporary relationships, with excellent use of the New York City backdrop.

The subject matter may be too sensitive for younger kids, especially those who have been exposed to divorce in real life; adolescents should find it both appealing and believable.

RING OF BRIGHT WATER (1969)

Color, 107 minutes

Cast: Bill Travers, Virginia McKenna, Peter Jeffrey, Jameson Clark, Helena Gloag, W. H. D. Joss, Roddy McMillan, Jean Taylor-Smith

Director: Jack Couffer

Screenplay: Couffer and Bill Travers, based on the book by Gavin Maxwell

Animal story/Comedy-drama

Rated G

Younger children: VG   Older children: VG

A delightful animal film, this is perfect fun for kids and their parents. Bill Travers (**Born Free**) plays Graham Merrill, a writer grown tired of the daily rat race in London. His new pet otter, Mij, has ruined his apartment, and with that, he decides to move to the Scottish coast to work on his book.

There, he becomes more and more interested in the doings of Mij and his mischief. While nothing much by way of plot happens from this point on, the footage of this playful otter in the beautiful coastal surroundings will capture your heart. Travers romances Virginia McKenna (his real-life wife), who plays a local doctor; inspiration finally comes to him as he begins his book on the upbringing of Mij.

With attractive people and an irresistible otter, *Ring of Bright Water* is an ideal family film. Both the performances and nature photography are top-notch.

ROBIN HOOD (1973)

Color, 83 minutes

Cast: Voices of Roger Miller, Brian Bedford, Monica Evans, Phil Harris, Andy Devine, Peter Ustinov, Terry-Thomas

Director: Wolfgang Reitherman

Screenplay: Larry Clemmons

Animated feature/Musical

Rated G

Younger kids: VG   Older kids: VG

This animated version of the Robin story casts each famous character as a different critter: Robin is a fox, Little John a bear, Friar Tuck a badger, and so on. The story is based on the familiar folk tale, with Robin infiltrating Prince John's archery contest disguised as a stork, romancing Maid Marian and freeing the enslaved inhabitants of Sherwood Forest.

Minstrel Allan-A-Dale (a rooster voiced by popular singer Roger Miller) sings most of the songs. Peter Ustinov and Terry-Thomas sound like they are having fun as the outlandish villains, while kids will readily recognize Little John as having the same gregarious voice as Baloo from *The Jungle Book*, Phil Harris.

Young viewers will enjoy the characterizations and slapstick sequences, even though this film lacks the cohesiveness of the great Disney animated features, not to mention the most important ingredient of the Disney classics: heart.

ROBIN HOOD: PRINCE OF THIEVES (1991)

Color, 138 minutes

Cast: Kevin Costner, Morgan Freeman, Mary Elizabeth Mastrantonio, Christian Slater,

Alan Rickman, Geraldine
McEwen
Director: Kevin Reynolds
Screenplay: Pen Densham and
John Watson
Swashbuckler/Action-adventure
Rated PG-13
Younger kids: No   Older kids:
OK

Kevin Costner (with a shaky half-
British accent) stars in this updated version of the enduring folk
tale. It's vastly different from previous tellings but still fairly enjoyable on its own terms, with some
exciting action scenes and a neat
surprise cameo at the end.

After escaping from a dungeon
during the Crusades with the help
of an aristocratic Moor (Morgan
Freeman), Robin returns home to
England and discovers that the vicious Sheriff of Nottingham (a
scene-stealing Alan Rickman) has
killed his father and taken over
his lands. Vowing vengeance,
Robin forms an army and takes
refuge in Sherwood Forest,
while finding time to romance a
distinctly modern and independent Maid Marian (Mary Elizabeth Mastrantonio).

This is a dark and gloomy rendition of the legend that fully
earns its PG-13 rating with some
graphic swordplay, sexual references, and partial nudity.

ROBINSON CRUSOE ON
MARS (1964)
Color, 110 minutes
Cast: Paul Mantee, Vic Lundin,
Adam West
Director: Byron Haskin
Screenplay: Ib Melchior and
John C. Higgins, suggested by
Robinson Crusoe by Daniel
Defoe
Science fiction/Adventure

Unrated
Young children: OK, with
advisories   Older children:
OK

Accompanied by a monkey, astronaut Mantee is stranded on Mars
when his spaceship is disabled and
his partner (West) is killed. He
manages to find ways to survive
and finally meets a slave escaped
from alien visitors. When the
aliens later attack, the two work
together to survive.

What seemed realistic to the
more credulous in 1964 looks just
like the same old hokum now,
with rocks that miraculously give
off oxygen, a cute monkey friend,
and an "alien" who's precisely as
human as the hero. Partly shot in
Death Valley, the film is convincingly desolate and handsomely
produced on its limited budget,
but teenagers of today are likely
to find the heavy-handed movie
obvious and slow. Younger children are much more likely to be
interested because of the monkey
if nothing else.

ROCK-A-DOODLE (1992)
Color, 77 minutes
Cast: Voices of Glen Campbell,
Ellen Greene, Christopher
Plummer, Charles Nelson
Reilly, Eddie Deezen, Phil
Harris, Sandy Duncan, Tony
Scott Granger, Sorrell Booke
Director: Don Bluth
Screenplay: David N. Weiss
Animated feature/Musical
Rated G
Younger kids: OK   Older kids:
NG

A strictly B movie, B standing for
Bluth. The story concerns a
rooster named Chanticleer (whose
mannerisms may remind one of

Elvis Presley), whose daily morning rock concerts bring forth the rising sun. On one fateful morning, an evil owl, The Grand Duke, disgraces Chanticleer and the rockin' rooster leaves the farm. This gives the Duke a chance to somehow control things with continuous thunderstorms.

A live-action little boy named Edmond has read about Chanticleer in a picture book and dreams himself into the story. Edmond is transformed into a cartoon cat by The Grand Duke and sets out to find Chanticleer, return him to the farm, and restore sunshine to his flooded homestead. The boy/kitten and some farm animals, followed by the Grand Duke, travel to the city to find Chanticleer, who is now a popular rock star. After a wild chase around a movie studio, the good guys return to the farm and save the day.

This must rate as a typical Bluth film, aimed at nondiscriminating 4- to 6-year-olds (one of the musical production numbers features the song "Tyin' Your Shoes"). Beautiful art direction and animation can't mask a poor screenplay and inconsistent direction.

THE ROCKETEER (1991)
Color, 108 minutes
Cast: Bill Campbell, Jennifer Connelly, Alan Arkin, Timothy Dalton, Paul Sorvino, Terry O'Quinn
Director: Joe Johnston
Screenplay: Danny Bilson, Paul De Meo, from a story by Bilson, De Meo, and William Dear, based on the graphic novel created by Dave Stevens
Science fiction/Adventure
Rated PG

Younger kids: Good   Older kids: Good

In the 1930s, hotshot test pilot Campbell finds a missing secret weapon, a jet pack that when strapped on his back, allows him to fly like a rocket. Enemy agents are after the pack, particularly dashing but bad-tempered movie star Dalton, who's modeled on Errol Flynn.

Kids will generally enjoy this movie; it's very attractive, the cast is appealing, and the special effects are excellent. However, until Campbell takes off as the Rocketeer, the movie is pretty talky. Also, the second half doesn't make as entertaining use of the flying pack as the first half does.

Although it's minor, a W. C. Fields character who encounters the hero's girlfriend, played by a pretty, well-endowed Jennifer Connelly, makes a wisecrack about her figure. It's this kind of thoughtless (and needless) moment that makes parents—especially parents of girls—wince.

This was based on a brief comic book series written and drawn by Dave Stevens, and expertly captures the visual appeal of the comic.

ROCKETSHIP X-M (1950)
Black & white, 78 minutes
Cast: Lloyd Bridges, Osa Massen, John Emery, Noah Beery, Jr., Hugh O'Brian, Morris Ankrum
Director: Kurt Neumann
Screenplay: Kurt Neumann
Science fiction/Adventure
Unrated
Younger kids: OK, with caution   Older kids: OK

The first rocket to the Moon is launched, but a swarm of meteors sends the craft off course, and it lands on Mars. The crew explores the Martian terrain, discovering that an advanced civilization there destroyed itself by atomic warfare.

Not only was this the first serious American movie about space travel (beating **Destination Moon** to the screen by a few months), but it was one of the first to graphically warn audiences about nuclear war. The dramatics are very dated today (no fault of the cast), but the scenes on Mars, filmed in California deserts, are eerily effective, largely thanks to the imaginative cinematography by Karl Struss.

Older kids who sneer through the first part might find themselves creeped out by the Martian sequences, and by the bleak ending.

ROCKY (1976)
Color, 119 minutes
Cast: Sylvester Stallone, Talia Shire, Burt Young, Carl Weathers, Burgess Meredith, Thayer David
Director: John G. Avildsen
Screenplay: Sylvester Stallone
Drama/Sports
Rated PG
Younger kids: OK   Older kids: VG

Rocky has become a modern-day classic of sorts and the very embodiment of an underdog-makes-good movie. Sylvester Stallone was an unknown when he made this film about a down-on-his-luck Philadelphia fighter and part-time loan shark's thumb-breaker named Rocky Balboa. Rocky gets the chance of a lifetime when he is selected to take on the heavyweight champ of the world, Apollo Creed (Carl Weathers).

The story was corny and old-fashioned when it was filmed, a retread of a thousand "chance of a lifetime" movie stories that came before it. But it works because of the affection that writer Stallone and director Avildsen bring to all of their characters, in the grimiest of situations and circumstances. Each one has surprising, hidden shades of warmth and humanity, and we are allowed to discover their dignity (along with them) as the story progresses.

Rocky is an especially wonderful character: shy, tender, proud, aware of his own limitations, a tough guy with the heart of a poet who is not afraid to wear it on his sleeve. The climactic bout between Rocky and Apollo is, by its very nature, quite brutal, but it's necessary to convey the difficulty of Rocky's ultimate dream to "go the distance."

Four sequels followed, and though some were financially successful, they grew increasingly mechanical; none was able to recapture the heart and spirit of the original film.

Any kid old enough to be interested in boxing—and in people—should find this film irresistible.

ROMEO AND JULIET (1968)
Color, 138 minutes
Cast: Olivia Hussey, Leonard Whiting, Milo O'Shea, Murray Head, Michael York, John McEnery, Pat Heywood, Natasha Parry, Robert Stephens, Keith Skinner, Richard Warwick, Dyson Lovell, Laurence Olivier
Director: Franco Zeffirelli
Screenplay: Franco Zeffirelli,

Masolino D'Amico, Franco
Brusati, based on the play by
William Shakespeare
Historical romance/Literary
classic
Rated PG
Younger children: No Older
children: VG (some nudity)

What could be sweeter or more
tragic than Shakespeare's young
lovers, who are forbidden to
marry? Romeo loves Juliet and
his ardor is matched by hers, but
their families will not allow it.
Their friends fight, setting off
more feuds between the Montagues and the Capulets. Juliet
seeks the help of a friar, who
gives her a potion that will simu-
late death. When Romeo thinks
she has died, however, he kills
himself. Juliet, upon awakening
and finding his body, does the
same.

Franco Zeffirelli's *Romeo and
Juliet* made Shakespeare accessible to young people, in part by
casting teenagers (Leonard Whiting and Olivia Hussey) in the title
roles. It's a rich, lush, action-filled
production that is pleasing to the
eye and the ear. (The music, especially the love theme by Nino
Rota, was enormously popular at
the time of the film's release.)
Purists may object because so
much of Shakespeare's dialogue
has been trimmed, but that must
be balanced against the beauty
and sincerity of the production as
a whole. Parents should know
that there is some nudity in addition to several sexual references.

ROMEO & JULIET (1996) (aka
**William Shakespeare's Romeo &
Juliet**)
Color, 120 minutes
Cast: Leonardo Di Caprio,

Claire Danes, Brian Dennehy,
John Leguizamo, Pete
Postlethwaite, Paul Sorvino,
Christina Pickles, Vondie
Curtis-Hall, M. Emmet Walsh,
Miriam Margolyes, Diane
Venora, Harold Perrineau,
Paul Rudd
Director: Baz Luhrmann
Screenplay: Luhrmann and Craig
Pearce, based on the play by
William Shakespeare
Drama
Rated PG-13
Young children: No Older
children: VG

Here is a brassy, high-tech, neo-
modernist *Romeo and Juliet.* Instead of its traditional setting of
Verona, Italy, the story now takes
place in Verona Beach, Florida.
There are televisions, swimming
pools, cars, and guns. The rivalry
between the Montagues and Capulets is depicted as a modern-
day blood feud. The style of the
film is post-MTV, with frenetic
cutting and editing tricks, all of it
designed to place this centuries-
old story into a contemporary,
cutting-edge context. Some of the
younger Montagues and Capulets
are portrayed as street toughs
who display some fairly anti-social
behavior. The images may be director Baz Luhrmann's, but all
the language in the film is Shakespeare's, verbatim.

Purists may pass on this version, but for many young people
this in-your-face adaptation with
two attractive and popular young
actors in the leads may have more
relevance (and resonance) than
any traditional production.

Leonardo DiCaprio and Claire
Danes are appealing as the young
lovers, although their famous balcony scene unravels with them

unconventionally treading water in the Capulet swimming pool! Even so, their passion is quite earnest, and their overall mastery of Shakespeare's substance and rhythm is superb.

This film may present Shakespeare on the far side, but its essence is true to its source material.

RONNIE AND JULIE (1997)
Color, 99 minutes
Cast: Teri Garr, Joshua Jackson, Margot Finlay, Alexandra Purvis, Tom Butler, Garwin Sanford
Director: Philip Spink
Screenplay: Richard Clark, Larry Sugar, and William T. Conway
Romantic drama
Rated PG
Young children: OK   Older children: VG

Shakespeare goes back to high school in this modest modern-day adaptation of *Romeo and Juliet*. This time the star-crossed lovers are the children of two families involved in a bitter campaign for mayor. Italy it's not, but the story rings true even for those who aren't familiar with the Bard's four-hundred-year-old tragedy.

For audiences who do recognize the parallels to the Montagues and the Capulets, however, the rewards are greater. Hockey takes the place of swordplay, for instance, but the theme remains the same.

So does the ending.

Families who feel that the Leonardo DiCaprio–Claire Danes version of the story is perhaps too violent or MTV-ish may prefer this modern variation on the theme.

ROOKIE OF THE YEAR
(1993)
Color, 103 minutes
Cast: Thomas Ian Nicholas, Gary Busey, Albert Hall, Amy Morton, Dan Hedaya, Bruce Altman, John Candy, Eddie Bracken, Daniel Stern
Director: Daniel Stern
Screenplay: Sam Harper
Comedy/Fantasy/Sports
Rated PG
Younger kids: VG   Older kids: VG

This fast-paced and likably loopy baseball fantasy tells the story of Henry Rowengartner, a young Chicago Cubs rooter. Because of his physical ineptitude, poor Henry is the object of much taunting among his contemporaries. Then one day, he fractures his arm. After it heals, he finds that he now can throw a baseball 100 miles per hour. Pretty soon, Henry is living out every Little Leaguer's dream as he is signed by his beloved Cubs. He becomes the team's top relief pitcher, and gets to whiff the likes of Bobby Bonds, Bobby Bonilla, and Pedro Guerrero.

Rookie of the Year fits like a batting glove as a perfect fantasy for its intended audience: all sports-loving youngsters who itch to know what it feels like to play in the pros.

The comedy is broad and likable. Actor Daniel Stern, who'll be familiar to many kids from his other movie roles, directed the film and gave himself the silliest part in the picture, as a dimwitted pitching coach. John Candy adds a lot of humor as an enthusiastic sportscaster.

The film's only serious aspect—the Mom's grubby, greedy boyfriend, who in one scene turns violent—is handled with dispatch.

A similar story was told in a vastly inferior film called *Roogie's Bump* (1954), with the team in question the Brooklyn Dodgers.

ROOTS (1977)
Color, 720 minutes
Cast: LeVar Burton, John Amos, Louis Gossett, Leslie Uggams, Ben Vereen, Richard Roundtree, Edward Asner, Cicely Tyson, Hari Rhodes, O.J. Simpson, Moses Gunn, Ren Woods, Beverly Todd, Ralph Waite, Lorne Greene, Maya Angelou, Thalmus Rasulala, Ji-Tu Cumbuka, Olivia Cole, William Watson, Lynda Day George, Vic Morrow, Robert Reed, Raymond St. Jacques, Gary Collins, Lawrence Hilton-Jacobs, John Schuck, Macdonald Carey, Lillian Randolph, Carolyn Jones, Lloyd Bridges, Georg Stanford Brown, Lynne Moody, Doug McClure, Burl Ives, Scatman Crothers, Sandy Duncan, Chuck Connors, George Hamilton, Brad Davis
Directors: Marvin Chomsky, David Greene, Gilbert Moses, and John Erman
Screenplay: Ernest Kinoy, James Lee, M. Charles Cohen, and William Blinn, based on the novel by Alex Haley
Historical drama
Unrated
Younger kids: OK, with caution Older kids: VG

A now legendary TV miniseries, *Roots* is based on Alex Haley's best-selling work, which traced his ancestral background to Kunta Kinte (Burton), a young African who was captured by slave traders in the 1760s and brought to America. The narrative continues for one hundred years, past the end of the Civil War, and follows Kinte through adulthood, as well as the lives of his daughter, Kizzy (Uggams), and her son, Chicken George (Vereen), the product of Kizzy's rape by a white slave owner.

Each generation fights the indignities and injustices of life under the yoke of slavery, and each generation passes on the story of its forefathers to the next. *Roots* was originally broadcast over eight consecutive nights on ABC, and in that short time it became a cultural phenomenon—as popular entertainment, as a heretofore little-explored chapter of African-American history, and as genealogical revelation. Much of the show is essentially a soap opera, and some critics took it to task for stereotypes, both black and white, that sacrificed historical veracity for high drama.

However, the scope of the narrative and the emotional touchstone of the slaves' plight are powerful and undeniably compelling. Given the subject matter, there is no avoiding the virtual catalogue of emotional and physical violence that is depicted—as we witness slaves being whipped, tortured, raped, and taken from their homes—which will upset children and adults alike.

This is, of course, part and parcel of the story and the times, and necessary to convey the terrors experienced by African-Americans of that era.

In 1979, a sequel, *Roots: The Next Generation,* aired, which was thematically far more complex than the original. It continued the saga from Chicken George all the way to Haley himself (played by James Earl Jones) and his encounters with Malcolm X (Al Freeman, Jr.) and American Nazi leader George Lincoln Rockwell (Marlon Brando), before discovering his own lineage.

ROVER DANGERFIELD
(1991)
Color, 74 minutes
Cast: Voices of Rodney Dangerfield (Rover), Susan Boyd, Ronnie Schell, Ned Luke, Shawn Southwick, Dana Hill
Directors: Jim George and Bob Seeley
Screenplay: Rodney Dangerfield
Animated feature
Rated G
Younger kids: OK, with reservations   Older kids: OK

The personality traits and voice of comedian Rodney Dangerfield are transferred to a cartoon canine in this feature-length cartoon. Rover is a wise-cracking Las Vegas dog, living the high life as pet of Connie, a chorus girl. Left alone with a jealous tough-guy boyfriend, Rover is thrown into the reservoir at Hoover Dam. He soon washes up in a peaceful farmyard, where the city dog tries to fit in and eventually falls in love. After various misadventures, he makes his way back to Vegas but quickly realizes his heart belongs with his true love, the farm collie named Daisy.

Handsome production can't disguise the producers' dual motivations. The film alternates between Rodney's sharp Vegas one-liners (for the adults) and a sappy barnyard storyline (for the kids). Young kids may go for the latter but be put off or confused by the former. Some of the humor and the harshness of the Las Vegas characters' lives (and skimpy costumes) are not really appropriate for the most impressionable young viewers. Youngsters unfamiliar with Dangerfield will not be thrilled.

RUDY (1993)
Color, 112 minutes
Cast: Sean Astin, Ned Beatty, Robert Prosky, Charles S. Dutton, Lili Taylor, Jon Favreau, Jason Miller
Director: David Anspaugh
Screenplay: Angelo Pizzo
Drama/Sports
Rated PG
Young children: OK   Older children: VG

If you have a soft spot for films like **Rocky** or **Hoosiers** (which was directed by David Anspaugh and written by Angelo Pizzo), chances are you'll respond to *Rudy*, another story of an underdog who makes good.

Rudy is based on the true story of Daniel E. "Rudy" Reuttiger, a young man who grew up with a dream of playing football at Notre Dame University. Rudy is a child of America's ethnic working class. No one in his family ever has attended a junior college, let alone a university as prestigious as Notre Dame. But Rudy is obsessed with Fighting Irish football. Even though it is expected that he will complete high school and join his father and brothers working in a steel mill, marry the girl next door, shrug his shoulders, and forget his Notre Dame fantasy, Rudy is determined to prove that dreamers can be doers. For after all, "Having dreams is what makes life tolerable."

Rudy is simple, direct, and unsubtle in its point of view. On rare occasion, it does become a bit sappy. But the film has as much heart as its title character, and for most of the way its emotions and feelings are genuine.

There is a smattering of strong language, hence the PG rating.

RUDYARD KIPLING'S THE JUNGLE BOOK (1994)
Color, 110 minutes
Cast: Jason Scott Lee, Cary Elwes, Lena Headey, Sam Neill, John Cleese, Jason Flemyng
Director: Stephen Sommers
Screenplay: Stephen Sommers, Ronald Yanover, and Mark D. Geldman, from a story by Yanover and Geldman based on the novel by Rudyard Kipling
Action-adventure
Rated PG
Younger kids: OK, with caution   Older kids: Good

Despite its title, the Disney studio's live-action version of the classic story that inspired its famous 1967 cartoon feature is much closer to Tarzan and Indiana Jones than it is to Kipling, with a decided emphasis on action and a modern sensibility.

The much-altered story has Mowgli (Jason Scott Lee), the boy who has grown up in the jungle under the care of animals, return to civilization to be with his childhood sweetheart Kitty (Lena Headey). But Kitty's father (Sam Neill), a British military officer, wants her to marry the slimy and brutal Captain Boone (Cary Elwes), unaware of the man's true nature. Boone eventually kidnaps her in an attempt to lure Mowgli back to the jungle to help him find a lost city of treasure.

Balanced against the melodramatic plot is the thoroughly winning performance of Jason Scott Lee, as a good-hearted and athletic Mowgli. The eye-filling Indian scenery is also a plus, and the climax, in a wondrous treasure city, is amazing. But the film has a few too many lulls, and those, combined with violent action scenes and a sprinkling of four-letter words, make this an iffy proposition for young children.

THE RUGRATS MOVIE
(1998)
Color, 79 minutes
Cast: Voices of E. G. Daily, Christine Cavanaugh, Kath Soucie, Cheryl Chase, Melanie Chartoff, Jack Riley, Michael Bell, Tress MacNeille, Joe Alaskey, Phil Proctor, Whoopi Goldberg, David Spade
Directors: Norton Virgien and Igor Kovalyov
Screenplay: David N. Weiss and J. David Stern
Animated feature
Rated G
Young children: VG, with caution   Older children: VG

Fans of Nickelodeon's long-running series *The Rugrats* are sure to enjoy the cast of characters in its first full-length feature. The basic story has to do with Tommy acquiring a baby brother and having to adjust to an intrusive new presence in his life. Along the way, Tommy, baby brother Dyl, and friends Chuckie, Phil, and Lil zoom away in one of Tommy's dad's inventions, a dragon-mobile, and get lost in the forest.

The Rugrats Movie is clever and funny, drawing on the same kids'-eye observations about life as the TV series, but even at 79 minutes, the film seems padded and over-long, as opposed to a typical half-hour television installment. A handful of songs helps to fill the time.

Parents of very young children should know that the kids are placed in peril a number of times; a ferocious wolf is on their trail, and their beloved dog, Spike, appears to die at one point. This is certainly more intense than anything the TV series ever presents to its young viewers, although every tense situation is quickly resolved, just as Tommy's dilemma of how to deal with his younger brother is cured by his dad giving him "sponsibility."

RUNAWAY (1984)
Color, 100 minutes
Cast: Tom Selleck, Cynthia Rhodes, Gene Simmons, Kirstie Alley, Stan Shaw, G. W. Bailey, Joey Cramer, Chris Mulkey
Director: Michael Crichton
Screenplay: Michael Crichton
Science fiction/Action
Rated PG
Young kids: Too scary Older kids: OK

In the near future, robots are widely used in industry and even in private homes; sometimes the robots malfunction, and that's when police sergeant Jack Ramsay (Selleck) steps in. He's an expert in dealing with malfunctioning robots, or "runaways." He comes into conflict with brilliant but deranged robotics scientist Luther (Simmons), who is creating a microchip that can turn any robot into a runaway. He has created a bullet that can zero in on an individual, plus deadly little robots that function like mechanical spiders. Jack has his work cut out for him.

This fast-paced movie features lots of exciting visual ideas and treats robots as the helpful machines they really are. (Not one robot in the movie, for example, looks like a human being.) The plot is elementary but serviceable, the effects are good, and Gene Simmons (from the rock group Kiss) makes a particularly hateful villain. The main weakness of the film is that the characters are thinly drawn and not terribly warm.

Younger kids will be scared by the creepy robot spiders and other killer devices, but older kids are likely to get caught up in the film as an action-adventure piece.

S

SAMSON AND DELILAH
(1949)
Color, 128 minutes
Cast: Victor Mature, Hedy
　Lamarr, George Sanders,
　Angela Lansbury, Henry
　Wilcoxon, Russ Tamblyn,
　George Reeves
Director: Cecil B. DeMille
Screenplay: Vladimir Jabotinsky,
　Harold Lamb, Fredric M.
　Frank, and Jesse Lasky, Jr.
Religion/Epic
Unrated
Younger kids: OK　Older kids:
　VG

Cecil B. DeMille was a master at
"improving" on the Bible by revel-
ing in sex, sin, and spectacle before
the requisite climactic salvation; this
film is a perfect example, making
the Old Testament story seem as exciting as a cliffhanging serial.

Victor Mature stars as Samson,
the strongman who leads the oppressed Danites in their fight
against the Philistines but falls in
love with a Philistine woman
named Semadar (Angela Lansbury). Semadar's treacherous sister, Delilah (Hedy Lamarr), also
has designs on Samson, and after
he rejects her, a riot ensues and
Semadar is killed. Vowing to destroy Samson, Delilah seduces
him, then drugs him and elimi-
nates the source of his strength by
chopping off his long hair. She delivers him to the Philistines, but
when they blind him and turn him
into a slave, she realizes that she

really loves him and helps to
free him.

Samson and Delilah may seem
corny and old-fashioned to adults
and even older children, but that's
part of its kitschy appeal, all
wrapped up in a sumptuous Technicolor package. Mature is perfectly cast as the brawny Samson,
and his fabled feats of strength—
battling a lion with his bare hands,
slaughtering thousands of soldiers
with the jawbone of an ass, and the
famous finale where he destroys a
temple by pushing apart its pillars—
are lots of fun, if not particularly believable (especially the lion fight,
with a wild animal that looks something like an old carpet), while the
sultry Lamarr makes a stunningly
beautiful and alluring Delilah. Their
steamy love scenes together were
hot stuff in their day and they're still
pretty sexy (although obviously not
explicit, this being a 1949 film).

For serious treatments of the
Bible, one should look elsewhere,
but for pure entertainment, this is
hard to beat. Kids of earlier generations couldn't wait to see how
Samson toppled the temple, and
this spectacular scene still packs a
punch today.

THE SANDLOT (1993)
Color, 101 minutes
Cast: Tom Guiry, Mike Vitar,
  Patrick Renna, Karen Allen,
  Denis Leary, James Earl
  Jones, Art La Fleur
Director: David Mickey Evans
Screenplay: Evans and Robert
  Gunter
Drama/Sports
Rated PG
Younger kids: OK   Older kids:
  VG

For some, baseball is more than
just a game: it's a way of life. This
sentimental film is set during the
summer of 1962, and tells the
story of a group of boys who play
ball day after day in a beloved
sandlot. They've developed into a
solid ball-playing unit and are
proud of their ability to function
as a team.

A new kid arrives in the neighborhood, and although he's shy,
he manages to join the team and
become a valued member. One
day the boy borrows his stepfather's prized possession, a ball au-
tographed by Babe Ruth, and the
horsehide is promptly belted over
a fence and into a yard presided
over by a notorious junkyard dog.

The Sandlot depicts an idealized but by no means unreal
American childhood, in which
playing baseball in the summer
sun becomes a sacred rite.
Younger viewers may not appreciate the film's sentimental
tone (or its heavy-handed narration), but they'll respond to the
various crises these kids encounter, from dealing with a vicious
dog to encountering his reclusive
(and therefore fearsome) owner.

There is some street language
and raucous juvenile behavior—
just enough to earn this film a
PG rating.

SANTA CLAUS (1985)
Color, 112 minutes
Cast: Dudley Moore, John
  Lithgow, David Huddleston,
  Burgess Meredith, Judy
  Cornwall, Jeffrey Kramer,
  Christian Fitzpatrick, Carie
  Kei Heim
Director: Jeannot Szwarc
Writer: David Newman
Fantasy
Rated PG
Younger children: OK   Older
  children: OK

This lavish film based on the legend of Santa Claus starts out so
well that it's a shame it veers off
course so badly in the second half.
The movie begins by telling a
charming version of Santa's story:
Centuries ago, a jolly woodcutter
(David Huddleston) and his wife,
known for gift giving at Christmas, get caught in a blizzard.
Finding their way to the North
Pole, they are introduced to magical elves (led by Dudley Moore as
Patch), who invite Santa to dis-
tribute toys made in their enchanted workshop.

Cut to the present day. Patch
tries out some new techniques for
toy production that fail miserably.
Dejected, he leaves the toy shop
and winds up in Manhattan as a
toy designer for evil businessman
B.Z. (John Lithgow), who has a
scheme to create "Christmas II"
on March 25. Here is where the
film goes down the chimney,
never to return.

Throw in a subplot about a boy
who doesn't believe in Christmas,
and you've got a mishmash of holiday clichés and special effects.
The movie is filled with eye-

candy, but what starts out as charming ends up crass.

There's too much of value here to dismiss *Santa Claus* (*The Movie* was dropped from the onscreen title) entirely; it's passable entertainment for kids. But what a shame, considering what this could have been. Santa deserves better; so do children.

THE SANTA CLAUSE (1994)

Color, 97 minutes
Cast: Tim Allen, Judge
  Reinhold, Wendy Crewson,
  Eric Lloyd, David Krumholtz,
  Peter Boyle, Larry
  Brandenberg, Mary Gross
Director: John Pasquin
Screenplay: Steve Rudnick and
  Leo Benevenuti
Comedy/Fantasy
Rated PG
Young kids: VG   Older kids:
  VG

Scott Calvin (Tim Allen) is a divorced businessman who has no time for his son, Charlie. When Santa Claus falls off his roof on Christmas Eve, Scott is forced to take his place, but he doesn't realize that by putting on the famous red suit, he will be completely transformed.

Not only does Scott become a better man, but he comes to appreciate the important things in life—especially a strong relationship with his son.

The Santa Clause begins as a very '90s movie, with a highly irreverent Tim Allen, caught up in his job and constantly having to appease his ex-wife, who's weary of his neglect (and excuses). Even when he arrives at the North Pole, Allen's character is a smart-aleck.

But in time, he becomes more and more Santa-like, and begins to learn what Santa Claus means to people around the world . . . and the things he's been neglecting in his own life.

The wonder of *The Santa Clause* is that in spite of its 1990s sensibilities, it manages to create both warmth and sentiment by the time it's over. It's a delightful film, filled with both laughs and surprises.

There are a few crude jokes, which earned this a PG rating. That too seems to go with the '90s territory, but on the whole it's terrific family entertainment.

SAY ANYTHING . . . (1989)

Color, 100 minutes
Cast: John Cusack, Ione Skye,
  John Mahoney, Lili Taylor,
  Amy Brooks, Pamela Segall,
  Jason Gould, Loren Dean,
  Bebe Neuwirth, Eric Stoltz,
  Chynna Phillips, Joanna Frank
Director: Cameron Crowe
Screenplay: Cameron Crowe
Comedy-drama
Rated PG-13
Younger kids: No   Older kids:
  VG

Kick-boxing enthusiast Lloyd Dobler (Cusack) has a crush on the school valedictorian, Diane (Skye). His friends advise him not to go after her but he persists . . . and she says yes. The story may sound like a standard teen romance, but this is a unique film with resonance. It takes youthful emotions and dreams very seriously, and the script invests its lead characters with three dimensions, making them likable, quirky, even dignified—and very real.

Most impressively, it extends the same courtesy to Diane's father (Mahoney), the central adult character, who loves his daughter and has problems of his own. The subject matter—and the sometimes eccentric, sometimes casual tone—may be over the heads of younger children, but it's ideal for the young adults at whom it's directed, who will certainly relate to Lloyd's unabashed longing for Diane and her conflicts about wanting him.

This is a far cry from the usual mindless teen sex romps and is highly recommended but not for younger children. The language and situations are only appropriate for adolescents.

SCARAMOUCHE (1952)
Color, 118 minutes
Cast: Stewart Granger, Eleanor Parker, Janet Leigh, Mel Ferrer, Henry Wilcoxon, Lewis Stone, Nina Foch, Richard Anderson, Robert Coote
Director: George Sidney
Screenplay: Ronald Millar and George Froeschel, based on the novel by Rafael Sabatini
Swashbuckler/Action-adventure
Unrated
Younger kids: OK   Older kids: VG

Scaramouche is another classic swashbuckler written by the prolific Italian novelist Rafael Sabatini, whose romantic tales of historical derring-do made him one of the masters of the genre. Stewart Granger stars as André Moreau, a playboy during the time of the French Revolution who clashes with master swordsman Noel, Marquis de Maynes (Mel Ferrer), after the latter kills Moreau's revolutionary friend. Determined to avenge his friend, Moreau disguises himself as a masked theatre clown called Scaramouche and trains to be a

swordsman, while also courting Noel's lover Aline (Janet Leigh).

Shot in eye-popping Technicolor by director George Sidney, a veteran of numerous MGM musicals, the film has the bouncy feel of a musical, with the energetic duels and sword fights staged like production numbers, most notably the dazzling six-minute showdown between Noel and Moreau, which is set in a theatre. Kids who like swashbucklers should thoroughly enjoy this one.

THE SCARLET PIMPERNEL (1935)
Black & white, 95 minutes
Cast: Leslie Howard, Merle Oberon, Raymond Massey, Nigel Bruce, Bramwell Fletcher, Anthony Bushell, Joan Gardner, Melville Cooper
Director: Harold Young
Screenplay: Robert E. Sherwood, S. N. Behrman, Arthur Wimperis, and Lajos Biro, based on the novel by Baroness Orczy
Adventure/Literary classic
Unrated
Young children: VG   Older children: VG

Many young people have seen Leslie Howard only in the rather wimpy, one-dimensional role of Ashley Wilkes in **Gone With the Wind.** Here is an opportunity to see this gifted British star in a more dashing part. He plays an English nobleman during the time of the French Revolution. On British soil he is Sir Percy, a foppish and vain courtier who appears to be a silly weakling. On the Continent, however, he secretly becomes the Scarlet Pimpernel, a valiant adventurer who saves the nobility of France from Robespierre's guillotine, always leaving behind a small red flower near the blade as his trademark.

Although only loosely adapted from the original novel, this is a memorable cloak-and-dagger adventure of intrigue and clever disguises that should please the entire family.

Leslie Howard returned to this role, more or less, in a World War II update called *Pimpernel Smith* (1941), which he also directed; the original story was remade for television in 1982 with Anthony Andrews. And the cartoon fans in your household may recall that this story was spoofed by Daffy Duck in a memorable Warner Bros. cartoon called *The Scarlet Pumpernickel.*

SCHINDLER'S LIST (1993)
Black & white, with color sequence, 195 minutes
Cast: Liam Neeson, Ben Kingsley, Ralph Fiennes, Caroline Goodall, Jonathan Sagalle, Embeth Davidtz
Director: Steven Spielberg
Screenplay: Steven Zaillian, from the book by Thomas Keneally
Drama
Rated R
Younger kids: No   Older kids: VG, with caution

Following the spectacular success of 1993's **Jurassic Park,** Steven Spielberg switched gears and astounded the public and critics alike with this film, a shattering adaptation of the Thomas Keneally book about Oskar Schindler (masterfully portrayed by Neeson), a charismatic German industrialist who builds an enamelware factory during World War II and uses cheap Jewish labor as his workforce. Without realizing it, he has prevented these men, women, and children from being sent to Nazi death camps. As the war continues, Schindler's exploitive attitude changes and the factory becomes a haven for Jews; by the war's end, Schindler has ultimately saved the lives of some eleven hundred people.

Schindler's List is one of the few fictional films that captures much of the full impact of the Holocaust. Filming in black and white for the first time, Spielberg abandoned much of his usual, carefully planned camera style, and created the stark feel of wartime documentary footage.

But parents must be aware that the film will be—to put it mildly—profoundly upsetting for children to watch. The violence of the Holocaust is extremely, unsparingly graphic and made even more powerful because it is conveyed with almost complete nonchalant indifference, which only heightens the horror. (For example, the Plaszow concentration camp's sadistic Nazi commandant Amon Goeth, brilliantly played by Ralph Fiennes, passes the time by randomly shooting Jews from his balcony window.) Schindler's awakening conscience provides the moral spine of the story, but even this evolution does not unfold in simple terms; the ambiguity of his character and his actions reflect the eternal clash of conscience, accountability, and necessity. This ambiguity even extends to Goeth who, in his own supremely limited way, tries for a few moments to relate to the Jews as being more than "rats."

Whatever the reasons—altruistic or selfish—for Schindler's actions,

487

the film shows, unforgettably, how one man did make a difference.

SCHOOL TIES (1992)
Color, 107 minutes
Cast: Brendan Fraser, Matt Damon, Chris O'Donnell, Randall Batinkoff, Andrew Lowery, Cole Hauser, Ben Affleck, Anthony Rapp, Amy Locane, Peter Donat, Zeljko Ivanek, Kevin Tighe, Michael Higgins, Ed Lauter
Director: Robert Mandel
Screenplay: Dick Wolf and Darryl Ponicsan
Drama
Rated PG-13
Younger children: No Older children: OK

Leaving his blue-collar home in Scranton, Pennsylvania, for an Eastern prep school in the 1950s, David Greene (Brendan Fraser), a young Jewish man on a football scholarship, decides to conceal his religion when he realizes his classmates are anti-Semitic. In his desire to fit in, he hides his Star of David in a Band-Aid box and plays football when he's promised his father to go to temple for Rosh Hashanah. When the truth accidentally comes out, David is shunned by his friends and his white-bread girlfriend, and then is almost expelled when he is accused of cheating. They refuse to believe that his football rival, Charlie Dillon (Matt Damon), a boy from a good Christian family, might be responsible.

The message of this movie is so loud and clear, it should have been sent by Western Union. This well-intentioned but heavy-handed and very predictable tale is interesting mostly for its cast of then-unknowns like Fraser,

Damon, Ben Affleck, and Chris O'Donnell.

Mild profanity and a nude shower fight make it inappropriate for younger kids.

SCROOGE (1970)
Color, 118 minutes
Cast: Albert Finney, Alec Guinness, Edith Evans, Kenneth More, Laurence Naismith, Michael Medwin, David Collings, Anton Rodgers, Suzanne Neve, Frances Cuka, Roy Kinnear, Mary Peach, Kay Walsh, Gordon Jackson
Director: Ronald Neame
Screenplay: Leslie Bricusse, based on the novella *A Christmas Carol* by Charles Dickens
Musical
Rated G
Young children: VG Older children: VG

Albert Finney, who once was hailed as "the second Olivier," is best known for his dramatic performances in films ranging from *Saturday Night and Sunday Morning, Two for the Road,* and *Tom Jones* to *The Dresser, Under the Volcano,* and *Miller's Crossing.* But he displayed his musical skill in *Annie,* in which he plays Daddy Warbucks, and *Scrooge,* a version of Charles Dickens' *A Christmas Carol.* Here, Finney plays the title character, Ebenezer Scrooge, an antisocial old coot who despises the concept of Christmas and is prone to pronouncing "Bah, humbug!" upon mere mention of the holiday. Through the course of the story, old Ebenezer is humanized as he is visited first by the ghost of Jacob Marley, his former business partner, and then by the

Ghosts of Christmas Past, Present, and Future.

It's difficult to mess up this timeless story, and *Scrooge* is a pleasant enough musical, with songs that work quite well within the framework of the picture, even if they don't linger in your memory. Finney sings and dances winningly, while Alec Guinness (whom youngsters will know best as Obi-wan Kenobi in **Star Wars**) makes a memorable Marley's Ghost.

THE SEA GYPSIES (1978)
Color, 101 minutes
Cast: Robert Logan, Heather Rattray, Mikki Jamison-Olsen, Shannon Saylor, Cjon Damitri Patterson
Director: Stewart Raffill
Screenplay: Stewart Raffill
Action-adventure
Rated G
Younger kids: Good   Older kids: Good

This is a first-rate family adventure in the vein of a film such as **The Adventures of the Wilderness Family,** which was written and directed by the same man, and also starred Robert Logan. The story this time deals with an around-the-world sailboat voyage undertaken by a father (Logan), his two daughters (Heather Rattray, Shannon Saylor), and the female magazine journalist (Mikki Jamison-Olsen) who's writing a story about the trip. The passenger list grows by one when they discover an orphaned stowaway (Cjon Damitri Patterson). When a storm hits, they're shipwrecked off the coast of Alaska and have to survive in the wilds while fending off whales, bears, and wolves.

The simple story is bolstered considerably by the refreshing scenery, and as with writer-director Raffill's other films, this is specifically geared for family viewing.

THE SEA HAWK (1940)
Black & white, 127 minutes
Cast: Errol Flynn, Brenda Marshall, Claude Rains, Donald Crisp, Flora Robson, Alan Hale, Henry Daniell, Gilbert Roland
Director: Michael Curtiz
Screenplay: Howard Koch and Seton I. Miller, based on the novel by Rafael Sabatini
Swashbuckler/Action-adventure
Unrated
Younger kids: OK   Older kids: VG

This classic Errol Flynn swashbuckler takes its title (and little else) from Rafael Sabatini's novel—the 1924 silent version is much more faithful—but still stands as one of the screen's great action-adventure epics. Flynn plays Captain Geoffrey Thorne, the leader of a band of British pirates who are at the service of Queen Elizabeth I (Flora Robson). After sinking a Spanish warship that was planning to attack England, Thorne convinces the Queen to let him wage a secret war against imperialistic Spain and discovers that a traitorous British official (Henry Daniell) is in league with the devious Spanish ambassador (Claude Rains).

Produced on a grand scale, this one has it all: a formidable cast, large-scale battle scenes on the high seas, sword fights galore, court intrigue, romance, and a great score by Erich Wolfgang Korngold. If your family has already acquired an interest in

Errol Flynn or pirate movies, *The Sea Hawk* should be considered a "must." It should be noted that it is quite long.

THE SEARCH (1948)
Black & white, 105 minutes
Cast: Montgomery Clift, Ivan Jandl, Aline MacMahon, Jarmila Novotna, Wendell Corey
Director: Fred Zinnemann
Screenplay: Richard Schweizer, in collaboration with David Wechsler, with additional dialogue by Paul Jarrico
Drama
Unrated
Young children: No   Older children: VG

This touching drama tells a simple, deeply human story of the most forgotten and voiceless victims of war: displaced youngsters who find themselves friendless outcasts with neither homes nor (in some cases) parents.

The time is post–World War II, and the story involves Karel Malik, a 9-year-old Czech refugee who has not set eyes on his mother for four years; he is not so much living as surviving in a camp for displaced children in Germany. It is for good reason that little Karel is wary; furthermore, his experiences have caused him to forget his identity. When he runs away from the camp, he is found and cared for by Ralph Stevenson (Montgomery Clift), an American G.I. Meanwhile, Karel's mother is searching the various D.P. camps in the hope of finding him.

The Search offers a potent tale of a young war refugee. At the very least, it may instill in youngsters a sense of how fortunate they are to be living out their own childhoods in peacetime. However, despite the manufactured happy ending (the film's one major flaw), the plight of little Karel surely will be too intense and intimidating for younger children.

Little Ivan Jandl, a nonprofessional actor, won a Special Academy Award for his unforgettable performance as Karel.

THE SEARCHERS (1956)
Color, 119 minutes
Cast: John Wayne, Jeffrey Hunter, Natalie Wood, Vera Miles, Ward Bond, John Qualen, Harry Carey, Jr., Olive Carey, Antonio Moreno, Henry Brandon, Hank Worden
Director: John Ford
Screenplay: Frank S. Nugent, based on the novel by Alan LeMay
Western
Unrated
Younger kids: OK   Older kids: VG

Generally acknowledged to be the best of John Ford's many masterly Westerns—and arguably the greatest of all the director's films—this powerful frontier saga also boasts one of John Wayne's most serious and impressive performances. Wayne is superb as Ethan Edwards, a loner and ex-Confederate soldier who, with his nephew Martin (Jeffrey Hunter), embarks on a relentless quest to find his young niece Debbie (played by Natalie Wood as a teen and her real-life younger sister Lana as a child), who's been kidnapped by Comanches. As the years drag on, Ethan becomes ever more obsessed with finding her, but Martin realizes, to his horror, that Ethan is a racist Indian-hater who intends to kill the now teenage Debbie since she's become a full-fledged "squaw" in his eyes. This leads to a shattering conclusion as the two men have an unforgettable showdown, and Ethan discovers his own humanity.

Filled with rich characterizations, thrilling action scenes, and majestic photography of Ford's beloved Monument Valley, the film is a marvelous Western adventure, but it's also much more: a genuine American classic that offers a searing study of prejudice and the redemptive power of love.

Young people who think of Westerns as clichéd shoot-'em-ups should give this one a try.

SEARCHING FOR BOBBY FISCHER (1993)
Color, 110 minutes
Cast: Joe Mantegna, Max Pomeranc, Joan Allen, Ben Kingsley, Laurence Fishburne, Michael Nirenberg, Robert Stephens, David Paymer, William H. Macy, Dan Hedaya
Director: Steven Zaillian
Screenplay: Zaillian, based on the book by Fred Waitzkin
Drama
Rated PG
Young children: OK   Older children: VG

This thoughtful, beautifully made drama tells the real-life story of a young boy named Josh Waitzkin, who in many ways is an average American kid. In fact, he wants to grow up to play second base for the New York Yankees. But Josh is significantly different from other kids: he is a budding chess prodigy. He may even follow in the footsteps of Bobby Fischer, the first American to become World Chess Champion, who after winning became a recluse.

Josh's sportswriter dad (Joe Mantegna) is proud of him and encourages him to pursue the game; his mother (Joan Allen) doesn't want her son to become obsessed with competition. One of his mentors (Laurence Fishburne), a chess hustler in the park, prefers that the boy play the game using his instinct, his gut, and his heart, but his new coach (Ben Kingsley), a famed chess teacher, attempts to toughen him up and teach him how to win at all costs.

This is an ideal film for parents to watch with their kids. Not only will *Searching for Bobby Fischer* entertain both generations; it offers a wealth of observations regarding the way parents raise and relate to their children in our highly competitive society. The film also explores the meaning of winning and losing.

It is an exceptionally fine film.

THE SECRET GARDEN (1949)
Black & white and color, 92 minutes
Cast: Margaret O'Brien, Herbert Marshall, Dean Stockwell, Gladys Cooper, Elsa Lanchester
Director: Fred M. Wilcox
Screenplay: Robert Ardrey
Literary classic
Unrated
Young children: OK, with caution   Older children: VG

THE SECRET GARDEN (1993)
Color, 101 minutes
Cast: Kate Maberly, Heydon Prowse, Andrew Knott,

Maggie Smith, Laura Crossley,
John Lynch, Walter Sparrow,
Irene Jacob
Director: Agnieszka Holland
Screenplay: Caroline Thompson
Literary classic
Rated G
Young children: VG, with
caution   Older children: VG

Mary Lennox, a cross and unhappy orphan, is sent to live at
Misselthwaite Manor, a remote
and somewhat spooky English
mansion, with her withdrawn
uncle. Over time, she begins to
thaw and makes adult friends of
the housemaid, Martha, and the
old gardener, Ben, and peer
friends with sickly Colin and the
Cornish lad, Dickon. With the
coming of spring, the three children work hard to rebuild a forgotten flower plot that hasn't
been tended in a decade, releas-
ing not only the plants but also
their own guarded emotions.

Twice the screen has produced
fruitful versions of Frances Hodgson Burnett's 1911 novel. MGM's
1949 film, the darker of the two,
stars Margaret O'Brien, the leading child actress of the 1940s.
Moody and subdued, Mary and
the movie walk hand in hand into
the light. (Early scenes in the
mansion are genuinely eerie, with
a strange howling down the hall
and an air of unpleasant mystery.)
Color is used only in the garden,
and then the screen seems bathed
in petals.

The 1993 adaptation is a far
greener vision, a sunny delight
that sometimes feels contrary to
repressive Victorian sensibilities.
The manor's forbidding atmosphere, itself a character in the
book, is almost missing. Notwith-
standing how pretty it all is, the

story shines through and reminds
us again to open our hearts.

These are both fine films, but
younger children may need some
hand-holding to get through them
at first. In the second version,
Mary's parents die offscreen, as
we hear the thunder of hoofbeats
and attack; while nothing is
shown, the effect is still upsetting.

**THE SECRET LIFE OF
WALTER MITTY** (1947)
Color, 105 minutes
Cast: Danny Kaye, Virginia
Mayo, Boris Karloff, Fay
Bainter, Ann Rutherford,
Thurston Hall, Konstantin
Shayne, Florence Bates,
Gordon Jones, Reginald
Denny
Director: Norman Z. McLeod
Screenplay: Ken Englund and
Everett Freeman, based on the
story by James Thurber
Comedy/Fantasy
Unrated
Younger children: VG   Older
children: VG

Browbeaten by everyone who
knows him, the meek proofreader
Walter Mitty (Danny Kaye) is
dominated by his mother, henpecked by his girlfriend, and bullied by his boss. To escape his
boring job and his miserable life,
Walter drifts into his imagination,
becoming hatmaker Anatole of
Paris, or perhaps a cowboy, the
Perth Amboy Kid. It's gotten so
Walter can't often tell what's real
and what isn't. So when he stumbles into a real mystery, complete
with jewel thieves, a villainous
Boris Karloff who pretends to
be a psychiatrist, and a beautiful
blonde, it's no wonder he's confused.

Although James Thurber, the

author, reportedly detested this film version of his well-known story, *The Secret Life of Walter Mitty* is an entertaining Danny Kaye vehicle, with all the necessary elements: multiple characters, foreign accents, musical numbers, fast-talking, silly movements. In short, it's a lot of fun and should appeal to everyone in the family. (Some may wince slightly at the now politically incorrect depiction of "Anatole of Paris.")

This is not to dissuade anyone from reading Thurber's gentler fable; in fact, if the film inspires a youngster to become acquainted with this great American humorist, so much the better.

THE SECRET OF NIMH
(1982)
Color, 83 minutes
Cast: Voices of Elizabeth Hartman, Dom DeLuise, Shannen Doherty, Wil Wheaton, John Carradine, Hermione Baddeley, Derek Jacobi
Director: Don Bluth
Screenplay: Bluth, Gary Goldman, John Pomeroy, and Will Finn, based on the novel *Mrs. Frisby and the Rats of NIMH* by Robert C. O'Brien
Animated feature
Rated G
Younger kids: OK   Older kids: OK

The first feature by animator-director-producer Don Bluth (who went on to make **An American Tail, The Land Before Time,** and **Anastasia**) is one of his best. This heartfelt story of a timid field mouse trying to save her home and family is filled with rich char-

acters, thrilling situations, and animated magic.

Mrs. Frisby needs to move her home before a farm tractor destroys it. With the help of Jeremy the crow, a bumbling if good-hearted friend, she seeks out the rats of NIMH, an advanced breed of intelligent rodents, formerly lab rats at the National Institute of Mental Health.

Serious adventure—including the possible loss of a home—takes precedence over comedy, so the film may be a tad too dark for the youngest members of your family. Older kids should be fascinated by the story. The character animation and background art are superb, as is Jerry Goldsmith's moody musical score.

THE SECRET OF ROAN INISH (1994)
Color, 102 minutes
Cast: Jeni Courtney, Eileen Colgan, Mick Laity, Richard Sheridan, John Lynch
Director: John Sayles
Screenplay: Sayles, based on the novella *The Secret of Ron Mor Skerry* by Rosalie Frye
Fantasy/Drama
Rated PG
Younger kids: VG   Older kids: VG

Young Fiona stays with her grandparents in an Irish fishing community and becomes fascinated by the stories and myths that have affected her family. One in particular involves the legend of the Selkie, a half-woman half-seal, and its connection to the loss of Fiona's little brother, Jamie, who was swept away to sea years earlier in the family's cherished cradle.

This is a small film but a

charming one, which parents can watch along with their children. Kids accustomed to loud, *Home Alone*-type antics might take a while to get used to the gentle tone that writer-director Sayles employs here. The magic doesn't come from special effects or loud explosions, but from the cinematography of Haskell Wexler and the amazing animals—seals and gulls—that give performances that seem every bit as real as those of the people onscreen. The mood, too, is interestingly somber and the lead actress, Jeni Courtney, is quiet and grave, a far cry from the mechanical cuties that usually dominate children's films.

SELENA (1997)

Color, 117 minutes
Cast: Jennifer Lopez, Edward James Olmos, Jon Seda, Constance Marie, Jacob Vargas, Lupe Ontiveros, Jackie Guerra, Richard Coca
Director: Gregory Nava
Screenplay: Gregory Nava
Musical biography
Rated PG
Younger children: No Older children: OK

Two sisters and their brother, growing up in Corpus Christi, Texas, are encouraged to play music and sing by their father (Edward James Olmos), a onetime musician who was discouraged in his career by prejudice against Mexican-Americans. Because of Selena's vocal talent, the family band takes off and spends years on the road building an audience. The budding star can barely speak Spanish, but she manages to charm the Mexican reporters who chart her rising success. Selena falls in love with the band's new guitarist, who their father regards as a punk; she asserts her independence by going off with him one night to get married. In time, her father makes his peace with his son-in-law and deals with letting go of his little girl. Meanwhile, Selena becomes a genuine star of Tejano music, appealing to a growing number of Mexican and American fans.

Until Selena came along in the late 1980s, no Mexican-American female had ever become a singing star; the Tejano field was strictly for men. But this talented young woman crossed all boundaries; she succeeded beyond even her father's vision and had begun to develop into an important figure in the music world when she was killed by the president of her fan club, a woman who had embezzled money from the young star.

For the most part, *Selena* is an inspiring account of young woman whose talent, hard work, and basic decency made her a role model for young Mexican-Americans. The music is infectious and lively, and the story moves right along, from the family's first stumbling efforts to make music to Selena's triumph at the Grammy Awards.

Parents who consider renting this video need to explain to their children beforehand the sadness of Selena's death, the work of an irrational and unbalanced woman. Despite this troubling outcome, the film presents many positive lessons on the value of hard work and the power of motivation. There is one mild profanity in the entire film and one minor sexual reference.

SENSE AND SENSIBILITY
(1995)
Color, 135 minutes
Cast: Emma Thompson, Alan
  Rickman, Kate Winslet, Hugh
  Grant, James Fleet, Harriet
  Walter, Gemma Jones,
  Elizabeth Spriggs, Robert
  Hardy, Greg Wise, Imelda
  Staunton, Imogen Stubbs,
  Hugh Laurie
Director: Ang Lee
Screenplay: Emma Thompson,
  based on the novel by Jane
  Austen
Drama/Literary classic
Rated PG
Young children: No   Older
  children: VG

In recent years, the writings of
Jane Austen have become popular subjects for screen adaptations, and this lavish, intelligent
version of her first published
novel is virtually impossible to
top. It tells of a newly impoverished family, the Dashwoods, in
early-19th-century England, and
the romantic involvements of
two very different sisters, Elinor
(Emma Thompson), who sup-
presses her feelings and is destined
for spinsterhood, and Marianne
(Kate Winslet), who is rash and
flirtatious. Despite their financial
plight, a trio of "eligible bachelors" enter their lives: the ever-
polite Edward Ferrars, Colonel
Brandon, a brooding older man,
and dashing, heroic John Wil-
loughby.

Sense and Sensibility is a sharply
observed commentary on the social
mores of the era and the manner in
which dissimilar personalities deal
with them—but with a contemporary awareness, which makes the
story relevant to the present day.
It's likely that older girls will respond best to this film, though
some of the wit and satire may go
over their heads.

Emma Thompson did a fine job
of adapting Austen's novel and
finding ways to make it especially
contemporary (without sacrificing
Austen's intentions). She won an
Academy Award for her effort.

**SESAME STREET PRESENTS:
FOLLOW THAT BIRD** (1985)
Color, 88 minutes
Cast: Voices of Carroll Spinney,
  Jim Henson, Frank Oz; Sandra
  Bernhard, John Candy, Chevy
  Chase, Joe Flaherty, Waylon
  Jennings, Dave Thomas, Bob
  McGrath, Alaina Reed,
  Roscoe Orman, Sonia
  Manzano, Linda Bove, Emilio
  Delgado, Loretta Long
Director: Ken Kwapis
Screenplay: Tony Geiss and Judy
  Freudberg
Comedy/Fantasy
Rated G
Young children: VG   Older
  children: OK

Sesame Street's beloved Big Bird
stars in this very entertaining film
about an eventful journey.

Big Bird is convinced that he
should leave Sesame Street and
live with "his own kind." He's
adopted by a family of dodo birds
in Ocean View, Illinois, but things
just don't work out . . . so the
eight-foot orphan tries to make
his way back home. When his
friends from Sesame Street learn
that he's disappeared, they start a
bird hunt to find their feathered
friend and make sure he's OK.
Bert and Ernie take to the skies
in a ramshackle biplane, while
Grover soars aloft as Super
Grover!

It would be hard to imagine a

film more likable than *Follow That Bird*. It's great fun from start to finish for the young and the young-at-heart. As with *Sesame Street* and the other Muppet movies, there are plenty of gags and ideas to amuse parents as well as kids, as well as some charming songs by Van Dyke Parks and Lennie Niehaus.

And of course, there's the Big Yellow Star himself, as innocent as he is endearing. If only there were more movie stars like him!

SEVEN BRIDES FOR SEVEN BROTHERS (1954)
Color, 103 minutes
Cast: Howard Keel, Jane Powell, Jeff Richards, Russ Tamblyn, Tommy Rall, Virginia Gibson, Julie Newmeyer (Newmar), Ruta Kilmonis (Lee), Matt Mattox, Jacques D'Amboise, Marc Platt, Nancy Kilgas, Betty Carr, Norma Dorgett, Ian Wolfe, Howard Petrie
Director: Stanley Donen
Screenplay: Albert Hackett, Frances Goodrich, and Dorothy Kingsley, based on the story *Sobbin' Women* by Stephen Vincent Benét, inspired by Plutarch's "The Rape of the Sabine Women" (*Life of Romulus*)
Musical
Unrated
Young children: VG · Older children: VG

This rip-roaring musical is a perfect blend of story, song, and dance, set in the mountain country of Oregon in 1850. One day Adam Pontipee (Howard Keel), the eldest of seven boisterous brothers, decides that it is time for him to find a wife, and rides into town to do so. His timing is unusually good, because an unattached young woman named Millie (Jane Powell) is ready for a change in her life, and agrees to be wed. But Adam fails to tell her the whole truth—that she'll be taking care of seven boisterous young men and will be more of a slavey than a bride. Determined to make the best of things, Millie insists that the Pontipee boys learn manners and sets about to civilize them. In time, Adam's brothers become convinced that they too should marry—but go about it the wrong way, by kidnaping their brides from town!

Seven Brides for Seven Brothers is considered one of the great dance movies of all time, and kids are sure to respond to its remarkable, rambunctious production numbers, staged by Michael Kidd. The brothers were played by some of the best dancers alive—including ballet star Jacques D'Amboise, Tommy Rall, Marc Platt, Matt Mattox, and the acrobatic Russ Tamblyn. Their leaps and bounds during the celebrated barn-raising sequence may lead to many replays.

But the beauty of *Seven Brides* is that the dancing is so perfectly integrated into its story and so well executed in every department.

Only the final moments of the film may require some explanation for younger viewers: it involves the concept of a shotgun wedding.

SEVEN CHANCES (1925)
Black & white, 56 minutes
Cast: Buster Keaton, T. Roy Barnes, Snitz Edwards, Ruth Dwyer, Frankie Raymond, Jules Cowles, Erwin Connelly
Director: Buster Keaton

Screenplay: Clyde Bruckman, Joseph Mitchell, and Jean Havez, based on *Seven Chances,* a comedy in three acts by Roi Cooper Megrue
Comedy/Silent classic
Unrated
Young children: VG   Older children: VG

Young viewers who've never seen Buster Keaton could scarcely do better than to start with this fast-paced feature, in which he plays a young man who will inherit a fortune only if he is married by 7:00 that evening! Jimmy desperately attempts to wed before the appointed hour and (having placed an item in the newspaper) eventually finds himself chased by thousands of eager prospective brides, in a memorable and hilarious chase scene.

The climax features another of Keaton's all-time great gag sequences. As he sprints away from the mob of harridans, he inadvertently starts an avalanche of rocks. Some are the size of grapefruits; others are quite a bit larger. Watching Buster dodge these boulders is one of the great moments in all of movie comedy.

Like all the best silent comedies, this one has universal appeal that should cut across all age barriers.

7 FACES OF DR. LAO (1964)
Color, 100 minutes
Cast: Tony Randall, Barbara Eden, Arthur O'Connell, John Ericson, Kevin Tate, Noah Beery (Jr.), Lee Patrick, Minerva Urecal, John Qualen, Royal Dano
Director: George Pal
Screenplay: Charles Beaumont, from the novella *The Circus of Dr. Lao* by Charles G. Finney
Fantasy/Western
Unrated
Young children: OK   Older children: OK

An elderly Chinese gentleman, Dr. Lao (Randall), rides a donkey into the Western town of Abalone and announces the impending arrival of his circus. The townspeople, however, find that the performers in the circus (mostly played by Randall in elaborate William Tuttle makeup) are shrewd commentators who show the onlookers the errors of their ways.

An unsettling blend of the best and worst of producer George Pal, who also directed, this is highly regarded by many and despised by others. It's undeniably sentimental, and the humor tends to be broad and corny, but when it works, it works wonderfully well. It has a light, frothy tone for much of its length and climaxes with a burst of stop-motion animation, the work of Jim Danforth.

Younger kids will like the frequent fantasy elements and the many disguises worn by Dr. Lao, but there will be long stretches where their attention will wander.

1776 (1972)
Color, 141 minutes
Cast: William Daniels, Howard da Silva, Ken Howard, Donald Madden, Ronald Holgate, David Ford, Ray Middleton, William Hansen, Blythe Danner, Roy Poole, Virginia Vestoff, John Cullum
Director: Peter H. Hunt
Screenplay: Peter Stone, from his musical stage play based on a Sherman Edwards concept

Musical
Rated G
Young children: VG   Older
  children: VG

This unusual musical is a fine piece of entertainment, a profound piece of Americana, and an engrossing history lesson. It does what the best historical dramas do, bringing the past to life with a sense of truth and immediacy . . . moreover, in this case, the drama is punctuated with wonderful, witty, expressive songs.

1776 is set in Philadelphia during America's first Congress, as representatives of the thirteen colonies debate the merits of becoming independent of Great Britain. In so doing, a host of names out of the history books come alive, including John Adams, Benjamin Franklin, and Thomas Jefferson. But these are no stick figures spouting platitudes and rhetoric; they are multidimensional characters with conflicting feelings. Their idealism is pitted against the realities of compromise and the determination to achieve freedom from England at all costs.

There is little or no action in the film, which was skillfully adapted from the hit Broadway play, so younger kids might be bored. Children who are old enough to have studied some of this history in school are the best candidates to fall under the spell of *1776*.

The film was released during the Vietnam War, when some citizens had embraced a love-it-or-leave-it brand of patriotism while others were deeming the Great American Experiment a failure. *1776* reminded flag-wavers that the United States was founded on revolution rather than the abstract concept of manifest destiny, while suggesting to those who were closing the book on the country that there still was much to be admired about America and its origins.

THE 7th VOYAGE OF SINBAD (1958)
Color, 87 minutes
Cast: Kerwin Mathews, Kathryn
  Grant (Crosby), Torin
  Thatcher, Richard Eyer
Director: Nathan Juran
Screenplay: Kenneth Kolb
Fantasy/Adventure
Unrated
Younger kids: VG   Older kids:
  VG

Here is a wonderful, old-fashioned Arabian Nights–style adventure yarn, in which heroic Sinbad finds a genie in a bottle, helps a beautiful princess, and does battle with a giant cyclops, a sword-wielding skeleton, and other monsters created by the legendary special-effects wizard Ray Harryhausen.

This is a favorite of '50s baby boomers, who'll love sharing it with their children. Older boys may look askance at some of the special effects, which date somewhat alongside their '90s counterparts, but there's a sense of wonder and innocence that few modern films could hope to recapture. And Bernard Herrmann's music score has seldom been topped.

THE SHAGGY D.A. (1976)
Color, 91 minutes
Cast: Dean Jones, Suzanne
  Pleshette, Tim Conway,
  Keenan Wynn, Jo Anne
  Worley, Dick Van Patten,
  Shane Sinutko, Vic Tayback,
  John Myhers, Richard

Bakalyan, Warren Berlinger, Ronnie Schell, Jonathan Daly, John Fiedler, Hans Conried
Director: Robert Stevenson
Screenplay: Don Tait, based on the novel *The Hound of Florence* by Felix Salten
Comedy/Fantasy
Rated G
Younger children: Good   Older children: Good

Director: Charles Barton
Screenplay: Bill Walsh and Lillie Hayward, suggested by *The Hound of Florence* by Felix Salten
Comedy/Fantasy
Unrated
Young children: OK   Older children: OK

Disney stalwart Dean Jones plays Wilby Daniels (the same role Tommy Kirk played in 1959's **The Shaggy Dog**), an attorney who, incredibly, falls under the same spell that turned him into an Old English sheepdog when he was a boy. His nemesis is John Slade (Keenan Wynn), another lawyer running against Jones for district attorney . . . and a rather unscrupulous opponent at that.

The plot here is simply a framework for sight gags and special effects sequences geared for kid appeal—including a pie-throwing spectacular. The sight of an enormous sheepdog doing human chores is about as surefire a laugh-getter as the Disney studio ever devised.

Snappier than the original 1959 feature, *The Shaggy Dog*, this one is good clean fun, with a cast of familiar comedy performers and character actors who know how to make the most of every scene.

THE SHAGGY DOG (1959)
Black & white, 104 minutes (also available in computer-colored version)
Cast: Fred MacMurray, Jean Hagen, Tommy Kirk, Annette Funicello, Tim Considine, Kevin Corcoran, Cecil Kellaway, Alexander Scourby, Roberta Shore

This unexpected comedy hit launched a long series of similar slapstick outings for the Disney studio. *The Shaggy Dog* was never a great film, but it had such appealing elements that audiences couldn't help responding. Those ingredients—chiefly, the idea of a teenage boy turning into a huge sheepdog—still work today, though the concept has by now been borrowed, reused, and remade so many times that this long, slower-paced movie may have been left in the shade.

Tommy Kirk (like his youthful costars a familiar face to all American kids at that time through Disney movies and TV shows) plays Wilby Daniels, a misfit teenager who inadvertently acquires a magic ring that carries with it a spell. He seems to have no control over how and when he will turn into a sheepdog from that time on, but being in the yard enables him to eavesdrop on their next-door neighbor and learn that Dr. Andrassy and his daughter are in fact spies who are planning to steal government missile plans. Confusion reigns supreme, however, since the Andrassys have a sheepdog which looks exactly like Wilby!

This relaxed film takes its time setting up both its story and its gag sequences, never straining too hard for credibility. (Though Wilby's father, played by the affable

Fred MacMurray, is said to be a postman, we never once see him at work.)

The Shaggy Dog's strongest assets are the dog itself, some entertaining sight gags, and the utter conviction of its stars, including the always likable Tommy Kirk. And like all Disney product of this period, the film is squeaky clean and suitable for all ages.

In 1976 the Disney studio made a belated sequel, **The Shaggy D.A.**, which is a much livelier film, and in 1988 and '89 there were two television remakes featuring Harry Anderson.

SHANE (1953)
Color, 118 minutes
Cast: Alan Ladd, Jean Arthur, Van Heflin, Brandon de Wilde, (Walter) Jack Palance, Ben Johnson, Edgar Buchanan, Emile Meyer, Elisha Cook, Jr.
Director: George Stevens
Screenplay: A. B. Guthrie, from the novel by Jack Schaefer
Western drama
Unrated
Young children: VG   Older children: VG

This all-time classic Western offers a picture of a heroic man, a character of almost mythic proportion called Shane. He's a drifter who is taken in by a homesteader and his wife, and slowly becomes involved in a local dispute between cattlemen and farmers. However, the plot dynamics are secondary. What is of importance is the vivid portrayal of the title character and the impact he has on a wide-eyed young boy named Joey. Indeed, much of the film is a depiction of Shane as seen through the eyes of Joey.

Shane may be an ex-gunfighter and saddle tramp, but he has a certain nobility. He is sympathetic and wise, a wonderful role model for Joey, whose father is honest and hard-working, but ordinary when compared to this laconic stranger.

He tells the boy, "I like a man who watches what's going on around him. He'll make his mark someday" . . . "Some like two guns, but one is all you need if you know how to use it" . . . and "A gun is a tool, no better or worse than the man who uses it."

Ultimately, Shane teaches Joey by example as he faces off against a vicious hired gun. In so doing, he illustrates how good men must stand up to evil, even if it means killing.

Shane is a tremendously entertaining and emotional film—never more so than when little Joey expresses his deepest feelings toward Shane. It also offers Alan Ladd (who plays Shane), a top star of the 1940s and '50s, what was to be his defining screen role.

It is an outstanding film to share with your family.

SHERLOCK, JR. (1924)
Black & white, 45 minutes
Cast: Buster Keaton, Kathryn McGuire, Ward Crane, Joseph Keaton
Director: Buster Keaton
Screenplay: Clyde Bruckman, Joseph Mitchell, and Jean Havez
Comedy/Silent classic
Unrated
Young children: VG   Older children: VG

This is Buster Keaton's most poetic film, a movie lover's delight in which Buster plays the title character, a luckless movie theater projectionist who has been falsely accused of stealing a watch owned by his girlfriend's father. While projecting a mystery drama titled *Hearts and Pearls* (also known as *The Lounge Lizard's Lost Love*), young Sherlock takes a nap—and summarily walks into the screen and becomes involved in the unfolding celluloid drama.

Only Buster could have conceived an idea in which he would walk directly into a movie screen—and only Buster and his technical team could have pulled it off so deftly. The special effects in this film, achieved decades before anyone ever heard of a computer, are still dazzling today.

Sherlock, Jr. is timeless and peerless, an endlessly innovative mixture of celluloid reality and fantasy. Woody Allen could not improve on its concept when he revised it more than sixty years later in *The Purple Rose of Cairo*.

SHE WORE A YELLOW RIBBON (1949)
Color, 103 minutes
Cast: John Wayne, Joanne Dru,
  John Agar, Ben Johnson,
  Harry Carey, Jr., Victor
  McLaglen, Mildred Natwick
Director: John Ford
Screenplay: Frank S. Nugent and
  Laurence Stallings, based on a
  story by James Warner Bellah
Western
Unrated
Younger kids: OK   Older kids:
  Good

With a silver mustache and gray streaks in his hair, John Wayne gives a dignified performance as an aging U.S. Cavalry captain who's forced to retire in this elegiac John Ford Western, the second of his so-called "Cavalry Trilogy" (between *Fort Apache* and *Rio Grande*). It's also the only one of the three filmed in color—in this case, softly glowing Technicolor photography which garnered an Oscar—and features striking compositions, which Ford claimed were inspired by Remington paintings.

Wayne stars as a career officer, stationed at a remote fort in 1876, who's assigned one last mission before retiring—to escort a superior officer's wife (Mildred Natwick) and her niece (Joanne Dru) from the fort, through hostile Indian territory, to the end of the stagecoach line. Along the way, there's plenty of action, rowdy humor (courtesy of a typically brawling Victor McLaglen), romance, and sentiment, all highlighted by the magnificent locations and color. The depiction of all the cavalrymen as heroic and all the Indians as savage may not be politically correct these days, but that was par for the course when this film was made, and this is a good, rousing Western.

SHIPWRECKED (1990)
Color, 91 minutes
Cast: Stian Smestad, Gabriel
  Byrne, Louisa Haigh, Trond
  Munch, Bjorn Sundqvist
Director: Nils Gaup
Screenplay: Gaup, Bob Foss,
  Greg Dinner, and Nick Thiel,
  based on the novel *Haakon
  Haakonson* by O.V. Falck-
  Ytter
Action-adventure
Rated PG
Younger kids: OK   Older kids:
  VG

Stian Smestad plays a young 19th-century Norwegian lad named

Haakon who becomes a cabin boy on a trade ship and gets mixed up with a notorious South Seas pirate named Merrick (Gabriel Byrne), who's aboard the ship and impersonating the British officer he killed. When the ship is wrecked during a storm, Haakon is washed up on a tropical island where he discovers a cave filled with treasure. It just so happens to be Merrick's booty, but when the pirate and his gang try to retrieve it, Haakon discovers his true identity and rigs a series of clever booby-traps to thwart him.

This handsomely produced Norwegian production (filmed in English) is a little-known but entertaining film that successfully captures the spirit of **Treasure Island** and marks a welcome return to such old-fashioned yarns about boys and buccaneers. Its violence earned it a PG rating, which means that the youngest children might find this too strong a brew.

SHORT CIRCUIT (1986)
Color, 98 minutes
Cast: Ally Sheedy, Steve Guttenberg, Fisher Stevens, Austin Pendleton, G. W. Bailey, Brian McNamara; voice of Tim Blaney (Number Five)
Director: John Badham
Screenplay: S. S. Wilson and Brent Maddock
Science fiction/Comedy-drama
Rated PG
Young children: OK Older children: OK

Five robot warriors are demonstrated to the military by Howard Marner (Pendleton), head of a robotics firm, and they work just fine. But lightning strikes Number Five, and it develops its own

personality and intelligence, wandering off base in search of adventure. The amiable robot is befriended by animal lover Stephanie (Sheedy), who later teams up with Newton (Guttenberg), the creator of the robots, to try to keep Number Five from being disassembled.

Clearly inspired by **E.T.,** this movie is good entertainment for younger children, who'll be endlessly delighted by Number Five, given amusing voice by Tim Blaney (though we could do without the impressions of movie stars).

Younger kids won't wonder over little details like why lightning brings Number Five to life and makes him benign, rather than frying his circuits and reducing him to a puddle of metal and plastic. Older kids may object to such fantasylike details and may consider the whole movie kid stuff beneath their notice.

Followed by a sequel, **Short Circuit 2.**

SHORT CIRCUIT 2 (1988)
Color, 110 minutes
Cast: Fisher Stevens, Michael McKean, Cynthia Gibb, Jack Weston, Dee McCafferty, David Hemblen; voice of Tim Blaney (Johnny Five)
Director: Kenneth Johnson
Screenplay: S. S. Wilson and Brent Maddock
Science fiction/Comedy thriller
Rated PG
Young children: OK Older children: OK

Ben Jahrvi (Stevens), who helped invent Number Five, the robot that came to life in **Short Circuit,** is trying to romance Sandy (Gibb), who's hired him to make toys based on Number Five. Ben and his partner, Fred (McKean), set up shop in an old factory where a crate soon arrives containing none other than Number Five himself.

Now calling himself Johnny Five, the cheerful robot pitches in to help, but soon all of them are entangled with the criminal plans of a trio of bank robbers.

It's disappointing that the writers couldn't find something more original for this sequel than a standard innocent-duped-by-crooks plot and unfortunate that director Johnson couldn't get the film down to a more reasonable length. But it has a number of bright moments, Johnny Five is still endearing, and there are even some traces of pathos, as when we learn the two books Johnny considers most important to him are *Frankenstein* and *Pinocchio*.

This will be enjoyed most by younger children.

SHOW BOAT (1951)
Color, 107 minutes
Cast: Kathryn Grayson, Ava Gardner, Howard Keel, Joe E. Brown, Marge and Gower Champion, Robert Sterling, Agnes Moorehead, Leif Erickson, William Warfield
Director: George Sidney
Screenplay: John Lee Mahin, based on the musical play by Jerome Kern and Oscar Hammerstein II from the novel by Edna Ferber
Musical
Unrated
Young children: OK Older children: VG

Edna Ferber's novel of life on a Mississippi showboat became a landmark Broadway musical in 1927. It was filmed in 1929 and 1936 (featuring the great Paul Robeson), but the picture-postcard MGM remake of 1951 is the best one to introduce to your family.

This rendering of *Show Boat* is a valentine to the classic musical itself and a time capsule of life a world away from our own. It begins on the *Cotton Blossom,* a riverboat that travels the Mississippi bringing show business to the entertainment-hungry citizens of riverfront towns. Captain Andy (Joe E. Brown) and his stern wife, Parthy (Agnes Moorehead), never intended for their daughter Magnolia (Kathryn Grayson) to become an entertainer on the showboat, but she has stage fever, encouraged by their resident star, the beautiful Julie (Ava Gardner). Complications begin when a dashing gambler named Gaylord Ravenal (Howard Keel) comes on board and sweeps Magnolia off her feet.

Everything about this film is beautiful: the depiction of life on the Mississippi, the riverboat itself, the handsome cast, and of course the songs, by Jerome Kern and Oscar Hammerstein II.

The subplot of Julie being hounded by the fact that she has black blood in her veins gives *Show Boat* great resonance beyond that of a mere escapist musical . . . and William Warfield's magnificent rendition of "Old Man River" gives full meaning to Edna Ferber's original intentions, to depict the variety of life along the Mississippi, where "colored folk work while the white folks play."

Show Boat is a wonderful experience to share with your family.

SILENT RUNNING (1971)

Color, 89 minutes
Cast: Bruce Dern, Cliff Potts, Ron Rifkin, Jesse Vint
Director: Douglas Trumbull
Screenplay: Deric Washburn, Michael Cimino, and Stephen Bochco
Science fiction
Rated G
Younger kids: OK   Older kids: OK

A neglected science fiction film, *Silent Running* features Bruce Dern as Lowell, a botanist aboard a spacecraft of the future that is carrying Earth's last forests and vegetation. When he is ordered to destroy it, he mutinies and sends it into deep space.

There isn't much story beyond the valuable environmental message the film is conveying, but it is a generally entertaining trip. Lowell is a little hard to warm up to, especially considering the fact that he prefers the company of robots to humans and has no regard for his shipmates. But Bruce Dern is just right as the man committed to saving Earth's last remaining natural beauty.

Children might be impatient with the slow pacing and the lack of any **Star Wars**–type battles, but the special effects are impressive and the endearing, waddling robot drones, Huey, Dewey, and Louie, who assist Dern are clearly forerunners of *Star Wars'* R2-D2. In fact, the most amusing scene is a poker game between Lowell and the drones he has programmed.

Parents should note that though G-rated, the film has one violent scene in which Lowell physically dispatches one of the other crewmen.

A SIMPLE WISH (1997)

Color, 89 minutes
Cast: Martin Short, Mara Wilson, Robert Pastorelli, Amanda Plummer, Francis Capra, Kathleen Turner, Ruby Dee, Teri Garr, Alan Campbell
Director: Michael Ritchie
Screenplay: Jeff Rothberg
Comedy/Fantasy
Rated PG
Younger kids: VG   Older kids: OK

Martin Short is funny (as always) as a flustered Fairy Godmother of the male variety who tries to help young Mara Wilson (who's adorable as ever) in her wish to get her father the stage part for which he's auditioning. Naturally, everything goes wrong . . . especially when he runs afoul of a "bad" witch (Kathleen Turner) who's up to no good.

The relationship between the single parent (Robert Pastorelli) and his kids is a sweet one, and the fact that his daughter wants a wish not for herself but for him is endearing.

A subplot involving Dad's audition for a musical play based on *A Tale of Two Cities* provides some enjoyment for older audience members, as it spoofs Andrew Lloyd Webber and his brand of musical theater (although the songs we hear sound quite good).

A Simple Wish is not a great film, but it's certainly entertaining. It might upset very young children because of the special-effect spells that are cast on the girl's father and other sympathetic characters. Older kids will have no such problems, but may find the going a bit too juvenile for their taste. Best moment: when

Short causes a pompous tenor (and Mara's father's rival) to get a frog in the throat, literally.

SINBAD THE SAILOR (1947)
Color, 117 minutes
Cast: Douglas Fairbanks, Jr., Maureen O'Hara, Anthony Quinn, Walter Slezak, George Tobias, Jane Greer, Mike Mazurki, Sheldon Leonard
Director: Richard Wallace
Screenplay: John Twist, based on a story by Twist and George Worthing Yates
Action-adventure/Fantasy
Unrated
Younger kids: Good   Older kids: VG

Douglas Fairbanks, Jr., does his father proud as the legendary Sinbad in this Arabian Nights fantasy filmed in glittering Technicolor. On his eighth voyage, Sinbad sails the seven seas in search of an island filled with the lost treasure of Alexander the Great. Along the way, he falls in love with a beautiful woman (Maureen O'Hara), who joins him on his voyage, and battles the wicked Emir of Daibul (Anthony Quinn) and a Mongolian sailor (Walter Slezak), who are also after the treasure.

This flamboyant and colorful swashbuckler is the kind of lighthearted, rainy Saturday afternoon kind of movie they just don't make anymore. It was Douglas Fairbanks Jr.'s homage to his father, the greatest swashbuckling adventure hero of the silent-movie era.

SINGIN' IN THE RAIN (1952)
Color, 102 minutes
Cast: Gene Kelly, Debbie Reynolds, Donald O'Connor, Jean Hagen, Cyd Charisse, Millard Mitchell, Douglas Fowley, Madge Blake, Rita Moreno
Directors: Gene Kelly and Stanley Donen
Screenplay: Betty Comden and Adolph Green
Musical
Unrated
Young children: VG   Older children: VG

This classic musical is set in Hollywood, as the moving picture industry was about to be shaken by the coming of sound. Silent stars with thick foreign accents or high-pitched voices were soon to be has-beens. *Singin' in the Rain* features a long-forgotten actress named Jean Hagen, who gives the performance of her career as one such movie goddess, whose squeaky voice doesn't match her blonde good looks.

There also is Donald O'Connor's hilarious, acrobatic song and dance routine, "Make 'Em Laugh," pert, young Debbie Reynolds and leggy Cyd Charisse, and of course Gene Kelly, who performs what may be the most famous of all American musical numbers, the film's title tune, with umbrella in hand on a rainy street.

Singin' in the Rain was not highly regarded when it first played in movie theaters, but its stature has swelled over the years and deservedly so. There is no finer musical to be found in all of movie history.

It embodies all the things that make vintage Hollywood musicals so special—and such treats to share with children—a sense of joy, a feeling of lightheartedness that makes you want to sing and dance along with the people onscreen. The songs, by Arthur Freed and Nacio Herb Brown, are still tuneful and fun to hear. What's more, in this case, the film is also extremely funny, one of the best comedy scripts ever written for what just happened to be a musical.

In fact, it is the comedy element that will likely draw younger children into *Singin' in the Rain.* The climactic "Broadway Melody" number may put some of them off, but if they give it a chance, you can congratulate them for having sat through a bona fide ballet.

SISTER ACT (1992)
Color, 100 minutes
Cast: Whoopi Goldberg, Maggie Smith, Harvey Keitel, Bill Nunn, Kathy Najimy, Wendy Makkena, Mary Wickes, Robert Miranda, Richard Portnow, Joseph Maher
Director: Emile Ardolino
Screenplay: Joseph Howard
Comedy
Rated PG
Younger kids: OK   Older kids: OK

Whoopi is Deloris Van Cartier, a sassy Reno lounge singer who witnesses a murder and then hides in a convent to elude the gangsters who are on her trail. While there, she takes over the convent choir, juicing it up with Motown songs and making it the hit of the neighborhood.

Here is a textbook "high concept" picture if there ever was one, with a predictable fish-out-of-water formula and plot points that a grown-up can see coming way before the characters do. Yet, surprisingly, it works, because of Goldberg's inherent likability and her ability to involve viewers in Deloris' personal change as she grows to accept and respect the nuns who live in the convent. Deloris has a profoundly positive effect on the nuns, too, especially meek Sister Mary Robert (Makkena), who reveals her talent for singing. The subplot involving the mobsters is much less interesting than the interaction between Deloris and the nuns because of the terrific supporting cast: imperious Maggie Smith, the hilarious Kathy Najimy (doing what she referred to as a perky Mary Hart impression), and best of all, veteran Mary Wickes at her sweet and sour best.

The film opens with a murder, followed by gunshots; there is some minimally offensive language and violence, on the order of hits to the groin. But this is a means to an end, a reason for Deloris to hide out in the convent.

The sequel, *Sister Act 2: Back in the Habit,* though amiable enough, was an unnecessary and all-too-predictable retread.

SIXTEEN CANDLES (1984)
Color, 93 minutes
Cast: Molly Ringwald, Anthony Michael Hall, Michael Schoeffling, Paul Dooley, Justin Henry, Gedde Watanabe, Blanche Baker, Carlin Glynn, Edward Andrews, Billie Bird, Carole Cook, Max Showalter, John Cusack, Joan Cusack, Jami Gertz, Beth Ringwald
Director: John Hughes
Screenplay: John Hughes
Comedy
Rated PG
Younger kids: OK   Older kids: VG

Molly Ringwald is the perfect everyteen in this comedy about Samantha, a young woman who is enduring every conceivable public and private humiliation, all on her 16th birthday. John Hughes' first film, made before he became a cottage industry, treats teen angst in a fresh and insightful way that young adults will have no problem relating to and, in some cases, will probably wince at in recognition. Some of the situations are a bit crude and rely too heavily on stereotypes (particularly a Japanese foreign exchange student and Samantha's visiting grandparents), while other characters, such as Anthony Michael Hall's geek and Samantha's father (Paul Dooley) are allowed to grow and deepen in unexpected ways.

The crudeness is also compensated by a lot of perceptive humor and on-target observations about the "class" system in school and the pressures of growing up in today's world. *Sixteen Candles* is also notable for the dialogue, which contains a lexicon of young adult slang, comparable in its own way to 1995's **Clueless.**

While there is nothing here in terms of content or language that a teenager wouldn't be exposed to in real life, that same material is not really suitable for (or pertinent to) younger kids.

SLEEPER (1973)
Color, 88 minutes
Cast: Woody Allen, Diane Keaton, John Beck, Mary Gregory, Don Keefer, John McLiam
Director: Woody Allen
Screenplay: Allen and Marshall Brickman
Comedy/Science fiction
Rated PG
Younger kids: OK   Older kids: VG

Brave New World meets Rip Van Winkle: Woody plays Miles Monroe, proprietor of a health-food store, who is frozen in suspended animation and awakens to find himself two hundred years in the future and wanted as an enemy of the government. This science fiction satire is one of Allen's so-called "early, funny" films. It is, indeed, one of his funniest and most endearing, with a rollicking jazz score and jokes and allusions that echo the best of silent comedies. (Examples: Woody dressing up as a robot in black and white tux, or stealing giant fruits and vegetables from a futuristic garden and slipping on an oversized banana peel.)

There is a serious underlying theme about the perils our society is heading for, as well as one-liners that will fly way over younger kids' heads, but the visual gags come at a fast and furious pace and can be enjoyed by young and old alike.

Parents might want to note some raunchy humor, particularly a silver orb, which, when rubbed, functions like a drug, and a chamber known as the "orgasmitron," which—well, you can figure it out.

SLEEPING BEAUTY (1959)
Color, 75 minutes
Cast: Voices of Mary Costa, Bill
Shirley, Eleanor Audley,
Verna Felton, Barbara Jo
Allen, Barbara Luddy, Taylor
Holmes, Bill Thompson,
Candy Candido
Director: Clyde Geronimi;
sequence directors Eric
Larson, Wolfgang Reitherman,
and Les Clark
Screenplay: Erdman Penner
(story adaptation), Joe Rinaldi,
Winston Hibler, Bill Peet, Ted
Sears, Ralph Wright, and Milt
Banta, from the Charles
Perrault version of "Sleeping
Beauty"
Animated feature
Unrated
Young children: VG   Older
children: VG

Sleeping Beauty was the most ambitious animated feature Walt Disney ever undertook. While returning to familiar fairy-tale territory, he wanted the film to look and sound different from anything the studio had ever done before. So it was filmed in widescreen Technirama and recorded in stereophonic sound; its songs were adapted from the works of Tchaikovsky, and it was designed, in large part, by the modern artist Eyvind Earle.

Still, what makes *Sleeping Beauty* so entertaining is the story itself. The character of Aurora (renamed Briar Rose when she's taken off to live a "normal" life, away from an evil curse) is pleasing and likable, so we care about what happens to her. We also can't help but like her three mischievous (and constantly bickering) fairy godmothers, Flora, Fauna, and Merrywether. The villainess, Maleficent, is fearsome indeed, and when in the climactic duel she transforms herself into a fire-breathing dragon, it may give pause to the youngest members of your family.

But like all good fairy tales, *Sleeping Beauty* has a happy ending—of which you can reassure your tiny tots. It also has color, magnificent pageantry, lovely music (including the memorable waltz "Once Upon a Dream"), and fanciful imagery to hold any audience's attention from start to finish.

SMALL CHANGE (1976)
Color, 104 minutes
Cast: Geory Desmouceaux,
Philippe Goldman, Claudio
Deluca, Frank Deluca
Director: François Truffaut
Screenplay: François Truffaut
and Suzanne Schiffman
Comedy-drama
Rated PG
Younger kids: Good   Older
kids: VG

Nobody made better or more honest films about childhood than French writer-director François Truffaut, and *Small Change* is one of his absolute best. Set in the small French town of Thiers, there's no real plot per se, but rather a tender and funny series of interwoven vignettes involving a group of schoolchildren (mostly nonprofessional actors) and their parents. It is an intelligent, witty, and compassionate film.

Such incidents as classroom and recess high jinks, sneaking into the local movie theater, a young boy's crush on a schoolmate and their first kiss, and a tiny tot falling out of a high-rise window, bouncing on the grass, and emerging unscathed are beautifully and delicately observed. There is also a serious subplot about an abused boy, whose mother is eventually arrested, which is treated in a very candid but understated manner, ending with a teacher delivering an impassioned speech to his students about the responsibilities of parenthood.

Originally Rated R, the film's rating was changed to PG on appeal. The subtitles contain some mild profanities, and there is some discreet and wholly natural nudity during a scene where a mother is breast feeding her newborn.

This is a charming ode to the joy and pain of childhood that can be thoroughly enjoyed by children as well as their parents.

SMALL SOLDIERS (1998)
Color, 99 minutes
Cast: Gregory Smith, Kirsten Dunst, Phil Hartman, Kevin Dunn, Jay Mohr, Denis Leary, David Cross, Ann Magnuson, Wendy Schaal, Robert Picardo, Dick Miller; voices of Tommy Lee Jones, Frank Langella, Ernest Borgnine, Jim Brown, George Kennedy, Bruce Dern, Clint Walker, Michael McKean, Christopher Guest, Harry Shearer, Christina Ricci, Sarah Michelle Gellar
Director: Joe Dante
Screenplay: Gavin Scott, Adam Rifkin, Ted Elliott, and Terry Rossio
Science fiction/Satire/Comedy
Rated PG-13
Younger kids: NG   Older kids: OK

Eager to please his cold-blooded new boss, a toy marketer (Mohr)—unbeknownst to his designer colleague (Cross)—purchases military surplus microchips to put into their new line of action figures. The son of a toy-store owner (Smith), who sees the figures on a delivery truck, urges the driver to let him have the first shipment. What the boy doesn't know is that the Commando Elite toys are programmed to go to war against Gorgonites—and destroy them. What's more, they have the ability to do so! A subsidiary story deals with the boy's troubled relationship with his parents and his puppy-love friendship with the girl next door (Dunst).

Using the latest in computer animation, *Small Soldiers* brings its toys to life with incredible realism—and director Joe Dante, a lifelong movie buff, has fun by casting veterans of the World War II action movie *The Dirty Dozen* as voices of these military marvels.

Unfortunately, the action gets fairly intense, and the threats frighteningly real—too real for younger kids, except for those who've been steeled against this by a steady diet of explosive action films. The adolescent characters in the story are appealing and believable.

SMILE (1975)
Color, 113 minutes
Cast: Bruce Dern, Barbara Feldon, Geoffrey Lewis, Nicholas Pryor, Michael Kidd, Colleen Camp, Joan Prather, Melanie Griffith, Annette O'Toole, Maria O'Brien
Director: Michael Ritchie
Screenplay: Jerry Belson
Comedy/Satire
Rated PG
Younger kids: No   Older kids: Good

Smile is a wicked satire of teenage beauty pageants, taking scathing shots at the American obsession with winning at all costs. Bruce Dern is terrific as "Big Bob," a glad-handing, cliché-spouting mobile-home salesman who's also the chief judge of the California State Young American Miss pageant. His perpetually upbeat outlook starts to crumble after his son, "Little Bob" (Eric Shea), is caught trying to take pictures of the contestants in their dressing rooms. Barbara Feldon is also great as the pageant's "perfect" organizer, a former Junior Miss herself, whose answer to every problem is to "keep smiling," but whose life—and marriage to a suicidal drunk (Nicholas Pryor)—is falling apart. And real-life choreographer Michael Kidd is devastating as a cynical choreographer whose career is in a slump and is brought in to try to teach the spectacularly untalented contestants how to dance.

Though the humor is sometimes cruel, the script is so hilarious and well observed that the characters are never reduced to stereotypes. What emerges is a caustic, yet good-natured social comedy. Some of the language and glimpses of nudity (when Little Bob is taking snapshots) would probably earn the film a PG-13 rating today, making it inappropriate for younger kids.

SNOW WHITE AND THE SEVEN DWARFS (1937)

Color, 83 minutes
Cast: Voices of Adriana Caselotti, Harry Stockwell, Roy Atwell, Billy Gilbert, Lucille LaVerne, Pinto Colvig, Scotty Mattraw, Otis Harlan, Moroni Olsen

Director: Ben Sharpsteen
Screenplay: Ted Sears, Otto Englander, Earl Hurd, Dorothy Ann Blank, Richard Creedon, Dick Richard, Merrill De Maris, and Webb Smith, adapted from *Grimm's Fairy Tales*
Animated musical/Fairy tale
Unrated
Young children: VG, with caution   Older children: VG

Does anyone need to be told the story of *Snow White and the Seven Dwarfs*? This Walt Disney version of the venerable tale has become part of our popular culture, and every child should be introduced to its charms.

Even in 1937, some critics complained that it was too scary for children: Snow White's flight through the woods, with every bramble seeming to threaten her . . . the transformation of the Queen into the Wicked Witch . . . the apparent death of Snow White, all gave fuel to accusations that Walt Disney was being cruel to kids.

But Disney believed that without evil there could be no good, that without a tangible threat there could be no happy ending—and he was right. Very young children may well be frightened by those still-potent scenes in *Snow White*, but if parents help them through those rough moments, the children will be rewarded, as they experience Snow White's journey from darkness to light, and share the incredible joy felt by the Dwarfs when all ends well.

Joy is the word that best describes *Snow White and the Seven Dwarfs*: it radiates a feeling of happiness that is positively contagious, whether it's during the impromptu dance scene after dinner or at the finale.

The songs are also part of our cultural landscape, and every child deserves to be introduced to "Whistle While You Work" and "Some Day My Prince Will Come."

The film may not play as well for older kids who are more accustomed to edgier modern cartoons. It's their loss.

SO DEAR TO MY HEART
(1949)
Color, 84 minutes
Cast: Burl Ives, Beulah Bondi, Harry Carey, Luana Patten, Bobby Driscoll
Director: Harold Schuster
Screenplay: John Tucker Battle, based on the book *Midnight and Jeremiah* by Sterling North
Drama/Animal story/Animation
Unrated
Younger kids: VG   Older kids: VG

Although not well known, this is as lovely and homespun a piece of Americana—Disney-style—as ever put on film, and one of Walt Disney's personal favorites. Set in 1903, the story centers on a young boy named Jeremiah (Bobby Driscoll) who adopts a black sheep and tries to train it so that he can enter it in a county fair competition.

That's about it for the plot; the considerable charm of the movie is in its wealth of period detail, its evocative atmosphere, and the warm emotions it elicits.

Framed as a series of memories from Jeremiah's scrapbook, the vignettes include: the boy feeding an apple to the great racehorse Dan Patch, whose train has stopped in his town; Jeremiah dancing with his beloved Granny (Beulah Bondi) and the kindly town blacksmith (Burl Ives); a dangerous trip to a swamp to gather honey from a beehive; and the colorful county fair competition. The shots of the little boy feeding the baby lamb a bottle of milk or sleeping with it in the barn are just too cute for words. There are also a few delightful animated segments in which a wise owl in Jeremiah's scrapbook comes to life and sings songs to demonstrate the value of hard work ("It's Whatcha Do with Whatcha Got") and persistence ("Stick-to-it-ivity"). The beloved folksinger Burl Ives also performs onscreen and introduces the lovely "Lavender Blue."

This nostalgic reverie is so sweet and gentle that from a contemporary point of view, it not only seems to be from another era but from another planet, yet even today's kids should succumb to its spell if they will slow down enough to give it half a chance.

SOMETHING WICKED THIS WAY COMES (1982)
Color, 94 minutes
Cast: Jason Robards, Jonathan Pryce, Vidal Peterson, Shawn Carson, Diane Ladd, Pam Grier, Royal Dano, Scott De Roy, Mary Grace Canfield
Director: Jack Clayton
Screenplay: Ray Bradbury, based on his novel
Period fantasy/Family melodrama
Rated PG
Young children: OK, but scary   Older children: OK

Young friends Will (Peterson) and Jim (Carson) are delighted when the strange Cooger &

Dark's Pandemonium Carnival arrives in Green Town, Illinois. However, the boys—but only the boys—soon learn that both Dark (Pryce) and Cooger (De Roy) have sinister supernatural powers and are definitely up to no good.

Ray Bradbury's novel had almost been filmed many times in the past; when it was finally entrusted to Clayton, director of **The Innocents,** and was scripted by the author himself, everyone expected something outstanding. The result was, instead, this disappointingly minor film, compromised and oddly unimaginative.

Generally, Bradbury's work has great appeal to young teenagers; often, they fall deeply in love with his fantasies and science fiction, so if any around your house have been bitten by the Bradbury bug, they may well insist on seeing this film—although they, too, may find it disappointing.

SOMEWHERE IN TIME (1980)
Color, 103 minutes
Cast: Christopher Reeve, Jane Seymour, Christopher Plummer, Teresa Wright, Bill Erwin, George Voskovec, Eddra Gale, William H. Macy, George Wendt
Director: Jeannot Szwarc
Screenplay: Richard Matheson, from his novel *Bid Time Return*
Fantasy/Romance
Rated PG
Younger kids: Of little interest   Older kids: OK

In a majestic old hotel, playwright Richard (Reeve) is surprised to see the portrait of a beautiful young woman; several years before, as an elderly woman, she'd unexpectedly given him a watch and whispered, "Come back to me." Based on advice from a professor he respects, Richard successfully wills himself back in time to the year 1912 (at the same hotel), where he meets the woman, actress Elise McKenna (Seymour). As they begin to fall in love, her manager, worried that this will interfere with her burgeoning career, has Richard kidnapped.

Younger kids will yawn their way through this romantic fantasy, but older kids will be drawn by its simple but heady romanticism. Girls have been known, in fact, to become devoted to the movie, taking it as a kind of personal talisman. Less credulous kids (and adults) will be bothered by some of the details, and if they don't focus in on the romance, will find it as tedious as younger kids do.

If you have a romantic teenager, you may be doing them a major favor by showing them this well-intentioned movie.

SON OF DRACULA (1943)
Black & white, 79 minutes
Cast: Lon Chaney (Jr.), Robert Paige, Louise Allbritton, Evelyn Ankers, Frank Craven, J. Edward Bromberg, Samuel S. Hinds, Adeline De Walt Reynolds
Director: Robert Siodmak
Screenplay: Eric Taylor, from a story by Curt Siodmak
Fantasy horror/Romantic suspense
Unrated
Young children: Marginal   Older children: OK

Katherine Caldwell (Allbritton) returns from a European trip to Dark Oaks, her Southern mansion. She is soon joined by the somber Count Alucard (Chaney), and to the shock of her longtime beau, Frank (Paige), she marries the Count one windy night. Of course, Count Alucard (read the name backward) is really the son of Dracula and a vampire himself—but even a vampire can be manipulated . . .

One of the most sophisticated and melancholy of the Universal horror movie series, *Son of Dracula* is also surprisingly effective in the usual ways. It makes full use of the list of vampire powers, and there are several imaginative, eerie scenes, as when Dracula's coffin drifts over the surface of a lake. Although Chaney wasn't physically suited to play a vampire—he looks rather well fed—his performance is very strong and effective otherwise.

This is among the few horror movies from this period (barring the Val Lewton films) with mature *ideas*; the film also has a surprisingly downbeat ending. These elements might make it a bit too much for younger kids, although there's nothing graphic about the movie at all. Older kids should enjoy this fast-paced, well-played movie.

SON OF FLUBBER (1963)
Black & white, 100 minutes
Cast: Fred MacMurray, Nancy Olson, Keenan Wynn, Tommy Kirk, Elliott Reid, Joanna Moore, Leon Ames, Ed Wynn, Ken Murray, Charlie Ruggles, William Demarest, Bob Sweeney, Paul Lynde, Stuart Erwin, Edward Andrews, Alan Hewitt, Jack Albertson
Director: Robert Stevenson
Screenplay: Bill Walsh and Donald Da Gradi, based on a story by Samuel W. Taylor and the *Danny Dunn* books
Comedy/Science fiction
Unrated
Young children: VG   Older children: VG

Walt Disney always resisted the temptation to make sequels—until **The Absent Minded Professor** proved to be such a success. Two years later, he and his team unveiled *Son of Flubber*. It isn't much in the story department, but it is packed with funny gags, clever special effects, and amusing actors—in fact, a cavalcade of familiar faces who know how to get the most out of every moment onscreen.

Fred MacMurray is back as Professor Ned Brainard. This time he's experimenting with something called dry rain, which is supposed to cause rainfall but mostly causes windows to shatter. Meanwhile, Biff Hawk (Tommy Kirk), son of bad guy Alonzo Hawk (Keenan Wynn), messes around with the Professor's equipment and comes up with flubbergas, which inflates members of the Medfield football team so they float down the field like human balloons! In the midst of this, the Professor's wife leaves him because she thinks he's interested in his onetime girlfriend, the alluring Desiree de la Roche (Joanna Moore).

Son of Flubber is just a silly retread of *The Absent Minded Professor*, but most of its gags are surefire, and the cast is great fun to watch. As with the earlier film, Walt Disney's effects team felt that they couldn't pull off their trickery in color and decided to shoot this film in black-and-white.

SON OF FRANKENSTEIN (1939)

Black & white, 95 minutes
Cast: Basil Rathbone, Boris
   Karloff, Bela Lugosi, Lionel
   Atwill, Josephine Hutchinson,
   Donnie Dunagan, Emma
   Dunn, Edgar Norton
Director: Rowland V. Lee
Screenplay: Willis Cooper
Science fiction–horror/Suspense
Unrated
Young children: Marginal   Older
   children: OK

When he arrives at his family's castle, Baron Wolf von Frankenstein (Rathbone) does not want to be associated with his father's misdeeds. However, evil, broken-necked shepherd Ygor (Lugosi) convinces him to seize the opportunity to restore the family name, and Wolf begins trying to revive the weakened Monster (Karloff). Unbeknownst to Frankenstein, Ygor intends to use the Monster for personal revenge.

This lively thriller is really only nominally a horror movie, as it rarely even tries to scare viewers; today, more people are irritated by child actor Dunagan than were ever scared by the Monster in this outing. However, it is entertaining, with a fine cast, unusual set design, and a bang-up finale involving a bubbling pit of molten sulfur. The Monster is just a lumbering piece of Gothic machinery this time, but Rathbone and Atwill are fine, and Lugosi delivers the performance of his life as the wickedly sardonic Ygor.

No more creepy than an average episode of *Goosebumps, Son of Frankenstein* is probably OK for monster-savvy kids of any age.

The next in the series was **The Ghost of Frankenstein.**

THE SON OF MONTE CRISTO (1940)

Black & white, 102 minutes
Cast: Louis Hayward, Joan
   Bennett, George Sanders,
   Florence Bates, Lionel Royce,
   Montagu Love
Director: Rowland V. Lee
Screenplay: George Bruce
Swashbuckler/Action-adventure
Unrated
Younger kids: OK   Older kids:
   Good

Louis Hayward and Joan Bennett, the stars of 1939's **The Man in the Iron Mask,** and Rowland V. Lee, the director of 1934's **The Count of Monte Cristo,** teamed up for this enjoyable adventure melodrama that has no official connection to Dumas but is fun all the same. The story finds the son of Edmond Dantes (Hayward) pretending to be a foppish Count, donning a mask and calling himself "The Torch" to aid the Grand Duchess of Lichtenburg (Bennett), who is trying to defeat the despotic General (George Sanders at his most dastardly), who has taken over her country.

Lively action and solid production values make this a good bet for swashbuckler fans of all ages.

SONS OF THE DESERT (1933)

Black & white, 68 minutes
Cast: Stan Laurel, Oliver Hardy,
   Charley Chase, Mae Busch,
   Dorothy Christy, Lucien
   Littlefield, John Elliott
Director: William A. Seiter
Screenplay: Frank Craven and
   Byron Morgan
Comedy
Unrated
Younger children: VG   Older
   children: VG

If you haven't laughed out loud in a while, you need to bring home *Sons of the Desert* and share it with your family. Many Laurel and Hardy buffs consider it the team's best feature film—and at 68 minutes, it's simple, clear, and to the point!

Stan and Ollie are henpecked husbands, all too easily browbeaten by their wives. As members of a fraternal lodge called Sons of the Desert, they long to attend the group's annual convention in Chicago, but know their wives won't consent. So they concoct an elaborate ruse about Stan having to accompany Ollie on a cruise to Hawaii for his health . . . then run off to Chicago.

Do you think the wives will discover their scheme? And what will happen when they do?

Sons of the Desert wastes no time building a reserve of laughs and setting its story into motion. It's prime Laurel and Hardy, and an ideal film to use to introduce youngsters to these beloved laughmakers.

SOUNDER (1972)
Color, 105 minutes
Cast: Cicely Tyson, Paul
  Winfield, Kevin Hooks,
  Carmen Mathews, Taj Mahal,
  Janet MacLachlan, James Best
Director: Martin Ritt
Screenplay: Lonne Elder 3rd,
  based on the novel by William
  H. Armstrong
Drama
Rated G
Young children: OK   Older
  children: VG

This lovely film poignantly charts the pains of a black sharecropper family as it strives to overcome bigotry and hardship in the Depression-era South. Rebecca and Nathan Lee Morgan are dutiful and loving parents who steadfastly refuse to allow poverty to adversely affect their bond with their children. Nonetheless, they are attempting to survive in an environment that is hostile to them simply because of the color of their skin. When Nathan Lee (Paul Winfield) is jailed for pilfering some food to feed his family, his eldest son, David Lee (Kevin Hooks), must take on the responsibilities of adulthood within the family structure.

Even if director Martin Ritt does romanticize these characters somewhat, their plight is unmistakably genuine. While the Morgan clan is depicted within a specific racial and cultural framework, their story—one of joy and suffering, love and familial responsibility—is a universal one that transcends race and era.

Sounder is a wonderful, moving film. It was especially notable in 1972, in the midst of the "blaxploitation" craze, and was one of the few films of that period to depict black Americans with dignity and humanity.

There are some painful and difficult moments in the story that might upset younger children, but the moral of the story—and the bond of the family—certainly compensate.

THE SOUND OF MUSIC (1965)
Color, 174 minutes
Cast: Julie Andrews, Christopher
  Plummer, Eleanor Parker,
  Richard Haydn, Peggy Wood,
  Charmian Carr, Heather
  Menzies, Nicholas Hammond,
  Duane Chase, Angela
  Cartwright, Debbie Turner,

Kym Karath, Anna Lee, Portia
Nelson, Ben Wright, Norma
Varden, Marni Nixon
Director: Robert Wise
Screenplay: Ernest Lehman, based
on the musical by Richard
Rodgers, Oscar Hammerstein
II, Howard Lindsay, and Russel
Crouse
Musical
Unrated
Young children: VG   Older
children: VG

"The hills are alive with the sound
of music . . ." and the movie screen
comes alive with this all-time family favorite.

The Sound of Music is the saga
of Maria (Julie Andrews, in one of
her signature roles), a novice nun
whose spirit and playfulness indicate that she may not have chosen
the ideal path in life. The time is
just before World War II, and
Maria becomes governess to the
seven children of widower Baron
Von Trapp, a retired Austrian
naval officer and stern disciplinar-
ian. Maria encourages the children
to sing, and before long the Von
Trapp Family is celebrated for its
musical performances. Then the
Nazis take over Austria.

The Sound of Music is a perfectly realized combination of
drama, emotion, and song. Young
and old will cherish Andrews'
bright screen presence, and the
great Rodgers and Hammerstein
songs: "My Favorite Things," "Sixteen Going on Seventeen," "Climb
Every Mountain," "Do-Re-Mi,"
and, of course, the title song.

The film also serves to introduce younger children to a bit of
recent history, illustrating how
the Nazis corrupted young people to serve their cause and

drove many loyal citizens out of
their homeland.

SOUTH PACIFIC (1958)
Color, 151 minutes
Cast: Rossano Brazzi, Mitzi
Gaynor, John Kerr, Ray
Walston, Juanita Hall, France
Nuyen, Russ Brown, Jack
Mullaney, Tom Laughlin,
Beverly Aadland, Ron Ely,
Doug McClure, Joan Fontaine
Director: Joshua Logan
Screenplay: Paul Osborn,
adapted from the musical by
Richard Rodgers, Oscar
Hammerstein II, and Joshua
Logan based on James A.
Michener's *Tales of the South
Pacific*
Musical
Unrated
Young children: VG   Older
children: VG

Some great stage musicals—**My
Fair Lady, West Side Story, The
King and I**—have become great
movie musicals as well. *South Pacific* was not so fortunate, but it
still retains enough of the Broadway show's content and sensibilities to make it worth seeing.

One of the main problems is
the casting. While Rossano Brazzi
and Mitzi Gaynor are perfectly
adequate as Emile De Becque and
Nellie Forbush, they lack the
charisma (or star power, if you
will) to make the most of these
roles, which were created on
Broadway by Ezio Pinza and the
great Mary Martin.

The story is set on a Pacific isle
during World War II, and involves parallel romances between
an older couple (De Becque, a
widowed planter, and Forbush, an
American nurse) and a younger
one (Lieutenant Cable, an Ameri-

can G.I., and Liat, a native girl). Cable is a wonderful character, a sympathetic, valiant, and honorable man who is heroically serving his country in time of need. (His death is one of the most powerful moments in *South Pacific* and one which children may find unsettling.)

The Rodgers and Hammerstein songs were, are, and always will be classics, from "There Is Nothing Like a Dame," "Bloody Mary," and "Happy Talk" through "Bali H'ai" and "Some Enchanted Evening." "You've Got to Be Carefully Taught," a punch-in-the-gut condemnation of racism and blind hatred, remains as potent and relevant today as back in 1949, when *South Pacific* premiered on Broadway.

SOYLENT GREEN (1973)

Color, 100 minutes
Cast: Charlton Heston, Leigh Taylor-Young, Chuck Connors, Joseph Cotten, Brock Peters, Paula Kelly, Edward G. Robinson, Whit Bissell
Director: Richard Fleischer
Screenplay: Stanley R. Greenberg, from the novel *Make Room! Make Room!* by Harry Harrison
Science fiction/Mystery
Rated PG
Younger kids: No   Older kids: OK

By the year 2022, overpopulation has caused worldwide poverty, serious food shortages, and intensely crowded cities. Police detective Heston shares his room with elderly Robinson, whose job it is to remember important things. When a millionaire is mysteriously murdered, Heston begins following a series of clues

that leads him to a conclusion that you and older kids will reach well before he does.

The movie has good intentions but at the same time trivializes its main theme; by concentrating on the Big Surprise, the central idea of overpopulation gets lost. There's also a standard big-studio slickness to the film that makes its artificiality all too obvious. There's some emphasis on sex, which makes the film inappropriate for younger kids, but it's really no stronger than today's prime-time television. It also has a rather unpleasant premise at its core. Older kids are likely to regard it as what it is: just another movie.

This was the final role for the great actor Edward G. Robinson, and he has a poignant death scene, made even more powerful when you realize that he knew he was dying when he filmed it.

SPACEBALLS (1987)

Color, 96 minutes
Cast: Mel Brooks, Rick Moranis John Candy, Bill Pullman, Daphne Zuniga, Dick Van Patten, George Wyner, Michael Winslow, Lorene Yarnell, John Hurt; voices of Joan Rivers, Dom DeLuise
Director: Mel Brooks
Screenplay: Brooks, Thomas Meehan, and Ronny Graham
Comedy/Science fiction
Rated PG
Younger kids: Good   Older kids: VG

Spaceballs may not be classic Mel Brooks, but his spoof of sci-fi films in general (including *Alien*, **2001: A Space Odyssey, Planet of the Apes,** and the **Star Trek** series) and **Star Wars** in particular is irresistibly goofy and certain to please kids.

Brooks plays two roles, including a Yoda takeoff named Yogurt who spouts lines like "May the Schwartz be with you" in a Yiddish accent, and Rick Moranis is a scream as Dark Helmet, a pipsqueak villain whose voice gets deeper whenever he puts on his enormous helmet. The supporting cast includes John Candy as a half-man, half-dog named Barf, Bill Pullman as a space cowboy named Lone Starr who's given the power of the Schwartz by Yogurt, Daphne Zuniga as Princess Vespa ("a Druish Princess"), and the voices of Joan Rivers as the robot Dot Matrix and Dom DeLuise as Pizza the Hutt.

The level of humor is generally sophomoric, but there are a number of inspired gags, such as when the villains buy a videotape of the movie so they can catch Lone Starr, only to keep fast-forwarding to the point where they're watching the tape, and a **Raiders of the Lost Ark** parody, where the heroes make a daring escape under a rapidly closing doorway but discover that it was actually only their stunt doubles who escaped.

There is a sprinkling of strong language, but it's fairly mild.

THE SPACE CHILDREN
(1958)
Black & white, 69 minutes
Cast: Michel Ray, Adam Williams, Johnny Crawford, Peggy Webber, Jackie Coogan, Sandy Descher, Richard Shannon, John Washbrook, Russell Johnson
Director: Jack Arnold
Screenplay: Bernard C. Schoenfeld
Science fiction/Suspense

Unrated
Younger kids: No   Older kids: OK

On an isolated stretch of the California coast, children of scientists and other workers at a nearby rocket base are confronted by a glowing alien, which resembles a twisted mass of brain tissue. (For no apparent reason, it keeps getting larger.) Although it looks menacing, its intentions are purely benign: to prevent mankind from spreading atomic war to space. Controlled by the alien, the children begin sabotaging the rocketry efforts.

This low-key, well-photographed but cheap movie is one of the lesser efforts from sci-fi specialist Jack Arnold, but in focusing so closely on children, it's definitely unusual for its period.

Younger children today may still find the alien a bit eerie, while older children will find the kids in the movie decidedly uncool. This is strictly for kids with a big appetite for vintage science fiction.

SPACE JAM (1996)
Color, 87 minutes
Cast: Michael Jordan, Bugs Bunny, Wayne Knight, Bill Murray, Theresa Randle, Larry Bird, Charles Barkeley; voices of Billy West, Danny DeVito, Bob Bergen, June Foray, Kath Soucie
Directors: Joe Pytka (live action); Bruce Smith and Tony Cervone (animation)
Screenplay: Leo Benvenuti and Steve Rudnick, and Timothy Harris and Herschel Weingrod
Live-action/animated Comedy/Sports
Rated PG

Younger kids: OK   Older kids: OK

The Looney Tunes All-Stars meet 1990s basketball superheroes in this comic fantasy that combines live action and animation. Real-life basketball superstar Michael Jordan plays himself, coming to the rescue of Warner Bros. cartoon characters who must win a life or death basketball game against alien life forms. The aliens have stacked the deck in their favor by sapping the athletic talents from NBA stars Larry Bird, Charles Barkley, Patrick Ewing, and others. Exaggerated cartoon action provides much of the humor and visual gags on the basketball court. An abbreviated subplot involves Bugs Bunny's new love interest, Lola, who's a match for him on the court and off.

Space Jam may not be a classic, but it's an entertaining (if over-produced) comic effort. It will be of greatest interest to basketball fans, but anyone can enjoy the high-energy high jinks of the simple story. The Looney Tunes characters are not at their best, and are overrendered and shaded in '90s high-tech fashion, but they still come through fairly well. Bill Murray adds his comic edge (which parents will particularly welcome) in the climactic game.

Jordan and his real-life basketball confreres are portrayed as pro-social good guys in the live-action footage. The "violence" which presumably earned this film a PG rating is about on a par with most contemporary TV cartoons.

SPARTACUS (1960)
Color, 184 minutes
Cast: Kirk Douglas, Laurence Olivier, Jean Simmons, Tony Curtis, Charles Laughton, Peter Ustinov, John Gavin, Nina Foch, Herbert Lom, John Ireland, Charles McGraw, Woody Strode, Joanna Barnes
Director: Stanley Kubrick
Screenplay: Dalton Trumbo, based on the novel by Howard Fast
Historical action-adventure
Unrated
Younger kids: No   Older kids: VG

Stanley Kubrick's film about the rebellious gladiator slave, Spartacus (Kirk Douglas), who led a slave revolt against the tyranny of Imperial Rome, is one of the great historical epics of all time. It won four Oscars, including Best Supporting Actor (Peter Ustinov) and Best Cinematography. Douglas and an all-star cast are excellent, the action scenes are superbly staged, and the exceptionally well-written script is miles ahead of the typical empty-headed Hollywood spectacle.

It clearly (and sometimes quite graphically) delineates the brutal treatment of the slaves, from the time of their purchase and training as gladiators to their subjugation at the hands of the decadent Roman emperors. It's also a touching romance, showing the bond that develops between Spartacus and the British slave (Jean Simmons) he falls in love with.

This is an intelligent historical adventure, though definitely not for the very young (the 1991 restored version received a PG-13 rating for its violent battle scenes and a bath scene between Laurence Olivier and Tony Curtis, in which Olivier speaks, in only slightly abstract terms, of his sexual preferences). There's even a famous shot of blood being spattered on the Senators after a violent fight scene—a shocking moment today, let alone in 1960! Older kids, however, can use this as a time machine to travel to the days of the Roman Empire.

SPICE WORLD (1998)
Color, 93 minutes
Cast: Spice Girls (Victoria Adams, Melanie Brown, Emma Bunton, Melanie Chisholm, Geri Halliwell), Richard E. Grant, Roger Moore, many guest stars
Director: Bob Spiers
Screenplay: Kim Fuller, from a story by Fuller and The Spice Girls
Musical
Rated PG
Young children: OK Older children: VG

Brit sensations The Spice Girls have a hard day's afternoon riding around London in their customized double-decker Spicebus en route to their first live performance on the BBC's venerable *Top of the Pops.* The femme Fab Five encounter little plot but have a very good time along the way. Grant is their neurotic manager (he's the only one who smokes in the movie), while Moore cheerleads them from a 007-esque hideout.

Music industry buddies like Elton John, Elvis Costello, and Bob Geldof appear in cameos, while Jackie O, Twiggy, Marilyn, *Charlie's Angels,* and *The Avengers* are all amusingly referenced.

The cheeky, individualistic Posh, Scary, Baby, Sporty, and Ginger are fun to watch in this amiable, lightweight movie, and their upbeat music (which they write themselves) cheerfully reflects their twin platforms of friendship and Girl Power. Female empowerment never wore such a glittery badge.

There is a subplot about a friend of the girls who's facing childbirth without the benefit of a husband and a bit of street language, but the picture is surprisingly "clean," and good fun for adolescent fans. Pop culture watchers will note that the film was made before Ginger Spice left the act—and before several of the Girls got pregnant.

SPLASH (1984)
Color, 111 minutes
Cast: Daryl Hannah, Tom Hanks, John Candy, Eugene Levy, Dody Goodman, Richard B. Shull, Shecky Greene, Howard Morris
Director: Ron Howard
Screenplay: Lowell Ganz, Babaloo Mandel, and Bruce Jay Friedman
Comedy/Fantasy/Romance
Rated PG
Younger kids: OK, with caution Older kids: VG

Splash is the enchanting tale of a shy, distracted man (Hanks) who falls in love with a dream woman (Hannah) who turns out to be a mermaid. It's a simple fantasy formula that is executed with charm and great humor, and has a sweetness that is rare in any modern comedy. Hanks and Hannah are perfect as boy and fish; there is definite sexual chemistry between the two characters (although nothing explicit is shown), but it is the innocence of their love which makes them so appealing.

The story goes on a bit too long, especially when the mermaid is put in jeopardy, leading to an obligatory chase towards the end, but even here, the genuineness of Hanks' and Hannah's unconditional love for each other makes the film absolutely believable.

There are a few risqué moments provided by John Candy as Tom's brother, a devotee of the *Penthouse Forum* and the kind of guy who drops coins on the ground to peek up women's dresses—but even he turns out to be a softie who believes in the power of true love.

SQUANTO: A WARRIOR'S TALE (1994)
Color, 101 minutes
Cast: Adam Beach, Mandy Patinkin, Michael Gambon, Nathaniel Parker, Eric Schweig, Donal Donnelly, Stuart Pankin, Alex Norton, Irene Bedard
Director: Xavier Koller
Screenplay: Darlene Craviatto
Adventure/Historical
Rated PG
Young children: OK, with caution Older children: VG

This is the story of Squanto (Adam Beach), the Native American credited with teaching the Pilgrims survival techniques that made the first Thanksgiving possible. Kidnapped by the English and brought to Great Britain to be exhibited publicly as one of the "marvels of the New World," Squanto escapes his captors and hides in a countryside monastery. Brother Daniel (Mandy Patinkin) befriends him and teaches Squanto

the English language. They exchange beliefs, Squanto sharing his knowledge of the land, the monks educating Squanto to European ways and customs. Squanto returns to America and becomes a valued link between the pilgrims and the Indian nation.

Squanto's story is a great one, filled with dangers, action, and a sense of wonder and respect for nature. Kids will be entertained, and even parents may learn a thing or two.

Young kids may also enjoy this, but there are some fairly dramatic moments and a degree of violence.

STAND AND DELIVER (1988)
Color, 105 minutes
Cast: Edward James Olmos, Lou Diamond Phillips, Rosana de Soto, Andy Garcia, Will Gotay, Ingrid Oliu, Virginia Paris, Mark Eliot
Director: Ramon Menendez
Screenplay: Menendez and Tom Musca
Drama
Rated PG
Younger kids: OK Older kids: VG

This is the inspiring drama of Jaime Escalante, the real-life teacher who taught math at an East Los Angeles school and got his students to study and pass the Advanced Placement Calculus Test. It's a film that sings the virtues of hard work, setting goals, and believing in yourself, but the character of Jaime Escalante is not a lovable guy on the order of Robin Williams in **Dead Poets Society.** He demands complete dedication from his students and works them like a taskmaster so that they can see and reach their full potential.

That the kids willingly comply with Escalante and eventually succeed is doubly impressive since these students have been essentially written off by the educational system. (They are even accused of cheating when their test scores are first noted!) Some of the details of the students' home lives are a little pat, but at its best, the film shows that intellectual achievement can be as satisfying and rewarding as anything in life.

Some strong language can be expected in this environment, but it rings true with the film's totally believable setting and characters.

STAND BY ME (1986)
Color, 87 minutes
Cast: Wil Wheaton, River Phoenix, Corey Feldman, Jerry O'Connell, Kiefer Sutherland, Casey Siemaszko, John Cusack, Richard Dreyfuss
Director: Rob Reiner
Screenplay: Raynold Gideon and Bruce A. Evans, based on the novella "The Body" by Stephen King
Comedy-drama
Rated R
Younger kids: OK, with caution   Older kids: VG

In the 1950s, four young boys go in search of a dead body in the woods and discover the true nature of friendship in this rose-colored look at growing up and facing the future.

The discussions of mortality and friendship among the four youngsters are often laid on thick and sometimes border on the sappy. Overall, however, there is a strong sense of the give-and-take byplay between kids and the constant one-upmanship, as well as topics of discussion that are worthy of *Seinfeld*. (Who would win in a fight: Superman or Mighty Mouse? And what exactly is Goofy?)

Parents should note the recurring theme of death that runs through the film (rather blatantly), not to mention the thugs led by scary Kiefer Sutherland and a supremely but very enjoyably gross story that one of the boys tells about a pie-eating contest that ends in mass vomiting.

The only reason for the R rating is the language, which contains a high quotient of four-letter words and sounds rather odd coming from children who supposedly live in the '50s.

STAND UP AND CHEER! (1934)
Black & white, 69 minutes (also available in computer-colored version)
Cast: Shirley Temple, Warner Baxter, Madge Evans, James Dunn, Sylvia Froos, John Boles, Arthur Byron, Ralph Morgan, Aunt Jemima, Nick (Dick) Foran, Nigel Bruce, Stepin Fetchit
Director: Hamilton MacFadden
Screenplay: Ralph Spence and Lew Brown, based on a story idea by Will Rogers and Philip Klein
Social issue musical
Unrated
Young children: VG   Older children: VG

Shirley Temple is one of an ensemble cast in this very offbeat—even strange—Depression-era musical fantasy offering the golden-haired toddler in a star-making turn singing "Baby, Take a Bow" with actor James Dunn. The story revolves around the premise that a famous Broadway producer and expert on female beauty is named U.S. Secretary of Amusement, in order to cheer up the population and make the Depression vanish. The newly appointed secretary is challenged by corrupt forces in Washington, D.C.—aren't there *always* corrupt forces in Washington, D.C.?—who want the Depression to continue in order to make certain private business deals prosper.

The ending includes a huge parade of American workers celebrating their victory over the Depression—purely a case of wishful thinking since the Depression would continue for several more years in real life. That is what's meant by "escapism," which was a service movies provided to the American public during this dark period. This is a valuable topic for discussion.

The film is a revue-style musical with lots of period allusions that will need to be explained to children, such as the Great Depression, the popularity of radio and vaudeville, child labor laws, and an African-American musical entertainer named Aunt Jemima. As such, it can serve as a piece of social history, but it should not be regarded as a "Shirley Temple movie" per se.

STARGATE (1994)
Color, 119 minutes (also available at 128m.)
Cast: Kurt Russell, James Spader, Jaye Davidson, Viveca Lindfors, Alexis Cruz, Mili Avital, Leon Rippy, John Diehl, Carlos Lauchu, Djimon Hounsou, French Stewart

Director: Roland Emmerich
Screenplay: Dean Devlin and Emmerich
Science fiction
Rated PG-13
Younger kids: No   Older kids: OK

Scientist Spader discovers how to use a big metal ring the government has been experimenting with: it's an instantaneous gateway to another solar system clear across the galaxy. When he goes through it, accompanied by a tough colonel (Russell) and a platoon of soldiers, he finds refugees from ancient Egypt under the centuries-old domination of an alien (Davidson) who thinks he is or may really be the Egyptian Sun God Ra.

Stargate is riddled with plot holes and improbabilities, big and small; for example, Spader can translate the Egyptian hieroglyphic for "galaxy"—even though there's no conceivable reason the Egyptians would *have* such a word. He's so smart (you can tell: he wears glasses) that he instantly recognizes the big ring as some kind of passageway—but so dumb he can't recognize the constellation Orion. (But of course, the script is so dumb that it thinks interstellar travelers would navigate by *Earth's* constellations.)

Blending science fiction and Egyptian motifs was hot stuff back around 1931 but looks more than a little shopworn now. The story is the standard Lost Race tale: civilized people find downtrodden but nice folks in the thrall of a tyrant, whom our heroes then help overthrow. Spader is very good, however, and the special effects are outstanding. It's two-bit brain candy, nothing more, from the same team that was to bring us **Independence Day** and *Godzilla* (1998).

Kids, on the other hand, are likely to get quite a charge out of the colorful movie, in spite of a lull in the middle of the story. It's hardly intellectually challenging, but as an adventure thriller with science fiction trappings, it will more than pass the time.

It was rated PG-13 for its action-violence and some language.

STAR KID (1998)
Color, 101 minutes
Cast: Joseph Mazzello, Joey
   Simmrin, Alex Daniels, Brian
   Simpson, Danny Masterson,
   Richard Gilliland, Corinne
   Bohrer
Director: Manny Coto
Screenplay: Manny Coto
Science fiction/Comedy/Action
Rated PG
Young children: Some scary
   scenes Older children: OK

Spencer Griffith (Mazzello) has a lot of problems: his family has only recently moved to generic small city Crystal Bluff, his dad, Roland (Gilliland), has little time for him, his slightly older sister, Stacey (Levitch), considers him a "fungus," Turbo (Simmrin), a bulgy bully at school, has made Spencer his favorite target, Spencer can't bring himself to talk to cute Michelle (Ekstrom), on whom he has a forlorn crush, and Spencer's beloved mom has been dead for two years.

But salvation is on its way from outer space: a device that's like an intelligent suit of armor lands in a junkyard near Spencer's home. In one of those perfect movie coincidences, he's the only one to see this happen. This Cyborsuit quickly learns English and invites Spencer to climb inside. He jumps at the chance, and while wearing it, he can leap tall buildings at a single bound, juggle automobiles, and maybe even fly. The suit still has something of a mind of its own, however.

This derivative movie is moderately entertaining, although too many of Spencer's problems exist solely to be solved by the advent of the Cyborsuit. The youngest children may have a problem with the Broodwarrior, which is spectacularly horrid-looking, but the friendly aliens are cute, so there's a trade-off. Teenagers are likely to regard the film as too young for them, and they're right.

STARMAN (1984)
Color, 115 minutes
Cast: Jeff Bridges, Karen Allen,
   Charles Martin Smith, Richard
   Jaeckel, Robert Phalen, Tony
   Edwards
Director: John Carpenter
Screenplay: Bruce A. Evans and
   Raynold Gideon
Science fiction/Romance
Rated PG
Younger kids: OK Older kids:
   OK

Lured by the friendly welcome contained on the *Voyager II* space probe, a spaceship visits Earth, only to be immediately shot down over Wisconsin. An alien life force drifts into the home of recent widow Jenny (Allen), and while she sleeps, uses DNA from a lock of her late husband's hair to build itself a human body (Bridges), which naturally looks exactly like her husband. Just as naturally, Jenny is stunned to find this "Starman" in her living room.

He's charming and friendly, and quickly learns English; Starman convinces Jenny to take him to a meteor crater in Arizona for a rendezvous with his mother ship. However, a scientist (Smith) and a NASA chief (Jaeckel) have tracked the alien, and are intent on capturing him.

This adult variation on **E.T. The Extra-Terrestrial** introduces (tame) sex to the equation, and gives Starman all sorts of "magical" powers, enabling him, for instance, to return a dead deer to life. It's really a chase movie/romance with a few fantastic touches, but it's quite well done for all that. Horror maestro Carpenter directs impersonally but well, and the film is modestly entertaining throughout.

It's perfectly acceptable for older kids, and with a little guidance, for younger ones, too. It's a very positive, upbeat film, anchored by Jeff Bridges' sensitive and appealing performance as the alien.

STARS IN MY CROWN (1950)
Black & white, 89 minutes
Cast: Joel McCrea, Ellen Drew, Dean Stockwell, Alan Hale, Lewis Stone, James Mitchell, Amanda Blake, Juano Hernandez, Ed Begley, James Arness
Director: Jacques Tourneur
Screenplay: Margaret Fitts, based on the novel by Joe David Brown
Drama/Western
Unrated
Younger kids: Good   Older kids: VG

Joel McCrea stars in this wonderful, though unheralded, family classic about a gentle parson who,

with his wife (Ellen Drew) and adopted son (Dean Stockwell), settles down in a small Southern town just after the Civil War. Using his wits and—when necessary—his fists, the parson has his hands full while dealing with local bullies, the town's resistance to a new doctor, a typhoid epidemic, and an attempted Ku Klux Klan lynching, not to mention trying to convert his stubborn atheist war buddy (Alan Hale).

Beautifully directed by Jacques Tourneur, the film is a vivid, honestly emotional, and superbly acted piece of Americana brimming with such old-fashioned virtues as kindness and warmth, offering valuable lessons of tolerance and understanding without ever feeling preachy or heavy-handed. Younger children can certainly watch this, but they will have to have certain things explained to them—like lynching.

STARRUCK (1982)
Color, 95 minutes
Cast: Jo Kennedy, Ross O'Donovan, Pat Evison, Margo Lee, Max Cullen, Melissa Jaffer, Ned Lander, John O'May, Dennis Miller, Norman Erskine
Director: Gillian Armstrong
Screenplay: Stephen Maclean
Musical
Rated PG
Young children: VG   Older children: VG

This spunky, charming musical is unlike any other film directed by Australian Gillian Armstrong, whose works (which include *My Brilliant Career*, **Little Women,** and *Oscar & Lucinda*) are generally more sedate and dramatic. It's a wonderfully original hybrid of old-fashioned Hollywood musicals—recalling especially the Judy Garland and Mickey Rooney let's-put-on-a-show-in-the-barn type—and modern sensibilities.

Starstruck is the story of Jackie Mullens (Jo Kennedy), a precocious young punkette who is determined to make it as a new wave singer. She sets out to do so with the help of Angus, her 14-year-old cousin (Ross O'Donovan), who becomes her manager.

What makes *Starstruck* so good for kids is the youthful exuberance and sheer likablity of Jackie and Angus. Then there are the wildly amusing production numbers and choreography. What they lack in slickness they make up for in energy and inventiveness.

STAR TREK: THE MOTION PICTURE (1979)

Color, 132 minutes (also available at 143m.)

Cast: William Shatner, Leonard Nimoy, DeForest Kelley, James Doohan, George Takei, Majel Barrett, Walter Koenig, Nichelle Nichols, Persis Khambatta, Stephen Collins, Grace Lee Whitney, Mark Lenard

Director: Robert Wise

Screenplay: Harold Livingston, from a story by Alan Dean Foster based on characters created by Gene Roddenberry

Science fiction/Adventure

Rated G

Young children: OK   Older children: OK

In the 23rd century, a strange force/machine is on its destructive way to Earth, so James T. Kirk (Shatner), who'd been bumped up to Admiral and given a desk job, is suddenly reassigned to the starship *Enterprise*, taking over from the disgruntled current captain, Decker (Collins). Kirk picks up his former first mate, Spock (Nimoy), from his home planet of Vulcan, and the ship sets out to once again save the universe.

Star Trek has become much more than a TV series; it's part of world pop history—the most successful science fiction franchise of all time. Four live-action TV series, a cartoon series, comic books, novels, and mountains of fan-written stories have turned Kirk, Spock, McCoy, and the others into cultural icons. (The same is happening to the crew from the second series, *Star Trek—The Next Generation*.)

This was a very troubled production; at the time of its release, it was the most expensive American movie ever made. Trekkies (some of whom prefer to be called Trekkers) flocked to the theaters, but most were disappointed; the movie is ponderously slow at times, the plot is familiar, and the characters don't interact enough. On the other hand, director Wise gave the film an epic scale and grandeur that set it apart from the TV show. This, unlike the many sequels that followed, really is a motion picture and not a glorified episode of the series. But the world really wanted glorified episodes, and that's what it's been given ever since.

There are thousands, probably millions, of families the world over in which the parents have weaned their kids on *Star Trek*. The positive values the series has always upheld, the comradeship between the characters and the courage to boldly go where no one has gone before—all these are virtues that children and adults alike can embrace. The *Star Trek* phenomenon comes by its fame and near-worship quite honestly.

This has also been released in a 143-minute version, which most viewers seem to prefer.

STAR TREK II: THE WRATH OF KHAN (1982)

Color, 113 minutes

Cast: William Shatner, Leonard Nimoy, DeForest Kelley, Ricardo Montalban, James Doohan, Walter Koenig, George Takei, Nichelle Nichols, Kirstie Alley, Bibi Besch, Merritt Butrick, Paul Winfield

Director: Nicholas Meyer

Screenplay: Jack B. Sowards, from a story by Sowards and Harve Bennett

Science fiction/Adventure

Rated PG

Younger kids: VG Older kids: VG

Years after being marooned on a dying world, evil Khan Noonian Sing (Montalban, in a charismatic performance) commandeers a starship and seeks revenge on Admiral James T. Kirk, the man who put him there. After the critical drubbing that **Star Trek: The Motion Picture** received, this film (based on the 1967 "Space Seed" episode, which also featured Montalban as Khan) steered the *Trek* franchise back on line and recaptured the spirit that made the original series so popular.

The emphasis here is on story and relationships, and the battle of wills between Kirk and the obsessed Khan gives the whole enterprise (no pun intended) gen-

uine tension. The special effects serve the story instead of overwhelming it, and the characters—especially Captain Kirk—are allowed to have quirks, foibles, and self-doubts.

There is some violence via space battles and one creepy scene when Khan plants tiny alien bugs into the brains of two Federation members, but anyone who has watched the TV series should know what to expect. This is a fun way for older fans of the series to pass on the *Trek* legacy to their kids.

STAR TREK III: THE SEARCH FOR SPOCK (1984)

Color, 105 minutes

Cast: William Shatner, Leonard Nimoy, DeForest Kelley, James Doohan, Walter Koenig, George Takei, Nichelle Nichols, Robin Curtis, Merritt Butrick, Christopher Lloyd, Robert Hooks, John Larroquette, James B. Sikking, Mark Lenard, Dame Judith Anderson, Grace Lee Whitney, Miguel Ferrer

Director: Leonard Nimoy

Screenplay: Harve Bennett, based on the TV series created by Gene Roddenberry

Science fiction/Space adventure

Rated PG

Young children: OK Older children: OK

After Mr. Spock dies while saving his crewmates, the *Enterprise* returns to Earth, where Dr. McCoy (Kelley) seems to be going crazy. Spock's father, Sarek (Lenard), explains to Kirk (Shatner) that before he died, Spock duplicated his mind in McCoy's brain. Furthermore, the Genesis Device that instantly terraformed an entire world has probably returned Spock to life; Kirk must reunite his friend's mind and body.

On the Genesis planet, Kirk's son David (Butrick) and Vulcan Lt. Saavik (Curtis) have indeed found a baby Spock, who is rapidly returning to his true age. Meanwhile, Klingon warlord Kruge (Lloyd) heads for the Genesis planet, hoping to use the Device as a weapon. Kirk and the *Enterprise* rescue McCoy from a detention center, steal the *Enterprise,* and set out for the Genesis planet themselves.

Regarded by Star Trek fans as one of the lesser entries in the series, partly because the film is centered on a question with an obvious answer—will Spock return?—this is still good entertainment, if strictly by the numbers. The special effects are good, but the Genesis planet sets are second-rate.

It's harmless enough for young children (especially for those already familiar with the series), and older children will probably have a good time.

STAR TREK IV: THE VOYAGE HOME (1986)
Color, 119 minutes
Cast: William Shatner, Leonard Nimoy, DeForest Kelley, James Doohan, Walter Koenig, George Takei, Nichelle Nichols, Jane Wyatt, Catherine Hicks, Mark Lenard, Robin Curtis, Robert Ellenstein, John Schuck, Brock Peters
Director: Leonard Nimoy
Screenplay: Steve Meerson, Peter Krikes, Harve Bennett, and Nicholas Meyer, from a story by Nimoy and Bennett
Science fiction/Adventure
Rated PG

Younger kids: VG   Older kids: VG

The fourth *Star Trek* movie finds the *Enterprise* crew traveling back into time (to 1986 San Francisco, to be precise) in order to capture humpback whales that are needed to communicate with alien forces threatening 23rd-century Earth. This is perhaps the most accessible of the *Star Trek* movies—and also the most enjoyable—because of its consistent comic tone and the story which pits Kirk, Spock, and company against the bizarre culture and customs of late-20th-century Earth.

The "save the whales" subplot is also the ultimate environmental message, which is perfectly in keeping with the messagey side of the original *Star Trek* series and adds to the good vibes all around. There is virtually no violence in this outing and only some mild profanity, which is treated as a joke, especially coming out of the unlikely mouths of Spock and Kirk. A treat for *Trek* devotees—or anyone else, for that matter.

STAR TREK V: THE FINAL FRONTIER (1989)
Color, 106 minutes
Cast: William Shatner, Leonard Nimoy, DeForest Kelley, James Doohan, Walter Koenig, Nichelle Nichols, George Takei, David Warner, Laurence Luckinbill
Director: William Shatner
Screenplay: David Loughery, from a story by Shatner, Harve Bennett, and David Loughery, based on the TV series created by Gene Roddenberry
Science fiction/Space adventure
Rated PG

Young children: Tense Older children: OK

A Vulcan mystic named Sybok (Luckinbill) takes several diplomats hostage. When Kirk (Shatner), Spock (Nimoy), and the others arrive at Nimbus III to settle the situation, Kirk learns to his shock that Sybok is Spock's heretofore-unmentioned half-brother. Sybok easily wins over everyone except Kirk to his cause of plunging through the Great Barrier at the center of the galaxy to reach the planet Sha Ka Ree, there to confront God Himself.

Clearly there is no way that the Star Trek team is going to do anything as potentially blasphemous as to encounter God, so one must wait patiently until the real identity of this powerful force is revealed. Which means sitting through the shoddiest special effects in *Trek* movie history, some embarrassing "group bonding" (Spock learns to sing!), and other unfortunate nonsense. Shatner proves to be a very good director of action, however, with a sense of scale and an eye for the epic. Too bad he chose to make his directorial debut with a third-rate script.

Die-hard *Star Trek* fans will undoubtedly want to watch this in any case.

STAR TREK VI: THE UNDISCOVERED COUNTRY
(1991)
Color, 109 minutes
Cast: William Shatner, Leonard Nimoy, DeForest Kelley, Ricardo Montalban, James Doohan, Walter Koenig, Nichelle Nichols, George Takei, Kim Cattrall, Christopher Plummer, Mark Lenard, Grace Lee Whitney, Brock Peters, Kurtwood Smith, Rosana DeSoto, David Warner, Iman, John Schuck, Michael Dorn, Christian Slater
Director: Nicholas Meyer
Screenplay: Meyer and Denny Martin Flitin, based on a story by Leonard Nimoy, Lawrence Konner, and Mark Rosenthal
Science fiction
Rated PG
Younger kids: VG Older kids: VG

The Federation offers an olive branch to the evil Klingons, whose world is on the verge of extinction, and the crew of the good starship *Enterprise* is sent to carry out the first tentative steps of peace. However, there are certain people who would rather not negotiate peace. Kirk, Spock, and company find themselves caught in the middle—and accused of murder.

A fitting valedictory to the films featuring the original cast of *Star Trek* (and unofficial proof that the best *Trek* movies are those ending with even numbers in the title). More than any of the previous *Trek* movies, this one really creates a family atmosphere among the crew of the *Enterprise* that heightens our affection for the characters after all of these years. (This, although Sulu has been given a promotion and now commands a ship of his own!) The timely parallel between the Klingon-Federation detente and the end of the Russian-American Cold War is amusingly handled, amid the usual philosophical rumblings of age, duty, and the potential of our race, adding warmth and humanity to the proceedings.

STAR WARS (1977)
Color, 121 minutes
Cast: Mark Hamill, Harrison
   Ford, Carrie Fisher, Alec
   Guinness, Peter Cushing,
   Anthony Daniels, Kenny
   Baker, Peter Mayhew, David
   Prowse, Phil Brown, Shelagh
   Fraser; voice of James Earl
   Jones
Director: George Lucas
Screenplay: George Lucas
Science fiction/Space adventure
Rated PG
Young children: OK   Older
   children: OK

When George Lucas was refused
the right to do a feature-length
Flash Gordon adventure, he decided to write his own space
opera, very loosely based on
Akira Kurosawa's movie *The
Hidden Fortress*. No one, certainly
not Lucas, expected the response
to be so overwhelming as to almost instantly make *Star Wars* the
box-office champion of all time.
Clearly, something in his sophisticated but naïve adventure spoke
to an entire generation of movie
fans.

Lucas not only drew on the Saturday matinee traditions of the
past, and opened the door to a
new era in special effects; he built
his story on time-worn elements
of mythology. It's not accidental
that the many copies and clones
of this film have fallen short.

The plot, for those who don't
already know, has young Luke
Skywalker (Mark Hamill) teaming up with rascally space pirate
Han Solo (Harrison Ford), a couple of robots, a Wookiee, and a
wise old warrior (Alec Guinness)
to rescue a princess (Carrie
Fisher) from a space prison. This
turns out to be a scheme on the
part of villainous Moff Tarkin
(Peter Cushing) and his black-
clad chief, Darth Vader (Prowse;
voice of James Earl Jones) to discover a secret rebel base.

Kids love this film for a variety
of reasons, not the least of which
is that Luke is a neglected, put-
upon boy who gets to prove his
manhood; girls respond to the
tough, independent character of
Princess Leia. Add to that the levels of fantasy, mythology, and
special effects—plus a sense of
humor—and you have not just a
kid-friendly movie but a phenomenon.

The only possible cause for
concern in *Star Wars* is the violence, but this is all space-era
shoot-'em-up stuff using laser
guns; there are lots of explosions,
but there is no blood.

In fact, the film was originally
rated G by the Motion Picture
Association of America. The distributor, 20th Century-Fox, went
back to the MPAA and asked for
a PG instead—so teenagers
wouldn't be turned off by the
"stigma" of seeing a G-rated film!

A few months before the release of **The Empire Strikes Back,**
the first *Star Wars* sequel, the
opening text of this movie was
changed so that the title now
seems to be "Chapter IV: A New
Hope." But don't worry: it's *Star
Wars*—only the very deepest-dyed
fans ever refer to this movie by
any other name.

In 1997, all three of the films
were reissued with spruced-up
special effects, the biggest changes
being made to the first film. This
version runs 4 minutes longer.

STATE FAIR (1945)
Color, 100 minutes
Cast: Jeanne Crain, Dana
   Andrews, Dick Haymes,
   Vivian Blaine, Charles
   Winninger, Fay Bainter,
   Donald Meek, Frank McHugh,
   Percy Kilbride, Henry (Harry)
   Morgan
Director: Walter Lang
Screenplay: Oscar Hammerstein
   II, Sonya Levien, and Paul
   Green, based on the novel by
   Phil Stong
Musical
Unrated
Young children: VG   Older
   children: VG

Here is the second (and very best)
of three versions of *State Fair,* a
candy-colored, agreeably idealized, and admittedly corny pan-
orama of middle America. It is
the story of the Frake family, an
Iowa farm clan making ready for
the upcoming state fair. Dad has
a pig he is grooming for competition, while mom is preparing her
favorite recipes, which she hopes
will win her blue ribbons. Daughter Margy and son Wayne are out
for fun, but they also just might
find romance.

State Fair is sheer escapism,
1940s-style, with a sunny disposi-
tion that's so alien to contemporary entertainment that kids may
think it came from another
planet. But it's so earnestly performed from the very first moment, when an old codger starts
singing about "our state fair,"
that it's pretty hard to resist.

Another major asset is the
score by Rodgers and Hammerstein—the only time they wrote
songs especially for a movie—
which includes "It Might as Well
Be Spring," "It's a Grand Night

for Singing," and "Isn't It Kind
of Fun."

State Fair was filmed without
songs in 1933, with Will Rogers,
Janet Gaynor, and Lew Ayres, and
was remade in 1962 with Pat Boone,
Bobby Darin, Ann-Margret, Tom
Ewell, and Alice Faye. Be sure to
avoid the latter, which is pretty
awful.

STEAMBOAT BILL, JR. (1928)
Black & white, 71 minutes
Cast: Buster Keaton, Ernest
   Torrence, Marion Byron, Tom
   Lewis, Tom McGuire
Director: Charles F. Reisner
Screenplay: Carl Harbaugh
Comedy/Silent classic
Unrated
Young children: VG   Older
   children: VG

Buster Keaton had a rather remarkable batting average in the
1920s, and this is another of his
great (and timeless) silent comedy features.

Buster plays William Canfield,
Jr. (also known as Steamboat Bill,
Jr.), a milksop who must demonstrate his manhood to his father,
a gruff Mississippi steamboat captain. The senior Canfield's craft,
the *Stonewall Jackson,* is old and
rickety, while the boat owned by
his rival is shiny and new. Compli-
cating matters is the fact that
young Canfield is in love with the
rival's daughter.

The highlight of *Steamboat Bill,
Jr.* is the famous finale in which
the riverfront town is overtaken
by a twister. Youngsters should
be reminded that this eye-popping
sequence was filmed before Hollywood had developed sophisticated special effects; most of what
you see is actually happening,
whether it's a building collapsing

or Buster leaning forward at an incredible angle to brace himself against the wind. In fact, it could be said that the most amazing special effect in *Steamboat Bill, Jr.* is Buster Keaton himself.

This sequence includes Buster's most famous—and hair-raising—stunt, in which the front of a building falls down all around him, with one small window leaving just enough room to clear his body and leave him erect. This was not done with any trickery at all: Keaton put himself at risk as a one-ton "prop" fell down with only inches to spare all around him.

Is it any wonder that contemporary action star Jackie Chan names Keaton as one of his heroes?

THE STING (1973)
Color, 129 minutes
Cast: Paul Newman, Robert
    Redford, Robert Shaw, Eileen
    Brennan, Charles Durning,
    Ray Walston, Eileen Brennan,
    Harold Gould
Director: George Roy Hill
Screenplay: David S. Ward
Comedy-drama
Rated PG
Younger kids: OK   Older kids:
    VG

Four years after their smash hit **Butch Cassidy and the Sundance Kid,** Paul Newman and Robert Redford reteamed with director George Roy Hill for this enormously entertaining caper comedy that proved to be an even bigger blockbuster and went on to win seven Oscars, including Best Picture and Best Director. In David S. Ward's ingeniously plotted script, Newman and Redford shine as brash con men in 1930s

Chicago who stage an elaborate "sting" on a ruthless racketeer (Robert Shaw) for $500,000, employing a small army of fellow scam artists to help pull it off.

The movie has lost some of its original luster and still feels a little long and slowly paced, but its double-crosses, triple-crosses, and the great twist ending still work. With its top-notch cast of veteran character actors, the splendidly evocative re-creation of its period, and Marvin Hamlisch's snappy adaptations of Scott Joplin's ragtime piano classics on the soundtrack, the movie is stylish, old-fashioned fun for young and old alike.

There is some material not suitable for younger children, including some brief violence.

THE STORY OF ROBIN HOOD AND HIS MERRIE MEN (1952)
Color, 83 minutes
Cast: Richard Todd, Joan Rice,
    Peter Finch, James Hayter,
    James Robertson Justice
Director: Ken Annakin
Screenplay: Lawrence E. Watkin
Swashbuckler/Action-adventure
Unrated
Younger kids: VG   Older kids:
    VG

Walt Disney takes a crack at the Robin Hood legend in this enjoyable production, which can hold its own with any other version and has the advantage of being filmed in the lush countryside of England. Richard Todd heads a fine cast and is quite convincing as the legendary, lighthearted hero, whether dueling with the wicked Sheriff of Nottingham (Peter Finch) or romancing the lovely Maid Marian (Joan Rice). Though the story follows the traditional plot in most regards, it has some delightful additions, such as the way that Robin and his Merrie Men send messages to each other by shooting whistling arrows throughout the forest and a scene where Robin steals the Sheriff's strongbox and donates it to the common people.

As with all of Walt Disney's British-made adventures of the 1950s and '60s, this one is well made, well cast, and consistent with the studio's family-entertainment credo. Somewhat forgotten in the wake of the studio's animated **Robin Hood,** it deserves to be better known.

STOWAWAY (1936)
Black & white, 86 minutes (also available in computer-colored version)
Cast: Shirley Temple, Robert Young, Alice Faye, Eugene Pallette, Helen Westley, Arthur Treacher, J. Edward Bromberg, Astrid Allwyn, Allan (Rocky) Lane, Robert Greig
Director: William A. Seiter
Screenplay: William Conselman, Arthur Sheekman, and Nat Perrin, based on a story by Samuel G. Engel
Comedy/Musical
Unrated
Young children: VG   Older children: VG

In this entertaining comedy with music, Shirley Temple plays Ching-Ching, the ward of a Chinese magistrate whose missionary parents were killed in an uprising. Through a series of incidents, she is left stranded without money or food. Eventually, the golden-haired tot befriends a handsome bachelor with a reputation for being a playboy, and then becomes an unintentional stowaway on a ship.

This is a wonderful adventure story geared to juveniles, but it also provides fun for older children and adults. In a convincing attempt to prove that this is one talented little performer, Shirley is allowed to speak several phrases in Chinese. She gets to imitate Al Jolson and Eddie Cantor, top entertainers of the period. With the help of a rag doll strapped to her toes, she even impersonates the dance team of Fred Astaire and Ginger Rogers! Needless to say, this emerges as one of Shirley's best talent showcases.

STOWAWAY IN THE SKY (1960)
Color, 82 minutes
Cast: Andre Gille, Maurice Baquet, Pascal Lamorisse; Jack Lemmon (narrator)
Director: Albert Lamorisse
Screenplay: Lamorisse (France), S. N. Behrman (U.S.)
Adventure
Unrated
Young children: VG   Older children: VG

For everyone who has seen and loved Albert Lamorisse's beguiling short fantasy *The Red Balloon* (1955) and hoped he'd do a similarly enchanting feature, here's the fulfillment of that wish.

Set in the turn-of-the-20th-century French countryside—or more precisely, *above* it—it's the story of an adventuresome grandfather and his stowaway grandson who take a voyage in an antique balloon over some of Europe's best scenery.

Lamorisse again directs his son Pascal as the boy, but the real star is the aerial display: the Eiffel Tower, a sailboat race to the Canary Islands, overhead views of Königsberg Castle and Strasbourg Cathedral, and a flock of flamingoes in flight, among many treats.

There's also some comedy, a few lessons to be learned along the way, and a melodious soundtrack, plus narration by Jack Lemmon.

Brie and a baguette would be very good with this movie.

STRANGE INVADERS (1983)

Color, 94 minutes
Cast: Paul Le Mat, Nancy Allen, Diana Scarwid, Michael Lerner, Louise Fletcher, Wallace Shawn, Fiona Lewis, Kenneth Tobey, June Lockhart, Charles Lane, Lulu Sylbert
Director: Michael Laughlin
Screenplay: Bill Condon and Laughlin
Science fiction/Comedy
Rated PG
Younger kids: Scary   Older kids: OK

In 1958, a flying saucer lands in Centerville, Illinois, and all the residents disappear. In 1983, after leaving her daughter Elizabeth (Sylbert) with her ex-husband, Charlie (Le Mat), Margaret (Scarwid) travels from New York to her home town of Centerville. When Charlie is attacked by aliens, he and tabloid reporter Betty (Allen) head straight for Centerville, where there turn out to be aliens aplenty, still living a 1950s lifestyle.

At once a tribute to 1950s science fiction thrillers and a gentle spoof of them, *Strange Invaders* still manages to work on its own terms as well. The leads are all attractive, the special effects are excellent (and at times hauntingly beautiful), and the score by John Addison particularly good. Its biggest problem is a slow pace.

Kids of today will, for the most part, not get the references to the past (including the presence of 1950s sci-fi hero Kenneth Tobey), but they'll probably enjoy the movie just for itself. For them, the references might well work backward: in years to come, they'll see films older than *Strange Invaders* that will remind them of this one.

STRICTLY BALLROOM (1992)

Color, 94 minutes
Cast: Paul Mercurio, Tara Morice, Bill Hunter, Barry Otto, Pat Thompson, Gia Carides, Peter Whitford, John Hannan, Sonia Kruger, Kris McQuade
Director: Baz Luhrmann
Screenplay: Luhrmann and Craig Pearce
Musical
Rated PG
Young children: OK   Older children: VG

Preteens and adolescents should go for this spunky Australian musical, set in the world of competitive ballroom dancing. That's because its young hero, a multitalented dancer named Scott Hastings (Paul Mercurio), is determined to rebel against his elders and the parochial little world they inhabit. Scott wishes to discover his own voice by dancing in a spontaneous, highly provocative, nontraditional manner.

After being abandoned by his partner, Scott decides not to

replace her with a sleek, well-schooled beauty. Instead, he selects Fran, an untrained, unattractive, yet supportive young woman who is fated to blossom under his instruction.

While all of this is utterly predictable, *Strictly Ballroom* spins its love story with great sincerity and charm . . . and balances it against a wild, colorful, often campy depiction of the ballroom dancing world. The result is highly unusual but impossible to dislike.

The dance scenes are particularly fluid and energetic.

STRIKE UP THE BAND
(1940)
Black & white, 120 minutes
Cast: Mickey Rooney, Judy
   Garland, Paul Whiteman and
   His Orchestra, June Preisser,
   William Tracy, Ann
   Shoemaker, Larry Nunn, Phil
   Silvers
Director: Busby Berkeley
Screenplay: John Monks, Jr.,
   Fred Finklehoffe
Musical
Unrated
Young children: VG   Older
   children: VG

Back in the late 1930s and early 1940s, Mickey Rooney and Judy Garland costarred in a series of spirited MGM musicals, including *Babes in Arms, Babes on Broadway, Girl Crazy, Thousands Cheer,* and *Strike Up the Band.* In each one Mickey and/or Judy would be faced with some sort of crisis, and eventually, a brilliant idea would pop into their heads: Why not organize a talent show, which would include all the singers, dancers, and musicians in their neighborhood or school? In-variably, these productions—supposedly mounted by a bunch of amateurs, on a limited budget—would take on the luster of a full-bodied Broadway musical.

While the teenagers depicted in these stories are light years removed from today's kids, the films remain fun to watch for their sheer exuberance and the talent on display.

The appropriately titled *Strike Up the Band* is as good as any of the Mickey-Judy musicals. Here, the two young dynamos head up a group of high school musicians who desire to compete in a national contest and turn their orchestra into a swing band. The film bears no relation to the 1928 George S. Kaufman–Morrie Ryskind–George and Ira Gershwin Broadway musical of the same name. But no matter. It's loaded with vitality and energetic musical numbers, and there's even a clever animated sequence, created by George Pal, in which a symphony is performed by some fruit puppets.

THE STUPIDS (1996)
Color, 94 minutes
Cast: Tom Arnold, Jessica
   Lundy, Bug Hall, Alex
   McKenna, Mark Metcalf, Matt
   Keeslar, Frankie Faison, Bob
   Keeshan, Christopher Lee
Director: John Landis
Screenplay: Brent Forrester,
   based on characters created by
   James Marshall and Harry
   Allard
Comedy
Rated PG
Younger children: VG   Older
   children: VG

This likably silly film (based on the popular children's books by

James Marshall and Harry Allard) introduces us to the Stupid family. They live a normal, suburban existence, and they love each other very much. They're just . . . well, stupid. In an escalating series of misunderstandings, dad Stanley is swept into a web of intrigue, and becomes the target of some deadly spies.

Trying to describe the plot of this film would be pointless. Suffice it to say that all four Stupids—Stanley and Joan, and their children, Buster and Petunia—have an uncanny knack for getting into trouble and not realizing it.

Young kids will love feeling superior to these hopeless dimwits, and older kids will enjoy catching the plays on words and story twists. The secret to the film's success is that all four leading actors play their parts with utter seriousness and never let down their guard for moment. And how can you dislike a film in which the leading character sings "I'm My Own Grandpa"?

There is some violence, mostly cartoonish in nature, but young children might be disturbed by some of the ruggedness of the climactic sequence.

SUBURBAN COMMANDO
(1991)
Color, 99 minutes
Cast: Hulk Hogan, Christopher Lloyd, Shelley Duvall, Larry Miller, William Ball, JoAnn Dearing, Jack Elam, Roy Dotrice, Michael Faustino
Director: Burt Kennedy
Screenplay: Frank Cappello
Action comedy
Rated PG
Younger children: OK   Older children: OK

This silly but entertaining family film stars wrestler turned actor Hulk Hogan as an intergalactic warrior who decides to hang out on Earth while his spaceship is being refueled. He rooms with a suburban Earth couple, meek Christopher Lloyd and mousy Shelley Duvall, and spends most of his time trying to figure out such earthly creations as video games and skateboards.

Additionally, the Hulkster outwits two cosmic bounty hunters and does battle with his greatest foe, General Suitor (William Bell), while teaching Lloyd how to stand up to his mean boss (Larry Miller), with the help of the alien visitor's super-power space suit.

Better made, better written, and better cast than many of Hogan's other video outings, this theatrical release is quite enjoyable. Some mild action-violence and raucous behavior earned it a PG rating.

SUMMER MAGIC (1963)
Color, 100 minutes
Cast: Hayley Mills, Burl Ives, Dorothy McGuire, Deborah Walley, Eddie Hodges, Jimmy Mathers, Michael Pollard, Una Merkel, Peter Brown
Director: James Neilson
Screenplay: Sally Benson, based on the novel *Mother Carey's Chickens* by Kate Douglas Wiggin
Musical
Unrated
Young kids: VG   Older kids: OK

Summer Magic is a cheerful, light-as-a-feather musical produced by Walt Disney. It barely has a story to hold it together, and the songs

536

(by the Sherman Brothers) are hardly memorable. But its likable cast and pleasant atmosphere manage to fill 100 minutes in harmless fashion.

Margaret Carey (Dorothy McGuire) is recently widowed and, with no money to speak of, is forced to move with her three children to a rundown house in Maine. The outgoing town postmaster, Osh Popham (Burl Ives) immediately takes an interest in the Carey clan and tries to help them get along. A key subplot has to do with the arrival of a snooty cousin (Deborah Walley) who comes to stay with the family.

Folksinger and actor Burl Ives is always a treat to listen to, and his best number here is "The Ugly Bug Ball."

For fans of Hayley Mills or anyone looking to pass the time in a congenial manner, *Summer Magic* will fill the bill.

THE SUMMER OF BEN TYLER (1996)
Color, 134 minutes
Cast: James Woods, Elizabeth McGovern, Len Cariou, Julia McIlvaine, Kevin Isola, Clifton James, Anita Gillette, Charles Mattocks; Judith Ivey (narrator)
Director: Arthur Allan Seidelman
Screenplay: Robert Inman
Drama
Rated PG
Young children: OK   Older children: VG

A *Hallmark Hall of Fame* production, this story is set in the midst of a scalding Southern summer in 1942 and tells of an idealistic lawyer who finds his ethics challenged when his mentor's son is brought up on drunk driving and manslaughter charges.

The old man has been like a father to attorney Temple Rayburn (Woods, in a fine performance). So when it's time to defend a man who feels like a brother to him, it's also time to question what is morally right versus what is legally right.

A subplot involves his taking in the mentally handicapped teenage son of his family's housekeeper. In addition to the legal dilemma he faces, he must now also battle racism and intolerance toward the disabled.

The difference between law and justice, between the well-meaning and those who actually do good, is what this absorbing courtroom drama is all about. Woods is superb in his portrayal of the man in the middle.

There is much here for families to absorb and discuss together.

SUMMER STOCK (1950)
Color, 109 minutes
Cast: Judy Garland, Gene Kelly, Eddie Bracken, Marjorie Main, Gloria De Haven, Phil Silvers, Ray Collins, Carleton Carpenter, Hans Conried
Director: Charles Walters
Screenplay: George Wells and Sy Gomberg, from a story by Gomberg
Musical
Unrated
Young children: VG   Older children: VG

Back in 1950, Judy Garland and Gene Kelly were MGM's two reigning musical stars, and this easygoing and entertaining property proved an ideal vehicle for them both. Garland plays Jane Falbury, a New England lass who happily resides on a farm and is engaged to marry a small-minded local. Jane's kid sister, Abigail (Gloria De Haven), is an actress and one day shows up with a gang of poverty-stricken performers who begin rehearsing a musical in the family barn. Kelly plays Joe D. Ross, the show's author, and of course, the end result is a production so lavish that it might as well have been prepared for Broadway.

Two now legendary musical numbers make *Summer Stock* extra special: Kelly's famous solo dance on a newspaper and Garland's stunning rendition of "Get Happy," one of her flashiest and most popular screen routines.

Summer Stock is good, clean fun, especially for young viewers who've already come to know and enjoy Garland and Kelly through other films.

SUPERGIRL (1984)
Color, 105 minutes
Cast: Faye Dunaway, Helen Slater, Peter O'Toole, Mia Farrow, Brenda Vaccaro, Peter Cook, Simon Ward, Marc McClure, Hart Bochner, Maureen Teefy, David Healy, Matt Frewer
Director: Jeannot Szwarc
Screenplay: David Odell
Science fiction
Rated PG
Younger kids: OK, but boring   Older kids: No

Floating in the cosmos, Argo City is the only part of Krypton to survive the destruction of the planet. Young Kara (Helen Slater), cousin of Kal-El, who became Superman/Clark Kent on Earth, is entrusted by her mentor, Zaltar (Peter O'Toole), with the Ome-

gahedron, which is really important. But she loses it, and the device winds up on Earth in the hands of petulant would-be witch Selena (Faye Dunaway), who immediately begins using its magical powers.

So Kara heads for Earth, adopting the secret identity of Linda Lee Danvers; since she has all the powers of Superman, she adopts a similar costume as Supergirl. She becomes friendly with Lucy Lane (Maureen Teefy), whose boyfriend is *Daily Planet* cub reporter Jimmy Olsen (Marc McClure). Kara is attracted to landscape gardener Ethan (Hart Bochner), whom Selena also wants, leading to a heightening of their conflict.

Once again, the creators of a movie based on a comic book toss out some of its tried-and-true elements in favor of fuzzy-headed fantasy; this only irked the fans of Supergirl. The movie cannot seem to find a consistent tone, being spoofy some of the time—particularly in Dunaway's flamboyant (but entertaining) performance—and more serious the rest.

In short, this is a bad movie, with poor effects, a mistreatment of a promising character, and no sense of itself. There are even a handful of four-letter words. The chances of kids enjoying it are very remote.

SUPERMAN (1978)
Color, 143 minutes
Cast: Christopher Reeve, Margot Kidder, Gene Hackman, Marlon Brando, Valerie Perrine, Ned Beatty, Jackie Cooper, Marc McClure, Susannah York, Trevor Howard, Harry Andrews, Jack O'Halloran, Maria Schell,

Terence Stamp, Sarah Douglas, Glenn Ford, Phyllis Thaxter, Jeff East
Director: Richard Donner
Screenplay: Mario Puzo, David Newman, Leslie Newman, and Robert Benton, based on characters created by Jerry Siegel and Joe Shuster
Science fiction/Superhero adventure
Rated PG
Young children: OK Older children: OK

The story begins on Superman's distant home world of Krypton, where his father Jor-El (Brando) is unsuccessful in persuading his fellow members of the ruling council that their planet will soon explode. Jor-El and his wife, Lara (York), send their infant son, Kal-El, to Earth and safety via an odd spaceship that looks like a Christmas tree ornament. (The special effects are excellent throughout, and won a special Oscar.)

Adopted by a farming couple (Ford, Thaxter) and given the name Clark, the boy from Krypton gradually develops powers and abilities far beyond those of mortal men. When Pa Kent dies, the adolescent Clark learns of his true origins from recorded messages left by the late Jor-El. Finally, he winds up in Metropolis, working as a reporter for the *Daily Planet* and keeping his identity as Superman a secret. He rounds up crooks, helps people, and in general performs miraculous, beneficial stunts—until he encounters supergenius criminal Lex Luthor . . .

This stirring, handsome movie gets almost everything right in adapting the famous comic book character created by Jerry Siegel and Joe Shuster (when they were teenagers) to the big screen. Christopher Reeve makes a splendid Superman, handsome, heroic, sincere, and unsophisticated without being naive. He's less impressive as Clark Kent—it's hard to imagine anyone would swallow his big handsome dork portrayal. Margot Kidder is a delightful Lois Lane: spunky, sassy, and daring. But while Gene Hackman's performance as Lex Luthor is terrific, the conception of Luthor seems wrong; in fact, everything centering on the villains plays like a sendup, a spoof of comic book material. Children who love comic books and the 1990s *Superman* TV cartoon series may find these comic bad guys more annoying and inappropriate than anything else.

Fortunately, they don't occupy much of the movie, which is made on a grand scale with an amazing cast. It's ideal family viewing.

This smash hit produced several sequels of diminishing quality; in fact, some of **Superman II** was shot simultaneously with this film. The main villains from the sequel are briefly seen here.

SUPERMAN II (1980)
Color, 127 minutes
Cast: Christopher Reeve, Gene Hackman, Margot Kidder, Terence Stamp, Ned Beatty, Jackie Cooper, Sarah Douglas, Jack O'Halloran, Valerie Perrine, Susannah York, Clifton James, E. G. Marshall, Marc McClure.
Director: Richard Lester
Screenplay: Mario Puzo, David Newman, and Leslie Newman, based on characters created by Jerry Siegel and Joe Shuster

Science fiction/Superhero adventure
Rated PG
Young children: OK   Older children: OK

General Zod (Stamp), Ursa (Douglas), and Non (O'Halloran), three murderous villains that Jor-El had imprisoned in the Phantom Zone (as seen in **Superman**), are accidentally freed when the Zone passes near Earth. Realizing they now have superpowers, the three head for Earth, intent on conquest. Unfortunately, it's at the same time that Clark Kent (Reeve), having fallen in love with fellow reporter Lois Lane (Kidder), has relinquished his own superpowers, in order to live with Lois as a normal human being. With the assistance of Lex Luthor (Hackman), the three villains wreak havoc on Earth, while Clark tries to regain his superstrength.

Far jokier than *Superman,* this sequel often ignores forty years of comic book history and gives the villains—as well as Superman himself—new, ridiculous, even contradictory superabilities. At times, though, the movie does rise to the level of the first, particularly in the spectacular, climax, when Superman battles the three villains in the streets of Metropolis. Reeve is more comfortable in his dual roles than he seemed to be in the first film; Kidder is the very embodiment of spunk; and Hackman is again excellent as a Luthor the likes of which never graced a comic book panel.

The more deeply your kids are into the Superman mythos, the more they'll find to complain about in this film, but they'll still enjoy it.

The villainy is particularly mean-spirited here, and the threats both to Superman and Metropolis are played menacingly enough to possibly upset younger kids.

SUPERMAN III (1983)
Color, 123 minutes
Cast: Christopher Reeve, Richard Pryor, Jackie Cooper, Marc McClure, Annette O'Toole, Robert Vaughn, Pamela Stephenson, Annie Ross, Margot Kidder.
Director: Richard Lester
Screenplay: David Newman and Leslie Newman, based on characters created by Jerry Siegel and Joe Shuster
Science fiction/Superhero comedy
Rated PG
Young children: OK   Older children: OK

This time, Superman's enemy is multinational businessman Ross Webster (Vaughn), who uses crooked computer expert Gus Gorman (Pryor) to try to gain control of the world coffee market. Superman (Reeve) thwarts this takeover attempt, so Webster decides to go after the Man of Steel himself. Lois Lane (Kidder) is on vacation, while Clark Kent returns to Smallville to find himself attracted all over again to his high school sweetheart, Lana Lang (O'Toole).

This was made on a much lower budget than either of the first two Superman features with Reeve, and it shows it badly. The effects are inadequate, and the costarring cast lacks the prestige and panache of the earlier films. The casting of Richard Pryor was seen as a gimmick at the time, but his (mostly adult) fans were disappointed to find that the character he played had none of this brilliant comedian's unique sensibilities. He was merely an actor here, playing a mediocre part.

But the real defect with *Superman III* is that director Lester and his screenwriters simply refuse to take the hero or his universe seriously, and their comedy approach is satiric, not affectionate. It's as if they decided that everything *bad* about the first two movies should be the basis of the third one. It did badly at the box office and essentially ended the Superman franchise, although another sequel limped into theaters several years later.

Very young children may not notice the trashing of the Superman legend; Superman is just too powerful a figure for kids to regard as a joke. But anyone older than 10 or so is likely to be very disappointed in this movie.

SUPERMAN IV: THE QUEST FOR PEACE (1987)
Color, 90 minutes
Cast: Christopher Reeve, Gene Hackman, Jackie Cooper, Marc McClure, Jon Cryer, Sam Wanamaker, Mariel Hemingway, Margot Kidder
Director: Sidney J. Furie
Screenplay: Lawrence Kohner and Mark Rosenthal, from a screen story by Kohner, Rosenthal, and Christopher Reeve, based on the characters created by Jerry Siegel and Joe Shuster
Science fiction/Superhero adventure
Rated PG
Young children: OK   Older children: OK

When tycoon Warfield (Wanamaker) takes over the *Daily Planet*, he makes his own daughter, Lacy (Hemingway), publisher, and she develops a crush on Clark Kent (Reeve). Meanwhile, a letter from a small boy convinces Superman to destroy all the nuclear weapons on Earth, which he does by flinging them into the sun. But then, hoping to revive the arms race, Lex Luthor (Hackman) and his bratty nephew, Lenny (Cryer), use one of Superman's hairs to create Nuclear Man, a supervillain.

Less of a deviation from the Superman mythos than *III*, and not as annoying, *IV* is still a disappointment. The sets and special effects are mediocre, and there's a general hangdog air about it. In fact, the film wasn't released in the United States for some time after it was completed, and then in a shortened version that cut out a second Nuclear Man from the plot!

Leading man Reeve helped devise the plot of this film, and it's clear that he still enjoys playing the Man of Steel. That sincerity gives the picture what little oomph it has.

SUPPORT YOUR LOCAL SHERIFF! (1969)
Color, 92 minutes
Cast: James Garner, Joan Hackett, Walter Brennan, Harry Morgan, Jack Elam, Bruce Dern, Henry Jones, Gene Evans
Director: Burt Kennedy
Screenplay: William Bowers
Comedy/Western
Rated G
Younger kids: Good   Older kids: VG

One of the sleeper hits of its era, this is a wry and very likable little Western that treads a fine line between comic action and outright parody. In a role that's reminiscent of the easygoing charmer he played on TV's *Maverick*, James Garner is in top form as Jason McCullough, a stranger passing through the wide open gold rush town of Calender, Colorado, on his way to Australia. In need of money, Jason accepts the sheriff's job (despite its three previous officer holders having recently bitten the dust) and makes the town drunk (Jack Elam) his deputy. Exerting as little energy as possible, he uses his wits (along with some ropes, rocks, and other nontraditional weapons) to clean up the town, outsmart the villainous patriarch (Walter Brennan) of the dastardly Danby clan, and woo the mayor's klutzy daughter (Joan Hackett).

The performances are a joy to behold in this affectionate, good-natured spoof that turns typical Western clichés on their ears while offering parodies of *My Darling Clementine*, *Destry Rides Again*, **High Noon,** *Rio Bravo,* and other classics of the genre. Kids won't have to have seen those films to appreciate the high spirits and sheer fun this movie has to offer.

SUSANNAH OF THE MOUNTIES (1939)
Black & white (originally released in Sepiatone), 78 minutes (also available in a computer-colored version)
Cast: Shirley Temple, Randolph Scott, Margaret Lockwood, Martin Good Rider, J. Farrell MacDonald, Maurice Moscovich, Moroni Olsen, Victor Jory
Director: William A. Seiter
Screenplay: Robert Ellis and Helen Logan, based on a story by Fidel La Barba and Walter Ferris, and the novel *Susannah, a Little Girl of the Mounties* by Muriel Denison
Drama
Unrated
Young children: VG Older children: VG

Shirley Temple delivers a sincere performance as Susannah, a young girl who has been orphaned during an Indian massacre and then adopted by two Canadian Mounties. Her adventures as she grows up at the Mounties' post in the always dangerous Northwest Indian Territory of the 1880s are the basis for this exciting adventure. At the time, the Canadian Pacific Railroad was being constructed, and one element of the plot deals with bad Indians stealing horses from the railroad. Some of the ways in which these Indians are depicted are straight out of old-fashioned cowboy-and-Indian dime novels; however, there are also solid portrayals of good Indians.

Shirley was 11 years old when she made this film, so her character even has a young boyfriend, the son of an Indian Chief who temporarily lives at the post. Because of her advancing age, Shirley had to rely on more than golden curls, dimples, and childlike charm to win the audience, and she does it credibly. Even so, her character sometimes is a bit too bossy to be a role model to any juvenile viewer.

THE SWAN PRINCESS (1994)
Color, 90 minutes
Cast: Voices of Michelle Nicastro, Jack Palance, John Cleese, Steven Wright, Howard McGillin, Steve Vinovich, Sandy Duncan
Director: Richard Rich
Screenplay: Brian Nissen
Animated feature/Musical
Rated G
Younger kids: OK   Older kids: No interest

A beautifully mounted animated production based on German fairy tale (Swan Lake), *The Swan Princess* will enchant young children but leave others wishing for more. Prince Derek and Princess Odette, destined to marry, are separated by evil enchanter, Rothbart, who has cast a spell on the princess. Banished from his kingdom years before for treason, Rothbart transforms Odette into a swan; only moonlight on her wings can restore her human form at night. Derek can defeat the spell with his love but must first battle the forces of black magic. Needless to say, good triumphs over evil and they live happily ever after.

All the visual elements are here, but they are flattened by the clichéd story and David Zippel's lackluster songs. Broadway-style musical numbers don't seem to belong in the midst of classical fairy-tale trappings, and the celebrity voices (John Cleese, Jack Palance, and Steven Wright) barely register. A pleasant film, but nothing more.

Followed by two direct-to-video sequels.

SWING KIDS (1993)
Color, 112 minutes
Cast: Robert Sean Leonard, Christian Bale, Frank Whaley, Barbara Hershey, Kenneth Branagh, Tushka Bergen, David Tom, Julia Stemberger, Jayce Bartok, Noah Wyle
Director: Thomas Carter
Screenplay: Jonathan Marc Feldman
Drama/Musical
Rated PG-13
Younger children: No   Older children: OK

Swing Kids is an odd, historically inaccurate film about swing-dancing, music-loving teenagers growing up in Nazi Germany.

The story focuses on three young men (Robert Sean Leonard, Christian Bale, Frank Whaley) whose passion for American pop music (Count Basie, Artie Shaw, Benny Goodman, etc.), zoot suits, and jitterbug dancing opposes the "Aryan" culture being propagated by the Hitler Youth movement. (Basie and some of the other key musicians of the time are black, which in Hitler's world was verboten.)

The story turns tragic as Nazi Youth propaganda and the Gestapo enter their lives and break them apart. The music and dancing sequences stand out and are the only reason to see *Swing Kids*. It's a pretty superficial slice of history and a story with too many holes in it to have much impact.

There is some violence and strong language, enough to earn a PG-13 rating.

SWING TIME (1936)
Black & white, 105 minutes
Cast: Fred Astaire, Ginger
  Rogers, Victor Moore, Helen
  Broderick, Eric Blore, Betty
  Furness, George Metaxa,
  Landers Stevens
Director: George Stevens
Screenplay: Howard Lindsay and
  Allan Scott, based on a story
  by Erwin Gelsey
Musical
Unrated
Young children: VG Older
  children: VG

Just about any Fred Astaire–
Ginger Rogers musical is guaranteed to produce a smile. *Swing
Time* is perhaps their very best, a
delightful romp in which Fred
plays Lucky Garnett, a dancer
and gambler who seems to be forever garbed in tuxedo and top
hat. At the outset, Lucky is late
for his wedding, and the father of
the bride demands that he set out
to earn an honest dollar and
prove that he is more than just
a shiftless good-for-nothing. Upon
meeting pert Penelope Carroll
(Ginger), a dance instructor,
Lucky finds that he is in love—
but not with his fiancée.

All of the musical numbers in
Swing Time are knockouts. The
Jerome Kern–Dorothy Fields
score is highlighted by "Pick
Yourself Up" (in which Penny/
Ginger attempts to teach Lucky/
Fred how to dance!), "A Fine Romance," and the lilting "The Way
You Look Tonight," which won
an Oscar. One of Astaire's all-
time best solos is the eye-popping
"Bojangles of Harlem," designed
as a tribute to the great black tap
dancer Bill "Bojangles" Robinson. (This is the only instance in
which Astaire performed on

screen in blackface, which was designed here as an homage, not a
caricature.)

If your kids have never seen
Fred and Ginger before, just show
them the "Pick Yourself Up"
number and see if they don't get
hooked.

SWISS FAMILY ROBINSON
(1960)
Color, 128 minutes
Cast: John Mills, Dorothy
  McGuire, James MacArthur,
  Janet Munro, Sessue
  Hayakawa, Tommy Kirk,
  Kevin Corcoran
Director: Ken Annakin
Screenplay: Lowell S. Hawley,
  based on the novel by Johann
  Wyss
Action-adventure
Rated G
Younger kids: VG Older kids:
  VG

Walt Disney's version of Johann
Wyss' classic adventure novel
about an 18th-century clan shipwrecked in the South Pacific is
jaunty family entertainment on a
grand scale. John Mills and Dorothy McGuire play the heads of the
Robinson family, who, along with
their three sons and numerous
pets, are stranded on a remote
tropical island after their ship is
destroyed by a storm at sea. On
the island, they build an elaborate
tree house and a rock fortress,
and befriend an old sea captain
and his granddaughter who are
also castaways, but their Pacific
paradise is threatened by the arrival of pirates.

Beautifully filmed on the island
of Tobago in the West Indies, this
is a wonderful film, brimming
with charm, good humor, and
high spirits. Purists could say, ac-

curately, that the original novel has been Disneyfied; for example, the pirate threats eventually pay off in a battle that becomes downright silly. Young viewers are likely to be uncritical, however, as this is the ultimate wish-fulfillment movie, showing how the Robinsons use their ingenuity to tame nature and create a paradise in their tree house and environment.

THE SWORD AND THE ROSE (1953)
Color, 93 minutes
Cast: Richard Todd, Glynis Johns, James Robertson Justice, Michael Gough, Jane Barrett
Director: Ken Annakin
Screenplay: Lawrence E. Watkin, based on the novel *When Knighthood Was in Flower* by Charles Major
Adventure/Historical
Rated PG
Younger kids: OK   Older kids: Good

This is an unusually serious historical Walt Disney drama dealing with the romance between Mary Tudor (Glynis Johns) and dashing commoner Charles Brandon (Richard Todd). Mary has Charles appointed Captain of the Guards and then tries to run away with him, but her brother, King Henry VIII (James Robertson Justice), forces her to marry the aged King of France (Jean Mercure), who soon dies. When Mary returns home, she discovers that the Duke of Buckingham (Michael Gough) is in love with her and has plotted to kill Charles, but Charles lives and comes to the rescue of his lady fair.

Although the film is largely fiction from a historical point of view, it was opulently filmed in England with a fine sense of period detail, and the story is an entertaining mix of action, romance, and royal intrigue. Young kids may well be bored, but older children—especially those with an interest in historical tales—might like it.

THE SWORD IN THE STONE (1963)
Color, 75 minutes
Cast: Voices of Ricky Sorenson, Sebastian Cabot, Karl Swenson, Junius Matthews, Alan Napier, Norman Alden, Martha Wentworth
Director: Wolfgang Reitherman
Screenplay: Bill Peet, based on the book by T. H. White
Animated feature/Fantasy/ Action-adventure
Rated G
Younger kids: VG   Older kids: VG

The legend of King Arthur and his fabled sword Excalibur are the subjects of this Disney cartoon feature. It isn't among the studio's best, but it's still pretty enjoyable for youngsters who enjoy tales of medieval knights. The story begins with a young scullery boy and knight's squire named Wart meeting up with Merlin the Magician, who grows fond of the lad and decides to educate him, with the help of his talking owl, Archimedes. They have a series of magical adventures, during which Merlin turns the boy into a fish, a squirrel, and a bird, and engages in a wizard's duel with a witch called Madame Mim. One day, Wart forgets to bring a sword for his knight's big jousting match and has to quickly find a replacement. Spotting a sword imbedded in a nearby stone, Wart easily slides it out, unaware that this is the legendary sword of which it has been prophesied that whoever can pull it out will become the next king.

The Sword in the Stone is fine entertainment for kids, with plenty of action and some amusing set pieces, including Wart's various animal incarnations and a scene in which Merlin makes the tea kettle and sugar bowl dance, and gets the dishes to wash themselves. Merlin's duel with Madame Mim is a comic and artistic highlight, as the two wizards duke it out by transforming into crocodiles, turtles, rabbits, worms, roosters, elephants, tigers, snakes, crabs, and rhinos, finally ending when Merlin turns himself into a germ to fell Mim's dragon. The finale, in which Wart pulls the sword from the stone is also nicely done, and surprisingly, is quite similar to the corresponding scene in John Boorman's classy, adult version of the story, *Excalibur* (1981).

T

TABLE FOR FIVE (1983)
Color, 122 minutes
Cast: Jon Voight, Richard
   Crenna, Marie-Christine
   Barrault, Millie Perkins, Kevin
   Costner
Director: Robert Lieberman
Screenplay: David Seltzer
Drama
Rated PG
Young children: OK   Older
   children: VG

A guilt-ridden dad, already distraught over being divorced, takes
his three kids on a Mediterranean
cruise, only to learn on vacation
that his ex-wife has died.

Voight's grief turns the trip into
a heart-stabber, as he palpably
shows the torn emotions of J. P.
Tanner, a man who used to be an
absentee father, now deep in des-
olation, trying to reunite with his
growing children.

Attempting to be both dad and
mom, he finds more trouble when
the late mother's new husband
decides to wrestle J. P. for custody rights. Embattled on all
fronts, the tears start to flow, and
so will yours.

Encourage your brood to bring
their own stock of Kleenex.

This is an excellent tearjerker,
with Voight in a moving performance as a man who's trying to
do the right thing. Some of the
issues he grapples with may be
too mature (or difficult) for young
children to deal with, however.

TAKE ME OUT TO THE
BALL GAME (1949)
Color, 93 minutes
Cast: Frank Sinatra, Esther
   Williams, Gene Kelly, Betty
   Garrett, Edward Arnold, Jules
   Munshin, Richard Lane, Tom
   Dugan
Director: Busby Berkeley
Screenplay: Harry Tugend and
   George Wells, based on a
   story by Gene Kelly and
   Stanley Donen
Musical/Sports
Unrated
Younger kids: VG   Older kids:
   VG

This baseball musical isn't one of
the top-drawer MGM musicals,
but it's still likable and entertaining, and offers an appealing
glimpse into the worlds of old-
time vaudeville and baseball.

The setting is the turn of the
20th century, and Gene Kelly,
Frank Sinatra, and Jules Munshin
are cast as Eddie O'Brien, Dennis
Ryan, and Nat Goldberg, who form
three quarters of the infield of the
Wolves, the reigning world champs.
In the off-season, O'Brien and Ryan
are vaudeville entertainers. When
they arrive at spring training, they
discover, to their chagrin, that K. C.
Higgins (Esther Williams), the new
owner of the Wolves, is a woman!
(This was as unlikely in 1949, when
the film was made, as it would have
been at the turn of the century.)

Take Me out to the Ball Game
is filled with spirited musical rou-

tines, from the title tune (sung by Kelly and Sinatra) to the comical "O'Brien to Ryan to Goldberg," a clever Tinker-to-Evers-to-Chance takeoff performed by Kelly, Sinatra, and Munshin.

With colorful characters and lively songs, this should appeal to kids of all ages.

A TALE OF TWO CITIES
(1935)
Black & white, 128 minutes
Cast: Ronald Colman, Elizabeth Allan, Edna May Oliver, Reginald Owen, Basil Rathbone, Blanche Yurka, Isabel Jewell, Walter Catlett, Henry B. Walthall, H. B. Warner, Donald Woods
Director: Jack Conway
Screenplay: W. P. Lipscomb and S. N. Behrman, based on the novel by Charles Dickens
Historic drama/Literary classic
Unrated
Young children: OK   Older children: VG

Dickens' masterpiece about Sydney Carton (perfectly played by Ronald Colman), an amiable young lawyer who becomes caught up in the defense of those being put to death during the French Revolution, may be too bleak and disturbing for sensitive young children, who might be frightened by the horrors of the Reign of Terror. Scenes of the blood-hungry rabble gathered around the guillotine and a dramatic sequence of the storming of the Bastille are quite chilling, even though no extreme violence is pictured.

Parents may wish to discuss the history of the French Revolution with younger family members before viewing the film to place the content into a clear framework. However, adolescents and teenagers will be more engrossed in the story, which is at once political, romantic, humanistic, and almost unrelenting in intensity. The story is told on a scale rarely achieved in modern-day moviemaking, with an intelligent script and a hand-picked cast. It is a fine example of how Hollywood could, on occasion, do justice to a great book without much compromise.

What makes this film so significant for young people is its inspiring philosophy of loyalty and friendship, and holding on to one's beliefs no matter what the consequences.

TALES FROM THE CRYPT
(1972)
Color, 92 minutes
Cast: Joan Collins, Peter Cushing, Roy Dotrice, Richard Greene, Ian Hendry, Patrick Magee, Barbara Murray, Nigel Patrick, Robin Phillips, Ralph Richardson, David Markham, Robert Hutton, Chloe Franks
Director: Freddie Francis
Screenplay: Milton Subotsky, from E.C. Comics stories by Johnny Craig, Al Feldstein, and William M. Gaines
Horror/Anthology
Rated PG
Young children: No   Older children: OK

In the early 1950s, William M. Gaines, head of E.C. Comics, began producing a series of horror comics that quickly became immensely popular. They were well written and well drawn, with a morbid but outrageous sense of humor that no one else seemed quite able to duplicate.

A series of paperback reprints

in the 1960s led directly to this film, which is very different from the much later TV series and movies. It's sleek, well produced, and not anywhere near so gleefully ghastly. In the first story, "All Through the House," a woman (Collins) who has just murdered her husband is herself pursued by a madman dressed as Santa Claus. In "Reflection of Death," a man (Hendry) awakens after a horrible automobile wreck and tries to return to his mistress; he's puzzled why everyone he passes screams in horror.

"Poetic Justice" deals with a nice old junkman (Cushing), beloved by the local children, who refuses to sell his property to a greedy father and son, so they come up with a vicious scheme. In "Wish You Were Here," a woman (Murray) uses a Chinese curio to wish her husband (Greene) back to life after he's killed in a car wreck, with terrible results. In "Blind Alley," a martinet (Patrick) takes over a home for the blind, then abuses and neglects the residents while lining his pockets. The residents plan their own form of revenge.

This was one of the unexpected hits of 1972, the most popular film in the history of Amicus Productions, the major rival to Hammer Films. It's a well-made, amusing movie, but with its grim goings-on, not suited for younger children. Older kids who already are familiar with the TV series might find this somewhat tame.

THE TALES OF HOFFMANN
(1951)
Color, 125 minutes
Cast: Robert Rounseville, Moira Shearer, Robert Helpmann, Leonide Massine, Pamela Brown, Frederick Ashton, Ludmilla Tcherina, Ann Ayars
Directors: Michael Powell and Emeric Pressburger
Screenplay: Powell and Pressburger
Opera/Ballet
Unrated
Young children: OK Older children: VG

From the creators of **The Red Shoes** comes an even more imaginative work of art, a fanciful one-of-a-kind visual and aural extravaganza based on Jacques Offenbach's 1881 French opera.

In a Nuremberg tavern, Hoffmann (the actual author of *The Nutcracker*) gloomily reminisces about his misadventures in love. There was lovely Olympia, a woman so perfect he couldn't see she was really a mechanical doll. There was seductive Giulietta in Venice, who tried to steal his reflection for her master, the Devil. And there was devoted but frail Antonia in Munich, who died when Hoffmann encouraged her to sing. Now he waits for the great ballerina Stella to arrive from the theater next door. Will he be thwarted again?

While these stories may not appear to be the stuff of which dreams are made, in fact this resplendent movie captivates from beginning to end. Endlessly inventive and with at least one superb aria in each act, it is a striking and offbeat accomplishment.

For children it will seem like a fairy tale. For adults it will be a highly stylized exercise in cinematic brilliance. For anyone who loves great music, dance, and color, it will be a memorable experience.

TALES OF TERROR (1962)
Color, 90 minutes
Cast: Vincent Price, Peter Lorre, Basil Rathbone, Joyce Jameson, Debra Paget, David Frankham
Director: Roger Corman
Screenplay: Richard Matheson, from works by Edgar Allan Poe: "Morella," "The Black Cat," "The Cask of Amontillado," and "The Facts in the Case of M. Valdemar"
Horror/Anthology
Unrated
Young children: Probably not   Older children: OK

This entry in Roger Corman's series of Edgar Allan Poe films consists of three stories, each starring Vincent Price. The first, "Morella," is a routine spirits-possess-the-living tale; the second, "The Black Cat," costars Peter Lorre and is a broad but funny comedy about the revenge of a habitual drunk; in the last, "The Facts in the Case of M. Valdemar," an evil hypnotist (Rathbone) mesmerizes a man on the moment of death and keeps him at that point for months.

Not the best of the Poe series, *Tales of Terror* is, however, the busiest, with three (actually four) stories to rush through in 90 minutes. The final story features a pretty gruesome makeup for Price, but it's only glimpsed, never clearly seen; otherwise, the film is OK for those kids from 10 up who are already into horror movies.

TALL TALE (1995)
Color, 96 minutes
Cast: Patrick Swayze, Oliver Platt, Roger Aaron Brown, Nick Stahl, Scott Glenn, Stephen Lang, Jared Harris, Catherine O'Hara, Scott Wilson
Director: Jeremiah Chechik
Screenplay: Steven L. Bloom and Robert Roddat
Fantasy adventure
Rated PG
Younger kids: OK, with caution   Older kids: OK

Tall Tale is a film that promises much more than it delivers. A revisionist look at some beloved American folk tales, it has an alarmingly downbeat tone.

Set in the Midwest at the turn of the century, the story focuses on young Daniel Hackett, who's tired of the hard work on his father's farm and intrigued with the modern era of electric lights and horseless carriages. His father is opposed to selling his land to ruthless developer J. P. Stiles. A shooting incident with Stiles leaves his father wounded, and Daniel takes off to protect the deed to the land.

Lost in the desert, Daniel encounters characters from his father's old tall tales—Pecos Bill (Patrick Swayze), Paul Bunyan (Oliver Platt), and John Henry (Roger Aaron Brown)—who agree to help Daniel and his neighbors against Stiles and his plans.

Slow-moving and melancholy, *Tall Tale* has some good performances (particularly by the folk heroes, including Catherine O'Hara in a much too brief appearance as Calamity Jane) but little else to recommend it.

Young viewers are likely to find it slow and generally unsatisfying. They're much better off watching Disney's animated versions of the stories of Pecos Bill, Paul Bunyan, and John Henry, which capture the wonder and delight of those enduring tall tales.

TAP (1989)
Color, 110 minutes
Cast: Gregory Hines, Suzzanne Douglas, Sammy Davis, Jr., Savion Glover, Joe Morton, Dick Anthony Williams, Terrence McNally, Sandman Sims, Bunny Briggs, Steve Condos, Jimmy Slyde, Pat Rico, Arthur Duncan, Harold Nicholas, Etta James
Director: Nick Castle
Screenplay: Nick Castle
Musical drama
Rated PG-13
Young children: OK, with caution   Older children: VG

This diverting film is a heartfelt tribute to the joys of tap dancing. Its scenario involves Max Washington (a perfectly cast Gregory Hines), a tap dancer turned jewel thief. He sees no future as a hoofer, and the story spotlights the way he is drawn back into the dancing life.

The story is serviceable, but it's little more than a framework for the dance sequences. For starters, Hines taps with an electricity and intensity that sets him apart from everyone else in the film. Sammy Davis, Jr., in his final film appearance, is a treat to watch as Little Mo. The cast is peppered with such old-time hoofers as Sandman Sims, Bunny Briggs, Steve Condos, Jimmy Slyde, Pat Rico, Arthur Duncan, and Harold Nicholas (of the Nicholas Brothers), all of whose characters are based on themselves.

Finally, the presence of young Savion Glover, who has since gone on to dance on Broadway in such shows as *Bring In Da Noise/ Bring In Da Funk,* offers proof that tap will not die off with these veterans.

There is some strong language, and adult situations relating to the film's inner-city setting, which earned this a PG-13.

TARANTULA (1955)
Black & white, 80 minutes
Cast: John Agar, Leo G. Carroll, Mara Corday, Nestor Paiva, Ross Elliott
Director: Jack Arnold
Screenplay: Robert M. Fresco and Martin Berkeley, from a teleplay by Fresco and Arnold
Science fiction/Monsters
Unrated
Young kids: OK   Older kids: Good

Reclusive scientist Carroll, trying to find a way to feed the growing population of the world, creates a growth serum that he tries out on various animals, including a desert tarantula. He's sidetracked when his dying assistant, who previously tested the drug on himself, injects Carroll with the serum, too. During their scuffle, a fire kills all the enlarged animals except the tarantula, which escapes into the desert and keeps on growing. Soon horses, cattle, and then people, begin disappearing. . . .

A tight, well-made film that isn't up to the level of its inspiration, **Them!,** it is still one of the best "giant bug" movies of the 1950s. Younger kids won't be as disturbed by this one as by **Them!,** partly because no kids are in danger, and partly because the spider is so huge that it's a remote menace. The variable special effects also diminish the power of the film to scare, but they're *just* good enough.

Incidentally, the pilot who na-palms the giant spider at the climax is Clint Eastwood.

TARZAN, THE APE MAN
(1932)
Black & white, 99 minutes
Cast: Johnny Weissmuller,
  Maureen O'Sullivan, Neil
  Hamilton, C. Aubrey Smith,
  Doris Lloyd
Director: W. S. Van Dyke
Screenplay: Cyril Hume and Ivor
  Novello, based on characters
  created by Edgar Rice
  Burroughs
Action-adventure
Unrated
Younger kids: OK Older kids:
  Good

MGM's first Tarzan production and the character's first full-length sound movie was also the first for the best of all the Tarzans, Johnny Weissmuller, the former two-time Olympic swimming champion who played Edgar Rice Burroughs' pulp-fiction jungle man in twelve movies. In this entry, Tarzan meets Jane (Maureen O'Sullivan) for the first time when she's captured by him after venturing into the jungle with her English father (C. Aubrey Smith) and her boyfriend (Neil Hamilton), who are in search of an ivory-rich elephants' graveyard. Naturally, Jane falls in love with the big ape (Tarzan, that is) and sets up a jungle love-nest with him and Cheetah the Chimp.

An entertaining film, to be sure, this may seem primitive in more ways than one to modern-day children. Beyond the British colonial attitudes toward natives and the 1930s view of womanhood, there is the obvious use of stock footage in many of the wild ani-mal sequences in addition to some fairly laughable attempts at special effects. However, the basic story is still solid—and (goodness knows) has been copied many times since—and the winning personalities of Weissmuller and O'Sullivan shine through.

TARZAN AND HIS MATE
(1934)
Black & white, 105 minutes
Cast: Johnny Weissmuller,
  Maureen O'Sullivan, Neil
  Hamilton, Paul Cavanagh
Directors: Cedric Gibbons (and
  Jack Conway, uncredited)
Screenplay: James Kevin
  McGuinness, Howard Emmett
  Rogers, and Leon Gordon,
  based on characters created by
  Edgar Rice Burroughs
Action-adventure
Unrated
Younger kids: No Older kids:
  Good

Tarzan and His Mate, the second entry of MGM's Johnny Weissmuller series, is hands down the best of all the Tarzan movies, featuring a strong story about ivory poaching, fierce action scenes, and excellent photography and special effects. The plot involves Jane's ex-beau (Neil Hamilton) returning to the jungle with a fellow hunter (Paul Cavanagh), bringing perfume and the latest Paris fashions to try to lure Jane (Maureen O'Sullivan) back to him. (This provides a fascinating subtext contrasting the jungle's "savagery" with his supposed "civilization.")

The two men are also searching for an ivory-rich elephant burial ground and trick Tarzan into helping them find it. Along the way, there's some furious action as Tarzan wrestles a lion, rides a rhino like a bucking bronco while stabbing it, fights with an alligator, and leads a herd of stampeding elephants in the rip-roaring climax. One of the vividly violent battle scenes features a native being tied to a tree as lions try to devour him!

The film is also marked by an intense eroticism—notable for its time, though considerably tamer today. The film ran into censorship problems when it was first released, mostly due to a notorious nude swimming sequence, which was cut but then later restored to the print. In the scene, Jane (doubled here by Olympic swimmer Josephine McKim) goes skinny-dipping with the clothed Tarzan, but the bubbles and underwater darkness obscure her body, apart from a few fleeting shots from behind and the side. Even without this scene, however, the film focuses on the primal relationship between the hunky jungle man and the erstwhile English Rose, who now runs around in various states of undress and wears a skimpy loincloth that exposes her hips and thighs. It's all handled in a perfectly innocent and nonprurient manner, and the amount of exposed flesh is less than kids see nowadays in a typical music video.

As always, native warriors are depicted in stereotyped fashion, but this film is not the place to seek social enlightenment. It's a source of robust adventure, too potent for young children but certain to entertain older kids.

TARZAN ESCAPES (1936)
Black & white, 89 minutes
Cast: Johnny Weissmuller, Maureen O'Sullivan, John Buckler, Benita Hume, William Henry, Herbert Mundin
Director: Richard Thorpe
Screenplay: Cyril Hume, based on characters created by Edgar Rice Burroughs
Action-adventure
Unrated
Younger kids: OK Older kids: VG

This third entry in the MGM Tarzan series with Johnny Weissmuller and Maureen O'Sullivan was actually filmed twice, but the first version (which was directed by O'Sullivan's real-life husband John Farrow) featured so many violent scenes of barbaric murders, giant devil bats, and other gruesome jungle horrors that children were supposedly terrified at preview screenings. So the studio made extensive edits and retakes, rendering the finished film more suitable for kids, but also narratively disjointed.

It also introduced a more domestic setting for Tarzan and Jane, giving them a cozy tree house replete with running water, an elephant-powered elevator, and a fan operated by Cheetah the chimp, who also provided a strong dose of juvenile comedy relief with his incessant cackling laugh and such antics as jumping onto the back of a zebra. What remains is a standard plot about a hunter trying to capture Tarzan and put him on display in England, but there are also traces of the original version during some vivid scenes involving the slaughter of native warriors and their violent falls from a cliff, human sacrifices in which victims are tied to a tree and launched into the air, a vicious knife fight between Tarzan and an antelope, and a grisly finale where the villainous hunter meets his death in a muddy swamp filled with huge lizards.

Some of this is still pretty potent today, and parents should bear that in mind.

TARZAN FINDS A SON!
(1939)
Black & white, 90 minutes
Cast: Johnny Weissmuller, Maureen O'Sullivan, Johnny Sheffield, Ian Hunter, Frieda Inescort, Laraine Day, Henry Wilcoxon
Director: Richard Thorpe
Screenplay: Cyril Hume, based on characters created by Edgar Rice Burroughs
Action-adventure
Unrated
Younger kids: Good   Older kids: Good

When a plane crashes in the jungle, Tarzan (Johnny Weissmuller) and Jane (Maureen O'Sullivan) rescue a baby and raise it as their own. (The unmarried jungle lovebirds were forbidden by Hollywood censors to have their own child since they were presumably living in sin.) Five years later, a search party arrives looking to establish the death of the child, who has come into a large inheritance in England. When they discover he's still alive, they plot to cheat him out of his fortune, but the scoundrels haven't counted on dealing with Tarzan.

After all the trouble MGM got into over the sexy **Tarzan and His Mate** and the violent **Tarzan Escapes,** they changed the series' tone entirely and geared it for family audiences, beginning with this entry, which introduced the character of Boy (played by Johnny Sheffield, who later starred in the *Bomba the Jungle Boy* series), and played up Cheetah the chimp's monkeyshines.

Though only moderately entertaining for adults, the result is a kids' fantasy come true, as Boy romps around the jungle and swings upside down on a vine, rides on the back of a baby elephant, gets caught in a giant spider web, and almost falls down a waterfall; inevitably, he is rescued by Tarzan. There are also some amusing moments where Cheetah milks a goat and the paternally challenged Tarzan tries to feed the baby a giant leg of raw meat. By this time in the series, the relationship between Tarzan and Jane was squeaky clean and his loincloth was much more revealing than her full-length jungle housedress.

TARZAN'S NEW YORK ADVENTURE (1942)
Black & white, 72 minutes
Cast: Johnny Weissmuller, Maureen O'Sullivan, John Sheffield, Virginia Grey, Charles Bickford, Paul Kelly, Chill Wills, Cy Kendall
Director: Richard Thorpe
Screenplay: Myles Connolly and William R. Lipman, based on a story by Connolly and characters created by Edgar Rice Burroughs
Action-adventure
Unrated
Younger kids: Good   Older kids: Good

The last entry in MGM's classic Tarzan series (and Maureen O'Sullivan's final appearance as Jane) is the campiest, but kids will love its mixture of outlandish action and animal antics. The story (which borrows heavily from **King Kong,** and which in turn influenced **"Crocodile" Dundee**) involves unscrupulous circus operators who come to Tarzan's jungle to trap some lions. When Boy (John Sheffield) demonstrates his skill at handling elephants, the villains try to do away with Tarzan and Jane, and abscond with Boy and his trained pachyderms. Tarzan immediately dons a suit and tie, and flies to Manhattan (or the "stone jungle" as he calls it). At first, he follows Jane's advice to let the law handle things, but when the bad guys find a loophole that allows them to keep Boy, the Ape Man takes matters into his own hands.

The premise of Tarzan in the big city makes for some cute moments. He's bewildered by telephones and radios, and steps into the hotel shower fully clothed. Later, when he takes the stand in court, he makes some clever observations contrasting the law of the jungle with that of civilization. Cheetah also gets a fair share of screen time, playing with water coolers and putting on Jane's makeup and nightgowns, but the scene where the mischievous chimp has a gibberish phone conversation with a black man (played by the wonderful character actor Mantan Moreland) is a tasteless and embarrassing example of the series' demeaning treatment of blacks.

TARZAN'S SECRET TREASURE (1941)

Black & white, 81 minutes
Cast: Johnny Weissmuller, Maureen O'Sullivan, John Sheffield, Reginald Owen, Barry Fitzgerald, Tom Conway
Director: Richard Thorpe

Screenplay: Myles Connolly and Paul Gangelin, based on characters created by Edgar Rice Burroughs
Action-adventure
Unrated
Younger kids: Good   Older kids: Good

The jungle high jinks of Cheetah and Boy (John Sheffield) get more screen time than Tarzan (Johnny Weissmuller) and Jane (Maureen O'Sullivan) in this juvenile adventure about a greedy band of explorers who invade Tarzan's backyard in search of gold. After Boy befriends a young native named Tumbo (Cordell Hickman), whose sick mother subsequently dies, the superstitious villagers blame Boy for the plague sweeping their land and try to kill him. Boy is rescued by a scientific expedition and unwittingly leads them back to the escarpment where Tarzan has discovered gold, but they're all captured by a savage tribe, and once again, it's up to Tarzan to save the day.

Although this is a relatively minor effort with a melodramatic plot, kids should enjoy it, as it affords plenty of opportunities for Weissmuller to show off his athletic abilities and swimming prowess. There's lots of silly comedy relief from Cheetah (who gets drunk in one scene) and some customary Irish blarney from Barry Fitzgerald as a kindly member of the expedition. Tarzan and Jane's immaculate jungle abode looks like something out of *House Beautiful,* replete with elaborate homemade kitchen appliances.

For once, the film's occasionally stereotyped treatment of the natives as savages is balanced by the nicely handled friendship between Boy and Tumbo.

TEENAGE MUTANT NINJA TURTLES (1990)
Color, 93 minutes
Cast: Judith Hoag, Elias Koteas, Josh Pais, Michelan Sisti, Leif Tilden, David Forman, Michael Turney, Jay Patterson, Raymond Serra, James Sato, Toshishiro Obata; voices of Robbie Rist, Kevin Clash, Brian Tochi, David McCharen, Michael McConnohie, Corey Feldman
Director: Steve Barron
Screenplay: Todd W. Langen and Bobby Herbeck, based on characters created by Kevin Eastman and Peter Laird
Fantasy action/Comedy-drama/ Martial arts
Rated PG
Young children: OK; probably unavoidable   Older children: OK

Evil ninja master the Shredder (Sato) is playing Fagin in New York City: he's recruited a gang of children to rob the city blind. Reporter April (Hoag) is unexpectedly befriended by four teenage mutant ninja turtles, streetwise reptiles who talk like junior high school dropouts, fight like Bruce Lee, and are named after classic painters: Raphael, Michelangelo, Donatello, and Leonardo.

They were regular turtles until mutated by atomic waste, and adopted by wise old rat Splinter, himself a mutation. When the Shredder kidnaps Splinter, the turtles, a vigilante (Koteas), and April team up to defeat the Shredder and his gang.

The beauty of the Turtles (who were introduced in a series of comic books) is that the youngest children take them as straight (if funny) heroes—brave, bold, and pizza-loving. Older children see them as originally intended, pretty sharp spoofs of superheroes. This cheesy-looking production is somewhat better, hipper even, than you'd expect, but mostly it follows well-worn grooves; it may miss some of the more promising aspects of Turtle Power, but it's still a sure bet to please kids.

Two sequels followed; the first, *Teenage Mutant Ninja Turtles II: The Secret of the Ooze* isn't even as interesting as the first, but the third, *Teenage Mutant Ninja Turtles III,* upped the ante, with a plot that involved time travel, lectures against violence, and very good exterior photography.

THE TEN COMMANDMENTS (1956)
Color, 220 minutes
Cast: Charlton Heston, Yul Brynner, Anne Baxter, Edward G. Robinson, Yvonne De Carlo, Debra Paget, John Derek, Cedric Hardwicke, H. B. Warner, Henry Wilcoxon, Nina Foch, Martha Scott, Judith Anderson, Vincent Price, John Carradine, Woody Strode
Director: Cecil B. DeMille
Screenplay: Aeneas MacKenzie, Jesse L. Lasky Jr., Jack Gariss, and Fredric M. Frank
Religion/Epic
Unrated
Younger kids: OK   Older kids: VG

With all due apologies to *Ben-Hur* (1959), Cecil B. DeMille's second version of *The Ten Commandments* (which he first filmed as a silent in 1923) stands for many as the apotheosis of 1950s Biblical epics—and it's certainly the most fun. Children may take it all quite seriously, but parents will chuckle at lines like "Oh Moses! You stubborn, splendid, adorable fool," a villainous Edward G. Robinson snarling, "Where's your messiah now?" and such campy scenes as the orgy of the Golden Calf. Indeed, the film has become a target for stand-up comics, yet it remains a stupendous example of the vanished genre of massive screen spectacle, featuring an all-star cast, a reported twenty-five thousand extras, colossal sets, and Oscar-winning special effects.

In the first of his many heroic, larger-than-life parts, Charlton Heston stars as Moses, whose life is traced from the time his mother set him afloat on the Nile, through his years as a young general in the Pharaoh's army, to his betrayal and exile, and finally, his deliverance of the Israelites and his receiving of God's commandments. The effects, though inevitably dated, were remarkable for their day and are still pretty effective. Among the highlights are sequences depicting the Plagues, Moses' staff turning into a serpent, the Burning Bush, the reception of the Ten Commandments on Mount Sinai, and the still impressive parting of the Red Sea.

Cecil B. DeMille might be considered corny, but he knew how to entertain an audience, and his best films still do just that. *The Ten Commandments* is extremely long, but it's seldom dull, and kids may find themselves getting hooked as the classic Biblical story is brought to life in such a colorful fashion.

TEX (1982)
Color, 103 minutes
Cast: Matt Dillon, Jim Metzler, Meg Tilly, Bill McKinney, Frances Lee McCain, Ben Johnson, Phil Brock, Emilio Estevez, Jack Thibeau
Director: Tim Hunter
Screenplay: Charles Haas and Hunter, based on the novel by S. E. Hinton
Drama
Rated PG
Young children: No Older children: VG

This is the first—and by far the best—of the films based on young-adult novels by S. E. Hinton that came to movie screens in the early 1980s. (The others are **The Outsiders** and *Rumble Fish*.) It is a simple, candid drama about 15-year-old Tex McCormick, a young man who for good reason is deeply troubled: His mother has died. His father, an itinerant rodeo performer, is constantly on the road and has no interest in providing for his sons. At the center of the story is Tex's relationship with Mason, his 17-year-old sibling, who is attempting to run their household, pay the bills, and deal with Tex's growing pains and increasing sense of desperation.

What makes Hinton's stories so appealing is that they depict adolescence from the adolescent's point of view. The pressures, misunderstandings, needs, desires, and insecurities of individuals entering adulthood all are present in ways that are cut-to-the-bone realistic, and this helps to make *Tex* an especially potent film for its intended audience.

that thing you do! (1996)
Color, 110 minutes
Cast: Tom Everett Scott, Liv
  Tyler, Johnathon Schaech,
  Steve Zahn, Ethan Embry,
  Tom Hanks, Charlize Theron,
  Bill Cobbs
Director: Tom Hanks
Screenplay: Tom Hanks
Musical/Comedy-drama
Rated PG
Young children: OK   Older
  children: VG

When rock 'n' roll was in its heyday, a young singing group could
(almost literally) be harmonizing
on a street corner on Saturday,
discovered on Monday, record a
couple of songs on Wednesday,
hear the "A" side of their 45 on
the radio on Friday, and have a
smash hit by the following Monday. One such scenario is depicted in *that thing you do!*, Tom
Hanks' appealing debut film as
writer-director.

The film is set in 1964, just as
The Beatles, The Rolling Stones,
and The Dave Clark 5 are leading
the British invasion on American
rock 'n' roll. Hanks tells the story
of the Oneders (pronounced
"Wonders," not "O-nee-ders"),
composed of four clean-cut young
men, each with a very different
personality, from Erie, Pennsylvania. The Oneders play at local
dances and appear in a pizza joint
in a town that has hardly changed
since the end of World War II.
Their rise to fame is strikingly
swift, and each member of the
band reacts differently to the sudden change in his life.

The song that catapults the
Oneders up the charts is titled
"That Thing You Do!" It's a
catchy, up-tempo tune that is

reminiscent of the early Beatles
and might easily have become a
hit had it been recorded in 1964.

that thing you do! is not a profound movie about the pitfalls of
life in the showbiz fast lane, but
it isn't meant to be. It's a sweet-
natured, entertaining look at
some one-hit wonders. Adults
who were around in the '60s will
respond to some of the knowing
references (and period detail)
here, but kids should also respond
to the universal appeal of the
story.

There's a smattering of four-
letter words, which accounts for
this film being rated PG.

THEM! (1954)
Black & white, 94 minutes
Cast: James Whitmore, Edmund
  Gwenn, James Arness, Joan
  Weldon, Fess Parker, Leonard
  Nimoy
Director: Gordon Douglas
Screenplay: Ted Sherdeman,
  based on a story by George
  Worthing Yates
Science fiction/Monsters
Unrated
Younger kids: Too
  intense   Older kids: VG

Mysterious deaths in the South-
western desert turn out to be the
result of eight-foot-long ants, mutated over generations by atomic
testing. As a team of scientists,
FBI agents, and the New Mexico
cop who was in from the beginning try to track down all the
giant insects, a colony of ants sets
up shop in the storm drains of
Los Angeles.

The first "giant bug" movie of
the 1950s is not only the best of
the breed but one of the best science fiction films of that sci-fi-
heavy decade. The premise is

built logically and structured for maximum suspense, even when the ants are nowhere to be seen. It's as dry and fast-paced as an episode of *Dragnet*, but has much more sympathetic characters. Younger children will be upset, partly because little kids are menaced by the ants at the opening and closing of the film, but also because the most likable character (Whitmore) ends up a victim of the giant insects.

The special effects are minimal, and sometimes the ants are not really very convincing, but the strong direction and taut script generally overcome that defect.

THE THIEF OF BAGDAD
(1924)
Black & white, 155 minutes
Cast: Douglas Fairbanks, Julanne Johnstone, Sojin, Anna May Wong, Snitz Edwards, Brandon Hurst
Director: Raoul Walsh
Screenplay: Elton Thomas (pseud. of Douglas Fairbanks)
Fantasy/Adventure/Silent classic
Unrated
Younger kids: Good Older kids: VG

"Happiness Must Be Earned," says the writing in the sky in this movie's first, storybooklike shot, setting the scene for a tale from the Arabian Nights, conceived and designed to be as fantastic as any fable ever spun on the printed page.

Douglas Fairbanks, the athletic star of such earlier silent-movie swashbucklers as **The Mark of Zorro,** *Robin Hood*, and **The Three Musketeers,** is in rare form here as the agile thief who's too quick-witted and fast on his feet for the people whose pocket he picks and food he pilfers. But when he sees the beautiful Princess (Julanne Johnston), he decides to set his sights higher than petty thievery and realizes that he must make himself worthy of this rare jewel. After disguising himself as a Prince, he embarks upon a lengthy quest to prove his mettle and return to her, not as a bogus prince, but as a genuine hero.

From the gargantuan sets (designed by the great William Cameron Menzies) to the broad, balletic acting style adopted by Fairbanks, *The Thief of Bagdad* is created in such a way as to take us all on a magic carpet ride away from reality.

It would be a shame to watch this film with modern eyes; its special effects have long since been surpassed. But its wonderful spirit, and the simplicity of its illusions, can still weave their magic spell if you approach the film with a willing sense of wonder and innocence.

Fairbanks battles a giant dragon, climbs a rope suspended in midair, flies on a magic carpet, and engages in all sorts of fantastic adventures in the course of this incredible film.

Seen in a good print, with appropriate music, this is the kind of movie that can win children over to the beauty and uniqueness of silent movies. It's a wonderful experience the whole family can share.

THE THIEF OF BAGDAD
(1940)
Color, 106 minutes
Cast: Sabu, Jon Justin, June Duprez, Conrad Veidt, Rex Ingram, Miles Malleson

Directors: Ludwig Berger, Tim Whelan, and Michael Powell
Screenplay: Lajos Biro and Miles Malleson
Adventure/Fantasy
Unrated
Younger kids: VG   Older kids: VG

This Arabian Nights tale is one of the greatest fantasies ever brought to the screen, a magical tour de force of extraordinarily imaginative sets, stunning special effects, and sumptuous Technicolor photography, all of which won Oscars. Some of these elements may seem a bit old-fashioned to modern eyes, but it's important to adopt a sense of wonder and belief, and get into the spirit of this fantasy adventure. Under the guidance of producer Alexander Korda, the film creates an intoxicatingly exotic fairy-tale atmosphere, replete with such wonders as a mechanical flying horse, a magic carpet, a giant genie, a huge spider that guards the all-seeing eye, and a six-armed dancing doll.

Sabu is delightful and winning as Abu the thief, and Conrad Veidt is deliciously wicked as the magician Jaffar, who turns Abu into a dog and blinds Ahmad, the Prince of Bagdad (John Justin) as part of his evil plan to win the heart of the Princess (June Duprez). All of the performances are marvelous, but Rex Ingram (a majestic and little-remembered African-American actor) is particularly memorable as the giant genie who grants Abu three wishes after being released from a bottle by him.

This is a perfect family film.

THE THING (FROM ANOTHER WORLD) (1951)
Black & white, 87 minutes
Cast: Kenneth Tobey, Margaret Sheridan, Robert Cornthwaite, Douglas Spencer, Dewey Martin, George Fenneman, James Arness
Director: Christian Nyby
Screenplay: Charles Lederer, from the novella "Who Goes There?" by Don A. Stuart (pseud. of John W. Campbell, Jr.)
Science fiction–horror/Suspense
Unrated
Young kids: No   Older kids: VG

Scientists and some military types find a crashed flying saucer, quick-frozen in Arctic ice. When the pilot of the wrecked spaceship thaws out of a giant block of ice, he (or it) sets out to reproduce by planting seeds, nourished with human blood . . .

A timeless classic in its field, *The Thing* is just as effective and terrifying today as it was when it was released. Fast-paced dialogue, strongly delineated characters, and escalating suspense will make this film a favorite of older kids who are already fond of science fiction. It's only very slightly dated, less so, actually, than the remake of 1982 (which is rated R). Younger kids are almost certain to be scared out of their wits, even if the movie is watched on a dim TV on a sunny afternoon.

Direction of the movie is credited to Christian Nyby, but all evidence strongly suggests that the film was actually directed by Howard Hawks, who took producing credit on it.

THINGS TO COME (1936)

Black & white, 96 minutes
Cast: Raymond Massey, Edward
  Chapman, Ralph Richardson,
  Margaretta Scott, Cedric
  Hardwicke, Sophie Stewart,
  Derrick De Marney, Ann
  Todd
Director: William Cameron
  Menzies
Screenplay: H. G. Wells
Science fiction/Epic
Unrated
Young children: OK Older
  children: OK

War breaks out in 1940 and continues unabated until 1966, leaving the world in ruins; a plague continues to kill thousands more. The city of Everytown is controlled by the tyrannical "Boss" (Richardson), who runs it with an iron fist. John Cabal (Massey), a scientist, arrives in a plane bringing promises of peace, but the Boss imprisons him. However, the tables are turned when Cabal escapes. Now the world is controlled by scientists and technicians, and becomes a gleaming paradise, led by Oswald Cabal (also Massey), a descendant of John. Theotocopulos (Hardwicke), a sculptor, leads a movement opposed to the rule of the Technocrats, protesting against Cabal's plan to send a couple into space.

This lavish film remains visually impressive, although the second half, set in 2036, looks more than a little silly. The opening segment, dealing with the Boss and his rule by force, is more interesting because it is less dated and because it has Richardson's powerful, convincing performance.

This was the first science fiction epic made in England. It was written by H. G. Wells himself and tends to be more than a little preachy. There's little in it to disturb children, but it's a very serious drama, and younger kids will be bored silly. Older children, especially those who are fond of *written* science fiction, will find more to interest them.

It's worth emphasizing to younger viewers that this film painted a world of the future; how closely does it resemble the world in which we live today?

A 1979 film called *The Shape of Things to Come* has nothing to do with this one, even though it bears the actual title of the Wells novel.

THIRD MAN ON THE MOUNTAIN (1959)

Color, 105 minutes
Cast: James MacArthur, Michael
  Rennie, Janet Munro, James
  Donald, Herbert Lom
Director: Ken Annakin
Screenplay: Eleanor Griffin,
  based on the novel *Banner in
  the Sky* by James Ramsey
  Ullman
Adventure
Unrated
Younger kids: Good Older
  kids: VG

This Walt Disney adventure film is one of the studio's best live-action films; why it isn't better known is something of a mystery. Set in 1865 and based on a true story, the film chronicles the efforts of an 18-year-old Swiss boy named Rudi (James MacArthur) who dreams of climbing the Matterhorn mountain (here called the Citadel), even though his father died years earlier while making the same attempt. After joining a climbing party led by Captain

Winter (Michael Rennie), Rudi acts recklessly and is forbidden to do any further climbing. But with the help of some friends, he trains in secret and proves himself worthy of making another attempt.

Breathtakingly photographed on Swiss locations, this is a fine coming-of-age story for young people, with plenty of excitement and a moral about facing challenges and learning to act responsibly. James MacArthur was one of Walt Disney's personal discoveries and starred in a handful of films for the studio in the late 1950s and early 1960s before settling in for a long run on the TV series *Hawaii Five-O*; he's also the oldest son in **Swiss Family Robinson**. His mother was the great actress Helen Hayes, who makes a cameo appearance near the beginning of *Third Man on the Mountain*.

35 UP (1991)
Color and black & white, 122 minutes
Director: Michael Apted
Documentary
Unrated
Young children: OK   Older children: VG

A uniquely fascinating long-term film experiment, *35 Up* reveals we are the people we're going to be when we're only 7 years old.

As a cultural experiment, British filmmaker Apted (best known as the director of such popular movies as *Coal Miner's Daughter* and **Gorillas in the Mist**) filmed interviews with a cross-section of British schoolchildren at age 7 (as an assistant to director Paul Almond), then age 14, again at 21 (at which time the results were shown as *21 Up*), 28 (released in 1984 as *28 Up*), and most recently at 35.

Idealistic youths grow up before our eyes, and become grownups with a variety of life experiences. Some turn out well. Some don't. Some try to achieve their goals and win. Some fail. And some refuse to be re-interrogated for the new edition.

The powerful subtext is the age-old battle between heredity and environment, and Apted's achievement is nothing less than to show the pageant of life.

By the way, it should be time for *42 Up*. What else will have happened to the kids?

THIS ISLAND EARTH (1955)
Color, 86 minutes
Cast: Jeff Morrow, Rex Reason, Faith Domergue, Lance Fuller, Russell Johnson, Douglas Spencer
Director: Joseph Newman
Screenplay: Franklin Coen and Edward G. O'Callaghan, from the novel by Raymond F. Jones
Science fiction/Suspense
Unrated
Younger kids: OK, with caution   Older kids: OK

A scientist (Reason) is recruited by mysterious benefactors who have established a scientific colony in a handsome mansion. Their leader, Exeter (Morrow), is friendly enough, but he's keeping a secret: he is the leader of a group of aliens who have come here to learn how to protect their planet Metaluna, which has been engaged in a lengthy battle with other aliens.

Even though this was skewered by *Mystery Science Theater 3000: The Movie, This Island Earth* remains one of the best examples of 1950s sci-fi, complete with aliens, flying saucers, and monsters (including the insectlike Mutant, which appears only briefly). Vivid, colorful, and exciting, it's safe enough for younger kids (who might find it boring at first), but older kids are likely to get involved—even if they find it old-fashioned.

THOROUGHLY MODERN MILLIE (1967)
Color, 138 minutes
Cast: Julie Andrews, James Fox, Mary Tyler Moore, Carol Channing, Beatrice Lillie, John Gavin, Jack Soo, Pat Morita, Philip Ahn
Director: George Roy Hill
Screenplay: Richard Morris
Musical
Unrated
Young children: VG Older children: OK

This thoroughly, unashamedly old-fashioned musical comedy tells the story of Millie Dillmount (Julie Andrews), a young woman who comes to New York City during the Roaring Twenties. Her aim is to find employment with a wealthy, good-looking boss, whom she will eventually marry. In order to accomplish this, Millie realizes she first must change her image. So she transforms herself from being prim and unstylish to a thoroughly modern Jazz Age flapper.

What follows are various shenanigans and plot twists, most of which involve Millie's new friend, pert orphan Dorothy Brown (Mary Tyler Moore), and a scheme to kidnap her into white slavery (!!!). Millie also hooks up romantically, not with an idealized rich businessman, but with an

Jimmy Smith (James Fox), a paper clip salesman who harbors a very special secret.

Some will find *Thoroughly Modern Millie* a wee bit precious, to say the least. For this reason, it will work best for younger viewers and diehard Julie Andrews fans.

THOSE MAGNIFICENT MEN IN THEIR FLYING MACHINES (1965)
Color, 132 minutes
Cast: Stuart Whitman, Sarah Miles, James Fox, Alberto Sordi, Robert Morley, Gert Frobe, Jean Pierre Cassel, Terry-Thomas, Irina Demick, Benny Hill, Flora Robson, Sam Wanamaker, Gordon Jackson, Millicent Martin, Red Skelton
Director: Ken Annakin
Screenplay: Annakin and Jack Davies
Action-adventure/Comedy
Unrated
Younger kids: Good Older kids: VG

The plot of this exhilarating look at the pioneer days of aviation is pretty well summed by its subtitle—*How I Flew From London to Paris in 25 Hours and 11 Minutes*—but it's the spectacular aerial footage and freewheeling slapstick comedy that makes it one of the most fondly remembered of all '60s roadshow blockbusters.

Set in 1910, the story involves an air race sponsored by a British newspaper publisher offering $50,000 in prize money. Among the participants are the publisher's daughter (Sarah Miles) and her fiancé (James Fox), an American cowboy (Stuart Whitman), an

Italian count (Alberto Sordi), a German cavalry officer (Gert Frobe), an amorous Frenchman (Jean-Pierre Cassel), and a villainous Englishman (Terry-Thomas) intent on sabotaging the others. The film is long, and kids are bound to get impatient during the buildup to the race, which doesn't even begin until almost 90 minutes in, but there are a number of humorous incidents along the way (such as a runaway plane, a duel in a hot air balloon, and a plane landing atop a moving train) and the antique aircraft themselves are very amusing oddball contraptions.

Once the race begins, it doesn't let up, and the movie really soars via some large-scale action scenes, hair-raising stunts, and the grandly panoramic photography of the British and French countrysides as the planes make their merry way across the English channel.

1001 ARABIAN NIGHTS
(1959)
Color, 76 minutes
Cast: Voices of Jim Backus (Uncle Abdul Azziz Magoo), Kathryn Grant, Dwayne Hickman, Hans Conried, Herschel Bernardi, Daws Butler, Alan Reed, The Clark Sisters
Director: Jack Kinney
Screenplay: Czenzi Ormonde
Animated musical
Rated G
Younger children: OK Older children: OK

The nearsighted Mr. Magoo's debut feature film can't compare to Disney's **Aladdin**, but is quite entertaining in its modest way. Magoo plays a lamp dealer who

also serves as protector of his love-sick nephew, Aladdin, in ancient Baghdad. A Wicked Wazir craves both Magoo's magic lamp and Aladdin's lady love, Princess Yasminda. Passing himself off as a long-lost brother, the Wazir tricks Magoo into giving him the lamp, which foils Aladdin and Yasminda's wedding plans. With the help of a flying carpet, Magoo saves the day by defeating the Wazir and reuniting the lovers.

This film is not nearly as funny as the UPA studio's award-winning Magoo shorts, but kids will enjoy the adventure storyline. The company's innovative art direction has been imitated since by many lesser TV cartoon studios, giving this feature a low-budget look, but the actual animation and storytelling is above par for a Magoo vehicle. Magoo, in fact, is almost a supporting player here, as Hans Conried's villainous Wazir steals the show with his greedy schemes.

THREE AGES (1923)
Black & white, 63 minutes
Cast: Buster Keaton, Margaret Leahy, Wallace Beery, Joe Roberts, Horace Morgan, Lillian Lawrence
Director: Buster Keaton and Eddie Cline
Screenplay: Clyde Bruckman, Joseph Mitchell, and Jean Havez
Comedy/Silent classic
Unrated
Young children: VG Older children: VG

Buster Keaton's *Three Ages* is a clever parody of the somber, moralistic silent-screen historical epics that had been popularized by D. W. Griffith. It consists of three love stories, set in the Stone Age, and in Roman and Modern times. In each, there is a beauty who is coveted by a hero (played by Buster) who is neither as wealthy nor as aggressive as his brutish rival.

One of the best bits in the film has the Stone Age Buster inventing golf. By the way, the Modern Age—meaning the 1920s—is labeled as an era of "speed, need, and greed." It sounds strangely contemporary!

Three Ages is loaded with funny comic antics, from Buster hitching a ride atop a dinosaur to a climactic scene in which he attempts to jump from one building rooftop to another. The result will have you shaking your head in amazement.

THE THREE CABALLEROS
(1945)
Color, 70 minutes
Cast: Aurora Miranda, Carmen Molina, Dora Luz; Voices of Sterling Holloway, Clarence Nash, Jose Oliveira, Joaquin Garay
Director: Norman Ferguson
Screenplay: Homer Brightman, Ernest Terrazzas, Ted Sears, Bill Peet, Ralph Wright, Elmer Plummer, Roy Williams, William Cottrell, Del Connell, and James Bodrero
Animated feature
Rated G
Younger kids: VG   Older kids: VG

Donald Duck takes a colorful tour through Latin America with his feathered friends Joe Carioca and Panchito in *The Three Caballeros,* a dazzling blend of animation and live action that was made by Walt Disney as a part of World War II's cross-cultural "Good Neighbor Policy." For his birthday, Donald receives a movie projector and some films about rare birds. Donald watches the story of Pablo the Penguin, who hates the cold and tries to sail to warmer climes. Another bird shown is the eccentric aracuan, who sings a crazy song and walks out of the screen to shake Donald's hand. Next up is the tale of Little Gauchito, a flying donkey. Donald then goes inside a pop-up picture book with his old parrot friend, Joe Carioca. They take a train to Brazil, where they samba down the street with a beautiful dancer and some musicians in a superb live-action/animated production number.

The visual gags then begin to accelerate at a dizzying pace and the screen explodes into mass of swirling colors and polka dots when the dancer kisses Donald. Things reach an even higher peak of lunacy when Panchito the rooster shows up, six-guns ablaze, and breaks into the rip-roaring "The Three Caballeros" number with Donald and Joe. When Donald smashes open a piñata, a storybook shows live-action scenes of Mexico as the animated trio hop onto a flying carpet and soar across the country, visiting Acapulco and Vera Cruz.

A follow-up to the featurette *Saludos Amigos* (1943), Disney's initial goodwill foray into South America, in which Donald Duck first met Joe Carioca, *The Three Caballeros* is fascinating for its historical and sociological elements as it is for its incredible technical expertise and brilliant animation.

The film's format, which dispenses with the need for a traditional narrative, seems to have liberated the imaginations of the Disney artists, who have created a kaleidoscopic eruption of Technicolor surrealism, containing some of the richest and most intense reds, purples, blues, and greens ever seen on a movie screen. The finale features a psychedelic montage of guitars, bright-red lips, flowers, and neon signs, segueing into slow-motion green-tinted live-actions shots of bathing beauties floating through the air, who then break into a Busby Berkeley–esque production number with Donald.

Although not as well known as some other Disney classics, *The Three Caballeros* represents the limitless possibilities of animation in its purest and most exuberant form, and is a must for aficionados of the art, as well as kids of all ages.

3 GODFATHERS (1949)
Color, 105 minutes
Cast: John Wayne, Pedro
  Armendariz, Harry Carey, Jr.,
  Ward Bond, Mae Marsh
Director: John Ford
Screenplay: Laurence Stallings
  and Frank S. Nugent, based
  on the story by Peter B. Kyne
Western
Unrated
Younger kids: Good Older
  kids: VG

Peter B. Kyne's touching story about three bandits on the run who find a newborn baby and care for it while fleeing across the desert is one of the most-filmed sagas in the history of Westerns. John Ford himself made a silent version and then remade it in this stirring Technicolor production. John Wayne gives a warm and

sympathetic performance as the lead bandit, who ultimately sacrifices himself in order to deliver the baby safely to the town of New Jerusalem on Christmas Eve.

The story is unabashedly sentimental, but there's also plenty of action—in a bank holdup and the subsequent chase by a posse—while scene after beautiful scene displays Ford's visual mastery, once again proving that no director ever had a better eye. Stunning tableaux of a swirling dust storm and silhouettes of the three lone outlaws trudging through the vast white sand as they're being pursued across the sun-baked desert have a poetic and haunting power that is palpable.

The film also has a strong spiritual element and is really a parable about the Three Wise Men, making it fine entertainment even for those who don't normally like Westerns.

THE THREE LIVES OF THOMASINA (1963)
Color, 87 minutes
Cast: Patrick McGoohan, Susan
  Hampshire, Karen Dotrice,
  Laurence Naismith, Jean
  Anderson, Wilfrid Brambell,
  Finlay Currie, Vincent Winter,
  Matthew Garber; voice of
  Elspeth March (as Thomasina)
Director: Don Chaffey
Screenplay: Robert Westerby,
  based on the novel
  Thomasina, the Cat Who
  Thought She Was God by Paul
  Gallico
Drama/Fantasy
Unrated
Younger children: OK, with
  caution Older children: VG

After Thomasina, the beloved cat of young Mary MacDhui (Karen

Dotrice), becomes deathly ill, Mary's father (Patrick McGoohan), the local veterinarian—a dour and distant widower—insists that the feline be put to sleep. Against the advice of her young friends, Mary bravely seeks the help of a mystical hermit, the beautiful Lori MacGregor (Susan Hampshire), who lives in the woods and is rumored to have a magical healing way about her. Through this quest, Mary, her father, and Thomasina are all healed, both physically and emotionally.

This is one of Walt Disney's most unusual films, set in the exquisite Scottish countryside at the turn of the 20th century. It is based on a much-loved book by Paul Gallico and narrated by Thomasina herself. The mystical elements of the story—including a trip to cat heaven, and the concept of death and rebirth—may be difficult for young children to fathom or contend with. Mary's father's behavior is also off-putting for much of the tale—but that's what makes his eventual transformation so satisfying.

A fine script and appealing stars give this film considerable charm. Adults will enjoy watching Patrick McGoohan and Susan Hampshire, while kids will certainly recognize Karen Dotrice (and in a smaller role, Matthew Garber) who one year later would play the Banks children in **Mary Poppins.**

THE THREE MUSKETEERS
(1921)
Black & white, 112 minutes
Cast: Douglas Fairbanks, Leon Barry, George Siegmann, Eugene Pallette, Boyd Irwin, Thomas Holding, Sidney

Franklin, Nigel de Brulier, Mary McLaren, Marguerite De La Motte, Barbara La Marr, Adolphe Menjou
Director: Fred Niblo
Screenplay: Lotta Woods, Edward Knoblock, and Douglas Fairbanks, from the novel by Alexandre Dumas
Adventure/Swashbuckler/Silent classic
Unrated
Young children: VG   Older children: VG

Douglas Fairbanks is one of the legendary stars of the silent screen. Throughout the 1920s he was movies' definitive swashbuckling hero. This rousing entertainment, in which Fairbanks plays D'Artagnan, a young adventurer who arrives from Gascony to join King Louis XIII's Musketeers, is as good a place as any to be introduced to his ebullient screen personality.

This *Three Musketeers* fits a tried-and-true formula that was to serve Fairbanks well. D'Artagnan poses and smiles as he forms his bond with Athos, Porthos, and Aramis, the title trio, and practically seems to be winking at the audience. He is charismatic and athletic, proving himself a swordsman supreme as he battles the bad guys and wins the fair maiden.

THE THREE MUSKETEERS
(1939)
Black & white, 73 minutes
Cast: Don Ameche, The Ritz Brothers, Binnie Barnes, Gloria Stuart, Pauline Moore, Miles Mander, John Carradine, Joseph Schildkraut
Director: Allan Dwan
Screenplay: M. M. Musselman,

William A. Drake, Sam Hellman, Sid Kuller, and Ray Golden, based on the novel by Alexandre Dumas
Swashbuckler/Musical/Comedy
Unrated
Younger kids: Good   Older kids: Good

If you and your kids have never encountered The Ritz Brothers, it's high time you did—and this is arguably their best movie vehicle. If you can get past the silly songs, including "We're King's Musketeers on Parade," this cheeky musical comedy version of the immortal Dumas swashbuckler is surprisingly faithful to the original story and still leaves ample room for the wild-eyed Al, Jimmy, and Harry Ritz to do their comic shtick. It's a combination the whole family can enjoy.

Sporting curly, shoulder-length hair, Don Ameche is quite dashing as D'Artagnan, while Binnie Barnes makes for an enticingly treacherous Milady de Winter. Gloria Stuart, who recently made a comeback in Titanic, is beautiful as the Queen whose missing emerald brooch sets the plot in motion. The Ritz Brothers play three lackeys who don the uniforms of the real musketeers and help D'Artagnan defeat the scheming Cardinal Richelieu (Miles Mander).

Though the Ritzs' brand of manic clowning is definitely an acquired taste, their material is cleverly integrated into the story. Director Allan Dwan, a veteran of lavish silent-screen spectacles, adroitly blends swordplay, action, romance, comedy, and songs into just over an hour and captures the novel's spirit in an exciting and entertaining film.

THE THREE MUSKETEERS
(1948)
Color, 125 minutes
Cast: Gene Kelly, Lana Turner, June Allyson, Van Heflin, Angela Lansbury, Robert Coote, Frank Morgan, Vincent Price, Keenan Wynn, Gig Young
Director: George Sidney
Screenplay: Robert Ardrey, based on the novel by Alexandre Dumas
Swashbuckler/Action-adventure
Unrated
Younger kids: OK   Older kids: Good

This extravagantly produced MGM version of the Dumas classic is like a Technicolor musical without the music, featuring zestfully choreographed sword fights and Gene Kelly gleefully bouncing his way through the role of D'Artagnan with acrobatic grace. The actual musketeers—played by Van Heflin (Athos), Gig Young (Porthos), and Robert Coote (Aramis)—are much duller than D'Artagnan, but Lana Turner has never appeared more beautiful than as Lady de Winter, and Vincent Price is marvelously malevolent as Richelieu.

The plot sticks fairly closely to the original story, with the musketeers coming to the aid of the bumbling King Louis XIII (Frank Morgan) against the treachery of Richelieu and de Winter, and the film is an entertaining, if superficial, adaptation. Violence is muted in this version of the story.

THE THREE MUSKETEERS
(1974)
Color, 105 minutes
Cast: Michael York, Oliver Reed, Richard Chamberlain, Frank Finlay, Faye Dunaway, Raquel Welch, Charlton Heston, Christopher Lee, Geraldine Chaplin, Jean-Pierre Cassel, Roy Kinnear, Spike Milligan
Director: Richard Lester
Screenplay: George MacDonald Fraser, based on the novel by Alexandre Dumas
Swashbuckler/Action-adventure
Rated PG
Younger kids: OK, with caution   Older kids: VG

Richard Lester's hugely enjoyable take on the classic novel is a rollicking combination of slapstick sight gags, exhilarating (and realistically bloody) swordplay, and gritty period detail, which manages to treat its material with reverence while simultaneously spoofing it. The all-star cast includes Michael York as the country bumpkin D'Artagnan, Richard Chamberlain as a stylish Aramis, Oliver Reed as an earthy Athos, and Frank Finlay as a comically vain Porthos, with strong support provided by Charlton Heston as the treacherous Cardinal Richelieu and Faye Dunaway as the seductive Milady de Winter.

This is a delightful movie with a unique and fresh approach to Dumas's novel, and in some opinions is the finest of its many film adaptations. The violence (not to mention the story intrigues) make this an iffy proposition for younger kids, but older ones should revel in its artful blend of comedy and adventure. It was followed by **The Four Musketeers**,

then years later by *Return of the Musketeers*.

THE THREE MUSKETEERS
(1993)
Color, 105 minutes
Cast: Charlie Sheen, Kiefer Sutherland, Chris O'Donnell, Oliver Platt, Tim Curry, Rebecca De Mornay, Gabriel Anwar, Hugh O'Conor, Julie Delpy
Director: Stephen Herek
Screenplay: David Loughery, based on the novel by Alexandre Dumas
Swashbuckler/Action-adventure
Rated PG
Younger kids: OK, with caution   Older kids: Good

Seventeenth-century France receives a resoundingly anachronistic depiction in this Disney-produced Brat Pack version of the venerable yarn. The story, dialogue, and characters have been modernized in a blatant appeal to the short-attention-span MTV generation, with an emphasis on nonstop action. Though Kiefer Sutherland, Charlie Sheen, Oliver Platt, and Chris O'Donnell are closer in age to the musketeers in Dumas's novel than actors who have appeared in previous film versions, they lack the stature and sense of heroic gallantry that the roles require. They do their best, however, and seem at least to be having fun—a feeling that young viewers may share.

The Austrian locations are handsome and a major asset, but the film's centerpiece is the broad, very entertaining performance of Tim Curry, who easily steals every scene he's in as the villainous Cardinal Richelieu.

There is some violence—and a

sprinkling of sexual innuendo—which parents should bear in mind before allowing young children to watch.

3 NINJAS (1992)
Color, 87 minutes
Cast: Victor Wong, Michael Treanor, Max Elliott Slade, Chad Power, Rand Kingsley
Director: Jon Turtletaub
Screenplay: Edward Emanuel, from a story by Kenny Kim
Action/Martial arts
Rated PG
Younger kids: OK Older kids: Good

This Disney action-comedy is highly derivative (borrowing elements from **Home Alone, The Karate Kid, Teenage Mutant Ninja Turtles,** and others) but proved to be a popular hit with its target audience of young boys, inspiring three sequels so far. The story is about three young brothers (Michael Treanor, Max Elliott Slade, Chad Power) who have been trained in the martial arts by their wise grandfather (Victor Wong), which comes in mighty handy when they're kidnapped by the nasty Ninja-master arms dealer (Rand Kingsley) whom their FBI father is pursuing.

Formulaic as it is, kids should get a kick out of it (pun intended), and anyway, the violence of the action scenes is fairly innocuous. The sequels that followed were pretty much copies of this film, with only minor variations . . . and diminishing results.

THREE SMART GIRLS (1936)
Black & white, 84 minutes
Cast: Deanna Durbin, Binnie Barnes, Alice Brady, Ray Milland, Barbara Read, Mischa Auer, Nan Grey, Charles Winninger, Ernest Cossart, Lucile Watson
Director: Henry Koster
Screenplay: Adele Comandini
Comedy with music
Unrated
Young children: VG Older children: VG

Fifteen-year-old Deanna Durbin makes her feature film debut in this charming comedy with music. And quite a debut it is. Durbin is billed as "Universal's new discovery," and the film's smashing success immediately transformed her into a major box-office attraction.

Although it's an "old movie," today's kids will have no trouble relating to the story of three girls who are told by their mother that their father (who is estranged from the family) is about to remarry. They haven't seen him in a decade, but they set out for New York just the same, determined to stop the marriage and reunite their parents.

The girls are winning, and the comedy is expert at every turn; in the midst of this, Durbin's beautiful soprano voice is showcased in several musical numbers. Again, contemporary kids may not be accustomed to hearing classical music, but this is as painless (or sugar-coated) a way of introducing them as ever devised.

The film was followed by a 1939 sequel, *Three Smart Girls Grow Up*.

THUMBELINA (1994)
Color, 94 minutes
Cast: Voices of Jodi Benson,
Carol Channing, Charo, Gary
Imhoff, June Foray, Gino
Conforti, Barbara Cook,
Gilbert Gottfried, John Hurt
Directors: Don Bluth and Gary
Goldman
Screenplay: Don Bluth, based on
the story by Hans Christian
Andersen
Animated feature/Musical
Rated G
Younger kids: OK   Older kids:
NG

Beautiful Don Bluth animation
can't mask this fairy tale gone
wrong. The film starts off the
right way: A lonely woman longing for a child is magically granted her wish with the arrival of Thumbelina, a grown woman no bigger
than her thumb. Thumbelina tries to
make her mother happy, but she
yearns to find others her size. Enter
Prince Cornelius, a winged sprite
who literally sweeps Thumbelina
off her feet. The convoluted story
has Thumbelina kidnapped by a
lovesick toad, rescued by a mischievous beetle, and given shelter
with a spinster field mouse.

Forgettable ballads (written by
Barry Manilow) and Las Ve-
gas-style production numbers do
nothing to help the confusing narrative. Because of Bluth's lush,
Disney-like animation style, audiences might expect the film to live
up to Disney standards, but it dis-
appoints at every turn. Bluth further blurs the lines by casting two
actors familiar to Disney fans in
major parts: Jodi Benson (the
voice of Ariel, the Little Mermaid) as Thumbelina and Gilbert
Gottfried (Iago, the parrot in

Aladdin) as Mr. Beetle. This is for
the younger ones only.

Note: The actual title of this
film is *Hans Christian Andersen's
Thumbelina.*

**THUNDERHEAD, SON OF
FLICKA** (1945)
Color, 78 minutes
Cast: Roddy McDowall, Preston
Foster, Rita Johnson, James
Bell, Diana Hale
Director: Louis King
Screenplay: Dwight Cummins
and Dorothy Yost, based on
the novel by Mary O'Hara
Animal story/Drama
Unrated
Younger kids: Good   Older
kids: VG

In this fine sequel to **My Friend
Flicka,** Roddy McDowall returns
as young Ken McLaughlin, the
horse rancher's son, who tries to
tame a beautiful but wild colt
foaled by Flicka and sired by a
violent albino stallion who has
been terrorizing the county and
stealing mares. When Thunderhead (who's nicknamed Goblin
because of his bright white coat)
demonstrates blazing speed, Ken
talks his parents (Preston Foster,
Rita Johnson) into letting him
train it to be a racehorse. He enters a local race in the hope of
winning $5,000 to pay for college
(and to fix up the ranch), but the
family also has to deal with the
return of the albino stallion.

Thunderhead has much of the
same appeal as its classic predecessor, including delightful animal
footage and gorgeous Technicolor
photography of Utah and Wyoming horse country, along with
such exciting action scenes as the
horse race and a climactic show-

down between Thunderhead and the albino stallion.

The magnificent landscape of the Rockies, with its canyons, lakes, and open pastures is wonderful to behold, and one can practically smell the fresh air and sweet country grass. Though made only two years after *My Friend Flicka,* Roddy McDowall seems much older than in that film, and the story deals effectively with his character's growing maturity (mirroring Thunderhead's similar growth). He bonds with his father and learns important lessons about patience, understanding, and dealing with adversity.

The fight between Thunderhead and the albino is fairly vivid and realistic, and includes some violent stomping action, which could frighten very young children, but it was monitored by the American Humane Association. This is an excellent family film.

TIGER TOWN (1983)
Color, 76 minutes
Cast: Roy Scheider, Justin Henry, Ron McLarty, Bethany Carpenter, Sparky Anderson, Ernie Harwell
Director: Alan Shapiro
Screenplay: Alan Shapiro
Drama/Fantasy/Sports
Unrated
Younger kids: OK   Older kids: VG

This moving made-for-TV movie stresses the importance of a child's need for a role model, be it a parent or a favorite athlete. Alex (Justin Henry) is a true-blue Detroit Tigers fan who is fiercely devoted to one ballplayer: Billy Young, an aging, slumping slugger. Alex also enjoys a loving relationship with his dad, an unemployed factory worker.

When Alex's father suddenly dies, Alex channels all his emotions into baseball, and begins to believe that whenever he attends a Tigers game and concentrates with all his might, Billy will respond with a base hit.

While the loss of Alex's dad may be too intense for the very youngest viewer, *Tiger Town* is extremely effective as a story about the power of positive thinking and a chronicle of a loving father-son union. This relationship flourishes in an often cruel and unfriendly world and, even more important, transcends the father's demise.

TIM BURTON'S THE NIGHTMARE BEFORE CHRISTMAS (see **The Nightmare Before Christmas**)

TIME AFTER TIME (1979)
Color, 112 minutes
Cast: Malcolm McDowell, David Warner, Mary Steenburgen, Charles Cioffi, Kent Williams, Andonia Katsaros, Patti D'Arbanville
Director: Nicholas Meyer
Screenplay: Meyer, from a story by Karl Alexander and Steve Hayes
Science fiction/Suspense thriller
Rated PG
Younger kids: Very tense   Older kids: OK

In 1893, Jack the Ripper (Warner) steals the time machine built by H. G. Wells (McDowell), and flees to San Francisco in 1979. When the machine automatically returns, Wells follows him, fearful of what his invention has unleashed. Quite at home in the violent world of 1979, the Ripper refuses to return to the 19th century, while Wells finds himself falling in love with a freethinking young woman (Steenburgen).

Partly because Meyer insists on trotting out all the expected clichés, *Time After Time* never rises to the charm and imagination of its premise. But there are still many amusing touches (such as Wells arriving in a museum display devoted to H. G. Wells), and all three leads (particularly Steenburgen) are excellent. And let's face it: the fundamental idea of the film is so compelling that the movie remains watchable in spite of itself.

Although the film is not very violent, the fact that it centers on Jack the Ripper and features prostitutes means it's definitely not for younger kids. Older kids, however, especially those who've begun reading the great science fiction novels of H. G. Wells, are likely to find the movie a lot of fun.

TIME BANDITS (1981)
Color, 110 minutes
Cast: Craig Warnock, David Rappaport, Kenny Baker, Malcolm Dixon, Mike Edmonds, Jack Purvis, Tiny Ross, David Warner, John Cleese, Sean Connery, Shelley Duvall, Katherine Helmond, Ian Holm, Michael Palin, Ralph Richardson
Director: Terry Gilliam
Screenplay: Michael Palin and Gilliam
Fantasy/Comedy
Rated PG
Younger kids: Use caution   Older kids: OK

Six dwarfs who work for the Supreme Being and who fancy themselves expert bandits steal a map of the Cosmos which shows all the "time holes." They fall into the bedroom of a young British boy, Kevin (Warnock), who then accompanies them on a series of time-traveling adventures. Among others, they meet a politely avaricious Robin Hood (Cleese), King Agamemnon (Connery), and Napoleon (Holm), while being pursued by the personification of Evil (Warner).

Two of the Monty Python team, Gilliam and Palin, created this cheerfully anarchic comedy, and a third Python (Cleese) appears in it as well. This will mean little to your kids, most likely, but might appeal to *you*. The movie is basically a series of blackout sketches, as the rambunctious dwarfs and the nice little boy are whisked from time to time throughout history.

Nothing about it should be taken seriously, even on its own terms, and if your older children are already comfortable with this kind of comedy, which blithely mixes lowbrow slapstick and college-level references, they're likely to have a good time.

THE TIME MACHINE (1960)
Color, 103 minutes
Cast: Rod Taylor, Yvette Mimieux, Alan Young, Sebastian Cabot, Tom Helmore, Whit Bissell, Doris Lloyd
Director: George Pal
Screenplay: David Duncan, from the novel by H. G. Wells
Science fiction/Adventure
Unrated
Younger kids: OK, with caution   Older kids: OK

In the late 19th century, a young researcher (Taylor) uses his self-built time machine to travel into the future. He ends up in the year 802,701, when the only human beings seem to be the indolent Eloi, who care nothing about books, and who wander among the ruins of civilization without noticing them. But underground live the Morlocks, a far more deadly remnant of humanity.

Time travel is one of the most intriguing of all science fiction ideas, and this film is a classic of its kind: rock-solid, high-minded, and energetic. Taylor is at once robustly heroic and intelligent, in refreshing contrast to today's sci-fi movies, where it often seems that the more ignorant a character is, the more likely he is to be the hero.

Some of the special effects (which won an Oscar) look cheesy today, and there is an unfortunate tendency toward whimsy, but otherwise this is good entertainment.

Younger children may be scared by the Morlocks (which are simultaneously eerie and silly), but the movie doesn't dwell on them. Older children could well be intrigued by the ideas in the movie.

(Ironically enough, the changes in Wells' story regarding the Morlocks and the Eloi were done to make the film more timely—but they've actually ended up dating it. The concept of an "all-clear" signal, used by the Morlocks to control the Eloi, is no longer contemporary.)

THE TIME OF THEIR LIVES (1946)

Black & white, 82 minutes
Cast: Bud Abbott, Lou Costello, Marjorie Reynolds, Binnie Barnes, John Shelton, Jess Barker, Gale Sondergaard, Robert Barrat, Donald MacBride, Ann Gillis, Lynne Baggett
Director: Charles Barton
Screenplay: Val Burton
Comedy/Fantasy
Unrated
Younger children: VG   Older children: VG

If your kids have already become fans of Abbott and Costello, they'll find this fantasy an interesting and enjoyable change of pace. If your kids have never seen Bud and Lou, they need no special introduction: this clever story stands on its own and doesn't call on any of the team's trademarked routines. In fact, Bud and Lou work separately through most of the film.

Lou plays a watch-tinker who lives in the Colonies during the Revolutionary War; his prized possession is a letter of commendation from General George Washington. He and the mistress of an estate (Marjorie Reynolds) are mistaken for traitors, after a mix-up with genuine conspirators, and shot. The soldiers dump their bodies in a well on her estate, and post a curse that condemns them to remain there for the rest of eternity. In time, the two of them emerge from the well and realize that they are ghosts.

In modern times, an ancestor of the original conspirator comes to examine the house, which he is renovating so that he can live there with his bride. The two ghosts see this as their chance. If somehow they can communicate with these people and get them to find Lou's letter from George Washington, it will prove that they were wrongly condemned and free their souls.

The Time of Their Lives is a delightful fantasy, with many clever twists, and a fine cast. Kids should find the premise as intriguing as their parents.

THE TINGLER (1959)
Black & white, with color
    sequence, 81 minutes
Cast: Vincent Price, Judith
    Evelyn, Darryl Hickman,
    Patricia Cutts, Pamela Lincoln,
    Philip Coolidge
Director: William Castle
Screenplay: Robb White
Science fiction–horror/Mystery
Unrated
Young children: Too
    weird Older children: OK

Dr. Chapin (Price) is convinced that fear is a living thing; the tingling in our spines when we're scared, he thinks, is an actual creature that grows and grows. It would crush our spines if we didn't scream. He's determined to prove that this wacky theory is true, and this being the kind of movie it is, he's right. Meanwhile, there are a couple of busy subplots about wives trying to murder their husbands, and husbands trying to murder their wives. And lots of waspish, sneering wisecracks.

For once, Price is not the villain, though he might as well be, since he's responsible for hauling the Tingler itself out of the back of a mute woman who died of fright. (She couldn't scream, see, so her Tingler reached full

flower—or whatever.) The Tingler itself resembles a cross between a cockroach and a trilobite, and at one point gets loose in a silent movie theater showing **Tol'able David.**

This sequence, near the end, was the entire reason for the film: producer-director Castle had found that gimmicks worked well for *Macabre* and **House on Haunted Hill,** and came up with a new one ("Percepto"), then built a film around it. In some theaters, selected seats were fitted with little motors that the projectionist could operate, buzzing the seats of patrons (not shocking them, despite what you might read elsewhere) during the silent-movie sequence. What a shame that Percepto is not adaptable to home movie viewing.

Very young children will be disturbed by the two-foot bug that is the Tingler itself, but it's not seen very often. And the one color sequence in which the mute woman sees a literal bloodbath is also pretty macabre. Older children are more likely to regard this movie more as a comedy than as a shocker, based on his ripe, funny performance, Vincent Price may well have had the same point of view.

TO KILL A MOCKINGBIRD
(1962)
Black & white, 129 minutes
Cast: Gregory Peck, Mary
    Badham, Philip Alford, John
    Megna, Brock Peters, Robert
    Duvall, Frank Overton,
    Rosemary Murphy, Paul Fix,
    Alice Ghostley, William
    Windom; Kim Stanley
    (narrator)
Director: Robert Mulligan

Screenplay: Horton Foote, from the novel by Harper Lee
Drama
Unrated
Younger kids: VG   Older kids: VG

This Hollywood classic stars Gregory Peck in the role with which he will always be identified: Atticus Finch, a quiet, noble small-town Southern lawyer who defends Tom Robinson (Peters), a black man accused of raping a white woman, Mayella Ewell (Wilcox). The trial becomes a pivotal event in a Depression-era Alabama town and in the lives of Atticus' children, Jem (Alford) and Scout (Badham), who discover the courage of their father in standing up to bigotry and small-mindedness. A second plot involving Boo Radley (Duvall, making his film debut), the son of mysterious neighbors who is supposed to be mad, parallels the Robinson trial and reinforces Finch's adage to Scout that one cannot truly understand another person until you have seen things from inside his skin.

To Kill a Mockingbird may, at first glance, seem too genteel for today's kids, but the film is surprisingly free of easy soapbox moralizing and concentrates instead on character and atmosphere, as the perceptions of race and class are filtered through Jem's and Scout's eyes and they come to grips with the hard realities of their own community and the world in general. The theme of personal honor is as important here as any overt examination of racism, and indeed, one of the most memorable moments comes when Mayella's father spits on Finch and he does nothing to retaliate. The lazy, quietly menacing character of the town is effortlessly captured, and securely anchoring it all is Peck, who creates an ideal hero worth emulating: restrained, self-effacing, confident, a man of integrity and true values.

TOL'ABLE DAVID (1921)
Black & white, 80 minutes
Cast: Richard Barthelmess, Gladys Hulette, Ernest Torrence, Warner Richmond, Walter P. Lewis
Director: Henry King
Screenplay: Edmund Goulding and King
Adventure/Silent classic
Unrated
Young children: VG   Older children: VG

This rich, atmospheric adventure centers on a rural Virginia teen who has to save his town and his sweetheart from marauding mountain men. Though tragedy strikes more than once, David's pluck saves the day (and the U.S. mail).

Based on the short story by Joseph Hergesheimer, this touching, often thrilling movie shows the evolution of a peace-loving soul who learns he must do more than just stand up for his rights. The story plays genuinely, and viewers of all ages may find more emotional power here than in most current fare.

A real period piece, its finely detailed portrait of long-gone Americana allowed director King to relive his own boyhood: he was born eight miles over the mountains from where the picture was filmed.

Silent star Barthelmess, once described by D. W. Griffith costar Lillian Gish as "the most beautiful face of any man who ever went before the camera," proves an ideal hero in a film that's sentimental but never saccharine.

TOM AND HUCK (1995)
Color, 92 minutes
Cast: Jonathan Taylor Thomas, Brad Renfro, Eric Schweig, Charles Rocket, Amy Wright
Director: Peter Hewitt
Screenplay: Stephen Sommers and David Loughery, based on the novel *The Adventures of Tom Sawyer* by Mark Twain
Adventure/Literary classic
Rated PG
Younger kids: OK   Older kids: Good

Yet another version of Mark Twain's classic about those mischievous rascals Tom Sawyer and Huckleberry Finn, this loose adaptation of *The Adventures of Tom Sawyer* has been given a very '90s Disney spin and is cast with teen heartthrobs Jonathan Taylor Thomas (Tom) and Brad Renfro (Huck). All of the book's familiar episodes are present, but the film's focus is more on action and suspense than humor and atmosphere, as Tom and Huck witness a murder and try to flee from Injun Joe (Eric Schweig).

Older kids will probably enjoy it, but younger children may be frightened by some of the scary incidents, which are treated in a fairly dark and realistic manner (as in Disney's 1993 production **The Adventures of Huck Finn**), and by the bloodthirsty villainy of Injun Joe.

TOM & JERRY: THE MOVIE (1993)
Color, 80 minutes
Cast: Voices of Richard Kind, Dana Hill, Anndi McAfee, Charlotte Rae, Tony Jay, Rip Taylor, Henry Gibson, Howard Morris
Director: Phil Roman
Screenplay: Dennis Marks
Animated feature/Musical
Rated G
Younger kids: OK   Older kids: No

Perhaps the filmmakers felt a "real" Tom & Jerry movie, inspired by the long-running series of MGM cartoon shorts, wouldn't be suitable family entertainment, so what we have here is "Tom & Jerry Lite." They talk, they sing, they help an orphan girl in distress. Not a falling anvil in sight.

Tom and Jerry have been so busy chasing each other, they fail to notice their master moving out and their house being demolished. Homeless, they team up for survival and soon meet up with Robyn, a little girl runaway in search of her father. Chased by wicked Aunt Figg, who bears a family resemblance to the evil Ursula of **The Little Mermaid**, Robyn's story becomes the film's melodramatic centerpiece, as cat and mouse help out in support.

The animation is strictly standard and nowhere near the quality of those vintage MGM shorts. Henry Mancini and Leslie Bricusse contribute an unmemorable score.

Slapstick cartoon mayhem was always Tom and Jerry's stock in trade. But after an opening chase sequence, this feature betrays these classic characters. Very young kids may enjoy it, but die-hard Tom and Jerry fans won't.

TOM BROWN'S SCHOOL DAYS (1940)
Black & white, 86 minutes
Cast: Cedric Hardwicke, Freddie Bartholomew, Gale Storm, Jimmy Lydon, Josephine Hutchinson, Billy Halop, Polly Moran
Director: Robert Stevenson
Screenplay: Walter Ferris, Frank Cavett, Gene Towne, and Graham Baker, based on the novel by Thomas Hughes
Drama/Literary classic
Unrated
Young children: VG Older children: VG

This Hollywood version of the British novel of two young boys' Victorian public school experience at Rugby is at times delightful and at other times archaic. The details of old-fashioned hazing and fagging (when upper-classmen demand favors from the younger boys) may arouse both curiosity and wonder, but today's youngsters should make strong connections with the recurring theme of friendship and bonding, as the young boys go through positive experiences that form their characters. They also benefit from their close relationship with an intelligent and understanding headmaster.

Children will relate to the boys' unfortunate times, such as when they are shamelessly bullied or when they get into trouble for cheating and other infractions. If the girls call for equal time, then you can also screen **The Trouble With Angels,** a lighthearted 1966 comedy about mischievous girls at a convent boarding school.

TOM BROWN'S SCHOOLDAYS (1951)
Black & white, 93 minutes
Cast: John Howard Davies, Robert Newton, Diana Wynyard, Hermione Baddeley, Kathleen Byron, James Hayter, John Charlesworth, John Forrest, Michael Hordern, Max Bygraves
Director: Gordon Parry
Screenplay: Noel Langley, based on the novel by Thomas Hughes
Drama/Literary classic
Unrated
Young children: VG Older children: VG

The British film version of Hughes' novel of Victorian public school life goes the 1940 American version one better by actually filming the story on location at Rugby. In this interpretation, the character of Tom Brown is presented as more lovable and more sensitive than in the earlier film. Perhaps that is because pre–World War II Hollywood often viewed the British as stereotypically reserved.

Here, the British are turning the cameras on themselves in order to record public school life as it was lived a century earlier. While both films draw similarly from the book, the atmosphere in this version is, of course, much more authentic.

TOMMY (1975)
Color, 111 minutes
Cast: Roger Daltrey, Ann-Margret, Oliver Reed, Elton John, Eric Clapton, Keith Moon, Pete Townshend, John Entwistle, Robert Powell, Tina Turner, Jack Nicholson, Paul Nicholas

Director: Ken Russell
Screenplay: Russell, based on the rock opera by Pete Townshend and The Who
Musical
Rated PG
Younger kids: OK, with caution   Older kids: OK

A frenetic, hyperactive adaptation of the Who's classic "rock opera," which tapped into the perils of late '60s spiritual freedom through the amazing journey of Tommy, a young boy who is struck deaf, dumb, and blind when he witnesses his war-hero father murdered by the lover (Reed) of his mother, Mrs. Walker (Ann-Margret). Tommy grows up (played by Daltrey), becomes pinball champion of the world and, once his senses are restored, a cult messiah.

Director Russell, well known for his visual and aural flamboyance, pumps up the volume, throws in bizarre camera angles and meat-cleaver editing, and tosses in everything but the kitchen sink to create a near psychedelic experience. The highlights: Elton John, in huge platform shoes, as the Pinball champ whom Tommy dethrones; Tommy's seduction by the Acid Queen (a very scary Turner); and Ann-Margret writhing on the floor in a cascade of soap suds, baked beans, and chocolate which explode out of a TV screen. Needless to say, this is a very literal interpretation of Townshend's story that plays up the themes of cultural exploitation and consumerism. It is undeniably energetic and watchable in a "Can you believe it?" kind of way, with performances that, to put it charitably, match the overall subtlety of the proceedings.

Those unfamiliar with *Tommy* or The Who may enjoy the movie as an eccentric period piece, and though there are some rough moments for kids (particularly the Acid Queen sequence), Russell's excesses may almost seem quaint compared with most music videos that kids watch today. Interestingly, Townshend himself updated *Tommy* for the Broadway stage in 1994 and, in doing so, considerably diluted a lot of the material's more angry content and themes.

tom thumb (1958)
Color, 98 minutes
Cast: Russ Tamblyn, June Thorburn, Peter Sellers, Terry-Thomas, Alan Young, Jessie Matthews, Bernard Miles, Ian Wallace, The Puppetoons
Director: George Pal
Screenplay: Ladislas Fodor, based on the Grimm Brothers fairy tale
Musical/Fantasy
Unrated
Young children: VG   Older children: OK

The very youngest family members should be enthralled by this delectable kiddie fairy tale/musical comedy. The story tells of Anna and Jonathan (Jessie Matthews, Bernard Miles), a kind, married couple who have not been blessed with a child of their own. So it is their great fortune when they are the recipients of an extra special present from the Forest Queen: the title character, a miniature boy who is just five and a half inches in height. Trouble turns up in the persons of the evil Ivan and his henchman, Tony, who plot to exploit tiny Tom.

Terry-Thomas and Peter Sellers make wonderful comic villains who are never *too* threatening. Russ Tamblyn, cast as Tom, is given ample opportunity to display his acrobatic dancing. There are delightful songs, clever special effects, and a host of extravagant musical numbers in which inanimate objects come to life and cavort with Tom Thumb. (These characters, known as Puppetoons, hark back to a series of animated shorts made in the 1930s and '40s by this film's producer-director, George Pal.)

By the way, the actual title of the film is *tom thumb,* with the lowercase lettering befitting the stature of the title character.

TOO MANY GIRLS (1940)
Black & white, 85 minutes
Cast: Lucille Ball, Richard Carlson, Eddie Bracken, Ann Miller, Hal LeRoy, Desi Arnaz, Frances Langford, Libby Bennett, Harry Shannon, Van Johnson
Director: George Abbott
Screenplay: John Twist, based on the musical by George Marion, Jr., Richard Rodgers, and Lorenz Hart
Musical
Unrated
Young children: VG   Older children: VG

Back in the 1930s, rah-rah, sis-boom-bah college musical comedies were extremely popular. Here is one of the very best, a briskly paced union of song, dance, romance, and laughs that was adapted from the hit Richard Rodgers–Lorenz Hart Broadway show.

The setting is Pottawatomie College, located in Stopgap, New

Mexico. The scenario involves wealthy Connie Casey, a new campus coed, and what happens when her dad hires a quartet of football stars to serve as her bodyguards.

Filled with good spirits and lively musical numbers, *Too Many Girls* is fun to watch, but the key to a young viewer's interest in it will be its featured performers Lucille Ball (who plays Connie) and Desi Arnaz (who's cast as Manuelito, one of the gridiron heroes). It was during this production that they met. *I Love Lucy* fans will especially enjoy Desi's furious conga drum dance, which is incorporated into the finale.

TOP HAT (1935)
Black & white, 101 minutes
Cast: Fred Astaire, Ginger Rogers, Edward Everett Horton, Erik Rhodes, Eric Blore, Helen Broderick, Donald Meek
Director: Mark Sandrich
Screenplay: Dwight Taylor and Allan Scott, based on the play *The Girl Who Dared (or A Scandal in Budapest)* by Alexander Farago and Aladar Laszlo
Musical
Unrated
Young children: VG   Older children: VG

Top Hat is, along with *Swing Time,* tops among Fred Astaire–Ginger Rogers musicals. It sparkles from its very first moments, as Astaire's character, a carefree chap named Jerry Travers, delightfully disturbs the peace at a boring London men's club by tapping his famous feet. The story goes on to involve Travers, a star of musical revues, and Dale Tremont (Rogers), the woman with whom he falls in love in a mistaken-identity scenario.

The film's score, composed by Irving Berlin, is loaded with gems. Among the highlights: "Isn't This a Lovely Day (to Be Caught in the Rain?)," with a rhythmic tap duet between Fred and Ginger. "Top Hat, White Tie and Tails" is a number that is the very personification of Astaire. The divinely romantic "Cheek to Cheek" is perhaps the most famous of all Astaire-Rogers dance numbers. And as always in these films, the musical numbers all have a purpose in the story, and express their chracters' feelings.

Some of the situations in *Top Hat* may be subtly risqué, and Erik Rhodes' character, Italian dressmaker Alberto Beddini, is both comically effeminate and a bit of an ethnic stereotype. Nonetheless, *Top Hat* exudes romance and innocence, and is the very essence of witty musical comedy, 1930s-style.

Finally, youngsters and their parents who are fans of *I Love Lucy* will enjoy spotting a very young Lucille Ball, cast in a tiny role as a flower shop clerk.

TO SIR, WITH LOVE (1967)
Color, 105 minutes
Cast: Sidney Poitier, Christian Roberts, Judy Geeson, Suzy Kendall, Lulu
Director: James Clavell
Screenplay: Clavell, based on a novel by Edward Ricardo Braithwaite
Drama
Unrated
Young children: No Older children: VG

This very popular film tells the story of Mark Thackeray, a young West Indian engineer who has been unable to secure employment in the field for which he has been trained. He finds work instead in a high school in the slums of London's East End. Here, he faces a classroom filled with alienated and recalcitrant youngsters who are constantly acting out their anger. Thackeray understands why the teens are so angstridden: They have been brought up by inattentive parents and shunted aside by an uncaring educational system.

So he ignores traditional teaching methods. He deals with them as if they are adults, opening up their world by taking them on field trips to museums and leading them in frank but necessary discussions relating to sex, marriage, and society. Despite several setbacks and hurdles, the teens—who basically are likable youngsters—grow, and learn, and mature under Thackeray's loving tutelage.

On a superficial level, *To Sir, With Love* seems to offer a pat solution to a complex issue. But it makes a solid case for the notion that adolescents will respond if someone takes the time to listen to them and treats them with respect.

Sidney Poitier was one of the top box-office stars in the world when he made this film. (Twelve years earlier, he was one of the unruly students giving teacher Glenn Ford a hard time in *The Blackboard Jungle*.) Having played a number of characters who had to battle racial prejudice, he now came full circle by playing a teacher whose presence is so commanding that the subject of race never comes up!

To Sir, With Love remains a highly entertaining film, following a tradition dating back to **Goodbye, Mr. Chips** and followed by such other inspired-teacher films as **Stand and Deliver** and *Dangerous Minds.*

TOY STORY (1995)
Color, 80 minutes
Cast: Voices of Tom Hanks, Tim Allen, Don Rickles, Jim Varney, Wallace Shawn, John Ratzenberger, Annie Potts, John Morris
Director: John Lasseter
Screenplay: Joss Whedon, Andrew Stanton, Joel Cohen, and Alec Sokolow
Animated feature
Rated G
Younger kids: OK   Older kids: VG

Toy Story made its mark as the first computer-generated cartoon feature ever released. But that would have been merely academic had it not captured the imagination of moviegoers young and old with its lively story and vivid characters.

The culmination of years of work—both technical and creative—by the folks at Pixar studios, led by John Lasseter, this film is told from the point of view of a boy's toys who live with their master in a typical boy's bedroom. Andy's longtime favorite has been Woody, a cowboy doll, but when he receives a present of a high-tech Buzz Lightyear figure, based on the latest TV sensation, Woody finds himself neglected overnight. A fight breaks out, and Buzz falls out the window. The other toys—including a Slinky dog and Mr. Potato Head—urge Woody to save the newcomer, leading to a series of adventures outside the safety of their home.

Toy Story is a marvel of imagination, full of clever gags and ideas, and built on a solid story framework. The fact that the toys are so frustrated and rarely happy is a subtext that will probably sail over the heads of most youngsters; they'll be too wrapped up in the fun and adventure of the film.

There is one sequence that gives some parents pause, when Woody winds up in the house next door, where a rotten kid has torn toys apart and created mutated versions by sticking and gluing different pieces together. It's a gruesome sight and a dose of black humor that most kids seem to love—but it might put off the youngest viewers.

Families who watch *Toy Story* over and over again should also seek out a cassette called *Tiny Toy Stories,* which includes the wonderful, award-winning Pixar short subjects that led to this first feature film. Those shorts also appear on the deluxe laserdisc version of the feature.

TRADING MOM (1994)
Color, 82 minutes
Cast: Sissy Spacek, Anna Chlumsky, Aaron Michael Metchik, Asher Metchik, Maureen Stapleton, Merritt Yohnka, Andre the Giant
Director: Tia Brelis
Screenplay: Tia Brelis, based on the short story "The Mummy Market" by Nancy Brelis
Comedy/Fantasy
Rated PG
Young children: OK   Older children: OK

A children's fantasy best suited for the younger ones, *Trading Mom* stars Sissy Spacek in four different "mommy" guises. When young Elizabeth Martin (Anna Chlumsky) complains to neighborhood witch lady, Mrs. Cavor (Maureen Stapleton), about her overworked mother, she suggests the Martin kids try a secret spell that will erase their memory of their mom, freeing them up to shop for another at the "Mommy Market" downtown.

Each child gets one choice: Elizabeth chooses Maman, a rich, selfish French matron, who treats the children as products rather than human beings. Brother Jeremy picks Mom, a sporting enthusiast, who wears the kids out with nonstop games and camping trips. Little Harry goes for Natasha, a gypsy circus performer, who converts the children into acrobats and welcomes the use of her children in dangerous circus acts. The kids learn the error of their ways and, when their memory is restored, are grateful for the Mom they have.

On paper this sounds like surefire material, but the film doesn't fulfill its promise; it's heavy-handed at every turn. Young kids may like it anyway, although it is rated PG for some crude humor.

TREASURE ISLAND (1934)
Black & white, 105 minutes
Cast: Wallace Beery, Jackie Cooper, Lewis Stone, Lionel Barrymore, Otto Kruger, Nigel Bruce, Douglass Dumbrille, Charles "Chic" Sale
Director: Victor Fleming
Screenplay: John Lee Mahin, based on the novel by Robert Louis Stevenson
Adventure/Literary classic

Unrated
Young children: VG   Older children: VG

One dark night a mysterious codger named Billy Bones gets drunk at an inn in Bristol, England. His loose tongue reveals the secret of a glorious cache of treasure, including gold and jewels. One of the listeners is a young boy named Jim Hawkins who eventually opens a sea chest and finds a map leading to the hidden riches. So begins one of the most exciting treasure hunts in the history of literature. Jim sets out on a ship headed for the South Seas, where he plans to locate the treasure island and then dig up the loot. Onboard the ship, he befriends a villainous, larger-than-life, one-legged pirate named Long John Silver, and together the two unlikely mates become engrossed in a thrilling, blood-chilling adventure.

Even though some of the action is intense, and Long John is an imposing character (with his eyepatch and wooden leg), this film is geared to appeal to a juvenile audience. Aside from Captain Hook and his crew in **Peter Pan** and the shipboard exploits in **Captain Blood,** there simply aren't enough good pirate adventures, especially ones that are targeted to young viewers. This one is a lollapalooza! The whole production is first-rate. The females in the family may miss the presence of any girls or women in the adventure, but this shouldn't keep them from becoming immersed in young Jim's fascinating search for treasure.

Jackie Cooper and Wallace Beery were two of the most popular stars of this period. If your family is familiar with the Little Rascals/Our Gang comedies, you may have seen Jackie in some of the most charming early 1930s episodes, involving schoolteacher Miss Crabtree. He went on to star opposite Beery in the classic tearjerker *The Champ*, and the great success of that film led to their being reteamed many times.

TREASURE ISLAND (1950)
Color, 96 minutes
Cast: Robert Newton, Bobby Driscoll, Basil Sydney, Walter Fitzgerald, Denis O'Dea, Ralph Truman, Finlay Currie, John Laurie, Frances de Wolff, Geoffrey Wilkinson, Geoffrey Keen
Director: Byron Haskin
Screenplay: Lawrence E. Watkin, based on the novel by Robert Louis Stevenson
Adventure/Literary classic
Unrated
Young children: VG Older children: VG

Walt Disney's first all-live-action feature boasts a spirited script and an extraordinary British cast (with the exception of Bobby Driscoll as young Jim Hawkins) that bring Robert Louis Stevenson's familiar novel to a new level of life. The script stays true to the novel, which relates the tale of a young boy's search for hidden treasure and his loyalty to a cutthroat, one-legged pirate. British star Robert Newton is perfectly cast as Long John Silver. His threatening, piercing glances send shivers down the spines of all who behold him, and his guttural "Aye, me hearties" voice calls for immediate obedience. Newton certainly chews the scenery, but with such gusto that he remains many people's image of the quintessential movie pirate.

The movie was shot in the rich Technicolor process, and the sumptuous photography showcases the fast-paced action in exotic settings, including sea battles set against tropical island backgrounds. What was considered to be "objectionable" violence was deleted from the 1975 reissue, but restored in the videotape/laserdisc released in 1992. The scene, a famous one in Stevenson's novel, involves Jim shooting a pirate at point-blank range from his perch in the crow's nest. It's a startling moment, but it's played for menace and adventure, not blood. Measured against today's liberal standards of violence, it's almost tame.

A TREE GROWS IN BROOKLYN (1945)
Black & white, 128 minutes
Cast: Dorothy McGuire, Joan Blondell, James Dunn, Lloyd Nolan, Peggy Ann Garner, Ted Donaldson, James Gleason, Ruth Nelson
Director: Elia Kazan
Screenplay: Tess Slesinger and Frank Davis, based on the novel by Betty Smith
Drama
Unrated
Young children: OK Older children: VG

Here is a poignant dramatization of the Betty Smith best-seller about Francie Nolan (Peggy Ann Garner), an intelligent and sensitive young teenager growing up amidst the poverty of Williamsburgh, Brooklyn, circa 1912. Francie yearns for a career as a writer; however, she is coming of age in an environment where self-expression is an extravagance, and youthful hopes are quickly squelched by the harsh realities of day-to-day life. Her perpetually worried mother, Katie (Dorothy McGuire), works tirelessly to support Francie and her kid brother, while Johnny (James Dunn), her idealistic dreamer of a dad, is an alcoholic singing waiter. Still, Francie struggles to keep her eyes on her goal and rise above her surroundings.

Adolescent girls will especially respond to Francie (especially since so much of the film is told from her point of view), but no viewer could fail to be touched by her loving relationship with her ne'er-do-well father, which is the foundation of the story.

A Tree Grows in Brooklyn is a poignant and beautiful film, a poetic look at people who seem absolutely, heartbreakingly real.

James Dunn and Peggy Ann Garner, cast as father and daughter, both won Academy Awards for their memorable performances. Garner, who never had a better screen role, was awarded a special citation as "outstanding child performer of 1945."

Tenement life has rarely been re-created so believably or with such sensitivity; the film marked an auspicious screen directing debut for Elia Kazan.

TREMORS (1990)
Color, 96 minutes
Cast: Kevin Bacon, Fred Ward, Finn Carter, Michael Gross, Reba McEntire, Bobby Jacoby, Charlotte Stewart, Tony Genaro, Ariana Richards, Richard Marcus, Victor Wong, Bibi Besch
Director: Ron Underwood

Screenplay: S. S. Wilson and Brent Maddock
Science fiction/Monster/Comedy
Rated PG-13
Younger kids: Too scary Older kids: Just scary enough

Buddies Bacon and Ward are more or less hanging around a desert valley when tunneling, carnivorous monsters, like colossal worms with pinchers, start attacking people. After a lot of hair-raising suspense, chases, and the like, the survivors learn that the monsters track their prey by sound, so they try to figure a way to safety.

This bright, sassy tribute to (and imitation of) the giant-monster movies of the 1950s has a winning cast, and some funny, well-written dialogue. The characters are very well drawn, the monsters convincing, and all the problems logically created and logically solved. It's just about an ideal movie of its type, all the way around.

The monsters, however, are definitely monsters, and there's some gruesome stuff and nerve-rattling suspense, so it's not for younger kids or, for that matter, the more sensitive older ones. If your 10- to 12-year-olds are ready for thrilling, funny monster action, they'll love this one.

TREMORS 2: AFTERSHOCKS (1995)
Color, 100 minutes
Cast: Fred Ward, Christopher Gartin, Helen Shaver, Michael Gross, Marcelo Tubert, Marco Hernandez, Jose Rosario
Director: S. S. Wilson
Screenplay: Brent Maddock and Wilson
Monster/Science fiction/Suspense

Rated PG-13
Younger kids: Too
   intense   Older kids: OK, for
   the initiated

Sort of famous for having defeated some giant, burrowing monsters (as shown in **Tremors**), Ward is nonetheless down on his luck, until more of the monsters turn up, menacing an oil field in Mexico. He's hired to deal with the creatures, and does fine until the creatures reproduce. What's more, their offspring don't burrow: they run about like giant, fanged turkeys, and no one knows how to handle these critters.

Although not as good as *Tremors*, this is a pretty effective sequel, especially for a movie that was released directly on video. The script and characters aren't as amusing, and it goes on too long, but Fred Ward is almost always a hell of a nice guy to spend a couple of hours with. The effects are more elaborate than in the original, with all those scampering monsters, but somehow not as convincing.

As with the original, if your kids can handle monster movie violence (and this is not particularly violent), they'll probably get a kick out of this one.

TRON (1982)
Color, 96 minutes
Cast: Jeff Bridges, Bruce
   Boxleitner, David Warner,
   Cindy Morgan, Barnard
   Hughes, Dan Shor, Peter
   Jurasik, Tony Stephano
Director: Steven Lisberger
Screenplay: Steven Lisberger
Fantasy/Adventure
Rated PG
Younger kids: OK   Older kids:
   OK

Computer expert Kevin (Bridges) has been fired from his job; while trying to help friends working against his former company, Kevin is disintegrated, then reintegrated in miniaturized form as a part of the pocket universe of the company's master computer system. What are mere video games in the real world are life-and-death battles in the world of the computer, and Kevin—now called Clu—seeks help from video warrior Tron (Boxleitner). Tron and others are working against the Master Computer Program (MCP) and its minion Sark (Warner) and are being helped by people in the real world.

Now known primarily for its early use of computer animation, and for marking a radical change of pace for the then tradition-bound Disney studio, *Tron* is moderately entertaining; the division between Good and Evil is as diagrammatic as the face of the MCP. Dividing the hero chores between Bridges and Boxleitner wasn't a good idea; Bridges is charming but ineffectual, Boxleitner skilled but bland. Warner, as usual, makes the most of his standardized villainous role.

Today's computer-savvy children might be interested in the "primitive" graphics, but are just as likely to be drawn into the story. Still, the movie continually promises more than it delivers, and children will recognize this, too, even as they enjoy the film the first time through.

THE TROUBLE WITH ANGELS (1966)

Color, 112 minutes

Cast: Rosalind Russell, Hayley Mills, June Harding, Binnie Barnes, Mary Wickes, Gypsy Rose Lee, Camilla Sparv, Kent Smith

Director: Ida Lupino

Screenplay: Blanche Hanalis, from the novel *Life with Mother Superior* by Jane Trahey

Comedy

Unrated

Young children: VG   Older children: VG

This cheerful comedy follows the misadventures of two mischievous teenage girls who are students at St. Francis Academy. Hayley Mills plays Mary Clancy, a reluctant boarder at the school, who is blessed with a series of "scathingly brilliant ideas" that test the patience of the nuns—particularly the stately Mother Superior (Rosalind Russell). With her fellow conspirator Rachel Devery (June Harding), the two play one comical prank after another. They substitute bubble bath powder for the sugar at the dining table where the sisters eat . . . then almost cause a fire when they secretly investigate the thrill of smoking cigars. In art class, their attempt to create masks of human faces ends in yet another comical disaster.

There is nothing mean-spirited about Mary and Rachel's escapades, and the film has a genuine spirit of fun. Girls will be especially drawn to the story, which in addition to the comedy also tackles such problems as being separated from one's family and contemplating the possibility of becoming a nun.

The Trouble With Angels was followed by a sequel: *Where Angels Go . . . Trouble Follows.*

20 MILLION MILES TO EARTH (1957)

Black & white, 74 minutes

Cast: William Hopper, Joan Taylor, Frank Puglia, John Zaremba, Thomas Browne Henry, Tito Vuolo, Bart Bradley

Director: Nathan Juran

Screenplay: Bob Williams and Christopher Knopf

Science fiction/Monster adventure

Unrated

Younger kids: OK   Older kids: OK

The first spaceship to Venus returns to Earth, crashing into the sea off Sicily. Meanwhile, a boy barters an odd object he finds by the sea to an old scientist, and the jelly-like mass opens to reveal a small, reptilian creature. It turns out it's from Venus, lives on sulfur, and grows at an astonishing rate. It's also very bad-tempered. At the climax, the giant monster runs amok in Rome.

The credits above don't indicate the real talent behind this film: Ray Harryhausen, master of stop-motion animation. The Venusian monster here is one of his most convincing, lively creations; it's not evil, just cranky when cornered, but that's enough to result in King Kong–like devastation. This also keeps the rapidly growing alien somewhat sympathetic, especially for children, who'll side with it from the moment it makes its tabletop advent.

Briskly paced with a well-structured story, this is Harryhausen's best black-and-white movie.

TWICE UPON A TIME (1983)
Color, 75 minutes
Cast: Voices of Lorenzo Music, Judith Kahan Kampmann, Marshall Efron, Julie Payne, James S. Cranna, Hamilton Camp
Directors: John Korty, Charles Swenson
Screenplay: Korty, Swenson, Suella Kennedy, and Bill Couturie
Animated feature
Rated PG
Younger kids: OK   Older kids: OK

Something like a feature-length "Fractured Fairy Tale," *Twice Upon a Time* is a funny, visually inventive animated adventure that can be appreciated by everyone in the family.

The fanciful story centers on a pair of eccentric characters from the land of Frivoli, the makers of sweet dreams, who inadvertently stop time, freezing the human beings of our dimension. The maniacal ruler of the Muckworks, a nightmare factory, seizes this opportunity to bomb mankind with nasty dreams—unless our unlikely heroes, the innocent doglike Ralph, superhero Rod Rescueman, aspiring actress Flora Fauna, and a prankster named MUM who speaks only in sound effects, can save the day.

An unusual cut-out animation technique and clever character designs give *Twice Upon a Time* a unique, offbeat feel. A witty script and smart dialogue is enhanced by an appealing voice cast. (Even the most rabid **Star Wars** fans may not know that George Lucas was the executive producer of this overlooked cartoon comedy feature.)

TWISTER (1996)
Color, 105 minutes
Cast: Helen Hunt, Bill Paxton, Jami Gertz, Lois Smith, Cary Elwes, Alan Ruck, Jeremy Davies, Joey Soltnick, Philip Seymour Hoffman
Director: Jan De Bont
Screenplay: Michael Crichton and Anne-Marie Martin
Disaster movie
Rated PG-13
Younger children: No   Older children: VG

When she was a child, Jo's father was whisked away by a tornado, so when she grows up, she decides to learn as much about these weather phenomena as she can. As the head of a team of eccentric scientists based in Oklahoma, an adult Jo (Helen Hunt) chases ferocious rainstorms and charts the development of tornadoes, hoping to gather enough data to aid in tornado prediction. When her ex-husband (Bill Paxton) shows up with his new fiancée, the lure of twister-chasing brings him irrevocably back to Jo. Together they track a "big one" and attempt to implant it with hundreds of tiny tracking devices, but the massive storms are as unpredictable as they are dangerous, and the expedition is fraught with danger.

Twister is the kind of movie often referred to as a "thrill ride," and indeed it offers the same sensation—and satisfaction—as a good run on a roller coaster. (This is supposed to make up for the dumb plotting and dialogue.) In a heart-pounding prologue, a little girl and her family are threatened by a twister. Indeed, her father is taken off—but when her *dog* is placed in peril and then rescued, it's a signal that the film doesn't intend to be overly reckless with our emotions! (There are also several knowing references to **The Wizard of Oz,** which featured the most famous twister in movie history.)

Even so, this is far too intense (and believable, at least in terms of special effects) for young kids. Parents will have to gauge how much their older kids can withstand in terms of excitement before allowing them to see *Twister.* The MPAA awarded it a PG-13 not because of sex, violence, or language, but for "intense depiction of very bad weather." No kidding.

2001: A SPACE ODYSSEY
(1968)
Color, 139 minutes
Cast: Keir Dullea, Gary Lockwood, William Sylvester, Leonard Rossiter, Daniel Richter; voice of Douglas Rain (HAL 9000)
Director: Stanley Kubrick
Screenplay: Arthur C. Clarke and Kubrick, suggested by Clarke's short story "The Sentinel"
Science fiction/Drama
Rated G
Young children: Confusing Older children: OK

This dazzling, unforgettable movie is one of the most influential films made since *Citizen Kane* and an ineradicable part of movie history. It often ends up on critics' lists of the ten best movies ever made, and it is not merely a deep personal favorite of thousands who saw it on its first release in 1968; it is part of their lives in a way that few movies ever are.

And yet it's hard to recommend as family viewing—not because there's anything racy or overly violent about the movie, but because so very much of the impact of this beautiful film is lost when watching it for the first time on a television screen. *2001: A Space Odyssey* demands to be seen in a theater.

In 1968, people were often confused by the movie. At the "Dawn of Man," a tribe of nearly human apes is on the verge of starvation. A large black slab mysteriously appears, and the frightened apes touch it. Later, the ape leader (Richter) remembers the slab while toying with some bones, and he makes the intuitive leap: the bones can be used to kill animals for food.

In the most audacious single cut in movie history, the film leaps forward four million years to the year 2001, when another black slab has been found buried beneath the surface of the Moon. When it is uncovered, it emits a single shrieking radio signal aimed at Jupiter.

Months later, aboard a ship heading for Jupiter, most of the crew is hibernating; Bowman (Dullea) and Poole (Lockwood) are the only ones awake and soon discover that HAL 9000, the self-aware, talking computer that controls their ship, is making serious errors. . . .

The greatness of *2001* doesn't lie in brilliant characters, scintillating dialogue, or even its then-unprecedented special effects. Rather, it's filmmaker Stanley Kubrick's vision, which is complex and multilayered. It's an interesting story and a fascinating speculation, with elements of biting satire; it's a variation on Homer's *Odyssey*; and it's a parable about the entire history of mankind. In fact, it's one of the few movies that can be analyzed legitimately any number of ways, even if they may contradict each other.

As far as entertainment for the family, it must be admitted that the movie is much more slowly paced than the action films disguised as science fiction of the 1990s, and many kids' attention is likely to wander, particularly if the movie is seen on television. However, for teenagers who are beginning to wonder about major questions, *2001: A Space Odyssey* can be as transcendental an experience as it was for kids their age in 1968.

A little-heralded but interesting sequel, *2010*, was made in 1984; while it lacks the complex layering of Kubrick's masterpiece, it's an ambitious and entertaining film in its own right.

U

THE UGLY DACHSHUND
(1966)
Color, 93 minutes
Cast: Dean Jones, Suzanne
  Pleshette, Charlie Ruggles,
  Kelly Thordsen, Parley Baer
Director: Norman Tokar
Screenplay: Albert Aley, based
  on the book by G. B. Stern
Comedy
Unrated
Younger kids: VG   Older kids:
  VG

In this cute live-action Disney
comedy, the ugly dachshund is
really a Great Dane who *thinks*
he's a dachshund, having been
abandoned as a puppy and raised
among a litter of dachsies. Dean
Jones (in the first of his many Disney movies) plays a commercial
artist named Mark whose wife,
Fran (Suzanne Pleshette), is devoted to her dachshund Danke.
When the dog has puppies, the
vet (Charlie Ruggles) talks Mark
into taking home a baby Great
Dane named Brutus, and the dog
quickly grows to mammoth pro-
portions and romps about the
house with the same reckless
abandon as his tiny "siblings."
The climax is a dog show for
which Mark tries to train Brutus
to act like the Great Dane it is.
  This is a featherweight sitcom
of a movie made in Disney's most
innocuous 1960s style, but its
wall-to-wall dog antics will delight
any canine fancier, and there's
something irresistibly funny about

seeing the giant Great Dane playing with the dachshunds and acting like one of them while
wreaking havoc in the house. The
climactic dog show sequence is
also quite amusing, and kids
should enjoy the whole silly thing.

THE UNINVITED (1944)
Black & white, 100 minutes
Cast: Ray Milland, Ruth Hussey,
  Gail Russell, Donald Crisp,
  Cornelia Otis Skinner,
  Dorothy Stickney, Barbara
  Everest, Alan Napier
Director: Lewis Allen
Screenplay: Jack Partos and
  Dodie Smith, from the novel
  Uneasy Freehold (aka *The
  Uninvited*) by Dorothy
  Macardle
Horror/Suspense
Unrated
Young children: OK, with hand-
  holding   Older children: OK

Brother and sister Milland and
Hussey buy an old mansion on
the Cornish coast of England and
become friendly with local girl
Russell, who has an uncanny connection with the building. Soon it
becomes clear that the house is
haunted by a malignant spirit—
though at times, the ghost seems
to be benign—that is drawn to
Russell.
  This intriguing, well-plotted
drama takes the existence of
ghosts for granted. However, the
ghost sequences are still very
spooky at times, and the subtle,

understated special effects are particularly convincing. The direction is careful and intelligent, the performances very good (including an icy turn by Skinner), and the mystery well conceived. While this isn't as frightening as **The Haunting** or **The Innocents,** it stands with them as one of the best ghost movies ever made.

Though the scenes with the vaporous ghosts are scary, even young children should get through them, provided there's a parent to cuddle up to. The movie is not romantic in the usual sense (though Milland does fall for Russell), but it does center on love in a way that might take teenagers by surprise, particularly those who are interested in Gothic romance novels. (Clue: it deals with parental love.)

UNSTRUNG HEROES (1995)
Color, 94 minutes
Cast: John Turturro, Andie MacDowell, Nathan Watt, Michael Richards, Maury Chaykin, Kendra Krull, Joey Andrews, Celia Weston, Anne DeSalvo, Candice Azzara
Director: Diane Keaton
Screenplay: Richard LaGravenese, based on the book by Franz Lidz
Drama
Rated PG
Young children: No   Older children: VG

Unstrung Heroes is an affecting coming-of-age film, set in the early 1960s, which beautifully captures a time and place. The primary character is 12-year-old Steven Lidz (Nathan Watt). He and his kid sister are an integral part of a happy, likably nutty Jewish family. His father, Sid (John Turturro), an eccentric inventor, is a genuinely sweet man; his mother, Selma (Andie McDowell), is aptly described as an "American beauty." Sid and Selma are wonderful, loving parents.

But then, Selma becomes seriously ill. Sid becomes preoccupied with his wife's condition and is insensitive to the needs of his son. So Steven turns to his two oddball uncles, who live in a crummy downtown hotel, for companionship: Arthur (Maury Chaykin), rotund, none-too-bright, but gentle and kind, and Danny (Michael Richards), a manic paranoid who sees political conspiracies lurking everywhere.

A boy's need for love and attention is the foundation of this story, which is told with both humor and understanding. The uncles are somewhat crazy, but they have a genuine fondness for Steven that helps him through some difficult times.

Unstrung Heroes may not be a great movie, nor does it offer any especially useful life lessons, but it is both touching and amusing, and offers a gallery of fine performances. It is based on author Franz Lidz's own experiences.

Older kids should enjoy it thoroughly; the sadness that hovers over the story with the mother's impending death makes it too difficult for young children.

V

VEGAS VACATION (1997)
Color, 95 minutes
Cast: Chevy Chase, Beverly
  D'Angelo, Randy Quaid,
  Ethan Embry, Marisol Nichols,
  Wallace Shawn, Miriam Flynn
Director: Stephen Kessler
Screenplay: Elisa Bell, from a
  story by Bell and Bob Ducsay
Comedy
Rated PG
Younger kids: No   Older kids:
  Good

In this fourth *Vacation* film (missing the *National Lampoon* imprim-
atur), Clark Griswold (Chevy
Chase) receives a bonus at work
for inventing a new food preser-
vative, and he treats the family to
a trip to Las Vegas. Naturally, the
vacation is filled with one comic
mishap after another. Clark loses
a fortune at the blackjack tables
and is plagued by a malicious
dealer (Wallace Shawn) . . . wife
Ellen meets Wayne Newton (himself) and ends up being wined and
dined by the singing star . . .
daughter Audrey (Marisol Nichols) is turned into a sexy showgirl
by her trashy cousin Vickie (Shae
D'Lyn) . . . and son Rusty (Ethan
Embry) imitates a slick gambler
so well that he's taken under the
wing of a high-rolling mobster
(played by the film's producer,
Jerry Weintraub).

Of course, Clark also is obliged
to pay a visit to his boorish redneck cousin Eddie (Randy

Quaid), who lives nearby at a nuclear test site.

Though filled with a typical
blend of low comedy and sexual
innuendo, this is generally toned
down and less tasteless than the
previous *Vacation* movies (hence
the PG rating), and there's something goofily amusing about it,
with top-notch comic support
from Quaid and Shawn, and a
funny cameo by Sid Caesar.

Adolescents should enjoy it and
won't be exposed to anything more
potent than what turns up on most
contemporary TV comedies.

A VERY BRADY SEQUEL
(1996)
Color, 90 minutes
Cast: Shelley Long, Gary Cole,
  Tim Matheson, Christine
  Taylor, Christopher Daniel
  Barnes, Jennifer Elise Cox,
  Paul Sutera, Olivia Hack,
  Jessie Lee, RuPaul
Director: Arlene Sanford
Screenplay: Jim Berg, Harry
  Elfont, Deborah Kaplan, and
  Stan Zimmerman, based on
  the TV series created by
  Sherwood Schwartz
Comedy
Rated PG-13
Young children: No   Older
  children: VG, with caution

The life of the Brady family is disrupted when a man (Tim Matheson) turns up claiming to be
Carol's long-lost first husband!
In truth, he's a con artist who

wants to get his hands on a sculpture the Bradys own, which—unbeknownst to them—is worth a fortune. Meanwhile, there's another kind of crisis brewing in the house because Greg and Marsha are forced to share a room.

There are some delightfully silly musical sequences and a handful of gags involving familiar guest stars in cameo roles.

As with the first Brady Bunch movie, this one imposes a '90s sensibility on a family stuck in the '70s. And like the first movie, some of its biggest laughs come from deliberately raunchy gags—in this case, the two oldest kids' highly uncomfortable realization that they are attracted to one another!

While this subplot is very funny from an adult point of view, it could be both disturbing and confusing to kids, and parents should be on the alert. There is just enough of this kind of humor here that the film should probably be off-limits to younger kids, even though they'll want to watch it.

VILLAGE OF THE DAMNED
(1960)
Black & white, 78 minutes
Cast: George Sanders, Barbara Shelley, Martin Stephens, Michael Gwynn, Laurence Naismith
Director: Wolf Rilla
Screenplay: Stirling Silliphant, Rilla, and George Barclay (pseud. of Ronald Kinnoch), from the novel *The Midwich Cuckoos* by John Wyndham
Science fiction/Suspense
Unrated
Younger kids: No   Older kids: OK

Everyone in a small English village (including animals) falls suddenly asleep one morning, and no one, including the concerned government, can find out why. A few months later, every woman in town capable of bearing a child is pregnant, including virgins. When born, the children strongly resemble one another, with thick blond hair and strange eyes—and they have telepathic powers, which they use with increasing ruthlessness.

The film never clearly establishes just where the children came from (in the novel, there's no doubt the "fathers" are aliens), but it's obvious why they are here: they intend to replace the human race.

Here is a fine example of what can be done with science fiction ideas that don't require special effects or a big budget. Furthermore, it's one of the few movies dealing with children whom kids in the audience won't identify with—because they're so creepy—but may find hypnotic just the same. (Who can ever forget those weird, piercing eyes?) Very nearly a sci-fi classic, older kids who like this brand of entertainment will be surprised and mesmerized.

Warning: Avoid the heavy-handed, violent, R-rated 1995 remake, starring Christopher Reeve.

VOYAGE TO THE BOTTOM OF THE SEA (1961)
Color, 105 minutes
Cast: Walter Pidgeon, Joan Fontaine, Barbara Eden, Peter Lorre, Robert Sterling, Michael Ansara, Frankie Avalon
Director: Irwin Allen
Screenplay: Irwin Allen and Charles Bennett
Science fiction/Suspense adventure

Unrated
Young children: OK   Older
   children: OK

Preposterous science fiction thriller in which icebergs sink and the Van Allen radiation belt *catches fire,* threatening all life on Earth. Who can save us all? Why, only Admiral Harriman Nelson (Pidgeon), his super-sub the *Seaview,* and his staff of well-known character actors—plus Frankie Avalon. Naturally, there's a saboteur aboard the sub as it races to set off the missiles that Nelson knows will snuff out the—uh, burning radiation. Giant squids, mine fields, and attacking submarines present hazards.

The long-running TV series based on this movie is still around and still thrilling younger children, the best audience for this absurd movie, which collects just about all submarine clichés into one flashy package, courtesy of the flamboyant filmmaker Irwin Allen.

Teenagers and adults will roll their eyes and glance at the clock, but kids from 8 to 12 will have a fine time.

W

WALKABOUT (1971)
Color, 100 minutes
Cast: Jenny Agutter, Lucien
  John, David Gulpilil, John
  Meillon
Director: Nicolas Roeg
Screenplay: Edward Bond, from
  the novel by James Vance
  Marshall
Adventure
Rated PG
Young children: OK, with
  caution   Older children: VG

This exquisitely rendered tale of
survival and coming of age begins
most harshly, when Mary and her
tiny brother, Peter, are left to
fend for themselves in the Outback after their dad tries to shoot
them and then kills himself (it's
only a plane crash in the book).

Thinking their only chance is to
trek fourteen hundred miles
across the North Australian desert to the town of Adelaide, the
city kids reluctantly embark, only
to be met by an Aborigine boy on
his walkabout, a six-month camp-
out required of bush boys as a rite
of passage into manhood.

Almost wordlessly, the three
journey together across magical,
dreamlike landscapes, learning
from each other, away from time
and society. For although the man-
child is supposed to stay on his
own, living off the land and sleeping on it, he knows he can't just let
these children die. His fateful decision changes all their lives forever.

Mysterious and eerie, with un-

expected moments of violence
and nudity, the film is unsettling,
often shocking.

But there simply isn't another
movie like it.

It's not really for younger kids,
although their curiosity might be
fired by the opening scenes. The
existential quality of the film may
ultimately raise more questions
than it answers but will give intelligent kids an unusual and worthwhile viewing experience.

THE WAR (1994)
Color, 125 minutes
Cast: Elijah Wood, Kevin
  Costner, Mare Winningham,
  Lexi Randall, Christine
  Baranski, Gary Basaraba,
  Raynor Scheine, Latoya
  Chisholm
Director: Jon Avnet
Screenplay: Kathy McWorter
Drama
Rated PG-13
Young children: No   Older
  children: OK

A well-intentioned story of a
Vietnam veteran (Kevin Costner)
returning home to his family in
the rural South, this parable is a
bit preachier than one might like.
Set in Mississippi in 1970, the
story mainly revolves around Stu
(Elijah Wood) and Lidia Simmons (Lexi Randall) and their
war with poor neighborhood kids
over a tree fort—a none-too-
subtle parallel with the Vietnam

war. Costner tries to teach Stu and Lidia the value of peace, harmony, and nonviolence—but it's hard for them to stomach when the neighbor kids are so genuinely mean.

The War has some strong moments and may reach impressionable adolescents—though even they will need a bit of a history lesson in order to understand the alienation of the Kevin Costner character and the problems of returning veterans.

The problem with *The War* is that it's long, slow, and unfocused; there are several climaxes, which wring your emotions dry. Even adults may find it difficult to digest, despite its good qualities and intentions.

The drama is quite intense at times—much too intense for kids under the age of 12.

WARGAMES (1983)
Color, 110 minutes
Cast: Matthew Broderick, Dabney Coleman, John Wood, Ally Sheedy, Barry Corbin, Juanin Clay, Maury Chaykin, Michael Madsen
Director: John Badham
Screenplay: Lawrence Lasker and Walter F. Parkes
Adventure/Drama
Rated PG
Younger kids: OK   Older kids: OK

A computer whiz (Broderick) tries to hack his way into the file of a new computer firm to play a game called Global Thermonuclear War. He accidentally breaks into the government's NORAD mainframe and nearly starts World War III by unwittingly playing the real thing. This is an ingenious and, of course, unset-

tling idea, and *WarGames* was one of the first major films (along with **Tron**) to explore the importance that computers were beginning to play in our lives. Broderick and Sheedy are believable and appealing as the teens who get in over their heads.

Unfortunately, the story falters along the way and gets too caught up in delivering an anti–nuclear war message; the threat of nuclear annihilation is milked for one too many climaxes. In addition, most of the adults and government officials in the film—with the exception of John Wood as the scientist who programmed the government's computer—are complete morons, which provides easy laughs and even easier scenarios for our intrepid teens to triumph over. (No doubt, kids will love this.) Nevertheless, the film is still an entertaining forum for parents to discuss the real threat of a nuclear war with their own children.

WAR OF THE WORLDS (1953)
Color, 85 minutes
Cast: Gene Barry, Les Tremayne, Ann Robinson, Robert Cornthwaite, Henry Brandon, Jack Kruschen, Sir Cedric Hardwicke (narrator)
Director: Byron Haskin
Screenplay: Barre Lyndon, from the novel by H. G. Wells
Science fiction/Suspense/Literary classic
Unrated
Younger kids: Maybe   Older kids: Good

Spaceships from Mars land en masse on earth. Hovering "war machines," equipped with two types of deadly rays, emerge and soon begin laying waste to the entire world. Gene Barry plays a scientist who's there when the first ship opens up, but there is little he can do against the unstoppable aliens.

Updated to the time of the production, H. G. Wells' classic novel is given robust treatment, with lively direction, plenty of action, an ominous mood, and a good cast. Some of the dialogue is dated, and kids are likely to smirk at some of the special effects (as when the wires holding up the war machines are visible), but they'll probably get involved just the same.

War of the Worlds is a serious—even grim—drama, with little relief once the attacks begin. People die (sometimes painfully), civilization is threatened, and it doesn't seem like make-believe. Younger kids may be scared by the intensity of the invasion and the doom-and-gloom prospects, but the finale, with its uplifting message, may ease some of their fears.

THE WATCHER IN THE WOODS (1980)
Color, 84 minutes
Cast: Bette Davis, Carroll Baker, David McCallum, Lynn-Holly Johnson, Kyle Richards, Ian Bannen, Richard Pasco, Frances Cuka
Director: John Hough
Screenplay: Brian Clemens, Harry Spaldin, and Rosemary Anne Sisson, from the novel by Florence Engel Randall
Juvenile mystery/Science fiction
Rated PG
Younger children: OK, but spooky Older children: OK

An American family moves into an old house in the English countryside, renting it from strange old Mrs. Aylwood (Bette Davis), who lives nearby. Seventeen-year-old Jan (Lynn-Holly Johnson) begins to have weird, perhaps supernatural adventures in the old house, which seem to have some connection with Karen, Mrs. Aylwood's daughter, who literally disappeared from the house many years before.

Jan and her younger sister, Ellie (Kyle Richards), decide to try to find out what happened to Karen, who may be trying to contact Ellie from beyond the veil of time.

The movie is handsomely produced, with a good cast, but the film has a patchwork feel to it—for good reason; the ending was reshot and the story cut by 15 minutes after a poor reception on its first release.

Younger children, who accept almost everything at face value, are more likely to enjoy this movie than older kids.

THE WATERBOY (1998)
Color, 88 minutes
Cast: Adam Sandler, Fairuza Balk, Henry Winkler, Kathy Bates, Jerry Reed, Larry Gilliard, Jr., Blake Clark, Clint Howard, Rob Schneider
Director: Frank Coraci
Screenplay: Tim Herlihy and Adam Sandler
Comedy
Rated PG-13
Young children: No Older children: OK

Adam Sandler steps into Jerry Lewis' wobbly shoes in this broad, obvious, likable comedy about a dim-witted young man who lives to serve—as the much-abused waterboy for football teams. He lives with his sheltering, smothering mama, and has no friends . . . until his new boss, a downtrodden coach for a Louisiana college (Henry Winkler) discovers that—with the proper motivation—Waterboy can run and tackle with great force. He determines to make Sandler a football star—in spite of Mama's objections.

Kids like Adam Sandler, and it's easy to see why; in this film, his underdog character is a natural magnet for young people, and the little-guy-makes-good story is as surefire as it was when Harold Lloyd took to the football field and became an unlikely hero in his silent-movie comedy classic *The Freshman.*

The main difference here is the use of four-letter words and sexual content. The *sh* word turns up twice in the very first scene! The *f* word is heard but once, much later on. And Sandler's budding relationship with girlfriend Fairuza Balk includes her introducing him to the joys of kissing (with tongue, he notes) and the pleasures of the flesh (unseen, thank goodness).

So while kids of all ages are bound to enjoy this popular movie, it does require that parents be willing to tolerate a dose of strong language and a dollop of sex. It's your call, folks.

WATERSHIP DOWN (1978)
Color, 92 minutes
Cast: Voices of John Hurt, Richard Briers, Michael Graham-Cox, Roy Kinnear, Sir Ralph Richardson, Zero Mostel, Denholm Elliott
Director: Martin Rosen
Screenplay: Rosen, from the novel by Richard Adams
Animated feature
Rated PG

Younger kids: No   Older kids: OK

Unlike most cartoon features, this one is not intended for young children. It is based on Richard Adams' best-selling book about a warren of rabbits seeking a new home.

The story begins with Fiver (voiced by Richard Briers), whose bizarre visions warn his band of impending doom. The rabbits, led by Hazel (John Hurt), attempt to find a new place to burrow, but encounter danger in the forms of a farm dog, a killer cat, and a dictatorial hare, General Woundwart (Harry Andrews).

Dramatic, violent, and even bloody at times, this is a heartfelt and realistic look at the world of animals in the wild. *Watership Down* is a faithful, intelligent adaptation that will satisfy the novel's fans and intrigue parents and teens looking for a story and a point of view more daring than average animated fare. There is mild comic relief in the form of daffy seagull named Keehar, voiced by Zero Mostel. Art Garfunkel sings the main theme, "Bright Eyes."

WAYNE'S WORLD (1992)
Color, 95 minutes
Cast: Mike Myers, Dana Carvey, Rob Lowe, Tia Carrere, Brian Doyle Murray, Lara Flynn Boyle, Kurt Fuller, Colleen Camp, Donna Dixon, Meat Loaf, Ed O'Neill
Director: Penelope Spheeris
Screenplay: Mike Myers, Bonnie Turner, and Terry Turner
Comedy
Rated PG-13
Younger kids: VG, with caution   Older kids: VG

Mike Myers and Dana Carvey bring their excellent, heavy metal–loving *Saturday Night Live* TV characters, Wayne and Garth, to the big screen. The duo hosts a cheap cable-access TV show called *Wayne's World* in their hometown of Aurora, Illinois, and find themselves courted by a sleazy TV executive (Lowe) who wants to turn the show into a network program. He also wants Wayne's singer girlfriend, Cassandra (Carrere).

The result is surprisingly enjoyable and surprisingly smart, mainly because of the relationship between Wayne and Garth. The two characters are extremely bright, resourceful, winning, and despite what they might think, likably naive; as Myers and Carvey play them, you cannot help but be in their corner.

Younger kids will enjoy the silliness and comic interaction between the two, not to mention their shared slang ("We're not worthy! We're not worthy!"), while older kids and parents will appreciate the sharper cultural references, from TV and movie parodies to jabs at product placement in movies, a fake multiple ending, and even a melodramatic moment that is accompanied by the subtitle "Oscar Clip."

Parents should note some raucous language (particularly, a scene involving the phrase "sphincter boy"), a variety of sexual references, and a scene where Myers prances about in his underwear that could be damaging to younger children and cause serious repercussions with the potential to topple our entire cultural ethos . . . *not!!*

WAYNE'S WORLD 2 (1993)
Color, 94 minutes
Cast: Mike Myers, Dana Carney, Tia Carrere, Christopher Walken, Kim Basinger, Ralph Brown, Ed O'Neill, Harry Shearer, James Hong, Drew Barrymore, Chris Farley
Director: Stephen Surjik
Screenplay: Mike Myers, Bonnie Turner, and Terry Turner
Comedy
Rated PG-13
Younger kids: OK, with caution   Older kids: OK

Wayne and Garth are back! This time Wayne is inspired by the ghost of Jim Morrison to put on a rock concert in his hometown of Aurora, naturally to be called Waynestock.

That's a promising start for a sequel, but this time around, some of the schwiiing is gone. The chemistry between Myers and Carvey is still strong, and the two remain endearing and lovable creations. There are a number of memorable movie parodies and bizarre moments—like a martial arts battle between Wayne and Cassandra's father and the appearance of a "better actor" to substitute for one who is delivering a monologue. But there are also a lot of gags that seem like stale retreads of things we saw in the first **Wayne's World,** along with ideas that don't quite go anywhere, like a man-hungry housewife, Honey Hornee (Basinger), who is hot for Garth, and a subplot involving a sinister record producer (Walken).

It's surprising that a movie that seems so aware of standard movie conventions couldn't take a few swipes at the inevitability of tired sequels.

The PG-13 rating is earned by raunchy language and sexual innuendo; how much of this you want to shield your children from seeing is your decision alone.

WAY OUT WEST (1937)
Black & white, 65 minutes
Cast: Stan Laurel, Oliver Hardy, Sharon Lynn, James Finlayson, Rosina Lawrence
Director: James W. Horne
Screenplay: Charles Rogers, Felix Adler, and James Parrott, based on a story by Jack Jevne and Rogers
Comedy/Western
Unrated
Younger kids: VG   Older kids: VG

Laurel and Hardy are at the peak of their considerable comedic powers in this rollicking Western spoof that's quite possibly the most perfect of all their features. The duo comes to Brushwood Gulch to deliver the deed to a gold mine to the daughter of a deceased friend but are tricked by a shifty saloon owner, irresistibly named Mickey Finn (and played by the incomparably hammy James Finlayson), into handing over the deed to him.

That's it for plot; the beauty of the film is in the sheer joy of watching Laurel and Hardy going through their exquisitely timed routines in the context of the Wild West setting, blissfully oblivious to the dangers that await them. Whether the boys are wading through a pothole-filled river with a mule, fighting with Finn over the deed, or singing "On the Trail of the Lonesome Pine" and going into a soft-shoe dance, the film has a relaxed and mellow mood that's simply refreshing.

There are so many subtle but hysterical gags—involving everything from tickling to Stan eating his hat and using his thumb as a lighter—that you and your kids will be giddy from laughter . . . and eager to see even more of Laurel and Hardy.

WEE WILLIE WINKIE (1937)
Black & white, 99 minutes (also available in computer-colored version)
Cast: Shirley Temple, Victor McLaglen, C. Aubrey Smith, June Lang, Michael Whalen, Cesar Romero, Constance Collier, Douglas Scott, Gavin Muir
Director: John Ford
Screenplay: Ernest Pascal and Julien Josephson, inspired by the story "Wee Willie Winkie" by Rudyard Kipling
Drama
Unrated
Young children: VG   Older children: VG

This is one of Shirley Temple's most exciting and exotic action pictures. As the plot unfolds, she and her mother arrive in northern India in 1897 to join her grandfather, a gruff military colonel who commands a British fort in the middle of dangerous rebel territory. In order to impress her grandfather, pint-sized Shirley turns into a brave soldier. She does so with the help of a few new friends, including a kindly sergeant, played by lovable character actor Victor McLaglen. Later, she even befriends the enemy rebel leader and helps to bring about peace between the warring factions.

One of the outstanding moments in the film is a deeply

touching scene where Shirley sings "Auld Lang Syne" to McLaglen as he lies on his death bed, unbeknownst to her. Younger children might find this sequence disturbing, particularly because the character has been such a good friend to the little girl. Otherwise, this is a terrific, lavishly produced adventure story and is notable for its depiction of the heathen rebel leader (Romero) not as a stock heavy but as a thoughtful human being. Credit director John Ford (who eleven years later cast a teenage Shirley in his Western classic *Fort Apache*) for breathing vigorous life into this entertaining tale.

WEIRD SCIENCE (1985)
Color, 94 minutes
Cast: Anthony Michael Hall, Kelly LeBrock, Ilan Mitchell-smith, Bill Paxton, Suzanne Snyder, Judie Aronson, Robert Downey, Jr., Robert Rusler, Vernon Wells, Michael Berryman, John Kapelos
Director: John Hughes
Screenplay: John Hughes
Comedy/Fantasy
Rated PG-13
Younger kids: No Older kids: No, but try and stop them

Teenage nerds Gary (Hall) and Wyatt (Mitchell-Smith) can't get dates, so they use Wyatt's computer to create an ideal woman—and, incredibly, she appears in the person of Lisa (LeBrock), who has magical powers which she uses to help the boys. But their nerdishness and Wyatt's crude older brother, Chet (Paxton), keep getting in the way.

The title should have been "Weird Fantasy," since there's no science here, just magic with a computer as the wand. It's a go-for-broke comic extravaganza, in which the basic idea of creating a perfect woman is dropped as soon as it's set up! LeBrock isn't bad, and Paxton and Hall fill their roles well, but the undisciplined movie is only intermittently funny.

For adults, that is. Teenage boys will probably giggle themselves into catatonia over the crude, often tasteless jokes. Writer-director Hughes has never been a critics' darling, but he does have a way of tapping into teen sensibilities, for better or worse. The film was popular enough to spawn, some years later, a cable-TV series of the same title. (However, this owes nothing at all to the old E.C. comic book of the same name.)

Trivia note: Occasionally, several people in Hollywood really do get much the same idea at much the same time. *Weird Science*, about teenagers tampering with technology, was released the same year as the similarly themed **Real Genius** and **My Science Project.** Not to mention **Back to the Future, Explorers,** and *Teen Wolf.*

WE'RE BACK! A DINOSAUR'S STORY (1993)
Color, 72 minutes
Cast: Voices of John Goodman, Rhea Perlman, Jay Leno, Walter Cronkite, Julia Child, Charles Fleischer, Yeardly Smith, Martin Short, Kenneth Mars
Director: Dick Zondag, Ralph Zondag, Phil Nibbelink, and Simon Wells
Screenplay: John Patrick Shanley
Animated Feature
Rated G

Younger kids: OK   Older kids:
   OK

Steven Spielberg produced this
forgettable animated feature,
based on a children's book by
Hudson Talbott. A hokey cartoon
premise sets up the action: kindly
Captain NewEyes, a time traveler
from the future, tunes his Wish
Radio in to hear kid's wishes.
When some modern-day youngsters wish to see a real dinosaur,
the Captain arranges this via a
special breakfast cereal (huh?),
which transports four friendly
prehistoric creatures to Manhattan. There, they get mixed up
with the plight of the Louie, a
runaway boy, and Cecilia, a poor
little rich girl, as well as evil
Captain ScrewEyes (NewEyes'
brother).

   The film has a wonderful central musical sequence, when the
dinosaurs wander into the Macy's
Thanksgiving Day parade and try
to fit in with the floats and giant
balloons. The whole film feels like
it's supporting this sequence, with
all sorts of trivial nonsense filling
up the time before and after.

   It's essentially a good-looking
film with nothing to offer. Younger
kids who like watching cartoon dinosaurs and do not require any context for fantastic situations will
enjoy it.

WEST SIDE STORY (1961)
Color, 155 minutes
Cast: Natalie Wood, Richard
   Beymer, Russ Tamblyn, Rita
   Moreno, George Chakiris,
   Simon Oakland, Ned Glass,
   William Bramley, John Astin,
   Tony Mordente
Directors: Robert Wise and
   Jerome Robbins
Screenplay: Ernest Lehman,

based on the musical *West
   Side Story* by Arthur Laurents,
   Leonard Bernstein, and
   Stephen Sondheim
Musical
Unrated
Young children: OK   Older
   children: VG

This Academy Award–winning musical drama of racial tensions and
violence erupting out of the poverty of New York's (then) Upper
West Side tenement neighborhood is one of the most celebrated of many reworkings of
Shakespeare's *Romeo and Juliet.*
The idea of setting this star-
crossed romance in a modern setting, amid the warfare of two
street gangs, the Jets (who are
Polish) and the Sharks (who are
Puerto Rican), was positively inspired. The lovers here are Maria,
whose brother Bernardo is the
head of the Sharks, and Tony,
whose ties are with the Jets.

   The music and dancing in *West
Side Story* are electric. The score
is now legendary, with one extraordinary number after the
next: the ever-hopeful "Something's Coming," "Maria," a romantic ballad that celebrates love
at first sight, the anticipatory "Tonight," "Cool," which bespeaks
the attitude of the Jets, and "I
Feel Pretty," which extols Maria's
blooming femininity.

   To kids weaned on music videos, where the editing and camerawork are visceral but the
participants don't necessarily do
much moving around, the fluid,
kinetic visuals of *West Side Story*
may come as a revelation. The
marriage of choreography and
camerawork here is incredibly exciting to watch, especially on a big
screen (though young people,

now as then, will have to get used to the idea of genuinely tough gang kids singing and dancing).

Despite all the romanticism, which will particularly appeal to starry-eyed adolescents, it must be emphasized that *West Side Story* is a tragic and occasionally violent story.

WESTWORLD (1973)
Color, 88 minutes
Cast: Yul Brynner, Richard Benjamin, James Brolin, Norman Bartold, Alan Oppenheimer, Victoria Shaw, Dick Van Patten, Steve Franken
Director: Michael Crichton
Screenplay: Michael Crichton
Science fiction/Action suspense
Rated PG
Young children: OK, but tense   Older children: OK

In the near future, ordinary guy Benjamin accompanies his pal Brolin to a new kind of amusement park, where the guests select from different "worlds" to inhabit for a few days. Our heroes pick Westworld, where only they and a few others are live people; the rest are all robots, programmed to provide harmless thrills.

But then something goes wrong. . . .

Westworld is timeless, bridging the gap between the science fiction movies of the 1950s and those of the '90s with unplanned ease. It's a little tense for younger children, but most of them will probably get through it just fine and have a good time doing so. Older kids will find some of it predictable but still enjoy the movie. Crichton is only a fair director, but his ideas are vivid, and the cast is appealing. As a robot

gunslinger, Brynner is, amusingly, dressed in the same costume he wore in *The Magnificent Seven.*

This was popular enough to generate a sequel of sorts, *Futureworld,* but that can be easily ignored.

WILLIAM SHAKESPEARE'S ROMEO & JULIET (see Romeo & Juliet [1996])

WHAT'S EATING GILBERT GRAPE (1993)
Color, 117 minutes
Cast: Johnny Depp, Juliette Lewis, Leonardo DiCaprio, Mary Steenburgen, Crispin Glover, John C. Reilly, Darlene Cates, Laura Harrington, Mary Kate Schellhardt, Kevin Tighe
Director: Lasse Hallstrom
Screenplay: Peter Hedges, from his novel
Drama
Rated PG-13
Younger children: No   Older children: Only the most mature

So what is eating Gilbert Grape (Johnny Depp)? Perhaps it's his family. He describes his obese mother as a "beached whale" who used to be pretty but ceased to care after his father committed suicide. She hasn't left the house in seven years. Or possibly it's his obnoxious 15-year-old little sister, who is obsessed with her teeth now that her braces are off. Or maybe it's Arnie (Leonardo DiCaprio in a knockout performance), his mentally retarded brother who "could go at any time" and who keeps climbing the town's water tower. "I want to be a good person," Gilbert says, but the odds seem to be against him even though he tries hard to take care of everyone. Mostly, he just wants out. Then he meets Becky (Juliette Lewis) who travels the country with her grandmother. Now, maybe Gilbert can see things differently.

What's Eating Gilbert Grape is serious and thoughtful, dealing with death, life, and responsibility. It reminds us that behind every oddball we encounter is, quite possibly, a story that explains why they act the way they do.

Probably not for most children because of its intensity and occasional sexual content, it is nevertheless an interesting and unusual film that might be right for a particularly mature older child.

WHAT'S UP, DOC? (1972)
Color, 94 minutes
Cast: Barbra Streisand, Ryan O'Neal, Kenneth Mars, Austin Pendleton, Madeline Kahn, Sorrell Booke, Michael Murphy, John Hillerman
Director: Peter Bogdanovich
Screenplay: Buck Henry, David Newman, and Robert Benton, based on a story by Bogdanovich
Comedy
Rated G
Younger kids: Good   Older kids: VG

Peter Bogdanovich's fond homage to the great screwball comedies of the '30s and '40s (particularly *Bringing Up Baby*) is a zany romp that, as its title implies, plays like a feature-length Looney Tunes cartoon. Ryan O'Neal makes like Cary Grant crossed with Harold Lloyd as a timid musicologist named Howard who comes to San Francisco with his shrill fiancée (a riotous Madeline Kahn) for a music fellowship competition. He gets mixed up with a seductive kook named Judy (Barbra Streisand) and a group of inept spies and jewel thieves who are after a plaid suitcase that's identical to the one Howard owns (containing the prehistoric rocks that demonstrate his theory on the origins of music). One hotel room fire and bullet-ridden soiree later, Howard and Judy find themselves on a bicycle, being chased through the steep city streets, during which a giant pane of glass is destroyed and they disrupt a Chinese parade and become part of a paper dragon, before the entire cast winds up in San Francisco Bay.

While somewhat self-conscious and intentionally imitative, this is quite a funny farce, with some uproarious scenes of door slamming and mistaken identity mayhem. It works itself up to a fine pitch of frenzy for a wild Keystone Kops–style chase sequence, a wacky courtroom finale, and the funny closing line where O'Neal spoofs his *Love Story* role. Even if Streisand and O'Neal aren't exactly Hepburn and Grant, they're still good, and the supporting cast is superb, particularly Kenneth Mars as an arrogant musicologist with a hilarious European accent and Liam Dunn as a pill-popping judge.

The original vintage screwball comedies are still better, but this is a reminder of the pleasures to be had from undiluted nonsense, and also a reminder of when Hollywood used to make G-rated films that weren't just cartoons or animal movies.

WHEN DINOSAURS RULED THE EARTH (1970)
Color, 96 minutes
Cast: Victoria Vetri, Robin Hawdon, Patrick Allen, Drewe Henley, Sean Caffrey, Magda

Konopka, Imogen Hassall, Patrick Holt
Director: Val Guest
Screenplay: Guest, from a story by J. G. Ballard
Prehistoric adventure/Science fiction
Rated G
Young children: OK   Older children: OK

Set (like *One Million Years B.C.*) in that never-never time when human beings and dinosaurs coexisted, this tells the adventuresome tale of Sanna (Victoria Vetri), who, as the movie opens, is about to be sacrificed to the sun because she's blonde. A cataclysm occurs; she escapes and is eventually accepted as a baby by a mother dinosaur. A real baby dino hatches and becomes Sanna's devoted friend. But the tribesman determined to sacrifice Sanna is on her trail.

There's no good way to judge movies like this. They're inherently absurd; the "primitive" people are for the most part gorgeous. Instead of English, they speak a created language of just a handful of words, as if they're too primitive to have an extensive vocabulary. These movies are really just excuses to show beautiful men and women in skimpy clothes.

Their other raison d'être is to show off special effects, which in this case are generally excellent, the work of the talented stop-motion animator Jim Danforth. (Hammer didn't provide as big a budget for Danforth as they did for Ray Harryhausen in *One Million Years B.C.*, so there are no grand scenes of monsters fighting each other.)

However, there is some strongly implied sex, which might bother parents more than it would kids, who'll consider all the scenes involving people as boring filler between monster action moments.

Note: Considering what it says on the banner that drifts down over the Tyrannosaurus rex at the finale of **Jurassic Park,** we can assume that Steven Spielberg liked this movie.

WHEN WORLDS COLLIDE
(1951)
Color, 83 minutes
Cast: Richard Derr, Barbara Rush, Peter Hanson, John Hoyt, Larry Keating
Director: Rudolph Maté
Screenplay: Sydney Boehm, from the novel by Philip Wylie and Edwin Balmer
Science fiction/Suspense
Unrated
Younger kids: OK   Older kids: OK

An astronomer discovers two planets heading toward our Solar System, and realizes that while one will pass near the Earth—causing catastrophic earthquakes and tidal waves, and then will go into orbit around the sun—the second will smash directly into our planet. The movie deals with the efforts of a group of Americans to create a "space ark" that will carry a handful of survivors to the new planet.

Obviously, this film cannot compare in spectacle with more recent movies like **Deep Impact** and *Armageddon*, but it's in there trying. The lack of an adequate budget undercuts the good intentions and effective melodrama of this George Pal production. (A dull cast doesn't help matters any.)

Younger kids will likely be

bored by the somewhat talky film, but older kids might be interested in how a tale like this was told in the "olden days" of the early 1950s.

WHERE THE RED FERN GROWS (1974)
Color, 97 minutes
Cast: James Whitmore, Beverly Garland, Jack Ging, Lonny Chapman, Stewart Peterson, Jill Clark, Jeanna Wilson, Bill Thurman
Director: Norman Tokar
Screenplay: Douglas Day Stewart and Eleanor Lamb, based on the novel by Wilson Rawls
Drama
Rated G
Younger children: VG   Older children: OK

This typical, almost generic, family film about a boy and his dogs is easy to watch and entertaining, if not terribly special.

Based on a well-known novel by Wilson Rawls, the film is set in the 1930s. Young Billy (Stewart Peterson) lives in Oklahoma with his grandpa (James Whitmore), mother (Beverly Garland), and two sisters, an optimistic farm family during the darkest days of the Depression. Billy's life brightens up with the addition of two hunting dogs that he raises to be champion raccoon chasers.

When one of them is killed in a fight with a mountain lion and the other dies shortly thereafter, the grieving boy learns lessons about life and the love of his family. *Where the Red Fern Grows* is well acted and produced—though older viewers may have the feeling they've seen it all before.

WHISTLE DOWN THE WIND (1962)
Black & white, 99 minutes
Cast: Hayley Mills, Alan Bates, Bernard Lee, Diane Holgate, Alan Barnes, Norman Bird, Diane Clare, Patricia Heneghan, Elsie Wagstaff
Director: Bryan Forbes
Screenplay: Keith Waterhouse, based on the novel by Mary Hayley Bell
Drama
Unrated
Young children: OK   Older children: VG

Hayley Mills is most fondly recalled for her performances in Walt Disney's **Pollyanna** and **The Parent Trap.** However, she made her first impression on-screen in *Tiger Bay,* cast as a lonely child who witnesses a murder and is summarily kidnapped. And she offers an equally riveting performance in *Whistle Down the Wind.*

Mills plays 15-year-old Kathy Bostock, who resides with her younger brother and sister on an out-of-the-way farm. One day, the children save some kittens from drowning and place them in their barn. When the youngest of the trio, 6-year-old Charles, wonders how the kittens will survive, a Salvation Army woman explains that Jesus will care for them. That evening, Kathy visits the animals and discovers that a bedraggled man (who actually is a murderer on the lam) has taken refuge in the barn. She and her siblings become convinced that he is in fact Jesus Christ.

Whistle Down the Wind is a touching drama of faith, childhood innocence, and the manner in which a kindly act might affect even the most desperate of men. It is one film that can be equally enjoyed by youngsters and their parents.

THE WHITE BALLOON
(1995)
Color, 85 minutes
Cast: Aida Mohammadkhani, Mohsen Kafili, Fereshteh Sadr Orfai, Anna Borkowska, Mohammad Shahani, Mohammed Bahktiari
Director: Jafar Panahi
Screenplay: Abbas Kiarostami
Comedy-drama
Unrated
Young children: VG   Older children: VG

You will not find any sort of political tract in *The White Balloon*, an endearing little film from Iran. Rather, the scenario involves a 6-year-old girl's desire to purchase a goldfish during the Iranian New Year. She persuades her mother to let her buy the fish, and her journey to do so becomes quite an odyssey. She is traumatized upon losing the money she is given to make the purchase and undergoes a series of wide-ranging experiences with the individuals she encounters.

The story told in *The White Balloon* is a universal one. Indeed, anyone who has ever found himself in big trouble as a child will relate to the girl's terror as she desperately attempts to retrieve the money.

And for those who only know Iranians from evening news reports, the film offers proof of the common humanity linking all people around the globe.

WHITE CHRISTMAS (1954)
Color, 120 minutes
Cast: Bing Crosby, Danny Kaye, Rosemary Clooney, Vera-Ellen, Dean Jagger, Mary Wickes, John Brascia, Anne Whitfield
Director: Michael Curtiz
Screenplay: Norman Krasna, Norman Panama, and Melvin Frank
Musical
Unrated
Young children: VG   Older children: VG

White Christmas really evokes the era in which it was made: almost a decade after the end of World War II, a time when veterans and their wives had put behind them all the hardships they once endured, and settled into a prosperous and comfortable peacetime.

Bing Crosby and Danny Kaye play a pair of ex–army buddies and present-day showbiz performers who come to the aid of their former, much-loved commanding officer. He has been mustered out of the service and is attempting (but failing miserably) to make a go of a New England inn. Along the way, Bing and Danny romance a pair of sisters, played by Vera-Ellen and Rosemary Clooney (the great pop singer who, of course, is the aunt of George). Scattered throughout are some top Irving Berlin tunes, including the title song, which became Crosby's holiday anthem, and "Sisters," which is introduced by the female stars and reprised by their male costars in drag.

Bing Crosby also starred, with Fred Astaire, in the less mushy, black-and-white musical *Holiday Inn* in 1942, in which "White Christmas" was introduced.

White Christmas is perfectly innocuous fare for the entire family to enjoy, ideally by a lit fireplace on Christmas Eve.

WHITE FANG (1991)
Color, 107 minutes
Cast: Klaus Maria Brandauer, Ethan Hawke, Seymour Cassel, Susan Hogan, James Remar
Director: Randal Kleiser
Screenplay: Jeanne Rosenberg, Nick Thiel, and David Fallon, based on the novel by Jack London
Action-adventure/Animal story
Rated PG
Younger kids: OK   Older kids: VG

Ethan Hawke gives a winning performance in this Disney adaptation of Jack London's coming-of-age classic. Set in the Klondike in 1898, the story centers on the adventures of young orphan Jack Conroy (Hawke) who, while trying to get to his late father's gold mine with the help of a Yukon guide (Klaus-Maria Brandauer), adopts a wolf-dog that had saved his life from a bear attack.

Though the film differs significantly from the book (as well as a vintage 1936 film version and a violent 1972 European adaptation) and often reduces White Fang to a peripheral character while softening his bite, this is a touching family film with spectacular locations and several exciting scenes, the violence consisting mostly of simulated animal attacks.

WHO FRAMED ROGER RABBIT (1988)
Color, 103 minutes
Cast: Bob Hoskins, Christopher Lloyd, Joanna Cassidy, Stubby Kaye, Alan Tilvern
Director: Robert Zemeckis

Screenplay: Jeffrey Price and Peter Seaman, based on the novel *Who Censored Roger Rabbit?* by Gary K. Wolf
Comedy/Fantasy/Animation
Rated PG
Younger kids: VG   Older kids: VG

In 1947 Hollywood, detective Eddie Valiant (Hoskins), investigates a murder in which cartoon character Roger Rabbit is the prime suspect. Soon Eddie is involved in all manner of intrigue and conspiracy, with characters both real and animated (and sometimes both). This amazing movie seamlessly combines live action and animation as live and cartoon characters interact with one another in clever and unprecedented ways.

The pacing is machine-gun fast, so kids will be riveted, but adults can enjoy it all, too, especially as old cartoon favorites pop up throughout the movie, from Daffy and Donald Duck (making their joint debut) to Betty Boop (rendered in black-and-white, naturally).

There is adult humor sprinkled throughout the picture—from a tough-talking baby star to the very presence of Jessica Rabbit, a supremely voluptuous female figure—which is why the film is rated PG. But the violence is literally cartoonlike and is executed with the visual panache of the shorts the film pays homage to.

WILD AMERICA (1997)
Color, 106 minutes
Cast: Jonathan Taylor Thomas, Devon Sawa, Scott Bairstow, Jamey Sheridan, Frances Fisher, Tracey Walter, Don Stroud, Danny Glover

Director: William Dear
Screenplay: David Michael
  Wieger, based on a story by
  Mark Stouffer
True-life adventure
Rated PG
Young children: OK, with
  caution Older children: OK

The year is 1967; the place is Ft.
Smith, Arkansas. The three Stouffer brothers—Mark, Marty, and
Marshall—are unhappy with their
lives. Their trucker father is always away, and their mother is always busy. Raised to love and
respect animals, the two older
boys announce their intention to
go off on their own and become
wildlife photographers. Younger
brother Marshall stows away in
their car so that he can get in on
the action, too. The adventure begins when they stalk wild animals
and find themselves in more dangerous situations than they ever
anticipated.

Wild America is aimed squarely
at adolescent audiences, and is
cast with appealing young actors.
Parents might find the plotting
too obvious, or clichéd, but
youngsters are likely to be less
critical. (Young siblings will certainly relate to the fact that 12-
year-old Marty is forever being
taunted and harassed by his older
brothers.) The boys' adventures
are exciting and believable,
though the film has several climaxes too many.

In real life, Marty Stouffer grew
up to become a respected wildlife
photographer and documentary
filmmaker.

Some use of language—and
scenes of peril—merit the PG
rating.

THE WILD CHILD (1971)

Black & white, 85 minutes
Cast: François Truffaut, Jean-
  Pierre Cargot, Jeati Daste,
  Paul Ville
Director: François Truffaut
Screenplay: Truffaut and Jean
  Gruault, based on the book
  *Memoire et Rapport sur Victor
  de ll'Aveyron* by Jean-Marc-
  Gaspar Itard
Comedy-drama
Rated G
Younger kids: OK Older kids:
  OK

The Wild Child tells the true story
of Jean Itard, a behavioral scientist who in the late 1790s tries to
civilize a young boy who was
raised alone in the woods. This is
a fascinating examination of
human nature, environment, and
the benefits (and/or limits) of ra-
tional thought. These are heady
subjects, indeed, for younger children, but for older children with
curious minds, there are many
springboards here for discussion.

At the core of the film is a man
of science trying to civilize a "savage" mind and the scientist's attempts to get through to the boy.
This is less a battle of wills (as in
The Miracle Worker) than a
grounding for debate over the ultimate benefits of science, but no
less interesting for it. The film is
shot in a very simple, almost documentarylike fashion, with Truffaut often reading narration from
Itard's own diary. This intensifies
the moments when the boy appears to be responding to the doctor's instruction, by playing a bell
and drum or reacting to certain
sounds. The child's fondness for
his primitive state is also conveyed, and the ambiguous ending

is eminently thought-provoking and conversation-worthy.

WILD HEARTS CAN'T BE BROKEN (1991)

Color, 89 minutes
Cast: Gabrielle Anwar, Cliff Robertson, Dylan Kussman, Michael Schoeffling, Kathleen York, Frank Renzulli, Nancy Atchison
Director: Steve Miner
Screenplay: Matt Williams and Oley Sassone
Biography/Romance
Rated G
Younger children: OK, with caution   Older children: VG

This is the story of a remarkable woman, Sonora Webster, who ran away to join the circus (more or less) as a child in the 1930s, acquired a father figure in the Buffalo Bill–like proprietor of the show, and found her specialty in riding a "diving horse" who would plummet from a high platform to a huge tank of water below. A misstep one day causes Sonora to go blind, but true to the tradition of show business, she decides to try to perform anyway—and in partnership with her well-trained horse, she does!

As unlikely a screen biography as one could find, the Disney studio's *Wild Hearts Can't Be Broken* is a lovely film for young and old alike, with an engaging lead performance by Gabrielle Anwar and solid support from Cliff Robertson as her mentor.

Although some animal lovers might be put off by the idea of a diving horse, those scenes were accomplished with movie magic, and the real horse was never required to play daredevil onscreen. The story takes place at a time when such stunts were widely accepted and enjoyed; in fact, one of this film's other strengths is its graceful depiction of life in the 1930s.

Most of all, one comes away with admiration for a courageous (if little-known) woman who refused to let a handicap keep her from doing what she loved to do.

WILLOW (1988)

Color, 125 minutes
Cast: Val Kilmer, Joanne Whalley, Warwick Davis, Jean Marsh, Patricia Hayes, Billy Barty, Pat Roach, Gavan O'Herlihy, Kevin Pollak
Director: Ron Howard
Screenplay: Bob Dolman and George Lucas
Fantasy adventure
Rated PG
Young children: No   Older children: VG

Reliably family-friendly Ron Howard (and producer George Lucas) score again with a tweaked fairy tale about three heroes: Madmartigan (Kilmer), a down-on-his-luck mercenary; Sorsha (Whalley), a warrior princess with a secret; and valiant Willow himself (Davis). Willow is a Nelwyn, a little person, who one day outside his village finds an abandoned infant who is in fact a golden child with the power to topple the evil kingdom of wicked Bavmorda (Marsh). He takes upon himself the dangerous task of delivering the baby to her place of destiny, aided by his unlikely comrades-in-arms.

Brisk dialogue and vivid action, supported by magical yet believable special effects, create a credible fantasy world that can sometimes be too much for tots to take (there's a particular two-headed Nasty Thing that could reappear in the kids' room at 2 A.M.). Much of the movie is intense, and for that reason this is probably best put aside until your kids are old enough for a full-blooded action-adventure fantasy.

Still, this huge movie is really about a small man with a big heart—a little person who's heroic and resourceful in spite of his short stature.

WILLY WONKA AND THE CHOCOLATE FACTORY

(1971)
Color, 98 minutes
Cast: Gene Wilder, Jack Albertson, Peter Ostrum, Roy Kinnear, Aubrey Woods, Michael Boliner, Ursula Reit
Director: Mel Stuart
Screenplay: Roald Dahl, from his novel *Charlie and the Chocolate Factory*
Musical/Fantasy
Rated G
Younger kids: OK Older kids: OK

Five lucky kids and their parents from points around the world win the chance to tour the spectacular candy factory of reclusive inventor and candy-man Willy Wonka. They soon discover all is not sweetness and light in the land of "pure imagination."

This genuinely odd musical fantasy has become a cult favorite over the years. There is much fun to be had, from Wilder's sly, eccentric lead performance to the wacky, surreal decor of Wonka's factory. Still, parents should be aware of the film's wicked, satiric streak—which shouldn't be surprising, coming from author Dahl—and the cruel fates that befall the kids on the tour (one girl ends up turning into a giant blueberry; one boy is atomized and then shrunk; another boy is sucked up a tube fed by a chocolate river). Along with these semi-gruesome incidents are messages about the dangers of gluttony, greed, and television that parents can certainly appreciate.

These messages are entertainingly conveyed through the songs of Wonka's helpers, the orange-skinned, green-haired Oompa-Loompas. Gene Wilder presides over the whole enterprise with a mischievous smile and a spring in his step.

THE WITCHES (1990)
Color, 91 minutes
Cast: Anjelica Huston, Mai Zetterling, Jasen Fisher, Bill Paterson, Brenda Blethyn, Rowan Atkinson, Charlie Potter, Jane Horrocks, Jenny Runacre
Director: Nicolas Roeg
Screenplay: Allan Scott, based on the novel by Roald Dahl
Fantasy/Comedy
Rated PG
Young children: OK, with caution Older children: OK

Young Luke (Fisher), now an orphan, has left America to live in England with his Norwegian grandmother, Helga (Zetterling), who has told him scary tales of witches—how they hate children and how to spot them. While staying at a seedy resort with Helga, he realizes that the seemingly benign Miss Ernst (Huston) is not only a witch, but the Grand High Witch of England, who is holding a witches' convention at the hotel. She plans to turn all the children of England into mice—and she starts with Luke and his pudgy friend, Bruno (Potter). Can two small mice stop the dastardly plans of all the witches of England?

A most unexpected film from the director of *Don't Look Now* and other stylish adult dramas, *The Witches* is a lot of fun, particularly for children. It doesn't avoid the scary stuff—Luke and Bruno are chased by a cat—and the witches, while often funny, are presented as genuine menaces. But this simply means the film doesn't condescend to children, who generally have little problem with such characters, as long as all is put right by the end.

Like the best children's films, *The Witches* is also entertaining for adults; if it doesn't quite measure up to the finest such films, it's still a worthy piece of work all the way around. The mice and the witches were the last work of the great Jim Henson.

THE WIZARD OF OZ (1939)
Color and black & white, 101 minutes
Cast: Judy Garland, Ray Bolger, Bert Lahr, Jack Haley, Frank Morgan, Billie Burke, Margaret Hamilton, Charley Grapewin, Clara Blandick, The Singer Midgets
Director: Victor Fleming
Screenplay: Noel Langley, Florence Ryerson, and Edgar Allan Woolf, based on the novel *The Wonderful Wizard of Oz* by L. Frank Baum
Musical/Fantasy/Literary classic
Unrated
Young children: VG   Older children: VG

Here is one movie that needs no introduction. Today's grade-school-ers are as familiar with *The Wizard of Oz* as their parents and grandparents. And inevitably, two or three decades into the future, they will be introducing this all-time classic to their own children.

Who has not been entranced by Judy Garland's heartfelt rendition of "Over the Rainbow" or been charmed by Ray Bolger, Jack Haley, and especially Bert Lahr (as the Scarecrow, Tin Man, and Cowardly Lion)? or hissed upon the appearance of Margaret Hamilton's Wicked Witch of the West?

This perfect screen adaptation of L. Frank Baum's fantasy celebrates the virtues of home and family, while taking its heroine (and Toto, too) on a fantastic journey, by way of tornado, from Kansas to the land of Oz. There is arguably no other film in history that has imbedded itself so thoroughly in our collective consciousness—in part because of its extraordinary imagination and in part because it touches on so many basic truths (about courage, common sense, bravery, friendship, and home sweet home).

Young children are quite properly put off, not only by the Witch and her flying monkeys, but by the first visions of the fearsome Wizard (and the Cowardly Lion's reaction to him). This is a film that may take time to grow into, and parents should respect their children's fears.

THE WOLF MAN (1941)
Black & white, 70 minutes
Cast: Lon Chaney, Jr., Claude Rains, Warren William, Ralph Bellamy, Patric Knowles, Bela Lugosi, Maria Ouspenskaya, Evelyn Ankers
Director: George Waggner
Screenplay: Curt Siodmak

Horror/Suspense
Unrated
Young children: Probably too
    strong   Older children: OK

*Even a man who's pure in heart
And says his prayers by night
Can become a wolf when the wolf-
bane blooms
And the autumn moon is bright.*

German emigré Curt Siodmak
wrote those lines, making him the
author of one of the best-known
poems in English. If you hear
those lines as a child, you're not
likely to forget them (though they
vary slightly from one movie to
the next), not because the poem
itself is so memorable, but because of its context: they explain
how genial Larry Talbot (Chaney), returning to his ancestral
home in Wales, is bitten by a
werewolf and so becomes one
himself. He sees a pentagram in
the palm of his next victim, and
the curse of lycanthropy drives
him to kill.

There's an air of sadness to *The
Wolf Man*, which is one reason it
has become one of the most famous horror movies of all time.
It's also briskly paced, well produced (with a vast, and nicely
creepy, studio forest wreathed in
fog), and has a top-notch cast. All
this combines with Chaney's ingratiating performance as Larry
Talbot and his animalistic vigor as
the Wolf Man (in great makeup
by Jack P. Pierce) to make this a
classic in its field.

Whether this is suitable for
young children has to be a parent's call, not ours. While most
horror movies of the 1940s are by
today's standards, mild, in terms
of gore and violence, there's an
aura of seriousness to *The Wolf
Man* that can make the film pretty
scary for younger children. It's a
tragic story; Talbot does nothing
to deserve his fate, and he comes
to a bad end; this is grim stuff,
and younger kids might be
haunted by the film. Older kids
might be, too, but they're usually
better prepared for this kind of
thing by the time they're 12 or so.

This was followed by *Frankenstein Meets the Wolf Man.*

THE WONDERFUL WORLD
OF THE BROTHERS GRIMM
(1962)
Color, 129 minutes
Cast: Laurence Harvey, Karl
    Boehm, Claire Bloom, Walter
    Slezak, Barbara Eden, Oscar
    Homolka, Arnold Stang,
    Martita Hunt, Tammy
    Marihugh, Yvette Mimieux,
    Russ Tamblyn, Jim Backus,
    Beulah Bondi, Terry-Thomas,
    Buddy Hackett, Otto Kruger
Directors: Henry Levin
    (biographical segments) and
    George Pal (fairy tales)
Screenplay: David P. Harmon,
    Charles Beaumont, William
    Roberts, from Hermann
    Gerstner's *Die Brüder Grimm*
    and fairy tales collected by
    Jacob and Wilhelm Grimm
Biography/Fairy tales/Animation
Unrated
Young children: OK   Older
    children: OK

In 19th-century Bavaria, Jacob
Grimm (Boehm) has a hard time
getting his brother Wilhelm (Harvey) to concentrate on their job
of writing the history of the family
of a local nobleman. Wilhelm is
much more interested in fairy
tales, which he collects and tells
to children. Several of these fairy

tales are dramatized: a woodsman (Tamblyn) wins the love of a princess (Mimieux); elves help a kindly cobbler (also Harvey) to meet an order; a cowardly knight (Terry-Thomas) and his squire (Hackett) battle a dragon.

Even if you don't know much about the real-life Grimm brothers, their story as presented here will seem phony and contrived, though the film, originally shown in Cinerama, is beautifully produced and shot on magnificent European locations. The highlights are the fairy tales, directed by George Pal; the giant bejeweled dragon (animated by Jim Danforth) of the third segment is impressive, but the most charming tale is that of the shoemaker and the elves.

Like many big-scale films of this period, the movie tends to be rather elephantine, but the fairytale segments will please children, and teenagers might like the special effects. Overall, though, it's very much an artifact of its times.

WUTHERING HEIGHTS
(1939)
Black & white, 104 minutes
Cast: Merle Oberon, Laurence Olivier, David Niven, Flora Robson, Donald Crisp, Geraldine Fitzgerald, Hugh Williams, Leo G. Carroll, Cecil Kellaway, Miles Mander
Director: William Wyler
Screenplay: Ben Hecht and Charles MacArthur, based on the novel by Emily Brontë

Drama/Literary classic
Unrated
Young children: OK Older children: VG

Even though it covers only half the original novel and veers from the narrative (particularly in its finale), this atmospheric adaptation of Emily Brontë's austere, eerie love story remains one of the screen's all-time great romantic epics. It is a superb production that represents Hollywood moviemaking at its zenith.

The setting is the Yorkshire moors, and the unfolding drama is emotionally complex. It is the story of the beautiful but class-conscious Cathy (Merle Oberon) and dashing, brooding gypsy Heathcliff (Laurence Olivier), lovers who are separated when she chooses to wed wealthy Edgar Linton. In the novel, Cathy loves both Heathcliff and Linton, and Heathcliff is alienated from any and all who are cultured. On-screen, however, Cathy is enamored of only Heathcliff, and she becomes the primary object of his wrath as she forsakes him and opts for a life of refinement and safety.

The screen version begs for comparison with Brontë's novel. Ultimately, both are compelling in their own way. And as Heathcliff, Laurence Oliver offers the first of his many unforgettable screen performances. Decades later, his mere presence can make women swoon.

X

X—THE MAN WITH X-RAY EYES (1963)
Color, 80 minutes
Cast: Ray Milland, Diana Van Der Vlis, Harold J. Stone, John Hoyt, Don Rickles, John Dierkes
Director: Roger Corman
Screenplay: Robert Dillon and Ray Russell
Science fiction/Medical melodrama
Unrated
Young children: Too mature   Older children: OK

In hope of helping surgeons and others, Dr. Xavier (Milland) is experimenting with eyedrops that will create X-ray vision. When his funding is cut, he tries out the eyedrops on himself; each successive dose increases the power of his X-ray vision, which steadily increases the seriousness of his problems.

A mixed bag, this film is typical of the work of Roger Corman at this time. His skill as a filmmaker and the seriousness of his intentions are constantly undercut by what he clearly regards as the necessity of pandering to the more sensational-minded members of his audience. Furthermore, the film's ambitions, which are considerable, are compromised because of his low budget: the effects just aren't good enough.

For the most part, it's acceptable family viewing. When Xavier sees through clothes, he does *not* see through underwear, or the "naked" people are hidden behind objects his vision does not penetrate. However, toward the end, Milland wears disturbing-looking contact lenses, and the very last shot will horrify younger kids—and maybe their parents.

X THE UNKNOWN (1957)
Black & white, 78 minutes
Cast: Dean Jagger, Leo McKern, William Lucas, Edward Chapman, John Harvey, Anthony Newley
Directors: Leslie Norman and Joseph Walton
Screenplay: Jimmy Sangster
Science fiction/Monster
Unrated
Younger kids: No   Older kids: OK

In a small region of Scotland, something emerges from a crack in the ground and begins seeking radioactive material. Anyone unlucky enough to be near the unknown entity dies of radiation—depicted with often gleeful gruesomeness. A scientist (Jagger) and a policeman (McKern) try to put a stop to the horrible events.

When we finally see the "thing," it's something of a letdown, being a mass of radioactive mud. However, the film is very well directed, and made in a documentarylike style that's often all too convincing. It's very suspenseful at times, and the scenes of people melting away are still disturbingly effective.

It's definitely too intense for younger kids, and even some older kids might be given the willies, but those with a taste for sci-fi and horror may like it a lot.

Y

YANKEE DOODLE DANDY
(1942)
Black & white, 126 minutes
Cast: James Cagney, Joan Leslie,
  Walter Huston, Irene
  Manning, Rosemary DeCamp,
  Richard Whorf, Jeanne
  Cagney, S. Z. Sakall, Walter
  Catlett, Frances Langford,
  Eddie Foy, Jr., George Tobias
Director: Michael Curtiz
Screenplay: Robert Buckner and
  Edmund Joseph, based on a
  story by Buckner
Musical biography
Unrated
Young children: VG Older
  children: VG

James Cagney is fondly recalled
for his tough-guy roles in such
gangster classics as *The Public
Enemy, Angels With Dirty Faces,
The Roaring Twenties,* and *White
Heat.* But he was also a marvelous
song and dance man, and he won
an Academy Award for his tour
de force performance in this four-
star flag-waver as George M.
Cohan, the legendary singer,
actor, dancer, songwriter, playwright, and all-around Yankee
Doodle Boy who was born on
the Fourth of July. *Yankee Doodle Dandy*, which came to movie
houses during World War II,
captures the mood of the moment as it unabashedly celebrates patriotism.

Cohan was born into a theatrical family and was virtually raised
in theaters and on the road. (His
famous curtain speech for The
Four Cohans was "My mother
thanks you, my father thanks you,
my sister thanks you, and I thank
you.") This movie traces his life
through a series of vignettes, from
childhood to retirement and a
fateful meeting with the President
of the United States. Throughout
the film we hear songs that Cohan
wrote and made famous: "Over
There," "Grand Old Flag," "Give
My Regards to Broadway,"
"Mary's a Grand Old Name," "45
Minutes from Broadway," and
the title tune.

The production numbers are
huge in scale and buoyant in
spirit. Once your family sees
Jimmy Cagney singing and dancing, they'll never forget him.

THE YEARLING (1946)
Color, 128 minutes
Cast: Gregory Peck, Jane
  Wyman, Claude Jarman, Jr.,
  Chill Wills, Margaret
  Wycherly, Henry Travers, Jeff
  York, Forrest Tucker, Clem
  Bevans, June Lockhart
Director: Clarence Brown
Screenplay: Paul Osborne, based
  on the novel by Marjorie
  Kinnan Rawlings
Drama
Unrated
Young children: VG Older
  children: VG

Many movies and books dealing
with a child's close relationship
with an animal are overly senti-

mental. *The Yearling* is a happy exception—a perceptive, dramatically potent tale of eleven-year-old Jody Baxter, played by Claude Jarman, Jr., who earned a special Academy Award for his performance. Jody is the child of a sympathetic but insolvent farm couple who are desperately struggling to maintain their meager existence. At the core of the story is Jody's growing attachment to a fawn, and the way the boy matures as he deals with his pet as it grows into a yearling.

The animal, of course, can never be domesticated; as it develops, it becomes increasingly destructive to the farm crops. The solution to this problem is as grim as it is inevitable . . . and leads to heartbreak both for Jody, and for us in the audience.

The Yearling earns its tears honestly, however. It is neither manipulative nor glib in its depiction of a boy's escape from the harshness of his life, and the crushing blow he must endure in order for his family to survive.

Beautifully made, sensitively acted, and respectfully adapted from Marjorie Kinnan Rawlings' classic book, *The Yearling* is an outstanding family film.

THE YEAR MY VOICE BROKE (1987)
Color, 103 minutes
Cast: Noah Taylor, Loene Carmen, Ben Mendelsohn, Graeme Blundell, Lynette Curran, Malcolm Robertson
Drama
Rated PG-13

FLIRTING (1990)
Color, 85 minutes
Cast: Noah Taylor, Thandie Newton, Nicole Kidman, Bartholomew Rose, Felix Nobis, Josh Picker
Drama
Rated R
Director: John Duigan
Screenplay: John Duigan
Young children: No   Older children: VG

The Year My Voice Broke and its sequel, *Flirting,* are charming and carefully observed coming-of-age dramas. *The Year My Voice Broke* is set in the early 1960s and tells the story of Danny Embling, a sensitive teen growing up in a small—and small-minded—Australian town. At the crux of the story are his friendship with, and infatuation by, a distraught and swiftly maturing girl, with resulting complications.

Flirting is set several years later, in an Australian boys' school where Danny has been sent off to study. He does not fit in with his regimented, inflexible environment and is unable to relate to his fellow students. He finds himself attracted to a sophisticated black African girl who attends a nearby school and is considered an outsider.

Although *The Year My Voice Broke* and *Flirting* focus on a familiar theme—a boy's transition from childhood to young adulthood—both films can be praised for the energy and intelligence they bring to the genre, and the naturalness of the performances. It was her work in *Flirting,* in fact, that brought Australian Nicole Kidman to the attention of Hollywood.

The Year My Voice Broke deals with mature situations that would be inappropriate (and not easily explainable) to younger children, while *Flirting* earned an R rating for its fairly candid moments of sexuality. But it would be a shame to shield your teenager from these films, which have genuine charm and understanding of human nature.

YELLOW SUBMARINE (1968)
Color, 85 minutes
Director: George Dunning
Screenplay: Lee Minoff, Al Brodax, Jack Mendelsohn, and Erich Segal
Animated feature/Musical
Rated G
Younger kids: OK   Older kids: VG

This feature length cartoon featuring The Beatles is a delight for the entire family. The Fab Four come to the rescue of Pepperland, a peaceful place under attack by the music-hating Blue Meanies. Traveling via Yellow Submarine, John, Paul, George, and Ringo are detoured through the musical Sea of Time, a Sea of Monsters, the Sea of Green, and a Sea of Holes where they encounter such fantastic characters as a Flying Glove, the Apple Bonkers, and a "Nowhere Man."

Kids will find lots to like in this imaginative fantasy: funny characters, favorite tunes, and a variety of inventive animation techniques. It's all played for laughs, with no real danger to frighten the small ones. Parents who were around when the Beatles phenomenon swept the world, will enjoy it even more, and may want to pass on their memories of John, Paul, George, and Ringo to their children.

Eleven classic Beatles songs are set to animation, including "All You Need Is Love," "Eleanor Rigby," "Lucy in the Sky with Diamonds," and "When I'm Sixty Four." Appealing, unusual art design by Heinz Edelman is a pleasant change from the usual Disneyesque approach to animated features. (A word or two to kids about the vogue for psychedelic artwork in the 1960s may be in order.)

YOU'LL NEVER GET RICH (1941)
Black & white, 88 minutes
Cast: Fred Astaire, Rita Hayworth, John Hubbard, Robert Benchley, Osa Massen, Frieda Inescort, Guinn Williams, Donald MacBride, Cliff Nazarro
Director: Sidney Lanfield
Screenplay: Michael Fessier and Ernest Pagano
Musical
Unrated
Young children: VG   Older children: VG

This solid musical was topical when it was released, as a key plot device involves the newly established military draft. However, its charm and wit make it just as entertaining today as it was on the eve of World War II.

The incomparable Fred Astaire stars as Robert Curtis, a musical comedy director who is mounting a hot new show. Unfortunately, he finds himself conscripted into the military, but he refuses to let his new status as a soldier—and a constant presence in the guardhouse—prevent him from completing work on the project. Meanwhile, Curtis becomes romantically entangled with stunning Sheila Winthrop (Rita Hayworth, who makes a ravishing dance partner for Astaire).

Youngsters may savor the

amusing presence of humorist-journalist-raconteur Robert Benchley, who is cast as Curtis' scheming producer—even if they do not completely comprehend his droll, sophisticated quips.

YOUNG FRANKENSTEIN
(1974)
Black & white, 108 minutes
Cast: Gene Wilder, Peter Boyle, Marty Feldman, Madeline Kahn, Cloris Leachman, Teri Garr, Kenneth Mars, Gene Hackman, Richard Haydn
Director: Mel Brooks
Screenplay: Gene Wilder and Brooks
Science fiction–horror/Spoof comedy
Rated PG
Young children: OK, with caution Older children: OK

Dr. Frederick Frankenstein—that's FRONK-on-steen, he insists—goes from America to Transylvania to claim an inheritance. Fired by the discovery of his ancestor's notebook ("How I Did It"), Freddy decides to restore the name of Frankenstein by creating a real human being from the bodies of the dead. Hampered with an idiot hunchbacked servant, Igor (Feldman), and a pretty but not very bright assistant (Garr), Freddy ends up creating another Monster (Boyle).

Hot on the heels of his outrageous Western parody, Blazing Saddles, writer-director Mel Brooks and his partner, Gene Wilder, created this scattershot but funny, loving spoof of the Universal Frankenstein series, mostly **Bride** and **Son of Frankenstein**. The references go far afield of horror films, however, and if this makes the film less cohesive, it doesn't hamper the laugh quotient. Boyle in particular is simply brilliant as the well-meaning Monster, especially in the "Puttin' on the Ritz" number.

While there's enough here to amuse those who've never seen the old movies at all, familiarity with them will increase appreciation of the film, not only as a comedy, but as an affectionate and accurate tribute to the originals. (The parody of the scene with the blind man from Bride of Frankenstein is especially uproarious if you know the real thing.) If your kids have been watching the old movies, but haven't seen this one, show it to them; they'll love it.

As with most Mel Brooks comedies, this one does have a fair share of double-entendre gags and sexual references, but they are fairly mild.

YOUNG PEOPLE (1940)
Black & white, 78 minutes (also available in a computer-colored version)
Cast: Shirley Temple, Jack Oakie, Charlotte Greenwood, Arleen Whelan, George Montgomery, Kathleen Howard, Minor Watson, Frank Sully, Mae Marsh
Director: Allan Dwan
Screenplay: Edwin Blum and Don Ettlinger
Comedy/Drama/Musical
Unrated
Young children: VG Older children: VG

Shirley Temple's last film as a "child star" places her in a conventional story of an orphan in show business. The yarn begins when two kindly vaudevillians adopt the infant daughter of their pal and raise her as their own

621

child. Years go by and the little girl successfully joins their song and dance act. Eventually the couple decides to introduce their daughter to a more normal lifestyle, so they leave the theater and settle down in a small Vermont town. However, as theater folk, they are greeted with suspicion and even derision by many of the townspeople.

At one moment in the story, a cruel child tells the little girl that she is adopted, which she had never been told by her loving parents. This scene might prompt children to wonder why this information would be withheld from the girl, calling for an explanation of changes in society's view toward adoption since the time this film was made.

It's also worth explaining that in days gone by, show people were held in disdain by many members of the public. Some boarding houses used to post a sign that read "No Dogs or Actors."

Shirley was 12 years old when she starred in this film, and her adolescence was apparent in her budding figure and mature reactions. No longer is this the little Shirley whose curls and dimples lit up theater screens during the Depression era. But Shirley still has musical talent and acting savvy to spare, and she benefits from the company of two outstanding character leads, sweetly funny Jack Oakie and lanky Charlotte Greenwood.

YOUNG SHERLOCK HOLMES (1985)
Color, 109 minutes
Cast: Nicholas Rowe, Alan Cox, Sophie Ward, Anthony Higgins, Susan Fleetwood, Freddie Jones, Nigel Stock, Roger Ashton-Griffiths, Earl Rhodes; voice of Michael Hordern
Director: Barry Levinson
Screenplay: Chris Columbus, based on characters created by Sir Arthur Conan Doyle
Period adventure/Mystery
Rated PG-13
Young children: Too scary at times Older children: OK

In 1870 at a British school, young John Watson (Cox) meets the slightly older Sherlock Holmes (Rowe), and the two become fast friends. Watson is constantly dazzled by Holmes' deductive skills (which aren't yet quite at their peak) and sense of adventure. Holmes literally crosses swords with his sinister fencing master Rathe (Higgins), while falling deeply in love with Elizabeth (Ward), whose father (Stock) is trying to invent a flying machine. Meanwhile, men who have no apparent connection with one another are being hit by darts, which cause them to have horrifying hallucinations and then die. Eventually, Holmes takes on the task of solving this mystery.

This handsome movie is based on an amusing premise. In Sir Arthur Conan Doyle's stories, Watson first met Holmes when both were grown men—but what if they had met when they were schoolboys? There are plenty of references to Holmes' later career, which will delight anyone who loves the original stories.

But, unaccountably, this fine idea is muddled by elaborate special-effects sequences (the hallucinations), an action climax that doesn't make sense, and moments that seem to have been inspired by **E.T. The Extra-Terrestrial** and **Indiana Jones and the Temple of Doom.** The result is something of a mess.

While teenagers are likely to feel that these scenes make the movie *more* appealing rather than less, even they may eventually regard the scenes as intrusive. *Young Sherlock Holmes* is a great disappointment that can score points only for good intentions.

Parents should heed the PG-13 rating, which applies mostly to the very intense and disturbing hallucination sequences.

Note: If you do watch this film, be sure to stay through the end credits.

YOU'RE NEVER TOO YOUNG (1955)
Color, 102 minutes
Cast: Dean Martin, Jerry Lewis, Diana Lynn, Nina Foch, Raymond Burr, Mitzi McCall
Director: Norman Taurog
Screenplay: Sidney Sheldon, based on a play by Edward Childs Carpenter, from a story by Fannie Kilbourne
Comedy
Unrated
Younger kids: Good   Older kids: Good

You're Never Too Young is one of the better films starring the team of Dean Martin and Jerry Lewis. Here, Jerry is a goofy apprentice barber named Wilbur who has a stolen diamond planted on him by a murderous thief named Noonan (played with memorable straight-faced menace by Raymond Burr). Wilbur later disguises himself as a 12-year-old in order to buy a half-fare train ticket for a trip home, but when a conductor becomes suspicious of Wilbur's age, he hides in the compartment of pretty schoolteacher Nancy (Diana Lynn), who falls for his ruse. When Wilbur discovers that Noonan is after him, he's forced to continue the masquerade at Nancy's school and develops a crush on her, much to the chagrin of her crooning beau (Dean Martin).

As he had previously done in *Living It Up* (1954), Lewis plays a tailor-made role that was actually originated by a female. (Ginger Rogers played the part of the bogus 12-year-old in Billy Wilder's very funny 1942 movie *The Major and the Minor,* just as Carole Lombard had played the supposedly dying small-town girl who's turned into an overnight celebrity in 1937's *Nothing Sacred*, which was remade as *Living It Up.*)

Jerry's regression to childhood (replete with an absurd kiddie sailor suit) gives him ample opportunities to indulge his riotous infantile predilections, which young kids will find very funny. His antics while hiding out at an all-girls boarding school are hilarious.

This is Jerry's show all the way and he makes the most of it, and even though Dean Martin has one of his most thankless roles as a bland straight man, there are plenty of well-staged slapstick action scenes for the team, and a wild water-skiing chase finale.

YOURS, MINE AND OURS (1968)
Color, 111 minutes
Cast: Lucille Ball, Henry Fonda, Van Johnson, Tom Bosley, Louise Troy, Ben Murphy, Jennifer Leak, Kevin Burchett, Kimberly Beck, Mitch Vogel,

Margot Jane, Eric Shea, Tim Matheson, Morgan Brittany (listed as Suzanne Cupito)
Director: Melville Shavelson
Screenplay: Shavelson and Mort Lachman, based on the book *Who Gets the Drumstick?* by Helen Beardsley
Comedy-drama
Unrated
Younger children: OK   Older children: VG

Here's a fine, funny film for all ages based on real-life family that puts the Brady Bunch to shame. Lucille Ball plays Helen North, a widow with eight children; Henry Fonda is Frank Beardsly, a widower with *ten* kids. They meet, fall in love, and marry—and chaos ensues. The melding of the two households into one makes for the many seriocomic situations: teenage romances, sibling rivalries, bathroom scheduling, etc. Toward the end, Helen and Frank give birth to their nineteenth child, and all are brought together as one happy family.

The film was a bit old-fashioned even in its day, but stands as a delightful, wholesome romp with good performances all around. Look for Tim Matheson as the oldest Beardsly child. Other notable young actors who went on to later fame include Tracy Nelson and Ben Murphy.

Fans of *I Love Lucy* (and who isn't?) shouldn't expect a wild, wacky Lucille Ball here; she plays her role fairly straight, except for one scene where she drinks too much at dinner. Still, she's as endearing and believable as ever.

Z

ZULU (1964)
Color, 138 minutes
Cast: Stanley Baker, Jack
  Hawkins, Ulla Jacobson,
  Michael Caine, Nigel Green,
  James Booth; Richard Burton
  (narrator)
Director: Cy Endfield
Screenplay: John Prebble and
  Endfield
Action-adventure/Historical
Unrated
Younger kids: No   Older kids:
  VG

Zulu is a spectacular account of
the battle that took place in South
Africa in 1879 between 105 British soldiers and four thousand
Zulu warriors. The meticulously
detailed chronicle begins when a
reverend (Jack Hawkins) learns
that Zulus have slaughtered
twelve hundred British soldiers
and plan to attack his missionary
station. The small British garrison
stationed there is led by Lts.
Chard (Stanley Baker) and Brom-
head (Michael Caine), who refuse
to abandon their posts and withstand a massive assault by the
Zulus.

One of the last great epics celebrating the British Empire, *Zulu*
is distinguished by its intelligent
script, its scrupulously realistic
portrayal of the horrors of war,
and its unstereoptypical depiction
of the Zulus as dignified warriors.
The movie's undoubted highlights
are its incredible scenes of battle,
which occupy virtually the entire
last half of the film and are brilliantly staged and photographed,
as well as being quite savage and
bloody, making it inappropriate
for younger viewers.

Zulu was followed, years later,
by a prequel, *Zulu Dawn*.

INDEX

Action

Batman (1966)
Batman (1989)
Batman Forever
Batman Returns
Batman & Robin
"Crocodile" Dundee
Independence Day
Jaws
Jumanji
Race the Sun
Runaway
Star Kid
Suburban Commando
3 Ninjas
Westworld

Action-adventure

Abbott and Costello Meet
  Captain Kidd
Across the Great Divide
The Adventures of Bullwhip
  Griffin
Adventures of Don Juan
The Adventures of the
  Wilderness Family
The African Queen
Africa—Texas Style!
Against All Flags
Alaska
Ali Baba and the Forty
  Thieves
An Arabian Adventure
Arabian Nights

At Sword's Point
Baby . . . Secret of the Lost
  Legend
The Bandit of Sherwood
  Forest
Batman (1966)
Batman (1989)
Batman Forever
Batman Returns
Batman & Robin
Beau Geste
The Black Arrow
Blackbeard the Pirate
The Black Cauldron
The Black Pirate
The Black Shield of Falworth
The Black Swan
The Buccaneer
The Call of the Wild
Captain Blood
Captain Horatio Hornblower
Captain Sindbad
The Corsican Brothers
The Count of Monte Cristo
The Crimson Pirate
The Crusades
Davy Crockett and the River
  Pirates
Davy Crockett, King of the
  Wild Frontier
Dick Tracy
Dragonworld
An Elephant Called Slowly
The Fighting Prince of
  Donegal
The Flame and the Arrow
The Four Feathers

The Four Musketeers
The Golden Voyage of
  Sinbad
The Goonies
The Great Escape
The Great Locomotive Chase
Gunga Din
Hatari!
Hercules (1959)
A High Wind in Jamaica
Indiana Jones and the Last
  Crusade
Indiana Jones and the
  Temple of Doom
In Search of the Castaways
Ivanhoe
Jack the Giant Killer
The Jungle Book
Kidnapped
Kim
King Solomon's Mines
Knights of the Round Table
The Last of the Mohicans
  (1936)
The Last of the Mohicans
  (1992)
Long John Silver
The Man Who Would Be
  King
The Mark of Zorro
Mighty Joe Young
Mutiny on the Bounty
Northwest Passage (Book
  1—Rogers' Rangers)
The Pathfinder
The Phantom
Prince Valiant
Raiders of the Lost Ark
Robin Hood: Prince of
  Thieves
Rudyard Kipling's The
  Jungle Book
Scaramouche
The Sea Gypsies

The Sea Hawk
Shipwrecked
Sinbad the Sailor
The Son of Monte Cristo
The Story of Robin Hood
  and His Merrie Men
Swiss Family Robinson
The Sword in the Stone
Tarzan Escapes
Tarzan Finds a Son!
Tarzan and His Mate
Tarzan's New York
  Adventure
Tarzan's Secret Treasure
Tarzan, The Ape Man
Those Magnificent Men in
  Their Flying Machines
The Three Musketeers (1948)
The Three Musketeers (1974)
The Three Musketeers (1993)
White Fang
Zulu

Adventure

The Abyss
Across the Great Divide
The Adventures of
  Huckleberry Finn
The Adventures of Mowgli
The Adventures of Robin
  Hood
The Adventures of the
  Wilderness Family
The Adventures of Tom
  Sawyer
The African Queen
Africa—Texas Style!
Against All Flags
Alaska
Ali Baba and the Forty
  Thieves
An Arabian Adventure

Arabian Nights
Around the World in 80 Days
At Sword's Point
The Bandit of Sherwood Forest
Battle for the Planet of the Apes
Beau Geste
Beneath the Planet of the Apes
The Black Arrow
Blackbeard the Pirate
The Black Cauldron
The Black Pirate
The Black Shield of Falworth
The Black Stallion
The Black Stallion Returns
The Black Swan
A Boy Ten Feet Tall
The Buccaneer
The Call of the Wild
Captain Blood
Captain Horatio Hornblower
Captain Sindbad
Clash of the Titans
Congo
The Corsican Brothers
The Count of Monte Cristo
Courage Mountain
The Crimson Pirate
The Crusades
Davy Crockett and the River Pirates
Davy Crockett, King of the Wild Frontier
Dragonslayer
Dragonworld
Drums Along the Mohawk
Elephant Boy
The Empire Strikes Back
Fantastic Voyage
Far From Home: The Adventures of Yellow Dog

A Far Off Place
The Fighting Prince of Donegal
First Men in the Moon
The Flame and the Arrow
Flight of the Navigator
Flipper
Fly Away Home
Follow the River
Forbidden Planet
The Four Feathers
The Four Musketeers
Free Willy
The Further Adventures of the Wilderness Family
George of the Jungle
Gold Diggers: Secret of Bear Mountain
The Golden Seal
The Golden Voyage of Sinbad
The Goonies
The Great Locomotive Chase
Greystoke: The Legend of Tarzan, Lord of the Apes
Gunga Din
Hatari!
A High Wind in Jamaica
Homeward Bound: The Incredible Journey
Homeward Bound II: Lost in San Francisco
Hook
Huckleberry Finn
The Incredible Journey
Indiana Jones and the Last Crusade
Indiana Jones and the Temple of Doom
In Search of the Castaways
Into the West
Iron Will
The Island at the Top of the World

Ivanhoe
Jack the Giant Killer
Jason and the Argonauts
Johnny Tremain
The Journey of Natty Gann
Journey to the Center of the
  Earth
The Jungle Book (1942)
Jurassic Park
Kidnapped
Kim
King Kong (1933)
King Kong (1976)
King Solomon's Mines
Knights of the Round Table
Ladyhawke
The Last of the Mohicans
  (1936)
The Last of the Mohicans
  (1992)
The Light in the Forest
The Little Ark
Long John Silver
Lost Horizon
The Lost World
The Lost World: Jurassic
  Park
The Magic Sword
The Man in the Iron Mask
  (1939)
The Man in the Iron Mask
  (1998)
The Man Who Would Be
  King
The Mark of Zorro
Mighty Joe Young
The Mummy's Hand
Muppet Treasure Island
Mutiny on the Bounty
Mysterious Island
The NeverEnding Story
Nikki, Wild Dog of the North
Northwest Passage (Book
  1—Rogers' Rangers)

The Odyssey
Operation Dumbo Drop
The Pathfinder
The Phantom
Prince Valiant
The Prisoner of Zenda
  (1937)
The Prisoner of Zenda
  (1952)
Raiders of the Lost Ark
Return of the Jedi
Robin Hood: Prince of
  Thieves
Robinson Crusoe on
  Mars
The Rocketeer
Rudyard Kipling's The
  Jungle Book
Scaramouche
The Scarlet Pimpernel
The Sea Gypsies
The Sea Hawk
The 7th Voyage of Sinbad
Shipwrecked
Sinbad the Sailor
The Son of Monte Cristo
Star Wars
The Story of Robin Hood
  and His Merrie Men
Squanto: A Warrior's Tale
Swiss Family Robinson
The Sword and the Rose
Tarzan and His Mate
Tarzan Escapes
Tarzan Finds a Son!
Tarzan's New York
  Adventure
Tarzan's Secret Treasure
Tarzan the Ape Man
The Thief of Bagdad (1924)
The Thief of Bagdad (1940)
Third Man on the Mountain
The Three Musketeers (1921)
The Three Musketeers (1948)

The Three Musketeers (1974)
The Three Musketeers (1993)
The Time Machine
Tol'able David
Tom and Huck
Treasure Island (1934)
Treasure Island (1950)
Tron
Walkabout
WarGames
White Fang
Wild America
Zulu

Animal story

The Adventures of Milo and
  Otis
Africa—Texas Style!
Air Bud
All Creatures Great and Small
The Amazing Panda
  Adventure
Andre
Babe
Babe: Pig in the City
The Bear
Beethoven
Beethoven's 2nd
Benji
Big Red
Black Beauty
The Black Stallion
The Black Stallion Returns
Born Free
The Brave One
Brighty of Grand Canyon
Buddy
Cheetah
The Day of the Dolphin
Doctor Dolittle
Dr. Dolittle
Dunston Checks In
Elephant Boy

An Elephant Called Slowly
Far From Home: The
  Adventures of Yellow Dog
Flipper
Fluke
Fly Away Home
Free Willy
The Golden Seal
Gorillas in the Mist
Gypsy Colt
Hatari!
Homeward Bound: The
  Incredible Journey
Homeward Bound II: Lost in
  San Francisco
The Horse Whisperer
The Incredible Journey
Lassie
Lassie Come Home
Legend of the Spirit Dog
Microcosmos
Misty
Monkey Trouble
My Friend Flicka
Namu the Killer Whale
National Velvet
Never Cry Wolf
Nikki, Wild Dog of the North
Old Yeller
101 Dalmatians
Operation Dumbo Drop
Paulie
Phar Lap
Prancer
The Red Pony
Ring of Bright Water
So Dear to My Heart
Thunderhead, Son of Flicka
White Fang
Wild America

Animated feature

Aaron's Magic Village
The Adventures of Ichabod
  and Mr. Toad

Aladdin
Alakazam the Great
Alice in Wonderland
All Dogs Go to Heaven
All Dogs Go to Heaven 2
An American Tail
An American Tail: Fievel
  Goes West
Anastasia
Antz
Arabian Knight
The Aristocats
Babar: The Movie
Balto
Bambi
Beauty and the Beast (1991)
Bebe's Kids
The Black Cauldron
A Boy Named Charlie
  Brown
The Brave Little Toaster
The Bugs Bunny/Road
  Runner Movie
a bug's life
Cats Don't Dance
Charlotte's Web
The Chipmunk Adventure
Cinderella
Dumbo
Fantasia
FernGully . . . The Last
  Rainforest
The Fox and the Hound
Fun & Fancy Free
Gay Purr-ee
A Goofy Movie
The Great Mouse Detective
Gulliver's Travels (1939)
Heidi's Song
Hercules (1997)
Hey There, It's Yogi Bear
The Hobbit
Hoppity Goes to Town
The Hunchback of Notre
  Dame (1996)

The Incredible Mr. Limpet
James and the Giant Peach
Jetsons: The Movie
The Jungle Book
Lady and the Tramp
The Land Before Time
The Lion King
The Little Mermaid
Little Nemo: Adventures in
  Slumberland
The Lord of the Rings
The Man Called Flintstone
Melody Time
Mulan
My Neighbor Totoro
The Nightmare Before
  Christmas
Oliver & Company
One Hundred and One
  Dalmatians
1001 Arabian Nights
The Pagemaster
The Pebble and the Penguin
Peter Pan
Pete's Dragon
The Phantom Tollbooth
Pinocchio
Pippi Longstocking
Pocahontas
Quest for Camelot
Raggedy Ann & Andy
The Rescuers
The Rescuers Down Under
Robin Hood
Rock-a-Doodle
Rover Dangerfield
The Rugrats Movie
The Secret of NIMH
Sleeping Beauty
Snow White and the Seven
  Dwarfs
Space Jam
The Swan Princess
The Sword in the Stone

The Three Caballeros
Thumbelina
Tom & Jerry: The Movie
Toy Story
Twice Upon a Time
Watership Down
We're Back! A Dinosaur's
  Story
Who Framed Roger Rabbit
Yellow Submarine

Ballet

Peter Rabbit and Tales of
  Beatrix Potter
The Red Shoes
The Tales of Hoffmann

Biography

Brian's Song
The Buddy Holly Story
Chariots of Fire
The Elephant Man
Funny Girl
Gandhi
Gorillas in the Mist
Great Balls of Fire!
Gypsy
The Jackie Robinson Story
Jim Thorpe—All-American
Korczak
Kundun
La Bamba
The Last Emperor
The Miracle Worker
Phar Lap
The Pride of the Yankees
Selena
Wild Hearts Can't Be Broken
The Wonderful World of the
  Brothers Grimm
Yankee Doodle Dandy

Charlie Chaplin movies

The Circus
City Lights
The Gold Rush
The Great Dictator
The Kid
Limelight
Modern Times

Comedy

Abbott and Costello Go to
  Mars
Abbott and Costello Meet
  Captain Kidd
Abbott and Costello Meet
  Dr. Jekyll and Mr. Hyde
Abbott and Costello Meet
  Frankenstein
Abbott and Costello Meet
  the Invisible Man
The Absent Minded
  Professor
The Addams Family
Addams Family Values
Adventures in Babysitting
The Adventures of Bullwhip
  Griffin
Air Bud
Airplane!
All of Me
American Graffiti
Angels in the Outfield (1951)
Angels in the Outfield (1994)
Around the World in 80
  Days
Auntie Mame
Babe
Baby Boom
Back to the Future
Back to the Future Part II
Back to the Future Part III
The Bad News Bears

Batman (1966)
Battling Butler
Bean
Beethoven
Beethoven's 2nd
Beetle Juice
The Bellboy
Big
Bill & Ted's Bogus Journey
Bill & Ted's Excellent
   Adventure
Blank Check
Block-Heads
The Bohemian Girl
The Brady Bunch Movie
Breaking Away
Bright Eyes
Buck Privates
Buck Privates Come Home
Bugsy Malone
The Cameraman
Captain January
Casper
Cat Ballou
Caveman
Cheaper by the Dozen
A Christmas Story
A Chump at Oxford
The Circus
City Lights
City Slickers
Clueless
College
Coneheads
The Court Jester
The Crimson Pirate
"Crocodile" Dundee
Cry-Baby
Curly Top
A Day at the Races
The Devil's Brother (aka Fra
   Diavolo)
Dr. Dolittle
Driving Miss Daisy

Duck Soup
Dunston Checks In
Emma
Explorers
Father of the Bride
Father of the Bride Part II
Ferris Bueller's Day Off
First Kid
The Flintstones
Flubber
Francis
Francis Goes to the Races
Freaky Friday
The Frisco Kid
From the Mixed-Up Files of
   Mrs. Basil E. Frankweiler
The General
George of the Jungle
Ghostbusters
Ghostbusters II
The Gods Must Be Crazy
The Gold Rush
Good Burger
The Goonies
Go West
The Great Dictator
The Great Race
Gregory's Girl
Gremlins 2: The New Batch
Groundhog Day
Hairspray
A Hard Day's Night
Harry and the Hendersons
Harvey
Help!
Here Comes Mr. Jordan
Hocus Pocus
Home Alone
Honey, I Blew Up the Kids
Honey, I Shrunk the Kids
House Arrest
Innerspace
I.Q.
It Happens Every Spring

It's a Mad Mad Mad Mad World
It Takes Two
I Wanna Hold Your Hand
Jack and the Beanstalk
Jingle All the Way
Jumanji
Jungle 2 Jungle
The Kid
A Kid in King Arthur's Court
Ladyhawke
A League of Their Own
Leave It to Beaver
Liar Liar
Life With Father
Life With Mikey
Li'l Abner
Little Big League
Little Giants
Little Miss Marker
The Little Rascals
The Little Shop of Horrors (1960)
Local Hero
The Long, Long Trailer
Look Who's Talking
The Love Bug
Madeline
Malcolm
Ma and Pa Kettle at Home
March of the Wooden Soldiers (aka Babes in Toyland)
The Mask
Matilda
Max Dugan Returns
McHale's Navy
Men in Black
Michael
The Mighty Ducks
Miracle on 34th Street (1947)
Miracle on 34th Street (1994)
Modern Times

The Money Pit
Monkey Trouble
The Monster Squad
Monty Python and the Holy Grail
Mouse Hunt
Mr. Deeds Goes to Town
Mr. Mom
Mrs. Doubtfire
Much Ado About Nothing
The Muppet Movie
Muppet Treasure Island
My Father, The Hero
My Science Project
National Lampoon's Christmas Vacation
National Lampoon's European Vacation
The Navigator
A Night at the Opera
North
The Nutty Professor
Oh, God!
One Fine Day
101 Dalmatians
Our Hospitality
Our Relations
Paper Moon
Parenthood
The Parent Trap (1961)
The Parent Trap (1998)
Pee-wee's Big Adventure
Please Don't Eat the Daisies
The Princess Bride
Radio Days
Raising Arizona
Real Genius
Rebecca of Sunnybrook Farm
Rhubarb
Richie Rich
Ring of Bright Water
Rookie of the Year
The Santa Clause

The Secret Life of Walter
   Mitty
Sesame Street Presents:
   Follow That Bird
Seven Chances
The Shaggy D.A.
The Shaggy Dog
Sherlock, Jr.
Short Circuit 2
A Simple Wish
Sister Act
Sixteen Candles
Sleeper
Small Soldiers
Smile
Son of Flubber
Sons of the Desert
Spaceballs
Splash
Star Kid
Steamboat Bill, Jr.
The Sting
Stowaway
Strange Invaders
The Stupids
Suburban Commando
Support Your Local Sheriff!
Those Magnificent Men in
   Their Flying Machines
Three Ages
The Three Musketeers (1939)
The Three Musketeers (1974)
Three Smart Girls
Time Bandits
The Time of Their Lives
Trading Mom
Tremors
The Trouble with Angels
The Ugly Dachshund
Vegas Vacation
A Very Brady Sequel
The Waterboy
Wayne's World
Wayne's World 2

Way Out West
Weird Science
What's Up, Doc?
Who Framed Roger Rabbit
The Witches
Young Frankenstein
Young People
You're Never Too Young

Comedy-drama

All Creatures Great and
   Small
Anne of Avonlea
Anne of Green Gables (1934)
Anne of Green Gables (1985)
Benny & Joon
Buffy the Vampire Slayer
Butch Cassidy and the
   Sundance Kid
Candleshoe
Casey's Shadow
Cocoon
Cocoon: The Return
The Courtship of Eddie's
   Father
David Copperfield
Dragonheart
Escape from the Planet of
   the Apes
The Front
Ghidrah, The Three-Headed
   Monster
Gremlins
Harriet the Spy
Hope and Glory
The Invisible Boy
Lilies of the Field
Limelight
Little Fugitive
A Little Romance
Matinee
Mermaids

The Muppet Christmas Carol
My Bodyguard
My Girl
My Girl 2
My Life as a Dog
Now and Then
On Golden Pond
The Outside Chance of
    Maximilian Glick
People Will Talk
Phantom of the Paradise
Pollyanna
Poor Little Rich Girl
Pride and Prejudice
Princess Caraboo
Rich Kids
Say Anything . . .
Short Circuit
Short Circuit 2
Small Change
Stand By Me
Teenage Mutant Ninja
    Turtles
that thing you do!
The White Balloon
The Wild Child
Yours, Mine and Ours

Disaster movie

Deep Impact
Twister

Disney studio animated features

Aladdin
The Aristocats
Beauty and the Beast (1991)
The Black Cauldron
The Fox and the Hound
A Goofy Movie
The Great Mouse Detective

Hercules (1997)
The Hunchback of Notre
    Dame (1996)
The Lion King
The Little Mermaid
Mulan
Oliver & Company
Pocahontas
The Rescuers
The Rescuers Down Under
Robin Hood

Walt Disney animated classics

Alice in Wonderland
Bambi
Cinderella
Dumbo
Fantasia
Fun & Fancy Free
The Adventures of Ichabod
    and Mr. Toad
The Jungle Book
Lady and the Tramp
Melody Time
One Hundred and One
    Dalmatians
Peter Pan
Pinocchio
Sleeping Beauty
Snow White and the Seven
    Dwarfs
The Sword in the Stone
The Three Caballeros

Documentary

Hoop Dreams
The Leopard Son
35 Up

Drama

Alice Adams
The Andromeda Strain
Apollo 13
The Baby-Sitters Club
Benji
The Bicycle Thief
Big Red
The Black Stallion
The Body Snatcher
Bopha!
Born Free
The Boy Who Could Fly
The Boy With Green Hair
Boyz N the Hood
The Brave One
The Brides of Dracula
A Bronx Tale
Captain Horatio Hornblower
Cat People
The Chosen
A Christmas Carol (1938)
A Christmas Carol (1951)
Contact
The Corn Is Green
Corrina, Corrina
The Crucible
Cry, The Beloved Country
  (1951)
Cry, The Beloved Country
  (1995)
The Curse of the Cat People
Dances with Wolves
A Day in October
Dead Poets Society
The Defiant Ones
The Diary of Anne Frank
Double Happiness
Driving Miss Daisy
An Early Frost
The Education of Little Tree
The Elephant Man
Ethan Frome

Fame
Field of Dreams
Flaming Star
Flirting
Fluke
Fly Away Home
Forrest Gump
The Four Hundred Blows
Friendly Persuasion
Gentleman's Agreement
Going in Style
Gone With the Wind
Goodbye, Mr. Chips
The Grapes of Wrath
The Grass Harp
Great Expectations
The Grey Fox
Greystoke: The Legend of
  Tarzan, Lord of the Apes
Gypsy Colt
The Haunting
Hedd Wyn
A Hero Ain't Nothin' But a
  Sandwich
Hester Street
High Noon
Home of the Brave
A Home of Our Own
Hoosiers
The Horse Whisperer
How Green Was My Valley
Ice Castles
Iceman
I Know Why the Caged Bird
  Sings
Imaginary Crimes
Imitation of Life (1934)
Imitation of Life (1959)
In the Heat of the Night
Inherit the Wind
Into the West
Intruder in the Dust
I Remember Mama
It's a Wonderful Life

Jack
Jane Eyre
The Journey of August King
Journey for Margaret
The Karate Kid
The Kid from Left Field
King of the Hill
Kramer vs. Kramer
Kundun
Lassie
Lassie Come Home
The Last Butterfly
The Last Emperor
The Learning Tree
Lies My Father Told Me
Little Big Man
Little Boy Lost
Little Buddha
Little Man Tate
The Little Princess
A Little Princess
Little Women (1933)
Little Women (1994)
Lucas
The Magnificent Ambersons
Malcolm X
The Man Without a Face
Man, Woman and Child
Marvin's Room
Mask
A Midnight Clear
Misty
Mr. Holland's Opus
My Ántonia
My Friend Flicka
The Nasty Girl
National Velvet
Never Cry Wolf
Norma Rae
Nothing But a Man
No Way Out
Now and Forever
Of Mice and Men (1939)
Of Mice and Men (1992)

Old Yeller
Oliver Twist
One on One
Our Little Girl
Our Town
The Outsiders
A Patch of Blue
Paths of Glory
Pelle the Conqueror
Persuasion
Places in the Heart
The Prime of Miss Jean
    Brodie
Radio Flyer
A Raisin in the Sun
Rebel Without a Cause
The Red Pony
Ring of Bright Water
Rocky
Romeo & Juliet (aka
    William Shakespeare's
    Romeo & Juliet)
Rudy
Schindler's List
School Ties
The Search
Searching for Bobby Fischer
The Secret of Roan Inish
Something Wicked This Way
    Comes
Sounder
Stand and Deliver
Stars in My Crown
The Summer of Ben Tyler
Swing Kids
Table for Five
Tap
Tex
Thunderhead, Son of Flicka
Tiger Town
To Kill a Mockingbird
Tom Brown's School Days
    (1940)
Tom Brown's School Days
    (1951)

To Sir, With Love
A Tree Grows in Brooklyn
Unstrung Heroes
The War
WarGames
Wee Willie Winkie
What's Eating Gilbert Grape
Where the Red Fern Grows
Whistle Down the Wind
Wuthering Heights
The Year My Voice Broke
The Yearling

Fantasy

The Adventures of Pinocchio
Alice in Wonderland
All of Me
Angels in the Outfield (1951)
Angels in the Outfield (1994)
An Arabian Adventure
Babe
Babe: Pig in the City
Baby . . . Secret of the Lost
    Legend
*batteries not included
Beauty and the Beast (1946)
Bedknobs and Broomsticks
Beetle Juice
Big
Bill & Ted's Bogus Journey
The Black Cauldron
The Blue Bird
Bogus
The Borrowers
The Boy and the Pirates
The Boy Who Could Fly
The Boy With Green Hair
Captain Sindbad
Casper
Chitty Chitty Bang Bang
A Christmas Carol (1938)
A Christmas Carol (1951)
Clash of the Titans

A Connecticut Yankee in
    King Arthur's Court
The Curse of the Cat People
Damn Yankees
Darby O'Gill and the Little
    People
The Dark Crystal
Dead of Night
Dick Tracy
Dragonheart
Dragonslayer
Dragonworld
Edward Scissorhands
Fairy Tale: A True Story
Field of Dreams
Finian's Rainbow
The 5,000 Fingers of Dr. T.
Flash Gordon
The Flintstones
Flubber
Freaky Friday
Ghostbusters
Ghostbusters 2
The Gnome-Mobile
The Golden Voyage of
    Sinbad
Gremlins
Gremlins 2: The New Batch
Hercules (1959)
Here Comes Mr. Jordan
Hocus Pocus
Hook
The Indian in the Cupboard
It's a Wonderful Life
Jack and the Beanstalk
Jack the Giant Killer
Jason and the Argonauts
Journey to the Center of the
    Earth
Jumanji
Kazaam
A Kid in King Arthur's Court
The Kid from Left Field
Kismet

Labyrinth
Ladyhawke
Legend
The Lion, the Witch and the
    Wardrobe
The Little Prince
Lost Horizon
The Love Bug
The Magic Sword
March of the Wooden
    Soldiers (aka Babes in
    Toyland)
Mary Poppins
The Mask
Matilda
Michael
Mighty Joe Young
Miracle on 34th Street (1947)
Miracle on 34th Street (1994)
The NeverEnding Story
The NeverEnding Story II:
    The Next Chapter
One Magic Christmas
Pee-wee's Big Adventure
Peter Rabbit and Tales of
    Beatrix Potter
The Princess Bride
Radio Flyer
A Rat's Tale
Return to Oz
Rookie of the Year
The Santa Clause
Santa Claus
The Secret Life of Walter
    Mitty
The Secret of Roan Inish
Sesame Street Presents:
    Follow That Bird
7 Faces of Dr. Lao
The 7th Voyage of Sinbad
The Shaggy D.A.
The Shaggy Dog
A Simple Wish
Sinbad the Sailor

Somewhere in Time
Splash
The Sword in the Stone
Tall Tale
Teenage Mutant Ninja
    Turtles
The Thief of Bagdad (1924)
The Thief of Bagdad (1940)
Three Lives of Thomasina
Tiger Town
Time Bandits
The Time of Their Lives
tom thumb
Trading Mom
Tron
Weird Science
Who Framed Roger Rabbit
Willow
Willy Wonka and the
    Chocolate Factory
The Witches
The Wizard of Oz

Historical

Amistad
The Autobiography of Miss
    Jane Pittman
The Crucible
The Crusades
Drums Along the Mohawk
The Emigrants
Gandhi
Glory
The Hunchback of Notre
    Dame (1939)
Johnny Tremain
Knights of the Round Table
The Last of the Mohicans
    (1936)
The Last of the Mohicans
    (1992)
The Light in the Forest
The Little Colonel

The Littlest Rebel
The New Land
The Pathfinder
Roots
Spartacus
Squanto: A Warrior's Tale
The Sword and the Rose
A Tale of Two Cities
Zulu

Horror

Abbott and Costello Meet
  Frankenstein
The Body Snatcher
Bride of Frankenstein
The Brides of Dracula
Cat People
The Curse of the Cat People
Curse of the Demon
The Curse of Frankenstein
The Curse of the Werewolf
The Devil Rides Out (aka
  The Devil's Bride)
Dr. Jekyll and Mr. Hyde
  (1931)
Dr. Jekyll and Mr. Hyde (1941)
Dracula
Dracula—Prince of Darkness
Frankenstein
Ghostbusters
Ghostbusters II
The Gorgon
The Haunted Palace
The Haunting
Horror of Dracula
The Hound of the
  Baskervilles (1939)
The Hound of the
  Baskervilles (1959)
House on Haunted Hill
House of Usher (aka The
  Fall of the House of
  Usher)

House of Wax
The Innocents
I Walked With a Zombie
Jaws
Kiss of the Vampire
The Masque of the Red Death
The Mummy (1932)
The Mummy (1959)
The Mummy's Curse
The Mummy's Ghost
The Mummy's Hand
The Mummy's Tomb
Mystery of the Wax Museum
The Phantom of the Opera
  (1925)
Phantom of the Opera (1943)
The Phantom of the Opera
  (1962)
Phantom of the Paradise
Phantom of the Rue Morgue
The Pit and the Pendulum
Poltergeist
The Premature Burial
Something Wicked This Way
  Comes
Tales From the Crypt
Tales of Terror
The Uninvited
The Wolf Man

Buster Keaton movies

Battling Butler
The Cameraman
College
The General
Go West
The Navigator
Our Hospitality
Seven Chances
Sherlock, Jr.
Steamboat Bill, Jr.
Three Ages

Laurel and Hardy movies

Block-Heads
The Bohemian Girl
A Chump at Oxford
The Devil's Brother (aka Fra
    Diavolo)
March of the Wooden
    Soldiers (aka Babes in
    Toyland)
Our Relations
Sons of the Desert
Way Out West

Literary classics

The Adventures of Huck
    Finn
The Adventures of
    Huckleberry Finn
The Adventures of Robin
    Hood
The Adventures of Tom
    Sawyer
Alice Adams
Anne of Avonlea
Anne of Green Gables
    (1934)
Anne of Green Gables
    (1985)
Black Beauty
A Christmas Carol (1938)
A Christmas Carol (1951)
A Connecticut Yankee in
    King Arthur's Court
The Curse of Frankenstein
David Copperfield
Dr. Jekyll and Mr. Hyde
    (1931)
Dr. Jekyll and Mr. Hyde
    (1941)
Emma
Ethan Frome
Fahrenheit 451

Frankenstein
Goodbye, Mr. Chips
The Grapes of Wrath
Great Expectations
Gulliver's Travels (1996)
Heidi
The Hound of the
    Baskervilles (1939)
The Hound of the
    Baskervilles (1959)
House of Usher (aka The
    Fall of the House of
    Usher)
The Hunchback of Notre
    Dame (1939)
The Hunchback of Notre
    Dame (1996)
The Innocents
Island of Lost Souls
Ivanhoe
Jane Eyre
Kidnapped
Kim
The Last of the Mohicans
    (1936)
The Last of the Mohicans
    (1992)
Life With Father
The Lion, the Witch and the
    Wardrobe
The Little Prince
The Little Princess
Little Women (1933)
Little Women (1994)
Lost Horizon
The Magnificent Ambersons
The Man in the Iron Mask
    (1939)
The Man in the Iron Mask
    (1998)
The Masque of the Red
    Death
Much Ado About Nothing
The Muppet Christmas Carol

My Ántonia
The Odyssey
Of Mice and Men (1939)
Of Mice and Men (1992)
The Old Man and the Sea
Oliver Twist
Our Town
The Pathfinder
Persuasion
The Pit and the Pendulum
The Premature Burial
Pride and Prejudice
The Prisoner of Zenda (1937)
The Prisoner of Zenda (1952)
Romeo & Juliet
The Scarlet Pimpernel
Scrooge
The Secret Garden (1949)
The Secret Garden (1993)
Sense and Sensibility
A Tale of Two Cities
Tom Brown's School Days (1940)
Tom Brown's School Days (1951)
Tom and Huck
Treasure Island (1934)
Treasure Island (1950)
War of the Worlds
Wuthering Heights

Martial arts

The Karate Kid
3 Ninjas

Marx Brothers movies

A Day at the Races
Duck Soup

Horse Feathers
A Night at the Opera

Monster

The Beast from 20,000 Fathoms
The Black Scorpion
The Blob
Creature from the Black Lagoon
The Creature Walks Among Us
The Deadly Mantis
Gamera, The Guardian of the Universe
Ghidrah, The Three-Headed Monster
The Giant Behemoth
Godzilla vs. King Ghidora
Godzilla, King of the Monsters
Godzilla 1985
Godzilla vs. the Thing
Gorgo
It Came From Beneath the Sea
King Kong (1933)
King Kong (1976)
King Kong vs. Godzilla
The Monster that Challenged the World
Mothra
The Quatermass Xperiment (aka The Creeping Unknown)
Revenge of the Creature
Tarantula
Them!
Tremors
Tremors 2: Aftershocks
20 Million Miles to Earth

644

When Dinosaurs Ruled the
  Earth
X the Unknown

Musicals

Aaron's Magic Village
The Adventures of Ichabod
  and Mr. Toad
Aladdin
Alakazam the Great
All Dogs Go to Heaven
All Dogs Go to Heaven 2
American Hot Wax
An American in Paris
An American Tail
An American Tail: Fievel
  Goes West
Anastasia
Anchors Aweigh
Annie
Arabian Knight
The Band Wagon
Babar: The Movie
Bathing Beauty
Beauty and the Beast (1991)
Bedknobs and Broomsticks
Bells Are Ringing
Billy Rose's Jumbo
Blue Hawaii
A Boy Named Charlie Brown
The Brave Little Toaster
Brigadoon
Bright Eyes
The Buddy Holly Story
Bugsy Malone
Bye Bye Birdie
Calamity Jane
Captain January
Carousel
Cats Don't Dance
Charlotte's Web
The Chipmunk Adventure

Chitty Chitty Bang Bang
A Connecticut Yankee in
  King Arthur's Court
Cover Girl
Curly Top
Daddy Long Legs
Damn Yankees
A Damsel in Distress
A Day at the Races
Dimples
Doctor Dolittle (1967)
Down Argentine Way
Easter Parade
Fame
FernGully . . . The Last
  Rainforest
Fiddler on the Roof
Finian's Rainbow
The 5,000 Fingers of Dr. T.
Flower Drum Song
Follow the Fleet
Footloose
Funny Face
Funny Girl
The Gay Divorcee
Gay Purr-ee
G.I. Blues
Gigi
Good News
A Goofy Movie
Grease
Great Balls of Fire!
Guys and Dolls
Gypsy
Hair
Hans Christian Andersen
A Hard Day's Night
The Harvey Girls
Heidi's Song
Hello, Dolly
Help!
Hey There, It's Yogi Bear
High Society
The Hobbit

Hoppity Goes to Town
In the Good Old
  Summertime
The King and I
Kismet
La Bamba
Li'l Abner
Lili
The Lion King
The Little Colonel
The Little Mermaid
Little Nemo
The Little Princess
Little Shop of Horrors
  (1986)
The Littlest Rebel
March of the Wooden
  Soldiers (aka Babes in
  Toyland)
Mary Poppins
Meet Me in St. Louis
Mrs. Santa Claus
The Music Man
My Fair Lady
My Sister Eileen
The Nightmare Before
  Christmas
Oklahoma!
Oliver!
Oliver & Company
One Hundred Men and a
  Girl
On the Town
Paint Your Wagon
The Pajama Game
The Pebble and the Penguin
Phantom of the Paradise
Pippi Longstocking
The Pirate
Poor Little Rich Girl
Quest for Camelot
Raggedy Ann & Andy
Rebecca of Sunnybrook Farm
The Red Shoes

Robin Hood
Rock-a-Doodle
Scrooge
Selena
Seven Brides for Seven
  Brothers
1776
Show Boat
Singin' in the Rain
The Sound of Music
South Pacific
Spice World
Starstruck
State Fair
Stowaway
Strictly Ballroom
Strike Up the Band
Summer Magic
Summer Stock
The Swan Princess
Swing Kids
Swing Time
Take Me Out to the Ball
  Game
Tap
that thing you do!
Thoroughly Modern Millie
The Three Musketeers (1939)
Three Smart Girls
Thumbelina
Tom & Jerry: The Movie
Tommy
tom thumb
Too Many Girls
Top Hat
West Side Story
White Christmas
Willy Wonka and the
  Chocolate Factory
The Wizard of Oz
Yankee Doodle Dandy
Yellow Submarine
You'll Never Get Rich
Young People

Religion

Kundun
Little Buddha
Samson and Delilah
The Ten Commandments

Romance

An American in
    Paris
Bells are Ringing
Brigadoon
Blue Hawaii
Bye Bye Birdie
Calamity Jane
Carousel
Cover Girl
Daddy Long Legs
Easter Parade
Flower Drum Song
Follow the Fleet
Forever Young
Funny Face
Funny Girl
G.I. Blues
Good News
High Society
In the Good Old
    Summertime
The King and I
The Little Mermaid
A Little Romance
Meet Me in St. Louis
The Mummy (1932)
My Girl
My Girl 2
Paint Your Wagon
Persuasion
The Princess Bride
The Prisoner of Zenda
    (1937)
The Prisoner of Zenda
    (1952)

Romeo and Juliet (1936)
Romeo and Juliet (1968)
Romeo & Juliet (aka
    William Shakespeare's
    Romeo & Juliet)
Ronnie and Julie
Sense and Sensibility
Seven Brides for Seven
    Brothers
Show Boat
Somewhere in Time
South Pacific
Splash
Starman
State Fair
Strictly Ballroom
Swing Time
Too Many Girls
Top Hat
Wild Hearts Can't Be
    Broken
You'll Never Get
    Rich

Satire

The Candidate
Cry-Baby
The Great Dictator
Gulliver's Travels
    (1996)
Mars Attacks!
Modern Times
The Nasty Girl
North
Small Soldiers
Smile

Science fiction

Abbott and Costello Go to
    Mars

Honey, I Blew Up the Kids
Honey, I Shrunk the Kids
House of Dracula
House of Frankenstein
Iceman
The Incredible Shrinking
  Man
Independence Day
Innerspace
Invasion of the Body
  Snatchers (1956)
Invasion of the Body
  Snatchers (1978)
Invisible Agent
The Invisible Boy
The Invisible Man
The Invisible Man Returns
The Invisible Man's Revenge
The Island of Lost Souls
It Came From Beneath the
  Sea
It Came From Outer Space
I Was a Teenage
  Frankenstein
I Was a Teenage Werewolf
Jurassic Park
King Kong (1933)
King Kong (1976)
King Kong vs. Godzilla
The Last Starfighter
The Little Shop of Horrors
  (1960)
Little Shop of Horrors (1986)
Logan's Run
Lost in Space
The Lost World
The Lost World: Jurassic Park
Man Made Monster
Mars Attacks!
Men in Black
The Monster Squad
The Monster That
  Challenged the World
Mothra

My Science Project
Mysterious Island
Planet of the Apes
The Power
Project X
The Quatermass Xperiment
  (aka The Creeping
  Unknown)
Quatermass II (aka Enemy
  from Space)
Quatermass and the Pit (aka
  Five Million Years to
  Earth)
Return From Witch
  Mountain
Return of the Jedi
Revenge of Frankenstein
Revenge of the Creature
Robinson Crusoe on Mars
The Rocketeer
Rocketship X-M
Runaway
Short Circuit
Short Circuit 2
Silent Running
Sleeper
Small Soldiers
Son of Flubber
Son of Frankenstein
Soylent Green
Spaceballs
The Space Children
Stargate
Star Kid
Starman
Star Trek: The Motion
  Picture
Star Trek II: The Wrath of
  Khan
Star Trek III: The Search for
  Spock
Star Trek IV: The Voyage
  Home
Star Trek V: The Final
  Frontier

Star Trek VI: The
  Undiscovered Country
Star Wars
Strange Invaders
Supergirl
Superman
Superman II
Superman III
Superman IV: The Quest for
  Peace
Tarantula
Them!
The Thing (from Another
  World)
Things to Come
This Island Earth
Time After Time
The Time Machine
The Tingler
Tremors
Tremors 2: Aftershocks
Tron
20 Million Miles to Earth
2001: A Space Odyssey
Village of the Damned
Voyage to the Bottom of the
  Sea
War of the Worlds
The Watcher in the Woods
Westworld
When Dinosaurs Ruled the
  Earth
When Worlds Collide
X—The Man With X-Ray
  Eyes
X the Unknown
Young Frankenstein

Silent classic

Battling Butler
The Black Pirate
The Cameraman
The Circus

City Lights
College
The General
The Gold Rush
Go West
The Kid
Modern Times
The Navigator
Our Hospitality
Seven Chances
Sherlock, Jr.
Steamboat Bill, Jr.
The Thief of Bagdad (1924)
Three Ages
The Three Musketeers (1921)
Tol'able David

Sports

Air Bud
Angels in the Outfield (1951)
Angels in the Outfield (1994)
The Bad News Bears
Breaking Away
Brian's Song
Casey's Shadow
Chariots of Fire
Cool Runnings
Field of Dreams
Hoosiers
Ice Castles
It Happens Every Spring
The Jackie Robinson Story
Jim Thorpe—All American
The Kid from Left Field
A League of Their Own
Little Big League
Little Giants
The Mighty Ducks
One on One
The Pride of the Yankees
Race the Sun
Rhubarb
Rocky

Rookie of the Year
Rudy
The Sandlot
Space Jam
Take Me Out to the Ball
    Game
Tiger Town

Suspense

The Birds
Colossus: The Forbin Project
Curse of the Demon
The Day of the Triffids
The Devil Rides Out (aka
    The Devil's Bride)
Earth vs. The Flying Saucers
Forbidden Planet
4D Man
From the Mixed-Up Files of
    Mrs. Basil E. Frankweiler
The Ghost of Frankenstein
The Gorgon
Horror of Dracula
House on Haunted Hill
The Incredible Shrinking
    Man
In the Heat of the Night
Invasion of the Body
    Snatchers (1956)
Invasion of the Body
    Snatchers (1978)
It Came From Outer Space
Kiss of the Vampire
The Mummy (1959)
The Mummy's Curse
The Mummy's Ghost
Mystery of the Wax Museum
The Power
Project X
Quatermass II (aka Enemy
    from Space)
Quatermass and the Pit (aka
    Five Million Years to Earth)

Son of Frankenstein
The Space Children
The Thing (From Another
    World)
This Island Earth
Time After Time
Tremors 2: Aftershocks
The Uninvited
Village of the Damned
Voyage to the Bottom of the
    Sea
War of the Worlds
When Worlds Collide
The Wolf Man

Swashbuckler

Adventures of Don Juan
The Adventures of Robin
    Hood
Against All Flags
Ali Baba and the Forty
    Thieves
An Arabian Adventure
Arabian Nights
At Sword's Point
The Bandit of Sherwood
    Forest
The Black Arrow
Blackbeard the Pirate
The Black Pirate
The Black Shield of Falworth
The Black Swan
The Boy and the Pirates
The Buccaneer
Captain Blood
Captain Sindbad
The Corsican Brothers
The Count of Monte Cristo
The Court Jester
The Crimson Pirate
The Fighting Prince of
    Donegal
The Flame and the Arrow

The Four Musketeers
The Golden Voyage of
  Sinbad
Kidnapped
Knights of the Round Table
Ladyhawke
Long John Silver
The Man in the Iron Mask
  (1939)
The Man in the Iron Mask
  (1998)
The Mark of Zorro
Prince Valiant
The Prisoner of Zenda
  (1937)
The Prisoner of Zenda
  (1952)
Robin Hood: Prince of
  Thieves
Scaramouche
The Scarlet Pimpernel
The Sea Hawk
The Seventh Voyage of
  Sinbad
The Son of Monte Cristo
The Story of Robin Hood
  and His Merrie Men
The Sword and the Rose
The Three Musketeers (1921)
The Three Musketeers (1939)
The Three Musketeers (1948)
The Three Musketeers (1974)
The Three Musketeers (1993)

Shirley Temple movies

Baby Take a Bow
Blue Bird
Bright Eyes
Captain January
Curly Top
Dimples
Heidi

The Little Colonel
Little Miss Broadway
Little Miss Marker
The Little Princess
The Littlest Rebel
Now and Forever
Our Little Girl
Poor Little Rich Girl
Rebecca of Sunnybrook
  Farm
Stowaway
Susannah of the Mounties
Wee Willie Winkie
Young People

War

The Great Escape
Hope and Glory
A Midnight Clear
Paths of Glory
Schindler's List

Western

Across the Great Divide
The Adventures of Bullwhip
  Griffin
Back to the Future Part III
Butch Cassidy and the
  Sundance Kid
By Way of the Stars
Calamity Jane
Cat Ballou
City Slickers
The Cowboys
Dances with Wolves
Davy Crockett and the River
  Pirates
Davy Crockett, King of the
  Wild Frontier
Flaming Star

Four Faces West
The Frisco Kid
The Grey Fox
High Noon
How the West Was Won
Little Big Man
The Man from Snowy River
Quigley Down Under
The Searchers

7 Faces of Dr. Lao
Shane
She Wore a Yellow Ribbon
Stars in My Crown
Support Your Local Sheriff!
3 Godfathers
Way Out West
Westworld